ON THE ROAD AROUND CALIFORNIA

A comprehensive guide to California by car

Fred Gebhart & Maxine Cass

A Thomas Cook Touring Handbook

PASSPORT BOOKS
a division of NTC *Publishing Group*

Published by Passport Books,
a division of NTC Publishing Group,
4255 West Touhy Avenue, ·
Lincolnwood (Chicago),
Illinois 60646-1975 U.S.A.

ISBN 0-8442-9015-7
Library of Congress Catalog Card
  Number: 94-67625

Published by Passport Books in conjunction with
the Thomas Cook Group Ltd

Managing Editor: Stephen York
Map Editor: Bernard Horton
Production Editor: Deborah Parker
Additional maps: Caroline Horton

Cover design by Greene Moore Lowenhoff
Cover illustration by Michael Benallack-Hart
Text typeset in Frutiger using Advent 3B2
  desk-top publishing system
Maps and diagrams created using GST
  Designworks
Text conversion by Riverhead Typesetters Ltd,
  Grimsby
Printed in Great Britain by Albert Gait Ltd,
  Grimsby

The Writing Team

Written and researched by
Fred Gebhart and Maxine Cass
Series and Book Editor: Melissa Shales
Additional research by Robert Holmes

Acknowledgments

The authors and publishers would like to thank
the following people and organisations for their
assistance during the preparation of this book:
Laurie Armstrong and Tami Bissell, Palm Springs
Desert Resorts CVB; Christopher P. Baker; Holly
Barnhill, The Biltmore Hotel; John Blades, Hearst
San Simeon State Historical Monument; Elaine
Cali, Anaheim Area VCB; Helen Chang, San Jose
CVB; Vivian Chastain, California State Automobile
Association (AAA); Mouse Cuzzocreo, Tuolumne
County VB; Dollar Rent a Car; Joanni Eyler, San
Luis Obispo County CVB; Janice Flippen, Ventura
VCB; Michael Forbes, Santa Barbara CVB; Lloyd
and Lou Gebhart; Hewlett Packard; Millie Howie,
Sonoma County CVB; Carol Infranca, Reno Sparks
CVB; Ken Jones, California Department of Parks
and Recreation; Dawn Keezer, Santa Cruz County
Conference and Visitors Council; Paul Lasley; Las
Vegas News Bureau; Maria Lenhart; Deane
Manning and Tim Gleason, Temecula Creek Inn;
Paul and Virginia McCarthy; Christine Morrison,
Recreational Vehicle Industry Association; Lois
Anne Naylor, Meredith Corporation; Anne North
and Laurie Allison, San Diego CVB; Elaine O'Gara;
Ann Parker, Santa Cruz Beach Boardwalk; Poi;
Jamie Lee Pricer, Palm Springs Life; Toby Pyle,
American Youth Hostels; Mary Ellen Quesada;
Sharon Rooney and Dawn Stranne, San Francisco
CVB; Judy Rowcliffe, Ritz-Carlton Hotels; Fred
Sater, California Office of Tourism; Sara Schmitz,
Kimton Group; Claire Simmons, Palm Canyon
Resort; Gary Sherwin, Los Angeles CVB; Terre
Stamoulis, Santa Monica CVB; Lucy Steffens,
Sacramento CVB; Diane Stracuzzi and Molly
Joest, Pebble Beach Company; Edna Texier;
Thomas Brothers Maps; Joe Timko, Coronado
Visitor Information; Tracey Vaughan, Monterey
Peninsula VCB; Keith Walklet, Yosemite Conces-
sion Services; Robert Warren, Shasta Cascade
Wonderland Association; Phil Weidinger, Lake
Tahoe Visitors Authority.

CONTENTS

HOW TO USE THIS BOOK

ROUTES AND CITIES

After spending the better part of a day in frenetic airports and crammed into airline seats, few people want to see just one city. This book reflects the way people actually travel, with detailed descriptions of the key cities and attractions in California and bordering ones of Nevada, linked by 31 **recommended routes**. Smaller cities, towns and attractions are described in order along each route.

The core of the book, pp. 53–347, consists of chapters describing either the larger cities or our choice of routes between cities and other attractions. Each chapter details one city or one route. We begin in Los Angeles, cover southern California and Las Vegas first, and then head northwards to the big national parks, San Francisco and lesser-known northern California.

The routes have been chosen to include as much interest along the way as possible. Where possible, more direct alternatives to the full scenic tour have been suggested. To avoid repetition, each route is described only once, but they are designed to be used in either direction, e.g. Los Angeles–Santa Barbara can be taken as easily from Santa Barbara to Los Angeles. Use the recommended routes as a menu from which to make up a tour which meets your requirements; mix, match and scramble them to suit your own time and interests.

WITHIN EACH ROUTE

Each route chapter begins with driving directions from the beginning to the end of the route.

→ Direct Route

This is the fastest, most direct, and sometimes, predictably, the most boring drive between hub cities. Freeways are used whenever possible.

～→ Scenic Route

This is the recommended route which avoids freeways whenever possible. Following ordinary highways complicates driving directions, but freeway designers generally had the good sense to by-pass the most scenic and interesting parts of the state. Road directions are specific; always be prepared for detours due to ceaseless road construction.

The driving directions are followed by sub-sections describing the more important towns and attractions along the way in more detail.You don't have to stop at every town en route, though most stops are listed. Ask at the local tourist office (usually the Convention & Visitors Bureau or Chamber of Commerce) for more information on attractions, lodging and dining.

Maps

Route maps show, in schematic form, the line of each route, but not its true direction or scale. Diagrams include the two end points, towns and other stops along the route, road numbers and distances. Their purpose is to summarise the driving directions in an at-a-glance form. **City maps**, maps of **national parks** and other scenic areas, and road maps for country areas such as **winery regions**, are provided throughout the text. The key on the inside back cover explains the symbols used in the maps and route diagrams. Additionally, the 8-page colour section at the end of the book provides a **road map** detailed enough for trip planning and on-the-road travel.

City and Town Descriptions

Whether the place is given a half-page description within a route chapter or merits an entire chapter of several pages to itself, we have concentrated on practical details: sources of tourist information; getting around by public transport, on foot or in your car, as appropriate; accommodation, eating and drinking; post and telephone communications; entertainment and shopping; and sightseeing, history and other points of interest. The largest cities have all this detail; in smaller places, some categories of information are less relevant and have been omitted or summarised.

Side Track

This heading is occasionally used to indicate departures from the main route or out-of-town trips to worthwhile sights, which may be described in full or highlighted in a paragraph or two.

Prices

It is impossible to keep up to date with specific price information, although we have given some sample indications under 'Cost of Living' in the Travel Essentials chapter, p. 15. However, we have rated accommodation and eating out by guideline categories throughout the book, as follows:

Accommodation
(per room per night)

Budget – under $35
Moderate – under $90
Expensive – under $150
Pricey – $150 and higher

Dining (meal for one person, exclusive of drinks, tip or tax)

Cheap – under $5
Budget – under $10
Moderate – under $20
Pricey – over $20

THE REST OF THE BOOK

Travel Essentials is an alphabetical section of general advice such as accommodation and food, and health and safety. **Driving in California** concentrates on advice for intending drivers, especially first-timers. **Background California** gives a brief taste of the fascinating geography and history of the state. **Touring Itineraries** provides suggestions for constructing itineraries that use the recommended routes to the full and take in as much, or as little, of California as you want.

The quickest way to find information on any place mentioned, large or small, is to consult the **Index**, pp. 348–350. This also indexes the colour planning map at the end of the book. The easiest way to look up a specific route is to consult the **Route Finder**, p. 8 or the **Routefinding Map**, pp. 6–7. **Driving Distances and Times** on p. 9 supplements the Route Finder information with indications of the length of journey you can expect between key places covered in this book.

ABBREVIATIONS USED IN THE BOOK

Abbreviations of hotel chains are listed on p. 10.

Bldg	Building (in addresses)	Jan, Feb	January, February, etc.
Blvd	Boulevard	km, kph	kilometres, kilometres per hour
Dr.	Drive	min(s)	minute(s)
Fwy	Freeway	Mon, Tues	Monday, Tuesday, etc.
hr(s)	hour(s)	Rd	Road
Hwy	US or State Highway, e.g. Hwy 60	St	Street
I-000	Interstate Highway, e.g. I-100	Ste	Suite (in addresses)

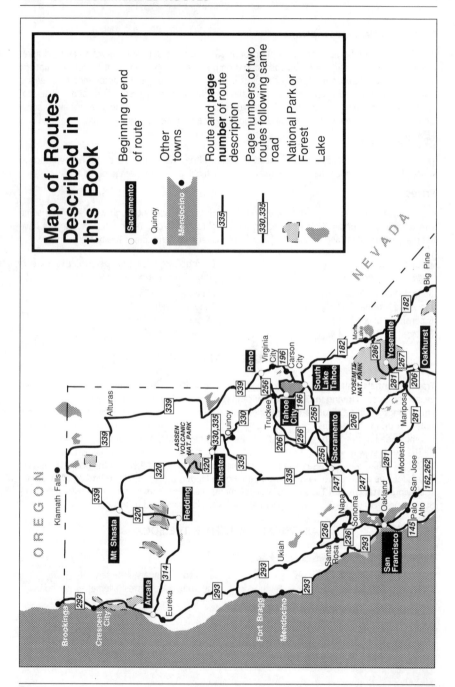

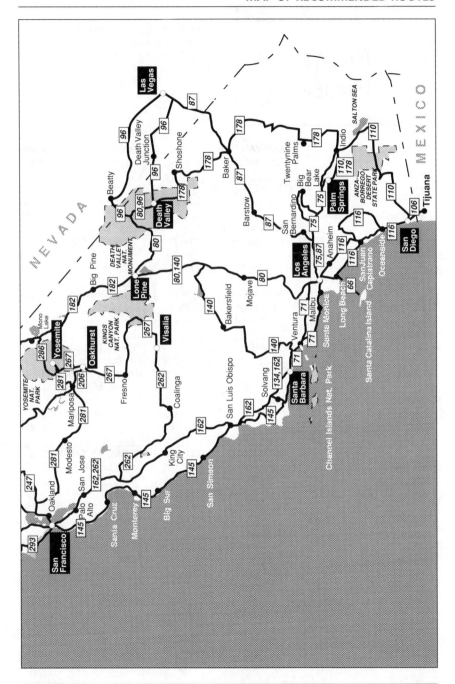

ROUTE FINDER

This table lists, in one alphabetical sequence, all the principal cities and other starting points in the book, and the routes connecting them, in both directions (e.g. Arcata to Redding is also listed as Redding to Arcata). References are to page numbers.

ARCATA to Redding 314–319

CHESTER to . . .
Lake Tahoe	330–334
Redding	320–329
Sacramento	335–338

DEATH VALLEY to . . .
Las Vegas	96–99
Los Angeles	80–86
Palm Springs	178–181

LAKE TAHOE
Lake Tahoe Circuit	196–205

Lake Tahoe to . . .
Chester	330–334
Lone Pine	182–195
Oakhurst	206–214

LAS VEGAS **90–95**
Las Vegas to . . .
Death Valley	96–99
Los Angeles	87–89

LONE PINE to . . .
Santa Barbara	140–144
South Lake Tahoe	182–195

LOS ANGELES **53–62**
Greater Los Angeles Routes	63–70

Los Angeles to . . .
Death Valley	80–86
Las Vegas	87–89
Palm Springs	75–79
San Diego	116–124
Santa Barbara	71–74

MT SHASTA to . . .
Reno	339–347

NAPA VALLEY to . . .
San Francisco	236–246

OAKHURST to . . .
Lake Tahoe	206–214

OREGON BORDER to . . .
San Francisco	293–313

PALM SPRINGS **173–177**
Palm Springs to . . .
Death Valley	178–181
Los Angeles	75–79
San Diego	110–115

REDDING to . . .
Arcata	314–319
Chester	320–329

RENO to . . .
Mt Shasta	339–347
Sacramento	256–261

SACRAMENTO **251–255**
Sacramento to . . .
Chester	335–338
Reno	256–261
San Francisco	247–250

SAN DIEGO **100–105**
San Diego Circuit	106–109

San Diego to . . .
Los Angeles	116–124
Palm Springs	110–115

SAN FRANCISCO **215–221**
San Francisco 49-mile Drive	223–227
San Francisco Bay Area Routes	228–235

San Francisco to . . .
Napa Valley	236–246
Oregon Border	293–313

San Francisco to . . .
Sacramento	247–250
Visalia	262–266
Santa Barbara (El Camino Real)	162–172
(Coastal Route)	145–161
Yosemite	281–285

SANTA BARBARA **125–128**
Santa Barbara Circuit	129–133
Santa Barbara County Routes	134–139

Santa Barbara to . . .
Lone Pine	140–144
Los Angeles	71–74
San Francisco (El Camino Real)	162–172
(Coastal Route)	145–161

SOUTH LAKE TAHOE to . . .
Lone Pine	182–195

VISALIA to . . .
San Francisco	262–266
Yosemite	267–280

YOSEMITE NATIONAL PARK **286–292**
Yosemite to . . .
San Francisco	281–285
Visalia	267–280

DRIVING DISTANCES AND TIMES

Approximate distances from major cities to surrounding places and main centres are given following the most direct routes. Driving times are meant as an average indication only, allowing for the nature of the roads but not for traffic conditions, which can be very variable (see the route descriptions throughout this book). They do not include allowance for stops or breaks en route.

Los Angeles to . . .

	Miles	Hours		Miles	Hours		Miles	Hours
Baker	200	4	Palm Springs	110	2¼	San Luis Obispo	200	4
Death Valley	315	6½	Sacramento	390	7	Santa Barbara	100	2
Las Vegas	300	5½	San Diego	130	2½	Tijuana	150	3
Lone Pine	210	4	San Francisco	450	10	Visalia	180	3½
Monterey	340	7	San Jose	350	7	Yosemite Village	320	7½

Las Vegas to . . .

	Miles	Hours		Miles	Hours		Miles	Hours
Baker	90	1½	Los Angeles	300	5½	San Diego	335	6½
Death Valley	160	3½	Palm Springs	285	5½	Visalia	360	7
Lone Pine	270	6	Reno	445	9			

Sacramento to . . .

	Miles	Hours		Miles	Hours		Miles	Hours
Alturas	300	6½	Napa	61	1½	Santa Barbara	430	8½
Arcata	295	6	Redding	170	3½	S Lake Tahoe	110	2
Chester	180	4	Reno	170	3	Tahoe City	120	2½
Crescent City	380	7½	San Diego	520	9½	Visalia	220	4½
Los Angeles	390	7	San Francisco	100	2	Yosemite Village	180	4
Monterey	220	4½	San Jose	130	2½			
Mount Shasta	240	4½	San Luis Obispo	325	6½			

San Diego to . . .

	Miles	Hours		Miles	Hours		Miles	Hours
Baker	245	4½	Palm Springs	140	3½	Santa Barbara	225	4½
Death Valley	360	7	Sacramento	520	9½	Tijuana	20	½
Las Vegas	335	6½	San Francisco	520	9½	Visalia	310	6
Lone Pine	300	6	San Jose	480	9			
Los Angeles	130	2½	San Luis Obispo	330	6½			

San Francisco to . . .

	Miles	Hours		Miles	Hours		Miles	Hours
Alturas	400	8½	Monterey	125	2½	San Jose	50	1¼
Arcata	280	7	Mount Shasta	310	5½	San Luis Obispo	260	5½
Chester	265	5½	Napa	60	1½	Santa Barbara	280	7½
Crescent City	365	5	Redding	230	4½	S Lake Tahoe	205	4
Lone Pine	395	8½	Reno	230	5	Tahoe City	200	4
Los Angeles	450	10	Sacramento	100	2	Visalia	250	5
Mendocino	145	3	San Diego	520	10½	Yosemite Village	195	4½

TRAVEL ESSENTIALS

For the Traveler: The information in the **Travel Essentials** and **Driving in California** sections of this book is intended to make traveling in California and nearby destinations a pleasant experience not only for Californians and their fellow US citizens, but also for visitors from Mexico, Canada, and the rest of the "wide world" who have come to California for a once-in-a-lifetime vacation.

Accommodations

California offers accommodations of every price level, from five-star hotels to youth hostels and campgrounds. Local tourist offices can provide lodging lists and telephone numbers, but generally can't make reservations. Where available, lodging services are noted in the text.

Accommodations can be extremely hard to find in major tourist destinations during the hight of the season, which is usually Memorial Day (last weekend in May) to Labor Day (first weekend in September), plus weekends and major public holidays. Three exceptions are Yosemite National Park, where peak season runs from late April through November; desert areas, where peak season runs from early November through April; and ski resorts, where "in" season prices arrive with the first good snowfall.

Thomas Cook or any other travel agent can handle room reservations when purchasing air tickets and local transportation. All-inclusive fly-drive arrangements, and "do-it-yourself packages" such as Thomas Cook's American Fly-Drive and American Options program, can provide hotel coupons, exchangeable at a range of hotel chains, which guarantee a prepaid rate at participating chains, although they do not guarantee rooms – it's up to you to phone ahead, or take a chance on availability. It's

particularly important to pre-book the first and last night's stay to avoid problems if flights are delayed.

Throughout the book we have indicated prices of accommodations in a comparative way by using terms such as "moderate" and "pricey"; see "How to Use This Book," p. 4, for an explanation of these descriptions in dollars.

Hotels and Motels

Hotel rates are quoted for single or double occupancy; children usually stay cheaply or for free with parents.

Once in the United States, you will find that most chain hotels and motels have toll-free reservation telephone numbers that can be

---

Hotel and Motel Chains

The following abbreviations have been used in the book to show which chains are represented in a particular town. Most cities and large towns have all except AY.

AY   American Youth Hostels
      (202) 783-6161
      (AYH information only)
BW   Best Western (800) 528-1234
CI   Comfort Inn (800) 228-5150
CM   Courtyard by Marriott (800) 321-2211
DI   Days Inn (800) 325-2525
ES   Embassy Suites (800) 362-2779
HI   Holiday Inn (800) 465-4329
HJ   Howard Johnson (HoJo)
      (800) 654-2000
HL   Hilton (800) 445-8667
HY   Hyatt (800) 233-1234
MA   Marriott (800) 228-9290
M6   Motel 6 (800) 437-7486
QI   Quality Inn (800) 228-5151
RA   Radisson (800) 333-3333
RM   Ramada (800) 228-2828
RI   Residence Inn (800) 331-3131
SH   Sheraton (800) 325-3535
TL   Travelodge (800) 578-7878
VI   Vagabond Inn (800) 522-1555

---

reached from anywhere in North America. The box on page 10 gives a selection of these, along with the abbreviations used in the text of this book

Advance reservations usually require a voucher or credit card number to guarantee the booking. Ask for discounts if you're disabled, a senior citizen, belong to an auto club, or traveling off season. When checking in, always ask if there's a cheaper room rate than the one you pre-booked. It's also practical to find lodging day by day, especially in off-peak seasons.

Motels are often the best bet. Literally, "motor hotels," motels are one- to three-story buildings with a modest version of a hotel's accommodations. Most belong to nationwide chains that enforce service and safety standards. Independent motels may not be quite as fancy, but offer even lower prices. Motels fill up fast during high season, but last-minute rooms are usually available in the off season, especially during the week. The AAA Tourbook for California and Nevada lists thousands of motels and hotels; thousands more are just as comfortable and affordable. Check the motels that line major highways entering most cities and towns. Special prices are often noted on a roadside sign. **Budget hotels**, especially in cities, tend to be dim, dirty, and dangerous. Look for a motel or youth hostel instead.

Bed and Breakfast

Anyone on a tight budget should avoid staying in a Bed and Breakfast, which is usually the most expensive lodging in the area. A California-style Bed and Breakfast is still a bedroom in a private home, but the accent is on luxury, not value. The typical style is a refurbished room in a Victorian mansion, complete with lace curtains, down comforter, fireplace, knickknacks atop antique furniture, and private bathroom facilities. If "Victorians" are in short supply, any ordinary house will do, so long as it's properly luxurious. Breakfasts vary. A few are so healthy and calorie-conscious a songbird could go away hungry. But the standard fare includes fruit juice, coffee or tea, an egg dish, homemade bread, and a sweet roll.

Camping

Camping usually means staying in a tent or a recreational vehicle (RV) in a rural campground. KOA, Kampgrounds of America, is a private chain of RV parks that accept tents. However if you're a serious outdoors person, KOAs won't be much of a wilderness experience. Many other campgrounds are public, most operated by the California Department of Parks and Recreation. Overnight fees range from $5 to more than $20, depending on location and season. Standard facilities include a firepit for cookouts, food storage locker, tent site, showers/toilets, and, during high season, guided hikes and evening educational programs.

Most state park campsites can be reserved in advance. In popular parks, they must be. MISTIX, PO Box 85705, San Diego, CA 92188-5706, tel: (800) 444-7275 or (619) 452-1950 outside the continental USA, handles reservations for all state parks as well as Joshua Tree National Monument, Sequoia/Kings Canyon National Parks, Whiskeytown National Recreation Area, and Yosemite National Park. Private campground information is available from **California Travel Parks Association**, PO Box 5648, Auburn, CA 95604, tel: (916) 885-1624.

Youth Hostels

American Youth Hostels (Hosteling International) was created for tight budgets. Most California hostels provide a dormitory-style room and shared bath for $8–$16 per night. Some have family rooms, all offer discounts to local attractions. The down-side: there are only 22 hostels in the entire state, most along the coast. Nevada's only hostel is in Carson City. And when two or more people are traveling together and can share a room, cheap motels may be even cheaper than hostels.

Airports

The three major California airports are Los Angeles International (LAX), San Francisco International (SFO), and San Diego International Airport/Lindbergh Field. Las Vegas'' McCarran International Airport and Reno Cannon International Airport serve Nevada.

Travelers Aid desks provide tourist information; **airport information** booths cover airport facilities, airport-to-city transportation and local accommodations, though no reservations are made.

All major airports have foreign exchange and banking services and car rental facilities. Public transportation to the nearest city is usually available, but seldom practical in terms of routes or time. Luggage carts are free for international arrivals at LAX and SFO; elsewhere, there is a $1 charge. Be prepared for long walks through terminals on arrival – moving walkways are few and far between.

Specific airport arrival information is given in the chapters dealing with the major airport cities.

Bicycles

Cycling is popular for countryside day touring in California – less so for overnight trips, due to geography. Bikes can be rented by the hour or the day in most wine country and beach areas as well as in Yosemite and other major parks. Urban drivers are not accustomed to sharing the street with cyclists, so try to avoid busy city streets.

For serious bikers (as cyclists are called in California), biking tours are available at all levels, from easy day trips to arduous adventures through Death Valley or over the Sierras. On-your-own bike tours are also possible, but beware of great distances and mountains between towns.

California State law requires cyclists of all ages to wear protective helmets while riding.

Borders

US Customs and Immigration has a reputation as one of the most unpleasant travel experiences the world has to offer, for citizens returning home as well as for first-time visitors. Visitors who overstay tourist and student visas are the largest single source of illegal immigrants to the United States. The smaller, but more visible flow of migrants slipping over the California border from Mexico makes illegal immigration a hot political and social concern.

C & I officials have *carte blanche* to ask any question, search anyone or anything, and do it in any manner they see fit, however unpleasant. In fact, most are polite to a fault, but the only defence against an inspector who got up on the wrong side of the bed is to have passport, visa, proof of financial support, and return ticket in order.

A car or RV can be a liability if crossing the border to Mexico: the diligent search can extend to your vehicle. Take a tourbus or the economical San Diego Trolley to visit Tijuana, and avoid the hassle.

California prices for alcohol, tobacco, perfume, and other typical duty-free items beat most **duty-free** shops. Follow the locals into chain supermarkets (Safeway, Lucky, Alpha-Beta, Boys, Raleys, and others) and discount stores (Target, K-mart, and Wal-Mart are the most common).

California agricultural inspection is another matter. Unprocessed plant, meat, and cheese products, especially fruits and vegetables, may not be brought into the state because of the danger of spreading agricultural pests. Canine Agricultural Inspectors, also known as the Beagle Brigade (though other breeds are also used), may perform the check at airport arrival halls. All road traffic must stop at agricultural inspection stations shortly after entering the state. There's a grateful thank-you for declaring and dumping forbidden products; a stiff fine for bringing even California-grown produce back into the state. During pest infestations, in-state prohibitions on transportation of fruit are indicated on billboard signs.

Importation of weapons, narcotics, or certain unapproved pharmaceutical products is prohibited. Carry doctors' prescriptions with documentation (such as a doctor's letter) to prove that medications are legitimate.

Buses

Greyhound Bus Lines, *Customer Service, 901 Main St, Dallas, TX 75202, tel: (800) 231-2222*, provides long-distance bus services between major cities. There are discounts for seniors (over 65), disabled travelers, and children (under 12) riding with a full-fare adult. The **Interna-**

tional **Ameripass** offers discounts for travelers not residing in North America. Greyhound passes are obtainable through some international travel agencies.

If you're buying tickets locally and are able to reserve at least three days in advance, they should cost less than $70, depending on distance traveled. Local transportation companies listed in the telephone directory under individual cities and towns provide local service. Thomas Cook publishes bimonthly timetables of US buses in the *Thomas Cook Overseas Timetable*, and a special edition devoted to US (and Canadian) buses and trains, containing much additional travel information, is published annually under the title *Thomas Cook North American Rail and Bus Guide* (full details of these and other publications under "Useful Reading" on p. 29).

Campers and RVs

It's the freedom of the open road, housekeeping on wheels, a tinkerer's delight, a large machine hurtling down slopes and plowing up grades. An RV, caravan, Winnebago or motorhome provides a kitchen and sleeping and bathroom facilities.

Fly-drive vacation packages usually offer the option of renting an RV. The additional cost to rent an RV can be offset by the economics of assured lodging for several people, space for meal preparation and eating, and the convenience of comfort items and souvenirs stored nearby. RVs are cramped, designed to stuff you and your belongings into limited space. The economics work only if advance planning assures that the pricey spur-of-the-moment allure of a hotel shower or unplanned restaurant meal won't overcome RV campers! Factor in the cost of gasoline — an RV guzzles three to four times more than a medium-sized car.

Always get operating manuals for the vehicle and all appliances before leaving the RV rental lot, and have someone demonstrate how *everything* works. Systems may be interdependent, or more complex than anticipated. Be prepared to pre-plan menus and allow additional time each morning and afternoon/ evening to level the RV (perfect leveling is

essential for correct operation of refrigerators) and hook up or disconnect electricity, water and sewer hoses, and cable television plugs. As at home, some basic housecleaning must be done; also allow time for laundry at RV parks.

Buy a pair of sturdy rubber washing gloves to handle daily sewer chores. Pack old clothes to wear while crawling under the vehicle to hook up and disconnect at each stop — many RVers carry a pair of overalls. Without hookups, water and electricity are limited to what you carry with you from the last fill-up or battery charge. If you camp in a park without hookups, locate the nearest restrooms before dark. Using showers and toilets in RV parks or public campgrounds will save time cleaning up the RV shower space and emptying the toilet holding tank. Have a strong torch (flashlight) handy.

When you move out on the road, expect anything that's not secured to go flying, or shake, rattle, and roll. Quickly get into a routine of allotted tasks and assign a quick-grab spot for maps, snacks, cameras, and valuables.

RV travel information: **Recreation Vehicle Industry Association (RVIA)**, *Dept. RK, PO Box 2999, Reston VA 22090-0999, tel: (703) 620-6003*. To plan RV camping, request *Go Camping America* from **Camping Vacation Planner**, *PO Box 2669, Reston VA 22090, tel: (800) 477-8669.*

Camping clubs offer RV information for members; some like the **Good Sam Club**, *PO Box 6060, Camarillo CA 93011, tel: (805) 389-0300*, offer roadside assistance for breakdowns and tire changing. Many camping clubs publish magazines or newsletters with tips on operating and driving an RV. For a hilarious insight into RV travel, find a copy of *Out West, 10522 Brunswick Rd, Grass Valley CA 95945, tel: (800) 274-9378*, a periodic tabloid with funny pictures of signs and stories about Western characters. The publisher packs his family and computer into an RV for several weeks at a time, and they deliver a flavorful picture of the best and the worst of home-on-wheels travel.

Campground directories list private RV park locations, directions, size, number of pitches, hookups, laundry, on-premises convenience stores, and showers. Private campground information is available from **California Travel Parks Association**, *PO Box 5648, Auburn, CA 95604; tel: (916) 885-1624*. Popular guides are *Trailer Life Campground & Woodall's Campground Directory (Western Edition), 28167 N Keith Dr., Lake Forest, IL 60045; tel: (708) 362-6700* ($13.70); *Wheelers RV Resort & Campground Guide, 1310 Jarvis Ave, Elk Grove Village, IL 60007; tel: (708) 981-0100,* ($15.50); *Kampgrounds of America (KOA) Directory, PO Box 30558, Billings, MT 59114-0558; tel: (406) 24-7444* ($3 or free at KOA campgrounds). The **AAA** has a directory and maps for Southern and Northern California campgrounds. See "Parks Information" in this chapter for campgrounds on state or federal land.

Children

California, with its many theme parks and natural attractions, is both ideal for traveling with children and welcoming. From museums to transportation, check for children's rates, often segmented by age, e.g., under 3 free, 6–12 years $3.00, 12–18 years $4.00. A student card must be shown to use student rates.

Traveling with children is never easy, but preparation helps. *Travel with Children*, by Maureen Wheeler, (Lonely Planet), is filled with useful tips. Kids get bored and cranky on long drives. Pack favorite games and books, and pick up a book of travel games. A traditional favorite is to count non-California license plates. The winner – always a child – gets a special treat later in the day. If the children are old enough, suggest that they keep a detailed travel journal. A journal will help them focus on California instead of what they might be missing back home. It will also help them remember details later to share with friends and teachers. Collecting anything, from postcards to admission tickets to travel brochures, adds a new dimension to travel.

Any driving destination in California is equipped for children of all ages, offering a range from diapers to video games. Most hotels and motels can arrange for babysitters, though the price may be steep. Many motel chains allow children under 12, 14, sometimes 18, to stay free in their parents' room. A rollaway child's bed, often called a cot, usually comes at no or low cost.

Meals can be difficult, but picnic lunches offer flexibility. It's also a good idea to carry a small cooler filled with ice, cold drinks, and snacks, especially in hot weather. Most towns have coffee shops with long hours, children's menus, and familiar fast-food names. If the children like McDonalds at home, they'll like Big Macs in California – and vice versa.

Climate

Climate is what you expect, weather is what you get. Expect rain (or snow) from October to April, sun the rest of the year. But don't be surprised to get rain in August, especially in the deserts. Drought years can bring water rationing instead of rain. *If you don't like the weather, drive ten minutes.* That's the comedian's answer to foul weather in California, and it often works. Uneven terrain creates patchwork weather patterns with no apparent rhyme or reason.

Summer fog is standard along the coast, but so are azure skies and a white-hot sun. Winter temperatures drop with altitude and distance north. In the south, summer temperatures climb with distance from the coast.

Summer is also fire season. Forest fires are often allowed to burn unchecked unless human lives or major property damage is threatened.

	LOS ANGELES	SAN FRANCISCO
JANUARY		
Highest	65°F/18°C	56°F/13°C
Lowest	45°F/7°C	46°F/7°C
APRIL		
Highest	71°F/22°C	61°F/16°C
Lowest	53°F/12°C	49°F/9°C
JULY		
Highest	83°F/28°C	64°F/18°C
Lowest	63°F/17°C	53°F/12°C
OCTOBER		
Highest	77°F/25°C	68°F/20°C
Lowest	57°F/14°C	54°F/12°C

Regular burning is a natural renewal process and necessary for the regeneration of many forest species. If a patch of forest has not burned in several years, deliberate fires, called controlled burns, are set during wet weather to burn out accumulated dead growth and prevent later conflagrations.

Fire is less benign in heavily populated Southern California. Hot, dry winds called Santa Ana winds blow from the mountains down toward the coast in late summer, boosting temperatures and cutting humidity to desert-like levels. A spark, an electrical storm, an accident, or an arsonist can send thousands of acres up in flames. Summer fires are usually followed by winter floods and mud slides, especially along coastal and mountain roads.

Clothing

San Francisco summers are often fogbound. Coastal breezes prevail year round. In any season, bring plenty of layers, from shorts for the beach to hats and jackets for the mountains. Cotton and wool, worn in layers, are California's unofficial state fibres. One layer is cool, several layers are warm. Adding and removing layers makes it easier to stay comfortable no matter how many times the weather changes in a single day.

What to pack is a constant question. An elegant restaurant requires jackets and ties for men. Most shops and restaurants require that shirts be worn. The bottom line is: when in doubt, leave it at home. California clothing prices are cheaper than almost anywhere outside the Third World. But bring good, broken-in walking shoes.

Consulates

Australia: *1 Bush St, 7th Floor, San Francisco, CA 94104, tel: (415) 362-6160*
611 N Larchmont Blvd, Los Angeles, CA 90004, tel: (213) 469-4300.
Canada: *50 Fremont St, Ste 2100, San Francisco, CA 94105, tel: (414) 495-7030.*
300 S Grand Ave, 10th Floor, Los Angeles, CA 90071, tel: (213) 687-7432.
France: *540 Bush St, San Francisco,CA, tel (415) 395-4330*

New Zealand: *10960 Wilshire Blvd, Ste 1530, Los Angeles, CA 90024; tel: (213) 477-8241.*
Republic of Ireland: *655 Montgomery St, San Francisco, CA 94104, tel: (415) 392-4214.*
South Africa: *50 North La Cienega Blvd, Ste 300, Beverly Hills, CA 90211, tel: (310) 657-9200.*
UK: *Ahmanson Center, East Bldg, Ste 312, 3701 Wilshire Blvd, Los Angeles, CA 90010, tel: (213) 385-7381.*
1 Sansome St, Ste 850, San Francisco, CA 94104, tel: (415) 981-3030.

Cost of Living

While California and Nevada have local sales taxes and hotel/lodging taxes, the combined levy is less than the VAT charged in most of Europe. Prices are always marked or quoted *without tax*, which is added at time of purchase (see 'Sales Taxes,'' p. 25. Gas prices are a special bargain, about $1.25 per US gallon (4 litres), or about $0.30 per litre. Motel rooms cost $30–$70 per night; hotels from $70 up. Restaurant meals, including soup or salad, main course, dessert, beverage, and tax are about $10–$20 per person for lunch; $20–$25 for dinner. Theme parks charge about $30 per adult; national and state parks $4-$6 per car; most museums $2–$5 per person.

Currency

US dollars are the only currency accepted in California and Nevada. Bill denominations are $1, $2 (very rare), $5, $10, $20, $50, $100, $1000 (rare), and $10,000 (rarer). All bills are the same color, green and white, and size. Take great care not to mix them up. The only differences, apart from the denominations marked on them, are the US president pictured on the front and the designs on the back. There are 100 cents to the dollar: coins include the copper 1-cent penny, 5-cent nickel, 10-cent dime, 25-cent quarter, 50-cent half-dollar (rare), and an extremely rare Susan B. Anthony dollar. Larger-sized dollar coins are common in Nevada casinos.

Outside foreign exchange offices, most Californians have only a vague idea that other currencies even exist. Banks can exchange foreign currency or travelers checks, but expect interminable delays (and extraordinary fees) as they telephone the main office in search of exchange rates and procedures. It is better to seek out one of the Thomas Cook locations noted in this book. However, travelers checks denominated in US dollars, from well-known issuers such as Thomas Cook, are acceptable everywhere and can be used like cash or changed easily. To report Thomas Cook travelers check losses and thefts, call 1-800-223-7373 (toll-free, 24-hour service).

For security reasons, avoid carrying large amounts of cash. The safest forms of money are US dollar travelers checks and credit or debit cards. Both can be used almost everywhere. If possible, bring at least one, preferably two, major credit cards such as **Access (MasterCard)**, **American Express**, or **Visa**. (Thomas Cook locations will offer replacement and other emergency services if you lose a MasterCard.)

Plastic is the only acceptable proof of fiscal responsibility. Car rental companies require either a credit card imprint or a substantial cash deposit before releasing a vehicle, even if the rental has been fully prepaid. Hotels and motels also require either a credit card imprint or a cash deposit, even if the bill is to be settled in cash.

Some shops, cheaper motels, small local restaurants, and low-cost gas stations, require cash. Automated teller machines, or **ATMs**, are a ubiquitous source of cash through withdrawals or cash advances authorized by debit or credit card. **Star** and **CIRRUS** are the most common international systems used in California, but check terms, availability, and PIN (personal identification number) with the card issuer before leaving home.

Customs Allowances

Personal duty-free allowances that can be taken into the United States by visitors are 1 US quart (approx. 0.9 liters) of spirits or wine, 300 cigarettes or 50 (non-Cuban) cigars, and up to $100 worth of gifts.

Foreigners returning home will be allowed to take in:

Australia: goods to the value of A$400 (half for those under 18) plus 250 cigarettes or 250 g tobacco and 1 litre alcohol.

Canada: goods to the value of C$300, provided you have been away for over a week and have not already used up part of your allowance that year. You are also allowed 50 cigars plus 200 cigarettes and 1 kg tobacco (if over 16) and 40 oz/1 litre alcohol.

New Zealand: goods to the value of NZ$700. Anyone over 17 may also take 200 cigarettes or 250 g tobacco or 50 cigars or a combination of tobacco products not exceeding 250 g in all plus 4½ liters of beer or wine and 1.125 liters spirits.

UK: The allowances for goods bought outside the UK and/or in UK duty-free shops are 200 cigarettes or 50 cigars or 100 cigarillos or 250 g tobacco + 2 liters still table wine + 1 liter spirits or 2 liters sparkling wine + 50 g/60 ml perfume + 0.5 l/250 ml toilet water.

Disabled Travelers

Access is the key word. Physically challenged is synonymous with disabled. Physical disabilities should present less of a barrier in the United States than in much of the world. State and federal laws, particularly the Americans with Disabilities Act (ADA), require that all businesses, buildings and services used by the public be accessible to handicapped persons, including those using wheelchairs. Every hotel, restaurant, office, shop, cinema, museum, post office, and other public building must have access ramps and toilets designed for wheelchairs. Most cities and towns have ramps built into street crossings and most city buses have some provision for wheelchair passengers. Even many parks have installed paved pathways so disabled visitors can get a sense of the natural world.

The bad news is that disabled facilities aren't always what they're meant to be or even what they're legally required to be. Museums, public buildings, restaurants, and lodging facilities are usually accessible, but special automobile controls for disabled drivers are seldom an option on rented vehicles.

Airlines are particularly hard on disabled passengers. US carriers can prevent anyone who is not strong enough to open an emergency exit (which weighs about 45 lb,

20.5 kg) or has vision/hearing problems from sitting in that row of seats – even if it means bumping them from the flight. Commuter airlines sometimes deny boarding to passengers with mobility problems on the grounds that they may block the aisle during an emergency.

Some public telephones have special access services for the deaf and disabled. Broadcast television may be closed-captioned for the hearing impaired, indicated by a rectangle around a double cc in a corner of the screen.

US Information: SATH (Society for the Advancement of Travel for the Handicapped), *347 5th Ave, Suite 610, New York, NY 10016, tel (212) 447-7284.*

UK Information: RADAR, *12 City Forum, 250 City Road, London EC1V 8AF; tel: (0171) 250 3222* publish a useful annual guide called *Holidays and Travel Abroad* which gives details of facilities for the disabled in different countries.

Discounts

Reductions on entrance fees and public transportation for senior citizens, children, students, and military personnel are common. Some proof of eligibility is usually required. For age, a passport or drivers license is sufficient. Military personnel should carry an official identification card. Students will have better luck with an International Student Identity Card (ISIC), from their local student union than with a college I.D.

The most common discount is for automobile club members. Tour guides from AAA (Automobile Association of America) affiliates in Northern and Southern California list hundreds of member discounts for California and Nevada. Always ask about "Triple A discounts" at attractions, hotels, motels, and car hire counters. Most recognize reciprocal membership benefits. Some cities will send high-season discount booklets on request, good for shops, restaurants, or lodging.

Drinking

Hollywood movies to the contrary, you must be 21 years old to purchase or to drink any kind of alcoholic beverage in California and Nevada. Licensed establishments, bars, lounges, saloons, or pubs, may be open between 11AM and 2PM. Though California's wine is one of the state's main agricultural products, wine may not be served at a restaurant owned by the winery owner. Beer, however, can be brewed and sold at a microbrewery, or brewpub, where the law requires that food must also be available. Convenience stores sell beer, wine, and sometimes spirits, but prices are high.

Laws against drinking and driving are very strict, and strictly enforced with fines and imprisonment. If stopped under suspicion of Driving Under the Influence (DUI), the police officer will ask you to choose between one of three tests: breath, blood, or urine. Any liquor, wine, or beer container in a vehicle (RVs excepted) must be full, sealed, and unopened – or you're asking for trouble.

Earthquakes

When a Californian asks if the earth moved, it's a serious question. More than 5000 earthquakes hit the state every year, but most are too mild to be felt. For Californians, quakes are no big deal – except on the rare occasions when they're catastrophic.

If the quake is mild, that is if dishes aren't bouncing off tables onto the floor and no one around seems upset, treat it like an amusement park ride. Thrill friends at home with stories of the narrow escape. Tremors strong enough to feel are so rare that there are "earthquake virgins" everywhere in the state.

If items start falling from shelves, lamps sway, or it becomes difficult to walk, take cover. Crawl under the nearest solid table for protection against falling objects. If there's no table handy, brace arms and legs in an interior doorway. Stay away from windows, bookcases, stairs, or anything else that could fall or break. *Don't* run outside. Glass, masonry, and live power lines could be falling.

If driving, pull off the road and stop. It's almost impossible to control a vehicle when the road won't hold still. If you're about to drive onto a bridge or overpass, don't, and if you're on one, get off as quickly as possible.

Once the quake is over, treat it like any other civil emergency. Make sure everyone is safe and provide all help possible to the wounded. And get ready for the next shake. There are always aftershocks.

Electricity

California (like the rest of the United States) uses 110 volt 60 hertz current. Two- or three-pin electrical plugs are standard throughout the country. Electrical gadgets from outside North America require plug and power converters. Both are difficult to obtain because local travelers don't need them.

Beware of buying electrical appliances in California for the same reason. Few gadgets on the US market can run on 220 v 50 hz power. Exceptions include battery-operated equipment such as radios, cameras, and portable computers. Tape cassettes, CDs, computer programs, and CD-ROMs sold in the United States can be used anywhere in the world.

US video equipment, which uses the NTSC format, is *not* compatible with the PAL and SECAM equipment used in most of the rest of the world. *Prerecorded* video tapes sold in the United States will not work with other equipment unless specifically marked as compatible with PAL or SECAM. *Blank* video tapes purchased in America, however, *can* be used with video recorders elsewhere in the world. Discount store prices on blank video cassettes are very reasonable.

Emergencies

In case of emergency, dial 911, free from any telephone. Ambulance, paramedics, police, fire department, or other public safety personnel will be dispatched immediately. See also under "Health" on the next page.

If you lose your Thomas Cook travelers checks, call 1-800-223-7373 (toll-free, 24-hour service).

Food

American pioneer traditions demand huge portions and endless refills of (admittedly weak) coffee. Copious consumption begins with breakfast. Thinly-sliced bacon and eggs cooked to order (fried, boiled, poached) come with hash browns (shredded fried potatoes) or

toast, a flat "English" muffin with butter and jam, or a bagel with cream (farmer's) cheese and lox (smoked salmon slices) is served alongside. Variations or additions include pancakes, French toast (bread dipped in egg batter and lightly fried), and waffles. Fresh fruit and yogurt, cereal, and oatmeal are other possibilities. A "continental breakfast" is juice, coffee or tea, and some sort of bread or pastry. Hotels and some restaurants offer Sunday brunch, usually 1100–1400, with all-you-can-eat self-service buffets heaped with hot and cold dishes. The economical Sunday brunch also includes coffee, tea, orange juice, and cheap "champagne" (sparkling wine).

Menus offer similar choices for lunch and dinner, the evening meal. Dinner portions are larger and more costly. Most menus offer appetizers (starters), salads, soups, pastas, entrées (main courses), and desserts. Californians expect salads to be fresh and crisp and sauces light and tasty. Cooking oils are not light on the palate, so avoid fried fish and ask instead for grilled seafood. Ice cream or sherbert is a lighter dessert choice.

For hearty eating, try a steak house where salad and a baked potato accompany a thick steak. Italian restaurants serve pizza, pasta, seafood, and steaks, with heavy doses of tomato and garlic. Mexican cooks use thin wheat or corn tortillas as the base for beans, rice, cheese, tomatoes, spicy sauce, meat, and other ingredients. The American-Chinese cuisine offered in Chinatowns is Cantonese with bean sprout chow mein and fried rice. More authentic Chinese dishes can be found with regional variations, from spicy Hunan to rich, meaty Mandarin. Bite-size dim sum (filled dumplings) or any variety of won ton soup make a filling lunch. Japanese, Vietnamese, and Thai food are other easy-to-find Asian cuisines. California's melting pot of cuisines in major cities includes Basque, French, German, Spanish, Cuban, Ethiopian, Salvadorean, and a hundred others.

Perhaps *beignets* or Chinese finger food came first, but America made fast food an international dining experience. Fast food is quick and economical. Food is ordered, paid for, and picked up from a service counter, all within a few minutes. Some fast-food outlets have drive-through service, where the driver pulls up to a window, orders from a posted menu, pays, and gets the meal, all without leaving the vehicle. Hamburgers, hot dogs, tacos, fried chicken, and barbecue beef are common offerings. McDonalds' golden arches and KFC's grinning chubby colonel are easy to spot. Other fast food chains include A & W, Arby's Roast Beef, Burger King, Carl's Jr., Del Taco, Jack-in-the-Box, Pizza Hut, and Taco Bell. All are cheap.

The budget rung of the price ladder includes chain restaurants such as Chevy's (Mexican), Denny's (common along freeways and usually open 24 hours), Fresh Choice (incredible choice of fresh salads, soups, and pastas), Olive Garden (Italian), Red Lobster (seafood), and Sizzler. Denny's are open for breakfast, the others for lunch and dinner only.

A new movement in California is certification of organically grown (without pesticides) produce. Be prepared to pay a premium for these fruits and vegetables.

Gambling

Gambling is illegal in California. Sometimes. The state has a highly advertised lottery, casinos on Indian Reservations, legal poker clubs in many areas, and bingo in Roman Catholic churches everywhere.

Casino gambling is legal in all of Nevada, which depends heavily on Californians driving across the border. The main gambling centers are Las Vegas and Reno, but every Nevada town has slot machines, video poker, and usually at least one casino. The odds *always* favour the house. See Las Vegas (p. 90) and Reno (p. 258) for more specifics.

Health

Hospital emergency rooms are the place to go for life-threatening medical problems. If a life is truly at risk, treatment will be swift and top notch, with payment problems sorted out later. For more mundane problems, 24-hour walk-in health clinics are available in urban areas and many rural communities. Payment, not care, is the problem.

Some form of **health insurance** coverage is almost mandatory in order to ensure provision of health services. Coverage provided by non-US national health plans is *not* accepted by California medical providers. The only way to ensure provision of health services is to carry some proof of valid insurance cover. Most travel agents who deal with international travel will offer travel insurance policies that cover costs in California and the rest of the country – at least $1 million of cover is essential.

Bring enough prescription medication to last the entire trip, plus a few extra days. It's also a good idea to carry a copy of the prescription in case of emergency. Because trade names of drugs vary from country to country, be sure the prescription shows the generic (chemical) name and formulation of the drug, not just a brand name.

No inoculations are required and California is basically a healthy place to visit. Common sense is enough to avoid most health problems. Eat normally (or at least sensibly) and avoid drinking water that didn't come from the tap or a bottle. Most ground water, even in the high Sierras, is contaminated with *giardia* and other intestinal parasites.

Sunglasses, broad brimmed sun hats, and sunscreen help prevent sunburn, sun stroke, and heat prostration. Be sure to drink plenty of non-alcoholic liquids, especially in hot weather.

AIDS (Acquired Immune Deficiency Syndrome) and other sexually transmitted diseases are endemic in California as they are in the rest of the world. The best way to avoid sexually transmitted diseases (or STDs, as they're usually called) is to avoid promiscuous sex or use protection when necessary.

In anything other than long term, strictly monogamous relationships, the key phrase is "safe sex." Use condoms in any kind of sexual intercourse – they're required in the legal brothels of Nevada and *very* strongly encouraged by prostitutes plying the sex trade illegally in California. Condoms can be bought in drug stores, pharmacies and supermarkets, and from vending machines in some public toilets.

Rabies is another endemic problem in California. It's most likely to afflict those who try to hand feed the squirrels, chipmunks, and racoons that haunt many parks, but end up being bitten instead. If bitten by an animal, go to the nearest emergency medical center. You must seek immediate treatment – if left too late rabies is untreatable.

Don't wear shorts for hikes through California's inviting coastal and foothill grasslands or forests. Instead, cover up with long trousers, long sleeved shirts, and insect repellent. The risk of contracting **Lyme Disease** from ticks that thrive in moist climates is rising by the year.

Lyme Disease is frequently misdiagnosed and usually mistaken for rheumatoid arthritis. Typical symptoms include temporary paralysis, arthritic pains in the hand, arm, or leg joints, swollen hands, fever, fatigue, headaches, swollen glands, heart palpitations, and a circular red rash around the bite up to 30 days later. Early treatment with tetracycline and other drugs is nearly 100% effective; late treatment often fails. Symptoms may not appear for three months or longer after the first infected tick bite, but the disease can be detected by a simple blood test.

Hiking

Walking is a favorite outdoor activity, especially in park areas. The same cautions that apply anywhere else are good in California: know the route; carry a map and basic safety gear; carry food and water. It's also wise to stay on marked trails. Wandering off the trail adds to erosion damage, especially in fragile forest and meadow areas. More importantly, many marijuana growers plant their fields off public trails in state and national parks, then guard the hidden growing areas with lethal booby traps or armed wardens.

Lyme Disease (see above) can be avoided by wearing long trousers and sleeves. The most common hiking problem is Poison Oak. This oak-like plant is usually a shrub, sometimes a vine, and always a trailside hazard. Variable leaf shapes make the plant difficult to identify, although the leaves always occur in clusters of three and usually look like rounded oak leaves. Leaves are bright, glossy green in spring and summer, bright red in fall, and dead in winter – but not forgotten.

All parts of the plant, leaves, stems, and flowers, exude a sticky sap that causes an intense allergic reaction in most people. The most common symptoms are red rash, itching, burning, and weeping sores. The best way to avoid the problem is to avoid the plant. Second best is to immediately wash skin or clothing that has come into contact with the plant in hot, soapy water. If you are afflicted, drying lotions such as calamine or products containing cortisone provide temporary relief, but time is the only cure.

Be aware of wildlife in remoter areas. **Mountain lions** (also called bobcats, cougars, and pumas in California) would rather run than attack, but can be vicious if defending a den or accidentally cornered. Avoid hiking alone and never let small children run ahead or fall far behind. If you meet a mountain lion, NEVER try to run or hide – you won't escape and either behavior signals that you're prey. Instead, be aggressive. Stand your ground. Try to appear larger by raising your arms or opening up a jacket. Should the lion approach, shout and throw sticks or stones. Show that you're ready to fight. In the extremely unlikely event that your are attacked, fight with all you've got. Wildcats are endangered species in North America and care should be taken to avoid hitting them while driving.

Bears are a more serious threat. They're large, strong and always hungry. They also understand that where there are humans there is usually food. Parks and campgrounds in bear country have detailed warnings on how to safely store food to avoid attack. When possible, hang anything edible (including toothpaste) in bags well above the ground or store in metal lockers. NEVER feed bears, they won't know when the meal is over. Shouting, banging pots, and throwing stones usually persuades curious bears to look somewhere else for a meal.

Few people in California ever see **snakes** outside a zoo. The only poisonous snake native to California is the rattlesnake, and only a handful of people each year across the entire USA die from rattlesnake bites, usually while trying to catch them. "Rattlers" are harmless if left alone (as all snakes should be). The markings vary with the species, but all have diamond-shaped heads and rattles in their tails. Most, but not all, rattle a warning. In the wild, look where you're walking; don't put hands or feet on ledges which you can't see; and before sitting down, make sure a rattler hasn't already claimed the spot.

Hitchhiking

In an earlier, more trustful era, hitchhiking was the preferred mode of transportation for budget travelers. Today, hitchhiking or picking up hitchhikers is asking for violent trouble, from theft to physical assault and murder. Don't do it.

Insurance

Experienced travelers carry insurance that covers their belongings and holiday investment as well as their bodies. Travel insurance should include provision for cancelled or delayed flights and weather problems, as well as emergency evacuation home in case of medical emergency. Thomas Cook and other travel agencies offer comprehensive policies. Medical cover should be high – at least $1 million. Insurance for drivers is covered in more detail in the "Driving in California" chapter, p. 32.

Language

English is the official language in California, but recently arrived immigrants speak dozens of languages. Spanish, Chinese (both Cantonese and Mandarin), Tagalog, and Vietnamese are spoken widely and often used on neighborhood billboards and in other advertising. Some hotels have bilingual signs in English/Spanish or English/Japanese.

How to Talk Californian

Alternate Means "alternative," not every other – sometimes a source of confusion when reading timetables.

Bed & breakfast Overnight lodging in a private home, usually with private facilities and almost always more expensive than nearby hotels and motels.

Buffalo wings Chicken wings, usually fried and served with a spicy sauce as an appetizer or bar food.

California cuisine Anything the chef wants it to be, as long as it's expensive, but usually based on fresh, organically grown foods.

Chili dog or *chili burger* Hot dog or hamburger covered with chili, onions, and cheese.

Chimichanga A pseudo-Mexican concoction of a fried tortilla filled with meat, beans, cheese, tomatoes, and lettuce.

Chips Usually made from potatoes, but in California they are often made from corn, taro, casava, rice, or other starches.

Corn dog Hot dog dipped in corn meal and fried. Usually served hot on a stick.

Dead head Fans of the band the Grateful Dead; also a term for hippies.

Designer water Pejorative term for bottled water.

Fajitas A Mexican dish, strips of grilled meat (beef, chicken, or pork) and grilled vegetables rolled in a hot tortilla.

(French) fries Deep-fried potatoes, cut into wedges, curls, flat ovals, waffles, or thin strips. Many local California eateries cook them with spicy Cajun flavoring.

Heart Smart Usually refers to foods in stores or restaurants that are low in cholestrol and/or fat.

Holiday A public holiday, such as Labor Day, not a private holiday, which is a *vacation.*

Lodging The usual term for accommodations.

Natural ingredients Food that has been grown, processed, and prepared without pesticides or other chemical additives.

Road kill Literally, animals killed by passing cars, but usually used to describe bad restaurant food.

Rug rat A small child.

Tailgate party A picnic, usually at a football game, held in the stadium parking lot.

YOUR RENTAL CAR AWAITS IN THE STATES.

Rent for three or more days, get one of the days

Free.

Compact through luxury cars.
Promo code: FCQ
UNLIMITED MILEAGE.

Budget® Rent a Car has more than 1,100 locations in the U.S., including over 120 in California alone. And with great rates on a wide variety of cars, you can drive whatever you want, wherever you want.

For reservations or information, contact your travel consultant or your local Budget reservation center. In the U.K., call Budget at **0800-181-181.**

FAR AND AWAY A BETTER DECISION.

HERE ARE SOME DETAILS YOU SHOULD KNOW: Mention promotion code **FCQ** when you reserve a compact through luxury size car for three or more days, and receive one day free. Offer is valid at participating U.S. Budget locations through December 15, 1995, and is subject to vehicle availability. Car must be returned to renting location, except in some metro areas. Local rental and age requirements apply. Discount applies to time and mileage only and is not available in conjunction with any other discount, promotional offer, or other special rate period. Offer will be prorated against the rate charges for the entire rental period. For example, a 10% discount will be applied on a 10-day rental. Refuelling services, taxes and optional items are extra. Additional driver, underage driver, and other surcharges are extra. Blackout dates may apply.

Advertisement

Even Californian English can cause visitors a few difficulties. A selection of commonly encountered terms that may be unfamiliar or have a different meaning are set out in the box on page 21. The next chapter, "Driving in California," also provides a glossary of driving terms for the non-US driver.

Luggage

Less is more where luggage is concerned. Porters don't exist outside the most expensive hotels and baggage carts are rare. Carts are free for international arrivals in San Francisco and Los Angeles, but must be rented in US currency everywhere else – even though there is no "bureau de change" until after customs and immigration. Luggage has to be light enough to carry. The transatlantic luggage allowance (scheduled flights) is two pieces, each of 70 lb (32 kg) maximum, per person.

Luggage must also fit in the car or other form of transport around California. Americans buy the same smaller cars as the rest of the world, not the enormous "boats" of the 1960s. If it won't fit in the trunk at home, don't count on being able to cram it into a Californian car.

Maps

The best all-around maps are produced by the **American Automobile Association** and distributed through its two California affiliates, the California State Automobile Association (northern and central California and Nevada) and the Automobile Association of Southern California (southern California). All three are known simply as AAA ("Triple A"). State, regional, county, and city maps are available free at all AAA offices, but only to members. Fortunately, most automobile clubs around the world have reciprocal agreements with AAA to provide maps and other member services. Be prepared to show a membership card to obtain service.

Rand McNally road maps and atlases are probably the best known of the ranges available outside the United States, in the travel section of bookshops and more specialist outlets.

The most detailed road maps available are produced by **Thomas Brothers**, tel: (800) 432-8430. Wire-bound Thomas Brothers maps are sold at most booksellers and larger airport shops around the state.

The possibilities are more confusing for back-country travel. **US Geological Survey** quadrangle (topographic) maps show terrain reliably, but **US Forest Service** maps, touted as the ultimate off-road guide, are often out of date because trails and logging roads come and go with alarming frequency. Even with the best of maps in hand, getting lost in the wilderness is a genuine possibility. If you are thinking of driving off the beaten track, always carry a topographic map and compass in addition to any other maps and guides. **Sierra Club** and **Wilderness Press** publish the most up-to-date and reliable back country maps and guides. Outdoor supply stores and good booksellers carry maps.

Before leaving civilization behind, compare every available map for discrepancies, then check with national forest or park personnel. Most are experienced back country enthusiasts themselves, and since they're responsible for rescuing lost hikers, they have a vested interest in dispensing the best possible information and advice.

Meeting People

Californians are friendly. However, this friendliness does not extend to inviting new acquaintances to their homes. Professional associations, sports clubs or interest clubs welcome visitors from abroad; contact well in advance for meeting times and venues. In the San Francisco Bay area, the **International Diplomacy Council**, *312 Sutter St, San Francisco, CA 94108; tel: (415) 986-1388* offers business and professional connections with some sightseeing and hospitality, for a fee, with in-person screening. Contact one month in advance. Sports events, casual restaurants, and bars can be meeting places, but most local people are wary of approaches by strangers.

California's melting pot and relatively liberal lifestyle let some locals indulge in colorful clothing and flamboyant jewelry. Be as cool as they are, and don't stare – a fixed or shocked stare is considered rude. Californians are very sensitive to comments about ethnicity and gender.

Opening Hours

Office hours are generally 9 AM–5 PM, Mon–Fri, although a few tourist offices also keep short Saturday hours. Most banks and other financial institutions are open 10 AM–4 PM Mon–Thur, 10 AM–6 PM on Fri, and 9 AM–1 PM Sat. ATMs are open 24 hours.

Small shops keep standard business hours. Large stores and shopping centers open at 9 AM or 10 AM Mon–Sat and close at 8 PM or 9 PM. Opening hours are slightly shorter on Sunday.

Many restaurants, museums, and legitimate theatres close on Monday, but most tourist attractions are open seven days a week.

Parks Information

For information on specific national and state parks, monuments, and seashores, see the appropriate description among the recommended routes throughout this book. For general information on National Parks, Monuments, and Seashore areas, contact the **National Parks of the West**, *Western Region Information Center, Fort Mason, Bldg. 201, San Francisco CA 94123, tel: (415) 556-0650.* For **California State Parks and Beaches** information, contact *State of California, Department of Parks and Recreation, PO Box 942896, Sacramento, CA 94296-0001, tel: (916) 653-6995 or (916) 445-6477*, Mon–Fri, 8 AM–5 PM. For reservations at most parks, beaches, and monuments, call **MISTIX**, *PO Box 85705, San Diego, CA 92188-5706; tel: (800) 444-7275, or (619) 452-1950* from outside the continental United States.

There is a charge for entry to national, state, and some regional parks. State parks charge daily use fees; national parks and monuments charge weekly fees. Campground fees are almost always additional. In winter, some state parks may not require fees.

Senior and disabled persons should ask if discounts apply. If visiting more than four or five national parks, monuments, or historical sites for which entrance fees are charged, purchase a **Golden Eagle Passport** for $25, which covers the holder and one other person. Blind and disabled travelers can obtain a free-of-charge

Golden Access Passport on arrival.

Passports and Visas

All non-US citizens must have a valid full passport (not a British Visitor's Passport) and, except for Canadians, a visa, in order to enter the United States. Citizens of most countries must obtain a visa from the US Embassy in their country of residence in advance of arrival. In the UK, Thomas Cook's Passport and Visa section – accessible via local Thomas Cook branches – can advise on and obtain US visas (which last the life of your passport).

British Citizens and New Zealand citizens can complete a visa waiver form, which they generally receive with their air tickets if the airline is a "participating carrier." Provided nothing untoward is declared such as a previous entry refusal or a criminal conviction, which would make application for a full visa mandatory, the waiver exempts visitors from the need for a visa for stays of up to 90 days. It also allows a sidetrip overland into Mexico or Canada and a return.

Note: Documentation regulations change frequently and are complex for some nationalities; confirm your requirements with a good travel agent or the nearest US Embassy at least 90 days before you plan to depart.

Police

To telephone police in an emergency, dial 911. There are many different police jurisdictions within California, each with its own force. The roads are patrolled by the California Highway Patrol (CHP). See also under "Security" on the next page and "Police" in the next chapter, "Driving in California."

Postal Services

Every town has a least one post office. Hours vary, although all are open Mon–Fri, morning and afternoon. Postal Service branches may be open Saturday or even Sunday. Some big hotels sell stamps through the concierge; large department stores may have a post office; and supermarkets such as Safeway sell stamps at the checkout counter. Some stamp machines are installed in stores, but a surcharge may be included in the cost. For philatelic sales, check major city telephone directories under US Postal Service.

Mail everything going overseas as Air Mail. If posting international letters near an urban area, mail should take about one week. Add a day or two if mailing from remote areas.

Poste Restante is available at any post office, without charge. Mail should be addressed in block lettering to your name, Poste Restante/General Delivery, city, state, post office's zip (postal) code, and United States of America (do not abbreviate). Mail is held for 30 days at the post office branch that handles General Delivery for each town or city, usually at the main office. Main General Delivery zip codes include:

    Los Angeles: 90086
    San Francisco: 94142
    San Diego: 92138
    Las Vegas: 89450
    Reno: 89501

Identification is required for mail pickup.

Public Holidays

America's love affair with the road extends to jumping in the automobile for holiday weekends. Local celebrations, festivals, parades, or neighborhood parties can disrupt some or all activities in town. In some areas, for example, children are on school break for the Chinese Lunar New Year or Cinco de Mayo (5 May). The following list of public holidays includes California and Nevada state days:

New Year (1 Jan); Martin Luther King Jr Day (third Monday in Jan); Lincoln's Birthday (12 Feb); Presidents' Day (third Monday in Feb); Easter (Sunday in Mar/Apr); Memorial Day (last Monday in May); US Independence Day (4 Jul); Labor Day (first Monday in Sept); California Admission Day (9 Sep); Columbus Day or Indigenous Peoples Day (second Monday in Oct); Nevada Day (31 Oct); Veterans Day (11 Nov); Thanksgiving Day (last Thursday in Nov); and Christmas (25 Dec).

Post offices and government offices close on public holidays. Some businesses take the day off, though department and discount stores use the opportunity to hold huge sales, well advertised in local newspapers. Gas stations remain open. Small shops and some grocery stores close or curtail hours.

Call in advance before visiting an attraction on a holiday as there are frequently special hours. National and state park campsites and lodging must be reserved in advance for all holidays. Accommodations may be discounted on Easter, Thanksgiving, and Christmas because most people stay at home or with family or friends on these days. Other holidays are "mobile" for Americans, so book early. The most festive holiday is 4 July, Independence Day, when most cities have public firework displays.

Sales Taxes

There is no Value Added Tax or Goods and Services Tax in California or Nevada. Both states charge sales tax for most products and services, itemized separately on every bill. In California, food products, newspapers and prescription drugs are not sales taxable. California sales tax ranges from 7.25% to 8.5%, depending on the locality. Nevada's general sales tax rate is 6.75%; 7% in Las Vegas.

Security

Throwing caution to the winds is foolhardy anytime, and even more so on vacation. The United States, by history and inclination, permits guns to circulate, both legally and illegally. Dial 911 on any telephone for free emergency assistance from police, fire and medical authorities.

Traveling Safely

Never publicly discuss travel plans or money or valuables you are carrying. Use caution in large cities, towns, and rural areas. Drive, park, and walk only in well-lit areas. If unsure of roads or weather ahead, stop for the evening and find secure lodging. Sightsee with a known companion, or in a group. Solo travel, in urban areas or in the countryside, is not recommended.

The best way to avoid becoming a victim of theft or bodily injury is to walk with assurance and try to give the impression that you are not worth robbing (e.g., do not wear or carry expensive jewelery or flash rolls of banknotes). Use a hidden money-belt for your valuables, travel documents, and spare cash. Carrying a wallet in a back pocket or leaving a handbag open is an invitation to every pickpocket in the vicinity. In all public places, take precautions – use a handbag with a crossed shoulderstrap and zip, wind the strap of your camera case around your chair or place your handbag firmly between your feet under the table while you eat.

Never leave luggage unattended. At airports, security officials may confiscate unattended luggage as a possible bomb. In public toilets, handbags and small luggage has been snatched from hooks, or from under stalls. Airports, bus, and train stations usually have lockers. Most work with keys; take care to guard the key and memorize the locker number. Hotel bell staff may keep luggage for one or more days on request, and for a fee – be sure and get receipts for left luggage before surrendering it.

Concealing a weapon is against the law. Some defensive products resembling tear gas are legal only for persons certified in their proper use. Mugging, by individuals or gangs, is a social problem in the United States. If you are attacked, it is safer to let go of your bag or hand over the small amount of obvious money – as you are more likely to be attacked physically if the thief meets with resistance. *Never resist.* Report incidents immediately to local police, even if it is only to get a copy of their report for your insurance company.

Driving Safely

Have car rental counter personnel recommend a safe, direct route on a clear map before you leave with the vehicle. Lock all valuables and luggage in the trunk or glove compartment so that nothing is visible to passersby or other drivers. Don't leave maps, brochures, or guide-books in evidence – why advertise that you're a stranger in town?

Always keep car doors and windows locked. Do not venture into unlighted areas, neighbor-hoods that look seedy, or off paved roads. Be leery about stopping if told by a passing motorist or pedestrian that something is wrong with your car, or if someone signals for help with a broken-down car. If you need to stop, do so only in well-lit or populated areas, even if your car is bumped from behind by another vehicle. If your car breaks down, turn on the flashing emergency lights, and if it is safe to get out, raise the hood and return to the vehicle. Do not split passengers up. Freeway telephone call boxes are normally spaced one-half mile apart. Lights on emergency vehicles are red or red and blue, so do not stop for flashing white lights or flashing headlights. Ask directions only from police, at a well-lit business area, or at a service station.

At night, have keys ready to unlock car doors before entering a parking lot. Check the surrounding area and inside the vehicle before entering. Never pick up hitchhikers, and never leave the car with the engine running. Take all valuables with you.

Sleeping Safely

When sleeping rough, in any sort of dormitory, train, or open campground, the safest place for your small valuables is at the bottom of your sleepingbag. In sleeping cars, padlock your luggage to the seat, and ask the attendant to show you how to lock a compartment door at night. If in doubt, it's best to take luggage with you. Be particularly conscious of your luggage and surroundings around airports and train and bus stations.

In hotels, motels, and all other lodging, lock all door locks from the inside. Check that all windows are locked, including sliding glass doors. Ground-floor rooms, while convenient, mean easier access by criminals intent on breaking in. Never leave the room at night without leaving a light on. Lights deter prowlers, and when you return, any disturbance to room contents will be visible.

Use the peephole to check before admitting anyone to your room. If someone claims to be on the hotel staff or a repair person, do not let the person in before phoning the office or front desk to verify the person's name and job. Money, checks, credit cards, passports, and keys should be with you, or secured in your hotel's safe deposit box. When checking in, find the most direct route from your room to fire escapes, elevators, stairwells, and the nearest telephone

Documents

Take a few passport photos with you and photocopy the important pages and any visa stamps in your passport. Store these safely, together with a note of the numbers of your travelers checks, credit cards, and insurance documents (keep them separate from the documents themselves). If you are unfortunate enough to be robbed, you will at least have some identification, and replacing the documents will be much easier. Apply to your nearest consulate (see "Consulates" in this chapter for addresses and phone numbers).

Shopping

Uniquely Californian souvenirs include California wines; tins of almonds; dates and other dried fruits; prepared mustards, oils, and condiments; sourdough French bread from San Francisco; and the ubiquitous t-shirts. Clothing can be a bargain, particularly at discount or factory outlet stores. Cameras and other photo equipment can be a fraction of UK prices, but do your homework on prices before you go, and shop around when you arrive.

Audiotapes cassettes, blank videotapes, CDs, computer programs, and CD-ROMs sold in the United States can be used anywhere in the world; most other electrical appliances use 110 volt 60 hertz current, not 220 v 50 hz power. One exception is battery-operated equipment such as radios, cameras, and portable computers.

For more information on electrical goods, see "Electricity" in this chapter.

Smoking

Lighting up is out in public buildings and on public transportation. All flights in the United States are nonsmoking, and some rental cars are designated as nonsmoking. Most hotels/motels set aside nonsmoking rooms or floors; Bed and breakfast establishments are almost all non-smoking. Restaurant dining regulations vary by locality; some forbid all smoking; others permit

it in the bars or lounges only; some have a percentage of the eatery devoted to smokers. Smoking is prohibited in most stores and shops. Always ask before lighting a cigarette, cigar, or pipe. When in doubt, go outside to smoke.

Solo Travel

Whether in urban or rural areas, it's always safer to travel with a companion. If you do choose to travel alone, always be aware of your surroundings and, as in any situation, use good judgement.

Telephones

The US telephone system is divided into local and long-distance carriers. Depending on the time of day and day of the week, it may be cheaper to call New York than to call 30 miles (48 km) away. After 5 PM Mon–Fri, and all weekend, rates are lower. Useful phone numbers are provided throughout this book.

Public telephones are everywhere, indicated by a sign with a white telephone receiver depicted on a blue background. Enclosed booths and wall-mounted or free-standing machines are all used. If possible, use public phones in well-lighted, busy public areas.

Dialing instructions are in the front of the local white pages telephone directory. For all long-distance calls, precede the area code with a 1. In emergencies, call 911 for police, medical, or fire department response. Dialing 0 reaches an operator. For local number information, dial 411. For long-distance phone information, dial 1, the area code, then 555-1212. There is a charge for information calls.

Pay phones take coins, and a local call costs from $0.20–$0.25 or more. An operator or computer voice will come online to ask for additional coins when needed. Most hotels and motels add a stiff surcharge to the basic cost of a call, so find a public telephone in the lobby.

Prepaid phone cards are a novelty in the United States and not widely available. Before you travel, ask your local phone company if your phone card will work in America. The United States has the cheapest overseas phone rates in the world, which makes it cheaper to fill pay phones with quarters than to reverse charges.

Also ask your phone company if your calling card will work to phone home. A credit card may be convenient, but only economical if you pay the bill immediately.

For comparison, local call rates:
coin $0.20–0.25
direct dial, calling card $0.35
operator-assisted, calling card $0.95

800 numbers are toll-free. Like all long-distance numbers, the 800 area code must be preceded by a 1, as in 1-800-123-4567. Some US telephone numbers are given in letters, as in 1-800-2LA-RIDE. Telephone keys have both numbers and letters, so find the corresponding letter and depress that key. A few numbers have more than seven letters to finish a business name. Not to worry, US or Canadian phone numbers never require more than seven numerals, plus three for the area code.

Dial an international operator on 00 for enquiries or assistance.

For international dialing, dial 011-country code-city code (omitting the first 0 if there is one)-local number; e.g., to call Great Britain, Inner London, from the States, dial: 011-44-171-local number. Some country codes:

Australia 61
New Zealand 64
Republic of Ireland 353
South Africa 27
United Kingdom 44

Time

California, Nevada, and Baja California (Tijuana) share a time zone, GMT –8 hrs, called Pacific

TIME IN CALIFORNIA (PST)	8 AM	12 NOON	5 PM	12 MIDNIGHT
TIME IN				
Auckland	4 AM	8 AM	1 PM	8 PM
Cape Town	6 PM	10 PM	3 AM	10 AM
Dublin	4 PM	8 PM	1 AM	8 AM
London	4 PM	8 PM	1 AM	8 AM
Mexico City	10 AM	2 PM	7 PM	2 AM
Sydney	2 AM	6 AM	11 AM	6 PM
Toronto	11 AM	3 PM	8 PM	3 AM

Standard Time (PST). From the first Sunday in April until the last Sunday in October, California pushes clocks forward to Pacific Daylight Time (PDT), GMT –7 hrs.

Tipping

Acknowledgment for good service should not be extorted. That said, tipping is a fact of life, to get, to repeat, or to thank someone for service.

Service charges are not customarily added to restaurant bills. Waiters and waitresses expect a tip of 15% to 20% of the bill before taxes are added on. In luxury restaurants, also be prepared to tip the maitre d' and sommelier a few dollars, up to 10% of the bill. Bartenders expect the change from a drink, up to several dollars.

Hotel porters generally receive $1 per bag; a bellperson who shows you to the room expects several dollars; in luxury properties, tip more. Room service delivery staff should be tipped 10–15% of the tariff before taxes, unless there's a service charge indicated on the bill. Expect to hand out dollars for most services that involve room delivery.

Some hotels will have a chambermaid name card placed in the room: it's a hint for a tip of a few dollars upon your departure, but never required. Ushers in theaters, arenas, and stadiums are not tipped; cinemas seldom have ushers, nor are tips expected.

Nevada casino personnel survive on tips. If you're successful, tip the dealer or croupier between hands, throws of the dice, or spins of the wheel with a few chips. A slot machine changeperson likes a small percentage of the pay off. Long-term keno players should tip runners an occasional $1.

Unless holding reserved show seats, $5–20 to the maitre d' should get better seats. If you're not happy with the original seats, indicate a preference and proffer a discreet $5–20 bill before sitting down, depending on the number in your party and the expense and popularity of the show. Showroom waiters expect $5–10 per couple or party for a cocktails show; $10–20 for a dinner show.

Toilets

There is nothing worse than not being able to find one! *Restroom* or *bathroom* are the common terms; *toilet* is acceptable; few people recognize *WC*. Most are marked with a figure for a male or a female; *Men* and *women* are the most common terms, though *caballeros* (or *señors*) and *damas* may be used in Spanish-speaking areas. Occasionally, a restroom may be used by both sexes.

Facilities vary from clean and well-equipped to filthy. Most businesses, including bars and restaurants, reserve restrooms for clients. Gas stations provide keys for customers to access restrooms. Public toilets are sporadically placed, but well marked. Parks and roadside rest stops have toilet facilities.

Tourist Information

To obtain information about traveling in California or Nevada, contact state tourism offices directly. To ensure that you'll get the information in time, make your requests well in advance. **California Trade and Commerce Agency**, *Division of Tourism, 801 K St, Ste 1600, Sacramento, CA 95814, tel: (916) 322-2881, fax: (916) 322-3402.* **Nevada Commission on Tourism**, *PO Box 30032, Reno, NV 89520, tel: (800) 638-2328.*

The US Tourism and Travel Administration (USTTA) maintains offices abroad, but serves the entire United States, and is often unresponsive to enquiries.

The State of California does not maintain tourism offices abroad. Write directly to: **California Division of Tourism** (address above). This book also gives addresses and telephone numbers of tourism offices in regions, cities, and towns along specific routes.

Trains

AMTRAK is the official passenger train transportation company in the United States, *tel: (800)-872-7245.* Main California routes run from Emeryville (near Oakland – bus connection to San Francisco) through Sacramento to Reno and beyond; along the coastal route north from Los Angeles through Emeryville to Oregon (and as far as Seattle); and from Los Angeles to San Diego. Trains do not stop at each town en route, so check if there is a stop at your destination. Seats may be reserved for an additional fee. CalTrain runs a commuter service from San Francisco to San Jose.

Train times for many AMTRAK and local services are published in the *Thomas Cook Overseas Timetable* (see under "Useful Reading" in this chapter).

AMTRAK sells a Far West Rail Pass, which gives 15 or 30 days of unlimited train travel on their system in California (and other Western states) at prices ranging approximately from $170–250. This is available from Thomas Cook and other international travel agencies.

The **California State Railroad Museum**, *111 I St, Old Sacramento, CA 95814, tel: (916) 448-4466* has an exquisitely restored collection of engines and railway cars from all eras. Tourist trains operate in California, but none provide regular transportation services. Service may be restricted by snow or high season, or offer only weekend service. **Napa Valley Wine Train**, *1275 McKinstry St, Napa, CA 94559, tel: (800) 427-4124,* offers dining in a 1917 Pullman Dining Car along the valley's heartland. **Roaring Camp & Big Trees Narrow Gauge Railroad**, *PO Box G-1, Felton, Santa Cruz County, CA 95018, tel: (408) 335-4484,* is a steam train through coastal redwoods, and **Santa Cruz, Big Trees, and Pacific Railway Company** (same contact information), is a broad-gauge, early 20th-century train from Roaring Camp in the redwoods to the seaside Santa Cruz Boardwalk. **Sacramento Rail Tours**, *Central Pacific Railroad Freight Depot, Front St, Old Sacramento, CA 95814, tel: (916) 445-4902,* conducts steam trains along the Sacramento River. On the **San Diego Railroad Museum Classic Train Ride**, *Santa Fe Depot, 1050 Kettner Blvd, San Diego,CA 92101, tel: (619) 595-3030,* has steam or diesel locomotives that depart from Campo in eastern San Diego County for Miller Creek, 8 miles (13km) away. **Sierra Railway** (Railtown 1897), *5th Ave, Jamestown, CA 95327, tel: (209) 984-3953,* runs a Gold Country steam train through the Sierra Nevada Foothills. The yellow **Skunk Train**, *California*

Western Railroad, PO Box 907, Ft. Bragg, CA 95437, tel: (707) 964-6371, is a Mendocino County diesel and steam logging locomotive with open observation cars. **Yosemite Mt Sugar Pine Railroad**, 56001 Hwy 41, Fish Camp, CA 93623, tel: (209) 683-7273, is steam-powered, just south of Yosemite National Park.

Travel Arrangements

Given that most of the world's international airlines fly into either Los Angeles or San Francisco, and the ease of renting cars at airports, California is an ideal destination for independently minded travelers. However, the many types of air ticket and the range of temporary deals available on the busy routes make it advisable to talk to your travel agent before booking, to get the best bargain.

In fact, taking a fly-drive package such as one of Thomas Cook's own, or one of the many others offered by airlines and tour operators, is usually more economical than making all your own arrangements. All include the air ticket and car hire element; some also follow set itineraries that enable them to offer guaranteed and prepaid en route accommodations at selected hotels. Programs such as Thomas Cook's America Fly-Drive or American Options allow the flexibility of booking the airline ticket at an advantageous rate and then choosing from a "menu" of other items, often at a discounted price, such as car rental, hotel coupons (which prepay accommodations but do not guarantee availability of rooms) and other extras such as excursions.

Useful Reading

Most international guidebook series feature a volume on California. *Thomas Cook Travellers: California*, by Robert Holmes, is available in bookstores in the UK (price £6.99), and in Ireland, Canada, Australia, New Zealand, and South Africa. In the USA the same title is available in the *Passport's Illustrated Guides* series, price $12.95.

Other useful Thomas Cook publications, if you are considering using trains or buses for any part of your trip, are the *Thomas Cook Overseas* *Timetable* (published every 2 months, £7.90 per issue) and the annual *Thomas Cook North American Rail and Bus Guide* (£6.95). (For more details of Thomas Cook publications see p. 63.)

If you are arranging your own accommodations as you travel, a comprehensive guide such as the *AAA Tourbook for California and Nevada* or one of the *Mobil Regional Guides* can often be obtained through specialist travel bookshops outside the USA.

Books you can buy in California include:

Automobile Club of Southern California regional guides: *Desert Area*; *Santa Barbara County*; *San Luis Obispo County*; *San Diego County*.

AAA A Photo Journey to San Francisco, by Maxine Cass, 1991, American Automobile Association, Heathrow, FL.

Adventuring in the California Desert, by Lynne Foster, 1987, Sierra Club Books, San Francisco.

Backroad Wineries of Northern California, by Bill Gleeson, 1994, Chronicle Books, San Francisco.

Backroad Wineries of Southern California, by Bill Gleeson, 1994, Chronicle Books, San Francisco.

The Best of the Gold Country, by Don & Betty Martin, 1992, Pine Cone Press, Columbia, CA.

California Road Atlas & Driver's Guide, 1994, Thomas Brothers Maps, Irvine, CA.

Northern California Handbook, by Kim Weir, 1994, Moon Publications, Inc., Chico, CA.

On Tap, by Steve Johnson, 1993, WBR Publications, PO Box 71, Clemson, SC 29633; tel: (803) 654-3360.

The Painted Ladies Guide to Victorian California, by Elizabeth Pomada and Michael Larsen, 1991, Dutton Studio Books, New York.

Park Guide, by Ariel Rubissow, 1990, Golden Gate National Park Association, San Francisco.

Roadside Geology of Northern California, by David Alt and Donald Hyndman, 1993, Mountain Press Publishing Co., PO Box 2399, Missoula, MT 59806; tel: (406) 728-1900.

San Diego on Foot, by Carol Mendel, 1990, Carol Mendel, PO Box 6022, San Diego, CA 92106.

Unknown California, ed. by Jonathan Eisen & David Fine, 1985, Collier Books, New York.

Wine Country California, by Sunset Books & Sunset Magazine, current edition, Lane Publishing Co., Menlo Park, Ca.

Wine Country: A History of the Napa Valley, by William Heintz, 1990, Capra Press, Santa Barbara.

For the techno-literati: CD-ROM *California Travel*, by Lee Foster, 1992, Ebook, Inc., *32970 Alvarado-Niles Rd, #704, Union City CA 94587; tel: (510) 429-1331.*

Weights and Measures

Officially, the United States is converting to the metric system. In truth, few people have changed. (A few road signs show both miles and kilometers.) The non-metric US measures are the same as Imperial measures except for fluids, where US gallons and quarts are five-sixths of their Imperial equivalents.

l foot	= 0.304 meters
l mile	= 1.6093 kilometers
l acre	= 0.4047 hectares
1 sq mile	= 2.59 sq km
1 ounce	= 28.35 gram
1 pound	= 0.4536 kilogram
1 US quart	= 0.94635 liters
1 US gallon	= 3.7854 liters
	= 0.83 imperial gallons

Temperature conversion:

$$°C \times 9/5 + 32 = °F$$
$$°F - 32 \times 5/9 = °C$$

What to Take

Absolutely everything you could ever need is available in California, so don't worry if you've left anything behind. California prices aren't much different than prices in other parts of the country, though they may be on the higher end of the range. It's a good idea to prepare a small first aid kit before you leave home with tried and tested insect repellent, sunscreen cream, and moisturizing lotion. Carry all medicines, glasses, and contraceptives with you, and keep duplicate prescriptions or a letter from your doctor to verify your need for a particular medication.

Other useful items to bring or buy immediately upon arrival are a waterbottle, sunglasses, a hat or visor with a rim, a Swiss Army pocket knife, a flashlight, a padlock for locking luggage, a money belt, a travel adapter, rope for a clothes line, an alarm clock, and a camera. Those planning to rough it should take a sleeping bag, a rain jacket, and plenty of layers in case it gets cold. Allow a little extra space in luggage for souvenirs.

DRIVING in CALIFORNIA

Accidents and Breakdowns

Holidays should be trouble-free, yet **breakdowns** can occur. Pull off to the side of the road where visibility is good and you are out of the way of traffic. Turn on the emergency flashers or turn signals, and, if it is safe, get out and raise the bonnet. Change a tyre only out of the traffic flow.

Dial 911 on any telephone to reach highway patrol, police, fire, or medical services. Emergency call boxes are placed about every half-mile on highways. Report your phone number, location, problem, and need for first aid.

Earthquakes are a rare but potentially devastating driving hazard – see p. 17 for specific advice.

If involved in a **collision**, stop. Call the California Highway Patrol (CHP) or police if there are injuries or physical damage to either vehicle. Show police and involved driver(s) your driver's licence, car registration, car insurance coverage, address and contact information. Other drivers should provide you the same information.

Collisions have to be reported to your car hire company. Injuries or death must be reported to the police or CHP within 24 hours. Collisions with injuries or death or accidents resulting in more than $500 in property damage to any vehicle must also be reported to the California Department of Motor Vehicles (DMV) within 10 days (report in person – local DMV offices are listed in the phone book).

Fly-drive travellers should bear in mind the effects of **jet-lag** on driver safety. This can be a very real problem. The best way to minimise it is to spend the first night after arrival in a hotel at the airport or in the city and pick up your hire vehicle the next day, rather than take the car on the road within hours of getting off the plane.

Car Hire

Hiring a car or RV (camper) gives you the freedom of the road with a vehicle you can leave behind after a few weeks. Whether booking a fly-drive package with an agency or making independent arrangements, plan well in advance to ensure you get the type and size of vehicle your heart desires. Free, unlimited mileage is common with cars, less so with RVs.

Sheer volume in airport rental car turnover means that in the USA it's usually cheaper to pick up the vehicle from an airport than from a downtown site, and to return it to the airport. A surcharge (called a drop fee) may be levied if you drop the car off in a different location from the place of hire. When considering an RV, ask about one-way and off-season rates.

You will need a valid credit card as security for the vehicle's value. Before you leave the hire agency, ensure that you have all documentation for the hire, that the car registration is in the glove box, and you understand how to operate the vehicle. For RVs, also get instruction books

---

Budget Rent a Car

Thomas Cook Publishing is pleased to be associated with Budget Rent a Car in the publication of this book.

Budget welcomes you to California with affordable rates and an exceptional variety of vehicles and services. With over 100 locations in California and over 1000 in the United States, you are never far from Budget Rent a Car.

To get the best out of your Budget rental, please observe the advice given in this chapter.

For reservations or information, contact the nearest Budget office or call toll-free 1-800-527-0700.

Don't forget to take advantage of the **Free Day** offer, exclusively for readers of this book, announced on p. 22.

---

and a complete demonstration of all systems and appliances and how they interconnect. Avoid hiring a car that exhibits a hire company name on a window decal, on the fender (bumper), or on licence plate frames. It's advertising for criminal attention.

Car size terminology varies, but general categories range from small and basic to all-frills posh: sub-compact, compact, economy, mid-size or intermediate, full-size or standard, and luxury. Sub-compacts are rarely available. Expect to choose between two- or four-door models. The larger the car, the faster it accelerates and consumes petrol. Some vehicles are equipped with four-wheel drive (4WD), unnecessary except for off-road driving (not covered in this book).

Standard features on US hire cars usually include automatic transmission, air conditioning (a necessity for summer and desert driving) and cruise control, which sets speeds for long-distance highway driving, allowing the driver to take feet off the accelerator.

Difficult Driving

Deserts

Tackling a desert is like approaching a snowy mountain: preparation is crucial. Insist that your car has air conditioning and a good heater. Winter in California and Nevada deserts is cold, and high deserts may get significant snow and rain. By February or March, daytime temperatures are high; in June, occasional thunderstorms unleash torrents of rain. Most of the time, deserts sizzle in the daytime. Plan to arrive at your desert lodging or campsite well before dark. Temperatures plummet after dark.

Basic precautions include making sure that the car's engine and cooling system are in good working order, tyres properly inflated, and the petrol tank filled. All travellers should carry extra water, snacks, a torch, and warm clothing in case of trouble.

If the car breaks down on a freeway, pull off and raise the bonnet. One person should walk to the nearest yellow emergency telephone, usually no more than ½ mile (1 km) away, call for help, then return to the car to wait. All other passengers should stay with the car until help arrives. Not only is the car likely to be the only shade within sight, but breakdown lorries will be looking for a stranded car, not a person walking along the freeway.

Carry at least 2–4 litres of bottled drinking water for each person in the car. If you're stranded or need to replenish a hiking water-bottle, the water will seem like gold. A warm sleeping-bag may come in handy should you need to camp out unexpectedly. If stranded in the desert (or mountains), stay with your vehicle – airborne searchers can spot a car or RV far more easily than a person.

Sandstorms can reduce visibility to nil. Pull over and park until the storm has passed in a spot above the surrounding terrain. RV drivers are sometimes tempted to park along the sides of the road or in dried-out river beds called washes. This is not safe. One of the worst hazards is the gullywasher, a sudden rainstorm which creates flash floods, washing down the river and carrying with it anything not cemented in place. In the national parks, always check with a warden for safe camping areas.

If venturing in the desert, have a sunscreen cream, sunscreen lip protection, lotion for dry skin, sunglasses, a hat and clothes that can be worn in layers. Also take a backpack to carry documents, water-bottle, snacks and extra clothes. Long underwear will be welcome in winter.

Skin can burn even in the desert winter; wear long trousers for comfort. Sandals risk footburn and are vulnerable to rattlesnakes and scorpions, both widespread in Western deserts. When hiking, wear comfortable boots with good traction.

Fog

Fog is frequent in some areas of California. In the Central Valley, locals call the impenetrable ground fog *tule fog*. It's treacherous to drive in, and results in several chain-reaction mass accidents each year. Never use bright lights in fog: it will blind oncoming drivers as well as anyone in front of you. Use low-beam headlights instead. Driving with parking lights only is illegal.

Winter

The Sierra Nevada Mountains are a formidable barrier, and never more so than during winter snowstorms. Visibility can be nil due to high winds and blowing snow. Some mountain passes simply close for the season (e.g. Tioga Pass in Yosemite National Park and the road through Lassen National Park). To find out whether California roads are open, subject to imminent closure, or require chains on vehicles, *tel: (800) 427-7623* for recorded information. Have the freeway and highway numbers along the proposed route ready, and enter them in sequence. For **Northern Nevada (Reno) road information**, *tel: (702) 793-1313;* **Southern Nevada (Las Vegas)**, *tel: (702) 486-3116.*

Caltrans Dist. 3, *PO Box 911, Marysville CA 95901; tel: (916) 741-4571*, has a leaflet on driving in winter. Because of slower speed limits and slippery roads, plan on more time to get to and through mountain areas. Local radio stations broadcast weather information.

Don't accelerate sharply when driving uphill. In California, the driver going uphill always has the right of way. If you get stuck, don't spin the wheels, but rock the car gently back and forward by changing gears; then use the left foot to brake while the right foot accelerates. Gently release the brakes.

When hiring a vehicle for winter mountain driving, ask that snow chains be included. After a snowfall, authorities post signs at checkpoints indicating chains are required. Failure to install chains can result in citation – or getting stranded in a snowdrift. In mountain areas, petrol station attendants or independent entrepreneurs will install, but not sell or rent, chains, for a fee. Pull over for installation, and get a receipt and the installer's badge number. The posted speed limit in areas where chains are required is 25–30 mph (40–48 kph).

Useful items are an ice scraper, a small shovel for digging out, warm sleeping bags, and extra clothing in case of long delays. Keep the petrol tank at least half-filled so you'll be able to go back should a road close unexpectedly. Keep warm and conserve fuel if stalled, but keep the car ventilated inside.

California operates **Sno-Parks** from 1 Nov to 30 May. Central Sierra Forest Service lands near cross country skiing and snowmobiling trailheads are cleared of snow for parking lots; some have snow playgrounds. Some overnight camping is permitted when the outside corners of the vehicle are staked with 8 ft (2.5 m) poles. Permits are $3 per day, $20 for the season, from **Sno-Park Program**, *PO Box 942896, Sacramento, CA 94296-0001; tel: (916) 653-8569.*

Distances

Point-to-point distances are vast in California and Nevada. One of the most-travelled routes, Hwy 101 from Los Angeles to San Francisco, is a 450 mile-drive (720 km) which takes 10 hours, non-stop. Plan on 50 miles per hour (80 kph) *direct* driving time, without stops, longer in cities and in the mountains. Use the sample driving distances and times on p. 9 as guidelines but allow for delays and stops.

Documentation

In California, your home country's driver's licence is valid. The minimum driving age is 18 in California; 16 in Nevada. Car hire companies may have higher age requirements, typically 21 or over (with additional charges for under-25 drivers).

Information

Automobile club membership in your home country can be invaluable. AAA clubs provide members of corresponding foreign clubs travelling to North America the reciprocal services that AAA members are eligible to receive abroad. Auto club services include emergency road service and towing; maps, tour guide books and specialist publications; touring services; road and camping information; discounts to attractions and hotels. The rule of thumb is, if it's free at home, it should be free in the USA, too. The AAA may charge for some services, like maps and tour books. Emergency breakdown road service may not be available to some non-North American club members. For information on reciprocal clubs and services, contact your own club or request *Offices to Serve You Abroad, American Automobile*

Association, 1000 AAA Drive, Heathrow FL 32746-5063; tel: (407) 444-7700. Carry your own club membership card with you at all times.

Motorcycles

If *Easy Rider* is still your idea of America, so be it. Motorcycles provide great mobility and a sense of freedom. Luggage will be limited, however; vast distances can make for long days in the saddle; and remember that potholes, gravel, poor roads, dust, smog, and sun are a motorcyclist's touring companions.

Hire motorcycles locally by finding a telephone directory listing. Helmets are required by law for both driver and passenger. By custom, most motor-cyclists turn on the headlight even in the daytime to increase their visibility. Cars can share lanes with motorcycles, though it's unsafe.

Parking

Public parking garages are indicated by a blue sign showing P with a directional arrow. Prices are posted at the entrance. Some city centre garages charge per 20 mins, at exorbitant rates, sometimes as much as $20.00 per hour. In civic centres, shopping and downtown areas and financial districts, coin-operated parking meters govern kerbside parking. The charge and time limit varies with the locality. Compare parking garage against meter charges for the most economic choice.

Kerbs may be colour-coded: *blue* is disabled parking; *white* is for passenger or post drop-off; *green* is limited time parking, as indicated on the kerb; *yellow* is a loading zone, generally for lorry deliveries; and *red* is no stopping or parking. No parking is allowed within 15 ft (4.6 m) of a fire hydrant, within 3 ft (0.9 m) of a disabled person sidewalk ramp, in a bus stop area, at an intersection, crosswalk (pedestrian crossing) or sidewalk, blocking a driveway or on a freeway except in emergencies.

If you park in violation of times and areas posted on kerb signs or poles nearby, or let the parking meter expire, expect to be issued with a citation – a ticket that states the violation, amount of a fine, and how to pay it. If you do not pay it, the car hire company may charge the

ticket amount (and any penalties) against your credit card. Fines range from a few dollars to several hundred dollars, depending on the violation and the locality.

Valet parking at garages, hotels, restaurants and events may be pricey, and the parking attendant will expect an additional tip of a few dollars when returning the car. Leave the car keys with the valet attendant, who will return them with the car.

Petrol

Petrol (gas) is sold in US gallons (roughly four litres per gallon). Posted prices including tax are shown in cents – as, for instance, 121.9 (= $1 and 21.9 cents) per gallon. Prices can vary from 100 to 175 cents per gallon, depending on location. In areas with many stations there can be strong price competition. Near urban areas, prices tend to be lower. In mountain or desert areas, prices can be astronomical. Some stations offer full service, filling the petrol tank, washing the windscreen and checking motor oil, usually for about $0.40 more per gallon. Most motorists use the more economical self-service.

Most US cars require unleaded petrol; due to environmental controls, leaded is not available in California. The three fuel grades are regular, super, and premium: use regular petrol unless the car hire company indicates otherwise. A few vehicles use diesel fuel.

When petrol stations are more than a few miles apart, normally a road sign will state the distance to the next services. Open petrol stations are well lit at night; many chains stay open 24 hours. Most stations accept cash, credit cards, and US dollar travellers' cheques. Cheaper stations may only accept cash or require advance payment; check before filling the petrol tank.

Police

Police cars signal drivers with flashing red or red and blue lights, and sometimes a siren. Respond quickly, but safely, by moving to the side of the road. Roll the driver's side window down but stay in the vehicle unless asked to get out. You have the right to ask an officer – politely – for identification, though it should be shown

---

Information–Motorcycles–Parking–Petrol–Police

immediately. Have your driver's licence and car registration papers ready for inspection when requested. Officers normally check computer records for vehicle registration irregularities and the driver for theft, criminal record, or other driving violations. If cited, do not argue with the officer, as a bad situation can only get worse.

The fine for littering the highway is $1000.

Road Signs

International symbols are used for directional and warning signs, but many are different from European versions; all language signs are in English, except street signs in special areas (e.g. San Francisco's Chinatown has bilingual signage), or near the Mexican border. Signs may be white, yellow, green, brown, or blue. (A selection of signs is included in the Planning Maps colour section at the back of this book.)

Stop, yield, do not enter, and wrong-way signs are *red* and *white*. *Yellow* is for warning or direction indicators. *Orange* is for roadworks or temporary diversions. *Green* indicates freeway directions. *Brown* is an alert for parks, campsites, hiking, etc. *Blue* gives non-driving information, such as radio station frequency for traffic or park information, or services in a nearby town. Speed limits and distance are primarily shown in miles, not kilometres. Dual-system signage is occasionally posted in National Parks and in extreme north-eastern California. Speed limit signs are *white* with black letters.

Traffic lights are red, yellow, and green. Yellow indicates that the light will turn red; stop, if possible, before entering the intersection.

A favourite (and highly illegal) Californian trick is to *jump* the red light, that is, enter the intersection when the signal is yellow and about to turn red. Police can cite you if you enter an intersection and you will not be clear of the intersection before the light turns red.

It is permitted to turn right at a red traffic light if there is no traffic coming from the left, i.e. as if it were a 'give way' sign, unless there is a sign specifically forbidding it (which is rare). A flashing yellow light, or hazard warning, requires drivers to slow down; flashing red means stop, then proceed when safe.

Road System

The US Interstate Highway System was built in the 1950s to streamline cargo transportation across the country. Federal funds maintain the interstates, which are usually the smoothest roads available. The **interstate** highways, designated I-(number) in the text, are the straightest and the usually least scenic route from point to point.

Freeways, often called expressways elsewhere in the USA, are motorways with controlled access. **Highways** have cross traffic interrupting the flow. East–west roads have even numbers, e.g., I-10, I-8, I-80; North–south roads are odd, e.g. I-5, Hwy 1, Hwy 101.

Rest areas, commonly along highways, have restrooms with toilets and public telephones, and are usually landscaped. Picnic tables are provided in scenic areas, and rest stops of historic or geographical interest post explanatory signs and maps. Use caution when leaving your vehicle at night and carry a torch (flashlight).

Local roads can range from satin-smooth to pitted, depending on local spending. Dirt roads indicated on maps or described this text may be treacherous. Ask at a petrol station about local road conditions before venturing on. Car hirers may prohibit driving on unpaved roads.

Rules of the Road

Lanes and Overtaking

Drive on the right. Vehicles are left-hand drive. The lane on the left, the *Number 1 Lane*, is fast; the right is slowest, and cars enter or leave traffic from the right (unless otherwise indicated by signs). Overtake other vehicles on the left side. A solid white line at least 4 ft (1.2 m) from the kerb is a special lane for bicycles, and should be labelled 'Bike Lane'. *Cars may and will pass you on both sides in a multi-lane road.* For many drivers from the UK, this is the most unexpected and confusing feature of US roads. Use direction indicators, but don't be surprised if other drivers don't bother. Never turn against a red arrow.

Make right turns from the right-hand lane after stopping at stop signs or traffic lights. Turn left from the most left-hand of lanes going in your direction, unless the turn is prohibited by a no-turn sign. Enter bike lanes only if making a right turn. Do not drive in areas marked for public transportation or pedestrians (e.g. cable car and trolley tracks in San Francisco).

Overtaking on a two-way road is permitted if the yellow line down the center in broken. Overtake on the left. Highways, especially in mountainous areas or long, narrow stretches of road, have occasional overtaking lanes. Overtake only when oncoming traffic is completely visible, and avoid overtaking in fog or rain. Two solid yellow lines means no overtaking, and no turning unless into a private driveway or for a legal U-turn. Driving or parking on sidewalks is illegal.

Main road drivers have the right of way over cars on lesser roads, but at the junction of two minor roads cars to your right have the right of way when arriving at the same time you do.

Freeway Driving

Lanes are numbered from left to right: number one is the extreme left-hand lane, number two the next lane to the right, and so on. An 'exit' or 'off ramp' is the ramp (slip road) leading off the freeway; an 'entrance' or 'on ramp' leads onto the freeway. 'Metering lights' are traffic lights controlling ramp access.

When freeway traffic does flow, it flows smoothly and quickly. 55 mph, the posted speed limit, is widely ignored; 70–75 mph is common in the fast (left) lane. The safest speed: match the general traffic flow in your lane, no matter how fast or slow.

When entering a freeway, *don't stop* on the ramp unless access is controlled by a traffic signal. Accelerate on the ramp and merge into the freeway flow. Cars that stop on the ramp are likely to be hit from the rear.

Freeways may have **carpool lanes**, for vehicles carrying several passengers; signs will specify the number of passengers required to access those speedier lanes, and the effective hours. Carpool lanes, also known as diamond lanes or HOV (high occupancy vehicle) lanes, are marked on the roadbed with a white diamond symbol. Special bus lanes will be marked.

Horns

Horns should be sounded only as a safety warning, and never near a hospital.

Pedestrians

Californians boast that pedestrians have the right of way, anywhere, anytime. Pedestrians can legally cross at intersections, even if crosswalks (pedestrian crossings) are not indicated. Some cities or towns may cite pedestrians for jaywalking. If a vehicle is involved in an accident with a pedestrian, the presumption of error always lies with the driver.

Speed Limits

The standard speed limit on freeways is 55 mph (88 kph) but 65 mph (104 kph) is allowed on a few rural freeway sections. Traffic may flow faster or slower than those limits, but the California Highway Patrol (CHP) and Nevada Highway Patrol can ticket anyone going faster than the limit. You may not see the patrols, as radar guns are used from a distance to track speeds.

Regardless of posted speed limits, police can invoke the *Basic Speed Law* that holds that no one can drive faster than is safe. The speed limit is 25 mph (40 kph) around schools and in most residential districts. At a railway crossing, the speed limit is 15 mph (24 kph) when you cannot see 400 ft (123 m) down the rails. Go 15 mph (24 kph) in any alley. To go much faster than the posted speeds for mountain driving and when taking bends is to court disaster.

Seat Belts

Seat belts must be worn in California by the driver and all passengers. Children under 4 years or weighing under 40 lb (18.2 kg) must ride in approved child safety seats. RV passengers behind the driver's area are not required to wear belts, but children should be safely seated while the vehicle is moving.

Vehicle Insurance

Californian law requires minimum third-party liability insurance coverage of $15,000 for death or injury to any person, $30,000 for death or injury to more than one person and $5000 for property damage. In practice, considerably more cover is desirable, and overseas visitors hiring a car are strongly recommended to take out top-up liability cover, such as the Topguard Insurance sold by Thomas Cook in the UK, which covers liability up to $1 million. (This is not to be confused with travel insurance, which provides cover for your own medical expenses – see p. 21.)

Car rental agencies will also ask the driver to take out collision damage waiver, or CDW (sometimes called loss damage waiver, LDW). Refusing CDW makes the renter personally liable for damage to the vehicle. CDW is strongly recommended for drivers from outside the USA, and often insisted upon as part of a fly-drive package. Sometimes it is paid for when booking the car hire abroad, sometimes it is payable locally on picking up the car. Occasionally special hire rates will include CDW. US and Canadian drivers using their own cars should ask their insurance company or auto club if their coverage extends to California and Nevada and meets California's minimum coverage requirements. If not, arrange for insurance before signing the car hire contract.

Vehicle Security

Lock it when you leave, lock it when you're inside, and don't forget the windows. Never leave keys, documents, maps, guidebooks and other tourist paraphernalia in sight. Be mindful of anyone lurking in the back seat or house part of the RV, especially at night. Watch other drivers for strange behaviour, especially if you're consistently followed. Never leave an engine running when you're not in the vehicle. Keep car keys with you at all times. And always park in well-lit areas.

Some California Driving Terms

big rig A large lorry, usually a tractor pulling one or more trailers.
boulevard stop Slowing at a stop sign, but not stopping
CHP California Highway Patrol, the state road police force.
CNG Liquified petroleum gas used as fuel.
crosswalk pedestrian crossing
connector A minor road connecting two freeways
curve bend
divided highway dual carriageway
DUI Driving Under the Influence of alcohol or drugs, aka Drunk Driving. The blood alcohol limit in California is 0.08% and *very* strictly enforced.
fender bumper
freeway motorway
garage or *parking garage* car park.
gas(oline) petrol
grade gradient, hill
highway trunk road
hood bonnet
metering lights Traffic signals controlling access to bridges, freeways, etc.

motor home motor caravan
pavement road surface. A UK 'pavement' is a *sidewalk.*
ramp slip road
rent hire
rubberneck(er) Slowing down to peer while driving past the scene of an accident or some unusual event.
RV (recreational vehicle) motor caravan
shoulder verge
sidewalk pavement
sig-alert An official warning of unusually heavy traffic, usually broadcast over local radio stations.
shift(stick) gear lever
switchback
tailgate Driving too closely to the vehicle immediately in front.
tow truck breakdown lorry
traffic cop traffic warden
trailer caravan
truck lorry
trunk boot
windshield windscreen
yield give way

Available in the UK only

American Options

Thomas Cook American Options – Travel for the independent traveller

Take off on an American dream holiday to California – tailor-made for you with the help of American Options.

Savour the natural beauty of the National Parks, taste the excitement of Las Vegas, the gambling city of the world, or head for the contrasting cities of Los Angeles, San Francisco and San Diego. With American Options, you can enjoy the freedom of designing your own holiday with all the ingredients you will need to appreciate a region that has something for everyone.

Book your transatlantic flights, then go as you please. Combine car hire with hotel vouchers or opt for the freedom of a motor home. Alternatively, see the major landmarks with one of our Californian self-drive tours, combining the security of pre-booked accommodation with detailed route information.

For those city stopovers, our mini-breaks are great value, offering local sightseeing and/or theme park entrances.

If you are on the road in California, American Options is a must.

To pick up a brochure, or make a booking, call in at your local Thomas Cook branch, where our staff will be happy to help. Alternatively, obtain further details by telephoning 01733 335524 from 0900 to 2000 Monday to Friday or 0900 to 1700 Saturday.

BACKGROUND CALIFORNIA

Geography

A restless state, a restless people. No more so than the soils they rest on. Earthquakes are perhaps California's best-known – and most feared characteristic. Upheavals for more than 23 million years have resulted in numerous faults, where plates of land mass scrape against each other, with jolting consequences.

California is a patchwork of awkward terrain. The state is 780 miles (1,255 km) long and 200 miles (320 km) wide, but California's only expanse of flat ground, the **Central Valley**, is just 400 miles (640 km) long by 50 miles (80 km) wide. Everything else is mountainous.

The highest and the lowest points in the continental United States, **Death Valley**, 282 ft (86 m) below sea level, and **Mount Whitney**, 14,494 ft (4,418 m) tall, are a scant 60 air miles (96 km) apart; the winding, 120-mile (192 km) driving journey takes all day.

The entire coastline, 1,264 corrugated miles (2,034 km), is hemmed in by the **Coastal Range**. Northern mountains are cloaked with dense forests, the southern slopes by explosively inflammable brush. The only break in the natural rampart is **San Francisco Bay**.

The eastern border is guarded by the **Sierra Nevada**, which rises gently through the foothills of **Gold Country**, then drops precipitously into **Nevada**. North and south of the Valley, a series of east–west peaks connect the Coast Range and the Sierras. Up to 50 ft (15 m) of snow blankets the Sierras every winter, closing some passes from November into June. The runoff roars through canyons up to 5000 ft (1500 m) deep every spring.

The climate is officially Mediterranean, though the winter rain/summer drought pattern is closer to North Africa than Greece or Italy. Rainfall varies from more than 100 inches (254 cm) in the northwest to less than 1 inch (25 mm) in the southeastern deserts. While primeval redwood forests hide in perpetual mists along the north coast, the southeast bakes in some of the highest desert temperatures ever recorded.

History

The Beginnings

Spain began weaving the veil of hyperbole that still surrounds California. Sixteenth-century conquistadors found empires to conquer and gold to loot in Central and South America. Sailing north, they found only the peninsula of lower, or Baja, California. The Indians were hostile, the landscape barren, and there was no gold. So they stretched the truth.

A 1510 Spanish romantic novel fancifully created Queen Calafia, ruler of an island filled with black Amazons who rode griffins into battle and fought with weapons of pure gold. The conquistadors named the unpromising peninsula 'California', deciding that fiction would serve better than truth.

The first European to see Alta, or Upper, California, died there. **Juan Rodriguez Cabrillo** landed at San Diego in 1542, then broke his leg on San Miguel Island and died, probably of gangrene. The survivors sailed north as far as Oregon, then retreated to Mexico. Spain declared it a futile exploration.

The English privateer **Francis Drake** was the first European to make his fortune in California. It was quasi-legal, but successful.

Drake hunted Manila galleons, lumbering Spanish treasure ships sailing from Manila to California then south to Mexico and safety. The hunt went so well that his ship's hull seams were splitting from the sheer weight of Spanish booty.

In 1579, Drake beached his ship, the *Golden Hinde*, for repairs. He probably landed at Drake's Bay, now part of Point Reyes National Seashore, just north of San Francisco. Drake then sailed home to a knighthood. Spain simply ignored California for another two centuries.

Spain's neglect was a reprieve for California's Native American population. The climate was mild; the terrain limited travel and warfare. Acorns were the staple food, usually made into porridge or bread. Deer and small game were abundant. Rivers and bays were so rich that coastal groups left heaps of discarded shells 30 ft (9 m) high. Once the Spanish arrived, the end came swiftly.

Gaspar de Portola and a Franciscan friar, **Junipero Serra**, led an expedition from Baja California north to San Diego in 1769. Serra stayed in San Diego to tend the sick and dedicate the first of 21 Missions in Upper California. Portola explored north along what would become El Camino Real, 'The King's Highway', the route now followed by Highway 101. California had joined the Spanish Empire.

When an advance party climbed a ridge between today's cities of Pacifica and Millbrae and found the way north blocked by a huge bay, Portola gave up. Only Juan Crespi, a monk, recorded in his diary the sighting of a bay sufficient to hold all the fleets of Europe – it was San Francisco Bay.

Portola returned to San Diego and sailed north with Serra to Monterey, reported to have ideal harbour conditions. Portola started a small fort, or Presidio; Serra founded another mission. More missions were established, including San Francisco in 1776, the year the United States declared independence from Great Britain.

The early 19th century saw the decline of Spain's empire, but the missions prospered. Vineyards, orchards, herds, and corn fields flourished. Buildings began to assume a familiar form: whitewashed stone or brick churches topped by red clay tiles, bordered by arched colonnades surrounding lush central gardens cooled by fountains.

The Californios

Prosperity didn't last. Mexico gained independence in 1821. Twelve years later, the 21 Missions were secularised and their vast estates sold to cattle ranchers. The Church's loss was California's gain.

The *ranchero*, or ranch, became the basic social, cultural, and economic unit. The era gave California a rose-tinted heritage of dashing *caballeros*, or landowners, and swirling *senoritas*, glamorous young women. It was one of the largest and most prosperous pastoral societies the world has ever seen.

Californios sold upwards of 75,000 hides a year for $2 each to Yankee traders. With no enforceable taxes, everything went into luxuries. Caballeros raised cattle and bought them back as expensive Boston boots. Senoritas slipped into gowns of fine Cantonese silk to dance on floors of packed dirt. English and American merchants, many of them originally sailors who jumped ship, managed the trade.

They managed the whaling and fur trades, too. New Englanders hunted whales migrating between Alaska and Baja California. Russia established a settlement at Fort Ross, north of San Francisco, and hunted sea otters to the brink of extinction.

Fur also brought the first Americans overland in the 1820s. In 1832, a young runaway named **Christopher 'Kit' Carson** helped map a trail from Santa Fe, New Mexico, to a dusty, lawless coastal village called Los Angeles. The next year, US Army Captain **Benjamin Bonneville** scouted California while on 'furlough' for a trapping expedition. The Hudson's Bay Company had been trapping and exploring California since 1829.

The first party of overland immigrants from the United States, later called 'pioneers', walked to California in 1841. The first wagon train made it over the Sierra Nevada in 1844. Then came the **Donner Party**. This group followed a guidebook written by a man who had never been to California. They were snowbound in the Sierra near Donner Summit, on what is now I-80, from November 1846 until February 1847. Forty of the original 87 survived by eating their livestock and their comrades.

The survivors arrived to find a new flag. Earlier settlers had been unhappy with a series of weak Mexican governors. When US Captain **John Fremont** appeared in early 1846 with 68 heavily armed troops, California's foreign population revolted. The rebels raised a flag over Sonoma carrying a star and a bear, and the California Republic was born.

The republic lasted one month. The USA declared war on Mexico in May; naval units

History   **41**

occupied every Californian port by July. The transition to American authority went smoothly. Californios still ruled society and local government, foreign merchants controlled the economy, and there was land to spare for immigrants.

The Gold Rush

In 1848, gold changed California forever. It was the first major supply of gold the world had seen since Spain looted the Aztec, Maya, and Inca empires in the 16th century. San Francisco grew from a windswept, fleabitten village of 812 into a hive of 25,000 in two years. The state population jumped from 10,000 to 100,000. Gold gave California the economic muscle to escape exploitation by financiers in New York and London; California grew its own crop of robber barons and a reputation as the land of eternal opportunity.

Spain and Mexico, the most experienced mining countries in the world, had owned California for three centuries without finding significant deposits of the precious metal. Americans of the era believed God intended gold for them alone; gold needed an American spark.

Even the timing of the discovery seemed divinely devised. **James Marshall** spotted gold flakes in a waterwheel raceway in January, 1848, just days before Mexico ceded California to the United States. America paid US$18.25 million for the entire southwestern quadrant of the continent. Miners pulled more than 30 times that much gold from California alone in less than a decade.

Nearly all the '49ers' went to what is now called Gold Country, the area along Hwy 49. (Discover this by following the Oakhurst–Lake Tahoe Route, p. 206). When military officials called a constitutional convention in 1849, delegates split along regional lines. The south opposed joining the United States, fearing (correctly) that land, not mines, would be taxed. The north wanted to join America to boost the gold market. The northern faction won; California became a state in 1850.

The Gold Rush meant fortune for successful miners and those who supplied the mines. Chinese labourers who were conscripted to work under the most appalling goldfield conditions called California 'Gold Mountain', hoping for fortune in a strange land. The influx of miners from around the world created shortages in everything from tea to tin. It meant ruin for the Californios. Inflation ravaged their finances. Drought devastated their herds. Worst of all, the upstart Americans demanded the millions of hectares owned by a few hundred Californio families. With the help of drumhead land commissions, most land ended up in American hands.

California never faltered. The gold fields played out, but a tide of Nevada silver turned incipient recession into boom. The Comstock Lode, beneath Virginia City, produced $400 million for San Francisco mining companies before deposits were exhausted in the 1880s.

Railroads were even more profitable. Sacramento merchants who backed the 1863 transcontinental railroad became known as the Big Four. **Mark Hopkins**, **Collis Huntington**, **Leland Stanford** and **Charles Crocker** built fortunes on questionable land schemes and outright fraud, but California boomed. San Francisco ruled a commercial empire that stretched from Alaska to Mexico and Utah to China.

Agriculture flourished, from the vegetable farms that nourished the cities to the vineyards that kept them drunk. Even the weather contributed. As gold and silver lost their lustre, farmers realised that California is the one part of North America where rain falls only in the winter. With later irrigation, the unique pattern of summer drought and winter relief made the state an agricultural powerhouse in everything from peas and cabbages to marijuana and oranges.

In the 1880s, the railroad, called The Octopus for its omnipresent power in state and local politics, dropped transcontinental fares to $1 per person. Real estate developers, farmers, and the City of Los Angeles began extolling the virtues of Sunny Southern California. Sunkist citrus campaigns promised California sunshine on every breakfast table. Nature provided the weather, but Californians designed the message, complete with alluring 'California Girl' posters. The lucky discovery of oil and production of automobiles made it inevitable that by the beginning of the 20th century people were pouring in, especially into the south.

The burgeoning population demanded water. Ridden with scandal and graft, an aqueduct was built in 1913 to pull water from the Owens Valley, east of the Sierra Nevada Mountains. Agricultural interests had seen the future – irrigation. Aqueducts carried water from the Colorado River to Southern California and the Central Valley. The Great Depression in the 1930s brought waves of rural farmers into California from dusty, drought-plagued Oklahoma and Arkansas. Many joined indigenous Mexican farmworkers who migrated to harvest seasonal crops.

World War II turned California's agricultural breadbasket into a wartime induction center and destination. Thousands of men shipped out to Pacific battlefields from San Francisco; naval operations brought an influx of military personnel and support services into San Diego and the San Francisco Bay Area.

Post-war California

After the war, soldiers and sailors returned in droves to settle in California's alluring coastal cities. The GI Bill provided veterans with a free education; many of them chose to study at the University of California Berkeley campus, where much of the war's atomic energy research had been conducted.

The new life and easy climate bred a unique artistic movement of protest in the 1950s. Beatniks, dressed in black, and given to free verse poetry recitals, came to earth in San Francisco's North Beach coffee-houses.

By the early 1960s, fieldworkers, primarily from Mexico, began to organise to protest at stooped-back farm labour. Strikes and produce boycotts had the desired effect on California's large agricultural corporations. Working conditions and wages improved. National civil rights legislation and court rulings dictated that schools must not only be desegregated, but that African American and Caucasian children would be bussed to non-neighbourhood schools to even out numbers.

By mid-decade, the first post-war generation had come of age. Higher education was no longer for the elite, but was state-funded. Free thinking, free speech, and so-called free love came together in the hippie movement. Tie-dyed clothing, flowers, beads, incense, bare feet, jeans, and no brassieres were trademarks of a scene which 'got into' drugs, smoked marijuana, and listened to music. After Liverpool and London, the world's music emanated from recording studios in Los Angeles and San Francisco, aided by cheap or free rock concerts.

Escalation of fighting in Vietnam in the late 1960s meant drafted soldiers again poured into California. War protesters on California campuses demonstrated in the streets, as the Vietnam military build-up brought prosperity to California's aerospace and communications technology industries.

The end of the Vietnam conflict in 1973 brought a wave of immigration from Vietnam and other parts of Indochina. Political turmoil in Central and South America in the 1970s brought new Latino, or Hispanic, immigrants to California's shores.

In 1978, Proposition 13 was approved by California voters. Property taxes were no longer to be used to fund social services or education. Some mental sanitariums emptied, homeless shelters were closed or reduced in size, and education was no longer fully funded.

Even as the aerospace industry stagnated with oversupply and the decline of Cold War enmities, California led the technology revolution. Silicon Valley, named after the essential mineral element required to produce computer chips, began in a rural area just north of San Jose. Several major biotechnology companies, including Genentech, granddaddy of them all, made the San Francisco area home. Multimedia is a recent wave to find a home in California – in San Francisco's South of Market district.

California's population has nearly doubled every generation since the 1849 Gold Rush, fuelled by hopeful waves of immigrants from around the globe. That sense of hope, forging boldly and successfully into the future, is as much a part of the way the world sees California as it is of how Californians see themselves.

TOURING ITINERARIES

Much of the pleasure of a driving holiday lies in tailoring your itinerary to match your tastes and interests. By dividing California into recommended routes, this book is intended to make it easy and pleasurable to plan your ideal tour. By linking several of our routes you can create a trip which will suit your tastes and you can be confident of following a tried and tested path which introduces you to the best that the route has to offer.

This chapter begins with some practical advice on tour planning, followed by two ready-made itineraries designed to show you as much as possible of California's variety in a two- or three-week trip. Feel free to vary our suggestions, using the full range of information contained in the route descriptions.

The remaining pages list features of California which you can use to create a self-planned 'themed' tour using the routes noted.

PRACTICAL HINTS

Here are a few tips to make practicable routes easier to plan and more fun to follow:

1. Use the most detailed maps available. The colour map section at the end of this book is useful for planning itineraries and will enable you to follow the routes while driving, but a more detailed road map will be invaluable, especially if you intend to vary the routes we have recommended. If you haven't already acquired a good road map or atlas, stop at the nearest AAA office as soon as possible after arriving in California and pick up maps for the areas you will be touring. For even more detail, buy a copy of Thomas Bros' *California Road Atlas & Driver's Guide* at any major bookseller.

2. Don't schedule too much driving each day. Allow a conservative 50 miles (80 km) per hour of freeway driving, 40 miles (64 km) each hour on secondary roads to allow for stretch breaks and the inevitable unplanned stops. It's better to have more time to explore along the way than be pressed to arrive by mealtime each evening. Each route description in this book gives information not only about mileage but also likely driving times.

3. Check weather and road reports. Most paved roads are open all year, but some major mountain passes, particularly Hwy 120 over Tioga Pass through Yosemite National Park and Hwy 44/89 through Lassen National Park, are closed from October/November until May/June. Other passes may be closed for several days following major storms. Fire, flood, and mudslide also close roads throughout California.

4. Unless accommodation is pre-booked, plan to arrive each night with enough time to find a place to sleep. In some areas, particularly Yosemite National Park, Sequoia/Kings Canyon National Parks, Hearst Castle, and small towns with few motels, advance bookings are essential.

5. Build in time at the end of the trip to get back to the departure city (usually Los Angeles or San Francisco) the day before a scheduled flight home. Airlines don't hold entire planes for one carload of late arrivals, and passengers travelling on cheap fares who miss a flight may be faced with buying a new ticket home – at full price.

6. Give serendipity a chance by not planning in too much detail. Allow time to spend an extra few hours – or an extra day – in some unexpected gem of a town, or to turn down an interesting side road. Anyone who wants their days preplanned in 15-minute increments will be happier on a fully escorted package coach tour than a self-drive holiday.

THE BEST OF CALIFORNIA

The following tours start and end in Los Angeles, but since they're circular, can be picked up in San Francisco or any other convenient spot.

The tours combine many recommended routes, with a few digressions and short-cuts added. Las Vegas and Reno are included because many fly-drive programs include stops in one or both of these gambling 'paradises.' Suggested overnight stops are in **bold type**. *Adapt the tours freely or use the same cut-and-paste idea to combine several routes for more personalised itineraries.*

14 Days

For those who want (or need) to 'do' California in one whirlwind bout of driving. It *can* be done, but allow a few days at home to recover before returning to work.

Day 1: **Los Angeles** (pp. 53–70).
Day 2: Los Angeles to Barstow, Baker, Shoshone, and **Death Valley**. (Los Angeles–Las Vegas, p. 87; Palm Springs–Death Valley, p. 178)
Day 3: Death Valley to Lone Pine, Whitney Portal, and **Bishop**. (Death Valley–Los Angeles, p. 80; Lone Pine–South Lake Tahoe, p. 182)
Day 4: Bishop to Lee Vining (Mono Lake) and **Yosemite**. (Lone Pine–South Lake Tahoe, p. 182; Yosemite National Park, p. 286)
Day 5: **Yosemite** (p. 286).
Day 6: Yosemite to Mariposa, Jamestown, Sonora, Columbia, Angels Camp, Plymouth, Diamond Springs, and **South Lake Tahoe**. (Yosemite National Park, p. 286; Oakhurst–Lake Tahoe, p. 206).
Day 7: Eastern shore of Lake Tahoe to Hwy 267 and Truckee, Reno, Virginia City, Carson City, and return to **South Lake Tahoe**. (Lake Tahoe Circuit, p.196)
Day 8: Western shore of Lake Tahoe to Tahoe City, Squaw Valley, and I-80, west to **San Francisco**. (Lake Tahoe Circuit, p. 196; Reno–Sacramento, p. 256; Sacramento–San Francisco, p. 247)
Day 9: **San Francisco** (pp. 215–227).

Day 10: San Francisco to Muir Woods, Point Reyes, Jenner, Guerneville, Healdsburg, and back to **San Francisco**. (San Francisco Bay Area Routes, p. 228; San Francisco–Napa Valley, p. 236)
Day 11: San Francisco to Gilroy, Castroville, Monterey, Big Sur, Hearst Castle (tour reservation required), **San Luis Obispo**. (San Francisco–Santa Barbara Coastal Route, p. 145.)
Day 12: San Luis Obispo to Santa Maria, Santa Ynez, Solvang, Buellton, **Santa Barbara**. (Santa Barbara–San Francisco Coastal Route.)
Day 13: Santa Barbara to **Los Angeles**, (p. 71.)
Day 14: **Los Angeles**.

21 Days

Three weeks is a more realistic time frame to see most of California. If possible, add another week to see the more remote and less travelled northern reaches of the state.

Day 1: **Los Angeles** (pp. 53–70).
Day 2: **Los Angeles**
Day 3: Los Angeles to **Palm Springs**, (p. 75.)
Day 4: Palm Springs to Indio, Twentynine Palms, Amboy, Baker, **Las Vegas** (Palm Springs–Death Valley, p. 178, as far as Baker, then via Los Angeles–Las Vegas, p. 87).
Day 5: **Las Vegas** (p. 90).
Day 6: Las Vegas to Pahrump, Beatty, **Death Valley**, p. 96.
Day 7: Death Valley to Lone Pine, Whitney Portal, and **Bishop**. (Death Valley–Los Angeles, p. 80, to Lone Pine, then Lone Pine–South Lake Tahoe, p. 182)
Day 8: Bishop to Lee Vining (Mono Lake) and **Yosemite**. (Lone Pine–South Lake Tahoe, p. 182 to Mono Lake, then into Yosemite, p. 286)
Day 9: **Yosemite** (p. 286).
Day 10: **Yosemite**
Day 11: Yosemite to Mariposa, Jamestown, Sonora, Columbia, Angels Camp, Plymouth, Diamond Springs, and **South Lake Tahoe**. (San Francisco–Yosemite, p. 281, to Mariposa, then Oakhurst–Lake Tahoe, p. 206)
Day 12: Eastern shore of Lake Tahoe to Hwy 267 and Truckee, Reno, Virginia City, Carson City, and return to **South Lake Tahoe**. (Lake Tahoe Circuit, p. 196)

Day 13: Western shore of Lake Tahoe to Tahoe City, Squaw Valley, and I-80, west to Hwy 20, Nevada City, Grass Valley, and **San Francisco** via I-80. (Lake Tahoe Circuit, p. 196, to Tahoe City; then Reno–Sacramento, p. 256 and Sacramento–San Francisco, p. 247)

Day 14: **San Francisco** (pp. 215–227).

Day 15: **San Francisco**

Day 16: San Francisco to Muir Woods, Point Reyes, Jenner, Gurneville, Healdsburg, and back to **San Francisco**. (San Francisco Bay Area Routes, p. 228; San Francisco–Napa Valley, p. 236)

Day 17: San Francisco to Gilroy, Castroville, Monterey, Big Sur, Hearst Castle (tour reservation required), **San Luis Obispo**. (San Francisco–Santa Barbara Coastal Route, p. 145)

Day 18: San Luis Obispo to Santa Maria, Santa Ynez, Solvang, Buellton, **Santa Barbara**. (Santa Barbara–San Francisco Coastal Route.)

Day 19: Santa Barbara to **Los Angeles**, p. 71.

Day 20: **Los Angeles** (pp. 53–70).

Day 21: **Los Angeles**.

THE MAJOR CITIES

Cities the world over have more in common than not. They're big, noisy, crowded, and busy, which can be alluring beacons or flashing warning signs. Here is a list of California's most popular cities (Nevada's, too) and what makes them that way.

The cities are listed in order of a circular tour, identifying the recommended routes from this book that connect them. So many cities in one tour might be indigestible, but by studying the chapters which describe the cities in full (also cross-referenced below) and the other recommended routes you can omit those places which don't interest you, and, if you wish, mix in some non-city routes for a taste of desert, mountain or coastal scenery.

Los Angeles

LA is arguably the cultural capital of the planet. Cultural purists from Paris to Beijing decry the surging forces of Hollywood, MTV, and American television emanating from California's biggest city, but they've never found a permanent antidote to Los Angeles' pounding, breathless rush at life. Neither has the rest of America, which has happily adopted LA's brash, youthful, suntanned, sycophantic self-image as its own. (Los Angeles p. 53. Los Angeles–San Diego p. 116.)

San Diego

In the four centuries since the outside world first touched California, San Diego has gone from a dusty, often-forgotten Spanish outpost town to the second largest city in the state (after Los Angeles). Balmy weather, titillating Mexico nearby, and sailboats galore make this coastal city the Med of California. Old Town recreates the city's Colonial period, Balboa Park offers one of the top zoos in the world, and Coronado is the premier water sports venue in California. (San Diego and San Diego Circuit, pp. 100–109; San Diego–Palm Springs, p. 110.)

Palm Springs

Palm Springs is a patch of green dropped in the midst of a major desert. But while golf courses and luxury resort homes continue to turn cactus-covered scrub into grass-covered velvet, they're adding to one of the most popular and enduring resorts ever perpetrated. Palm Springs began as an exclusive winter hideaway for Hollywood stars and their friends in the 1920s. Today, it's among the most visited and talked about holiday refuges in the world. (Palm Springs, p. 173.) For Palm Springs to Las Vegas take either Palm Springs–Los Angeles route (p. 75) to San Bernardino and then Los Angeles–Las Vegas route (p. 87), or the Palm Springs–Death Valley route (p. 178) as far as Baker, and again joining the Los Angeles–Las Vegas route.

Las Vegas

Las Vegas is the gambling capital of the world, with more flash and glitter per square metre than any other patch of urban landscape on earth or in imagination. What Disney did for children, casino designers have done for adults, twisting reality into caricature so complete that the unreal seems perfectly normal. A volcano erupts on demand, showgirls turn dazzling smiles on every bald pate and pot belly in the audience, and the elusive jackpot is always just one more turn of the cards away. (Las Vegas p. 90; Las Vegas to Reno by following Las Vegas–Death Valley, p. 96, and Death Valley–Los Angeles, p. 80, as far as Lone Pine, and then Lone Pine–South Lake Tahoe, p. 182, and finally to Reno via the Lake Tahoe Circuit, p. 196.)

Reno

This is Las Vegas' smaller brother. Vegas has more glitter, but Reno has outdoor and historical attractions that Las Vegas can only try to build. Gambling is Reno's biggest lure, but winter and summer sports in the nearby Sierra Nevada mountains and Lake Tahoe attract a more outdoor-oriented crowd than Las Vegas. Wild West aficionados can find a wealth of history in abandoned gold and silver mines nearby. (For a description of Reno and the journey to Sacramento, see Sacramento–Reno Route, p. 256.)

Sacramento

California's state capital, Sacramento has been a centre of trade, commerce, and politics since the 1849 Gold Rush. Downtown neighbourhoods are filled with gracious Victorian mansions, many now converted into offices for the attorneys, lobbyists, consultants and others attracted by the largest state budget in America. Old Sacramento, the original city along the Sacramento River, sports paddlewheel river boats, old-time trains, carriage rides, and summertime Dixieland jazz. (Sacramento, p. 251; Sacramento–San Francisco p. 247.)

San Francisco

San Francisco is a mutual appreciation society. Citizens proudly proclaim their city's beauty, their cultural superiority over the modern Philistines of Los Angeles, and their undying devotion to peace, love, and a good time. It's mostly untrue, except for the physical beauty of the place, but there's enough truth left to make San Francisco one of the most popular cities in America to visit. And revisit. (San Francisco p. 215; San Francisco to Monterey via Santa Barbara–San Francisco Coastal Route, p. 145.)

Monterey

Monterey has aged gracefully from California's first capital under Spanish and Mexican rule to a scenic seaside holiday community with spectacular urban shoreline. The water is too cold for serious swimming, but sea kayaking is a popular way to get close to the sea lions and sea otters of Monterey Bay. Golfers flock to championship courses at Pebble Beach, scuba divers to the dense kelp forest just off shore, and ordinary tourists to the quiet streets and peaceful mission that were once key players in international politics. (For Monterey, and route to Santa Barbara, see Santa Barbara–San Francisco Coastal Route, p. 145.)

Santa Barbara

Nestled between sheer mountains and the sea, Santa Barbara embodies the myth of Southern California. The weather is idyllic (continental America's only commercial banana plantation is nearby), the setting stunning (movie makers originally chose Santa Barbara over Hollywood), the population young (a major university helps), and the pace of life purposefully slow (many of Los Angeles' rich and famous come here to relax). A one-time opera diva said it all by naming her estate 'Lotusland'. (Santa Barbara, p. 125; Santa Barbara–Los Angeles route p. 71.)

THE TOP TEN SIGHTS

Here are the top 10 places visitors to California actually visit, according to statistics compiled by the State Office of Tourism. They're less crowded during the winter months, but anyone who is looking for a crowd won't go wrong by sticking to these attractions.

1. **Hollywood** and **Universal Studios/Hollywood** Tinsel Town at its best. (Greater Los Angeles Routes, p. 63.)
2. **Disneyland** and **Knotts Berry Farm** Top theme parks, but stick to Knotts for adrenalin and Disney for cute. (Greater Los Angeles Routes, p. 63.)
3. **San Francisco** Everybody's favourite city. (City chapter p. 215.)
4. **San Diego** and **Tijuana** The perfect climate

and a splash of foreign colour. (San Diego chapter, p. 100.)

5. **Palm Springs** Where the rich go to play. (Palm Springs chapter, p. 173.)
6. **Las Vegas** Where the would-be rich go to play. (Las Vegas chapter, p. 90.)
7. **Yosemite** Scenery so stunning that 50,000 people a day can't ruin it. (Yosemite chapter, p. 286.)
8. **Napa/Sonoma Wine Country** The best promoted wine regions in California with some of the best wines in the world. (San Francisco–Napa Valley route, p. 236.)
9. **The Redwoods** The biggest living things on earth (Sequoia National Park) and the tallest living things on earth (Redwood National Park). (Visalia–Yosemite route, p. 267, for Sequoia and San Francisco–Oregon Border Route, p. 293, for Redwood.)
10. **Santa Cruz/Monterey/Big Sur** Stereotypically perfect cliffs, crashing surf, and fog-shrouded forests come to life. (Santa Barabara–San Francisco Coastal Route, p. 145.)

TOP PARKS AND MONUMENTS

California's National Parks and monuments are listed first, followed by other parks, reserves, beaches, and shores administered by Federal or State authorities.

Channel Islands National Park, *12 miles (19 km) offshore of Ventura, about 60 miles (96 km) north of Los Angeles, via Hwy 1 or Hwy 101; tel: (805) 658-5730.* Four islands are boat-accessible; park headquarters in Ventura. Unique plant and animal species thrive, especially foxes, seals, sea lions, dolphins, whales and birds. (Los Angeles–Santa Barbara, p. 71.)

Death Valley National Monument, *87 miles (140 km) south-east of Lone Pine via Hwys 136 and 190, or 160 miles (256 km) from Las Vegas via I-15, and Hwys 127 and 178; tel: (619) 786-2331.* Sand dunes, dried seabeds, coloured rocks, alluvial fans, and an abandoned borax works compete for attention in the desert's blistering desolation. (Los Angeles–Death Valley, p. 80, and Las Vegas–Death Valley, p. 96.)

Lassen Volcanic National Park, *200 miles (320 km) north of Sacramento, via Hwys 99, 70, and 89; tel: (916) 595-4444.* Geothermal areas with sulphur works, steaming hot springs, and Rim of Fire volcanic desolation. (Redding–Chester route, p. 320.)

Presidio Of San Francisco National Park, *tel: (415) 556-0560.* (San Francisco chapter, p. 226).

Redwood National Park, *320 miles (512 km) north of San Francisco via Hwy 101: tel: (707) 464-6101.* Coastal redwoods, tallest trees in the world, have sheltered for up to two millenia in this damp coastal strip extending from north of Eureka to Crescent City. (San Francisco–Oregon Border route, p. 293.)

Sequoia and Kings Canyon National Parks, *south of Yosemite National Park, 52 miles (83 km) east of Fresno via Hwy 180 to Kings Canyon; 35 miles (56 km) east of Visalia via Hwy 198 to Sequoia; tel: (209) 565-3134.* Combined national parks showcase the Giant Sequoia (redwood) tree in groves on the western side of the Sierra Nevada Mountains. (Visalia–Yosemite route, p. 267.)

Yosemite National Park, *31 miles (50 km) north-east of Mariposa via Hwy 140; tel: (209) 372-0264.* Yosemite Valley meadows buttressed by the granite monoliths Half Dome, El Capitan and Sentinel Rock. *Via Hwy 120,* Tioga Pass (closed in Winter), travel east across the Sierra Nevada Mountains by alpine meadows and crystalline lakes *to Hwy 395.* (Yosemite, p. 286.)

Anza-Borrego Desert State Park, *85 miles (136 km) north-east of San Diego via I-8, Hwys 79 and 78; tel: (619) 767-5311.* The largest state park in the continental USA, with spectacular sweeping vistas, dramatic dunes, washes, wildflowers, palm groves, and wildlife. (San Diego–Palm Springs route, p. 110.)

Bodie State Historic Park, *7 miles (11 km) south of Bridgeport on Hwy 395, then 13 miles (21 km) east on Bodie Rd; tel: (916) 525-7232.* Unrestored, unimproved 1880s ghost town with

---

Top Ten Sights–Top Parks and Monuments

weathered buildings. (Lone Pine–South Lake Tahoe route, p. 182.)

California State Capitol Museum, *Capitol Mall and 10th St, Sacramento; tel: (916) 324-0333.* State Capitol building, restored to its turn-of-the century appearance. (See Sacramento chapter, p. 251.)

Columbia State Historical Park, *4 miles (6 km) north of Sonora via Hwy 49; tel: (209) 532-4301.* The best-restored Gold Rush town in California. (Oakhurst–Lake Tahoe, p. 206.)

El Pueblo de Los Angeles State Historic Park; *tel: (213) 628-1274.* The city's oldest section has 27 museums, adobes, and other buildings showing Los Angeles' ethnic diversity. (Greater Los Angeles Routes, p. 63.)

Fort Ross State Historical Park, *12 miles (19 km) north of Jenner on Hwy 1; tel: (707) 847-3286.* Coastline site of the original Russian settlement of California with a reconstructed fort and Orthodox chapel. (San Francisco–Oregon Border, p. 293.)

Golden Gate National Recreation Area, San Francisco Bay environs; *tel: (415) 556-0560.* Alcatraz, San Francisco's historic ships and much of its waterfront, the Marin Headlands, Muir Woods National Monument's redwoods and ferns, are highlights of this piecemeal chequerboard of historic and natural areas. (San Francisco Bay Area Routes, p. 228.)

Hearst (Castle) San Simeon State Historical Monument, *41 miles (66 km) north of San Luis Obispo on Hwy 1; tel: (800) 444-7275.* Newspaper magnate William Randolph Hearst spent 28 years building and furnishing this partially-finished hilltop castle/residence. (Santa Barbara–San Francisco Coastal Route, p. 145.)

Joshua Tree National Monument, *26 miles (42 km) north-east of Palm Springs via I-10 and Hwy 195*; tel: (619) 367-7511. Named after the spindly, spiky-leaved plants which prevail in the higher, wetter Mojave Desert in the western

half, the monument's arid eastern half is Colorado desert. (Palm Springs–Death Valley, p. 178.)

Mono Lake Tufa State Reserve, *10 miles (16 km) south-east of Lee Vining via Hwys 395 & 120; tel: (619) 647-6331.* Million-year old saltwater lake surrounded by jagged towers of minerals which originally formed under water. (Yosemite, p. 286.)

Monterey State Historic Park, *210 Olivier St; tel: (408) 649-2118.* California's first capital, with ten historic buildings from early California. (See Santa Barbara–San Francisco Coastal Route, p. 145.)

Old Sacramento State Historic Park, *Front St, on the Sacramento River; tel: (916) 445-7373.* The original centre of Gold Rush-era Sacramento, with original buildings, now restored, and the **State Railroad Museum**. (Sacramento chapter, p. 251.)

Old Town San Diego State Historic Park, *San Diego Ave and Twiggs St; tel: (619) 264-7777.* San Diego from Mexican and early American days, adobes, and demonstrations. (San Diego chapter, p. 100.)

Pinnacles National Monument, *130 miles (208 km) from San Francisco via Hwys 101 and 25; tel: (408) 389-4485.* Rosy-coloured boulders, crags and spires are witness to seismic activity aeons ago. (San Francisco–Visalia, p. 262.)

Point Lobos State Reserve, *3 miles (5 km) south of Carmel on Hwy 1; tel: (408) 624-4909.* A mosaic of bold headlands, irregular coves, and one of the richest underwater habitats in the world. (Santa Barbara–San Francisco Coastal Route, p. 145.)

Point Reyes National Seashore, *A 30-mile (48 km) long peninsula, just north of San Francisco on Hwy 1; tel: (415) 663-1092.* Winding roads twist over ridges formed by earthquakes, through deer-filled forests, to the Pacific Ocean. (San Francisco Bay Area Routes, p. 228.)

Prarie Creek Redwoods State Park, *50 miles (80km) north of Eureka on Hwy 101; tel: (707) 488-2171.* Coastal redwoods with the tallest trees in the world and the world's largest herd of wild Roosevelt elk. (San Francisco–Oregon Border, p. 293.)

Samuel P. Taylor State Park, *15 miles (24 km) west of San Rafael on Sir Francis Drake Blvd; tel: (415) 488-9897.* Quiet groves of coastal redwoods filled with ferns next to open grasslands. (San Francisco Bay Area Routes, p. 228.)

Torrey Pines State Beach & Reserve, *12 miles (19km) north of San Diego, west off I-5; tel: (619) 729-8947 or (619) 755-2063.* Unique pines, hang-gliding, beach. (San Diego–Los Angeles, p. 116.)

Weaverville Joss House State Historic Park, *50 miles (80 km) west of Redding on Hwy 299; tel: (916) 623-5284.* Stunningly restored, the oldest continuously used Chinese temple in California. (Arcata–Redding, p. 314.)

WINE COUNTRY TOURS

Southern Wine Country

Temecula *60 miles (96 km) from San Diego, via I-5, Hwy 76, and I-15, or 90 miles (144 km) south-east of Los Angeles via Hwy 1, I-5, I-710, Hwy 1, I-5, Hwy 74, and I-15; Temecula Valley Vintners Association; tel: (909) 699-3626.* Compact, it is a popular day trip from San Diego. Weekend crowds cause traffic congestion. Most wineries impose tasting fees.

Cooling afternoon breezes, a 1500-ft (462 m) elevation, winter morning fog and granite soils produce a wide range of drier varietals – except Pinot Noir. (San Diego–Los Angeles Route, p. 116.)

Santa Barbara County Wineries in the **Santa Ynez Valley** *north of Santa Barbara via Hwys 154 and 246 and the* **Santa Maria Valley**, *north on Hwy 101; Santa Barbara County Vintners' Association; tel: (805) 688-0881.* Look for winemaker/owners behind tasting counters of thirty-some wineries. The Santa Ynez Valley's rolling green hills are dotted with vineyards, horse farms, and cow pastures. Santa Maria Valley winery buildings hide behind their vineyards.

The east-west 'transverse' mountain range differs from all others in California. Summer fog and cooling breezes venture far inland, causing a long growing season in a cooler climate. Try the Chardonnay or Pinot Noir, and savour some of the state's best wines. (Santa Barbara County Routes, p. 134.)

Edna Valley Wineries, *10 miles (16 km) south of San Luis Obispo, on Hwy 227 near Hwy 101. Edna Valley Vintners; tel: (805) 541-5868.* A limited number of wineries follow in the tradition of Mission San Luis Obispo, where wine production made it the richest in its heyday. Pacific Ocean breezes a few miles west cause cool summers and balanced Chardonnays. (Santa Barbara–San Francisco El Camino Real, p. 162.)

Paso Robles Wineries, *20 miles north of San Luis Obispo via Hwy 101. Paso Robles Chamber of Commerce; tel: (805) 238-0506.* Hot summers and blending from many of the area's vineyards produce the full range, from sweet whites to medium dry reds and ultra sweet Muscat Canelli dessert wine. Reds are flavourful. Most wineries charge a tasting fee. (Santa Barbara–San Francisco El Camino Real, p. 162.)

Wine Country North

Napa Valley, *45 miles (72 km) north-east of San Francisco, Hwy 29 runs 22 miles (35 km) up the valley. Napa Valley Vintners Association; tel: (707) 963-0148.* Queen Victoria's 1838 coronation coincided with the first Napa Valley plantings. Hot summers, eight microclimates, and more than 20 soil types create diverse vintages.

Summer weekend traffic snakes up Hwy 29 and its parallel road, the biker-favoured Silverado Trail. Vigilant police nab drunken drivers, especially during treacherous morning fog. The **Napa Valley Wine Train**, *tel: (800) 427-4124*, provides a 3-hour area overview from tracks paralleling Hwy 29. (San Francisco–Napa Valley, p. 236.)

Sonoma County, *north of San Francisco via Hwy 101*. Wineries are dispersed in several valleys: Russian River, Anderson Valley and Dry Creek. **Sonoma County Wine & Visitors Center**, *Rohnert Park; tel: (707) 586-3795*. Wine tasting, winemaking videos, lodging and itinerary planning information.

Thick coastal fog blankets many county wineries until mid-afternoon. Cooler southern and western areas produce excellent Chardonnay, Pinot Noir, and Gewürztraminer. The warmer north-west favours Sauvignon Blanc, Zinfandel, and Cabernet Sauvignon. (San Francisco–Napa Valley, p. 236.)

Mendocino County, *100 miles (160 km) north of San Francisco on Hwy 101*, **Ukiah-Hopland**, *and Hwy 128, the* **Anderson Valley**. *Mendocino County Vintners Association; tel: (707) 468-1343*. Rocky, rolling hills and unirrigated vineyards produce intensely-flavoured wines. Chardonnay and Pinot Noir are found county-wide; other varietals vary with proximity to cooling coastal breezes.

Drive through the Anderson Valley from oak-lined hills near Hwy 101, through apple orchards and vineyards, to redwood groves near the Pacific Coast. (San Francisco–Oregon Border, p. 293.)

Amador/Sierra Foothills, *Hwy 49, east of Plymouth; Amador Vintners Association; tel. (209) 245-6942*. Volcanic soil, winter snowfall and elevation produce dry wines. This **Shenadoah Valley** area is a scenic and tasty detour off the Hwy 49 Gold Rush route. (Oakhurst–Lake Tahoe, p. 206.)

Monterey County, *via 101, Monterey Wine Country Associates; tel: (408) 375-9400; Santa Cruz Mountains Winegrowers Association; tel: (408) 479-9463*. Wineries scatter from Santa Clara across the Santa Cruz Mountains and through Monterey County. (Santa Barbara–San Francisco El Camino Real, p. 162.)

CALIFORNIA MISSIONS

The history of the California Missions, founded by the pioneering Fr Junipero Serra in the earliest days of the European settlement of California, is outlined in the feature on pp. 131–133. The sites of the missions, stretching from San Diego in the south to Sonoma, north of San Francisco, form a historic trail which provides a themed itinerary through coastal California. The key routes to follow are Santa Barbara–San Francisco Coastal Route, p. 145, the El Camino Real, p. 162, and San Francisco Bay Area Routes, p. 228, though some mission sites lie off these routes.

Touring with Thomas Cook – Victorian-style

California became a popular destination for the Thomas Cook travellers as soon as the company opened up the USA to British travellers. Cook's first round-the-world tour of 1872–73 took in California, and in 1876 the company ran the first tour to California in its own right. The journey was by Pullman Cars on the transcontinental railroad from the eastern ports – a distance of 3000 miles to Merced, California, where passengers transferred to stage-coach to visit Yosemite Valley (which was to become part of the world's first National Park in 1890). Tourists explored Yosemite by stage-coach or in the saddle, before rejoining the train to San Francisco for four days' sightseeing. All the elements of a present-day tour of California were already there in Cook's inaugural 1876 expedition – even visits to the Napa Valley vineyards. Only Los Angeles, which began to grow in the 1880s, and Disneyland, which came much later, were not included.

LOS ANGELES

Los Angeles embodies the best and the worst of California. The weather is very nearly perfect, the beaches are broad, the mountains tempting. Unfortunately, the lure works too well. It sometimes seems that the entire world has moved to Los Angeles for the fine weather. Beaches disappear beneath immense crowds, mountains vanish behind a brown pall of smog, and roadways become parking lots.

Those same crowds create the vibrancy and the energy that make Los Angeles the de facto capital of California. But no one calls it Los Angeles. It's LA, pronounced, and sometimes written, as El Lay, pun intended. Most Californians live in Greater Los Angeles, giving LA, Orange, Riverside, and San Bernardino Counties immense political and economic power. Entertainment industries centred around Hollywood have made the city one of the most influential cultural centres on the planet. Loved and hated, usually in the same breath, LA is a California original.

Tourist Information

The **Los Angeles Convention & Visitors Bureau (LACVB)**, *685 S. Figueroa St, Los Angeles, CA 90017; tel: (213) 689-8822*, is open Mon–Sat, 0800–1700.

The **Hollywood Visitor Information Center**, *6541 Hollywood Blvd (Janes Square), Hollywood, CA 90028; tel: (213) 689-8222*, is open Mon–Sat, 0900–1700.

The **Anaheim Area Convention & Visitors Bureau**, *800 W. Katella Ave, PO Box 4270 Anaheim, CA 92803; tel: (714) 999-8999*, is open Mon–Fri, 0900–1700.

The **Long Beach Convention & Visitor Council**, *One World Trade Center, Suite 300, Long Beach, CA 90831-0300; tel: (310) 436-3645*, is open Mon–Fri, 0900–1700.

The **Santa Monica Visitor Center** *1400 Ocean Ave, Santa Monica, CA 90401; tel: (310) 393-7593* is open daily, 1000–1600.

The **West Hollywood Convention & Visitors Bureau**, *9000 Sunset Blvd, Suite 700, West Hollywood, CA 90069-5807; tel: (800) 368-6020*, is open weekdays.

Weather

LA is a temperate desert, with warm weather and low humidity all year. Winters (Nov–Apr) seldom drop to freezing. Summers are hot inland, cooler near the coast. The rainy season is Nov–Mar, usually sporadic rainy days followed by sunshine.

Daily weather reports include air pollution forecasts. Expect occasional health advisories (warnings) to stay indoors and avoid physical exertion, particularly in summer and autumn when smog levels peak. Air quality is better near the coast, worst in the inland valleys.

Arriving and Departing

Airports

Los Angeles International Airport (LAX) is on the coast south-west of downtown, about 30 mins from the city centre and 10 mins from airport hotels. Taxi to downtown, $27.50. Door-to-door shuttle, $14. Bus connections (RTD, Rapid Transit District) are possible, but service is slow and irregular. Free shuttles to rental car locations and airport hotels.

International flights arrive and depart from Bradley International Terminal. Free shuttles to other terminals for domestic connections. Board the 'A' bus under the LAX Shuttle sign outside the arrival area on the ground level. Shuttles are white with blue-and-green trim. Ground transport information is available at white kiosks outside all baggage claim areas.

Burbank and **Van Nuys** (San Fernando Valley), **Long Beach**, and **John Wayne Orange County Airport** serve domestic flights.

By car

One of LA's busiest freeway interchanges is that between the Santa Monica (I-10) and the San Diego (I-405) for airport traffic. Surface streets are almost always faster.

To get **downtown**, take Century Blvd to Airport Blvd, turn left to La Tijera Blvd, veer right. Cross under the 405, continue to La Cienega Blvd, turn left to Slauson Ave, right to La Brea Ave, left to Stocker Ave, left to Crenshaw Ave and on to the I-10 eastbound.

To go **north**, toward Santa Monica, follow signs out of the airport to Sepulveda Blvd (Highway 1) northbound.

To go **south**, toward Long Beach, Disneyland and San Diego, take Century Blvd to the 405 southbound. For the beach cities (Manhattan, Hermosa and Redondo Beach) and Palos Verdes, follow signs to Sepulveda southbound.

To go **east**, toward Norwalk and northern Orange County, follow signs for Sepulveda southbound and the Century Freeway (I-105) eastbound.

Getting Around

All 9 million people who live in Greater Los Angeles seem to be driving all day and most of the night. It's nearly impossible to navigate LA without a car and equally impossible to explore most neighbourhoods with one. Drive to an area, park, explore on foot, then drive on.

Avoid walking more than a few blocks in South Central, East LA, and anywhere buildings are protected with bars, grates, and rolls of concertina or barbed wire. Parks and dimly lit areas are unsafe after dark.

Taxi stands are located at airports, Union Station (train station), bus terminals, and major hotels. Otherwise, taxis are dispatched by radio and must be ordered in advance. Passing cabs rarely stop when hailed.

Public Transport

Popular myth says LA grew up with the automobile. In real life, it grew up with public transport. The Red Line was once the most efficient streetcar system in America, but LA outgrew its rail network before World War II. The automobile took over.

Two generations later, public transport is trying for a come back. In some areas, it's even succeeding. **Union Station** is LA's public transport hub.

The Los Angeles County Metropolitan Transit Authority (**MTA**), *tel: (213) 626-4455*, is trying to wean Angelenos out of cars and into public transport. LA has the largest passenger bus system in the United States, but few commuter routes are useful for sightseeing.

At 25 cents a ride, **DASH**, *tel: 1-800-2-LA-RIDE*, the Downtown Area Short Hop shuttle system, is the top transport system in the state. Four lines link major business, shopping and tourist areas between Chinatown, the University of Southern California (USC), the Harbor Freeway and Little Tokyo.

Best bets for downtown sightseeing: stay at the Biltmore or another downtown hotel (convenient but expensive) and use DASH; or park at Union Station and pick up DASH across Alameda St at El Pueblo de Los Angeles State Historical Park. DASH maps are available at hotels, LACVB Visitor Centers, and Metro Rail stations.

Metro Rail, *tel: (213) 626-4455*, is a 300-mile (480 km) rail system due for completion by 2001. Two lines are in operation. The **Blue Line** connects downtown LA and downtown Long Beach from 0600–2100 daily. The **Red Line** runs 4.4 miles (7 km) underground between Union Station and MacArthur Park. The **Green Line**, with service to LAX, is scheduled to open in 1995.

Driving in Los Angeles

Best source of maps is any branch of the **Automobile Club of Southern California**. Apply in person, checking the phone book for addresses. ACSC's free 'Travel $aver' newsletter lists special member attraction and lodging discounts.

The 1994 Northridge Earthquake crumbled vital freeway links, but most had re-opened by summer 1994. Unlike the San Francisco Bay Area, which still hasn't decided what to do with freeways damaged in the 1989 Loma Prieta quake, Los Angeles never questioned the need to rebuild.

Angelenos don't talk about how far away a place is, but how long it takes to get there. Timing depends on the hour and the number of accidents along the way. Traffic is slowest during commuting hours (0600–1000 and

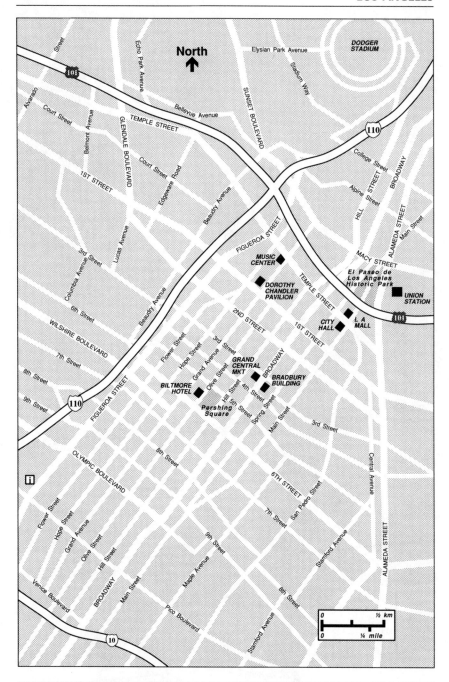

Downtown Los Angeles Map

LOS ANGELES

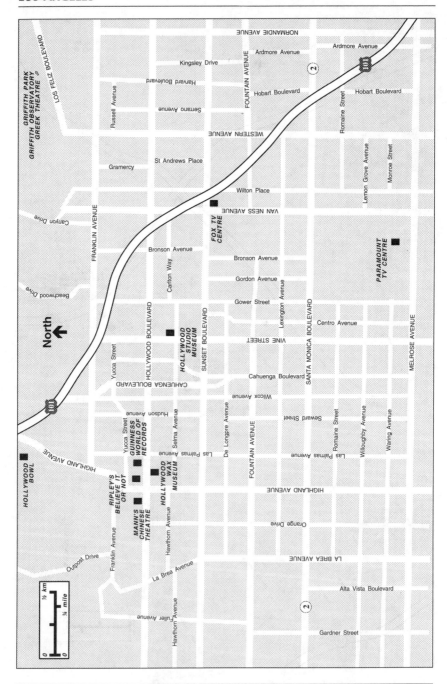

1500–1900), weekend evenings, holidays, and special events.

Radio is the best source for current road conditions. Station KNX, 1040 on the AM dial, has frequent and detailed traffic reports.

Lay out your route before leaving for the next stop. It's also a good idea to plan an alternative in case traffic backs up – with someone other than the driver designated to navigate.

Freeways

The Los Angeles freeway tradition began on 30 Dec 1940. Native American Chief Tahachwee and state Public Works Director Frank W. Chark smoked a peace pipe and the Kawie tribe signed over land that became the 8.2-mile (13 km) Pasadena Freeway. Half a century later, LA has more than 560 miles (896 km) of freeways, the most extensive network of controlled access highways in the world.

Locals avoid them whenever possible. Freeway routes may be more direct than surface streets, but it's hard to get off again to skirt traffic hold-ups.

Freeways are almost always referred to by name instead of number:

Freeway name	Freeway number
Glendale	2
Golden State/Santa Ana	5
Santa Monica/San Bernadino	10
Garden Grove	22
Orange	57
Pomona	60
Marina	90
Artesia/Riverside	91
Ventura/Hollywood	101
Pasadena/Harbor	110
Century	105
Simi Valley/San Fernando Valley	118
Ventura	134
Hollywood	170
Foothill	210
San Diego	405
San Gabriel River	605
Long Beach	710

Surface streets are usually, but not always, arranged in a grid. One-way streets are common downtown but not in other areas.

Left-turn lanes, however, are rare. Plan routes to avoid left turns. The alternative is waiting for traffic break, usually as the light turns from green to red, leaving just enough time for two or three cars to slip through before cross-traffic thunders through.

Living in Los Angeles

Accommodation

LA probably has more chain hotels than any other city in the world, from top international names like Four Seasons, Kempinski, Peninsula, and Regent to Motel 6 and other budget choices. Expect temporary local shortages, downtown during major conventions at the Convention Center, or in Hollywood during film industry events, but the city last ran out of rooms during the 1984 Olympics.

If possible, stay where you're visiting. Changing hotels occasionally will save hours of driving frustration.

It's also smart not to plan a long drive for the day you arrive on an intercontinental flight. Try to spend the first night in an airport hotel, then get an early driving start the next morning.

Most **Downtown** hotels charge high business rates during the week with equally high weekend discounts. The expensive Biltmore, facing Pershing Square, has the best location for exploring downtown. The equally expensive Hotel Intercontinental is within walking distance of the Music Center and MOCA, the Museum of Contemporary Art. Allow an extra $20 per night for parking.

The **West Side** – Bel Air, Beverly Hills, Hollywood and West Hollywood – is the world capital of glitz. The Beverly Prescott overlooks the residential end of Beverly Hills and Rodeo Drive with a hot-spot restaurant, Rox, and prices to match. Other top-end names include Century Plaza, Peninsula, Regent Beverly Wilshire, and Mondrian.

Moderate West Side hotels are clustered in Hollywood, now the area's low rent district. Try the Hollywood Celebrity Hotel, the Hollywood

Palm, the Hollywood Roosevelt (a Radisson) and Regency Plaza Suites.

Beach area hotels also run toward the expensive end. Top of the line is the Ritz-Carlton Marina del Rey, on the water about 10 mins from the airport. Shutters on the Beach and the Loews Beach Resort, both in Santa Monica, are only slightly less expensive. Palos Verdes Inn, 30 mins south on Highway 1 in Redondo Beach, is a more moderate choice. In Long Beach, the *Queen Mary* has become a moderately-priced floating hotel.

AY have 3 youth hostels in the Los Angeles area: HI-Los Angeles/San Pedro, *PO Box 5345, San Pedro, CA 90731, tel; (310) 831-8109*, and HI-Los Angeles/Santa Monica, *1436 Second St, Santa Monica, CA 90401, tel; (310) 393-9913.* For details of the *AY* hostel in the Disneyland area, see p. 67.

Eating and Drinking

Big-name restaurants are as expensive here as anywhere in the world, and as mercurial. For the latest and hippest, check *LA Magazine* and the *Los Angeles Times* food section.

If the budget doesn't allow for dinner at the likes of Spago, Geoffrey's, Water Grill, or DC3, lunch is 20% cheaper. At the very least, buy a drink in the Rendezvouz Lounge on the ground floor of the Biltmore Hotel. It's the cheapest way to sample the 1920s splendour of LA's Golden Age.

For more realistic eating, check the restaurant section in *Westways* magazine from the Automobile Club of Southern California, available on newsstands.

It's hard to go wrong with budget-to-moderately priced ethnic restaurants. The **Grand Central Market**, *317 S. Broadway*, downtown, has cheaper and more authentic Mexican food than Olvera Street.

Local restaurants in Chinese, Japanese, Korean, and Vietnamese neighbourhoods are also good bets. In the Westside, **Canter's**, *419 N. Fairfax Ave, near Beverly Blvd*, and **Nate 'n Al**, *414 N. Beverly Dr., near Santa Monica Blvd* delicatessens are worth searching out. Moderate rather than low prices, but portions are so big that doggie bags are standard.

Brewpubs, like other restaurants, come and go. Check the telephone book Yellow Pages under 'Breweries' for the current batch.

Communications

There are more than 100 post offices in greater Los Angeles. Mail can be addressed to hotels.

Money

Thomas Cook Foreign Exchange branches: *452 North Bedford Drive, Beverly Hills; tel: (310) 274-9176.*
Hilton Hotel Center, 900 Wilshire Blvd, Los Angeles; tel: (213) 624-4221.
111 West Ocean Blvd, Long Beach; tel: (310) 491-0158.
Bank of Los Angeles , 8901 Santa Monica Blvd, West Hollywood; tel: (310) 659-6092.
Travellers' cheque refunds available at all above.

Entertainment

LA is the heart of the USA's music, club, and comedy scenes. For current best bets, check *LA Magazine* and *LA Weekly*, a tabloid available in most music and CD shops. Local newspapers list daily cinema offerings.

The **Music Center**, *135 N. Grand Ave, Downtown, tel: (213) 972-7211*, is the centre for performing arts, with **The Ahmanson Theatre** as the main stage; the 750-seat **Mark Taper Forum** is known for experimental theatre. The 3200-seat **Dorothy Chandler Pavilion** houses the Philharmonic, Opera, and Academy Awards.

Other major stages: **The Ahmanson at the UCLA James A. Doolittle Theatre**, *1615 N. Vine St, CA 90028 Hollywood; tel: (213) 972-7372;* **Pantages Theatre**, *6233 Hollywood Blvd, CA 90028, Hollywood; tel: (213) 464-7521;* and the **Schubert Theatre**, *2020 Ave of the Stars, Westwood, CA 90067; tel: (310) 201-1500.*

Shopping

If Angelenos sometimes seem born to shop, blame it on opportunity. Major department stores include The Broadway, Bullocks, Nordstrom's, Robinson-May Co., and Saks Fifth Avenue, all with multiple locations.

Rodeo Drive, between Santa Monica Blvd and Wilshire Blvd in Beverly Hills, is perfect for anyone who can spend $1000 on a pair of shoes without breathing hard. Beverly Hills provides 2hrs of free parking so that the rest of us can gape at this epitome of conspicuous consumption.

Third Street Promenade, in Santa Monica, and **Santa Monica Place** offer more realistic prices and 200-plus shops. The **Beverly Center**, *8500 Beverly Blvd*, is one of the hottest malls for shopping and eating. **Century City Shopping Center & Marketplace**, *10250 Santa Monica Blvd*, is a major lure for Westside shoppers.

Westside is also the place for sexy swimsuits and lingerie, from mass-produced **Frederick's of Hollywood**, *6608 Hollywood Blvd*, to handmade silks and leathers at **Trashy Lingerie**, *402 N. La Cienega Blvd*.

Discount Outlets are expanding. The **Cooper Building**, *860 S. Los Angeles St*, has more than 50 discount outlets, but parking is tight. The **Citadel**, *5675 E. Telegraph Rd, Commerce, CA 90040 (off I-5, 9 miles S. of downtown LA); tel: (213) 888-1220*, has four dozen factory outlets in a castle-like former tyre factory.

Sightseeing

The LACVB has divided Greater Los Angeles into five areas: Downtown, Hollywood, Westside, Coastal and Valleys. We've added Long Beach, Catalina Island and Greater Los Angeles are covered separately (see pp. 63–70).

Downtown

Downtown streets are crowded and parking expensive. Union Station has the cheapest parking, Pershing Square the most convenient.

Broadway is a study in contrasts. At street level, a cacophony of entrepreneurs from around the globe sell everything from discount electronics to cheap clothing, bolstering LA's reputation as America's largest Third World city. One floor up, architectural details from the Roaring '20s reflect the era when LA first began flexing its financial muscle.

The **Biltmore Hotel**, *506 S. Grand Ave*, and **Union Station** have been restored to their original grandeur. For other downtown gems,

take a Los Angeles Conservancy self-guided walking tour; *tel: (213) 632-CITY*.

Union Station, *800 N. Alameda St*, **City Hall**, *200 N. Spring St*, and the **Bradbury Building**, *304 S. Broadway*, have played starring roles in innumerable cinema and television productions. **El Pueblo de Los Angeles Historic Park**, *845 N. Alameda St; tel: (213) 628-1274*, is the centre of historic Los Angeles, founded in 1781. The park includes LA's oldest building, **Avila Adobe** (1818), the original town park, first fire house and 25 other historic buildings. **Olvera St** was closed to traffic in 1930 and turned into a traditional Mexican marketplace. Guided tours Tues–Sat.

The **Grand Central Market**, *317 S. Broadway*, is the city's oldest and largest food market. More than 50 stalls sell fresh produce (great for stocking picnic lunches) and prepared food. Mon–Sat, 0900–1800, Sun 1000–1700. Best spots to enjoy the picnic are **Pershing Square**, **California Plaza**, and the **LA Mall**, *Fletcher Bowron Square*.

LA's cultural diversity is reflected in the **Music Center**, *135 N. Grand Ave*, home to opera, traditional and experimental theatre, symphony concerts and the Academy Awards.

Hollywood

The corner of Hollywood Blvd and Highland Ave is the centre of **Hollywood**, but expect more museums, souvenir stands and lingerie shops than living Hollywood heroes. Park at any of the secure lots along Hollywood Blvd.

Nearly 2000 bronze stars still glitter along the **Walk of Fame**, *Hollywood Blvd between Sycamore Ave and Gower St, and Vine St between Yucca St and Sunset Blvd*, but watch out for chewing gum on the pavement. The **Hollywood Roosevelt Hotel**, *7000 Hollywood Blvd*, has an outstanding collection of cinema nostalgia and historic photographs.

The only way to be sure of seeing today's stars is to catch them at work. **Hollywood on Location**, *8644 Wilshire Blvd; tel: (213) 659-9165*, publishes a list of public locations for cinema, television and advertising shoots around 0900 each morning. Admission is free, the list is not.

Shopping–Sightseeing **59**

Souvenir shops also sell maps showing locations of stars' homes. Don't forget that movie stars, like most Angelenos, go off to work every day.

Three of Hollywood's grandest cinema palaces have survived. The **Egyptian Theatre**, *6712 Hollywood Blvd*, has become a triplex. Across the street, more than 150 famous hand-, foot- and hoofprints are preserved in the courtyard of **Mann's Chinese Theatre**, *6925 Hollywood Blvd*. It's worth the price of a ticket to **El Capital Theatre**, *6838 Hollywood Blvd*, just to see the restored combination of Italian Baroque and East Indian decor.

The largest Hollywood landmark is the white 'Hollywood' sign at the top of Beachwood Canyon, near the corner of Beachwood and Franklin. The classic cinema view of the 15-metre letters is from **Griffith Observatory**, *2800 E. Observatory Rd, Griffith Park*. The **Hollywood Bowl**, *2301 N. Highland Ave*, and the **Greek Theatre**, *2700 N. Vermont Ave*, draw sellout crowds for outdoor concerts with Eric Clapton, the LA Philharmonic and every musical taste in between.

Westside

The **Westside** has all the symbols of grace and glamour that Hollywood once boasted, including the walled mansions of **Beverly Hills** and **Rodeo Drive** shopping palaces for the solid of bank account.

Melrose Ave (Doheny Dr. to La Brea Ave) is lined with the most fashion-forward shops and shoppers you're likely to see anywhere. The transportation of choice is long and chauffeured or sporty and red; the reality is the same mix of slightly dented imports that crowd most LA streets.

La Brea Ave, south of Melrose, is lined with galleries, art studios, bookstores, coffee-houses and some of LA's trendiest eateries. Nearby blocks of **Santa Monica Blvd** house chic salons and clothing shops.

Nighthawks still head for **Sunset Strip** (Sunset Blvd just east of Beverly Hills) for the hippest music, comedy clubs and food. **Century City** is a more staid entertainment venue on what used to be the back lot of Twentieth Century Fox cinema studios. Today, it houses the densest concentration of entertainment industry companies in the world, first-run cinemas, shopping palaces, up-market eateries and posh hotels.

Coastal

Coastal LA is a 72-mile strip of surf and sand from **Malibu** south to **Long Beach**. Most of the stretch is lined with walking, cycling, and skating paths isolated from automobile traffic. Public piers provide fishing access and a view of surfers as they ride crashing waves toward shore. **Pacific Coast Highway**, PCH, is the main north–south artery along the coast. PCH runs inland south of Santa Monica, but local streets hug the coastline.

Surfrider's Beach, just north of Malibu Pier, the original California surfing beach, is still popular. The Spanish Colonial Revival **Adamson House**, *23299 PCH, Malibu, CA 90265; tel: (310) 456-8432*, behind Surfrider, is the finest extant example of California decorative tile work.

The rugged **Santa Monica Mountains** rise just across PCH from the beach. The **Santa Monica Mountains National Recreation Area**, *30401 Agoura Rd, Suite 100, Agoura Hills, CA 91301; tel: (818) 597-9192*, is laced with hiking trails and remote canyons filled with exclusive homes. Summer wildfires sweep the steep hillsides; winter rains trigger mud slides which close roadways for a few days every winter.

The **Santa Monica Pier** has an antique carousel and bumper cars, plus more adult pastimes like fishing and dining. The **Third Street Promenade** is an indoor/outdoor pedestrian shopping and restaurant mall.

Venice Beach is a seven-day circus. **Oceanfront Walk** is jammed with bicycles, skaters, walkers, and gawkers from late morning until dusk. The lure is sun, sand and a constant stream of musicians, comedians, jugglers, mime artists and dancers concentrated around Windward Ave.

Muscle Beach, just south of Windward, is the original outdoor body-building studio. Mr and Ms Universe wannabes pump iron and build bulk in public. Pickup basketball games are popular on nearby public courts – and very physical.

Marina del Rey is the world's largest man-made harbour. For great sunset views, follow Via Marina to the end of the breakwater. The best weekend meal in town is Sunday brunch at the Ritz-Carlton Hotel. Expensive, and worth it. Reservations required.

Los Angeles Airport is just south of Marina del Rey. Next come the beach cities of **Manhattan, Hermosa**, and **Redondo**, fronted by miles of beach. Each city has its own pier, a focal point for open air restaurants, volleyball, cycling, skating, or just watching the world swirl past.

Palos Verdes Blvd climbs the shoulder of the **Palos Verdes Peninsula** from Redondo Beach. The peninsula is littered with ordinary multi-million dollar homes, walled estates, and spectacular coastline views. Most land is private, but marked public paths lead down from Paseo del Mar to sheltered coves.

On the south side of the peninsula, **Point Vicente** Interpretive Center is a favourite spot to watch whales migrating south to Baja California in autumn and north to Alaska in spring.

Wayfarers Chapel, 2 miles south of Point Vicente, is a glass-walled chapel overlooking the Pacific. The 1951 church is a memorial to 18th-century mystic and theologian Emanuel Swedenborg.

Palos Verdes forms the north side of Los Angeles and Long Beach harbours. The best view across **Worldport LA**, the busiest harbour on the west coast of North America, is from **Point Fermin**, a city park at the southern tip of the Palos Verdes peninsula.

Long Beach

Long Beach forms the south side of the harbour. The SS **Queen Mary** is permanently docked at *1126 Queens Hwy; tel: (310) 435-3511*. The bridge, engine room, and first class public areas are a museum; lounges and restaurants have been reopened; and first class cabins have been restored as moderate hotel rooms.

Economic revival has created soaring new office towers and hotels amidst refurbished towers from the 1920s. **Ports O' Call Village** is

a marine-themed shopping centre with free parking, helicopter tours and harbour cruises. **Planet Ocean** covers the exterior of the Long Beach Sports Arena with the world's largest mural, life-sized paintings of whales and other local sea life. The **Belmont Brewing Company**, *25 39th Place, Long Beach, CA 90803; tel: (310) 433-3891*, is at the foot of Belmont Pier, in the midst of miles of golden beaches and grassy parks extending south to Orange County.

The Valleys

The Santa Monica Mountains separate the **valleys**, San Fernando, San Gabriel and Santa Clarita, from the LA basin. 'The Valley' is usually San Fernando, the biggest. All three are famous for vast dormitory towns, traffic, and smog.

Mission San Gabriel, *537 W. Mission Dr., San Gabriel, CA 91776; tel: (213) 282-519*, named one valley in 1771. The compound includes the mission church, with original furnishings and decorations, the oldest cemetery in Los Angeles County, the original quadrangle, and original cisterns, vats, aqueducts, and cannon. Open daily, 0930–1615.

Mission San Fernando, Rey de España, *15151 San Fernando Mission Blvd, Mission Hills, CA 91345; tel: (818) 361-0186*, was damaged in the 1994 Northridge earthquake. Church, gardens, cemetery, workshops, museum and ranch foreman's house are open daily, 0930–1600.

Museums

Decades as the economic powerhouse of California has left Los Angeles with dozens of major **museums**. The **Armand Hammer Museum of Art**, *10899 Wilshire Blvd, 90024, Westside; tel: (310) 443-7000*, covers five centuries of Western European art. The **J. Paul Getty Museum**, *17985 PCH, Malibu, CA 90265, Coastal; tel: (310) 458-2003*, housed in a Greek-style villa, specialises in Greek and Roman antiquities, pre-20th century Western Europe and photography. Parking reservations required. The **Los Angeles County Museum of Art**, LACMA, *5905 Wilshire Blvd, 90036 Westside; tel: (213) 857-6111*, is a five-building complex with worldwide painting, sculpture,

Sightseeing   **61**

costumes, textiles and decorative arts, pre-historic to contemporary.

Next door, the **George C. Page Museum**, *5801 Wilshire Blvd, Westside, 90036; tel (213) 936-2230*, features Ice Age fossils from the La Brea Tar Pits, just outside.

Beit Hashoah–Museum of Tolerance, *9786 W. Pico Blvd, Westside, 90035; tel (310) 553-8403*, focuses on the history of intolerance and prejudice in the USA and the Holocaust. One of the busiest museums in a multicultural, often-violent city.

The **Gene Autry Western Heritage Museum**, *4700 Western Heritage Way, Hollywood, 90027; tel: (213) 667-2000*, in Griffith Park, covers Western North America from the 16th century, not singing cowboys.

Hollywood is rife with museums: the **Hollywood Bowl Museum**, *2301 N. Highland Ave, 90028, tel: (213) 850-2058;* the **Hollywood Studio Museum**, *2100 N. Highland Ave, 90028, tel: (213) 874-2276;* **Max Factor Museum of Beauty**, *1666 N. Highland Ave, tel: (213) 463-6668;* **Frederick's of Hollywood Lingerie Museum**, *6608 Hollywood Blvd, 90028, tel: (213) 466-8506;* the **Guinness World of Records Museum**, *6764 Hollywood Blvd, 90028, tel: (213) 463-8506;* the **Hollywood Wax Museum**, *6767 Hollywood Blvd, 90028, tel: (213) 462-8860;* and **Ripley's Believe It or Not Hollywood**, *6780 Hollywood Blvd, 90028, tel: (213) 466-6335.*

Walking Tours

The **Los Angeles Conservancy**, *tel: (213) 632-CITY*, a non-profit group dedicated to preserving and revitalising the city's architectural roots, sponsors 2-hr **downtown** tours every weekend. Self-guided tour maps are also available. Most tours start from the historic Biltmore Hotel: Art Deco, Terra Cotta, Marble Masterpieces, Little Tokyo, Broadway Theaters (luxury cinema palaces) and glamorous Hollywood flats.

The **Beverly Hills Visitors Bureau**, *tel: 1-800-345-2210*, has a self-guided tour of the USA's ultimate city of self-indulgence. The route starts in the business district, spans Rodeo Drive shopping, and passes some of the city's more magnificent mansions.

The historic cinema capital of **Hollywood** has the greatest variety of walking tours. Tours sponsored by the Hollywood Heritage historical society visit the city's oldest restaurant, first nightclub, site of the first Academy Awards, and several original movie palaces. *Tel: (213) 874-4005.*

A self-guided 'Windows on Hollywood' tour, *tel: (213) 469-9151*, highlights Hollywood Blvd storefronts that have become showcases of entertainment industry memorabilia.

University of California Los Angeles Visitor Center, *tel: 310-206-8147*, offers self-guided or 90-minute guided tours of the bustling **UCLA** campus.

Television and Movie Studio Tours

Television and movie studio tours take advance planning, but are relatively easy to arrange. Tickets for the most popular TV shows can be hard to get.

Audiences Unlimited, *Fox Television Center, 5746 Sunset Blvd, Hollywood; tel: (818) 506-0067*, is the exclusive ticket agent for most ABC, CBS, MTM, and Universal Studios TV programmes.

CBS Television City, *7800 Beverly Blvd, LA; tel: (213) 852-2624*. Box office is open 0900–1700 daily.

NBC Television, *3000 W. Alameda Ave, Burbank; tel: (818) 840-3537*, box office is open 0800–1700 weekdays. Studio tours 0900–1500 weekdays, 1000–1600 Saturdays.

Paramount Television, *860 N. Gower Ave, Hollywood; tel: (213) 956-5575*, box office ispen 0800–1600 weekdays. Studio tours 0900–1400 weekdays.

Audiences Unlimited handle tickets for **Warner Bros Studios**, *4000 Warner Blvd, Burbank; tel: (818) 954-1744*. Studio tours 0900–1400 weekdays. Reservations required at least 48 hours in advance. Paramount and Warner offer the best behind-the-scenes look at TV and cinema production.

Universal Studios, *100 Universal City Plaza, Universal City, CA 91608; tel: (818) 508-9600*, is a movie theme park with a perfunctory tram tour of the back lot. For a fuller description, see p. 67.

GREATER LOS ANGELES ROUTES

LOS ANGELES CIRCULAR DRIVE

Allow at least half a day for this 53-mile tour of Los Angeles. Visiting all the museums and attractions could stretch to an exhausting week.

The route begins and ends at Union Station for convenience, but you can pick it up at any point. The route can be taken in either direction, but the directions given reduce left turns. Try to drive the Hollywood section before 1500, when left turns are banned for the commuting period.

Civic Centre

From Union Station, cross Alameda St to Los Angeles St at the edge of **El Pueblo de Los Angeles State Historic Park.** Park at Union Station to explore the park and **Olvera St.**

Follow Los Angeles St over the freeway to Temple St. The **Federal Building** is on the left, **Los Angeles Mall** on the right.

Continue along Los Angeles St to First St. Turn right. **Civic Center** city and state government buildings are on the right. The retro-futuristic **City Hall** tower is on the right near Main St. The **Los Angeles Times Building** is across the street. The **Music Center** is on the right at Grand Ave.

Pass the Music Center and take the First St overpass. First St becomes Beverly Blvd. Beverly continues 2 miles (3 km) through a mix of Korean and Hispanic residential neighbourhoods. Veer left around an Art Deco building just after Commonwealth Ave. Stay on Beverly, headed west. (This is a good area to avoid after dark.)

At Western Ave, turn right into a Japanese neighbourhood. Turn left ½ mile (1 km) later onto Melrose Ave. The **Paramount Studio Main Gate** is on the right, opposite Windsor Blvd. Trendy businesses begin appearing around Highland Blvd; trendies control the 2 miles (3 km) between La Brea and La Cienega.

Turn left at La Cienega. Four blocks south, at Beverly Blvd, is **Beverly Center,** one of the hottest shopping centres in LA. Turn left onto Beverly Blvd 1.3 miles (2 km) ahead, and then turn right onto Fairfax Ave.

CBS Television City is across the street on the left. The **Farmers Market** is next to CBS, at Fairfax and Third St. The market has plenty of free parking and a variety of restaurants for lunch and dinner. Popular with CBS employees.

Turn left onto Third St. Follow Third to Highland Ave, turn left. Highland is a divided parkway, lined with large, expensive homes and equally large, expensive cars parked along narrow traffic lanes.

Cross Melrose, 1 mile (1.6 km) beyond, and Santa Monica Blvd, another ½ mile (1 km). There are no street signs announcing **Hollywood,** just a sudden rash of billboards hyping would-be movie stars, mostly female, alluring and half-dressed.

Hollywood

Hollywood High School is on the left a half-mile (1 km) beyond Santa Monica Blvd. On the right is the **Max Factor Museum.** Cross Hollywood Blvd for a cluster of novelty museums: **Ripley's Believe It or Not, Guinness World of Records** and the **Hollywood Wax Museum.**

The next major intersection is Franklin St and the **First Methodist Church.** Two very long blocks beyond is Milner St and the **Hollywood Screen Museum,** on the right.

If you're not visiting the museum, move into the left lane to avoid entering the Hollywood Freeway. Follow signs left to the **Hollywood Bowl** and the **Hollywood Bowl Museum.**

Leaving the Bowl, turn right onto Highland. Continue back to Hollywood Blvd and turn left. Pass Ripley's, Guinness, and the Wax Museum again in the first block.

If left turns are not allowed, continue one block to Hawthorne Ave, turn right to Orange Ave, turn right to Hollywood Blvd, turn right at the **Hollywood Roosevelt Hotel. Mann's Chinese Theatre** is across the street. Continue east on Hollywood Blvd past **Frederick's of Hollywood** to Vine St. The **Pantages Theatre** is just ahead. Turn right onto Vine St. Follow Vine a

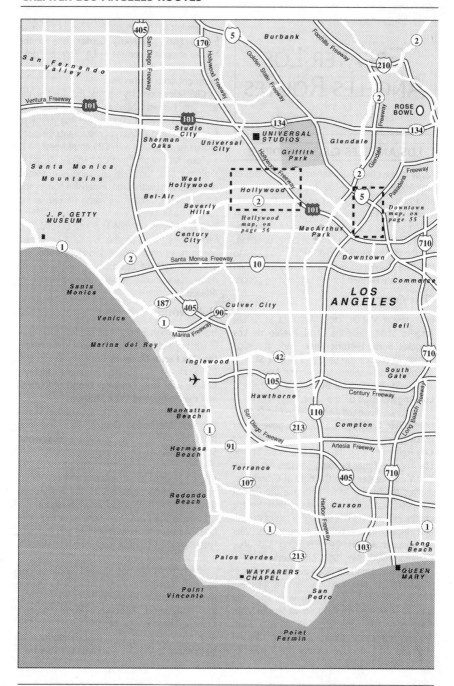

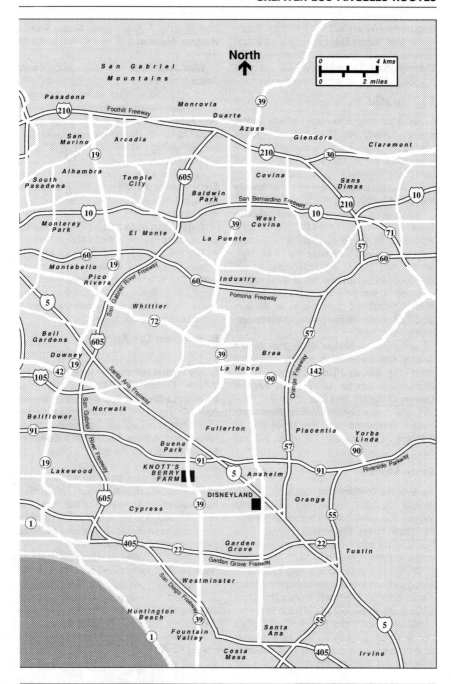

long block to Sunset Blvd and turn right. Follow Sunset west. **Sunset Strip** begins near the border between West Hollywood and Beverly Hills. The **Comedy Store**, **The Whiskey Club** and other hot spots are easy to miss during the day.

Beverly Hills

Sunset turns into a divided parkway before entering **Beverly Hills**. There isn't much to see beyond high walls, closed gates, and luxuriant landscaping. A triangular park at the corner of Sunset and Beverly Dr. is a convenient spot to watch expensive cars wheel into the **Beverly Hills Hotel**, across the street.

The other end of the park is formed by **Rodeo Drive**. Turn left onto Rodeo Dr., a wide, calm residential street. There's plenty of street parking, but don't overstay the 2-hr limit. Beverly Hills police are notoriously under-employed and highly protective of their enclave.

Rodeo Dr. **shopping** begins at **Santa Monica Blvd** and continues three blocks to **Wilshire Blvd**. Follow signs for free parking at **Via Rodeo**, Rodeo and Wilshire.

Turn right at Wilshire Blvd. The **Regent Beverly Wilshire Hotel** is directly across the street. The **Beverly Hilton** is on the left at Wilshire and Whittier Dr. The **Los Angeles Country Club** golf course abuts the Beverly Hills–LA border 1 mile beyond. Wilshire drops down toward **Westwood** and the **University of California, Los Angeles**, 1½ miles (2.4 km) away.

Santa Monica

The **Wilshire Corridor** continues west, passing beneath the I-405 freeway and on to **Santa Monica**. Four miles (6.4 km) beyond Westwood, the **Third Street Promenade** extends three blocks to the left: metered parking on nearby streets and multi-storey car parks.

Wilshire ends at Ocean Ave, Hwy 1. Turn left. A long park and promenade follows the cliff top in both directions. The **Santa Monica Pier** is four blocks south at the foot of Colorado Ave.

Follow Ocean to Pico Blvd. Turn left. Follow Pico one block to Main St. Turn right. Main is another trendy neighbourhood of restaurants, galleries, and clothing stores, but far more relaxed than Melrose Ave. **Santa Monica Heritage Museum** is ½ mile (1 km) south on the left.

Windward Circle is 1 mile south. **Venice Beach** is one short block down Windward Ave. To return downtown, drive to Windward Circle, follow Grand Ave one block to Dell Ave. Turn right, cross Venice Blvd (one-way to the beach) to Venice Blvd toward downtown. Turn left. **Venice High School** is on the right beyond Lincoln Blvd.

At Centinella Ave, turn left. The turnoff for the **Santa Monica Airport** and the **Museum of Flying** is 1 mile north. At Ocean Park Blvd, turn right. The road veers left, becomes Gateway Blvd, and crosses under the I-10 Freeway. At Pico, turn right and pass under the San Diego Freeway.

Two miles beyond the I-405, turn left onto Avenue of the Stars. **Century City** is straight ahead. One mile beyond, turn right onto Santa Monica Blvd. Beverly Hills is less than ½ mile ahead. The **Peninsula Hotel** is near the corner of Santa Monica Blvd and Laskey Dr.

Downtown Los Angeles

Turn right onto Wilshire Blvd. Rodeo Dr. and the Beverly Wilshire Hotel are ½ mile east along the Wilshire Corridor. **LACMA** and the **Page Museum/La Brea Tar Pits** are 2 miles beyond Rodeo Dr. The offices of **Variety** magazine, the entertainment industry daily, are on the right at Wilshire and Masselin Ave. The **RTD Customer Service Center** is on the left at Wilshire and La Brea.

The trimmed palm trees, lawns, bandshells, and fountains of **Lafayette Park** and **MacArthur Park** mark what was the edge of suburban LA in the 1920s and '30s. MacArthur Park is currently the southern end of the MTR Red Line. Avoid the parks between dusk and mid-morning.

Continue on Wilshire over the 110 to **Figueroa St**. Turn left one block to Sixth St, turn right. The round towers of **Arco Plaza** are on the left at Flower St. At Grand St, the **Biltmore Hotel** is on the left. The open plaza opposite the Biltmore is **Pershing Square**.

At Broadway, turn left. Many of the 1920s movie palaces are still standing, though few are still used as cinemas. At Third St, the **Bradbury**

Building is on the right, the **Million Dollar Theatre** on the left.

Cross the I-101 freeway. Continue through **El Pueblo de Los Angeles** to Sunset Blvd. Turn right. Drive four blocks to Alameda St. Turn right. Union Station is on the left.

UNIVERSAL STUDIOS

Universal Studios Hollywood, *100 Universal City Plaza, Universal City, CA 91608; tel: (818) 508-9600,* is part movieland theme park, part studio tour, and part pseudo-reality. Despite the Hollywood name, Universal Studios is firmly anchored to the edge of the San Fernando Valley, just off the Hollywood (Hwy 101) Freeway. Take the Lankersham exit from the Hollywood (Hwy 101) or Ventura (Hwy 134) freeways on the southern edge of the San Fernando Valley and follow the signs. No free or overnight parking.

Rather than hiding the illusions of cinema production, Universal openly uses the tricks of its trade to create a very upbeat, but disarmingly real-seeming atmosphere – real enough that promoters say it has become the fourth most popular man-made attraction in the USA.

Although the park is part of the immense Universal Studios production complex, there is very little sense of active film or television production. What Universal does offer is a splendid sense of the theatrical, all tied to some Universal Studios' film, television production or character. Universal is divided into five sections: the **entrance and ticket booth** area; **Entertainment Center**; **Studio Center**; the **Studio Tram** ride; and **Universal CityWalk**. Each is progressively more engaging.

The hilltop entrance area is purely functional: buy tickets; pick up park maps and guides; rent prams or wheelchairs; ask questions. The park really begins at **Entertainment Center**. Mock cinema sets portray Baker Street, the Moulin Rouge, stereotypical Western and New York streets, and Cape Cod, all with appropriate souvenir shops. Periodic film-based stage shows are aimed squarely at children and young teenagers: a musical from *An American Tail*, adventure from *Conan the Barbarian*, stunt performers from *Miami Vice* and the Wild West.

Los Angeles Theme Parks

All of Los Angeles has been accused of being a gigantic theme park, but even in LaLa Land, some places are less real than others. The top three contenders are Universal Studios Hollywood, Knott's Berry Farm, and the original Disneyland. Adult admission prices were $25–30 in mid-1994, plus parking. None of the parks allow food or drink to be brought in and all charge exorbitant prices at snack bars, restaurants and souvenir shops.

Anaheim-Buena Park hotels are easiest for Disneyland or Knott's Berry Farm visits. The Disneyland Hotel is an obvious – and expensive – choice. There are better deals at nearby *HI, SH, HN* and *MA*, all moderately priced. Most have free shuttles to Disneyland. Nearby motels are busy during the summer months and holiday weekends, but have unadvertised budget-priced specials the rest of the year.

Best bet for Knott's Berry Farm is the Buena Park Hotel & Convention Center next door. Disney and Knott's are about 20 mins apart. *AYH* have a youth hostel in the area: *1700 North Harbor Blvd, Fullerton; tel: (714) 738-3721.*

The nearest **Thomas Cook foreign exchange** branch is at *City Shopping Center, 8 City Blvd East, Ste 83, Orange; tel: (714) 978-9979.*

Integrated sound, visuals, and limited motion produces impossible kinetic effects from *Back To The Future*. Special seats that rock and shake, gigantic 270° curved cinema screens, 10,000 watts of sound, and special visual effects fool all five senses into believing that you're hurtling through time, twisting between the snapping teeth of an oversized dinosaur, or smashing through solid barriers.

Shaded escalators drop down the hillside to **Studio Center**, on the valley floor. Several sound stages (immense warehouse-like buildings used for filming) have been converted into cinema-based attractions. *Backdraft* recreates the explosive fire effects seen in the film, some of them hot enough to singe the front rows.

ET, cycling gently through space and the skies above LA, is more suitable for young children.

'Cinemagic' explains some of the visual and aural tricks used to produce *Back to the Future*, Alfred Hitchcock's *Vertigo* and current TV shows.

The **Studio Tram** is a 45-min ride through Universal's back lot. The route passes sets (New York streets, New England streets, Parisian streets) that have appeared in hundreds of productions, famous sets like the house in *Psycho*, a collapsing bridge, an earthquake, an avalanche and more. Anyone expecting to see how films are made, however, will be sorely disappointed. To see the actual craft of cinema and television, visit Paramount or Warner Bros.

The kicker at Universal isn't even part of the theme park. **Universal CityWalk** is a theme park Los Angeles street scene, open to the public. The enclosed pedestrian mall is complete with automobiles poking through building facades, talking carousel animals, a magic club, Museum of Neon Art and a Wolfgang Puck restaurant with reasonable prices. It's the best place in town to see LA as it envisages itself.

KNOTT'S BERRY FARM

Knott's Berry Farm, *8039 Beach Blvd, Buena Park, CA 90620; tel: (714) 220-5200),* is about 40 mins south of downtown LA in northern Orange County. Easiest access is south off the Santa Ana (I-5) or Riverside (Hwy 91) freeways onto Beach Blvd (Hwy 39). From beach areas, take Beach Blvd north. No free or overnight parking.

Knott's is the USA's original theme park, based on the Wild West, characters from the 'Peanuts' syndicated newspaper cartoon series, and some of the most exciting roller coasters around. It began as a family-owned berry farm in 1920. When the Depression hit Southern California, the Knott family started selling home-made boysenberry pies and chicken dinners. By the 1940s, the family had added wagon rides through their burgeoning berry fields to occupy the 4000 or so visitors who showed up for dinner every Sunday. A replica

ghost town followed, then amusement park rides.

Ghost Town is a reproduction of an 1880s California mining town. Much is authentic, like the Butterfield stage coach that bounces over carefully placed ruts, and the wrist-numbing fatigue of panning for real gold. Many of the building facades are authentic relics from abandoned mining towns. So are the hundreds of artifacts in the Western Trails Museum and the genuine Denver & Rio Grande railroad.

There's also a fair bit of unreality, most of it from 1950s-era Hollywood Westerns: the stoic American Indian statues spotted around the concrete Painted Desert; the bare, gartered leg swinging from an upper-storey window of the Old Trails Hotel; the cheerful Wagon Camp immigrants bound for California without a care in the world.

Fiesta Village is a romantic paean to early Spanish California, although the style portrayed has more to do with Mexico than Spain. The high point (literally) is Montezooma's Revenge, an upside down and backwards thrill ride that hits 55 mph in less than five seconds. A fun theme area for the historically insensitive.

The Roaring '20s recreates a California amusement park from the 1920s. Twin highlights are the Buffalo Nickel Penny Arcade, the largest arcade of its kind west of the Mississippi River, and the Boomerang, a high-energy roller coaster that hurtles riders through six upside down loops – three times forward and three times backwards. The Boomerang is the most crowded ride in the park.

Roaring '20s also features an indoor ride with full-sized dinosaurs and LA's only remaining outdoor show with dolphins and sea lions.

Camp Snoopy is headquarters for the Charles Schulz cartoon beagle, Snoopy, and his 'Peanuts' gang: Linus, Lucy and Charlie Brown. The area is patterned after a High Sierra children's camp, complete with waterfalls, pontoon and suspension bridges, play houses and wandering shows. Cartoon characters pose for photos with kids of all ages.

Wild Water Wilderness is the newest theme area, based on a turn-of-the-century river wilderness area. Highlights are Bigfoot Rapids,

California's longest man-made rapids, and Mystery Lodge, a new attraction that explores mystical Indian beliefs from the Pacific Northwest.

A shopping area outside the park offers a variety of Western-themed items, including the entire Knott's line of jams and preserves. And Mrs Knott's Chicken Dinner Restaurant still serves more than 1½ million chicken dinners every year.

DISNEYLAND

Disneyland, *1313 Harbor Blvd, Anaheim, CA 92803; tel (714) 999-4565,* calls itself the Magic Kingdom for a good reason. Neither expense nor effort are spared to keep the real world at bay. Disneyland has more police than the entire city of Anaheim, less litter than any street corner in Singapore, and a work force that has never publicly talked about job actions.

Disney built a worldwide success with the not-so-simple magic of making people feel good. It's a world based on American cinema from the 1930s, when anything was possible, brought to life in a 1950s theme park, supported by 1990s technology. Despite immense crowds, long queues, high prices and blazing summer temperatures, few leave disappointed.

Easiest access is south off the Santa Ana (I-5) freeway on Harbor Blvd. Turn right into the main parking lot. No free or overnight parking.

Crowds start lining up outside the gates more than an hour before opening. Main Street opens 30 mins before the rest of the park, both to ease the backup outside and to build excitement as the magic moment approaches.

Main Street is archetypal Small Town America from the early 20th century, complete with horse-drawn carriages, silent films and friendly policemen in tall hats.

To the left is **Adventureland**, with its Jungle Cruise, Swiss Family Robinson Tree House and talking parrots.

New Orleans Square is a Bowdlerised version of the queen of Mississippi River towns, complete with friendly ghosts and amusing pirates.

Frontierland brings back the likes of Davey Crocket, Huckleberry Finn, and river boats that once plied the waterways of North America. And

perish the thought that Huck Finn's river raft didn't run on a strict timetable.

Fantasyland has its own capitol, Sleeping Beauty's Castle, patterned after an equally unreal fairytale castle in Bavaria. Everything else in Fantasyland is equally fantastic, from Dumbo the flying elephant to a not-very-wild ride with Mr Toad.

Life doesn't get much stranger than **Toontown**, where crooked cartoon buildings, bounding automobiles, and falling strong boxes are the stuff of everyday reality.

Tomorrowland is probably closer to real life than any other place in the park. Michael Jackson clutches his crotch while fighting intergalactic villains, robots throw spaceships through impossible manoeuvres, and submarines glide through polluted oceans littered with bits of plastic that look something like fish.

The best times to visit Disneyland, or any other theme park, is midweek during the wintertime. The worst time is a summer weekend when everyone else is on holiday, too. There are ways to beat the crowds, however. Arrive early. Decide which attractions or rides you want to see most, then go there first, before the crowds arrive. And if your number one must-do happens to be Captain Eo (Michael Jackson), Star Tours (a Star Wars-type adventure), or the Matterhorn (rollercoaster), get ready for a long wait.

SANTA CATALINA ISLAND

Tourist Information

Catalina Island Chamber of Commerce and Visitor's Bureau, *PO Box 217, Avalon, CA 90704; tel: (310) 510-1520.* Visitor centre on the Green Pleasure Pier, central Avalon.

Arriving and Departing

Boat crossings take 1–2 hrs from San Pedro, Long Beach, Newport Beach, Dana Point, Oceanside, and San Diego. Most departures are from San Pedro and Long Beach. **Catalina Cruises, Inc.,** *320 Golden Shore, Long Beach; tel: (800) 228-2546,* has the largest ships and 2-hr crossings. **Catalina Express,** *next to the Queen Mary, Long Beach and Berth 95 (foot of Vincent Thomas*

Bridge), San Pedro; tel: (310) 519-1212, has the quickest trip, 55 mins.

Island Express helicopter service, from the same locations; *tel: (310) 510-2525,* takes 15 mins. **Island Hopper Catalina Airlines,** *Lindbergh Field, San Diego; tel: (800) 339-0359,* takes 60 mins. The island's airport is the **Airport-in-the-Sky,** *PO Box 2734, Avalon, CA 90704; tel: (310) 510-0143.* Don't miss the view from the coffee shop patio.

Getting Around

Most of Catalina (the 'Santa' is usually dropped) is protected and undeveloped. Motor vehicles and other pollution sources are religiously controlled. A handful of residents have cars; a few taxis are available at blackmail prices.

Visitors rent golf carts, sometimes called 'autoettes', cycle (rentals are available), or walk. Avalon is easily walkable, though hills are steep.

Cyclists and walkers need free permits to explore beyond Avalon, available from the **Santa Catalina Island Conservancy Visitor Office,** *125 Claressa Ave; tel: (310) 510-1421.* Or take a coach or water tour. The largest tour operator on the island is **Discovery Tours,** *Box 737, Avalon, CA 90704; tel: (310) 510-2500.*

Accommodation

The Visitor's Bureau lists lodgings, but can't make bookings. **Catalina Reservations,** *tel: (310) 510-3000,* books all price ranges. Reservations are essential. For quaint Victorian charm, try **The Hotel Catalina,** *tel: (800) 540-0184,* moderate. The most elegant and expensive choice is **Hotel Metropole,** *tel: (800) 300-8528.*

Tent campsites are near Avalon, Black Jack, Little Harbor, Two Harbors and Parson's Landing. Camping is by permit and advance booking only. For Avalon bookings, *tel: (310) 510-8368.* For island campsite bookings, *tel: (310) 510-2800.*

Eating and Drinking

The **Marlin Club,** *tel: (310) 510-0044,* the oldest bar in town, is now restored to 1946 splendour.

Seafood bars along Avalon Bay are fast, cheap, and popular. There's no shortage of restaurants in all price ranges. Best and most expensive is the **Hotel Villa Portofino,** *111*

Crescent Ave; tel: (310) 510-0508. **Buffalo Nickel,** *tel: (310) 510-1323,* moderate, and **Pirrone's,** *tel: (310) 510-0333,* expensive, are other favourites.

Many restaurants and bars offer live entertainment during the summer season. **The Casino** provides concerts and daily cinema showings. Check the visitor centre for schedules.

Sightseeing

Europeans first saw Catalina in the mid-16th century. Some 350 years later, chewing gum magnate William Wrigley bought all 76 square miles (197 square km) to build a posh summer resort on Avalon Bay. Wrigley's heirs gave 86% of the island to the Santa Catalina Island Conservancy in 1975.

With almost no cars or development, Catalina remains a piece of Southern California from the uncluttered past – if you don't count Avalon beaches on summer weekends. The weather matches LA's, but with far less smog.

The Casino, *Casino Way,* on the north side of Avalon Bay, *tel: (310) 510-7400,* is the most obvious landmark. The round, blindingly white Art Deco building opened in 1929 with a ballroom and the world's first cinema designed expressly for sound films. The cinema and ballroom, both recently restored, are still open. Despite its name, it has always been an entertainment palace, not a gambling hall.

Just offshore is the **Underwater Park at Casino Point,** a magnet for snorkelers and scuba divers. Glass-bottom boat and semi-submersible tours are also available. Non-divers can take carefully supervised scuba tours after a brief diving course. Reefs and kelp forests around the island lure certified divers all year.

The **interior** of Catalina looks much as early Spanish explorers saw it: steep slopes, cliffs plunging into the blue Pacific, and a few rolling mountain tops – plus wild pigs, goats, deer and buffalo. Fourteen buffalo were brought to Catalina in 1924 for production of *The Vanishing American.* Today, about 200 head graze wild.

The **Catalina Island Museum,** at the Casino, covers island history, geography, flora, fauna and pottery.

LOS ANGELES to SANTA BARBARA

This can be one of the most pleasant 2-hour drives through Southern California, or one of the most frustrating. Traffic and weather make the difference. The direct route, Hwy 101 through the San Fernando Valley, is subject to traffic delays. The scenic route, Hwy 1, occasionally slows or closes due to autumn wild fires and winter floods and mudslides. The two routes join at Oxnard and continue north to Santa Barbara. Under normal circumstances, Hwy 1 takes 30 mins longer.

ROUTE

➡ Direct Route

The direct route from Los Angeles to Santa Barbara follows Hwy 101 95 miles (152 km) from downtown to downtown. With no traffic delays, the trip takes just under 2 hrs. Rush hour, an accident, a Dodgers baseball game, an event at Universal Studios, or any other traffic delay can stretch the trip toward 4 hrs.

From Union Station (downtown LA), take the Hollywood Freeway (Hwy 101) northbound towards Ventura and Santa Barbara. The freeway passes Hollywood, with the Capitol Records Tower on the left, then crosses over Cahunga Pass in the **Santa Monica Mountains**, past Universal City on the right (see p. 67 for the Universal Studios theme park), and heads down into the San Fernando Valley. Commuter traffic is extremely heavy in both directions, morning and evening.

Highway 101 veers left (west) 3 miles (5 km) beyond Universal City and becomes the Ventura Freeway. The Hollywood Freeway, Hwy 170 beyond the Hwy 101 interchange, continues

north. Take the Ventura Freeway (Hwy 101) exit toward Ventura and Santa Barbara.

The freeway runs westward along the northern edge of the Santa Monica Mountains through Studio City, Sherman Oaks, Encino, Tarzana and Woodland Hills. One district blends into the next, but all are part of the City of Los Angeles. The broad expanse of The Valley, as San Fernando Valley is almost always called, disappears northward into the smog. Most Valley residents commute to work elsewhere in the LA area.

Continue on Hwy 101 through **Woodland Hills, Calabasas, Agoura Hills, Westlake Village, Thousand Oaks, Newbury Park**, and down the hill. The sweeping turns of **Conejo Grade** offer broad vistas down into Ventura County, but no parking places. The city of **Camarillo** lies at the bottom of the Grade.

The coastal plain of Ventura County was, and largely remains, an agricultural area. Citrus, especially lemons, strawberries, peppers, tomatoes, beans and a dozen other crops are a year-round business. The population is heavily Hispanic. Continue on Hwy 101, parallel to the Santa Barbara Channel coastline, through **Ventura** to Santa Barbara.

〰 Scenic Route

The scenic route to Santa Barbara follows Hwy 1 along the coast to Oxnard, where it joins Hwy 101 and the direct route to Santa Barbara.

Pick up the Los Angeles Circular Drive (see p. 63) at the end of Wilshire Blvd in Santa Monica. Continue north along Hwy 1. Every time one of the multi-million dollar homes is hit by surf, fire, or mudslide, owners rush to rebuild, often more lavishly than before. Some of the most luxurious homes are just south of Point Dume, the point north of Malibu.

Follow Hwy 1 north to the end of the freeway in **Oxnard**. Signs lead through Oxnard to the Ventura Freeway (Hwy 101) and Ventura.

SANTA MONICA MOUNTAINS

The **Santa Monica Mountains Recreation Area** (SMMRA) stretches 18 miles (24 km) north along the coast beyond **Point Dume**. The entire area is dotted with wide public beaches, broad parking lots and summer lifeguard stations.

Mugu Lagoon, just north, is a spreading marsh and bird sanctuary, part of the Point Mugu Naval Air Station and the adjoining Pacific Missile Test Center – hilltops above the beach are bristling electronic gear. Unannounced visitors are *not* welcome.

VENTURA

Ventura is a small Mission town with broad beaches and suburbs spreading in all directions. **Tourist Office: Ventura Visitors & Convention Bureau**, *89-C S. California St, Ventura, CA 93001; tel: (805) 648-2075.* The visitor centre is open Mon–Fri, 0830–1700.

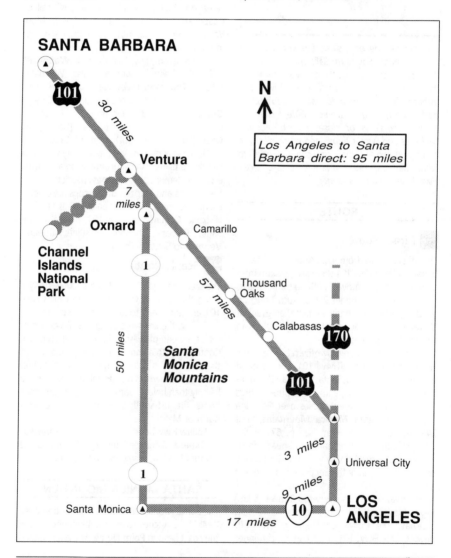

Getting Around

The **Buenaventura Trolley**, *21 S. California St, #402, Ventura, CA 93001; tel: (805) 643-3103* follows three routes that connect Ventura Harbor and several major hotels with the downtown area.

Accommodation

This covers the entire range. All chain hotels are represented, as well as the **Ventura Beach RV Resort**, *800 W. Main St, Ventura, CA 93001; tel: (805) 643-9137*, just north of downtown.

Eating and Drinking

The best bet downtown is the budget **Shields Brewing Co.**, *24 E. Santa Clara St; tel: (805) 643-1807*. Every shopping centre has its share of cheap fast food outlets. For seafood, try a restaurant at Ventura Harbor.

Sightseeing has two focal points, the downtown district and Channel Islands National Park, 12 miles (19 km) offshore (see below).

The walkable downtown has plenty of parking on the west end of Main St near museums and **Figueroa Plaza**, a pedestrian street filled with fountains and colourful tiles.

Ortega Adobe, *215 W. Main St; tel: (805) 648-5823*, is the original home of the giant Ortega Chile Company. The 1857 adobe is typical of early Ventura homes.

Mission San Buenaventura, *211 E. Main St; tel: (805) 643-4318*, was founded in 1782. A peaceful garden, crowded museum, and gift shop are next to the church, completed in 1809.

The **Albinger Archaeological Museum**, *113 E. Main St; tel: (805) 648-5823*, is an archaeological dig covering a full city block. Indoor and outdoor exhibits chronicle five different cultures on the site over the past 3500 years.

The **Ventura County Museum of History & Art** is across the street at *100 E Main St; tel: (805) 653-0323*. Highlights include Chumash Indian artifacts, tools once used by oil wildcatters in the area, early farm implements and a must-see collection of quarter life-size historical figures.

The **San Buenaventura City Hall** is just uphill from the opposite end of downtown, *501 Poli St; tel: (805) 654-7800*. The outside is sheathed in white ceramic tile, the interior has a marble lobby and grand stairway, mahogany and walnut panelling, and a stained glass dome. Tours are available.

In between, private and commercial buildings dating back to the 1870s line **Main St**. Most have been converted to antique stores and small boutiques.

The **'C' Street Surfing Museum**, *342 S. California St; tel: (805) 643-2742*, at Surfer's Point, has historic surfing gear.

Follow Hwy 101 north along the coast. Ten miles (16 km) north of Ventura is **La Conchita**, the only commercial banana plantation in the continental United States.

Many of the sunny slopes around **Carpinteria** are sown in flowers, grown for nursery stock and seed. Blooms are best in springtime. **Carpinteria State Beach** has one of the state's largest concentration of public beach camping facilities.

The structures visible out to sea are **oil platforms**. Beaches from Ventura north beyond Santa Barbara are littered with globules of tar, nearly all of it from natural oil seeps. Chumash Indians once used the natural beach tar to seal their boats.

If you accidentally pick up some tar, charcoal or cigarette lighter fluid is a effective foot and shoe cleaner. Tar stains on clothing are all but impossible to remove.

‒ ‒ ‒ ‒ ‒ ‒ ‒ ‒ ‒ ‒ ‒ ‒ ‒ ‒ ‒ ‒ ‒ ‒ ‒

 Side Track from Ventura

CHANNEL ISLANDS NATIONAL PARK

Channel Islands National Park (CINP) is a calm marine sanctuary on the edge of an exploding mainland population. The park protects an island chain that looks almost close enough to touch on clear days. In reality, the closest island is 11 miles (18 km) off the coast, the most distant, 40 miles (64 km).

Park Headquarters and Visitor Center are at *Ventura Harbor, 1901 Spinnaker Dr., Ventura, CA 93001; tel: (805) 658-5730*.

The eight Channel Islands are submerged

mountain peaks stretching 120 miles (192 km) from Santa Barbara to San Diego. CINP covers the four northernmost islands, **San Miguel**, **Santa Rosa**, **Santa Cruz**, and **Anacapa**, offshore from Santa Barbara to Ventura, and **Santa Barbara Island**, off Los Angeles. The other islands, San Nicholas, Santa Catalina (see p. 69), and San Clemente, are under private or military control.

The Channel Islands have been cut off from the mainland since the last Ice Age, long enough for distinct species of plants and animals to evolve. The islands are home to tens of thousands of birds; enormous kelp forests and offshore waters support countless seals, sea lions, fish, dolphins and whales.

All the islands were used as ranches in the last century, but were largely abandoned after World War II. Today, the islands and their inhabitants represent a fragile balance between wind, surging tides and limited water. At least part of all five islands are open, but access and conditions are deliberately difficult, to reduce human impact.

No food or water is available on any of the islands; visitors must bring their own, whether for a day visit or overnight camping. There is no shade or shelter from sun, wind and fog. Bring clothing for both hot and cold weather.

Visitors are responsible for their own transportation to CINP. **Island Packers**, next to the Visitor Center at *1867 Spinnaker Dr., Ventura, CA 93001; tel: (805) 642-1393* is the sole concessionaire. Boat trips depart Ventura Harbor daily. The company can provide almost any service from a half-day cruise-by to hiking excursions, snorkelling or scuba diving trips and ferry service for campers.

Anacapa, closest to the mainland, is actually three islets. East Anacapa is the most popular, with campsites, swimming, and a self-guided nature trail. West Anacapa is closed to protect bird nesting grounds.

Santa Cruz is the largest island in the park, 96 square miles (249 square kilometres). Mountains, plains, canyons and ample water support a large wildlife population. Landing requires a special permit; contact the CINP Visitor Center.

Santa Rosa is open to the public, but most visitors are interested in the beaches and diving

or snorkelling in dense kelp forests just offshore.

San Miguel is a low plateau, famous for unique foxes inland and the seals and sea lions on rocky beaches. Juan Cabrillo, the Spanish discoverer of California, died from a fall and was buried on the island in 1543.

Santa Barbara, off Los Angeles, is the only park island without a water supply. Spring wildflower displays on the desert landscape are magnificent, especially after a wet winter.

Private boats may anchor off CINP islands, but landing permits are required to go ashore. For San Miguel, Santa Rosa, and Santa Cruz; *tel: (805) 964-7839*. Santa Cruz is privately owned, so permission must also be obtained from the landowners. Contact the Visitor Center for information.

Park rangers conduct guided walks on San Miguel and Santa Rosa; reservations and landing permits must be arranged in advance at the Visitor Center.

Primitive camping is allowed on Anacapa, San Miguel, Santa Rosa, and Santa Barbara; reservations are required through the Visitor Center. All food and water must be brought in, all trash must be taken out.

_ _ _ _ _ _ _ _ _ _ _ _ _ _ _ _ _ _ _ _

OXNARD

Tourist Information: Oxnard Convention and Visitors Bureau, *400 Esplanade Dr., Ste 100, Oxnard, CA 93030; tel: (805) 485-8833*.

Oxnard, 15 miles (24 km) beyond Camarillo, is a small farming community that has grown into a thriving dormitory town for Los Angeles, to the south, and Ventura/Santa Barbara, to the north.

Look for some of the most authentic Mexican food in the area in small taquerias downtown, near the central park. The **Carnegie Art Museum**, *424 S. C St; tel: (805) 385-8157* focuses on 20th century California painters. The **Ventura County Maritime Museum**, *2731 S. Victoria Ave; tel: (805) 984-6260*, at **Channel Islands Harbor**, has a small collection of ship models and artwork covering maritime history from ancient times to the most modern cargo ships. The harbour is a major small-boat anchorage and shopping area.

LOS ANGELES
to
PALM SPRINGS

This route is an efficient 1½-hour mad dash from Los Angeles glitz to the glitter of the Palm Springs desert resorts, or a chance to explore some of the mountainous hinterlands of Southern California by adding a scenic two-day loop. Overnight at Big Bear Lake.

The scenic route leaves the Interstate 10 direct route at Redlands for a winding loop drive through mountains to an all-season lakeside resort. The combined route then continues south-east on I-10 to the Hwy 111 turnoff for Palm Springs and the Coachella Valley.

➡ Direct Route

Take Hwy 101 1 mile (1.6km) east from Union Station in downtown Los Angeles. Turn onto I-10, the San Bernardino Freeway, and continue east 94 miles (150 km) to the Hwy 111 turnoff at West Palm Springs Village. Continue south-east on Hwy 111 11 miles (18 km) to the city of Palm Springs.

There are few attractions and few reasons to stop along our route between Los Angeles and Redlands, an area of dormitory communities for Los Angeles, Riverside and San Bernardino. Lodging, including most chain hotels, is available along I-10, and accommodation and dining in all price ranges is available in the scenic route Big Bear Lake resort area.

Once an area of endless citrus groves, walnut orchards and small farms, its modern face is suburbs lined by hills – and some trees. The San Bernardino Freeway passes **Alhambra, Monterey Park**, and **Rosemead**. **El Monte** was the westward terminus of the Santa Fe Immigrant Trail in the mid-1850s. I-10 passes **Covina** and **West Covina**, then crosses Hwys 57 and 71. **Pomona** is south. California State Polytechnic

University has an equine training school, the **W.K. Kellogg Arabian Horse Center**; *tel: (909) 869-2224*. The horses perform in occasional shows.

⤳ Scenic Route

The scenic route adds 94 miles (150 km) to the direct route. Take Hwy 101 1 mile (1.6 km) east from Union Station in downtown Los Angeles. Turn onto I-10, the San Bernardino Freeway, and continue east.

North of I-10 is the **Adobe de Palmares**, *491 E. Arrow Hwy, Pomona, CA 91767; tel: (909) 620-2300*, open Sun 1400–1700, an 1854 furnished adobe which was once a stop for stage-coaches and freight-hauling mule teams. Just east is **Claremont**.

Continue directly along the I-10 to **Redlands**, or turn north onto I-215 for **San Bernardino** 56 miles (90 km) from downtown Los Angeles. Rejoin I-10 via Hwy 30 and Redlands.

Take Hwy 30 north from Redlands, or east from San Bernardino, and follow signs to Hwy 330 for the loop around Big Bear Lake. Almost immediately the road enters the **San Bernardino National Forest**. Beyond City Creek Forest Station, Hwy 330 twists and winds up to **Running Springs** at 6030 ft (1855 m), where Hwy 18, the **Rim of the World Drive**, forks westward towards Lake Arrowhead and eastward to **Big Bear Lake**. Go east on Hwy 18. Within one mile (1.6 km) is a turnoff to Arrowbear Lake. Continue on Rim of the World Drive for 5 miles (8 km) to **Lakeview Point** at 7117 ft (2189 m), with a panoramic view of Big Bear Lake and snowclad mountains. Four miles (6.4 km) later at a big stone dam is the junction of Hwys 18 and 38. Take Hwy 38 along Big Bear Lake's North Shore Drive. In winter, spot **bald eagles** at Grout Bay, near Fawnskin. Stop 3 miles (5 km) east at the **Big Bear Ranger Station**; *tel: (909) 866-3437* for a driving tour brochure to the log cabins and mines of the Holcomb Valley, site of the original gold discovery in the region. Turn right just beyond the Big Bear City Airport on Greenway Dr.

Continue for ½ mile (I km) to **Big Bear Blvd**, Hwy 38. **Big Bear City**, the **City of Big Bear Lake**, and **Snow Summit** and **Bear Mountain**

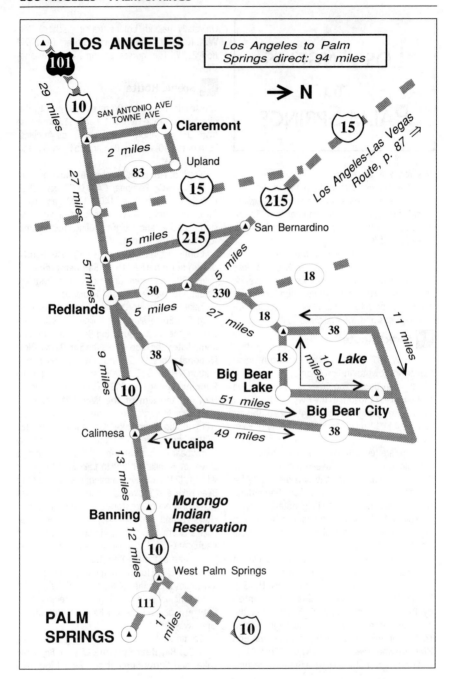

LOS ANGELES

Los Angeles to Palm Springs direct: 94 miles

→ **N**

101

29 miles

10

SAN ANTONIO AVE/ TOWNE AVE

Claremont

2 miles

83

Upland

15

215

15

Los Angeles-Las Vegas Route, p. 87 ⇗

27 miles

5 miles

215

San Bernardino

5 miles

5 miles

18

30

330

Redlands

5 miles

27 miles

18

18

38

11 miles

5 miles

38

18

10 miles

Lake

9 miles

10

Big Bear Lake

51 miles

Big Bear City

Calimesa

Yucaipa

49 miles

38

13 miles

Morongo Indian Reservation

Banning

10

12 miles

West Palm Springs

111

11 miles

10

PALM SPRINGS

ski areas, with lodging and services, are to the right.

The route continues on Hwy 38 to the left (east), then turns right and becomes **Greenspot Blvd**. Hwy 38, a state scenic highway, winds 50 miles (80 km) through the mountains toward Redlands. Juniper and pines line the road near 8443 ft (2598 m) Onyx Summit, 9 miles (14.4 km) along the loop's return route. The highway follows the Santa Ana River for several miles. Stop at **Barton Flats Visitors Center** for information and permits for hiking trails in the **San Bernardino National Forest** and **San Gorgonio Wilderness** and nearby campsites.

Hwy 38 leaves the national forest just beyond **Mountain Home Village** for the relative flatness of **Mentone** and Redlands. Alternatively turn left to **Yucaipa** and rejoin the I-10 at **Calimesa**.

Continue to Palm Springs on I-10 past Calimesa. To the east is the **Edward-Dean Museum of Decorative Arts**, 9401 Oak Glen Rd, Cherry Valley, CA 92223; tel: (909) 845-2626, open Tues–Fri 1300–1630, Sat–Sun 1000–1630, showing fans, paperweights, and other collections. At **Beaumont**, I-10 curves due east. The San Bernardino Mountains are to the north (left); the San Jacinto Range is to the south (right).

Banning is on the west side of the **Morongo Indian Reservation**.

I-10 begins to descend towards the desert. Take the **Main Street** exit in **Cabazon** to **Dinosaur Delights**, tel: (909) 849-8309, huge rampant statues of dinosaurs near a lorry stop. For bingo, card games, and satellite betting, visit **Casino Morongo**; tel: (800) 252-4499.

Continue south-east on I-10 33 miles (53 km) to the Hwy 111 turnoff at **West Palm Springs Village** and go 11 miles (18 km) south-east to the city of **Palm Springs** (p.173).

CLAREMONT

Tourist Information: Claremont Chamber of Commerce and Visitors Center, 205 Yale Ave, Claremont, CA 91711; tel: (909) 624-1681, has information on accommodation and colleges.

Claremont, a multi-university town, is an educational centre whose architecture mixes ivy-covered buildings and early 20th-century Craftsman-style homes. **Rancho Santa Ana Botanic Garden**, 1500 College Ave, Claremont, CA 91711; tel: (909) 625-8767, open 0800–1700, has 85 acres (34 ha) of native California plants, spectacular in spring. The **Raymond M. Alf Museum**, 1175 W. Base Line Rd, Claremont, 91711; tel: (909) 624-2798, open Sept–May, displays fossils and paleontology. For Western US music, visit the **Kenneth G. Fiske Musical Instrument Museum**, 450 N. College Way, Claremont, CA 91711; tel: (909) 621-8307.

Montclair and **Upland** are further east. Aircraft buffs should detour 8 miles (13 km) south on Euclid Ave to the **Planes of Fame and Jet Fighter Museums**, 7000 Merrill Ave, Chino Airport, Chino, 91710; tel: (909) 597-3722, displaying World War II planes, an 1896 glider, and P-59-era to F-104 fighters.

SAN BERNARDINO

For details of San Bernardino, see the Los Angeles–Las Vegas route, p. 88.

REDLANDS

Tourist Information: Redlands Chamber of Commerce, 1 E. Redlands Blvd, Redlands, CA 92373; tel: (909) 793-2546, provides general information on the city, and suggests walking and drive-by tours of Victorian buildings.

San Bernardino Asistencia, 26930 Barton Rd, Redlands, CA 92373; tel: (714) 793-5402, open Wed–Sat 1000–1700, Sun 1300–1700, is a replica of the 1830s outpost of Mission San Gabriel Arcangel, complete with several rooms and a functioning chapel. The **Lincoln Memorial Shrine**, 125 W. Vine St, Redlands, CA 92373; tel: (909) 798-7632, open Tues–Sat, and Feb 12 (Lincoln's Birthday) 1300–1700, is literally a collection of US President Abraham Lincoln memorabilia, including photos, books and manuscripts.

Some Redlands Victorians, the **Heritage Homes**, are open for tours on a limited basis. Drive by the **Edwards Mansion**, 2064 Orange Tree Ln., Redlands, CA 92374; tel: (909) 793-2031, a multi-storey mansion with a steeple-shaped look-out and garden gazebo. Modelled on a French château, the **Kimberly Crest House and Gardens**, *PO Box 206, 1325 Prospect Dr., Redlands, CA 92373; tel: (909) 792-2111*, is open Thurs–Sun 1300–1600. Paper company heirs owned the 1897 mansion for 74 years, playing host to a relative, actress Carole Lombard, during the 1930s. Tiffany lamps, colourful examples of the best American stained glass art, are plentiful. The 1890 Queen Anne-style **Morey Mansion**, *190 Terracina Blvd, Redlands, CA 92373; tel: (909) 793-7970*, is open Sun 1200–1500. The great house, filled with inlaid golden oak woodwork, was the centre of a San Francisco shipbuilder's orange-growing ranch. The **Historical Glass Museum**, *1157 N. Orange, PO Box 921, Redlands, CA 92373; tel: (909) 797-1528 or (909) 793-7190*, housed in a 1903 Victorian mansion, displays early 20th-century American glassware. Victorian-era lunch and tea are served at **Lavender Blue**, *22 E. State St, Redlands, CA 92373; tel: (909) 793-0977*.

BIG BEAR LAKE

Tourist Information: Big Bear Lake Resort Association, *PO Box 2860, Big Bear Lake, CA 92315; tel: (714) 866-7000*, has area visitor information.

Southern Californians use the **Big Bear Lake** resort area as a getaway, so avoid 100,000 visitors on holidays and the crowds on all summer and winter weekends.

Big Bear was named after the then-numerous grizzly bears which roamed the area in the 1840s. In 1860, William Holcomb discovered the largest gold deposits ever found in Southern California. Gold and silver strikes drew other miners to the area in the 1860s, replacing trappers who had sought grizzly, deer, beaver and birds in the mountain forests. In summer ranchers grazed cattle, which fed the mining settlements, in the high country.

Six feet (2 m) of snow fall annually. In 1884, a dam formed 5-mile (8 km) long Big Bear Lake, and fish were transplanted from Lake Tahoe. Resorts sprouted, and Rim of the World Drive was built in 1915 to provide smooth access to the area. **Bear Mountain**, *tel: (909) 585-2519*, and **Snow Summit**, *tel: (909) 866-5766*, ski resorts have winter alpine skiing. **Bluff Lake Nordic Center**; *tel: (909) 866-3621*, and the **US Forest Service**; *tel: (909) 866-3437*, have cross-country skiing information. Other winter activities include: **snowmobiling**, *tel: (909) 585-8002*; **sleigh rides**, (Victoria Park Carriages; *tel: (909) 866-7137)*; and a scenic **sky chair ride**; *tel: (909) 866-5766*.

Summer visitors ride horses, bicycles and mountain bikes, swim, fish, row, canoe, paddle, sail, jet ski, water ski, windsurf, golf, and hike.

YUCAIPA

Tourist Information: Yucaipa Valley Chamber of Commerce, *35144 Yucaipa Blvd, PO Box 45, Yucaipa, CA 92399; tel: (909) 790-1841*.

South-east of Redlands at an elevation of 2622 feet (807 m), **Yucaipa** was home to Serrano Indians at the time of first Spanish contact in the late 18th century.

The 1842 **Sepulveda Adobe**, *32183 Kentucky St, Yucaipa, CA 92399; tel: (909) 795-6352*, the area's oldest building, has furnishings brought around Cape Horn. The 1858 **Yucaipa Adobe**, *33900 Oak Glen Rd, Yucaipa, CA 92399; tel: (909) 790-3120*, open Tues–Sat 1000–1700, Sun 1300–1700, is furnished with antiques. The **Mousely Museum of Natural History**, *35308 Panorama Dr., Yucaipa, CA 92399; tel: (909) 790-3163 or (909) 798-8570*, exhibits seashells and fossils. Enjoy apple products at 1867 **Parrish Pioneer Ranch**, *38561 Oak Glen Rd, Yucaipa, CA 92399; tel: (909) 797-1753*, open 1000–1800, which has an apple processing shed and animal park. Nearby **Los Rios Ranch**, *39610 Oak Glen Rd, Yucaipa, CA 92399; tel: (909) 797-1005*, open Aug–Dec 0900–1700, offers apple wine tasting and orchard tours.

BANNING

Tourist Information: The Banning Chamber of Commerce, *123 W. Ramsey, PO Box 665, Banning, CA 92220; tel: (909) 849-4695*, has area information.

The **Malki Museum**, *11-795 Fields Rd, Banning, CA 92220; tel: (909) 849-7289,* is staffed by Native Americans who explain the significance of the Cahuilla's and other tribes' cultural objects. **Gilman Ranch Historical Park**

and Wagon Museum, *16th and Wilson Sts, Banning, CA 92220; tel: (909) 922-9200,* was a ranch and stage-coach stop and now has a large wagon museum, open Mar–Nov, Sat–Sun, 1200–1600.

LOS ANGELES to DEATH VALLEY

Travel 299 miles (478 km) away from the bustle of Los Angeles, by forests, mountain ranges, and military testing areas. From the spine of the Sierra Nevada Mountains, turn east over dry Owens Lake, climbing through multi-coloured mountains to the entrance to Death Valley National Monument. Break up the trip with an overnight in Lone Pine before plunging into Death Valley.

Death Valley's varied desert wilderness, raw and primeval in every season, deserves two to three days to allow for backtracking along the north–south road's 79 miles (126 km) of natural attractions. Powdery white dunes, mountains streaked with colour, pinkish dawn, borax mining ruins, a palm oasis and a volcanic crater are juxtaposed with the lowest, hottest spot in North America.

ROUTE

From Union Station, take Sunset Blvd 0.3 mile (0.5 km) to Figueroa St. Turn right for one long block, and continue east on Hwy 110, the Pasadena Freeway, for 2 miles (3.2 km), passing Dodger Stadium on the left.

Go north-west on I-5, the Golden State Freeway, for 25 miles (40 km), through **Glendale, Burbank, San Fernando** and **Sylmar**. Turn right onto Hwy 14, the Antelope Freeway, 34 miles (54 km) to **Palmdale**.

Continue north on Hwy 14 through **Lancaster, Mojave,** and **Red Rock Canyon State Park**. Four miles (6.4 km) north of Homestead take Hwy 395 north through **Olancha** to **Lone Pine**.

To enter **Death Valley National Monument**, take Hwy 136 from Lone Pine south-east and

east over Towne Pass, then descend via Hwy 190 into the monument by **Stovepipe Wells** as far as the junction of Hwys 190, 374 and 267. From this junction, the Death Valley National Monument tour goes 35 miles (56 km) north to **Scotty's Castle** and **Ubehebe Crater**, and south on Hwy 190 to the **Furnace Creek Ranch**.

LOS ANGELES OUTSKIRTS

Put downtown Los Angeles behind, leaving Union Station via Sunset Blvd. Nine short blocks north-west, turn right onto Figueroa St. One block later, enter Hwy 110 going north.

Two miles (3.2 km) later, while passing through Elysian Park, home of the Dodgers baseball team, leave Pasadena Freeway for I-5 going north.

To the left, 3½ miles (5.6 km) beyond, is **Griffith Park**, *Park Ranger Visitor Center, 4730 Crystal Springs Dr, Los Angeles, CA 90027; tel: (213) 665-5188,* with the **Griffith Observatory**, *2800 E. Observatory Rd, Los Angeles, CA 90027; tel: (213) 664-1191,* the **Los Angeles Zoo**, *5333 Zoo Dr., Los Angeles, CA 90027-1498; tel: (213) 666-4090* and the **Gene Autry Western Heritage Museum**, *4700 Western Heritage Way, Los Angeles, CA 90027; tel: (213) 667-2000.*

Just west of Griffith Park off Hwy 134 is **Forest Lawn-Hollywood Hills**, *6300 Forest Lawn Dr, Los Angeles, CA; tel: (213) 254-7251,* a kitschy mortuary with replicas of American and Mexican monuments and statues of US presidents. Get a map at the cemetery gate; actress Bette Davis' epitaph, on the left side of the Courts of Remembrance entrance, reads: 'She Did It The Hard Way'.

One mile (1.6 km) past Hwy 118, take San Fernando Mission Blvd left ½ mile (1 km) to **Mission San Fernando, Rey de España** (see Los Angeles, p. 53), open despite damage in the 1994 Northridge Earthquake.

West (left) of I-5 is the Los Angeles Reservoir. North of the Hwy 210 junction and Balboa Blvd exit are the **First and Second Los Angeles Aqueducts,** terminus of the 250 mile (400 km) aqueduct system that Los Angeles City Engineer William Mulholland orchestrated in 1907–1913

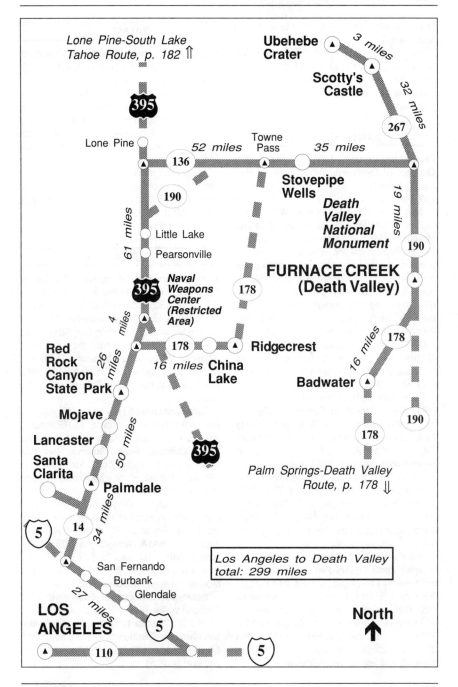

Lone Pine-South Lake Tahoe Route, p. 182 ⇑

Ubehebe Crater

Scotty's Castle

3 miles

32 miles

395

267

Lone Pine

Towne Pass

52 miles   35 miles

136

190

Stovepipe Wells

Death Valley National Monument

19 miles

190

Little Lake

Pearsonville

61 miles

FURNACE CREEK (Death Valley)

395

Naval Weapons Center (Restricted Area)

178

4 miles

178

Ridgecrest

178

Red Rock Canyon State Park

26 miles

178

16 miles China Lake

16 miles

Badwater

190

Mojave

178

Lancaster

50 miles

395

Santa Clarita

Palmdale

Palm Springs-Death Valley Route, p. 178 ⇓

5

14

34 miles

San Fernando

Burbank

Glendale

Los Angeles to Death Valley total: 299 miles

LOS ANGELES

27 miles

5

North ↑

110

5

to drain Owens Valley water (see Lone Pine to South Lake Tahoe, p. 182).

Five miles (8 km) north of Mission San Fernando, turn right onto Hwy 14, the Antelope Valley Freeway. The road leaves the heavily-populated San Fernando Valley for the forested mountains.

SANTA CLARITA

Tourist Information: Santa Clarita Valley Chamber of Commerce, *23920 Valencia Blvd, Ste. 125, Santa Clarita, CA 91355; tel: (805) 259-4787.*

Take San Fernando Rd off Hwy 14 for 2 miles (3.2 km) to the **William S. Hart County Park and Museum**; *24151 North Newhall Ave, Newhall, CA; tel: (805) 254-4584.* 'Two Gun Bill' Hart, a silent cinema cowboy actor, built a ranch house with walls that could be removed or shifted for scenes in some of his 75 films. Today the ranch raises bison and farm animals; hikers can tackle the trails. Hart's hilltop mansion is a Western-theme museum, open for free tours Wed–Sun 1100–1600 in summer, curtailed hours the rest of the year. California's first commercially successful oil well and refinery were established close by in 1876.

A few miles north on Hwy 14 is the right turn onto Placerita Canyon Rd. Continue 2 miles (3.2 km) to **Placerita Canyon State and County Park**, *19152 W. Placerita Canyon Rd, Newhall, CA; tel: (805) 259-7721.* Hike and picnic beneath the oaks. In 1842 Francisco Lopez pulled gold from the roots of a wild onion he dug from underneath the still-preserved 'Oak of the Golden Dream', commencing California's first commercial gold rush. The chaparral landscape was a 1930s location for Westerns and *Cisco Kid* films.

There's more rugged cinema scenery in **Vasquez Rocks County Park**, 2 miles (3.2 km) north of Hwy 14 on Agua Dulce Rd, then right for 0.3 mile (0.5 km). Craggy golden sandstone rocks shelter picnic tables and hiking trails.

Twenty-nine miles (46 km) along Hwy 14 is 3179-foot (978 m) **Soledad Pass**. Hwy 14 crosses the San Andreas Earthquake Fault before it descends and approaches **Palmdale**.

PALMDALE

Tourist Information: Palmdale Chamber of Commerce, *38260-A 10th St East, Palmdale, CA 93550; tel: (805) 273-3232.*

At the edge of the Mojave Desert, Palmdale is a flat expanse of red-roofed housing estates which sprung up in the past decade as cheap housing for workers willing to commute to Los Angeles or locally-employed aircraft assembly and maintenance workers.

Budget and moderate lodging is available; *HI* and *RM* are among hotel chains in Palmdale. The **Super 8 Motel**, *200 W. Palmdale Blvd, Palmdale, CA 93550; tel: (800) 232-1212 or (805) 273-8000* is moderate.

LANCASTER

Tourist Information: Lancaster Chamber of Commerce, *44335 Lowtree Ave, Lancaster, CA 93534; tel: (805) 948-4518 or (805) 949-1212.*

North on Hwy 14 is **Lancaster**. Moderate lodging is available, including *BW*. Fifteen miles (24 km) east of Hwy 14 among the buttes is the **Antelope Valley Indian Museum**, *15701 East Avenue M, Lancaster, CA 93534; tel: (805) 942-0662,* built into the rocks; call ahead for opening hours.

Take West I Ave off Hwy 14 for 10½ miles (16 km) until it becomes Lancaster Rd. Continue 3 miles (5 km) to the entrance of the **Antelope Valley California Poppy Reserve**; *tel: (805) 724-1180 or (805) 942-0662,* for 1700 acres (688 ha) of the orange state flower which blooms profusely March–May.

Captain Chuck Yeager broke the sound barrier, and most other US aircraft have been tested, at **Edwards Air Force Base**, near Rosamond. **NASA Ames-Dryden Flight Research Facility**, *PO Box 273, Edwards Air Force Base, CA 93523; tel: (805) 258-3460,* is open Mon–Fri for free advance-booked tours.

Rosamond Chamber of Commerce, *2564 Diamond St, Box 365, Rosamond, CA 93560; tel: (805) 256-3248.* **Burton's Tropico Gold Mine and Museum**; *Rosamond Blvd, Rte 1 Rosamond, CA 93560; tel: (805) 256-2618,* has a museum and gold panning.

MOJAVE

Tourist Information: Mojave Chamber of Commerce, *15836 Sierra Hwy, Mojave, CA 93501; tel: (805) 824-2481.*

Colourful rock formations appear as Hwy 14 approaches the town of **Mojave**. In the 1880s, Mojave marked the end of the 165-mile trek by twenty-mule teams from the Death Valley Harmony Borax Works. Fill the petrol tank. After evolving 200 million years ago, California's (endangered) state reptile is preserved in a walk in-only **Desert Tortoise Natural Area**, *Box 453, Ridgecrest, CA 93556; tel: (619) 446-4526*, 10 miles (16 km) north-east of Mojave and California City.

RED ROCK CANYON STATE PARK

Tourist Information: Red Rock Canyon State Park, *Box 26, Cantil, CA 93519; tel: (805) 942-0662.*

Red Rock Canyon State Park is 25 miles (40 km) north-east of Mojave on Hwy 14. Inhabited by sabre-tooth tigers, mastodons, and rhinoceros millions of years ago, the park now shelters hawks, coyotes and roadrunners among its massive glowing rocks. The one-time way station for stage-coaches is now used as another Western film set and offers 50 primitive campsites and hiking trails.

RED ROCK CANYON TO LONE PINE

Continue north on Hwy 14 three miles (5 km) north of Freeman, then go right on Hwy 178 for 14 miles (22 km) to the **China Lake Naval Weapons Exhibit**, *Main Gate, N.A.W.S, Ridgecrest, CA 93555; tel: (619) 375-6900*, open Mon–Fri 0730–1630.

The **Maturango Museum**, *100 E. Los Flores Ave, Ridgecrest, CA 93555; tel: (619) 375-6900*, open Tues–Sat 1000–1700, Sun–Mon 1300–1700, Wed 1000–2200, has Northern Mojave Desert exhibits and petroglyphs.

There's plenty of moderate accommodation available with the military base nearby. For area information, contact the **Ridgecrest Area Convention and Visitors Bureau**, *100 W.*

California Ave, Ridgecrest CA 93555; tel: (619) 375-8202.

Return to Hwy 14, or take Hwy 395 from Inyokern north-west to the junction with Hwy 14. Continue north on Hwy 395 through **Pearsonville** and **Little Lake**, with black lava mountains on the east and a lake on the west. Three miles (5 km) north of Little Lake, postpiles and volcanic cinder cones indicate where to take Cinder Cone Rd right. Follow BLM signs for 1 mile (1.6 km) to parking and the narrow trail to **Fossil Falls**, two waterfalls flowing over lava amid rock climbers' canyons.

Criss-crossing the Los Angeles Aqueduct, continue north on Hwy 395 by **Coso Junction**, **Dunmovin** and **Haiwee Reservoir** to sand dunes near **Olancha**. Ahead and to the right is the dry bed of Owens Lake, drained by Los Angeles, and **Lone Pine** (Lone Pine–South Lake Tahoe, p. 182).

Fill the petrol tank in Lone Pine and prepare for the long drive to Stovepipe Wells in Death Valley. Note: In the morning the sun will be in your eyes as you drive east.

LONE PINE TO DEATH VALLEY

From Lone Pine, take Hwy 136 18 miles (29 km) south-east past the dry white salt flats of Owens Lake to the Hwy 190 junction. Ruined silver mines are scattered north amidst the Inyo Mountains' rocky clutter.

Twenty-one miles (33 km) further on, **Father Crowley Point** at 4000 ft (1231 m) offers a magnificent north-east vista of the multi-coloured red and ochre Panamint Range above the off-white Panamint Dunes. Gold and silver inspired the 'pan-a-mint' name during an 1870s boom.

Descend 8 miles (13 km) east to Panamint Springs' limited facilities. Panamint Dunes Rd is for very intrepid walkers, as cars cannot go beyond the first few miles. The 250-ft (77 m) high Panamint Dunes are framed by mountains. Yellow Panamint daisies line the roadside. A dry lakebed crosses Hwy 190. Ahead, the Panamint Range's Cottonwood Mountains are up a steep 13% slope. Pull into the vista point on the right-hand side for a view of the Panamints.

Enter **Death Valley National Monument** at

4596-ft (1414 m) Towne Pass , with its 'Burro Crossing' road sign.

DEATH VALLEY NATIONAL MONUMENT

Tourist Information: Death Valley National Monument, *Death Valley, CA 92328; tel: (619) 786-2331.* The Visitor Center is at Furnace Creek. An excellent guidebook is the *Road Guide to Death Valley*, Barbara and Robert Decker, Double Decker Press, 4087 Silver Bar Rd, Mariposa, CA 95338.

Accommodation

The national monument has about 1500 pitches spread over nine campsites. Check with rangers for backcountry camping suggestions. All lodging is full over winter and spring holidays and during the Death Valley '49ers Encampment, on the second weekend in November.

Three lodgings are operated by **Furnace Creek Inn & Ranch Resort**, *PO Box 1, SR 190, Death Valley National Monument, CA 92328; tel: (800) 528-6367.* The pricey 125-room **Furnace Creek Inn**, *tel: (619) 786-2345,* is open mid-Oct–mid-May. The 224-room **Furnace Creek Ranch**, *tel: (619) 786-2345,* open all year, moderate to expensive, has restaurants, a general store, RV parking, pricey petrol, and a post office. Not all 83 rooms at year-round, moderate, **Stove Pipe Wells Village**, *tel: (619) 786-2387,* have drinking water, but there's a restaurant, store, and petrol station.

Eating and Drinking

Meals and snacks are expensive at the Furnace Creek and Stovepipe Wells stores. In winter, dates from the Furnace Creek Ranch oasis are sold on site. Both the Inn and Ranch have restaurants. Bring a supply of water with you and never walk even a few steps in the desert without a water bottle and small snack.

There are hiking trails and lay-bys throughout the monument. In this desert country, temperature and climate can be extreme, calling for tip-top condition for your vehicle and for thorough preparation for human travellers. Always take water, food, warm clothes, sun protection, a good map and wear comfortable walking shoes.

Sightseeing

Hwy 190 descends 3000 feet (923 m) in the 7 miles (11 km) from Towne Pass to the **Emigrant Ranger Station**. Scrub brush covers the valley floor. If it's open, stop at the ranger station for a brochure and map; weather reports are posted on a signboard at the Emigrant Campground across the road.

There's another ranger station at **Stovepipe Wells**; *tel: (619) 786-2342,* elevation five feet (1.5 m), which was Death Valley's first tourist resort in 1926. **Stovepipe Wells Village**, with a motel, is on the right; a 200-pitch campsite is on the left, a mecca for RVs during the Nov–Apr season. The general store and petrol station are near by an old blacksmithy. The main attraction is **Sand Dunes** to the north-east.

Follow Hwy 190 for 2 miles (3.2 km), then walk on the golden dunes. Early in the day tracks of animals like bobcats, coyotes, kangaroo rats, and lizards, bird patterns from roadrunners or ravens, and the serpentine patterns of side-winder rattlesnakes carpet the sand. Near sunset, the dunes cast deep, almost lunar, shadows.

Three miles (5 km) east is the **Devil's Cornfield**, where arrowweed clumps together over salty sand, looking uncannily like corn. Just beyond is a T-junction. Scotty's Castle is 36 miles (58 km) north; Furnace Creek and most of the monument's attractions are south on Hwy 190 and Badwater Rd.

The northern drive passes the Cottonwood Mountains on the left. Alluvial fans and vast, eroded mountainsides etched by ancient water mark the darker Grapevine Range on the right. At 33 miles (53 km) is the **Grapevine Ranger Station**; *tel: (619) 786-2313.* **Scotty's Castle** is 3 miles (5 km) east on Hwy 267. Guided tours of the 25-room Moorish-style mansion are offered daily. Early in the century Walter Scott, a US Midwesterner turned Death Valley prospector, conned businessmen into investing in his schemes. One arrived from Chicago to see for himself. Albert Johnson appraised the situation and ended up building the 'Castle', elegant with wrought iron detail, leatherwork, fine furniture and tapestries.

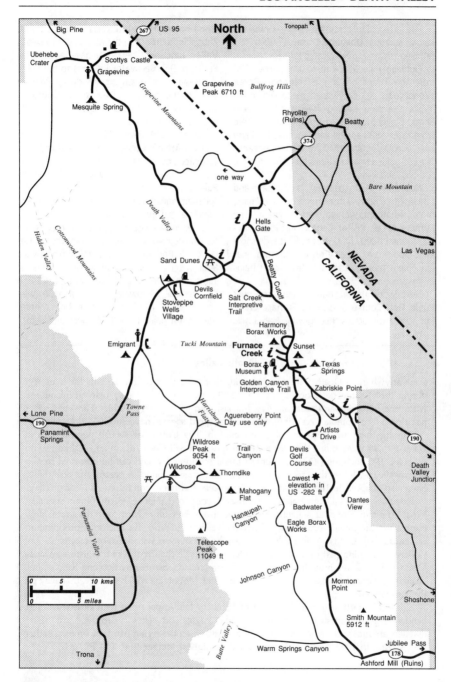

North ↑

Big Pine
267 US 95
Tonopah

Ubehebe
Crater

Scottys Castle
Grapevine

Mesquite Spring

Grapevine Mountains

Grapevine
Peak 6710 ft

Bullfrog Hills

Rhyolite
(Ruins)
Beatty

374

Death Valley

one way

Bare Mountain

Hidden Valley

Cottonwood Mountains

Sand Dunes

i

Hells
Gate

i

NEVADA
CALIFORNIA

Las Vegas

Devils
Cornfield

Stovepipe
Wells
Village

Salt Creek
Interpretive
Trail

Beatty Cutoff

Harmony
Borax Works

Emigrant

Tucki Mountain

**Furnace
Creek** i

Borax
Museum

Golden Canyon
Interpretive Trail

Sunset

Texas
Springs

Zabriskie Point

i

Lone Pine

190

Panamint
Springs

Towne
Pass

Harrisburg Flats

Aguereberry Point
Day use only

Artists
Drive

190

Wildrose
Peak
9054 ft

Wildrose

Thorndike

Trail
Canyon

Mahogany
Flat

Devils
Golf
Course

Lowest
elevation in
US -282 ft

Badwater

Eagle Borax
Works

Dantes
View

Death
Valley
Junction

Panamint Valley

Telescope
Peak
11049 ft

Hanaupah
Canyon

Johnson Canyon

Mormon
Point

Shoshone

0   5   10 kms
0   5 miles

Smith Mountain
5912 ft

Butte Valley

Trona

Warm Springs Canyon

Jubilee Pass

178

Ashford Mill (Ruins)

Five miles (8 km) north-west of the Grapevine Ranger Station is **Ubehebe Crater**, a 600-ft (185 m) deep red and grey volcanic funnel.

Eighteen miles (29 km) south on Hwy 190 from the T-junction is the **Harmony Borax Works** ruins. Ronald Reagan made a name in 1950s television touting Twenty Mule Team Borax, the product raked up and refined here from 1883–1889 and hauled 165 miles (264 km) over hideous terrain to Mojave with mule teams. The self-guided tour overlooks the barren terrain, wagons, and kilns.

Next door is Furnace Creek, a date palm and tamarisk tree oasis with a campground, RV park, motel, restaurants, general store, and petrol. The **Furnace Creek Visitor Center**, *tel: (619) 786-2331,* open 0800–1700, has a good slide show and bookstore. The **Borax Museum** has equipment used by the mule teams and trains in the area.

Next door is the incongruous **Furnace Creek Public Golf Course**. The luxury **Furnace Creek Inn** is on a rise across the highway. Half a mile

(1km) south, Hwy 190 veers south-east past **Zabriskie Point** out of the Monument to **Death Valley Junction** (See Las Vegas–Death Valley Route, p. 96). **Badwater Rd** forks to the right.

Twelve miles (19 km) down Badwater Rd (Hwy 178) on the left is the **Devil's Golf Course**, a chunky, dried seabed that is blindingly white with almost pure salt.

Twenty-eight miles (45 km) from Furnace Creek is **Artist's Drive**, a 9-mile (14.4 km) one-way circuit over a narrow, roller coaster-style dirt road. Halfway, there is a turnoff to the **Artist's Palette**, where the mountains to the east are splashed horizontally with colour: lime green, magenta, red, rust, purple and gold.

Back on Badwater Rd, retrace the route south for 4 miles (6.4 km) and continue another 8 miles (13 km) to **Badwater**. At 282 ft (87 m) below sea level, it's the lowest point in North America. Temperatures have been as high as 134°F (56 °C). Ironically, Badwater is less than 70 miles south-west of 14,494-ft (4460 m) Mt. Whitney, the highest point in the USA south of Alaska!

Death Valley

Look anywhere in Death Valley and an arid, almost lunar landscape assaults the eyes. Yet during the Pleistocene Epoch, 2 million–12,000 years ago, the valley held an inland sea. More than 380 wetland areas survive, brackish and often barely visible. (Furnace Creek's palm oasis is a notable exception). Uniquely adapted species have survived the millenia.

Among them are 5 species of desert pupfish. The Cottonball Marsh pupfish lives in water 6 times more saline than sea water. In spring, at Salt Creek, 6½ miles (10.4 km) south on Hwy 190, inch-long (2.5 cm) pupfish breed purposefully, and can be observed from a boardwalk parallel to the creek. Springsnails, like cousins found in oceans and aquariums, have also adapted to the dry climate, salty waters and harsh conditions of Death Valley.

Extremes prevail. Death Valley receives an average of 1.9 inches (5 cm) of rain annually. What little moisture does reach the area arrives from the Gulf of Mexico to the south. High thermals create thunderhead clouds above the valley in summer; the release of precipitation can cause flash floods. Afterwards the desert briefly blooms with wildflower carpets.

Breezes pushing east from the Pacific Oean have little chance of taking moisture as far as Death Valley. Three mountain ranges, the Sierra Nevada, San Bernardino and San Gabriel, create a rain shadow, exacerbated by the Panamint Mountains which gird Death Valley on the western side.

Sidewinder rattlesnakes and scorpions inhabit the landscape, along with kit foxes, desert banded geckos, skittish bighorn sheep, golden eagles and yellow warblers. Most desert dwellers are most active before sunrise or at dusk, when the frying pan heat simmers rather than sizzles. In 1913 Death Valley recorded its highest temperature, 134°F (56°C).

LOS ANGELES to LAS VEGAS

This may be the most boring 293-mile (469 km) drive most Californians make, but they make it by the millions every year. The twin lures are the gambling pits of Las Vegas and a well-marked freeway route that makes it almost impossible to get lost along the way. And with few features to distract you, either natural or man-made, for most travellers there's little reason not to drive straight through in a single day. Nevertheless, there are some places of interest along the way, principally San Bernardino and Barstow.

Be prepared, however, for serious desert driving. Observe the precautions advised in 'Desert Driving', p. 33. Once beyond the urban confines of San Bernardino, it's a good idea never to allow the petrol tank to fall below half-filled. In summer, cars without air-conditioning should not make the drive in the daytime, when desert heat and sun can very literally become deadly.

The Mojave Desert, from San Bernardino to near the Nevada border, is relatively high, wet, and cool – for a desert. The Colorado Desert, from the Nevada Border and on to Las Vegas, is low, dry, and hot. In winter, daytime temperatures can reach 30°C, yet the nights are freezing. Summer temperatures regularly hit 45°–50°C, but the nights can still be freezing.

ROUTE

From **Union Station** in downtown Los Angeles, turn left on Alameda St. Cross Hwy 101 (the Santa Ana Freeway) and immediately turn left to enter the freeway southbound. Merge onto I-10 eastbound, the San Bernardino Freeway, toward San Bernardino, 1 mile (1.6 km) later.

I-10 traverses over 50 miles (104 km) of small (and not so small) towns to I-15. Take I-15 northbound to by-pass **San Bernardino**, or to visit San Bernardino continue to the I-215 turn-off and turn north onto I-215.

Fourteen miles (22 km) north of San Bernardino, I-15 joins I-215 and becomes the Mojave Freeway as it begins climbing toward **Cajon Summit** (4260 ft; 1291 m). Breaks in the dry streambeds and rock formations on each side of the freeway trace the path of the **San Andreas Fault** on its route to the Pacific Ocean north of San Francisco. The freeway crosses the fault 4 miles (6 km) north of the Devore-Glen Helen exit and continues up to the summit.

Driving on smooth highway, it's easy to forget that this pass was once a precipice – *cajon* means 'box' in Spanish. The natural amphitheatre leading to the summit forms a box opening to the south. Travellers coming from the Mojave Desert found themselves looking over the edge of a cliff; those approaching from the coast had to climb the same sheer walls.

Native Americans in the area obligingly showed some of the easier routes to the Hudson Bay Company and American explorers in the 1820s, although some of the first white settlers had to dismantle their wagons at one point, lower them over a cliff, and reassemble them at the bottom before continuing on. By 1855 a train route had been blasted through the mountains.

From the summit, the freeway gently descends 11 miles (18 km) to **Victorville**. The **Roy Rogers–Dale Evans Museum**, *15650 Seneca Rd, off I-15; tel: (619) 243-4547*, is filled with personal and professional memorabilia from the famous Hollywood cowboy/cowgirl duo. The freeway cuts 31 miles (50 km) through the Mojave desert to **Barstow**.

Eight miles (13 km) beyond Barstow is the **California Agricultural Inspection Station**. All traffic coming into California must stop for inspection. Fruits and vegetables may not be brought into the state without special permit.

The 52 miles (83 km) between the Inspection Station and the tiny town of **Baker** is everything a desert ought to be: waterless wastelands filled with tenacious (and usually prickly!) brush that looks dead most of the year, dry lakes, sand

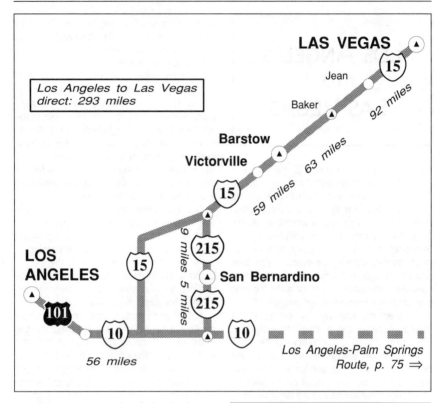

dunes, and cacti. Much of the land may eventually be included in a proposed Desert National Park being debated in the US Congress at the time of writing.

Baker also marks the western edge of the East Mojave National Scenic Area (see Palm Springs–Death Valley route, p. 178), a high desert area of sand dunes 600 ft (182 m) tall, dry lake beds, and ancient mountains eroded into grotesque formations. **Mountain Pass**, at 4730 ft (1433 m) is the highest point on the route to Las Vegas.

The **Nevada Border** is easy to spot: just beyond are the neon signs of the first casinos, Whiskey Pete's and the Primadonna. The last two offer free coffee from 2200–0600 to combat fatigue and the high accident rate on the dreary 45-mile (72 km) run into Las Vegas. The first freeway exits for the parade of Las Vegas casinos known as The Strip (see p. 90) are **Russel Road** and **Tropicana Blvd**.

SAN BERNARDINO

Tourist Information: San Bernardino Convention and Visitors Bureau, PO Box 920, San Bernardino, CA 92402; tel: (800) 669-8336 or (909) 889-3980.

Accommodation and Food

Accommodation covers the entire range. All chain hotels are represented except AY. For food, the entire range is represented, usually within sight of the freeway.

Sightseeing

San Bernardino is 67 miles (107 km) miles east of Los Angeles along I-10. The elevation gradually rises to 1000 ft (308 m), as San Bernardino's namesake mountains draw near. The city is the gateway to recreational areas in the nearby San Bernardino Mountains, including Lake Arrow-

Ghost Towns

The deserts of California and Nevada are littered with ghost towns, most of them founded on some exhausted gold or silver mining boom. Some towns, such as Virginia City (p. 203) are alive and even growing again. A few, like Calico, have been resurrected as tourist attractions. But most ghost towns are well and truly dead, abandoned when the mineral deposits that sparked them into life played out.

When prospectors staked their first claims to mine a new mineral discovery, other miners flocked in for a share of the wealth. Tent cities sprang up almost overnight, complete with general stores, bars, barber shops, brothels and occasionally, a church. In most cases, it was a false alarm, with the mineral deposits too small to support a town.

Occasionally the claims were rich enough to support a real town, with buildings of wood, sometimes even of brick, complete with electricity, telephones and newspapers. But in the end, economics always prevailed. When the mines were exhausted and finally closed, the miners moved on, and the town slowly began to return to the desert.

---

head and Big Bear Lake (see Los Angeles–Palm Springs route, p. 75). Most visitors pass through the city on the way to somewhere else. San Bernardino is the last major city before Las Vegas, and has the best petrol prices before the end of the journey.

The **California Theatre of the Performing Arts**, *562 W. 4th St, San Bernardino, CA 92402; tel: (800) 228-1155 or (714) 882-2545*, is one of five extant Art Deco theatres in the state. Musical productions are performed in the 1928 Spanish Colonial-style building.

BARSTOW

Tourist Information: Barstow Chamber of Commerce, *222 E. Main St, Suite 216, Barstow, CA 92311; tel: (619) 256-8617*.

Accommodation and Food

Barstow sits at the junction of three major highways with several military installations nearby, so there's a surprising choice of accommodation for such a small town. *BW, HI, HJ, QI,* and *VI* are all represented. For eating and drinking, fast food and chain restaurants are the best bets.

Sightseeing

Barstow is popularly known as the windiest and loneliest town in California. It's the kind of place where the most exciting night-time noises are the crashes and bangs of freight cars being shunted through a major railroad yard on the edge of town. It's also a heavily used stop for petrol, food, and overnight lodging.

The **Calico Early Man Archaeological Site**, *15 miles (24 km) north-east via I-15 and Minneola Rd; tel: (619) 256-5102*, was begun by Dr Louis Leakey in 1964. More than 12,000 stone tools dating back around 200,000 years have been found in the area, making it the oldest prehistoric tool site yet found in the Western Hemisphere. The site and visitor centre are open Wed–Sun.

Calico Ghost Town, *11 miles (18 km) north-east via I-15; tel: (619) 254-2122* is a 19th-century silver mining ghost town brought back to life with a mine tour, museum, Playhouse Theater (period melodrama), and narrow gauge train.

The biggest attraction in Barstow is the **California Desert Information Center**, *831 Barstow Rd; tel: (619) 256-8313*. The centre features exhibits on the natural history and environment of the Mojave Desert.

The **Factory Merchants Outlet Plaza**, *4 miles (6 km) south of Barstow near the Lenwood Road exit* is a good spot to pick up discount coupons for Las Vegas casinos and other attractions. The Nevada Commission on Tourism also produces a free 132-coupon *Discover Nevada Bonus Book, Capitol Complex, Carson City, NV 89710; tel: (800) 237-0774*.

LAS VEGAS

Glitter and glamour have made Las Vegas one of America's most popular tourist spots for nearly five decades. Every time the lure of bright lights, lively shows, and crowded casinos begins to fade, the city reinvents itself. The latest turn is toward family attractions – amusement rides, theme parks, shows and casinos built around adventure themes or cartoon characters. Don't take the change too literally. Vegas, as locals call it, remains a gambling town. The family entertainment theme is a play for parents, not children. The average adult visitor, casinos say, leaves $500 in the gambling halls.

Tourist Information

Las Vegas Convention and Visitors Authority (LVCVA), *3150 S. Paradise Rd, Las Vegas, NV 89109; tel: (702) 892-0711*, is open Mon–Fri 0800–1700. Brochure racks at the airport, car rental offices, hotels, restaurants, souvenir shops and museums are always full.

The monthly **Las Vegas Advisor**, *5280 S. Valley View Blvd, Ste B, Las Vegas, NV 89118; tel: (702) 597-1884*, is packed with tips on bargain meals, special lodging and show deals, casino coupons and gambling strategies. $45 per year or $5 per single issue.

Arriving and Departing

McCarran International Airport is 5 miles (8 km) south of downtown and just south of the Strip. Taxi to Strip hotels averages $10, mini-bus is $3.50 single.

I-15 is the primary road access from California. **AMTRAK** has daily train service from Los Angeles. The station is at the *Union Plaza Hotel, 1 Main St.; tel: (800) 872-7245.*

Getting Around

The millions of dollars in cash changing hands each day makes casinos extremely conscious of

security. **The Strip**, the 3-mile (6 km) line of nearly 30 flashy casinos along Las Vegas Blvd South, and **Glitter Gulch**, the downtown casino strip on Fremont St between Main St and Las Vegas Blvd, are extremely safe, day or night.

Car parks are less safe late at night. Use the free valet parking offered by every hotel. Tip the attendant $1 when picking up the car.

Away from casino areas, Las Vegas is no different from any other major US city. Avoid late night strolls.

The other major source of trouble are hustlers, male and female, who work casinos, conventions, and tours. Don't invite strangers, no matter how alluring, to your room. Too many are expert at drugging and robbing newfound 'friends'. Prostitution is legal, regulated, and less expensive at brothels in neighbouring Nye County, less than an hour's drive west on Hwy 95 or Hwy 160.

Public Transport

Citizens Area Transit (CAT); *tel: (702) 228-7433*, provides bus service. Buses run along the Strip all night, but frequency drops between 0100–0700. Buses serve downtown 0530–0130. Kerbside bus stops are marked with CAT signs.

Motorised **Strip Trolleys** serve strip casinos every 30 mins until 0200. Ask the casino doorman for the nearest trolley stop.

Traffic can be extremely slow on the Strip, especially from mid-afternoon through late evening. For long north-south driving, use Paradise Rd, east of the Strip, or Industrial Rd, west. Traffic moves more smoothly on I-15 and downtown.

Living in Las Vegas

Accommodation

Vegas is the hotel capital of the USA, with nearly 100,000 rooms. Every chain is represented, most of them several times.

The LVCVA has hotel listings, but cannot make bookings.

Tourist Las Vegas has two sections, the Strip and Downtown. New Strip hotels tend to be the most expensive, downtown hotels cheaper.

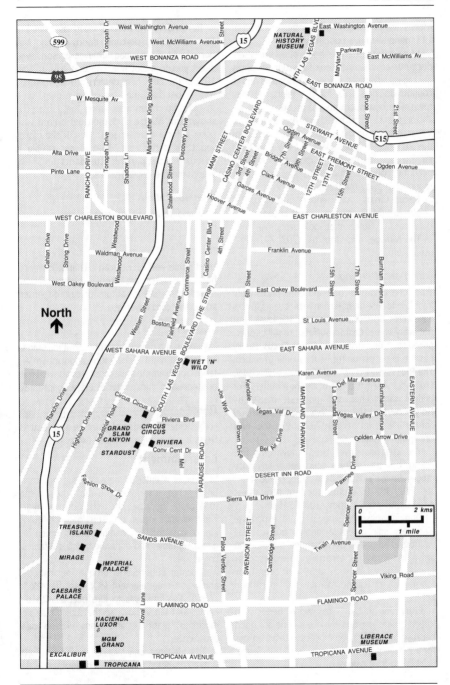

Motels away from both areas, often just west of I-15, generally have budget prices.

Most casinos have a hotel attached where discounts are the rule. Look for room and show packages, advertised in local newspapers and in coupon booklets free for the taking all over town. The best discounts are on Sun–Thurs.

For the best prices, check the current *Las Vegas Advisor* or the Sunday travel section of the *Los Angeles Times*. Once in Las Vegas, keep an eye out for casino coupon booklets and discount coupons in *What's On* and other tourist give-away magazines.

Circus Circus, *north end of the Strip; tel: (702) 734-0410,* is the lowest-priced major hotel/casino. Hotels that look expensive, such as **The Mirage**, *mid-Strip; tel: (702) 791-7111,* usually are.

Eating and Drinking

Traditionally, casino food and drink prices were kept low to lure gamblers. In recent years, prices have crept up toward more realistic levels. But not everywhere. **Casino buffets** are still budget-priced to attract customers. **Circus Circus** usually has the cheapest buffet, with quality to match. **The Rio**, *Flamingo Rd and Valley View Blvd; tel: (702) 252-7777,* has one of the best buffets. For budget sandwiches and moderate meals, try **Holy Cow!**, *2423 Las Vegas Blvd South, at Sahara Ave; tel: (702) 732-2697,* the only brewpub in Vegas.

The city has never been known for fine dining, but steaks are a good bet in any price range. **Binion's Horseshoe**, *128 Fremont St; tel: (702) 382-1600* offers the best steak value, a full dinner for $2 from 2200–0545.

Drinking has also grown more expensive. Gamblers still get free drinks, but cocktail waitresses are often overextended and slow to arrive. Many casinos, especially older ones, offer special drink values such as 50-cent beer. Look for specials on casino marquees or in coupon books.

Everything in Las Vegas works better with 'green grease', or **tips**. Service is generally good because most Vegas employees depend on tips for the bulk of their livelihood – minimum wage, or close to it, is common.

Bartenders and **cocktail waitresses** get $1–$2 each round; **skycaps, doormen,** and **bell persons** $1–$2 per bag. **Change persons** who direct you to a slot machine that pays off get 10% of the take. Give **dealers** a chip when you win, a bet half the size of your own, or a sizeable tip when you leave the table. The **showroom Maitre d'** doesn't get a tip if your ticket is for a reserved seat. If he or she moves you to a better seat, $5–$10 per couple is adequate. **Valet parking attendants** get $1–$2 every time the car is delivered.

Communications

Mail and faxes can be sent to and from any hotel.

Money

Most banks and casinos can exchange currency, but bank rates are slightly better. Casinos provide terminals for automatic cash dispensers and credit card advances.

Weather

Las Vegas is a desert, blisteringly hot in summer and cold at night. Dehydration and sunburn are serious problems in any season. Locals wear hats outdoors and drink water at every opportunity.

Dress

Forget cinema images of black tie and sequins. Dress is casual with very rare exceptions.

Entertainment

Las Vegas *is* entertainment, a neon tribute to tinsel riches. It's easier to gamble than to buy toothpaste because chemists close at night while casinos never do. The 'get rich quick' lure of easy money, whirling wheels, green felt gambling tables and glittering hotels is a fantasy come to life.

Mobster Bugsy Siegel brought resort hotels and resort entertainment to Vegas after World War II. The idea was to lure people with big names and fancy shows so they could play slot machines, blackjack and craps with a clear conscience.

The idea not only worked, it fed on itself. Hotels competed to present the biggest and the flashiest shows. Visitors came in growing numbers, feeding the spiral. Every year, the Strip, and now Downtown, grew brighter, the shows bigger, the casinos slicker with new games. Fantasy became reality.

Casinos

The new megahotel/casino complexes provide the ultimate in escapist fun. **The Mirage**, *tel: (702) 791-7111* or *(800) 627-6667*, has a volcano that erupts every 15 mins from dusk to dawn and a $25-million theatre to showcase disappearing white tigers and other illusions by **Siegfried and Roy**. Next door, **Treasure Island**; *tel: (702) 894-7111* or *(800) 944-7444* stages a fiery pirate battle every 90 minutes, complete with sinking ship, while the Cirque de Soleil stretches the limits of contortion and acrobatics in a custom theatre.

Excalibur; *tel: (702) 597-7777* or *(800) 937-7777* has 14 towers striped in red, blue and gold, a moat and drawbridge, and hourly battles between Merlin and a dragon. Players enter the **MGM Grand**; *tel: (702) 891-1111* or *(800) 929-1111*, through a lion's mouth, with a theme park somewhere beyond his right foot. Downtown, **Fremont St** is being arched by millions of tiny bulbs to create a 1500-ft (455 m) tunnel of light with fanciful figures parading through the open air at night.

Gambling is the money machine behind the flash. The industry calls it 'gaming' to ease prickly consciences.

Either way, it starts with slot machines at the airport (don't: locals say the payoff is terrible). Hotels place casinos between registration counters and guest room elevators. Rows of slots stand like sentries almost everywhere – gas stations, supermarkets, pharmacies, even wedding chapels.

The State of Nevada regulates casinos and gambling, but the only sure way to make money in a casino is to own one. The easier the game, the better the odds for the house. The house edge, or advantage, ranges from about 45% for Keno to ½% or less for expert blackjack and video poker.

Casinos warn against playing without knowing the rules, and they're right. Casinos give free lessons covering the basics. **The Gambler's Bookstore**, *630 S. 11th St; tel: (800) 634-6243* offers textbooks and advanced strategies.

The best guide on how to win (or how to lose less), is *Bargain City: Booking, Betting, and Beating the New Las Vegas* by LVA publisher Anthony Curtis. The $11.95 book is available in Vegas bookstores or by mail from the *Las Vegas Advisor*.

Slot machines account for about 60% of casino profits. Each casino sets its own odds. Most hold 4½%–12% of the bets that flow through each machine. Bigger casinos generally give slightly better odds than smaller ones, and the percentage payoff is slightly better with dollar machines than those that take quarters.

The US government also gets a cut. Winnings over $1200 are subject to income tax withholding, currently 30%. Win $1199, and you can take it all. Win $1200, and Uncle Sam leaves you with just $840.

Shows

Shows are Vegas' number two attraction. Traditional productions such as the **Folies Bergere**, *Tropicana; tel: (702) 739-2411*, **Splash**, *Rivera; tel: (702) 794-9301*, and **Enter the Night**, *Stardust; tel: (702) 732-6111* feature lavish sets, singing, dancing and topless showgirls. Some play covered versions in the early evening, topless shows later. Prices usually include two drinks.

The newer 'family shows' eschew bare breasts for costume extravaganzas such as **King Arthur's Tournament**, *Excalibur; tel: (702) 597-7600* and **Winds of the Gods**, *Luxor; tel: (702) 262-4900*, to mixed reviews. Magic shows are gaining in popularity. The best is **Lance Burton**, *Hacienda; tel: (702) 739-8911*.

The supershows are the most popular and the most expensive: **Siegfried and Roy**, *The Mirage, tel: (702) 792-7777*, and the **Cirque de Soleil**, *Treasure Island; tel: (702) 894-7111*.

Casinos also present **lounge acts**, usually musical performers or comedians.

Some casino attractions start early. **Circus Circus**; *tel: (702) 734-0410* or *(800) 634-3450* stages free circus acts throughout the day. The casino theme park, **Grand Slam Canyon**, has adventure rides. The best free attraction is the pirate battle, *Treasure Island; tel: (702) 894-7111 or (800) 944-7444*, every 90 mins from mid-afternoon. Best seats to watch the pirates win are at the north end of the Battle Bar, or on the wooden walkway near the British ship. Claim a spot at least 45 mins early.

The **Mirage** has three free attractions: an erupting volcano on the street; a rain forest in the casino; and a glass-walled habitat where Siegfried and Roy's rare white tigers frolic. The dolphin habitat has an admission charge.

The **Imperial Palace**, *tel: (702) 731-3311 or (800) 634-6441*, has an outstanding collection of automobiles once owned by famous people. **Caesar's Palace**, *tel: (702) 731-7110 or (800) 634-6001*, opens onto an up-market shopping mall with Roman decor, including statues that come to life on the hour.

Excalibur, *tel: (702) 597-7777 or (800) 937-7777*, stages hourly battles between Merlin and a dragon. A medieval-themed amusement area is inside, downstairs. Egyptian-themed **Luxor**, *tel: (702) 795-8118 or (800) 288-1000*, has an entertainment centre with three Egyptian-themed interactive attractions, a 'cruise' on the river Nile that passes scale models of famous tombs, and a stunning reproduction of King Tut's tomb. All have admission charges.

The **MGM Grand**, *tel: (702) 891-1111 or (800) 929-1111*, has an amusement arcade and shops based on MGM cartoon characters and a movie/adventure theme park with an entry fee.

The best way to experience Las Vegas is to walk, especially from dusk to early evening when the crowds are thick. Every Strip casino attempts to outdo its neighbours, from Caesar's Palace with its pseudo-Roman fountains and statues, to the fantasy castle of Excalibur and the tikis with glowing eyes guarding the Tropicana.

Glitter Gulch earns its name once the sun goes down. Downtown casinos are packed together so closely that the neon signs blend into a general glitter that turns night-time into an amusement arcade.

Museums and Tours

There's a surprising amount to do that is unrelated to casinos and gambling. **The Guinness World of Records**, *2780 Las Vegas Blvd South; tel: (702) 792-0640*, offers feats from the Guinness record books.

Las Vegas Natural History Museum, *900 Las Vegas Blvd N.; tel: (702) 384-3466*, has animated dinosaurs as well as traditional exhibits of birds, marine life, and animals from around the world.

The Liberace Museum, *1775 E. Tropicana Ave; tel: (702) 798-5595*, is devoted to antiques, pianos, jewellery, costumes, and cars owned by the millionaire entertainer.

Lied Discovery Children's Museum, *833 Las Vegas Blvd N.; tel: (702) 382-5437*, has 100 hands-on exhibits on science, the arts, the humanities, and everyday living.

Nevada State Museum and Historical Society, *700 Twin Lakes Dr.; tel: (702) 486-2502*, covers the history, cultures, geography, and wildlife of southern Nevada in a rambling Spanish Colonial-style building.

Old Las Vegas Mormon Fort State Historic Park, *Washington Ave and Las Vegas Blvd; tel: (702) 486-3511*, is a recreation of the original Mormon settlement and brick fort that began Las Vegas.

Wet 'N. Wild, *2600 Las Vegas Blvd; tel: (702) 737-3819*, grows in popularity with the heat. The water park includes flumes, a water roller coaster, and just plain swimming. Discount coupons are in most tourist throw-away papers.

Many of Vegas' top attractions are outside the city. **Ethel M's Chocolate Factory**, *2 Cactus Garden Dr., Henderson; tel: (702) 433-2500* is on the route to Hoover Dam. The factory has a self-guided tour with free samples at the end. A botanical garden has 350 species of cacti.

Also in Henderson is **Kidd's Marshmallow Factory**, *8203 Gibson Rd; tel: (702) 564-5400*, a self-guided tour of the marshmallow making process. Every visitor gets a free bag of gooey puffs after the tour.

– – – – – – – – – – – – – – – – – – –

⌒ Side Tracks from Las Vegas

Lake Mead National Recreation Area, 20 miles (32 km) east of Las Vegas, has six major recreation areas around the lake formed by

Hoover Dam. The **Alan Bible Visitor Center**, *4 miles (6 km) north-east of Boulder City on Hwy 93; tel: (702 293-8906*, has information and maps for the entire lake area.

Hoover Dam is 8 miles (13 km) beyond Boulder City on Hwy 93, *tel: (702) 293-8367*. Built in 1935, the 726-ft high dam (220 m) is one of the engineering and visual marvels of the world. Power from the dam drives every neon sign in Las Vegas. There are daily tours of the dam and gigantic hydroelectric turbines.

Watching enormous fountains playing along the Strip, it's easy to forget that Las Vegas is a desert. **Red Rock Canyon National Conservation Area**, *15 miles (24 km) W. of Las Vegas on Hwy 159 (W. Charleston Blvd); tel: (702) 363-1921*, is a scenic desert reserve with red and white sandstone cliffs, cacti, wild burros, and a 13-mile (21 km) one-way scenic drive. The Visitor Center, at the head of the scenic drive, is open 0830–1630 daily.

Valley of Fire State Park *(tel: (702) 397-2088)*, 50 miles (80 km) north-east of Las Vegas, I-15 to Hwy 169, has unique sandstone formations in brilliant red. The area is also known for petroglyphs, pictures chipped into the rock by Native American inhabitants. One of the best hiking and petroglyph trails is a one-hour loop to **Mouse's Tank**, named for a 19th-century Indian leader who successfully resisted capture for years in the rugged canyons. The Visitor Center is open 0830–1630 daily.

Las Vegas History

About 20,000 years ago Las Vegas was a marsh, dominated by mammoths. By the time humans arrived, marsh had become the Mojave Desert, relieved only by scattered artesian springs – including Las Vegas. The oasis lay unseen by outsiders until Mexican traders arrived in 1829. They named the springs Las Vegas, 'the meadows' in Spanish, after the abundant grasses. Water and forage shortened the arduous route between Santa Fe, New Mexico and Los Angeles. John Fremont stopped at Las Vegas on his way to California in 1844. Mormon settlers arrived a decade later. Part of their original 'Mormon Fort' survives near the intersection of Las Vegas Blvd North and Washington Ave.

Railroad developers decided to stop in Las Vegas. Work began in 1904, and the first train ran through new railroad yards on Jan 30 1905. The Plaza Hotel, at Main and Fremont Sts, occupies the site of the original Union Pacific depot. The depot is still in use, the only railroad station in the world inside a hotel-casino.

Las Vegas was the first US state to legalise casino gambling. It was also the last to make it illegal. The strict prohibition took effect in 1910. It lasted less than three weeks. That's how long it took not-so-secret casinos to open their doors. The underground industry flourished until 1931, when the state legislature legalised gambling to support schools. The same year, thousands of Hoover Dam construction workers flooded Las Vegas. The newly legal casinos became an instant success.

After World War II, a casino building boom erupted. The two lane road leading from Los Angeles into Las Vegas became The Strip, and mobster Benjamin 'Bugsy' Siegel, decided to build a Miami-style 'carpet joint'. He thought a posh hotel-casino with carpets could lure more gamblers than his rough, Western-style competitors. The Flamingo opened on New Years Eve 1946 and proved him right. Siegel was murdered six months later, but Vegas casinos have grown steadily more plush and more profitable since.

Did organised crime run post-war Las Vegas? Probably. Nevada folklore says the Mob was in control until the 1960s. That's when billionaire Howard Hughes arrived with enough money to buy a casino. Once Hughes blazed the way, other investors recognised the immense profits that honest gambling could produce.

LAS VEGAS to DEATH VALLEY

The full 155-mile (248 km) scenic route from Las Vegas to Death Valley National Monument takes about 3½ hrs without stops. The journey from Las Vegas to Pahrump, Beatty, Rhyolite, and into Death Valley crosses some of the starkest, hottest and most picturesque desert in North America. Summer and winter, start with a full petrol tank and carry plenty of water and food in case of a breakdown. If the vehicle does break down, raise the bonnet and wait for help to arrive. Walking for help in the desert can be a particularly nasty way to commit suicide.

For a quicker trip, follow the new highway from Pahrump to Death Valley which opened in the summer of 1994. The shorter route does not yet appear on most road maps, but cuts the journey to 124 miles (198 km) and 2½ hrs.

→ Direct Route

From Las Vegas, follow I-15 south approximately 9 miles (14 km) to **Hwy 160**. Turn right onto Hwy 160 toward **Pahrump**. Hwy 160 winds up through rugged desert mountains to Mountain Springs Summit at 5493 ft (1664 m). In winter, watch for snow and ice on the upper reaches of the highway; in summer, the cooler mountain breezes are a welcome respite from the heat in Las Vegas and the even higher temperatures yet to come in Death Valley. From the summit, Hwy 160 runs 30 miles (48 km) down to the Pahrump Valley and the green oasis of **Pahrump**.

From Pahrump, take the new highway west to **Death Valley Junction**. For specific directions, stop at any petrol station on the way into Pahrump. The new road should begin to appear on maps and road signs by mid-1995.

The highway crosses a series of low mountain ranges opening onto broad valleys. As recently as

the last Ice Age, the entire area was part of a vast lake system that extended south to the present line of the I-15 and Soda Lake, in the East Mojave National Scenic Area. Today, mountains and valleys alike are barren and untouched, the shapes changing magically as light and shadow creep across the landscape with the advancing sun.

Follow Hwy 190 north into **Death Valley National Monument**, to **Zabriskie Point**, 24 miles (38 km) beyond Death Valley Junction.

From Zabriskie Point continue another 5 miles (8 km) north to **Furnace Creek**.

〰 Scenic Route

Follow the direct route as far as Pahrump. From there, follow Hwy 160 27 miles (43 km) north to the intersection with Hwy 95.

The highway skirts the western slope of the **Spring Mountains**, a bustling mining area from the 1870s through to the early years of this century. Almost every road leading east toward the mountains or west into the flatlands ends in an abandoned mine or mining town. Most were abandoned so long ago that even the names have been forgotten, but a few are still recognisable by stone and concrete foundations beneath the blowing sands and slow-growing greasewood bushes.

Turn left onto Hwy 95. The **Amargosa Valley** and the tiny settlement of **Lathrop Wells** are 16 miles (26 km) north. Lathrop Wells, at the junction of Hwys 95 and 373 (running north from Death Valley Junction) has two claims to fame: an enormous lorry stop and an equally enormous collection of brothels. The latter cater for long-distance lorry drivers and tourists driving in from Las Vegas, an hour south along Hwy 95, as well as Californians who leave I-15 at Baker, 108 miles (173 km) south. To the east of the settlement is the **Amargosa Desert**. The **Funeral Mountains** are just across the California border.

From Lathrop Wells, follow Hwy 95 to **Beatty**, 29 miles (46 km) north. The highway follows the course of the Amargosa River, an on-again, off-again river that occasionally runs as much as 12 in. (30 cm) wide near Beatty. The river sometimes thunders down the usually dry bed for a few hours following heavy winter rains, but the

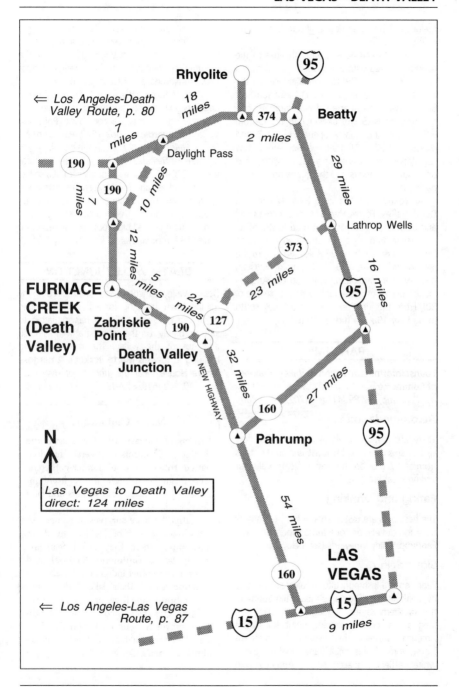

Rhyolite

⬅ Los Angeles-Death Valley Route, p. 80

Beatty

18 miles

7 miles

Daylight Pass

374

2 miles

29 miles

190

190

10 miles

7 miles

Lathrop Wells

373

12 miles

FURNACE CREEK (Death Valley)

Zabriskie Point

5 miles

24 miles

23 miles

95

16 miles

127

190

Death Valley Junction

32 miles

NEW HIGHWAY

27 miles

95

160

N

Pahrump

Las Vegas to Death Valley direct: 124 miles

54 miles

LAS VEGAS

160

⬅ Los Angeles-Las Vegas Route, p. 87

15

15

9 miles

majority of the water flow is about 40 ft (13 m) below the surface.

Mountains and deserts on both sides of the river are littered with abandoned mining camps and ghost towns. The town of **Carrara**, on the east side of Hwy 95, 9 miles (14 km) south of Beatty, was headquarters for a large marble quarry 3 miles (5 km) deeper into the Carrara Hills. Town and quarry opened in 1913 and closed in 1924. All that remains are a few foundations and traces of a cable railway that once carried workers into the quarry and marble back out.

At Beatty, turn left onto Hwy 374 toward **Death Valley**. Follow Hwy 374 for 2 miles (3 km) and turn right on a good dirt road to **Rhyolite**.

After visiting Rhyolite, retrace your route to Hwy 374 and continue 25 miles (40 km) to the junction with Hwy 190. At this point you can head west towards Lone Pine and Los Angeles along the Los Angeles–Death Valley route (see p. 80). From the junction to Furnace Creek south along Hwy 190 is a further 19 miles.

PAHRUMP

Tourist Information: Pahrump Valley Chamber of Commerce, *on Hwy 160 downtown, PO Box 42, Pahrump, NV 89041; tel: (702) 727-5800.*

Accommodation

There are a few motels in Pahrump, but few visitors spend the night. Most are on day trips from Las Vegas, on the way to Death Valley or visiting local brothels.

Eating and Drinking

The best bets are restaurants in local casinos or fast food outlets, or, for a more expensive meal, Pahrump Valley Vineyards (see below).

Sightseeing

Pahrump is a lush agricultural valley surrounded by bleak deserts. The name means Big Spring in the southern Paiute language; the valley was long an important stopping point for Native American travellers because of its abundant water, forage, and small game. In the 1870s, white settlers displaced Native Americans to plant vast orchards, truck gardens, and vineyards. They sold fruit, vegetables and wines to the railroad town of Las Vegas, as well as to the innumerable mining towns that sprang up across Western Nevada and Eastern California.

Most of those early fields have disappeared beneath golf courses and housing estates, but winemaking has made a comeback. **Pahrump Valley Vineyards**, *PO Box 1540, Pahrump, NV 89041; tel: (702) 727-6900,* is the only winery in the state of Nevada. The winery is open daily for tours, 1000–1630, or by appointment. It also has Pahrump's best and most expensive restaurant, open for lunch and dinner. Look for a white Spanish-style building with a four-storey tower and a blinding cobalt blue roof surrounded by 40 acres (16 ha) of vineyards, just off Hwy 160.

DEATH VALLEY JUNCTION

Death Valley Junction was once a company mining town and stop for a train line hauling borax out of Death Valley. It has managed to survive, barely, on the tourist traffic flowing in and out of the Valley. The most imposing building in town is **Marta Becket's Amargosa Opera House**, *near the junction of Hwys 127 and 190; tel: (619) 852-4316.* The opera house, once the city hall, is a backdrop to Becket's solo dance/mime performances Nov–May.

The **Amargosa Hotel**, next door, *tel: (619) 852-4441*, is usually open for accommodation and meals. More facilities should open as travellers from Las Vegas discover the new, shorter route into Death Valley.

ZABRISKIE POINT

The scenic viewpoint, made famous by Italian cinema director Federico Fellini, is just to the left of the highway beyond a parking lot.

The heavily eroded layers of multi-coloured rock surrounding the left-leaning snaggle tooth of Zabriskie Point are hardened mud and sand laid down between 3 and 9 million years ago when Death Valley was a broad lake, and the steady water supply supported mastodons, camels and huge predator cats.

The best time to view Zabriskie Point is in the soft light of dawn, when the entire badlands vista is thrown into sharp pink relief by the rising sun. Plan to arrive at the parking lot at least 45 mins before dawn to watch the spectacle of changing colours and shapes emerge from the shadows of night. The magical colours vanish by the time the sun is fully visible above the horizon.

BEATTY

Tourist Information: Beatty Chamber of Commerce, *on Hwy 95, PO Box 956, Beatty, NV 89003; tel: (702) 553-2225.*

Accommodation and Food

There are a handful of small motels and cafes in Beatty, but no chain outlets. Best bet for eating and drinking is the **Exchange Club**, which is also an unofficial tourist office.

Sightseeing

Beatty was founded in 1904, one of more than a dozen mining towns that blossomed in what was called the Bullfrog mining district – gold was found in veins of green rock, which reminded miners of bullfrogs. Only Beatty survived, mostly a matter of luck and a steady water supply from Amargosa River.

The town prospered as a freight and commercial centre for the entire district. By 1906, it had more than 1000 people, three railroads, a bank, and dozens of merchants. The Bullfrog boom subsided in 1909, but Beatty continued as a railroad town and supply centre. By the time the last railroad closed in 1940, the town had grown to become the first town of any size north of Las Vegas along Hwy 95.

As tourism into Death Valley increased, Beatty discovered that it was the northeastern gateway into the National Monument, a role Pahrump is likely to usurp for travellers from Las Vegas. Beatty is the best spot to fill up on petrol before entering Death Valley, where prices rise as quickly and as high as the temperature.

RHYOLITE

Late in the summer of 1904, two penniless prospectors discovered gold in the trackless mountains northeast of Death Valley. In early 1905, a town was laid out near some of the richest mines and Rhyolite appeared almost overnight. By 1907, it had 12,000 inhabitants, three railroads, three ice plants, four newspapers, an opera house, a board of trade and a telephone exchange. Residential neighbourhoods spread across the sagebrush for blocks from the city centre. A modern city had appeared even before the local mines had ever turned a profit. Most of them never did.

A financial panic swept America late in 1907 and Rhyolite collapsed. By 1910 the population was down to 700. By 1920, it had become a ghost town – buildings, offices, schools and banks open to the ceaseless desert winds. All that remains today is an abandoned railroad station, a house built entirely of empty bottles (often the most easily available building material in desert mining towns), and a few tottering walls.

How much longer the few surviving ruins will survive is open to question. Modern mining methods are far more efficient than the early 20th century processes. An Australian operator has reopened mining operations just a hillside away from Rhyolite. Vibrations from the open pit blasting and digging operation are shaking what remains of the old town to pieces.

SAN DIEGO

San Diego spans two cultures – US and Mexican. Spanish is spoken as much as English; burritos and tacos are as everyday as burgers and hot dogs. Of all California's coastal cities, San Diego has the most temperate weather and the most sun. Mountains are visible from North County to Baja, Mexico, and to the east where San Diego's rugged, forested backcountry begins. Sailing, deep-sea fishing, snorkelling and scuba diving occupy San Diegans on the water; sun lures the shirtsleeves and shorts crowd to an all-year Mediterranean climate.

With a decline in the presence of the US Navy and the aerospace industry which supported the economy for 40 years, San Diego is now looking to tourism and NAFTA-induced manufacturing just across the border in Mexico to continue its prosperity.

Angelenos (citizens of Los Angeles) use San Diego as a getaway. For locals and visitors alike, San Diego is also the gateway to Mexico.

Tourist Information

San Diego Convention & Visitors Bureau, (SDCVB), Dept. 700, 401 B St, Ste 1400, San Diego, CA 92101-4237.

Visitor Information Center, 1st Ave and F St, 11 Horton Plaza, is open Mon–Sat 0830–1700, Sun 1100–1700 (Jun–Aug); tel: (619) 236-1212.

Coronado (Island) Visitor Information Center, 1111 Orange Ave, Ste A, Coronado, CA 92118, is open Mon–Fri 0900–1700, Sat–Sun 1000–1600; tel: (800) 622-8300 or (619) 437-8788.

Arriving and Departing

Airport

San Diego International Airport/Lindbergh

Field is 3 miles (5 km) northwest of downtown; tel: (619) 231-5220. Bus (San Diego Transit) no. 2 to downtown, $1.50. San Diego taxis charge $1.60 per mile from Lindbergh Field. Check with the airport for shuttles to downtown, Mission Valley hotels, or elsewhere.

Station

From Los Angeles' Union Station, it's a 3-hr rail journey to San Diego's **Santa Fe Depot**, Kettner and Broadway. Eight trains run daily; fare $24 one-way, $31 round trip. Guarantee seats with a $6 custom coach reservation fee ($12 round trip), paid upon booking with **AMTRAK**, tel: (800) 872-7245. You can take the South Line San Diego Trolley from the Santa Fe Depot south to Mexico and walk across the border to Tijuana.

Roads

Interstate 5 (I-5), which runs south from Canada to Mexico, is called the **San Diego Freeway** between Los Angeles and San Diego. Allow 2½ hours; more between 0700–0830 or 1530–1730 rush hours. I-8 is the main east-west artery into San Diego. Freeway traffic flows well, though downtown freeway on-ramps are poorly marked.

Weather

Coastal San Diego is blessed with a dry subtropical Mediterranean climate all year round. Temperatures range from 4° to 21°C. Days are sunny, with less than 0.3 m of annual rainfall between Dec and Mar. Carry a pullover for cooler evenings and spring morning fog. Air quality varies from crystal-clear to pollution-brown, but the sun is always strong.

Getting Around

San Diego's compact and walkable **Downtown** is centered around the **Gaslamp Quarter District-Horton Plaza**. Avoid auto-guardian scams and unwanted approaches from denizens of this slightly sanitised skid row by parking in well-lit public parking lots at night. Avoid neighbourhoods to the east of the Gaslamp Quarter, where there's nothing to see anyway.

Not far from downtown is the city's cultural

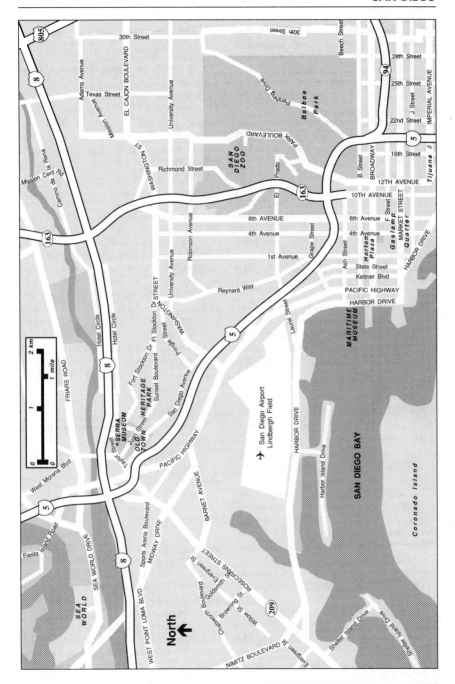

mecca, **Balboa Park**. Museums, speciality gardens, theatres and the **San Diego Zoo** nestle amidst tropical and desert-loving flora.

Shelter and **Harbor Islands** connect with the mainland by causeways; a high, sloping toll bridge connects posh **Coronado Island** with the mainland.

The **Cabrillo Monument** towering atop **Point Loma** at the bay channel entrance marks the Spanish discovery of San Diego in 1542. In 1769, the first Roman Catholic mission north of present-day Mexico was founded a few miles inland. Local Indians, most forcibly converted, lived close to the Franciscan fathers' mission. **Old Town San Diego State Historic Park**, (north-east of Downtown, off I-8) preserves adobes (whitewashed, thick mud brick buildings) and stores from the secularised Mexican Rancho era of 1821–1848, as well as dwellings built after the 1848 American take-over.

Public Transport

Buses and trolleys combine to service San Diego. The **San Diego Trolley System South Line** provides inexpensive transportation to the San Ysidro international border station just across from Tijuana, Mexico.

The **Transit Store**, *449 Broadway, open Mon–Sat from 0830–1730; tel: (619) 233-3004*, has information on bus and trolley routes and Day Tripper passes for in-town, south county and rural areas. Town bus fares are $1.50, including free 1-hr transfers. Trolley tickets sold from self-service machines cost $1–$1.75 (exact change required).

The **South Line Trolley** runs north from San Ysidro International Border to downtown, turns west to the Santa Fe AMTRAK train depot, and continues north. Service runs every 15 mins (10 mins during rush hour), 0505–0015, from County Center Station south; additional services operate on Saturday night. By 1995, the route should extend from the Mexican border to San Diego's Old Town.

The **Bayside Line Trolley** connects with the South and East Line Trolley routes, then skirts Harbor Dr. near Seaport Village and the Gaslamp Quarter.

One- or 4-day **Day Tripper** passes provide unlimited use of bus and trolley lines and the San Diego–Coronado Ferry for $4 and $12 respectively.

Daily **Old Town Trolley Tours** stop at ten points of interest over a 2-hr period, starting at 0900. Narration and free reboarding makes the $15 adult and $7 (6-12 year) child's ticket a bargain, since parking space is limited and costly; *tel: (619) 298-8687*.

Hop on at one of 12 stops along the free **Balboa Park Tram** route to visit museums, theatres, and the San Diego Zoo.

Ferries

The **San Diego–Coronado Ferry** has been plying the bay for a century. Today, cars use the San Diego–Coronado Bay Bridge, and pedestrians and cyclists catch the ferry from the **Broadway Pier** or Coronado **Ferry Landing Marketplace**. Ferries depart each 30 minutes, from 0900 daily; the service continues until 2200 or 2300 (Fri and Sat). The 15-min crossing, $2 single ($0.55 for bicycles) is a mini-harbour tour; *tel: (619) 595-1490*.

Mission Bay **Harbor Hopper Ferry** is a water taxi making nine stops around the Mission Bay marinas northwest of Lindbergh Field and Old Town. Adult return fare is $6; all-day pass, $10; *1875 Quivira Way, #C5, San Diego, 92109; tel: (619) 925-4677*.

Hornblower and **Invader** offer bay and dining cruises from the Broadway Pier; *tel: (619) 234-8687*.

Harbor Excursion offer harbour cruises, dining, and Coronado Ferry transit from the Broadway Pier; *tel: (800) 442-7847*.

Driving

Many downtown streets are one-way; plan driving routes in advance. Harbor Dr. skirts the bay. Broadway, Market St and Imperial Ave are the main west–east arteries. Numbered streets, from 1st to 12th Ave and 13th St to 50th St, run east, beginning at Horton Plaza. Lettered streets begin three blocks north of Broadway and end at L St, just north of Imperial Ave.

Parking meters around downtown and Harbor Dr. take only quarters. Park free for 3 hrs in the well-lit Horton Plaza car park with a plaza merchant validation for purchases or dining. Weekend parking is congested in Balboa Park and Old Town.

The next chapter, San Diego Circuit, provides a ready-made driving tour of the main sights of the city area.

Living in San Diego

Accommodation

San Diego County boasts 45,000 rooms; 6100 are in Mission Valley's Hotel Circle, a 10-min drive via I-8 and I-5 from downtown. Nov–Mar is low season, with prices 15–40% less than in summer. Most beachfront lodging is pricey in any season. Downtown lodging is limited; with a vehicle, Mission Valley is the best option.

The **SDCVB Official Visitors Guide** lists some accommodation, but does not make bookings. Ask for automobile club, senior citizen and youth discounts upon arrival.

San Diego Hotel Reservations, Inc., *7380 Clairemont Mesa Blvd, Ste 218, San Diego, CA 92111; tel: (800) 728-3227 or (619) 627-9400*, makes bookings for 250 hotels and motels.

San Diego Bed & Breakfast Directory, *Box 3292, San Diego. CA 92163; tel: (800) 424-8303 or (619) 297-3130*, books 30 county homes and inns at moderate-to-pricey rates.

Hotel Circle properties, like the Polynesian-theme **Hanalei Hotel**, *2270 Hotel Circle North, San Diego, CA 92108;* tel: (800) 882-0858, are moderate to expensive and are close to Old Town (across the road), downtown (10 mins), La Jolla (8 mins) and the San Diego Mission and Mission Bay (3 mins in opposite directions).

Two 'grande dame' downtown hotels have been restored to Victorian splendour. Have a drink in the **Horton Grand Hotel** glassed-in lobby; *311 Island Ave, San Diego, CA 92101; tel: (800) 542-1886*, expensive; or stay across from Horton Plaza at the **U. S. Grant Hotel**, *326 Broadway, San Diego, CA 92101; tel (800) 237-5029*, also expensive.

AY is more economical: **HI-San Diego**, *500 W. Broadway, San Diego, CA 92101; tel: (619) 525-1531*, budget. **HI-Elliott Hostel**, *3790 Udall St San Diego, CA 92107; tel: (619) 223-4778*, budget.

Eating and Drinking

San Diegans take Mexican food for granted. There's also Harbor Island seafood, Cajun (spicy Louisiana) cuisine, pub food, Greek, Indian, Chinese, French, steak and potatoes, or a combination.

The Official San Diego Visitors Guide, San Diego Magazine, San Diego Home/Garden, and several give-aways, *San Diego Reader, San Diego This Week* and *Guide to San Diego's Downtown*, list both ethnic and American restaurants. Warm, sunny weather encourages **Sunday brunches**, an economical way to fill up and sample cheap California sparkling wine.

Fri and Sat nights, **Mystery Café Dining Theatre** waiters interact with the audience to solve a comic whodunit; **Imperial House Restaurant,** *505 Kalmia St, San Diego, CA; tel: (619) 544-1600*, pricey. Find truly posh beef at the **Prince of Wales**, *Hotel Del Coronado, Coronado, CA 92118; tel: (619) 435-6611*, pricey.

Try the foot-tall 'motherlode sandwich' at **Claim Jumper**, *12384 Carmel Mountain Rd, San Diego; tel: (619) 485-8370*, budget. **La Salsa** is a Southern California chain with authentic-tasting burritos and choice of hot condiments; *Horton Plaza, tel: (619) 234-6906*, cheap. Moderate **Charley Brown's**, *880 E. Harbor Island Dr., Harbor Island, San Diego, CA 92101; tel: (619) 291-1880*, a replica of an 1880s steamboat, serves beef and seafood.

The Gaslamp Quarter is crowded, especially on weekends, but come dark, pubs and restaurants jump. **Brewski's Gaslamp Pub-Bistro and Brewery**, *310 5th Ave; tel: (619) 231-7700*, spills onto the sidewalk; budget. Try the ribs at **Buffalo Joe's BBQ Grill & Saloon**, *600 5th Ave; tel: (619) 236-1616;* moderate. There's rotisserie chicken at **Dakota Grill & Spirits**, *901 5th Ave; tel: (619) 234-5554*, moderate. Indulge in late afternoon reduced 'happy hour' prices on drinks and snacks.

Try the range of 'Mexican' cuisine in Old Town, from ersatz cardboard American to tortillas that taste like those south of the border. At **Casa de Bandini**, dine to mariachi music on the patio of an 1829 adobe hacienda;

tel: (619) 297- 8211, moderate. At **Old Town Mexican Cafe y Cantina**, a woman in the window makes tortillas by hand, *2489 San Diego Ave, San Diego, CA 92110; tel: (619) 297-4330*, budget. Find cheap and tasty chicken, burritos, tacos, and combination entrées at **Carne Estrada's**, *2502 San Diego Ave, San Diego, CA 92110; tel: (619) 296-1112*.

Money

There are **Thomas Cook Foreign Exchange** branches at *University Towne Center, 4525 La Jolla Village Dr., Ste D1B, San Diego; tel: (619) 457 0841* and *177 Horton Plaza, San Diego; tel: (619) 235 0900*. Both also handle travellers' cheques refunds.

Entertainment

Comedy flourishes at **Improvisation** ('Improv'), *832 Garnet Ave, Pacific Beach; tel: (619) 483-4522*. Dixieland music, and rowdy casualness prevail at **Dick's Last Resort**, *345 5th Ave; tel: (619) 231-9100*. Check local newspapers for comedy, music, lounge act entertainment and Tijuana tours.

Balboa Park's **Old Globe Theatre** offers 12 annual productions of Shakespeare and contemporary works in three theatres; *tel: (619) 239-2255*. Free outdoor Sunday concerts begin at 1400 at **Spreckels Organ Pavilion**; *tel: (619) 235-1100*. Horton Plaza's **Times ArtsTix** sells cash-only, half-price, day-of-performance, theatre, dance, and music tickets, Horton Plaza; *tel: (619) 238-3810*.

Shopping

Horton Plaza has major department stores: **Nordstrom**; *tel: (619) 239-1700*; **Robinsons-May**; *tel: (619) 544-9810*; **The Broadway**; *tel: (619) 231-4747*; and the more economical **Mervyn's**; *tel: (619) 231-8800*. Across First Ave is **Paladion**'s couture boutiques; *tel: (619) 232-1627*. Find a Stetson at **Western Hats**; *5th Ave and Broadway.*

Seaport Village has waterfront shops, restaurants, a carousel and buskers; *W. Harbor Dr. at Kettner Blvd; tel: (619) 235-4013*. **Bazaar del Mundo**, *Old Town; tel: (619) 296-3161*, has Mexican crafts. **Fashion Valley** mall has 100 shops, department stores and eateries, with parking: *Mission Valley; tel: (619) 297-3381*.

For bargains, shop at **Kobey's Swap Meet** (Thurs–Sun); *3500 Sports Arena Blvd: tel: (619) 226-0650*, or the **San Diego Factory Outlet Center**, *4410–4520 Camino de la Plaza, San Ysidro; tel. (619) 690–2999*. Tijuana shopping is just across the border.

Sightseeing

San Diego, California's second and America's sixth largest city, is bursting at the seams with people. Metropolitan area population currently numbers about 2½ million, living in a sprawling area with ultra-swank beach towns, mountains, high desert, bays, flower fields, and Hispanic influences. **Tijuana, Mexico** is 10 miles (16 km) south of downtown San Diego (see San Diego Circuit, p. 108).

San Diego Bay long ago fixed the city's character as a 'Navy' town, though global stand-down has decreased the naval influence in recent years. The 1992 America's Cup competition sealed San Diego's love affair with the sea.

The city's most famous attraction is the **San Diego Zoo**. Located in Balboa Park, the zoo pioneered natural flora habitats for animals. Regarded as one of the world's leading zoos, it is home to over 4000 animals, and incorporates a Children's Zoo.

The area has beaches, marinas, parks, hills, cliffs, islands, winter whale watching, boating and sprawl. Local residents speak of Mission Bay, Ocean Beach, Downtown, Point Loma, Balboa Park, La Jolla, Mission Valley, Old Town, etc. Neighbourhoods run from elegant, tree-lined Hillcrest, formerly called 'Banker's Hill', to run-down brick flophouses south of downtown San Diego.

Sleepy San Diego grew little after 18th Century colonisation by Spanish soldiers and missionaries. A natural harbour led San Francisco businessman Alonzo Horton to locate his enterprises nearby in the late 19th century. San Francisco sugar baron John D. Spreckels bought Coronado Island from a pair of railroad speculators who had gone bust in the 1887 depression. The downtown and Coronado developed side by side, though the island became a tented summer resort playground until the World War I. An influx of naval personnel during World War II determined the personality of a community that, until a few years ago, was defined by the military and aerospace.

A pleasant climate and marine life drew scientists to Scripps Institution of Oceanography (La Jolla) and Sea World Research Institute (Mission Bay). The Salk Institute (La Jolla), named after the discoverer of polio vaccine, is engaged in cutting-edge genetic research.

Museums

Many San Diego museums cluster in **Balboa Park** along Pan American Plaza and pedestrian-only **El Prado**. **San Diego Aerospace Museum**, *tel: (619) 234-8291*, includes displays of the Flying Tigers, the Eagle Squadron, and Miramar Air Station 'Top Gun' pilot helmets. Among 66 historic aircraft is the best-preserved of 19 Mann-Egerton aircraft delivered to the USA in 1917 and a Supermarine Spitfire Mk. XVI. Sixty **San Diego Automotive Museum** vehicles include horseless carriages, motorcycles, taxis and sports cars; *tel: (619) 231-2886*.

Other park attractions include the **Model Railroad Museum**, *tel: (619) 696-0199*, (operating model trains, local railroad artifacts); the **Museum of Photographic Arts**, *tel: (619) 239-5262*; the **Reuben H. Fleet Space Theater & Science Center**, *tel: (619) 238-1233* (interactive science exhibits and IMAX cinema); the **Natural History Museum**, *tel: (619) 232-3821* (desert ecology, stroke a live tarantula); the **Museum of Art**, *tel: (619) 232-7931* (lunch in the outdoor **Sculpture Garden Cafe**); the **Museum of Man**, *tel: (619) 239-2001* (3.5-million year old skeleton, tortilla making and Mexican weaving); and the **Timken Art Gallery**, *tel: (619) 239-5548* (European painters, Russian icons).

A one-week **Passport to Balboa Park**, good for all but the Timken, costs $13 from museums, Horton Plaza Times ArtsTix booth, or Balboa Park Visitors Center; *tel: (619) 239-0512*.

The lush vegetation of **Balboa Park Gardens** includes more than 400 species of trees, 67 varieties of palms and 160 different roses, plus cacti, lilies, ferns and bamboo. Horticulturalists conduct free 1-hr garden walking tours each Saturday at 1000, Mid-Jan–mid-Nov. **Offshoot Tours**, *in front of the Botanical Building; tel: (619) 235-1114*. Reservations are not required.

The **San Diego Maritime Museum**, *1306 N. Harbor Dr.; tel: (619) 234-9153*, includes the 1863 three-masted *Star of India* sailing ship, the 1904 steam yacht *Medea*, and the 1898 San Francisco ferryboat, the *Berkeley*. The *Berkeley* has a working boiler room, and an upper deck with stained glass windows and patterned seats. America's Cup memorabilia is mid-decks.

Old Town San Diego State Historic Park, *4002 Wallace St, San Diego, CA 92110; tel: (619) 220-5422*, is a group of original and reconstructed adobes illustrating the Mexican and early American settlements from 1821 to 1872. Some buildings are restaurants and souvenir shops. **La Casa de Estudillo** is furnished as it was from 1830–1849 when it was the city's socio-political centre. Costumed rangers sometimes make tortillas, hand-dip candles and blacksmith at **Machado y Stewart Adobe**. **Seeley Stables** has buggies, wagons, Western tack and pioneer gear. There's a stagecoach and Gold Rush equipment at the **Wells Fargo Museum**; *tel: (619) 294-5549*.

Heritage Park boasts six Victorian buildings and a Jewish Temple; *tel: (619) 694-3049*.

The mission-style **Junipero Serra Museum**, *2727 Presidio Dr.; tel: (619) 297-3258*, named after the founder of California's Missions, sits at the site of the Spanish **Presidio** (garrison).

The **Stephen Birch Aquarium-Museum**, *Scripps Institution, 2300 Expedition Way, La Jolla, CA 92093-0207; tel: (619) 534-3474*, has interactive oceanographic, meteorologic, and natural history exhibits.

Walking tours

Self-guided tours are described in *San Diego on Foot*, by Carol Mendel, *PO Box 6022, San Diego, CA 92016*. **Gaslamp Quarter Foundation**, *410 Island Ave, San Diego, CA 92101; tel: (619) 233-5227* (Sat tours, $5). **Old Town San Diego State Historic Park Walking Tour**; *tel: (619) 293-0117* (free, daily at 1400, beginning at Robinson-Rose Bldg at north side of the Plaza).

SAN DIEGO CIRCUIT

SAN DIEGO 59-MILE DRIVE

The 59-mile scenic drive requires at least a day to visit San Diego, La Jolla, and Coronado Island. Watch for a white seagull on blue and yellow signs every ¼ mile (0.4 km).

Downtown to Point Loma

Begin downtown at the foot of Broadway, drive north on Harbor Dr. past the Broadway Pier and Cruise Ship Terminal to the **Maritime Museum**'s three ships.

Continue north on Harbor Dr. past **Lindbergh Field**. Take **Harbor Island** exit to the island's north side for a **San Diego skyline** view. Return to Harbor Dr. by staying in the right-hand lane while crossing the bridge, and go through the road loop. Turn left onto Scott St, then left on Shelter Island Dr. to **Shelter Island** marinas, sportfishing, hotels, and seafood.

Return to Scott St, and turn right onto Talbot St, left onto Canon St, and left again onto **Catalina Blvd (Hwy 209)**. Head 3½ miles (5.6 km) south to Point Loma and **Cabrillo National Monument**; tel: (619) 557-5450. The white statue of Juan Rodriguez Cabrillo, the 1542 European discoverer of San Diego Bay, stands high above a panoramic view of the ship channel, Coronado Island, and the coastline to Mexico's mountains.

Walk up the 1855 winding stairway of **Old Point Loma Lighthouse**. Hike the 2-mile (3.2 km) **Bayside Trail** by old coastal defences, chapparal, and cliffside vistas. From Dec–Feb, watch **grey whales** migrate south from the Arctic Ocean.

Sunset Cliffs and Sea World

Return north on Catalina Blvd and turn left at Hill St. Turn right at **Sunset Cliffs Blvd** to see tidepools, beaches and surfers below. Go left on Newport Ave to fish or bird-watch at **Ocean Beach Municipal Fishing Pier**.

Take Sunset Cliffs Blvd across the San Diego River to the 4600-acre (1862 ha) **Mission Bay Park**. Quickly turn right at the Sea World Dr. exit and park to see **Sea World's** killer whales. Return to the Sea World Dr. exit and go north on Ingraham St. Cross two bridges to Crown Point Dr. to watch windsurfers and catamarans.

Turn left at Lamont St (which becomes Soledad Rd at the Beryl St intersection). Pass Kate Sessions Park, then turn left onto Soledad Mountain Rd, and right on La Jolla Scenic Dr. to **Mount Soledad Park** and 360° vistas.

La Jolla and Pacific Beach

Go right on Via Capri, left on Hidden Valley Rd., left on Frontage Rd., and right at the stoplight. At the next stoplight, turn left onto North Torrey Pines Rd. It's easy to get lost, but the route winds past the **University of California San Diego** campus, famous for modernistic outdoor sculpture, and the **Salk Institute**. Look seaward for hang gliders launched from Torrey Pines glider port.

Reverse direction on Torrey Pines Rd and turn at Expedition Way for the **Stephen Birch Aquarium-Museum**.

Turn left onto Torrey Pines Rd., then left onto La Jolla Shores Dr. The **La Jolla** shoreline, walkable at high tide, attracts UCSD students and the affluent. Restaurants are trendy. Visit the **Mingei International Museum of World Folk Art**, University Towne Centre, 4405 La Jolla Village Dr.; tel: (619) 453-5300. Turn right on **Prospect St**, La Jolla's major shopping area.

Go right on Coast Blvd, then walk down the stairway to **Sunny Jim Cave** through La Jolla Cave and Shell Shop. Westward at street level is **La Jolla Cove Park**.

To drive by La Jolla's elegant homes, continue south on Coast Blvd, right on Olivetas St, left onto Nautilus, right onto La Jolla Scenic Dr., and left onto La Jolla Mesa Dr.

When the street name changes to Mission Blvd, you're in **Pacific Beach**, where grunion (smallfish) 'run' Mar–Aug, and one of the main

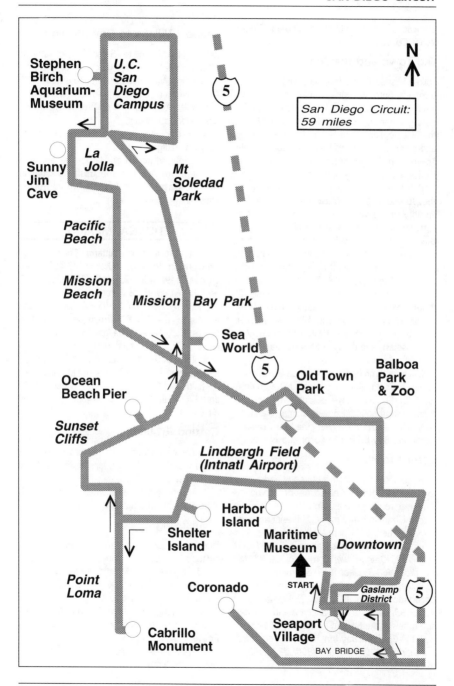

N ↑

San Diego Circuit: 59 miles

Stephen Birch Aquarium-Museum
U.C. San Diego Campus
Sunny Jim Cave
La Jolla
Mt Soledad Park
Pacific Beach
Mission Beach
Mission Bay Park
Sea World
Ocean Beach Pier
Old Town Park
Balboa Park & Zoo
Sunset Cliffs
Lindbergh Field (Intnatl Airport)
Harbor Island
Shelter Island
Maritime Museum
Downtown
Point Loma
Coronado
START
Gaslamp District
Cabrillo Monument
Seaport Village
BAY BRIDGE

attractions is the 74-ft (22.8 m) tall **Giant Dipper Roller Coaster**.

Old Town and the Zoo

Follow Mission Blvd 2 miles (3.2 km) south and turn left onto W. Mission Bay Blvd. At the interchange, follow signs for Sports Arena Blvd, driving under the I-8 overpass and turning left at the first stoplight. Turn left on Rosecrans St, go under the I-5 overpass to Taylor St, and enter **Old Town San Diego State Historic Park** and **Heritage Park** on the right.

Return to Taylor St and go up Presidio Dr. to the **Junipero Serra Museum**. Continue on Presidio Dr. Turn left on Arista St and right at Fort Stockton through **Mission Hills**, an early San Diego suburb. For well-heeled **Hillcrest**, turn right on Goldfinch, then left onto Washington St.

Head towards Downtown by turning right onto First Ave for 1½ miles (2.4 km), then left on Laurel St, which, five blocks east, becomes **El Prado** when it enters **Balboa Park**. Park **buildings** are Spanish and Mexican Colonial style, built for 1915 and 1935 expositions. Visit the **museums** and the world-famous **San Diego Zoo**.

Drive south on Park Blvd. It becomes 12th Ave at the park's boundary. Go left on J St, turn right on 17th St, and move quickly onto the I-5 freeway southbound. Exit almost immediately to Hwy 75 which goes over the **San Diego–Coronado Bay Bridge** to **Coronado Island**.

Coronado Island

The resort community's most famous landmark is the Victorian **Hotel Del Coronado**, complete with red roofs, cupolas, and resident ghosts. Queen Elizabeth II and many US Presidents have stayed at the 'Del', where Marilyn Monroe, Jack Lemmon and Tony Curtis starred in *Some Like It Hot; 1500 Orange Ave, Coronado, CA 92118; tel: (800) 468-3533 or (619) 522-8000;* pricey.

Bike, sunbathe, walk, play golf, tennis, or sail. **Coronado Touring**, *1110 Isabelle Ave; tel: (619) 435-5993*, begins a tour of the island's history and hotels at the Edwardian Spreckels Mansion, now the **Glorietta Bay Inn**, *1630 Glorietta Blvd, Coronado, CA 92118; tel: (800) 283-9383 or (619) 435-3101;* moderate to pricey.

Seaport Village to Downtown

Return via the bridge to I-5 northbound. Take the 19th St turnoff, go three blocks north to Martin Luther King Way, then turn left and drive to 12th Ave. Drive six blocks north, turn left on B St, then left on 4th Ave, and right on Broadway towards the waterfront.

At Pacific Hwy, go left ½ mile (1 km) to **Seaport Village**.

Continue southeast on Harbor Dr., and turn left onto 5th Ave into the **Gaslamp Quarter Historic District**. Turn left onto F St. **Horton Plaza** is one block ahead.

TIJUANA, MEXICO

Tourist Information: Tijuana Tourism and Convention Bureau, *PO Box 43-4523, San Diego CA 92143-4523; tel: (800) 252-5363, and Ave Paseo de los Heroes 108, Tijuana, B.C. Mexico; tel: (52) 66 84-05-37.* For in-person assistance, the **State Tourism Dept.** has two offices: *Calle 1* at *Avenida Revolucion*, which also provides Tourist Protection legal help, is open Mon–Fri. 0900–0700; *tel: (52) 66 88-05-55*; headquarters is several miles south at *Plaza Patria* on *Blvd Diaz Ordaz*, open Mon–Fri 0800–1500 and 1700–1900, Sat, 0900–1400; *tel: (52) 66 81-94-94*.

Getting Around

Try friendly bargaining with taxi drivers to lower the average round-town fare from $6. Local buses cost about $0.25.

US currency *may* be accepted; some Spanish is helpful, though English is understood.

Sightseeing

Due to car insurance technicalities and returning customs procedures, non-US citizens should avoid driving into Mexico. Book a guided Tijuana tour (request SDCVB listings), or take the San Diego Trolley or drive to the San Ysidro border crossing. Downtown Tijuana is less than 1 mile (l.6 km) across the border via the **Pedestrian Route**.

Non-US citizens may need a visa for entry into Mexico and a multiple-entry visa to return to the

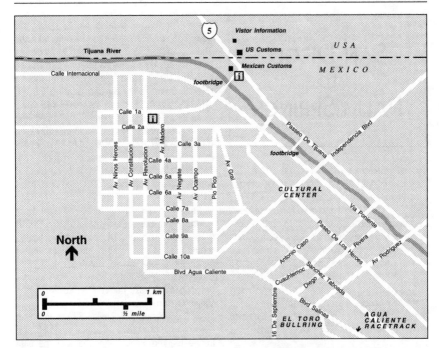

USA. Check with embassies or consulates for requirements.

Tijuana is the colourful gateway to Baja California, and a glimpse of what California *might* have been had history taken a different course. Now Mexico's fourth largest city, Tijuana abuts the US border 10 miles (16 km) south of San Diego.

Tijuana has shed its sleazy image with the relative economic prosperity that has come in the wake of factories which cheaply assemble raw materials from the US and export finished products.

Shop, dine and enjoy nightlife along seven blocks of downtown Tijuana's **Avenida Revolución**. You can bargain in small shops; prices are fixed in department and larger stores.

Jai Alai, played in Fronton Palacio, Calle 7 and Avenida Revolucion, is a throwback to Spain's Basque culture 200 years ago. Lightning scoops of long wrist-strapped baskets propel balls through a game reputed to be the world's fastest; *tel: (619) 231-1910 or in Tijuana, tel: (52) 66 85-16-12.*

Two **bullfighting** venues alternate in offering Sunday entertainment May–Sept, at 1600. In San Diego, Mexicoach Five Star Tours; *tel: (619) 232-5049,* sells ($14–$40) tickets to **El Toreo** and **Plaza Monumental** bullrings.

Watch **greyhound racing** at **Agua Caliente Racetrack**, daily except Tues or spring **horse racing**, Mar–early Jun; *tel: (619) 231-1910, or in Tijuana (52) 66 81-78-11.*

Mexitlan, a block from the Tijuana River's Pedestrian Bridge, has more than 150 scale models of Mexican architectural sites, temples, and monuments; *tel: (619) 531-1112, or (52) 66 38-41-01 in Tijuana.*

The **Tijuana Cultural Center**, open daily, is a Mexican history, archaeology and art museum with an OMNIMAX theatre showing a film on Mexican culture; *tel: (52) 66 84-11-11.*

Nuestra Señora de Guadalupe Cathedral, *Calle 2 and Avenida Niños Héroes*, is one of the finest viewpoints over the old downtown district. The twin towers of the classic church overlook everything except modern skyscrapers.

SAN DIEGO to PALM SPRINGS

Coastal California is never far from the mountain ranges which define climate, precipitation, animal life and flora. Nowhere in the state is it possible to go so quickly from sea level over deeply forested mountains, through rough-hewn canyons, to desert, to saline sea, to a date palm oasis. Urban surroundings are left far behind when rugged mountains appear 15 miles east of San Diego.

This route traverses the Anza-Borrego Desert State Park, and is particularly attractive during the spring wildflower season. Allow 2–3 days to do justice to the full 170 miles (272 km).

ROUTE

From Horton Plaza in downtown San Diego, take E St 7 blocks east, turn left headed north on 11th Ave for 5 blocks, then follow signs onto Hwy 163 (which starts in Balboa Park). Continue onwards for 3 miles (4.8 km), then follow signs to turn east onto I-8.

After driving 3½ miles (5.6 km) east on I-8, take the Fairmount Ave exit. Go through the underpass under I-8, north to Twain Ave/San Diego Mission Rd. Turn left onto San Diego Mission Rd. The bright, white facade of **Mission San Diego de Alcala** is on the right.

Return to I-8. Take the Spring St exit south ½ mile (l km), following the red San Diego Trolley Line to La Mesa Blvd. One block right is the weekend-only **La Mesa (Railroad) Depot Museum**, *4695 Nebo Dr., La Mesa, CA; tel: (619) 697-7762*, which is housed in an engine, freight car and caboose.

Return to I-8, which begins to climb quickly towards the mountains. By **El Cajon**, at 14 miles (22 km), rugged, rolling mountains are visible

ahead. For Indian-operated bingo, poker, pai gow, and satellite horse-race betting, take the 2nd St turnoff and drive right 2 blocks to Jamacha Rd. Take Jamacha Rd for a ½ mile (0.8 km), then turn left and follow Dehesa Rd about 6 miles (9.6 km) to the **Sycuan Gaming Center**, *5469 Dehesa Rd, El Cajon; tel: (619) 445-6002*. At 21 miles (33.6 km) on I-8, the speed limit becomes 65 mph (104 kph). At 23 miles (37 km), the elevation is 1000 ft (308 m). At 27 miles (43 km), pull off at **Alpine** to sample American-style breads, rolls, cakes, biscuits and pastries at **Alpine Village Bakery**, *2109 Alpine Blvd*, open 0700–1900 daily.

Return to I-8. Thirty miles (48 km) from Horton Plaza, the highway has risen to 2000 ft (616 m) in elevation. The surrounding golden mountains, which house the Viejas Indian Reservation, look sparse, dry and craggy. This is part of the Cleveland National Forest. For more Indian gaming, take the Willows Rd exit to the **Viejas Casino**.

At **Sweetwater**, 35½ miles (57 km) from San Diego and 2900 ft (879 m) above sea level, stop at the marked viewpoint to gaze at the blue Pacific Ocean, 40 miles (64 km) to the west. Across the road are huge sandstone boulders.

Watch for the turnoff at 38 miles (61 km), and turn north on Hwy 73 for 4 miles (6.4 km) as cows graze bucolically beneath oak trees.

Turn left onto Hwy 79, a winding road through chaparral and forested hills. At 44 miles (70.6 km) is **Cuyamaca Rancho State Park**, *12551 Hwy 79, Descanso, CA 92016; tel: (619) 765-0755*. The Kumeya'ay Indians, who lived in the yellow pine and oak tree forest of the Peninsular Mountain Range before Spanish explorations, called the region 'the place where it rains'. Colourful foliage appears in fall; in winter, there's often snow.

In summer, Cuyamaca Rancho State Park is a relief from the heat. Eight miles (13 km) beyond the park entrance is **Lake Cuyamaca**, summer venue for fishing – and lakeside dining. A vista point at 59 miles (94.4 km) shows valleys and mountain ranges running west to east, and the Salton Sea further east.

You can ride mountain bikes, birdwatch, fish the Sweetwater River or Lake Cuyamaca, and

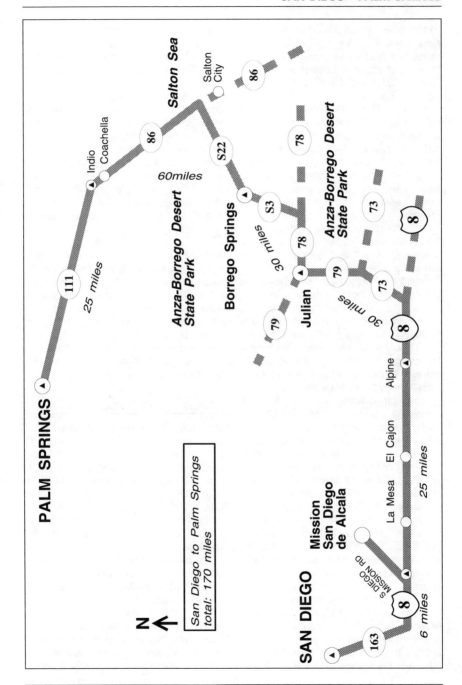

San Diego to Palm Springs
total: 170 miles

Salton Sea

Salton City

86

86

Indio
Coachella

S22

60miles

Anza-Borrego Desert State Park

78

78

Borrego Springs

S3

30 miles

Anza-Borrego Desert State Park

73

8

111

25 miles

78

79

79

Julian

79

73

30 miles

8

PALM SPRINGS

Alpine

8

El Cajon

25 miles

La Mesa

Mission
San Diego
de Alcala

6 miles

S DIEGO RD
MISSION RD

163

8

SAN DIEGO

N

hike on more than 100 miles (160 km) of trails. Kumeya'ay artifacts are displayed in the Dyar House park headquarters museum. Stonewall Mine site photographs interpret an important Southern California gold mine. For campsites *tel: (800) 444-7275.*

Julian is at 61 miles (98 km), an 'alpine' town between the coast and the eastern deserts. Leaving Julian's forests, take Hwy 78 north and east at 15–25 mph (24–40 kph) down winding Banner Grade and the folds of a canyon sandwiched in layers by ancient earthquakes. Yucca trees, with creamy yellow blossoms topping awkward stalks, dot the slopes of chaparral-covered mountains.

At 75 miles (120 km), cross county road S2 at Scissors Crossing. To the right is the Great Southern Overland Stage Route of 1849, also called Earthquake Valley.

Enter Anza-Borrego Desert State Park 1 mile (1.6 km) beyond. Thorny, spindly ocotillo, cholla cacti and yucca grow along the roadside.

After another 4½ miles (7 km), turn left onto County road S3, Yaqui Pass Rd, and continue 7 miles (11 km) north, then turn left onto Borrego Springs Road and continue 5 miles (8 km) into **Borrego Springs**, an enclave surrounded by **Anza-Borrego Desert State Park** (ABDSP).

Leave Borrego Springs and drive part of the Erosion Trail. Starting at Christmas Circle in Borrego Springs, take State Road S22 east for 27 miles (43 km) towards the Salton Sea.

To the left, the land forms red alluvial fans. At 4½ miles (7 km), S22 turns left onto Pegleg Road, and faces Coyote Mountain and the white marble-girded Santa Rosa Mountains.

Two miles (3.2 k.m) further, the road turns east again. At 8.7 miles (14 km) re-enter ABDSP. Font's Point turnoff is at 10.2 miles (16.3 km); a hint of badlands is visible on the right. Watch for heavy winds hurling sand across the road. Light-coloured hills on the left were formed by California's most active fault, the San Jacinto.

The blue **Salton Sea** appears over a rise at 16.6 miles (26.6 km). The wild, eroded, surreal landscape rushes by the straight, well-paved road. Be alert for road dips, cyclists on the road and RVs. The Torres Martinez Indian Reservation is between the highway and the sea.

Enter an area of flatlands at 23½ miles (37.6 km), and turn left going north on Hwy 86, at 27 miles (43 km). Proceed along at Hwy 86 for 32 miles (51 km), to the junction of Hwy 111 at **Indio.**

At 38 miles (61 km) appear vineyards, grapefruit trees and date palm orchards. The Santa Rosa Mountains on the left act as a backdrop. Hwy 86 becomes one lane each way, and can clog with lorries.

At 44 miles (70 km), Hwy 86 turns left until it ends in Indio, just past Coachella, at Hwy 111. Turn left onto Hwy 111, at 58½ miles (93.6 km), and continue 21 miles (34 km) north-west through the Coachella Valley to **Palm Springs.**

Weather and Survival

While San Diego is temperate year-round, it snows in mountain areas in winter. Most of the year, deserts are very hot from dawn until sunset but chill at night. Occasional winter snowfall dusts deserts white; spring wildflowers, especially after an unusually rainy winter, are spectacular, and accessible.

Carry bottled water, warm clothing, sun coverups, and hats. If travelling in winter, carry tyre chains. Petrol is expensive along this route.

MISSION SAN DIEGO DE ALCALA

Mission Basilica San Diego de Alcala, *10818 San Diego Mission Rd, San Diego, CA 92108-2498; tel: (619) 281-8449.*

The mission parish, actually a minor basilica since 1976, was moved to this site in 1774, five years after its founding as the first 'Upper' California mission by Fr Junipero Serra. Burned by restive Native Americans in 1775, and rebuilt by 1780, it was later repaired after an 1803 earthquake.

The bell tower holds two large bells cast in 1802 and 1894. A self-guided tour includes Serra's rectory, lushly-planted gardens with modern religious statues, and a one-room museum with a few religious and Indian artifacts. An archaeological site contains monastery ruins. The blindingly white façade of Mission San Diego is softened by lush plantings of bougainvillea and bird-of-paradise flowers.

JULIAN

Tourist Information: Julian Chamber of Commerce, *PO Box 413, Julian, CA 92036: tel: (619) 765-1857.*

Accommodation

Julian Bed & Breakfast Guild, *PO Box 1711, Julian, CA 92036; tel: (619) 765-1555.* **The Julian Hotel**, *PO Box 1856, Julian, CA 92035; tel: (800) 734-5854*, on Main Street, is a Victorian survivor from 1897, still a bed and breakfast establishment. Budget to moderate, with rates better in mid-week.

Sightseeing

Julian, at 4235 ft (1303 m), is between the coast and the eastern deserts, cooler than either in summertime. Deer and mountain lions reside in nearby hills.

In 1869 a large gold strike brought settlers. A 90-min guided tour of the 1870 **Eagle & High Peak Mines**, *Eagle Mining Company, PO Box 624, Julian, CA 92036; tel: (619) 765-0036*, open daily 0900–1600, includes 1000 ft (308 m) of tunnel, engines, tools and a rock and mineral display.

San Diegans make weekend pilgrimages to backcountry Julian to sample homemade **apple pies** and fresh apple juice along the wooden sidewalks of the 3-block long Main Street. A few wooden storefronts survived the gold bust. Have an American-style ice cream soda or banana split at the old-fashioned wooden soda fountain at the **Julian Drug Store**. Annual festivals include a **Wildflower Festival** in early May; a Fourth of July **Quilt Show**, the **Fiddle, Banjo, Guitar and Mandolin Contest** in September, and **Apple Days** in October.

ANZA-BORREGO DESERT STATE PARK

Tourist Information

Anza-Borrego Desert State Park, *PO Box 299, Borrego Springs, CA 92004; tel: (619) 767-5311.* The Visitor Center, about 1 mile (1.6 km) from Christmas Circle in Borrego Springs (open daily 0900–1700, Oct–May, and weekends and holidays, 1000–1500, from Jun to Sept), is built into a rocky hillside. A slide show offers a four-season introduction to ABDSP. Just outside the centre is a labelled cactus garden and a desert pupfish pond.

Borrego Springs Chamber of Commerce, *622 Palm Canyon Dr., Borrego Springs, CA 92004; tel: (619) 767-5555.*

Accommodation and Food

Campsites for tents and RVs are scattered throughout ABDSP. To reserve campsites within a mile of the Visitor Center, *tel: (800) 444-7275.* Other campsites are first come, first served.

The Borrego Springs Chamber of Commerce provides a town accommodation list, but does not make reservations. A mile from the Visitor's Center in Borrego Springs is **Palm Canyon Resort & RV Park**, *221 Palm Canyon Dr., Borrego Springs, CA 92004; tel: (800) 242-0044 or (619) 767-5341*, moderate, with a Western Town decor, large rooms, a pool, and proximity to the park. Its **Smoke Tree Restaurant** serves steak. Moderate.

La Casa del Zorro, *3845 Yaqui Pass Rd, Borrego Springs CA 92004; tel: (800) 325-8274*, is where General George Patton trained tank troops for Sahara warfare at the then-simple adobe. Palm and pepper trees cast shade during hot weather. The Butterfield Dining Room's wall murals show local history. Moderate to pricey.

For a cheap breakfast, there's **The Coffee Book Store**, *590 Palm Canyon Dr., Ste 202; tel: (619) 767-5080*, open daily 0600–1600. Browse softback novels or natural history works while sampling giant bran, lemon-poppy or orange-chocolate chip muffins.

Sightseeing

California's largest state park is well-known for a magnificent annual wildflower bloom for a few weeks during Feb–Apr. Accommodation, camp-sites and parking areas fill up. For the ABDSP Spring Wildflower Hotline *tel: (619) 767-4684.* There are few paved roads in the park; check at the Visitor Center for road conditions and trail closures. Summer temperatures can climb to 50°C!

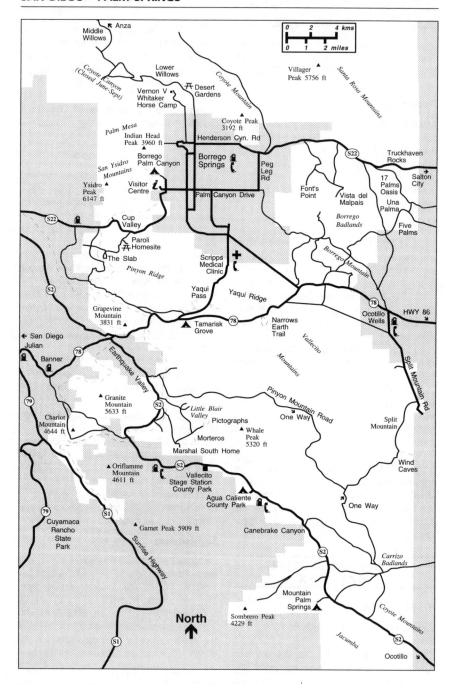

Photographers hover as canyon light constantly shifts on this varied-hued desert, from red to russet, orange, deep green, pale green, dun, grey, or purple. Eroded mountains, extending in every direction, have an etched appearance.

Named after the 'borrego', or Peninsular bighorn sheep seen leaping from rock to rock, ABDSP was home to ancient Indians, and later, to miners, oilmen, cattlemen and homesteaders. Cacti bristle with spines, and, for a few weeks each year, bloom in bright pink, red or yellow bursts. Lizards, dragonflies, coyotes, and occasional birds rustle in the low bushes. In many canyons, palm trees make surprising oases near rushing, half-hidden streams. From the **Font's Point** overlook, colourful 'badlands', treacherous, desiccated, eroded mountain canyons, stretch to the horizon.

Accessible **Borrego Palm Canyon Trail**, is 1 mile (1.6 km) from the Visitor Center. This brochure-guided trail, though only 1½ miles (2.4 km) long, is rocky, and takes more than an hour. Bighorn sheep, quail, rabbits, and roadrunners may appear. Along the trail, encounter huge boulders, dry streambeds, Indian grinding rocks, natural black stains on rocks, or 'desert varnish'.

California Fan Palms, the largest palms in North America and California's only native palm, wait in a pool towards the trail's end.

The Visitor Center has additional information on hiking the trails. The Erosion Road Auto Tour accesses Font's Point and the Borrego Badlands Overlook, site of ancient mastodons roaming the savannah.

SALTON SEA

Tourist Information: Salton Sea State Recreation Headquarters, *PO Box 3166, North Shore, CA 92254; tel: (619) 393-3052.*

The Salton Sea, 35 miles (56 km) long and 15 miles (24 km) wide, is one of the world's largest inland saltwater areas.

A pervasive sulphur stench comes from the shallow sea. The sea filled in 1905 when irrigation water from Colorado River canals overflowed. Agricultural runoff and evaporation continues to leave salt residue.

SAN DIEGO to LOS ANGELES

The South Coast between San Diego and Los Angeles is the sunny playground of 'beach blanket films'; a haven for the rich and tanned; a carpet of flower fields; and, inland, within easy reach, a compact wine region. Dining and shopping are art forms with appropriately elevated prices. This route's atmosphere and ambience are as much of a draw as its attractions. Choose from a 2½-hour direct non-stop route, or plan 2–3 days for either of two scenic routes.

ROUTE

→ Direct Route

The 120-mile (192 km) direct route takes I-5 between downtown San Diego and Los Angeles and Hwy 101 from I-5 to Union Station.

From the **Santa Fe Depot** at Broadway and Kettner Blvd in San Diego, take Broadway to 1st Ave, turn left, cross under I-5, go left at Hawthorn, then follow signs onto I-5, northbound. After crossing I-8, Mission Bay waterways are to the left.

Continue northwest on I-5 past Mission Viejo, Laguna Hills, Irvine, site of a University of California campus, Santa Ana and Anaheim (see Greater Los Angeles Routes, p. 63), to Union Station.

Scenic Route

The 115-mile (184 km) scenic route takes I-5 from San Diego to Capistrano Beach, then continues north on Hwy 1 to I-710, then follows I-5, reaching Union Station via Hwy 101.

Most of this section of coast has a true seafront road one block from the Pacific Ocean.

Not always scenic, it has many stop signs and lights. To experience one town or area 'at the seaside', leave the highway and drive west. Traffic is slow and congested at weekends and holidays. Speed limits are enforced.

To visit **La Jolla**, take the Grand Ave turnoff to Pacific Beach, or Ardath Rd 4 miles (6.4 km) north of the I-8 and I-5 junction. (See also the San Diego 59-mile Drive, p. 106.)

Take the Via de la Valle exit west from I-5 for **Del Mar**.

To visit **Encinitas**, take the Encinitas exit west from I-5.

Take the Carlsbad Village Dr. exit and go west to State St, downtown to visit **Carlsbad**.

Oceanside's main attraction is its harbour and pier. For the harbour, take the exit after Nevada St, make the loop from I-8 to Hill and 6th Sts, then continue west to Pacific St; the harbour is to the north.

At **Capistrano Beach**, 62 miles (99 km), Hwy 1 swings left of I-5 to follow the coastline. I-5 turns north-east to **San Juan Capistrano**. Take the Ortega Hwy exit from I-5 for the mission.

At Capistrano Beach, leave I-5, and continue along the coast on the Pacific Coast Highway, Hwy 1 beginning at **Dana Point**.

The 30 miles (48 km) of beach cities between Capistrano Beach and Long Beach are among the most affluent in the world. Million-dollar homes are on display along any street near the shore. Beaches are jammed in summer; parking meters are *de rigeur*. Traffic crawls on weekends, holidays, and when schools are out, Jun–early Sept. If California has a riviera, this is it.

Very Scenic Route

For a very scenic 170 miles (272 km) tour which includes the Temecula Wine Region, take I-5 from San Diego north to Oceanside. Go east on Hwy 76, then turn left on I-15 and drive to Temecula. Continue north on I-15, then turn left on Hwy 74, and drive through the Cleveland National Forest to San Juan Capistrano. Take I-5 to Capistrano Beach, continue north on Hwy 1 to I-710, then follow I-5 to downtown Los Angeles via Hwy 101.

For an excursion to California's most compact wine area, turn right on Hwy 76 at Oceanside.

Eighteen miles (29 km) north-east, turn left to go north on I-15 to Temecula. Take the Front St exit from I-15 for Old Town Temecula.

Continue north on I-15 for 13 miles (21 km) to **Lake Elsinore State Park**; *tel: (714) 674-3177*, for biking, hang-gliding, paragliding, boating, fishing, and swimming.

Turn left onto Hwy 74, which climbs quickly to show great lake vistas. Drive the 22 miles (35 km) of constant bends at 25–40 mph (40–64 kph). The **Lookout Roadhouse** serves barbecue ribs for lunch and dinner.

The road rises to 2666 ft (820 m) at the summit. Thirty miles (48 km) from Temecula, enter the **Cleveland National Forest**, which has several campsites. Hwy 74 finally descends to San Juan Capistrano.

Weather

The South Coast has a mild, Mediterranean climate all year. If visiting the Temecula Wine Region, be prepared with warmer clothing for morning fog and cooler mountain evenings. Winery tasting rooms are chilly.

Tourist Information

The **San Diego Convention & Visitors Bureau**, *Dept. 700, 401 B St, Ste 1400, San Diego CA 92101-4237; tel: (619) 236-1212*, has general county information. **San Diego North County Convention & Visitors Bureau**, *720 N. Broadway, Escondido CA 92025; tel: (800) 848-3336 or (619) 745-4741*. Other towns en route provide specific information.

LA JOLLA

Tourist Information: La Jolla Town Council, *1055 Wall St, Ste 110, La Jolla, CA 92038; tel: (619) 454-1444*.

Thomas Cook foreign exchange branch: *University Towne Center, 4525 La Jolla Village Dr., Ste D1B; tel: (619) 457 0841*.

La Jolla's shoreline, caves, shopping, and dining are close by. Visit the **Mingei International Museum of World Folk Art**, *4405 La Jolla Village Dr., San Diego, CA 92122; tel: (619) 453-5300*.

To the right of I-5 is the brilliantly white 203-ft (62.5 m) neo-Gothic **Mormon Temple** with twin spires. Public entry is forbidden.

Interstate 5 bisects the **University of California, San Diego** campus; *tel: (619) 534-2230 or (619) 534-2208*. To visit the campus, famed for biomedical research, outdoor **Stuart Collection of Sculpture**, and an inverted pyramid library building, take the La Jolla Village exit left. The **Stephen Birch Aquarium-Museum**, the **Scripps Institute of Oceanography** and the **Salk Institute** are nearby.

🌊 Side Track from La Jolla

To visit **Torrey Pines State Reserve**; *tel: (619) 755-2063*, with the rarest pine tree in North America (Torrey Pine), continue north on I-5 for 3½ miles (5.6 km), take Carmel Valley Rd west to North Torrey Pines Rd, and turn left. Eight walking trails on pine-covered bluffs lead through chaparral, sage, badlands, and marshlands. The adobe-style Torrey Pines Lodge has a museum and visitor centre. Brilliant sunsets in Oct–Nov, January whale-watching, and springtime flowers tempt nature lovers. To join hang gliders at **Torrey Pines State Beach**, *tel: (619) 452-3202*. There is no camping or lodging at the reserve and beach.

DEL MAR

Tourism Information: Del Mar Chamber of Commerce, *1401 Camino del Mar, Ste 101, Del Mar, CA 92014; tel: (619) 755-4844*.

The seaside town offers Jul–Sept thoroughbred horse racing at the **Del Mar Racetrack**, *2260 Jimmy Durante Blvd; tel (619) 256-1355 or (619) 755-1411*, founded by Bing Crosby in 1937. **Del Mar Plaza**, *1555 Camino Del Mar; tel: (619) 792-1555*, has a mascot cat which greets centre shoppers. **Skysurfer Balloon Co.**, *tel: (619) 481-6800*, and **California Dreamin**, *tel: (619) 438-3344* launch hot air balloons from Del Mar. For a seaside stay just north of Del Mar, query the **Solana Beach Chamber of Commerce**, *210 W. Plaza, Solana Beach, CA 92075; tel: (619) 755-4755*.

Route–La Jolla–Torrey Pines–Del Mar

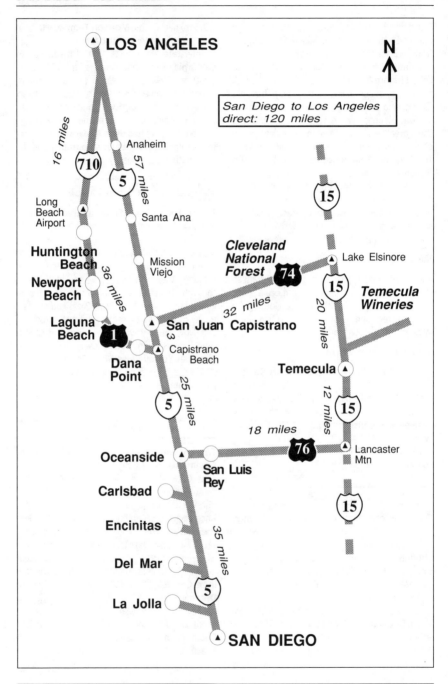

LOS ANGELES

N ↑

San Diego to Los Angeles
direct: 120 miles

Anaheim

16 miles

710

5

57 miles

Long
Beach
Airport

Santa Ana

Huntington
Beach

Mission
Viejo

36 miles

Newport
Beach

Laguna
Beach

1

Dana
Point

Capistrano
Beach

3

San Juan Capistrano

Cleveland
National
Forest

74

Lake Elsinore

15

15

Temecula
Wineries

32 miles

20 miles

Temecula

12 miles

15

5

25 miles

18 miles

76

Lancaster
Mtn

Oceanside

San Luis
Rey

15

Carlsbad

Encinitas

35 miles

Del Mar

15

5

La Jolla

SAN DIEGO

ENCINITAS

Tourist Information: Encinitas Chamber of Commerce, *345-H N. First St, Encinitas, CA 92024; tel: (619) 753-6041.*

Encinitas, 5 miles (8 km) north, and 25 miles (40 km) from San Diego, is known as the 'flower capital of the world' and as a surfing mecca.

Interstate 5 runs through **San Elijo Lagoon County Park and Ecological Reserve**; *tel: (619) 565-3600.* Go east or west on Manchester Ave to access the reserve's 7 miles (11 km) of hiking trails and birdwatching in the low-lying wetlands. To camp at **San Elijo State Beach**; *tel: (619) 753-5091* (information) or *(800) 444-7275* (reservations). **Surfers** flock to **Cardiff State Beach**, on the coast at Encinitas. **Sea Cliff Park** has ocean views; you can play volleyball at **Moonlight Beach**.

The 'flower capital' ships **poinsettias** and **gladioli** around the USA. May brings spring flower tours.

Take Encinitas Blvd east, then turn right to **Quail Botanical Gardens**, *230 Quail Gardens Dr.; tel: (619) 436-3036,* open daily 0800–1700, except the first Mon. of the month. The large gardens are known for hibiscus, bamboo and native California plants. Visit quiet ocean view gardens at the **Self-Realization Fellowship**, *K St and First Ave,* open Tues–Sat 0900–1700, Sun 1100–1700. Monks and students meditate surrounded by peaceful greenery.

During Feb–Nov, you can make an appointment to see monarch butterflies at the **Butterfly Vivarium**, *450 Ocean View Ave; tel: (619) 944-7113.*

CARLSBAD

Tourist Information: Carlsbad Convention & Visitors Bureau, *PO Box 1246, Carlsbad, CA 92018-1246; tel: (619) 434-6093.* For hotel information and bookings *tel: (800) 227-5722.* The **Visitors Information Center** is in the Old Santa Fe Train Depot, *Carlsbad Village Dr.,* open Mon–Fri 0900–1700, Sat 1000–1600, and Sun 1000–1400.

McClellan-Palomar Airport takes small feeder flights from larger airports in the region.

Accommodation

The Carlsbad CVB makes bookings in all price ranges; *tel: (800) 227-5722.* Chains represented in Carlsbad include *BW, M6,* and *RM.* Camp at **Carlsbad State Beach**; tel: (619) 729-8947. **La Costa Resort and Spa**, *Corona Del Mar Rd, Carlsbad, CA 92009; tel: (800) 854-5000,* has spa treatments, golf, and tennis for the affluent; pricey. The **Pelican Cove Inn**, *320 Walnut Ave; tel: (619) 434-5995,* is a modern bed and breakfast near downtown; moderate–pricey.

Sightseeing

Flowers, lagoons, Old European-style architecture, antique shops and a posh spa characterise **Carlsbad**, 'the village by the sea.'

Carlsbad is named after the famous Bohemian spa of Karlsbad. John Frazier, a farmer, dug a well along the railroad line in 1883. The waters were said to be therapeutic. A self-guided Historical Society brochure explaining the turreted, half-timbered **Alt Karlsbad Hanse House**, *2802 Carlsbad Blvd; tel: (619) 729-6912,* and other older buildings is available from the CVB. The Queen Anne-style Victorian mansion known as the **Schutte House** is said to harbour two ghosts, a draw for **Neiman's** restaurant inside, *2978 Carlsbad Blvd; tel: (619) 729-4131.*

Flowers bloom in April. The **bird-of-paradise** was commercially developed in Carlsbad. Ranunculus, gladioli, and watsonia are seasonally profuse. **Lego Family Park**, resembling Legoland in Billund, Denmark, will open in 1999.

Jet ski, windsurf, or water ski at **Agua Hedionda Lagoon**; *tel: (619) 434-2837.* Watch weekly car races at **Carlsbad Raceway**, near Palomar Airport Rd; *tel: (619) 727-1171,* where drag racers join motocross and oval track enthusiasts.

OCEANSIDE

Tourist Information: Oceanside Visitors and Conference Center, *928 N. Hill St, Oceanside, CA 92054; tel: (800) 350-7873 or (619) 721-1101.*

Oceanside Pier is home to the **California**

Surfing Museum, *308 N. Pacific St; tel: (619) 721-6876*. A local tram costs $0.25.

Extending north 6 miles (10km) is **Camp Pendleton**, a Marine Corps amphibious training base; *tel: (619) 725-5566*, with self-guided tours of the Landing Vehicle Track Museum. **San Onofre Surf Beach** adjoins the **San Onofre Nuclear Generating Station**, just south of **San Clemente**. **San Onofre State Beach**; *tel: (714) 492-4872* and **San Clemente State Beach**; *tel: (714) 492-3156* have camping. Richard Nixon's Western White House was in San Clemente. **San Clemente Chamber of Commerce**, *1100 N. El Camino Real, San Clemente, CA 92672; tel: (714) 492-1131*.

SAN JUAN CAPISTRANO

Tourist Information: San Juan Capistrano Chamber of Commerce, *31682 El Camino Real, San Juan Capistrano, CA, 92675; tel: (714) 493-4700*. For information on the month-long March swallows' return celebrations; *tel:*

(714) 248-2049. Advance booking is necessary.

Eating and Drinking

The Rio Grande Bar & Grill across from the mission in the old train depot; *tel: (714) 496-8181*, serves a delicious budget Sunday brunch. In the same complex are old railway carriages, 2–3 across, housing the AMTRAK station and the Capistrano Depot Bar. Try cheap burgers and patty melts at **Cafe Capistrano**, *corner of Camino Capistrano and Ortega Hwy*, across from the mission.

Sightseeing

San Juan Capistrano is fabled for a mission to which swallows return each Mar 19. The compact downtown includes the mission, antique dealers, and the adobes and train depot of Los Rios (National) Historic District.

Mission San Juan Capistrano, *31882 Camino Capistrano, San Juan Capistrano, CA 92675; tel: (714) 248-2048*, open daily 0800–1700, is named after a Hungarian saint who

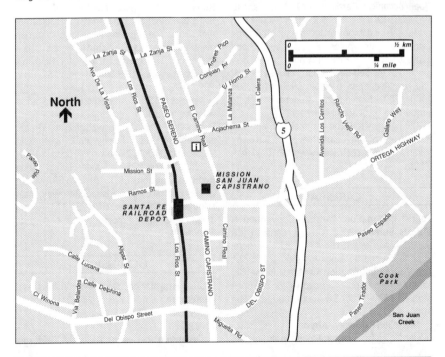

turned back Turkish invaders in 1387. When local people wanted to rebuild the mission ruins in the early part of the century, the swallows' annual return on St Joseph's Day, Mar 19, was the focal point of fund-raising.

The large mission site has a carnival atmosphere. Coin-operated machines dispense feed for pigeons ('doves' on signs); every tree and plant is labelled, and children scamper everywhere. Ruins of candle- and soap-making are designated, 'This is part of Orange County's First Industrial Complex.' Between the clutter are three small museums with artifacts from the Indian, Spanish and Mexican eras and restored mission work rooms. **Fr Serra's Chapel** has bright Indian motif wall borders and a 300-year-old gold-covered cherrywood altar.

The **Old Barn Antiques Mall**, *31792 Camino Capistrano; tel: (714) 493-9144*, open daily 1000–1700, is a co-operative of antique dealers. See fine American antique jewellery, silver, glass, china, saddles, dolls, books and Orange County fruit box labels. The 31-structure **Los Rios Historic District** includes adobe houses, an animal petting farm, *tel: (714) 831-6550*, and the 1894 **Santa Fe Railroad Depot**.

DANA POINT

Tourist Information: Dana Point Chamber of Commerce, *24671 La Plaza, Ste 2, Dana Point, 92629; tel: (714) 496-1555*. Reach Hwy 1 at **Doheny State Beach**; *tel: (714) 496-6171*, where good weather draws surfers. Go left on Harbor Dr. to **Dana Point Harbor**, for windsurfing, parasailing, sailing or deep sea fishing.

At the harbour's west end cove is the **Orange County Marine Institute**; *tel: (714) 496-2274*, offering free tours of a 121-ft replica of the brigantine *The Pilgrim*. Richard Henry Dana, author of *Two Years Before the Mast*, sailed to this area aboard the original ship. Dana Point is also home to California's official tall ship, the 1849 replica of the revenue cutter *C.W. Lawrence; tel: (800) 432-2201*.

Pricey and truly deluxe is the **Ritz-Carlton Laguna Niguel**, *3353 Ritz-Carlton Dr., Dana Point, CA 92629; tel: (800) 241-3333 or (714) 240-2000*, actually located at Monarch Beach

just north of Dana Point Harbor. Flower-landscaped gardens on bluffs above a 2-mile (3.2 km) long beach set the tone for flawless service. Sunday brunch in the Lounge at a window table takes advantage of the great view. Pricey.

LAGUNA BEACH

Tourist Information: Laguna Beach Visitor Information Center, *252 Broadway, Laguna Beach, CA 92652; tel: (800) 877-1115*, provides information and makes free bookings for hotels and restaurants.

Getting Around

The **Laguna Beach Municipal Bus System**; *tel: (714) 497-0746*, runs from Dana Point up PCH and north of town to the hills and an ocean vista from **Top of the World Viewpoint**.

Accommodation and Food

The Visitor Information Center runs a free accommodation and restaurant referral service. Lodging rates are moderate–pricey. Most desirable are locations near the beach. The *BW* chain is represented. **Ruby's Autodiner**, *30622 S. Coast Hwy; tel: (714) 497-7829*, along PCH is one of a chain of red and white '40s-style diners with all-American burgers, fries, and milkshakes, served on an outdoor ocean view terrace.

Shopping

More than 90 shops, art galleries, and speciality boutiques mass along Gallery Row in North Laguna to Forest Ave, downtown. Modern or rustic wood, each shop building is different.

Sightseeing

Laguna Beach hugs the coast for the next 9 miles (14.4 km). Shopping and tourism are this getaway's *raison d'etre*. Upmarket clothing boutiques, art galleries, and restaurants are its lifeblood. The dress code is casual chic. Local people live in gated, fenced, security-controlled 'cottages.'

Laguna Beach, started as a Plein Air School artists colony in 1917, has continued its association with art. The **Festival of Arts and**

Pageant of the Masters, in which human models enact tableaux of famous paintings, takes place each July–Aug; *tel: (714) 494-1145*. The **Laguna Art Museum**, *307 Cliff Dr.; tel: (714) 494-6531* is a glass-facade building filled with changing exhibitions of modern art.

From the museum, take Cliff Dr. along Heisler Park, for outstanding views or lawn bowling. At Fairview St, walk down a beautiful path to the water and the **Laguna Beach Marine Life Refuge**. Play basketball, surf, bodysurf, body board, or explore tidepools at **Main Beach**; scuba or snorkel at **Diver's Cove**; mountain bike or hike in **Aliso/Wood Canyon Regional Park**; rollerblade, fish, play golf, tennis, or volleyball, all near PCH. Injured sea lions are nursed back to health at **Friends of the Sea Lions Marine Mammal Center**, *20612 Laguna Cyn. Rd; tel: (714) 497-0716*.

Out of Town

The **Sherman Library and Gardens, 2647 E.** *Pacific Coast Hwy, Corona del Mar, CA 92625; tel: (714) 673-2261*, 1030–1600 daily, a self-described 'horticultural paradise', is a botanical garden with cacti, rose and shade plant areas supplemented by a tropical plant conservatory, all laid out among gazebos and walking paths. For budget lunches on The Terrace *tel: (714) 673-2261*.

NEWPORT BEACH

Tourist Office: Newport Beach Conference and Visitors Bureau, *366 San Miguel Dr., Ste 200, Newport Beach, CA 92660; tel: (714) 644-1190 or (800) 942-6278*.

Newport Beach claims more than 10,000 yachts in its marinas. A 6-mile (9.6 km) finger of land forms an area of protected lagoons. No beachfront manse costs less than $1 million. Many streets are one-way with turns prohibited. **Newport Pier** and **Balboa Pier** are the two magnets for beach bunnies. **Balboa Pavilion,** *400 Main St, Balboa, CA 92661; tel: (714) 673-5245*, is the Newport terminal for Catalina Island cruises, sailing and whale-watching boats. **Gondola Company of Newport**, *3400 Via Oporto, Ste 103B, Newport Beach, CA 92663;*

tel: (714) 675-1212, offers 1-hr cruises of the bay and canals. Main attractions at the free **Newport Harbor Nautical Museum**, *1714 W. Balboa Blvd; tel: (714) 673-3377*, are a collection of ships in bottles and photographs of old yachts. Browse among 200 shops in the open-air **Fashion Island** mall, *1045 Newport Center Dr., Newport Beach, CA 92660; tel: (714) 721-2000*.

HUNTINGTON BEACH

Tourist Office: Huntington Beach Conference and Visitors Bureau, *2100 Main St, 92648; tel: (800) 729-6232 or (714) 969-3492*, the city beach park extends for miles of biking and jogging. Expensive beach parking meters are enforced daily, 0500–2000. The **International Surfing Museum**, *411 Olive St; tel: (714) 960-3483*, has board paraphernalia.

To the east side of the Pacific Coast Highway is **Bolsa Chica Ecological Reserve**, a restored saltmarsh providing shelter to many bird species. A flat walking path winds around the reserve, open daily 0600-2000. The city is also known as 'Little Saigon' for its Vietnamese population.

Just south of Long Beach is **Seal Beach**. Down Main St is a pedestrian pier, while an old trolley car houses the small **Red Car Museum** on Electric Ave.

SAN LUIS REY

Mission San Luis Rey de Francia, *4050 Mission Ave, San Luis Rey, CA 92068; tel: (619) 757-3651*, was restored from the 1798 ruins to its present white splendour. An excellent, extensive museum testifies to the 'King of the Missions' history as the largest building in the state during the mid-19th century. The Franciscan friars directed over 2000 Luisano Indians in planting oranges, olives and grapes; cattle and sheep were herded in the hills nearby. The original deed signed by US President Abraham Lincoln in 1865, restoring the California missions to the Roman Catholic Church, is kept at the mission. Votive candles flickering in the Madonna Chapel convey a medieval atmosphere.

Beyond the mission, the speed limit drops to 40 mph (64 kph) as produce stands begin to appear on Hwy 76. Sixteen miles (25.6 km) from Oceanside is the turnoff for **Pala Mesa Resort**, *2001 Old Hwy 395, Fallbrook, CA 92028; tel: (800) 722-4700*, a golf resort set in boulder-strewn hills, pricey. Six miles (9.6 km) on the other side of the I-15–Hwy 76 junction is **Mission Antonio de Pala**, an auxiliary mission and museum; *tel: (619) 742-3317*. Huge boulders appear along I-15, 25 miles (40 km) from Oceanside; Temecula is a few miles north.

TEMECULA

Tourist Information: Temecula Valley Chamber of Commerce, *27450 Ynez Rd, Ste 104, Temecula, CA 92591; tel: (909) 676-5090*, has information on town activities. **Temecula Valley Vintners Association**, *PO Box 160, Temecula, CA 92593-1601; tel: (909) 699-3626*, has winery brochures.

Accommodation

The Temecula Creek Inn, *44501 Rainbow Canyon Rd, Temecula, CA 92592; tel: (800) 962-7335 or (909) 694-1000*, nestled in a valley among oaks, is close to both Old Town and the wineries. Large rooms with Indian artifacts displayed in wall cases overlook a lush golf course. Expensive.

    Loma Vista Bed & Breakfast, *33350 La Serena Way., Temecula, CA 92591; tel: (909) 676-7047*, sits on a bluff overlooking the wine country. All rooms are named after wine varietals. Expensive. The chains are represented by *BW, CI, M6* and *RM*.

Eating and Drinking

Temet Grill *at the Temecula Creek Inn; tel: (909) 676-5631*, has fine dining overlooking the golf course. An extensive local wine list permits sampling by the glass before setting off for the wineries. It's expensive, with cheerful ambience.

    Baily Wine County Café, *27644 Ynez Rd; tel (909) 676-9567*, is operated by a winery. A local favourite is the south-western-style grilled cheese sandwich plate (budget–moderate). **Claim Jumper**, *29540 Rancho California Rd; tel: (909) 694-6887*, has huge sandwiches, especially the 'motherlode' (budget). Pizza,

Mexican food, and various Asian cuisines are represented in the area. Many wineries have attractive picnic areas.

Sightseeing

Temecula began as a Butterfield Stage Coach stop in the mid-19th century. A few wooden storefronts survive in **Old Town Temecula** on the west side of I-15. Many are antique shops. There are a dozen wineries in Temecula's wine country nearby. Hot air balloons provide a bird's eye view of the vineyards, especially attractive when hills are green in spring.

    Antique shops, gift shops, and small restaurants are strung along 6 blocks of Front St. Among Old Town's historic buildings are the **Machado Store**, now The Shire, with antique and gift shops, *28656 Front St; tel: (909) 676 9233*, and the 1885 brick **Temecula Mercantile** on Main St. **Old Town Temecula Greeters** provide walking tours; *tel: (909) 676-4614*.

    The **Temecula Valley Museum**, *41950 Main St, (909) 676-0021*, displays Indian, Spanish period and ranch artifacts, open Wed–Sun 1100–1600.

TEMECULA WINERIES

San Diegans and Angelenos consider the Temecula Wine Country their backyard. It's a popular day trip for locals; watch for heavy traffic and erratic driving, particularly on weekends.

    The **Temecula Shuttle** conducts wine country tours, *28657 Front St, no. A; tel: (909) 695-9999*. Contact the **Temecula Chamber of Commerce** for information on companies offering **hot air ballooning** over the vineyards.

    Exit I-15 at Rancho California Rd, and go east. Vineyards appear 4 miles (6.4 km) later, on gently rolling hills. Most wineries are along **Rancho California Rd**. Be prepared to pay for wine tasting and keep the wineglass. Allow at least 3 hrs for tasting.

    Morning fog, a 1600-ft (462 m) elevation, and afternoon breezes make this wine region cooler than the San Diego Coastline or the deserts to the east. Varietals run the gamut from Chardonnay and Riesling to Cabernet Sauvignon. Only Pinot Noir does poorly.

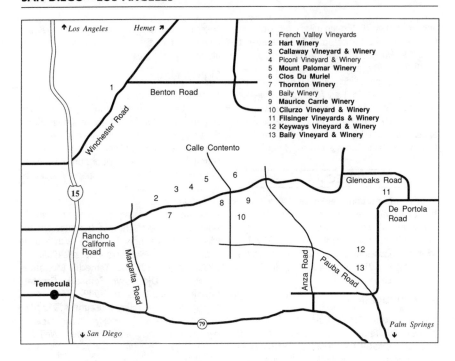

1 French Valley Vineyards
2 **Hart Winery**
3 **Callaway Vineyard & Winery**
4 Piconi Vineyard & Winery
5 **Mount Palomar Winery**
6 **Clos Du Muriel**
7 **Thornton Winery**
8 Baily Winery
9 **Maurice Carrie Winery**
10 **Cilurzo Vineyard & Winery**
11 **Filsinger Vineyards & Winery**
12 **Keyways Vineyard & Winery**
13 **Baily Vineyard & Winery**

Hart Winery, *32500 Rancho California Rd; tel: (909) 676-6300*, up a short dirt road, is a family-owned business which experiments with rarer varietals, and specialises in drier wines of all kinds. Next door is the largest Temecula producer, **Callaway Vineyard & Winery**, *32720 Rancho California; tel: (909) 676-4001*, where tasters tend to linger over a wide range of white wines. A picnic area is outside. Most of **Clos Du Muriel** wine is from grapes grown elsewhere.

Next along the left side of the road is **Mount Palomar Winery**, *33820 Rancho California Rd; tel: (909) 676-5047*, which conducts tours of the wine-making process and equipment. Enjoy wine with a picnic for a view of the vineyards and orange groves.

Thornton Winery, *32575 Rancho California Rd; tel: (909) 699-0099* on the south side, produces *méthode champenoise* sparklers. A herb garden enhances outdoor tasting at its **Café Champagne Wine Bar**.

Maurice Carrie Vineyard & Winery, *34225 Rancho California Rd; tel: (909) 676-1711*, has covered picnic umbrellas, childrens' swings, a deli, and free wine tasting.

Baily Vineyard & Winery, *36150 Pauba Rd; tel: (909) 676-9463*, boasts very dry, elegant reds and whites at the 'vineyard in the sky'. Follow signs up a very bad dirt road to **Santa Margarita Winery**, *Madera del Playa; tel: (909) 676-4431*, to taste dry, aged cabernet sauvignon.

Old-fashioned, hearty wine is still made by 1968 Temecula wine pioneer, Vince Cilurzo, a lighting director for television's *Jeopardy*. **Cilurzo Vineyard & Winery**, *41220 Calle Contento; tel: (909) 676-5250*, has chairs arranged in a semi-circle for tasters in a cavernous room with family and show business photos on the walls.

Filsinger Vineyards, *39050 DePortola Rd; tel: (909) 676-4594*, produces the only Gewürztraminer in the Temecula region, in addition to fine Cabernet Sauvignon. **Keyways Winery & Vineyard**, *37338 De Portola Rd; tel: (909) 676-1451*, has buttery white wines, and a tasting room with a car and other knick-knacks inside.

SANTA BARBARA

Santa Barbara was California's first cinema capital when Hollywood was nothing more than empty pastures. It's somehow fitting that the city's unique Spanish Colonial architectural style is as false as those early cinema epics – the graceful whitewashed arches, iron grillework, and red tiles are no older than the hurried reconstruction following a disastrous earthquake in 1925.

But life in Santa Barbara is too pleasant to worry about the petty details of historical accuracy. The weather is idyllic, the beaches protected, and a semicircle of sheer mountains rises almost within touch of downtown. Sidewalk cafés, long lunches and extended dinners are a way of life barely interrupted by the mundane necessities of earning a living. When the cinema makers moved to Hollywood, they left their hearts, and often their homes, in Santa Barbara. The former resort community has grown into a full-fledged city surrounded by dormitory communities, but the relaxed style of living still makes Santa Barbara a favourite getaway for the rest of Southern California.

Tourist Information

Santa Barbara Conference & Visitors Bureau (SBCVB) *510 State St, Suite A, Santa Barbara, CA 93101; tel: (805) 966-9222.*

Visitor Information Center: *1 Santa Barbara St (Cabrillo Blvd near Stearns Wharf); tel: (805) 965-3021,* open Mon–Sat 0900–1700, Sun 1000–1700; and *504 State St,* open Mon–Fri 0900–1700.

Weather

Weather is mild and sunny all year, with occasional coastal fog north of town. Summer temperatures hit 25°C near the coast and 30°C inland. Winter frost is rare, but evenings can drop to 10°C.

Arriving and Departing

Airport

Santa Barbara Municipal Airport is 8 miles (13 km) north of downtown in the town of Goleta; *tel: (805) 967-5608.* Taxi to downtown, $12.50.

Getting Around

Most of Santa Barbara is flat and walkable, but too spread out to tour on foot. The major areas of interest are the beach (south of Hwy 101), Old Town (the old downtown), and Santa Barbara Mission (off upper Mission St). Drive or ride public transport, and then explore on foot.

Public Transport

Electric shuttles travel State St between Stearns Wharf and downtown and along the waterfront on Cabrillo Blvd between the harbour and the Zoo. Free **bus ferries** run every 10–15 mins on State St, every 30 mins on the waterfront, Sun–Thu 1000–1700 and Fri–Sat 1000–2000.

Santa Barbara Metropolitan Transit District (MTD) buses run daily except on public holidays, but frequency can be a problem. The **MTD Transit Center**, *1020 Chapala St (near Carrillo St); tel: (805) 683-3702,* has information, schedules, change and fare tokens.

The **Santa Barbara Airbus**, *5755 Thornwood Dr., Goleta, CA 93117; tel: (800) 423-1618* or *(800) 733-6354,* runs 14 daily round trips between Santa Barbara and Los Angeles International Airport.

Driving

Driving is gloriously uncongested after Los Angeles. Some north–south downtown streets are one-way. Public parking is plentiful downtown; the first 90 mins are free. Recreational vehicles are not allowed in multi-storey car parks.

Living in Santa Barbara

Accommodation

Santa Barbara has been a popular – and expensive – resort city since the 1870s. Prices climb in direct proportion to the proximity of a location to the Pacific or to the surrounding mountains.

Top of the line are the **Four Seasons Biltmore**, on the beach, and the **San Ysidro Ranch**, in the hills of Montecito. Prices drop inland and reach more reasonable levels in Goleta, just north of Santa Barbara. Rooms below $50 per night are rare. Confirmed bookings are essential for weekends and a good idea for the rest of the week.

The SBCVB publishes lodging lists, but cannot make bookings. **Accommodations Santa Barbara**, *tel: (800) 292-2222*, and **Hot Spots**, *tel: (800) 793-7666*, book all price levels. The **Santa Barbara Bed & Breakfast Innkeepers Guild**, *tel: (800) 776-9176*, books bed and breakfast. Bookings are free.

Camping is available at county and state parks 15–30 mins drive from Santa Barbara. RV parks are located in the city.

Eating and Drinking

Santa Barbara is a culinary haven for Los Angeles refugees. Zealous chefs work wonders with local fish, wild mushrooms, avocados, citrus fruits, vegetables, and wines. Their patrons may have more dollars than taste buds, but the results can be spectacular.

Ethnic restaurants are perennial favourites, from traditional taquerias to gourmet fare from around the world. **La Super-Rica Taqueria**, *622 N. Milpas St; tel: (805) 963-4940*, serves budget-priced Mexican food for gourmets. The **Original Enterprise Fish Company**, *225 State St; tel: (805) 962-3313*, grills some of the best fish in the area. Moderate. **Main Squeeze**, *138 E. Cañon Perdido St; tel: (805) 966-5365*, is a budget trip around the world, from sizzling curries and authentic Mexican to organic California sprouts.

Entertainment

Santa Barbara has a busy arts scene, from resident theatre and music companies to touring shows from around the world and trendy nightspots. The *Santa Barbara News-Press* and the *Santa Barbara Independent* newspapers list current events.

Major venues include the **Arlington Center for the Performing Arts**, *1317 State St; tel: (805) 963-4408*, a 1930s cinema palace recreating a starlit Spanish village; the **Grenada Theatre**, *1216 State St; tel: (805) 966-2324;* the **Lobero Theatre**, *33 E. Cañon Perdido St; tel: (805) 963-0761*, California's oldest theatre in continuous operation; and the **University of California, Santa Barbara**, in Goleta; *tel: (805) 893-3535*.

The outdoor **Arts & Crafts Show**, *along E Cabrillo Blvd east from State St; tel: (805) 962-8956*, is part entertainment, part museum, and part shopping. Artists and artisans display, sell, and talk up their wares every Sunday.

Events

Santa Barbara's climate and ambience create a party atmosphere; events range from a New Year's Day **hang-gliding contest** to the **International Film Festival** in March. The May **'I Madonnari' Italian Street Painting Festival** allots space in the Old Mission courtyard for chalk drawings, many of them oversized and of museum quality.

California's penchant for colourful dress is nowhere more evident than at June's **Summer Solstice Parade**. One of the state's most authentic festivals is the city-wide, five-day **Old Spanish Days Fiesta** in August, complete with lace- and mantilla-swathed *señoritas* and dashing *caballeros* listening to mariachi bands at El Paseo.

Summer is sports time, including **Semana Nautica**, Jun, the **Outrigger Championships**, Jul, **Pacific Coast Open Polo Tournament**, Aug, and the **Lawn Bowling Tournament**, Sept.

Shopping

Santa Barbara lives for, and by, shopping. **El Paseo**, *800 block of State St near de la Guerra St*, is a decades-old maze of whitewashed passages and courtyards mimicking an Andalusian village – good for expensive gifts, clothing, speciality shops, studios, galleries and restaurants.

Paseo Nuevo, bordered by State and Chapala Sts and Ortega and Cañon Perdido Sts, is updated Spanish shopping chic. The block between Nordstrom and The Broadway depart-

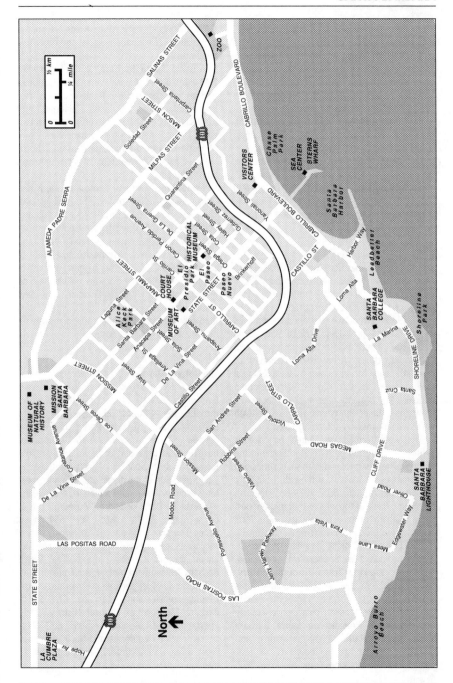

ment stores is filled with boutiques, restaurants, art galleries, and performance spaces.

Brinkerhoff Ave, a two-block street between Haley and Ortega Sts 1½ blocks west of State St, is a historic district lined with original Victorian homes. Most of the residences have been turned into antique or speciality gift shops.

La Cumbre Plaza, *3800 block of State St*, north of downtown, is the city's largest shopping centre, with two department stores, more than 60 small shops, and an enormous car park.

Factory outlets are concentrated on the 600 and 1100 blocks of State St, the light industrial area around Haley and Olive Sts, and on lower Milpas and Salsipuedes Sts.

Sightseeing

Red tile roofs and stucco walls are *de rigeur*, from the old Mission to downtown bank buildings and shopping complexes. Every element has been carefully crafted.

A 1925 earthquake flattened downtown Santa Barbara, providing a clean slate for a hastily-summoned architectural review board. The board's choice was a distinct mishmash of Mediterranean, Moorish, and Spanish Colonial that endures to this day – flame-coloured bougainvillea draping over arched doorways, fountains in quiet courtyards, red tiles beneath olive trees, palms and spreading oaks.

The waterfront is dominated by **Stearns Wharf**, an extension of State St jutting into the harbour. The wharf is lined with small shops and restaurants, with space near the end for fishing. The **Sea Center**; *tel: (805) 962-0885*, features life-sized models of the whales that migrate past Santa Barbara each year, aquaria with local fishes, and a touch tank to feel sea creatures.

Old Town, a 12-block area east of State St, was the original 1782 Spanish fort, or Presidio, and town. **Walking Tours Through History**, *tel: (805) 967-9869*, offer 2½-hr guided tours through the historic district. Highlights include the **Presidio**, the Moorish palace-style **County Courthouse**, **El Presidio de Santa Barbara State Historic Park**, several museums, and numerous historic adobe buildings. A self-guided **Red Tile Walking Tour**, *tel: (805) 962-*

6464, follows a similar route. Maps are printed in the SBCVB 'Destination Guide' and other free brochures.

Mission Santa Barbara, *2201 Laguna St; tel: (805) 682-4713*, was the 10th California mission, founded in 1786. The twin towers are a Hollywood vision of early California, not surprising since it was the only Mission that early cinema set designers had ever seen. Mission museum, grounds, gardens and church are open for self-guided tours. It is still used as a parish church.

Hope Ranch, west of Santa Barbara, is one of America's more luxurious housing estates. The grounds include a private country club and golf course, landscaped lagoon, polo, football and baseball fields, miles of riding trails, and splendid ocean views. **Montecito**, just south of Santa Barbara, claims the highest per capita income in America. Famous locals include Michael Jackson, Michael Douglas, Jane Seymour, Ronald Reagan and more movie stars than ever lived in Hollywood. Most mansions are hidden behind guarded gates.

Museums

The **Botanic Garden**, *1212 Mission Canyon Rd; tel: (805) 682-4726*, is devoted to native flora. Five miles (8 km) of walking trails wander through the gardens. **El Paseo de Santa Barbara State Historic Park**, *123 Cañon Perdido St; tel: (805) 966-9719*, includes buildings that were part of the original Presidio Real, the last Spanish military outpost in California. Some buildings are original, most have been excavated and rebuilt in recent years.

Santa Barbara Historical Museum, *136 E. de la Guerra St; tel: (805) 966-1601*, is an adobe complex with one of California's finest collections of regional history from pre-European contact to the present. The **Santa Barbara Museum of Art**, *1130 State St; tel: (805) 963-4364*, specialises in American, 19th-century French, and Asian art. The **Santa Barbara Museum of Natural History**, *2559 Puesta del Sol Rd; tel: (805) 682-4711*, concentrates on California and North American West Coast natural history, including a walk-through blue whale skeleton.

SANTA BARBARA CIRCUIT

Allow 3 hrs for this 30-mile driving tour, longer if you plan to visit the museums or other sights along the way. The circular route begins and ends at El Presidio de Santa Barbara State Historical Park, or can be started at any convenient point. The route can be taken in either direction, but begins on a one-way section of Santa Barbara St.

ROUTE

Begin at the corner of Santa Barbara and Ortega Sts. To explore **El Presidio de Santa Barbara State Historical Park**, use metered street parking or one of ten city car parks (the first 90 mins are free) in the area and explore on foot. **Casa Covarrubias** and the adjoining **Historic Adobe** are on the corner to the left.

Drive north along Santa Barbara St. The **Santa Barbara Historical Society Museum** is on the left near the corner of De La Guerra St. The buildings of **El Presidio de Santa Barbara Historic Park** are on the left, just beyond the corner of Cañon Perdido St. The original presidio wall is marked by bands of coloured paving stones crossing Cañon Perdido and Santa Barbara Sts. Only the **Canedo Adobe** and **El Cuartel**, on the extreme left, are original. The padre's quarters, chapel and commander's quarters are recent reconstructions. Most of the original Presidio is being excavated.

Continue up Santa Barbara St. The **Santa Barbara County Courthouse** is on the left between Figueroa and Anapamu Sts. The whitewashed Moorish palace-style building was opened in 1929. Interior corridors are lined with Tunisian tiles, floors are red terracotta, lighting is from hammered iron Spanish lanterns, doors are solid carved wood, and furniture is heavy leather studded with brass. The Board of

Supervisors' chambers and other public areas are covered with murals depicting local history. Admission to the 85-ft (26 m) bell tower observation deck is free.

The spreading oaks and lawns of **Alameda Plaza** stretch on both sides of Santa Barbara St between Sola and Micheltorena Sts. The Plaza is perfect for picnics, with tables, benches, and children's play equipment.

Alice Keck Memorial Garden, to the right between Micheltorena and Arrellaga Sts, is a miniature botanical garden. Within its one square block are two streams, a pond, pathways, gazebo and half a dozen plant communities. Several bed and breakfasts are within walking distance of the garden.

Continue four blocks north to Mission St. Turn right: **Mission Santa Barbara** lies 1 mile up Mission St. The 1786 Mission is called 'Queen of Missions' for its elegant facade. Pre-Hollywood cinema studios at State and Mission Sts filmed the Mission for hundreds of Westerns in the 1910s. Parts of the original Mission water system are still in use. The large park surrounding the Mission includes a spectacular **rose garden** that is in bloom nearly all year.

Follow Mission Canyon Rd uphill to Foothill Rd (Hwy 192). The **Museum of Natural History** is just beyond the Mission. Houses become larger, more expensive, and more exposed to wildfires as the road climbs. Turn left onto Foothill and one of Santa Barbara's more exclusive residential areas.

Continue on Foothill to San Marcos Pass Rd (Hwy 154). Turn left toward Hwy 101. At State St (end of Hwy 154), turn right and bear right into **Hope Ranch** and Las Palmas Dr. The large shopping centre near State St and Hwy 101 is **La Cumbre Plaza**.

The stately palm trees along Las Palmas Dr. were planted in the early 1900s, but Hope Ranch homes are modern. Las Palmas becomes Robles Dr., then Marina Dr., then Cliff Dr. Expansive homes block most ocean views, but Arroyo Burro Beach County Park has public parking and a small swimming beach.

Follow Cliff Dr. to Shoreline Dr. Turn right. Shoreline turns right at the **Santa Barbara Lighthouse** (closed to the public) to follow the

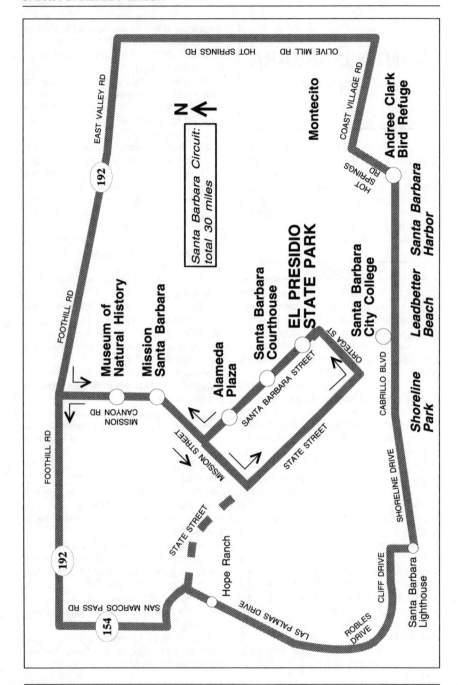

coastline. On clear days, the **Channel Islands** (see p. 73) are sharply outlined near the horizon. **Shoreline Park** and **Leadbetter Beach** are popular for sports and sunning, especially with students from **Santa Barbara City College**, on the hill to the left.

Shoreline continues behind **Santa Barbara Harbor** and becomes **Cabrillo Blvd** at the foot of Castillo St. Cabrillo is lined with small motels and restaurants on one side and broad beaches on the other.

Stearns Wharf juts into the ocean at the foot of **State St**, with **Chase Palm Park** continuing to the east. The **SBCVB Visitor Center** is at the foot of **Santa Barbara St.**

Continue along Cabrillo Blvd, parallel to East Beach and the ocean beyond. The **Santa Barbara Zoo** and **Andree Clark Bird Refuge** are on the left.

Cross beneath Hwy 101, turn right onto Hot Springs Rd, continue straight into **Montecito** and **Coast Village Rd**, Santa Barbara's version of Rodeo Dr. At Olive Mill Rd turn left. Olive Mill turns into Hot Springs Rd, which ends at East Valley Rd (Hwy 192). Turn left.

Montecito could be the permanent subject for *Lifestyles of the Rich and Famous*. Mercedes and BMWs look like the vehicle of choice for quick trips to the supermarket. Modest homes start around $1 million, seaside and mountain estates regularly hit eight figures.

Most homes are invisible behind high walls and electrified gates. **Lotusland**, *695 Ashley Rd; tel: (805) 969-9990*, the estate and gardens once owned by socialite opera singer Gana Walska, is open for tours by reservation between mid-Feb and mid-Nov.

East Valley Rd changes names frequently as it winds between gnarled oaks and hidden estates. Shortly after it becomes **Foothill Blvd**, turn left onto **Mission Canyon Rd**. Follow Mission Canyon past Mission Santa Barbara to State St. Turn left. **State St.** is Santa Barbara's main street, lined with a succession of small shops, department stores, and public buildings. The **Santa Barbara Museum of Art** is at the corner of Anapamu St, the public library just beyond on Anapamu. The main entrance to **El Paseo** shopping arcade is two blocks south on State

St near Carillo St. Parts of El Paseo were built in the 1820s. At Ortega St, turn left. Santa Barbara St, and the end of the route, is two blocks ahead.

CALIFORNIA MISSIONS

Mission Santa Barbara is one of 21 Missions whose sites run along the coast. This is a convenient place to list and index them. For more on their history, see next page.

San Diego de Alcala (I-8, San Diego), was relocated about 10 miles (16 km) from its original site. Two large early 19th-century bells adorn a gleaming white double belfry (San Diego–Palm Springs Route, p. 110.)

In the hills around **San Luis Rey de Francia**, 1798, 27,000 cows once grazed. (San Diego–Los Angeles p. 116.)

Legend holds that swallows return each March 19 to **San Juan Capistrano**, 1776, once the only mission with a seaport (Dana Point) between San Diego and San Francisco. (San Diego–Los Angeles, p. 116.)

San Gabriel Arcangel (San Gabriel), 1771, has an outdoor display of wood and adobe models of all the missions. (Nearest route: Los Angeles–Death Valley, p. 80.)

San Fernando Rey de España (San Fernando), 1787, partially damaged in the 1994 Northridge Earthquake, has an extensive museum collection of early mission (native) baskets. (Los Angeles–Death Valley, p. 80.)

San Buenaventura (Ventura), 1782, has the missions' only wooden bell in its museum. (Los Angeles–Santa Barbara, p. 71.)

Santa Barbara, 1786, 'Queen of the Missions', was rebuilt after early 19th-century earthquakes in a classical Roman style. Pink paint on the church facade gives it a Hollywood look. A peaceful courtyard garden and nearby civic rose garden perfectly display Santa Barbara's ideal growing climate.

Santa Ines (Solvang), 1804, at the edge of a town surviving on tourism, is an oasis of calm with a fine collection of 18th-century religious paintings. (Santa Barbara County Routes, p. 134.)

La Purisima Concepcion (Lompoc), 1787, a state historic park, is the best-restored of all the

California Missions

Conversion and colonisation came hand in hand to Alta (Upper) California in 1769. Peaceful coastal natives had worshipped nature spirits and respected elders according to tribal custom for millennia. Spain's desire to explore, settle, plough and convert new territory led Franciscan friars to set sail from Baja California in the company of a provincial governor and military escort.

Two boats sailed up the Baja California peninsula toward San Diego Bay. Father Junipero Serra, father-president of the Franciscan missionaries, proclaimed San Diego as the site for the first mission. The Franciscans established 21 missions between 1769 and 1823. As with European monasteries, each was no more than a day's journey from the next. The missions' route was *El Camino Real*, the King's Road, a south–north passage through mountains and plains from San Diego to San Francisco Solano in present-day Sonoma. Today, El Camino Real is Hwy 101 (see p. 162).

The Spanish wanted to quickly settle an area while providing adequate defence against hostile natives or European claimants to the land. Simultaneously, the friars would convert the local populace to Roman Catholic Christianity, serving the triple end of saving souls, preventing hostilities by local natives, and providing a workforce for the mission activities.

The missions were designed to be self-sustaining, raising crops and cattle for food and hides. The semi-arid mountain ranges close to the coast resembled the climate and land in Spain – vineyards thrived, cows grazed and citrus and olives flourished. Most of the missions became prosperous, some shipping wine to Mexico City and hides back to Spain.

A typical mission compound had a church, cemetery, water cistern, kitchen, the clergy's and the servants' quarters, guest rooms, a library, winery, soap making and tallow rendering vats, a tannery, blacksmithy, weavers, carpenters, potters, gardens (including a medicinal herb garden), a fountain, young unmarried native women's quarters, storerooms, barracks, and cannon. The buildings were adobe, whitewashed plaster covering stone and mud bricks. Adobe walls were several feet (m) thick. Little kept out the dust, but the walls provided some insulation against summer heat. Wooden beams provided building supports and red terracotta tiles covered roofs.

Cloistered walkways lined the central patio and gardens to form a quadrangle. Candles and animal fat lamps provided illumination. Bells tolled for prayer times and daily activities. The church nave was a simple rectangle painted with bright colours and occasional images of saints. Some missions had bell towers.

Earthquakes, always destructive to the mud brick adobes, periodically turned one mission building or another to ruins. Disease brought by outsiders decimated native populations; several instances of native defiance to the civilian and religious settlements ended in blood – and ultimately the loss of native sacred sites and communities. The natives came to live near or inside the mission, working in fields, kitchens or workshops, and learning the rudiments of Christian religion.

The missions were secularised in the 1830s after Mexican independence from Spain. Lands were sold to ranchers and soldiers. Mission adobe bricks were carted away to build rancho adobes. Most of the missions fell into ruins, and were largely ignored for the next century. Today, all 21 missions are open to the public. Few of them have all of the *original* buildings extant; most have been totally or partially rebuilt, re-roofed, and repainted. Some are more evocative or charming than others; some mission museums are more complete. It's worth a visit to at least one mission to sense the hard struggle of the missionaries to tame a dry land and its inhabitants, a world away from Spain.

missions. Every building, room and plant is labelled, tanned hides lie about, and donkeys stay in a corral (p. 145).

San Luis Obispo de Tolosa, 1772, is set among huge trees in an urban pedestrian area, centre of downtown dining and musical entertainment (p. 145).

San Miguel Arcangel (Paso Robles), 1787, sits beside a dusty stretch of Hwy 101, with a magnificent cacti garden and a brightly-painted church interior. Its multiple-bell detached belfry has become a symbol for the missions (p. 162).

San Antonio de Padua, 1771, was famous for horses.

Nuestra Señora de la Soledad, 1791, Our Lady of Solitude, still sits in the small dusty agricultural town of Soledad (p. 168).

San Carlos Borromeo (Carmel), 1770, called Carmel Mission, is Fr Serra's burial place and was the chain's headquarters. An excellent museum presents mission-era life; the lush courtyard gardens are sunny and peaceful (p. 156).

San Juan Bautista, 1797, is the largest mission and site of the mission scenes in Alfred Hitchcock's *Vertigo* (p. 168).

Santa Cruz, 1791, barely survived denizens of a nearby red light district, to be felled by a tidal wave and neglect. In 1931 it was rebuilt to half-scale. (p. 161).

Santa Clara de Asis (Santa Clara), 1777, rebuilt on the University of Santa Clara campus, has original mission bells from the King of Spain (p. 172).

San Jose, 1797, in downtown San Jose, was redone in rococo (p. 170).

San Francisco de Asis (San Francisco), 1776, known now as Mission Dolores, is one of the best-preserved mission building with a cemetery for early Native Americans and notable San Franciscans. The mission withstood earthquakes in 1906 and 1989 due to its fortress-like construction: 36,000 adobe bricks reinforce 4-ft thick walls (p. 227).

San Rafael Arcangel (San Rafael), 1815, was established as a hospital for the San Francisco mission (p.233).

San Francisco de Solano (Sonoma), 1823, was the last of the missions. Within a decade the missions yielded to secular use (p. 246).

California Missions

SANTA BARBARA COUNTY ROUTES

Allow at least a full day for the 71-mile (114 km) Scenic Route from Santa Barbara north through the Santa Ynez Mountains to the Danish town of Solvang, and back. Combining this with the Wineries Circuit can stretch the route to 2½ days. Solvang offers the greatest choice for overnight accommodation.

SCENIC ROUTE

The route can be driven in either direction, but the ocean views from the crest of Hwy 154 are best in the morning. Sunsets from beach parks west of Santa Barbara can be spectacular.

At Buellton you have the choice of turning south back towards Santa Barbara and the beach parks, or north to Los Alamos and back to Santa Barbara via Los Olivos.

The Wineries Circuit (p. 137) intersects with the route at several points between Santa Ynez and Los Olivos and can be combined with the Scenic Route..

The Scenic Route begins near Hope Ranch, at the intersection of Hwy 101 and Hwy 154 (San Marcos Pass Rd). Take Hwy 154 4 miles (6 km) uphill to the junction with Hwy 192. Continue up Hwy 154 24 miles (38 km) towards San Marcos Pass, Lake Cachuma, and Santa Ynez.

San Marcos Pass Rd is the only route through the rugged **Santa Ynez Mountains** into the lush **Santa Ynez Valley** in northern Santa Barbara County. The road snakes 9 miles (14 km) up mountainsides covered with **chaparral**, a mixture of dense, low growing brush that periodically explodes into intense wildfires in the dry autumn months. The slopes are carpeted with the soft green of new growth after late winter rains.

A large vista point near the summit looks back along the Santa Barbara coast, from Point Conception east to Ventura and south beyond the Channel Islands. San Marcos Pass is 2225 ft (674 m) above sea level.

Lake Cachuma, a major water supply and recreation area for Santa Barbara, comes into view 4 miles (6 km) beyond the vista point. The lake is named for the Native Americans who once lived throughout the Santa Barbara area.

Lake Cachuma County Park, *tel: (805) 568-2460*, beside the artificial lake, has shaded campsites and picnic tables. Swimming is prohibited, but two large swimming pools are open in the summer. Fishing is allowed year round; boats for hire, fishing licences, bait and tackle are available. Two-hour boat cruises of the lake's wildlife and bird populations begin at the park marina.

The highway dips towards the **Santa Ynez Valley** just beyond the head of Lake Cachuma. The area was first mapped in 1798 when a party from Mission Santa Barbara set out to find a site for a new mission midway between Santa Barbara and Mission La Purisima in Lompoc. The site, in what is now Solvang, became Mission Santa Ines in 1804.

The valley is a succession of rolling hills, green in winter, golden brown in summer, sprinkled with stands of oak and eucalyptus trees. Dozens of side-roads serve the extensive cattle and horse ranches, croplands that are being replaced by growing numbers of vineyards and citrus groves.

Most wineries welcome visitors. So do most horse farms – with advance notice. American Paints, Andalusians, Arabians, Icelandics, Miniatures, Peruvian Pasos, Quarter Horses and Thoroughbreds are all raised in the valley. The **Solvang Chamber of Commerce**, *tel: (805) 688-3317*, has a current list of ranches that welcome visitors by prior arrangement. At the junction of Hwys 154 and 246, turn left onto 246. The town of **Santa Ynez** is 3 miles (5 km) ahead.

From Santa Ynez, continue west along Hwy 246. **Solvang** is 3 miles (5 km) beyond Santa Ynez.

From Solvang continue 3 miles (5 km) down Hwy 246 to the intersection of Hwy 101 and **Buellton**. The town has several motels and RV parks, but is best known as 'the home of split pea soup,' the huge **Pea Soup Andersen's Restau-**

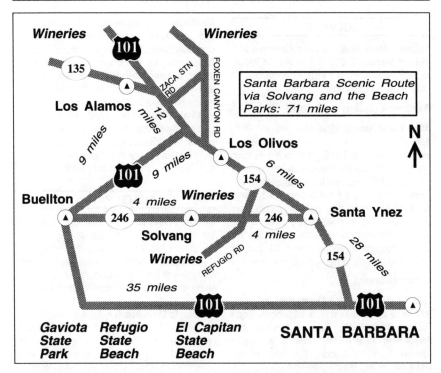

Santa Barbara Scenic Route via Solvang and the Beach Parks: 71 miles

rant. The soup is filling, and anyone who can beat the gluttony record (over 20 bowls at one sitting) eats for free.

To visit the beach parks, turn south onto Hwy 101 towards Santa Barbara. Hwy 1 turns north towards Lompoc 8 miles (13 km) later. One mile (1.6 km) beyond the Hwy 1 turnoff, the freeway plunges into a short tunnel through the final slopes of the Santa Ynez Mountains. A **rest area** is ½ mile (1 km) beyond the tunnel. A concise natural history display describes the different flora and fauna zones north and south of the Santa Ynez Mountains, a formidable natural barrier that once separated Southern California from the rest of the state. Continuing along Hwy 101, you pass **Gaviota State Park**, **Refugio State Beach** and **El Capitan State Beach**.

The **University of California, Santa Barbara (UCSB)** is 12 miles (19 km) south on Hwy 217, west of Hwy 101 in Goleta. **Santa Barbara**, and the junction with Hwy 154, is 10 miles (16 km) beyond the UCSB turnoff.

SANTA YNEZ

Like other valley towns, Santa Ynez is schizophrenic, trying to serve its traditional role as a country town and supply centre for nearby farms while it welcomes a growing number of tourists.

Feed and supply stores are booming. So is tourism, encouraged by false-front, old-west style buildings in the business district. The **Parks-Janeway Carriage House**, *3596 Sagunto St; tel: (805) 688-7889*, has one of the finest collections of horse-drawn vehicles and accessories in the West. The **Santa Ynez Valley Historical Museum**, *3596 Sagunto St; tel: (805) 688-7889* features articles made or used by area residents from the Chumash through to the early 20th century.

Glider Rides take off from the Santa Ynez Airport, just south of the highway; *tel: (805) 688-2517*. Commercial pilots take passengers on swooping, sometimes acrobatic motor-less glides above the valley.

SOLVANG

Tourist Information: Solvang Conference & Visitors Bureau, *PO Box 70, Solvang, CA 93463; tel: (800) 468-6765.* The **Visitor Centre**, *1511 A Mission Dr.,* is open daily.

Accommodation and Food

Alisal Guest Ranch, *1054 Alisal Rd; tel: (805) 688-6411,* is one of the best and most expensive resorts in California. The 20 or so motels in town are moderate, but reservations are essential for weekends, holidays, and the summer months.

Food and drink are big business in Solvang. Three dozen restaurants span the gamut from cheap fast food to pricey white linen dining. Danish is the most common theme, all-you-can-eat smorgasbords among the most popular meals. Bakeries outperform most restaurants.

Entertainment

The best show in town is **Theaterfest**, *tel: (805) 922-8313,* an open-air replica of London's Globe Theatre. **The Pacific Conservatory of the Performing Arts** (PCPA) presents a six-play summer repertory season. The summer rep and a winter rep season play at Allan Hancock College in Santa Maria, 40 miles (64 km) north. Open-air shows can be cold, but PCPA is one of the top acting companies in America.

Sightseeing

Solvang began as a Danish college and cultural centre in 1914, then grew into a small agricultural town. A 1947 magazine article describing the Danish-style buildings sparked a tourist boom.

The permanent population is about 4800, but thousands of visitors from around the world jam sidewalks every day to soak up the feel of old-time Denmark. What they get is a theme-park version of reality, complete with 19th-century half-timbered buildings, gas streetlamps, red-and-white flags fluttering from every house peak, horse-drawn streetcars, pastries, and enough Danish souvenirs to stock Disneyland.

Elverhoy Museum, *1624 Elverhoy Way; tel: (805) 686-1211,* has Danish artifacts and memorabilia in a typical 18th-century Danish farmhouse. **The Honen**, *tel: (805) 686-0022,* with replicas of early 20th-century horsedrawn streetcars from Copenhagen, provide guided tours and transportation to the Elverhoy Museum. **Hans Christian Andersen Park**, *off Atterdag Rd,* three blocks north of Mission Dr., has broad lawns and picnic areas.

Mission Santa Ines, *1760 Mission Dr.; tel: (805) 688-4815,* has been restored to its original beauty. The Mission, museum, and grounds are open for tours. A side door from the church leads to a quiet garden off the tour track.

BEACH PARKS

Gaviota State Park lies 2 miles (3 km) south of the rest area on the beach side of Hwy 101. The beach park has tent camping, RV spaces and a pier, but does not accept reservations. It's packed on weekends and during the summer, but almost empty during the week from autumn until late spring.

Refugio State Beach is 9 miles (14 km) south of Gaviota. The campsite, just behind the beach, was renovated in 1994. A quiet lagoon, a sandy beach backed by palm trees, and a small store open in the summer round out the facilities. In the quiet winter months, Refugio looks like an isolated tropical refuge – but the water is closer to 15°C than 25°C.

El Capitan State Beach is 2 miles (3 km) south of Refugio. The beach is small, but dozens of rocky tidepools make it a favourite for families with children. Chumash Indians also enjoyed El Capitan, both for the shellfish that lived in tidepools and the edible nuts produced by stands of pinon pine trees up the canyon.

LOS OLIVOS

The town was once an important stage-coach and rail stop. But around the turn of the century San Francisco and Los Angeles financiers decided to route major rail lines and roads nearer the coast and present-day Hwy 101. The town withered, but never died.

Accommodation is easy: **Los Olivos Grand Hotel**, *2860 Grand Ave; tel: (805) 688-7788* is romantic, but the only choice in town. Expensive.

The choice of **eating and drinking** is slightly wider. **Mattei's Tavern**, *Railway Ave, ½ block west of the Hwy 154–Grand Ave intersection; tel: (805) 688-4820,* the original stage-coach stop, has rebounded as a popular restaurant. **Remington's Restaurant**, in the Grand Hotel, is the other choice. Both places are moderate to expensive

LOS ALAMOS

The town was founded as a stage-coach stop and retains strong ties with its western heritage and the neighbouring farming families. Many of the older buildings have been reborn as antique stores and art galleries.

Accommodation: The **Union Hotel** and the adjoining **Victorian Mansion** have been restored to their 19th-century glory, down to the wooden sidewalk in front and the brilliant yellow, gold, and white colour scheme on the Mansion. Decor and furnishings are 1890s, but service and comfort are strictly 1990s. Expensive.

SANTA BARBARA WINERIES CIRCUIT

Tourist Information: Contact the **Santa Barbara County Vintners' Association**, *PO Box 1558, Santa Ynez, CA 93460; tel: (805) 688-0881,* for maps and brochures. Information is also available at most hotels and tourist attractions in Southern and Central California.

Day circuits are slightly shorter out of Santa Maria than from Santa Barbara, but the most distant winery is barely 2 hrs from either city via Hwy 101. A two-day trip is more relaxed, with an overnight in the Santa Ynez-Los Alamos area.

Begin the circuit in the same way as the Scenic Route, as far as the Hwy 154–246 intersection. Follow Hwy 246 1 mile (1.6 km) to **The Gainey Vineyard**, *3950 E. Hwy 246, Santa Ynez; tel: (805) 688-0558.* Gainey charges for tasting, but the shaded picnic tables surrounded by rolling vineyards are free. Bring your own food, or pay a small premium at the tasting room deli. Tours are also free.

If time is tight, a tour of four more Santa Ynez

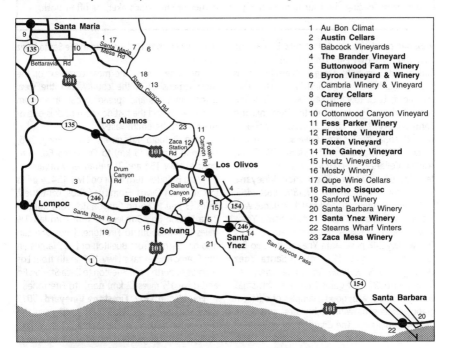

1 Au Bon Climat
2 **Austin Cellars**
3 Babcock Vineyards
4 **The Brander Vineyard**
5 **Buttonwood Farm Winery**
6 **Byron Vineyard & Winery**
7 Cambria Winery & Vineyard
8 **Carey Cellars**
9 Chimere
10 Cottonwood Canyon Vineyard
11 **Fess Parker Winery**
12 **Firestone Vineyard**
13 **Foxen Vineyard**
14 **The Gainey Vineyard**
15 Houtz Vineyards
16 Mosby Winery
17 Qupe Wine Cellars
18 **Rancho Sisquoc**
19 Sanford Winery
20 Santa Barbara Winery
21 **Santa Ynez Winery**
22 Stearns Wharf Vinters
23 **Zaca Mesa Winery**

Santa Barbara Wineries

Santa Barbara County has more than 30 wineries, most of them on Santa Ynez Valley side roads off Hwys 154 and 246, or near Foxen Canyon Rd in the Santa Maria Valley. Wine was made in the area from Mission days until Prohibition (1919), but the first modern commercial vineyards weren't planted until the late 1960s.

The lack of winemaking history ensures that every Santa Barbara vintner is working here by choice, not tradition. With no traditions to break, Santa Barbara winemakers are probably more free to experiment than their counterparts anywhere else in the state. Geography doesn't leave them much choice. The Santa Ynez Mountains run east–west, unlike any other coastal mountains in Western North America. This 'transverse range' creates valleys open to the Pacific that funnel summer fog and cool breezes far inland. Fog and winds keep summer temperatures relatively low, which makes for one of the longest grape growing seasons – and some of the most flavourful grapes – on the West Coast.

Vineyards in the Santa Maria Valley, closest to the Pacific, have the most fog and lowest temperatures. Temperatures climb inland, towards the south-west and the Santa Ynez Valley. Both valleys are famed for Chardonnay and Pinot Noir, which do best in cooler climates, but warmer, more protected vineyards are producing a steady succession of award-winning Cabernet Sauvignons and Merlots as well.

About half the wineries offer tours and tasting, but don't expect the kind of grand establishments that dot Napa or Sonoma Valleys. Northern California wineries have had decades to grow and consolidate. Most Santa Barbara wineries have produced fewer than 20 vintages. They're still small, family-owned and informal. The person behind the tasting counter or leading the tour is most likely the owner or the winemaker, or often both.

wineries points you back to Santa Barbara on Hwy 154. Take Hwy 246 5 miles (8 km) to Alamo Pintado Rd. Turn right. Drive 7 miles (11 km) as Alamo Pintado becomes Grand Ave. At Hwy 154, turn right, back towards San Marcos Pass and Santa Barbara. The tour visits the **Buttonwood Farm Winery**, *1500 Alamo Pintado Rd, Solvang, tel: (805) 688-3032;* **Carey Cellars**, *1711 Alamo Pintado Rd, Solvang, tel: (805) 688-8554;* **Austin Cellars**, *2923 Grand Ave, Los Olivos, tel: (805) 688-9665;* and **The Brander Vineyard**, *2401 Refugio Rd, Los Olivos, tel: (805) 688-2455.*

With more time, mix and match wineries with the Scenic Route and town visits to Santa Ynez, Solvang, and Los Olivos, or concentrate on wine. Follow Hwy 246 past Santa Ynez to Refugio Rd, turn left, go 1 miles (1.6 km) to **Santa Ynez Winery**, *343 N. Refugio Rd, Santa Ynez; tel: (805) 688-8381.* Self-guided tours of this small winery are free, with good examples of different grape varieties, growing techniques, and wine-making equipment. The Chardonnay vineyard in front of the tasting room was planted in 1967, the oldest commercial vineyard in the Santa Ynez Valley.

The wines aren't the most complex (or the most expensive) in the county, but the view across vineyards and spreading oak trees from picnic tables and the tasting room deck is one of the best in the entire valley.

Take Refugio Rd north. Cross Hwy 246, continue 3 miles (5 km) to Ontiveros Rd. Turn right to Hwy 154 and The Brander Vineyard.

From Brander, turn right on Hwy 154, 4 miles (6 km) to Los Olivos. From Los Olivos, continue 2 miles (3 km) to Foxen Canyon Rd. Turn right to Zaca Station Rd., 6 miles (10 km). Turn left 1½ miles (2 km) south to Firestone. (Firestone can also be reached from Buellton or Los Alamos on the Scenic Route: take Hwy 101 south from Los Alamos or north from Buellton to Zaca Station Rd and drive 1½ miles (2 km) north to Firestone.)

Founded in 1972, **Firestone Vineyard**, *5017 Zaca Station Rd; tel: (805) 688-3940,* was the first major winery in the Santa Ynez Valley. Today, it's the largest and most successful winery in Santa Barbara County. It's also the only local winery that can compete with better-known Napa and Sonoma facilities for the sheer size of the winery, tasting room, tours, and sales. As with many successful wineries, prices can be on the high side. To keep its wines selling, Firestone introduced Prosperity Red and White table wines during the depths of the early 1990s recession. Prosperity became one of the best values in California wine, and a successful inducement to visit Firestone to sample higher-priced labels. Tours, tasting, and picnicking are free.

After leaving Firestone, turn left onto Zaca Mesa Rd 3 miles (5 km) to **Fess Parker Winery**, *6200 Foxen Canyon Rd; tel: (805) 688-1545.* Owner Fess Parker is better known for his early roles as Davey Crockett and Daniel Boone in Walt Disney TV and cinema productions than for his wines. There is a charge for tasting, but the landscaped picnic grounds are free.

Continue 3 miles (5 km) up Foxen Canyon Rd to **Zaca Mesa Winery**, *6905 Foxen Canyon Rd; tel: (805) 688-9339.* The new redwood-sided winery and tasting room is a favourite stop for summer bicyclists who collapse in the deep shade and soft lawn beneath ancient oaks – 'Zaca' means 'peaceful resting place' in the Chumash language. Families like Zaca Mesa for the oversized toy box that keeps children busy while the adults taste. And the wines have been winning awards since the late 1970s. Reds, especially Pinot Noir, Syrah, and Merlot, are slightly more successful than Chardonnay, but it's hard to find a bad bottle.

Continue 7 miles (11 km) up Foxen Canyon Rd. The narrow, bumpy road winds through the San Rafael Mountains, actually little more than rugged, densely wooded hills, into the Santa Maria Valley.

Foxen Vineyard, *Rt. 1, Box 144A, Foxen Canyon Rd, Santa Maria; tel: (805) 937-4251,* is a small family-owned winery. There are no tours, but the tasting room, a converted barn, is open for tasting on weekends until wines sell out. The vineyard, road, and canyon are named after Benjamin Foxen, an English sailor who settled the area in 1837. Foxen sided with America in the short war with Mexico over California in the mid-

1840s. He guided Capt. John Fremont's troops through the Santa Ynez Mountains to avoid ambush at Gaviota Pass, near the coast, and to attack Santa Barbara from the rear.

Continue up Foxen Canyon Rd 2 miles (3 km) to **San Ramon Church**, a white chapel overlooking the road on the right. Turn right to **Rancho Sisquoc Winery**, *Rt 1, Box 147, Foxen Canyon Rd, Santa Maria; tel: (805) 934-4332.* This is actually a huge working cattle ranch along the Sisquoc River, but a small though increasing portion of the ranch is planted with grapes, cooled by the Pacific Ocean 20 miles (32 km) west. The first Sisquoc vineyard was planted in 1968, the second commercial wine venture in Santa Barbara Country. Relatively few people make the rough road pilgrimage to Sisquoc. Winery and tasting room have been built into existing ranch buildings, surrounded by barns, workshops, and the owner's home. An enormous picnic area, shaded by trailing grape and wisteria vines, looks more like a small town park than one of the most successful small wineries in the state.

Annual production is only 5000 cases, compared to 50,000 cases at Zaca Mesa and 80,000 at Firestone, but the winery consistently earns gold medals for every variety. Most of the wines are a bargain, especially Sauvignon Blanc, Sylvaner, and Johannisberg Riesling. Reds are outstanding, but more expensive.

Return to Foxen Canyon Rd and turn right onto Tepusquet Rd. Continue 2 miles (3 km) to **Byron Vineyards and Winery**, *5230 Tepusquet Rd, Santa Maria; tel: (805) 937-7288.* The road to Byron skirts low, dry hills flanking the Susquoc River. Winter floods occasionally close Tepusquet Rd and afternoon winds can whip up sharp gusts any time of the year. Byron is owned by Napa giant Mondavi Winery, but original owner Byron Brown remains as winemaker. He concentrates on Pinot Noir and Chardonnay, taking advantage of the early morning summer fog and generally cooler temperatures than are found at Rancho Sisquoc and the Santa Ynez Valley.

To complete the route, take Tepusquet Rd south to Santa Maria Mesa Rd, turn right, drive 5 miles (8 km) to Betteravia Rd, and 7 miles (11 km) to Hwy 101.

Santa Barbara Wineries Circuit   **139**

SANTA BARBARA to LONE PINE

From Santa Barbara's playland, this two-day route winds through the Los Padres National Forest to the agricultural southern Central Valley, and follows the Kern River east to the spine of the Sierra Nevada Mountains. The 298-mile (477 km) drive provides a quick overview of California's regions: seaside resort, mountain forest, agricultural heartland, recreational lake and rugged mountains. Plan to spend the night in Ojai, Bakersfield, or Isabella Lake.

ROUTE

Take Hwy 101 east from Santa Barbara towards Los Angeles. Turn north on Olive Mill Rd towards **Montecito**; after 1 mile (1.6 km), it becomes Hot Springs Rd, continuing for 1 mile (1.6 km) to Hwy 192, East Valley Rd. Turn right on Hwy 192 going south.

At the Ventura County line, turn left on Hwy 150. Continue around **Lake Casitas** for 15 miles (24 km). At the Hwy 33 junction, drive east for 3 miles (5 km) to **Ojai**.

From Ojai, take Hwy 33 north for 58 miles (93 km) to the Hwy 166 junction. Turn right on the Westside Hwy, joint Hwys 166/33, for 14 miles (22 km) to **Maricopa**.

Continue 23 miles (37 km) east on Hwy 166, over I-5 to Hwy 99. Turn right onto Hwy 99 at **Mettler**, and continue north 24 miles (38 km) to downtown **Bakersfield**.

Continue on Hwy 178 north-east along the **Kern River**, to **Isabella Lake**, **Onyx**, and south-east along **Freeman Canyon** to **Freeman Junction**. Take Hwy 14 north for 3 miles (5 km) to the junction with Hwy 395, then continue north to **Lone Pine** along the same route as Los Angeles–Death Valley (see p. 80).

SANTA BARBARA TO OJAI

The Santa Barbara seaside is set against magnificent mountains, the southern extension of the Santa Ynez Range in the Los Padres National Forest. The rich, famous, wannabes and even President Clinton like the stretch of coastal scenery just south of the city. The Santa Barbara Circuit (see p. 129) includes part of Montecito.

As you drive south on Hwy 192, avocado and flower nurseries line the roadside and the mountains rise on the left. Mansions and estates are screened by gates and old trees; catch an occasional glimpse of how the truly rich live. From everywhere, creeks run from the mountains to the ocean. Two miles (3.2 km) down Hwy 192 on the right is Birnam Wood Golf Club. Beyond is upper Summerland, with the Clintons' vacation beaches to the right.

Hwy 192 curves right and becomes Toro Canyon Rd for ½ mile (0.8 km), then returns to Foothill Rd. The Summerland-Carpinteria area is known for flowers, especially cymbidium (orchids). **Stewart Orchids**, *3376 Foothill Rd, Carpinteria, CA 93013; tel: (805) 684-5448,* open Mon–Fri 0800–1600, Sat 1000–1600, has huge orchid greenhouses. Just down Foothill Rd is the **Santa Barbara Polo and Racquet Club**, *3375 Foothill Rd, Carpinteria, CA 93013; tel: (805) 684-8667 or (805) 684-6683,* open Sundays 1300 Apr–Oct, which stages exciting polo matches.

Foothill Rd, Hwy 192, ends at the Ventura County border. Turn left on Hwy 150, and drive east over the 969-ft (298 m) West Casitas Pass and 1143-ft (351 m) East Casitas Pass to **Lake Casitas**. The lake is surrounded by oak-covered hills and provides water to Ventura County. No swimming is permitted in the reservoir, but the 750-pitch campsite **Lake Casitas Recreation Area**, *11311 Santa Ana Rd, Ventura, CA 93001; tel: (805) 649-2233* has boating, rowing, sailing, and fishing for bass, rainbow trout and channel catfish. There is a viewpoint at the lake's north end. Just before Hwy 150 joins Hwy 33, there's a good view of an ancient dry seabed at **Burnham Wash**.

Hwy 150, Baldwin Rd, continues 5 miles (8 km) east to **Ojai** (pronounced 'oh-high').

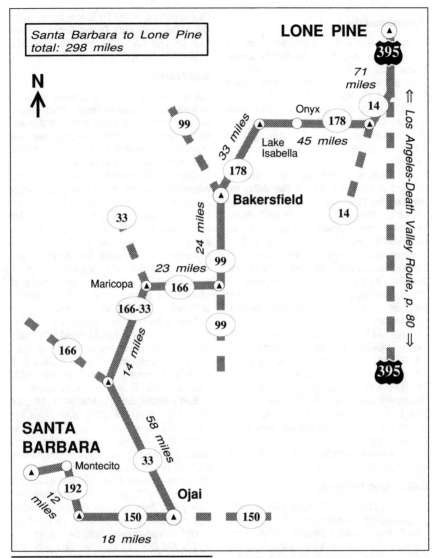

Santa Barbara to Lone Pine
total: 298 miles

N

LONE PINE

395

71 miles

⇑ Los Angeles–Death Valley Route, p. 80 ⇓

14

Onyx

178

33 miles

99

Lake Isabella   45 miles

178

24 miles

Bakersfield

33

14

23 miles

Maricopa   **166**

99

166-33

99

14 miles

166

58 miles

SANTA BARBARA

Montecito

33

Ojai

192

12 miles

150

150

18 miles

OJAI

Tourist Information: **Ojai Valley Chamber of Commerce**, *338 E. Ojai Ave, PO Box 1134, Ojai, CA 93024; tel: (805) 646-8126*, open Mon–Fri 0930–1630, Sat–Sun 1000–1600, has sightseeing, dining and lodging information, but does not make bookings.

Getting Around

Park and take the Ojai Trolley to downtown sights and dining. The **Ojai Trolley**, *tel: (805) 965-0353*, makes daily, 45-min circuits of the City of Ojai, from 0830–1730, for $0.25. Be prepared for an animated driver commentary on the citizens who use this service daily!

Accommodation

In this resort area, most of the accommodation is moderate to expensive. The 20-room **El Camino Lodge**, *406 W. Ojai Ave, Ojai, CA 93023; tel: (805) 646-4341*, is the most economical. **Casa Ojai**, *1302 E. Ojai Ave, Ojai, CA 93023; tel: (800) 255-8175*, is a moderate 45-room *BW* across from the **Ojai Valley Trail** (9 miles to Ventura). The **Capri Motel**, *1180 E. Ojai Ave, Ojai, CA 93023; tel: (805) 646-4305*, is another moderate choice.

Golf clubs and tennis togs have been the standard at the posh 212-room **Ojai Valley Inn and Country Club**, *Country Club Rd, Ojai, CA 93023; tel: (800) 422-6524*, since 1923. Pricey. The resort offers horseback riding and guided hiking and mountain biking at Rancho Dos Rios, a wilderness area 1 mile (1.6 km) south. Frank Capra's Shangri-La also offers a pricey health spa, **The Oaks at Ojai**, *122 E. Ojai Ave, Ojai, CA 93023; tel: (805) 646-5573*, with aerobics, body conditioning, yoga, and a reducing regimen programme.

Three bed and breakfast inns offer moderate lodging. **Ojai Manor Hotel**, *210 E. Matilija, Ojai, CA 93023; tel: (805) 646-0961*, has six rooms with common facilities in Ojai's oldest building, an 1874 schoolhouse. The 1887 **Theodore Woolsey House**, *1484 E. Ojai Ave, Ojai, CA 93023; tel: (805) 646-9779*, has six rooms. Spanish hacienda-style **Casa de La Luna**, *710 S. La Luna, Ojai, CA 93023; tel: (805) 646-4528*, has seven rooms, gardens, and an art gallery with oils, watercolours, and prints.

Eating and Drinking

For breakfast basics, try **Bill Baker's Bakery**, *457 E. Ojai Ave, Ojai, CA 93023; tel: (805) 646-1558*, open 0530 except Mon. Most breads are hearty German-style, but all avoid sugar and oil. Advertising 'no grease' is the budget Asian cultural mix of **Chu's Teriaki & Egg Roll House**, *11566 N. Ventura Ave, Ojai, CA 93023; tel: (805) 646-1177*. **Lanna Thai Cuisine**, *849 E. Ojai Ave, Ojai, CA 93023; tel: (805) 646-6771*, has budget lunch and dinner.

The **Ranch House**, *102 Besant Rd, Ojai, CA 93023; tel: (805) 646-2360*, has weekend prime rib and seafood. Pricey. Try Sunday brunch at the Ojai Valley Inn's **Vista Dining Room**, *Country Club Rd, Ojai, CA 93023; tel: (805) 646-5511, 1130–1430*. Pricey.

Sightseeing

Ojai is a summer weekend getaway for Santa Barbara and Ventura residents. What attracts them is the cooler mountain weather and an arts scene in a Spanish mission-style downtown. The Ojai Valley nestles within mountain ranges laced with hiking trails and rugged camping.

Ojai Valley's mountain hideaway attracted wintertime residents from the US East Coast in the 1870s. In 1917 a glass manufacturer, Edward Libbey, built the Ojai Valley Inn and Country Club and encouraged the Spanish-style buildings along Ojai Ave, Hwy 150, in downtown Ojai. A red-tiled roof crowns the **Arcade**'s chic clothing boutiques and bookstores. A 65-ft (20 m) campanile, Ojai's symbol, houses the **post office** in the centre of town – visitors over 14 years old can go up to see the view.

Drive all the way through town on Hwy 150, Ojai Ave; 1½ miles (2.4 km) beyond is Dennison Grade (slope), where the view inspired Frank Capra to film *Lost Horizon* in 1937. Ojai is known for its 'pink moment', a rosy hue which glows from the surrounding mountains at sunset.

Bart's Books, *302 W. Matilija St, Ojai, CA 93023; tel: (805) 646-3755*, open Tues–Sun 1000–1730, is *al fresco* – read and browse among the 100,000 volumes. When (very infrequent) rain falls, tarpaulins are pulled over the bookshelves. Music plays in the background. Rarer, more valuable books and first editions sit in the History Room or the Bookhouse and Gallery. Paperback books are left out after hours – patrons leave the money in a collection box.

Ojai Valley Museum, *109 S. Montgomery St, PO Box 204, Ojai CA 93024; tel: (805) 646-2290* or *(805) 646-0445*, open Wed–Mon 1300–1700 and housed in a historic firehouse, has local Native American objects, and good exhibits on the rancho era, oil discovery, firefighting, and railroads. For a totally different collection, there's the **Attitude Adjustment Shoppe**, *1129 Maricopa Hwy, Ojai, CA 93023; tel: (805) 646-1109*, which claims to have the world's largest collection of US beer steins (300-plus). There are many art galleries in town. Up to 15,000 weekend visitors peruse the **Sunday artists' outdoor display** of paintings, water-colours and pottery along Ojai Ave near **Libbey Park**.

The **Ojai Festival**, *tel: (805) 646-2094*, the first weekend of June, has presented classical and modern music for a half century. The **Ojai Shakespeare Festival**, *tel: (805) 646-9455*, performs two plays in repertory in early August. In October, there's **A Bowlful of Blues**, *tel: (805) 646-7230*, with country, urban, zydeco and gospel blues music, and the **Ojai Studio Tour Weekend**, *tel: (805) 646-8126*, when artists show off their work venues. The **Ojai Arts Center**, *113 S. Montgomery St, Ojai, CA 93023; tel: (805) 646-0117*, displays local artists' work and sponsors performances.

Ojai also attracts philosophical thinkers. **Krishnamurti Library**, *1130 McAndrew Rd, Ojai, CA 93023; tel: (805) 646-2726*, was the philosopher's residence from 1922 to 1986. The **Krotona Institute of Theosopy**, *2 Krontona Hill, Ojai, CA 93023; tel: (805) 646-2653*, has lovely views and a library on comparative religions and the occult.

The actively inclined can take in the April **Ojai Tennis Tournament**, *tel: (805) 646-7241*, 1800 players competing in the USA's oldest same-site amateur tournament. There are several 2–4 mile (3–6 km) trails around town; for longer wilderness hikes, contact **Los Padres National Forest**, Ojai Ranger District, *1190 E. Ojai Ave, Ojai, CA 93023; tel: (805) 646-4348*.

OJAI TO BAKERSFIELD

The route continues north on Hwy 33, passing Matilija Reservoir on the left. Six miles (10 km) from Ojai is **Wheeler Hot Springs**, *16825 Maricopa Hwy, Ojai, CA 93023; tel: (800) 227-9292*, a Hollywood favourite since the 1920s, with natural hot and cold sulphur baths, a spa, skin treatments, live music on weekends, and a creekside restaurant. Pricey. Just up the road is **Wheeler Gorge Campground**, *tel: (800) 283-2267*.

Hwy 33 continues north, a serpentine, two-lane road, 25 miles (40 km) from 1500-ft (462 m) **Wheeler Springs** to **Pine Mountain Summit** at 5084 ft (1564 m). In winter, the area has snowfall, though the roads remain open – carry tyre chains. Six miles (9 km) beyond the summit is **Ozena Ranger Station**, at the junction with Lockwood Valley Rd.

Leaving Los Padres National Forest, the highway continues north for 20 miles (32 km), descending through **Cuyama Valley** past **Ventucopa** to the Hwy 166 junction. Drive east, then north, for 14 miles (22 km) on the Westside Hwy, Hwy 166/33, past Reyes Station, to **Maricopa**. 1½ miles (2.4 km) north is the site of **Lakeview Gusher No. 1**, *Petroleum Club Rd*, where in 1910, an oil well spewed crude oil at the rate of 100,000 barrels per day for 18 months.

From Maricopa, go east on Hwy 166 24 miles (38km) and cross over I-5, to **Mettler**. Take Hwy 99 north to **Bakersfield**.

BAKERSFIELD

Tourist Information: **Bakersfield Convention and Visitors Bureau**, *1033 Truxtun Ave, Bakersfield, CA 93301; tel: (805) 325-5051*. **Kern County Board of Trade**, *2101 Oak St, PO Bin 1312, Bakersfield, CA 93302; tel: (805) 861-2367*.

Accommodation

Most of the major chains are represented, at moderate prices. **Rio Bravo Tennis & Fitness Resort**, *11200 Lake Ming Rd, Bakersfield CA 93306; tel: (805) 872-5000*, has rooms along Lake Ming. Moderate.

Eating and Drinking

Chalet Basque, *200 Oak St, Bakersfield, CA 93304; tel: (805) 327-2915*, closed Sun–Mon, has the traditional, filling, multi-course meal typical of US Basque cuisine. Moderate. **Patrick's at the Ice House**, *3401 Chester Ave, # H, Bakersfield, CA 93301; tel: (805) 321-9584*, closed Sun, in an historic ice house building, serves continental meals. Moderate.

Sightseeing

Bakersfield is an agricultural and petroleum

centre at the southern end of the San Joaquin Valley. John Steinbeck's *The Grapes of Wrath* described the hard lives of migrants from the dusty, dried farms of the upper South (Oklahoma, Arkansas, Texas) during the Great Depression of the 1930s. Two-thirds of those migrant crop harvesters, pejoratively but historically called 'Okies', ended up in Kern County, the Central Valley area which includes Bakersfield. Those migrants brought music; today, Bakersfield is the country music capital of California.

In 1899, James and Jonathan Elwood struck oil only 13 ft (4 m) beneath the earth's surface, just north of Bakersfield. Oildale, centre of the Kern River Oil Field, became California's biggest petroleum-producing area for many years.

The **Kern County Museum**, *3801 Chester Ave, Bakersfield CA 93301; tel: (805) 861-2132,* open Mon–Fri 0800–1700, Sat 1000–1700, has an excellent Pioneer Village section, with 60 buildings from the years 1880–1930. Among them are a cook wagon, log cabin, shepherd's hut, a Mexican adobe, and a general store. The 1891 W.A. Howell House has a turret, stained glass windows, and speaking tubes for inter-storey communication. There's also a 74-ft (23 m) oil drilling derrick. Next door is the **Lori Brock Children's Museum**, *3803 Chester Ave, Bakersfield, CA 93301; tel: (805) 395-1201,* with interactive arts and science exhibits.

For the background on local migrant history during the Great Depression, visit the **Dust Bowl Room**, Kern County Library, *8304 Segrue Rd, Lamont, CA 93241; tel: (505) 845-3471,* about 5 miles (8 km) south-east of downtown Bakersfield. North-east of the town off Hwy 178 is the **California Living Museum**, *14000 Alfred Harrell Hwy, Bakersfield, CA 93306; tel: (805) 872-2256,* open Tues–Sun, with native California plants and a wildlife zoo.

BAKERSFIELD TO LONE PINE

Continue east on Hwy 178, past the **Mesa Marin Raceway**, *tel: (805) 366-5711,* home for NASCAR stock car and USAC midget car races. 1.5 miles (2.4 km) beyond on the left is the Alfred Harrell Hwy, with access to **Lake Ming**, *1110 Golden State Ave, Bakersfield, CA 93301; tel:*

(805) 861-2345, for sailing, boating and water skiing, as well as the **California Living Museum** and **Hart Park**, *tel: (805) 861-2345,* for boating and picnicking along the Kern River.

Hwy 178 enters Sequoia National Forest, climbing into the mountains. On the left, the **Kern River** froths beneath the Lower Kern Canyon's granite walls.

The Kern River, with its several forks, is the longest river in the state. Several sections are designated as a Wild and Scenic River. Rafting and kayaking is popular, but dangerous, on the Lower Kern River.

Hwy 178 crosses over the river, and follows the south shore of **Lake Isabella**, *tel: (619) 379-5646.* Lake Isabella Dam, completed in 1954, is 185 ft (57 m) high and the reservoir covers 14 square miles (36 sq. km). Windsurfing and boating are favourite activities for those not tackling the Class III–V rapids on the Kern River on the north side of the lake. For information and booking of the 800-place lakeside campsite, call **MISTIX**; *tel: (800) 283-2267.*

Staging area for **rafting** and **kayaking** trips is **Kernville**, 11 miles (18 km) north of this route via Hwy 155. Outfitters include: **Sierra South**, *11300 Kernville Rd, Kernville, CA 93238; tel: (619) 376-3745,* and **Mountain & River Adventures**, *11113 Kernville Rd, Kernville, CA 93238; tel: (619) 376-6553.* Accommodation and dining are available in town. For local history and a glimpse of 1940s films made in this scenic area visit, **Kern River Valley Historical Society Museum**, *tel: (619) 376-4628.*

Continue on Hwy 178 around the south side of Lake Isabella. The **South Fork Wildlife Area** and the Nature Conservancy's **Kern River Preserve** protect birds nesting among cottonwood and willow trees. With the Dome Land Wilderness to the north and the Scodie Mountains to the south, Hwy 178 continues for 33 miles (53 km), finally crossing the Sierra Nevada Mountains and the California Aqueduct to join Hwy 14 at Freeman Junction. Seven miles (11 km) north, Hwy 14 joins Hwy 395. Continue north on Hwy 395, past Olancha's sand dunes and the dry Owens Lake bed to **Lone Pine**, following the same route as Los Angeles–Death Valley (see p. 80).

SANTA BARBARA to SAN FRANCISCO COASTAL ROUTE

Highway 1, the scenic coast route between Southern and Northern California, is one of the most breathtaking and (in summer) crowded roads in the state. Allow at least two full days for the 367 miles (587 km) from Santa Barbara to San Francisco with an overnight near San Luis Obispo. Better still, allow three to four days, with stops in San Luis Obispo, San Simeon, and Santa Cruz–Monterey. San Luis Obispo and Santa Cruz have the best petrol prices. At San Luis Obispo you can switch to the alternative, inland, Santa Barbara–San Francisco route, El Camino Real (see p. 162), in either direction.

For the finest views, take Hwy 1 southbound: the ocean-side lane often seems to hang over empty space. Driving northbound is noticeably less thrilling, but more comfortable for vertigo sufferers.

ROUTE

Follow Hwy 1/101 north from Santa Barbara toward San Francisco. Hwy 1 turns toward **Lompoc** just beyond **Gaviota State Park**, 41 miles (66 km) north of Santa Barbara. The highway crosses the Santa Ynez Mountains before dropping into the **Lompoc Valley**.

Chumash Indians occupied the valley and nearby coastal areas long before the Spanish arrived to found **Mission La Purisima Concepcion** in 1787. Today, the area supports rich range land, fields, oil wells, and **Vandenburg Air Force Base**, the west coast headquarters for US military missile and space programmes. Five-hour base tours are usually available on the first Tuesday of every month, starting at 0845. For information and reservations, contact the Lompoc Valley Chamber of Commerce (see next page).

From Lompoc, Hwy 1 runs through the Purisima Hills and Vandenburg AFB to the **Santa Maria Valley**. The valley stretches 20 miles (32 km) from the chaparral-covered Sierra Madre Mountains to drifting sand dunes along the coast. The Chumash lived in mountain canyons among stands of oak and sycamore trees, not the dry, sandy valley. Early American settlers headed for the same canyons. Later settlers were stuck with valley land, which turned out to be fertile, easy to plough, and highly productive. Modern crops include alfalfa, grain, fruits, vegetables, and flowers.

Beyond **Guadalupe**, the road climbs an immense mesa, or flat-topped hill, covered with groves of gum trees and oil refineries, then descends sharply into the agricultural **Cienega Valley** and the beach cities of **Oceano, Grover City, Pismo Beach**, and **Shell Beach**. Several local and state parks provide coastal access.

Hwy 1 rejoins Hwy 101 at Pismo Beach. Continue north for 12 miles (19 km) to **San Luis Obispo** or, for a scenic detour, take the **Avila Beach** exit, 5 miles (8 km) north of Pismo Beach. The road follows San Luis Obispo Creek through lush oak forests and deep meadows. Return to Hwy 101 and turn north toward San Luis Obispo, 7 miles (11 km).

Follow Hwy 1 toward **Morro Bay**, 13 miles (21 km) north. The highway passes seven extinct volcanic cones amidst rolling farm and pasture land. The weather is noticeably cooler and foggier nearer the coast.

Past Morro Bay, the road gives views of **Estero Bay**. The broad crescent of sand stretches 6 miles (10 km) north to **Cayucos**. From Cayucos follow the road north 3 miles (5 km) to **Cambria**. Continue north past public beaches. Walking, hunting for semiprecious moonstones or jade, surfing, windsurfing, and fishing are better choices than swimming – the water is chilly and currents are dangerous.

Continue 5 miles (8 km) north to **Hearst Castle**. On the ocean side of the highway is a fine county park and fishing pier, open for day use only. **San Simeon** is a small settlement that was the administrative and warehouse centre for the grandiose hilltop castle above.

The 65 miles (104 km) of road from San Simeon to **Big Sur** runs between the sea and the Santa Lucia Range of mountains. From Big Sur to **Carmel** is a further 25 miles (40 km). Turn off Hwy 1 here to visit **Monterey, Pacific Grove** and the **Monterey Peninsula**.

Returning to Hwy 1 from the peninsula, follow the road another 3 miles (5 km) north to **Elkhorn Slough** and **Moss Landing**. The slough, 7 miles (11 km) long, is a sanctuary and research reserve. The meandering channels are home to tens of thousands of birds as well as seals, deer, foxes, otters, bobcats, and other animals. The only way to explore is by kayak or canoe:contact **Elkhorn Slough Foundation**, *1700 Elkhorn Rd, Watsonville, CA 95076; tel: (408) 728-2822.*

Moss Landing, first a produce port, then a whaling harbour, is now a commercial fishing and pleasure boat centre. Moss Landing Rd is lined with antique and second-hand shops. The PG&E steam power plant, built about 1948, is still among the largest in the world.

The coast north is filled with public beaches. Some are broad and easily accessible, others are accessible only by rough tracks twisting down small canyons. Cars parked beside the road usually indicate a favourite surfing or nude beach hidden below. Hwy 1 broadens to four lanes beyond Moss Landing and continues north to **Aptos, Soquel, Capitola**, and **Santa Cruz**.

Ano Nuevo State Reserve, *New Year's Creek Rd, Pescadero, CA 94060; tel: (415) 879-0595*, 20 miles (32 km) north of Santa Cruz, is a rare mainland breeding ground for the endangered northern elephant seal. It's the only place in the world where humans can leave their cars and walk among 2–3-ton (1.8–2.7-tonne) elephant seals in their natural habitat. Males arrive Nov–Dec and begin fighting for dominance. Females appear in January, give birth, and mate again before leaving a month or so later. A few seals remain all year. Winter access is by guided tour only.

HI-Pigeon Point Lighthouse Hostel, *Pigeon Point Rd, Pescadero, CA 94060; tel: (415) 879-*

0633, 6 miles (10 km) north of Ano Nuevo, is an 1872 lighthouse converted into an *AY* youth hostel. The high point (literally) is a hot tub perched on the rocky cliffs above surging surf, the perfect spot to enjoy spectacular sunsets– when the fog allows. AY's **HI-Point Montara Lighthouse Hostel**, *16th St at Hwy 1, Montara, CA 94037; tel: (415) 728-7177*, is 25 miles (40 km) north of Pigeon Point. In between are small beaches – estuary parks at **Pescadero** and **Pomponio**. Birding is best in winter.

The coastline beyond Pt Montara is lined with khaki-coloured bluffs, sandy beaches, and rocky reefs. **Pacifica**, 7 miles (11 km) north of Montara, is the self-proclaimed Fog Capital of California. Fishing is generally good from the Pacifica Pier. Hwy 1 climbs the spine of the San Mateo Peninsula just north of Pacifica, heading for Hwy 280, **Daly City** and **San Francisco**.

LOMPOC

Tourist Information: Lompoc Valley Chamber of Commerce, *111 South I St, Lompoc, CA 93436; tel: (805) 736-4567.*

Accommodation

Vandenburg Air Force Base helps keeps motels busy all year, including *ES* and *QI*. Advance bookings are always wise.

Sightseeing

More than 1000 acres (400 ha) of flower nursery fields blaze with changing colours during the blooming season, May–Sept. Growers produce over 200 types of seed, including asters, calendula, cornflowers, larkspur, lavender, lobelia, marigolds and sweet peas. **Civic Center Plaza**, *C St and Ocean Ave*, has a large, labelled display garden. The Chamber of Commerce publishes a free, self-guided driving map of flower fields.

La Purisima Mission State Historic Park, *2295 Purisima Rd, Lompoc, CA 93436; tel: (805) 733-3713*, is 3 miles (5 km) north-east of Lompoc, off Hwy 246. Mission La Purisima Concepcion de Maria Santisima, to use the original name, is the most authentically restored of the 21 California missions. The mission was

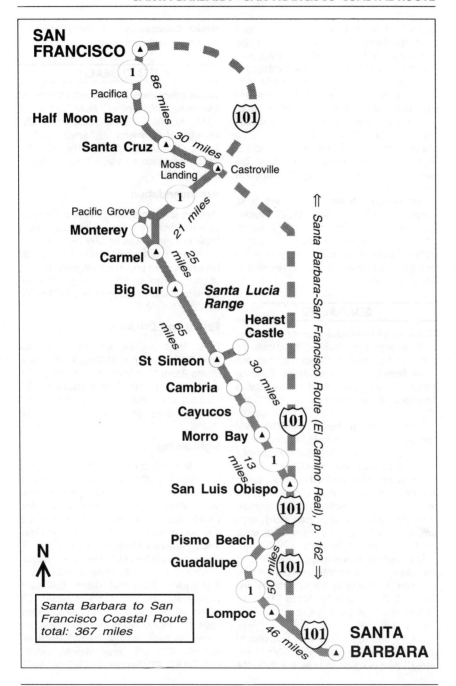

SAN FRANCISCO

Pacifica

86 miles

Half Moon Bay

Santa Cruz

30 miles

Moss Landing — Castroville

1

Pacific Grove

Monterey

21 miles

Carmel

25 miles

Big Sur

Santa Lucia Range

Hearst Castle

65 miles

St Simeon

Cambria

30 miles

Cayucos

Morro Bay

13 miles

1

San Luis Obispo

Pismo Beach

Guadalupe

50 miles

1

Lompoc

46 miles

SANTA BARBARA

⇐ Santa Barbara-San Francisco Route (El Camino Real), p. 162 ⇒

N
↑

Santa Barbara to San Francisco Coastal Route total: 367 miles closed in 1834 and the land sold to local ranchers. Union Oil Company bought the property in 1933, then gave the mission ruins and 900 acres (364 ha) to the state. Buildings and furnishings reflect the 1820s, the height of La Purisima's glory. The replanted kitchen and medicinal gardens reflect the cuisine (garlic, chilis, beans, maize, tomatoes and squash) and the medical care of the era. The mission farm is stocked with early 19th-century animals, including burros and four-horned 'churro' sheep. The park also has 12 miles (19 km) of walking and equestrian trails.

The **Lompoc Museum**, *200 South H St, Lompoc, CA 93436; tel: (805) 736-3888*, houses an extensive collection of Native American artifacts emphasising the Chumash. Another gallery documents Lompoc's history from the founding of La Purisima to the development of Vandenburg AFB.

GUADALUPE

Guadalupe is a time capsule. Turn-of-the-century brick buildings along Main St still display the names of the Mexican, Chinese, Basque, and Italian farmers who erected them. Towering monuments still crown the traditional **Italian Cemetery**, at the intersection of Hwys 1 and 166.

Santa Maria Barbecue is still a local speciality. In the last century, cattle ranchers staged spring round-ups to gather their half-wild stock and brand the new calves. Their traditional feast was beef grilled over red oak coals, served with bread, beans and salad. Local eateries still serve thick steaks seasoned with salt, pepper, and garlic, cooked over open coals, sliced paper-thin, and served with spicy beans. Salad, salsa, and bread round out the menu.

The **Nipomo Dunes** begin south-west of Guadalupe, a sea of sand 18 miles (29 km) long by 2 miles (3 km) wide, stretching north to Pismo Beach. Cecil B. DeMille filmed *The Ten Commandments* in the dunes near West Main St (Hwy 166).

For the best view of the wild, undeveloped coastline, park at the end of West Main St and walk 2½ miles (4 km) south to **Mussel Rock**. The

Nature Conservancy, *tel: (805) 545-9925*, conducts guided dune walks.

PISMO BEACH

Tourist Information: Pismo Beach Chamber of Commerce, *581 Dolliver, Pismo Beach, CA 93449; tel: (805) 773-4382*. Also **Grover City Chamber of Commerce**, *177 South Eighth St, Grover City, CA 93433; tel: (805) 489-9091*. Visitor information is available 24 hours a day on AM radio 530.

Accommodation

There are about four dozen choices in the beach cities area, from expensive bed and breakfasts to familiar chains, including *BW*, *HJ*, and *M6*. Chambers of Commerce provide lodging lists, but cannot make bookings. Campsites are open all year; advance bookings are required during the summer and holiday weekends. Call **MISTIX**, *tel: (800) 444-7275*.

Eating and Drinking

Pismo Beach has the greatest choice. The perennial favourite is **F. McLintock's Saloon & Dining Room**, *750 Mattie Rd; tel: (805) 773-1892*, moderate. **Sea Cliffs Restaurant**, *2757 Shell Beach Rd, Pismo Beach, CA 93449; tel: (805) 773-3555*, offers expensive continental choices.

Sightseeing

Pismo Beach is best known for the pismo clam, a tasty local bivalve that visitors once scooped from the broad beach by hand – newspaper accounts tell of 45,000 clams harvested in one day. Decades of overharvesting have cut the take to a maximum of ten per person per day. **Pismo True Value Hardware Store**, *tel: (805) 773-6245*, sells licences and hires out clamming equipment.

Most of the sand stretching south to Mussel Rock is part of **Pismo State Beach**, *3220 South Higuera St, Suite 311, San Luis Obispo, CA 93401; tel: (805) 549-3312*. It's one of the few areas in California where off-road vehicles are allowed to roam freely (inside two fenced-off sections). ATVs (All Terrain Vehicles) can be rented at **BJ's ATV Rentals**, *tel: (805) 481-5411,*

Pismo Dunes Sports, *tel: (805) 489-4288*, and **Sand Center**, *tel: (805) 489-6014*. ATVs cannot be driven outside specified areas.

Pismo also has a dune preserve, beach campgrounds, and trees filled with Monarch butterflies. The **Monarch Butterfly Grove** is just south of North Beach Campground, between Pismo Beach and Grover City; *tel: (805) 489-1869*. The butterflies hang in clusters from the branches of gum and Monterey pine trees Nov–March, part of a seasonal migration that takes them as far north as Canada and as far south as Central Mexico.

On cold days, the fragile insects clump together like shingles for warmth and protection from rain. On warm days, they search for flowers and nectar. When the weather cools, they return to cluster in the trees. In spring, the migration continues.

Pismo Beach also has a 1200-ft (396 m) pier, popular with fishermen. Passenger vehicles can drive onto the beach from entrance ramps at the foot of Grand Ave in Grover City and Pier Ave in Oceano. State park rangers collect an entrance fee and warn of high tides or other potential problems. Driving on wet, hard-packed sand is no problem, but stopping in soft, dry sand is a good way to get stuck.

AVILA BEACH

Tourist Information: San Luis Obispo County Visitors & Conference Bureau, *1041 Chorro St, San Luis Obispo, CA 93401; tel: (805) 541-8000*. The tiny town faces **San Luis Bay**, 1 mile (1.6 km) beyond Sycamore Hot Springs. **Front St** is five blocks of small restaurants, boutiques, and fishing supply shops. Fishermen flock to **Avila Pier** for red snapper, perch, halibut, and crabs. Sportfishing boats bring back salmon, halibut, albacore, and rockcod.

Port San Luis, *at the end of Avila Beach Dr.; tel: (805) 595-5400*, is home to more than 100 fishing boats, one of the largest commercial fleets in Central California. **Point San Luis Lighthouse**, *at the tip of Point San Luis beyond Port San Luis*, guided the ships that plied these rocky waters from 1890 to 1975. The lighthouse can be visited on guided hikes with the *Nature*

Conservancy, Box 15810, San Luis Obispo, CA 93406; tel: (805) 541-8735. The easy return walk is about 2½ miles (4 km). The lighthouse, nestled amidst windswept pines, overlooks kelp beds, sea otters, sea lions, the remains of a 19th-century whaling station, and in winter, migrating whales. Coach tours of **Diablo Canyon Nuclear Power Plant**; *tel: (805) 595-7647* are available with advance reservations. The 3-hr tour visits the plant's marine biology lab, intake/discharge structure, and control room simulator where technicians are trained.

Avila Hot Springs, *250 Avila Beach Dr., San Luis Obispo, CA 93405; tel: (805) 595-2359*, is just off the freeway. The spa was once a boozy stop for W.C. Fields, Charlie Chaplin, Clark Gable, and other Hollywood stars on their way to Hearst Castle (see p. 154). During Prohibition, 1919–1933, spirits were smuggled ashore at Avila Beach, divided up at the spa, and driven to Los Angeles and San Francisco along Hwy 101. Today, Avila is a sedate, moderately-priced family resort, RV park and picnic ground, complete with a hot outdoor mineral pool, private spa pools, and massage treatments.

Sycamore Mineral Springs, *1215 Avila Beach Dr., San Luis Obispo, CA 93405; tel: (805) 595-7365*, is just under 1 mile (1.6 km) beyond Avila Hot Springs. Sycamore is an expensive, full-service spa with private rooms built into a shaded hillside. Each room has a spa on a private deck or balcony. Day guests use outdoor hot tubs secreted around the hillside. Sycamore also has one of the area's best restaurants, **The Gardens of Avila**; *tel: (805) 595-7365*, serving moderate–expensive California cuisine.

SAN LUIS OBISPO

Tourist Information: San Luis Obispo Chamber of Commerce, *1039 Chorro St, San Luis Obispo, CA 93401; tel: (805) 781-2777*.

Arriving

Most visitors arrive by car, but **AMTRAK**, *tel: (805) 541-5028 or (800) 872-7245* offers daily northbound and southbound rail services.

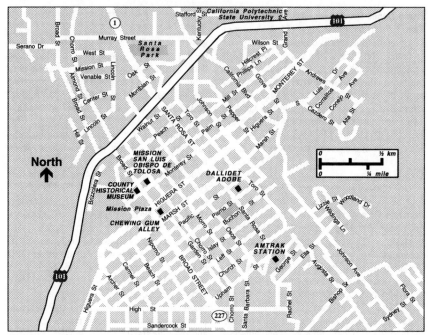

Accommodation

San Luis is the traditional stopping point between Southern and Northern California. It has *BW, ES, HJ, TL,* and *VI,* as well as fine bed and breakfasts and independent motels. The Chamber of Commerce has lodging lists, but cannot make bookings.

The florid pink and white building at the south end of town is the moderate–expensive **Madonna Inn**, *100 Madonna Rd, San Luis Obispo, CA 93405; tel: (805) 543-3000 or (800) 543-9666*. The inn was created by local construction magnate Alex Madonna and decorated by his wife Phyllis. The Jungle Rock Room, for example, has zebra-striped beds, rock walls and a shower made of rocks weighing up to 200 tons (182 tonnes). Cave Man, Safari, Love Nest, Fabulous 50s, and other rooms are equally unusual.

Eating and Drinking

A thriving university community gives SLO more than its share of good eating and drinking spots. Best bet is the **Farmers Market**, *600–900 blocks of Higuera St*, 1830–2100 every Thursday. Local growers sell fresh fruit and produce while local restaurants hawk everything from traditional hot dogs to sandwiches, barbecue, burritos, biscuits, ice cream, and candies. Buskers provide plenty of planned (and spontaneous) entertainment and most Higuera St merchants stay open late. Parking is free on side streets or in nearby shopping malls. Municipal car parks at Palm and Morro Sts, and Marsh and Chorro Sts are nearly as convenient.

Popolo, *1255 Monterey St; tel: (805) 543-9543*, offers cheap seasonal sandwiches and salads with an Italian accent. **Café Roma**, *1819 Osos St; tel: (805) 541-6800*, has excellent, but pricey, Northern Italian food in the historic **Park Hotel** near the restored Spanish-style railroad station. The **SLO Brewing Co.**, *1119 Garden St; tel: (805) 543-1843*, offers gigantic sandwiches and sausages to match at least four beers brewed on the ground floor. The budget eatery is a favourite with students as well as downtown professionals. **SLO Maid Ice Cream and Deli**, *728 Higuera St; tel: (805) 541-3117*, has budget and sinfully enticing desserts and sandwiches.

Sightseeing

The town is usually called San Luis (pronounced 'lou-is', not 'lou-ee') and abbreviated SLO, as in 'slow', the preferred pace of life in this university and farming town. Winter rains turn oak-dotted hills surrounding SLO a vibrant green. The colours turn tawny in summer, but morning and afternoon breezes keep temperatures comfortable.

San Luis was founded in 1772 as the fifth California mission. The town remained an isolated farming community until the railroad arrived in 1894. Residents, a mix of farmers, academics, craftspersons and small business owners, have staunchly resisted most trappings of urban life. The town centre still has tree-lined streets and commercial buildings that seldom top four floors. The Chamber of Commerce **Heritage Walks** brochure outlines four walks in different historic districts. Attractions range from the mission to Chinese stores, one of the best collections of Art Deco commercial buildings in California, and neat clapboard houses from the early 20th century. The **SLO Trolley** runs a circular route seven days a week serving nearly all of the major tourist attractions.

One major attraction not on the official map is **Chewing Gum Alley**, *Higuera St to Marsh St between Garden and Broad Sts.* Brick walls are covered with names, graffiti, and freeform designs, all executed in well-used chewing gum. No one seems to know why this particular alley has been singled out for oral appliqué, but it's a piece of living art that changes slightly almost every night.

Mission San Luis Obispo de Tolosa, *Chorro and Monterey Sts; tel: (805) 543-6850,* remains the heart of SLO. The mission became a courthouse and jail after Mexican independence, but was returned to the Roman Catholic Church when California was annexed by the United States in 1848. It was restored to something approaching its original appearance in the 1930s, complete with whitewashed walls, red tile roof, and wooden benches.

Opposite the mission is **Murray Adobe**, its shady courtyard a popular public sitting area. Just downhill is **Mission Plaza**, a wide, shaded park joining the mission and the business district. San Luis Obispo Creek winds through the plaza, which is a popular lunch spot. Live music from nearby restaurants wafts through the trees, providing free concerts most of the year.

The **San Luis Obispo County Historical Museum**, *696 Monterey St (opposite the mission); tel: (805) 543-0638,* has an eclectic collection of regional memorabilia from Native American artifacts to the mid-20th century. The museum is housed in the sandstone and granite Carnegie Library Building, built in 1904.

About half of SLO's population attends **California Polytechnic State University**, *2 miles (3 km) north of the city centre; tel: (805) 756-1111,* usually called Cal Poly, which emphasises agriculture, architecture, business, and engineering. For visual and performing arts presentations, *tel: (805) 756-1421;* for other activities, *tel: (805) 756-2476.* Campus highlights include **Poly Canyon**, an outdoor laboratory for experimental architecture and construction techniques, and the **Botanic Garden and horticulture greenhouses**. For student-led tours, *tel: (805) 756-2792.*

MORRO BAY

Tourist Information: Morro Bay Chamber of Commerce, *895 Napa St, Suite A-1, Morro Bay, CA 93442; tel: (805) 772-4467.*

Accommodation

There are 40-some choices in Morro Bay, including *BW*. Rooms are tight during the summer and holiday weekends.

Eating and Drinking

Morro Bay's large commercial fishing fleet docks behind restaurants along The Embarcadero – order fresh fish. One of the best choices is the **Great American Fish Company**, *1185 Embarcadero, Morro Bay, CA 93442; tel: (805) 772-4407,* moderate.

Sightseeing

Originally a shipping port for coastal farmers, Morro Bay is now a fishing port and a holiday destination for beachcombers, birdwatchers, fishermen, walkers, and shoppers. Morro Rock, which dominates the Bay and town, is the last volcanic cone between SLO and the sea.

Morro Bay, the beaches to the north, and the estuary to the south, are a **bird sanctuary** and a must-see for birdwatchers. The focal point is **Morro Rock**, 578 ft (191 m) tall. After four centuries of mining for construction, The Rock is a shadow of its former self, but still covers about 50 acres (20 ha) at the base. Follow the Embarcadero north beyond the PG&E power-plant and swing left onto **Coleman Dr.**, the causeway to The Rock. The beach to the north is popular for walking, fishing, and surfing. The harbour side of the causeway is a pleasant spot to watch the harbour. Morro Rock itself is a wildlife refuge, protecting endangered peregrine falcons nesting on the upper slopes.

The Embarcadero is the main tourist area as well as the fishing centre. The commercial fishing fleet docks near the north end; a string of art galleries, speciality shops and restaurants stretches south. Bay cruises, sport fishing, and whale-watching trips leave from the Embarcadero. The **Friday Night Market**, 1800–2030, *at the North T-pier*, features fresh fish, oysters, and crabs from the boats, handicrafts, fresh fruit and produce, and entertainment. The **Morro Bay Aquarium**, *595 Embarcadero; tel: (805) 772-7647*, has more than 300 live specimens. The aquarium also houses the **Morro Bay Marine Rehabilitation Center**, where injured marine mammals are nursed back to health.

Bay Taxi, *1215 Embarcadero; tel: (805) 772-1222*, provides water taxi service to the sand spit separating Morro Bay from the Pacific Ocean. The 4-mile (6 km) strip of sand is popular for birdwatching, clamming, picnicking, walking and surf fishing. **Tiger's Folly II**, *1205 Embarcadero; tel: (805) 772-2257*, provides 1-hr narrated tours of the bay and estuary.

The south end of the Embarcadero, near the **Morro Bay Estuary**, is a large park with picnic and playground facilities as well as quiet spots to watch birds, passing boats, and the sun setting beyond the sandspit. At 2300 acres (931 ha), the estuary is one of the largest unspoilt coastal marshes in California and a major stop on the Pacific Migratory Bird Flyway. Permanent resi-

dents include great blue herons, which nest in gum groves at the water's edge. Hire a canoe at the **Morro Bay State Park Marina**, *tel: (805) 772-8796*, for the best views.

Morro Bay State Park, *Morro Bay, CA 93442; tel: (805) 772-7434*, covers 1965 acres (795 ha) of rolling hillside behind the estuary. Camping and picnicking areas adjoin a picturesque 18-hole public golf course. The **Museum of Natural History**, *Morro Bay State Park, Morro Bay, CA 93442; tel: (805) 772-2694*, overlooks the bay from a high rocky outcropping. Exhibits cover the geology, geography, and human history of the Central Coast. To reach the park, follow Main St south from Morro Bay to the museum.

To explore the other side of the estuary, follow Main St to State Park Rd. Turn right to South Bay Blvd. and right again onto Santa Ysabel Ave and Baywood Park.

Baywood Park, Cuesta-by-the Sea and **Los Osos** are called the **South Bay** because no one, including residents and real estate agents, knows where one community ends and the next begins. The California grizzly bears after which Los Osos was named disappeared decades ago, but the fight is on to save **El Molino Elfin Forest**, 90 acres (36 ha) of moss-covered pygmy oaks in Baywood Park. **Los Osos Oaks**, *south side of Los Osos Valley Rd, 5 miles (8 km) east of South Bay Blvd.*, offers a ½-mile (0.8 km) self-guided trail through similarly stunted oaks. The leafy trail wanders among drooping branches, mushrooms, wild cucumbers, and other plants that flourish in heavy shade – including poison oak. **Sweet Springs**, *north side of Ramona Ave, ½ mile (0.8 km) west of 4th St*, begins in a grove of gum trees favoured by wintering Monarch butterflies, then continues through marshland to the shore of Morro Bay. It's an excellent spot to watch for butterflies and shore birds.

From Sweet Springs, take Pine Ave south to Los Osos Rd. Turn right (west). Follow Los Osos to the end, where it becomes Pecho Valley Rd. Continue 4 miles (6 km) to the white frame headquarters of **Montana de Oro State Park**, *tel: (805) 528-0513*. The name means 'mountain of gold' in Spanish, but the 8000-acre (3238 ha) park was named for the mounds of California poppies, wild mustard, and other wildflowers that carpet the coastal hillsides every spring. The park offers camping and more than 50 miles (80 km) of walking trails. One of the most popular walks is **Hazard Canyon**, ½ mile (0.8 km) from gum forests along Pecho Valley Rd to tidepools along the rocky beach. **Bluff Trail** follows the edge of the twisted cliffs with Morro Rock in the distance. Several paths lead down to tidepools hidden in secluded coves.

Take South Bay Blvd north to Hwy 1 and continue north back through Morro Bay.

CAYUCOS

Tourist Information: Cayucos Chamber of Commerce, *80 North Ocean Ave, Cayucos, CA 93430; tel: (805) 995-1200.*

There isn't much in Cayucos beyond a few dozen houses dusted with blowing sand, a 400-ft (132 m) fishing pier, and a broad beach that is usually empty. Several small budget motels are clustered along the south end of Ocean Ave. The north end of Ocean Ave, near the pier, is lined with restored buildings from earlier in the century. Look for small cafés, antique stores, boutiques, and fishing shops.

Hwy 1 turns inland just beyond Cayucos through open, rolling dairy pastures to **Harmony**, 8 miles (13 km) north. Once a thriving dairy town, Harmony has been reborn as an arts and crafts centre, with a claimed population of 18 – just about what it was when the Harmony Valley Cooperative Dairy was founded in 1907. Restored dairy buildings shelter glass blowers, sculptors, potters, clothing designers, a winery, restaurants, and a wedding chapel.

CAMBRIA

Tourist Information: Cambria Chamber of Commerce, *767 Main St, Cambria, CA 93428; tel: (805) 927-3624.*

Accommodation

Cambria is the main tourist centre for Hearst Castle, 30 miles (48 km) north. *BW* is the only chain. Rooms are scarce during the summer and

over holiday weekends. **Bed and Breakfast Homestay**, *PO Box 326; tel: (805) 927-4613*, books area bed and breakfasts.

Eating and Drinking

The best value is **The Hamlet Restaurant at Moonstone Gardens**, *across from Moonstone Beach, 3 miles (5 km) north; tel: (805) 927-3535.* The combination restaurant, cactus garden and nursery offers tasty budget lunches and moderate dinners indoors or out, depending on the weather.

Sightseeing

This bustling tourist and retirement village is surrounded by rugged beaches that are favourites with beachcombers and fishermen. The original town centre, now called **East Village**, is about 1 mile (1.6 km) east of Hwy 1 in a narrow, tree-lined valley. The newer section, **West Village**, is next to Hwy 1 a short drive north. Most businesses are located along **Main St**, which connects the two sections.

East Village has most of the prosaic establishments such as banks, petrol stations, and a post office. Several gift, speciality and art outlets are located on Burton Dr., near the intersection with Main St and the town's only stop sign. In West Village, Main St is lined with restaurants, galleries and antique shops. One of the best-known establishments is the **Toy Soldier Factory**, *789 Main St; tel: (805) 927-3804*, filled with detailed miniature soldiers and thousands of other painted pewter figures.

SAN SIMEON ACRES

Tourist Information: San Simeon Chamber of Commerce; *9255 Hearst Dr, San Simeon, CA 93452; tel: (805) 927-3500.*

The tiny town is closer to Hearst Castle and prices are higher. **San Simeon State Beach**; *tel: (805) 927-4509*, has camping. There is usually space in winter, but advance bookings through MISTIX; *tel: (800) 444-7275*, are needed for summer and holiday weekends.

The best choice is **El Chorlito**, *9155 Hearst Dr, tel: (805) 927-3872*, serving tasty Mexican dishes.

HEARST CASTLE

Tourist Information: Hearst-San Simeon State Historical Monument, *750 Hearst Castle Rd, San Simeon, CA 93452; tel: (805) 927-2020.* Advance tour bookings are vital spring–autumn, weekends and holidays. Call **MISTIX**, *tel: 800-444-4445.* Walk-in space is usually available mid-week, mid-Nov–mid-Mar.

The official name for Hearst Castle was La Cuesta Encantada, The Enchanted Hill. Built by newspaper baron William Randolph Hearst between 1919 and 1947, the 144-room Spanish Renaissance palace was the model for Xanadu in Orson Welles' 1941 film *Citizen Kane*. Welles' cinematic portrait was accurate, including the portrayal of Marion Davies, Hearst's mistress, who was *de facto* Queen of Hearst Castle.

Hearst, the only child of mining and political powerhouse George Hearst, turned the money-losing *San Francisco Examiner* into a chain of opinionated, publicity-mongering and fabulously profitable newspapers.

After World War I, America's most influential man decided to build America's most impressive home. Hearst hired Julia Morgan, the first female engineering graduate of the University of California, Berkeley, and the Ecole des Beaux-Arts in Paris.

She gave Hearst exactly what he wanted, whether it was a cathedral facade for *La Casa Grande*, the main house, a dining room hung with Sienese silk banners and lined with medieval choir stalls, or bedrooms built around ceilings pulled from European monasteries. Every room and hallway was (and still is) filled with priceless works of art that most museums couldn't afford to buy – Hearst could, and did. After Hearst died, the family gave the castle to the State.

Hearst provided non-stop parties for the entertainment and political elite. The guest list included Charlie Chaplin, President Calvin Coolidge, Winston Churchill, Greta Garbo, Clark Gable, Charles Lindbergh, Louis B. Mayer, Laurence Olivier, George Bernard Shaw, Shirley Temple, and hundreds more. It was, quipped regular visitor Cary Grant, 'a great place to spend the Depression.'

It's also a great place to spend a couple of hours or a couple of days. There are four escorted tours of the castle, each about two hours of climbing staircases and walking long corridors. Don't cram all four tours into one day. After the first few hours, one Baroque tapestry or Gothic statue starts looking like any other.

Tour One is a good first-time look at the ground floor of the main house, the cinema ('home movies' with Hollywood's most famous stars in mufti), a guesthouse, the Greco-Roman outdoor pool, and the Art Deco indoor pool.

Tour Two covers the upper levels of the main house, including Hearst's private Gothic suite, family living quarters, libraries, and kitchens.

Tour Three covers another guesthouse and the 'new wing' of 36 lavish bedrooms.

Tour Four includes the spectacular gardens (the topsoil was trucked up to what was a barren, treeless knob of stone), a hidden terrace, the wine cellar, guesthouse, and pools, but is offered only April–Oct.

Tours leave from the **Visitor Center** at the foot of the hill. Even if tours are fully booked, the centre is worth a stop for the art conservation workshops and an excellent exhibit on Hearst and his castle.

BIG SUR

Tourist Information: Big Sur Chamber of Commerce, *PO Box 87, Big Sur, CA 93920; tel: (408) 667-2111.* Headquarters for the four area state parks is at **Pfeiffer-Big Sur State Park**, *Big Sur, CA 93920; tel: (408) 667-2315.* The mailing address for individual businesses is *Big Sur, CA 93920.*

Accommodation

Campsites are the only budget lodging in Big Sur, but they fill up early on weekends and during the summer. Book state parks and **Plaskett Creek** (US Forest Service) through **MISTIX** *tel: 800-444-7275.* Private campsites are situated at **Limekiln Creek**, *tel: (408) 667-2403,* **Ventana**; *tel: (408) 667-2331,* **Riverside**; *tel: (408) 667-2414,* and **Big Sur**; *tel: (408) 667-2322.*

Big Sur's few hotels are moderate–pricey, with the emphasis on the high end. **Deetjens Big Sur Inn**, *tel: (408) 667-2378,* is a rambling, relaxed inn 61 miles (98 km) north of Hearst Castle. The **Ventana Inn**, *tel: 408-667-2331*, 4 miles (6 km) north, is a modern, rough-hewn resort on the inland side of Hwy 1. The spectacular rooms are pricey, but restaurant views are equally good and far more affordable. The **Post Ranch Inn**; *tel: (408) 667-2200*, is out of sight across the road from Ventana. Modernistic rooms with similar views and prices.

Eating and Drinking

The best values are in and around **Big Sur Valley**. **Deetjens** is famous for filling breakfasts. **Ventana Inn** and **Post Ranch Inn** have great but pricey meals. **Nepenthe**, *1 mile (1.6 km) south of Ventana-Post Ranch; tel: (408) 667-2345*, is a multi-level arts and food centre with better views than food.

Sightseeing

Big Sur begins somewhere near **Piedros Blancos Lighthouse** (closed to the public) and the increasingly wild cliffs north of San Simeon, then quietly fades away near Point Lobos Reserve, south of Carmel. It's the wildest, twistiest, and most scenic stretch of Hwy 1, but lay-bys are rare – the early 20th-century convicts who carved the road into sheer cliffs high above the crashing surf took little interest in scenic views. Food, petrol, and lodging are expensive, but parks and public beaches invite camping, picnics, and lonely walks.

Hwy 1 is seldom lonely, especially in summer. The two-lane road is crowded with RVs and city-trained drivers traumatised by the tight turns and switchbacks. If you can make the drive from Nov–April, traffic is lighter. In summer, allow *at least* 4 hrs for the 98 miles (157 km) from Hearst Castle to Monterey.

Nature is the biggest draw in Big Sur, presenting an ever-changing panorama of mountains and ocean. Hwy 1 is the only highway, but there are numerous walking trails into the mountains and down to the ocean. Annual winter landslides can block trails and Hwy 1 for months at a time.

Big Sur Valley, 66 miles (106 km) north of Hearst Castle, is as close as the area comes to urban blight, but there are no flashy boutiques,

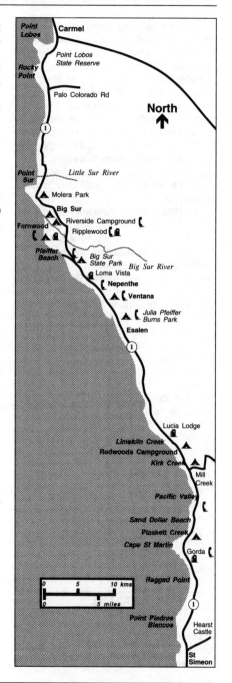

Big Sur

no shopping malls, no cinemas, not even any traffic signals. The 6-mile (10 km) stretch includes most of Big Sur's famous inns and restaurants as well as the tiny town of **Big Sur**.

Esalen Institute, *50 miles (80 km) north of Hearst Castle; tel: (408) 667-3000* is the Ferrari of New Age Retreats; an introductory weekend starts around $300. Outsiders are welcome to sample the retreat's famed outdoor hot tubs, 0100–0300 every morning. Eight miles (13 km) north is **Julia Pfeiffer Burns State Park**, a small, quiet park with picnic tables and a pleasant walk down to **McWay Cove**, a good place to watch for sea otters.

The **Henry Miller Memorial Library**, *tel: (408) 667-2574*, 3 miles (5 km) north of the park, is a collection of clutter about the writer/artist. **Nepenthe** and **Ventana-Post Hill** are just north. **Pfeiffer Big Sur State Park** is 2 miles (3 km) beyond the inns, with the **Big Sur Lodge**, area information, and the largest campsite in the area. **Point Sur State Historic Park**, *tel: (408) 625-4419*, the 19th-century lighthouse that warned ships away from the rocky coast, tops Point Sur, 8 miles (13 km) north of Pfeiffer Big Sur. Guided tours must be booked in advance.

Big Sur trails off into expensive homes on the outskirts of Carmel, about 15 miles (24km) north of Pt. Sur. **Point Lobos State Reserve**, *Rte. 1, Box 62, Carmel, CA 93923; tel: (408) 624-4909*, displays what the houses have hidden, 6 miles (10 km) of aquamarine coves, reddish cliffs, endless tidepools, stands of stately Monterey cypress trees, and open, rolling meadows bursting with spring wildflowers. The reserve opens onto the **Monterey Bay National Marine Sanctuary**, which extends south beyond Big Sur. Inshore waters are open to scuba diving by permit. The reserve is criss-crossed by walking trails, but the number of people in the park is limited. In summer, arrive early or wait in long queues on Hwy 1.

CARMEL

Tourist Information: Carmel Valley Chamber of Commerce, *PO Box 288, Carmel Valley, CA 93924; tel: (408) 659-4000*. The **Tourist Information Center** is at *Ocean and Mission Sts.*

Accommodation

Carmel has dozens of motels, hotels, inns, and bed and breakfasts. BW is the only chain. Lodging is more reasonable in Monterey, 8 miles (13 km) north.

La Playa Hotel, *PO Box 900, Carmel, CA 93924; tel: (408) 624-6476*, has lush gardens, large cottages, and a memorable restaurant. **Highlands Inn**, *PO Box 1700, Carmel, CA 93921; tel: (408) 624-3801*, just south of Point Lobos, is classic luxury with stunning ocean views. The **Tickle Pink Inn**, *155 Highland Dr, Carmel, CA 93923; tel: (408) 624-1244*, has equally stunning views at slightly lower prices. All three are pricey.

Eating and Drinking

The **California Market**, *Highlands Inn; tel: (408) 624-3801*, is as fabulous (and as moderate) as the Inn is expensive. **Hog's Breath Inn**, *San Carlos, between 5th and 6th Sts; tel: (408) 625-1044*, moderate, owned by former Carmel mayor Clint Eastwood, is a must-see for the presiding hog heads. Carmel is rife with 'cuisine'; ask for the hottest new restaurants.

Sightseeing

There are three Carmels: **Carmel-by-the-Sea**, the seaside village that most people know as Carmel; **Carmel Valley**, 10 miles (16 km) inland; and **Carmel Highlands**, just south of Pt Lobos. Carmel began as a mission and artists' colony; high priced shopping and golf are the biggest modern attractions.

Mission San Carlos Borromeo del Rio Carmelo, *3080 Rio Rd; tel: (408) 624-3600*, was California's second mission, founded in Monterey in 1770 and moved to Carmel a year later to distance Native American mission women from Presidio soldiers. Mission founder Junipero Serra is buried at the foot of the altar. The baroque stone church was completed in 1794 and abandoned after secularisation. Most of the existing buildings and gardens were rebuilt in the 1930s, but the reconstruction conveys a sense of ancient peace and tranquillity. The silver altar furnishings, Spanish vestments, and Native artifacts in the mission museum are all originals. Serra's starkly simple priest's cell is reproduced from period paintings and illustrations. Self-guided tours are free, but donations are appreciated. The church, now a basilica, is not open for tours during mass.

Carmel Beach City Park is an alluring crescent of sand the colour of white flour against aquamarine Carmel Bay, but the water is too cold and the undertow too fierce for swimming. **Carmel River State Beach**, just south of town, is less crowded, but high surf can be dangerous. The nearby marsh and bird sanctuary is home to hawks, kingfishers, cormorants, herons, pelicans, sandpipers, snowy egrets, and migrating flocks of ducks and geese.

In summer and most warm-weather weekends Carmel-bound traffic backs up on Hwy 1. The town centre, **Ocean Ave** and its side streets, is filled with antique, art, and knicknack shops interspersed with t-shirt emporia, restaurants, ice cream parlours, and hordes of people. All that's lacking is adequate parking, street signs, street addresses, street lights, and traffic signals.

The rest of Carmel deserves more attention. The area between 5th and 8th Sts and Junipero and the city beach is packed with unique shingled cottages, 'dolls' houses' loaded with gingerbread, and fake adobe homes. The most imposing buiding is the medieval-looking **Tor House**, *26304 Ocean View Ave, Carmel, CA 93921; tel: (408) 624-1813.* Poet Robinson Jeffers hauled the golden granite boulders for his three-storey home from the beach below with horse teams. The family still live in the house; access is by guided tours on Fridays and Saturdays.

Take Ocean Ave west. Just before the city park, turn right onto the **17-Mile Drive**. Security guards collect a fee at the entry gate. The drive (actually less than 17 miles long) is privately owned. Del Monte Corporation, of tinned food fame, was the original owner, turning a forest and a barren expanse of dunes into one of the

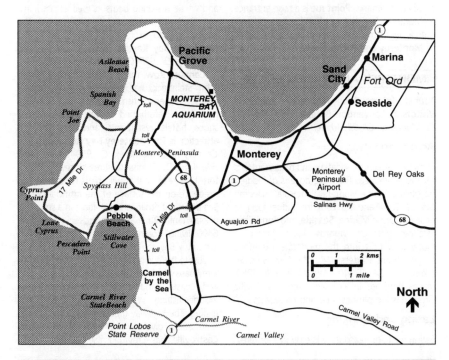

Carmel–Monterey Peninsula Map

most exclusive housing, golfing, and resort estates in the world. The road passes the **Pebble Beach Golf Links, Cypress Point Club, Spyglass Hill Golf Course**, and **The Links at Spanish Bay**, as well as innumerable multi-million dollar mansions half-glimpsed behind dense stands of cypress and tall walls. Most courses are open for public play with advance bookings: contact **The Pebble Beach Co**, *PO Box 567, Pebble Beach, CA 93953; tel: (408) 649-2789*. Two pricey hotels, **The Lodge at Pebble Beach** and the **Inn at Spanish Bay**, *tel: 800-654-9300*, have impressive restaurants as well as luxury accommodation. A bagpiper pipes the sun down each day at Spanish Bay.

But the best reason to pay for driving to Monterey instead of taking Hwy 1 for free is the coast, lined with golden boulders and cypress trees and alive with birds, seals, and sea otters. **Stillwater Cove** is an undisturbed haven for scuba divers. **The Lone Cypress**, clinging to a seemingly bare rock (and largely supported by guy wires) is one of California's most photographed landmarks. **Point Joe** is a false entrance to Monterey Bay that has lured scores of ships onto a jagged reef. The Drive exits into the towns of **Monterey** and **Pacific Grove**.

MONTEREY AND PACIFIC GROVE

Tourist Information: Monterey Peninsula Visitors & Convention Bureau, *380 Alvarado St, Monterey, CA 93940; tel: (408) 648-5354*.

Accommodation

The VCB has accommodation and restaurant lists for the entire area. There are dozens of lodging possibilities on the Monterey Peninsula, including *BW, CI, DI, HI*, and *M6*. Look for budget lodging near Fort Ord in **Marina**, **Seaside**, and **Sand City**. Establishments on **Munras Ave**, Monterey's motel row, drift into the moderate–expensive range. **Room Finders**, *140 West Franklin St, Monterey, CA 93940; tel: (408) 646-9250*, makes bookings in all price categories. Pacific Grove has the plushest bed and breakfasts.

Eating and Drinking

Eating well and reasonably is easy in Monterey.

Happy Hour, 1600–1900, brings half-priced drinks and free food. Many restaurants offer bargain-priced 'early bird specials' for dinner before 1900.

The Poppy, *444 Alvarado St; tel: (408) 646-1021*, is a budget breakfast and lunch house that was the model for the Golden Poppy Café in John Steinbeck's *Sweet Thursday*. On Fisherman's Wharf, **Rappa's**, *at the end of the pier; tel: (408) 372-7562*, is a solid seafood choice with great early bird specials. On Cannery Row, **Beau Thai**, *807 Cannery Row; tel: (408) 373-8811*, is a local favourite for budget Thai food.

Sightseeing

Monterey was the capital of California under Spanish, Mexican, and American flags. Today, it's a busy tourist town. **Monterey State Historic Park**, *20 Custom House Plaza, Monterey, CA 93940; tel: (408) 649-7118*, offers a self-guided walking tour of three dozen historic buildings dating back to 1794. Allow half a day. **Fisherman's Wharf** is home to charter fishing and whale-watching boats as well as sea lions. Sea otters also play around the pier and bay. The easiest way to explore the bay is by kayak, **Monterey Bay Kayaks**, *693 Del Monte Ave, Monterey, CA 93940; tel: (408) 373-5357*.

Cannery Row, made famous by local writer John Steinbeck, has been reborn to process tourists instead of fish. Decrepit fish canneries have been refurbished or replaced to house shops, hotels, restaurants, and bars. The top attraction is **The Monterey Bay Aquarium**, *886 Cannery Row, Monterey, CA 93940; tel: (408) 648-4888*. Don't miss the three-storey giant kelp forest, so realistic that wild birds have taken up residence on the surface of the artificial ocean. Sea otters eat, frolic, and eat again in a split level display tank. Other exhibits include more than 6400 living ocean creatures, most native to Monterey Bay.

Just to the north of Monterey are **Fort Ord**, an army base which is in the process of closing, and vast coastal sand dunes. Favourite activities include fishing, walking, surfing, and hang-gliding. The highway gradually turns inland and sand dunes give way to fields of artichokes. **Castroville** has crowned itself the artichoke

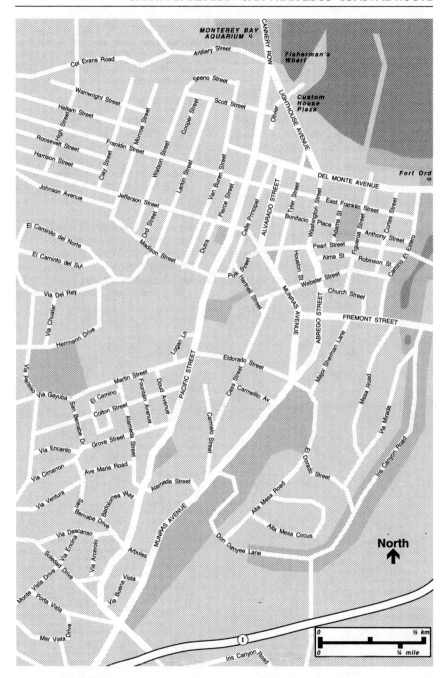

North

capital of the world and roadside stands sell fresh produce in season.

SANTA CRUZ

Tourist Information: Santa Cruz County Conference and Visitors Council, *701 Front St, Santa Cruz, CA 95060; tel: (408) 425-1234*; and **Santa Cruz Beach Boardwalk**, *400 Beach St, Santa Cruz, CA 95060; tel: (408) 423-5590.*

Accommodation

The Santa Cruz area is well-supplied with accommodation, including *AY, BW, CI, HI, TL,* and numerous bed and breakfasts.

Eating and Drinking

As a university town, Santa Cruz is filled with reasonably priced food and entertainment. **The Boardwalk** has the largest concentration of restaurants in the area. **India Joze**, *1001 Center St; tel: (408) 427-3554*, is a local institution with

great pastries as well as budget Asian dishes. **Santa Cruz Brewing Co. and Front Street Pub**, *516 Front St; tel: (408) 429-8838*, and **Seabright Brewery**, *519 Seabright Ave; tel: (408) 426-2739*, serve popular beers and budget food.

Sightseeing

Holidaymakers started going to Santa Cruz during the 1890s and never really stopped. A University of California campus added an ivory tower element, followed by back-to-the-land refugees from San Francisco and Silicon Valley electronics wizards. The combination keeps local politics in a ferment, while massage parlours do a booming business.

Don't miss **The Boardwalk**, *south of the Municipal Wharf*. The 1924 **Giant Dipper** roller coaster is usually rated among the country's top ten. The lovingly restored 1911 **Charles Looff Carousel** has handcarved horses, chariots, and a 19th-century pipe organ. Coaster and carousel are National Historic Landmarks. New rides

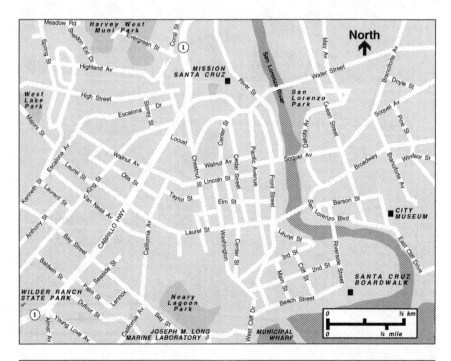

induce more terror, while the **Cocoanut Grove** ballroom still swings to 1930s and 1940s dance tunes. The CVC *Walking Tour of the Historical Santa Cruz Boardwalk* brochure is a handy guide to the boardwalk then and now. The boardwalk is open daily Memorial Day–Labor Day, weekends and holidays the rest of the year.

Just in front of the Boardwalk is **Santa Cruz Beach**, with sugary white sand and towel-to-towel bodies during the summer and spring school break. There is more room eastward, near the mouth of the San Lorenzo River and beyond, below East Cliff Dr. The **Santa Cruz Surfing Museum**, *in the lighthouse on West Cliff Dr, northwest of town; tel: (408) 429-3429*, overlooks prime surfing territory. Exhibits go back to the 1930s and 15-ft (5 m) redwood boards weighing 100 lb (45 kg).

Enough of historic Santa Cruz was demolished by the 1989 Loma Prieta earthquake to shake the city from the National Register of Historic Places. Enough remains to make a comfortable walking tour by following the CVC *Historic Santa Cruz Walking Tours and Museum Guide*. The **Santa Cruz Mission Adobe**, *off Mission Plaza; tel: (408) 425-5849*, is one of the county's few original adobes, now a California museum, circa 1840. All that remains of **Mission de Exaltacion de la Santa Cruz**, *126 High St*, is memories and a half-size replica built in 1931. The original was destroyed by earthquakes in the mid-19th century. The **Santa Cruz City Museum**, *1305 East Cliff Dr.; tel: (408) 429-3773*, covers local human and natural history. **Joseph M. Long Marine Laboratory**, *at the end of Delaware Ave near Natural Bridges State Park; tel: (408) 459-4308*, is a University of California marine research laboratory and museum. **Wilder Ranch State Park**, 2 miles (3 km) north of town on the west side of Hwy 1, *1401 Coast Rd; tel: (408) 426-0505*, a Victorian ranch and dairy farm museum, has 5 miles (8 km) of deserted coastline.

SANTA CRUZ WINERIES

The Santa Cruz Mountains, east of this route, produced some of California's finest wines in the last century. Modern vintners have drifted south from Napa and Sonoma, often landing on vineyards abandoned or destroyed during Prohibition. Most wineries are too small to maintain permanent tasting rooms, but the premium Zinfandels, Pinot Noirs, and Chardonnays sell out quickly. For current information on tours and tastings, contact the **Santa Cruz Mountains Winegrowers Association**, *PO Box 728, Soquel, CA 95073; tel: (408) 476-7288*.

One of the most colourful wineries in the state is Bonny Doon Vineyards, *10 Pine Flat Rd., Santa Cruz, CA 95060; tel: (4087) 425-3625*, where the winemaker-owner produces homespun but highbrow philosophy, and Rhone-style wines with names like Le Cigare Volant, Old Telegram, and Le Sophiste. Grappas and fruit brandies round out an eclectic product line which consistently wins prizes for quality.

HALF MOON BAY

Tourist Information: Half Moon Bay/Coastside Chamber of Commerce, *225 South Cabrillo Hwy, Half Moon Bay, CA 94019; tel: (415) 726-5202*.

Half Moon Bay is the largest coastal town on the southern San Mateo Peninsula, the tongue of land extending north between the Pacific and San Francisco Bay. It's a perplexing place, a San Francisco suburb, an old-fashioned farming town, a surfing community, and a shopping destination for local art and artefacts. Just north is **Pillar Point Harbor** and **Princeton by-the-Sea**. Most accommodations are Bed and Breakfasts. The Chamber of Commerce has current lists but cannot make bookings.

Princeton began as a whaling station and survived as a commercial fishing and whale-watching port. **Barbara's Fish Trap**, on the harbour, *281 Capistrano Rd; tel: (415) 728-7049*, is a long-time favourite with San Franciscans. Just north is **Fitzgerald Marine Reserve**; *tel: (415) 726-6203*. At high tide, the reserve looks like any other patch of rocky coastline, but low tide reveals broad rock terraces filled with tidepools waiting to be explored. Guided tours are sometimes available.

SANTA BARBARA to SAN FRANCISCO (EL CAMINO REAL)

Hwy 101 is the most direct route from Santa Barbara to San Francisco. The route roughly follows the Spanish Colonial route, El Camino Real, the King's Highway, connecting the 21 California Missions from San Diego to Sonoma (see p. 131).

ROUTE

Follow Hwy 101 north from Santa Barbara to San Francisco. The entire route is at least four lanes, almost all freeway. Allow one long day for the 345-mile (552 km) drive without sightseeing. San Luis Obispo is the traditional overnight stop, but if time allows, stretch the journey to overnight at Buellton, San Luis Obispo, and Salinas. Best petrol prices are in San Luis Obispo, King City and Salinas.

From Santa Barbara, Hwy 101 follows the coastline past **El Capitan State Beach**, **Refugio State Beach**, and **Gaviota State Beach** before turning inland to **Buellton** and the low pass through the western end of the Santa Ynez Mountains to Santa Maria. See Santa Barbara County Route, p. 134. Alternatively, from the end of the Santa Barbara Wineries Circuit at Betteravia Rd (p. 137) and Hwy 101, turn north toward Santa Maria.

Continue north on Hwy 101 toward **San Luis Obispo**, 12 miles (19 km). The beach cities and San Luis Obispo are covered in the Santa Barbara–San Francisco Coastal Route, p. 145.

From San Luis Obispo, take Hwy 101 north toward Atascadero, Paso Robles and King City.

Just north of San Luis Obispo is **Cuesta Grade**, one of the steepest hills on the entire length of Hwy 101. Beyond the grade, the highway runs gently down to **Atascadero**, set 16 miles (26 km) north of San Luis Obispo among the rolling hills, oak trees and cattle herds of northern San Luis Obispo County. Continue north on Hwy 101 toward Paso Robles and Mission San Miguel or sample at more than two dozen local wineries.

SANTA MARIA VALLEY

Santa Maria is 28 miles (45 km) north of Buellton. The town is the economic centre of the **Santa Maria Valley**, one of the most productive vegetable growing and ranching areas in California.

The **Santa Maria Museum of Flight**, in a hangar at the municipal airport, *3015 Airpark Dr.; tel: (805) 922-8758*, has a collection of working World War II aircraft and associated equipment. The airport was a major flight training centre during World War II.

Nipomo, 4 miles (6 km) north of Santa Maria, was originally a private ranch. The ranch headquarters became a major stopover between the missions in Santa Barbara and San Luis Obispo. The area is clothed with tens of thousands of blue gum eucalyptus trees, originally planted in the mistaken belief they would yield high-grade hardwood timber.

Maison Deutz, *453 Deutz Dr., Arroyo Grande, CA 93420; tel: (805) 481-1763*, is 8 miles (13 km) north of Nipomo on the eastern side of Hwy 101. A large sign marks the turnoff for northbound traffic, but there is no sign for southbound traffic. Other area wineries are located inland between Arroyo Grande and San Luis Obispo.

This California scion of the famous French champagne house produces sparkling wines by the *méthode champenoise* that are winning medals around the world. The cool climate and chalky soil is very similar to Deutz' home territory in Ay, France. The winery is open daily for tours and tasting. The tasting charge includes a full flute of wine and an hors d'oeuvre plate that could make a light lunch. Non-alcoholic drinks are also available.

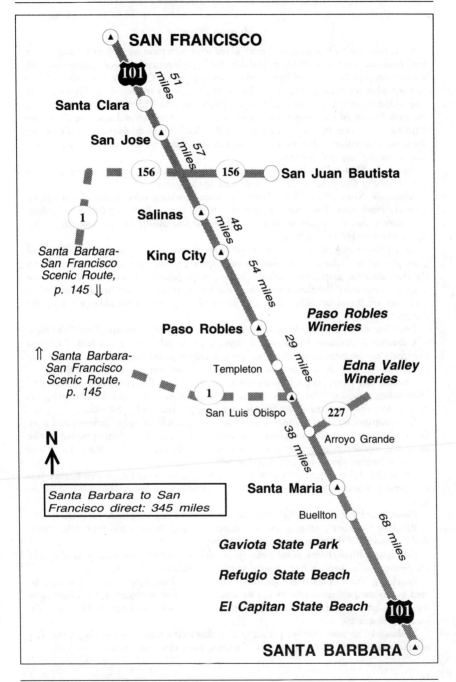

SAN FRANCISCO

101
51 miles

Santa Clara

San Jose
57 miles

156   156 San Juan Bautista

1

Salinas

*Santa Barbara-
San Francisco
Scenic Route,
p. 145* ⇓

King City
48 miles

54 miles

***Paso Robles
Wineries***

Paso Robles
29 miles

⇑ *Santa Barbara-
San Francisco
Scenic Route,
p. 145*

Templeton

***Edna Valley
Wineries***

1

San Luis Obispo

227

N
↑

Arroyo Grande
38 miles

*Santa Barbara to San
Francisco direct: 345 miles*

Santa Maria

Buellton
68 miles

Gaviota State Park

Refugio State Beach

El Capitan State Beach

101

SANTA BARBARA

Californian Wine

The old rule about white wine with fish and red wine with meat worked well enough when both food and wine were utterly predictable. But today's recipes are more interesting, with a wider range of flavours and ingredients – and not just in California. It's more useful to find out what the wine actually tastes like than whether it's red or white. Here's a quick look at the major types of wine and grapes you're likely to find in California. A warning: the basic flavour of each grape is changed by where it is grown and how the winemaker turns juice into wine. No two wines taste exactly alike. No two drinkers experience exactly the same taste, either. If it doesn't taste good to you, it doesn't taste good, no matter how long or loudly 'experts' declaim.

Blanc de Blancs Literally, 'white from whites,' a sparkling wine made of all white grapes, usually Chardonnay. The most delicate sparking wine.

Blanc de Noirs 'White from blacks', a white sparkling wine made of red grapes, normally Pinot Noir. The juice is separated from the skins, which contain the red colour, immediately after the grapes are crushed. A blanc de noir usually has a stronger fruit taste than a blanc de blancs, but both are dry.

Blush These pink wines vary in colour from almost white to almost red. The most popular is white Zinfandel. Like blanc de noirs sparkling wine, the juice is separated from the skins after the grapes are crushed. The longer the juice is left with the skins ('on the skins' in winespeak), the darker the colour and the more intense the flavour. Most blush wines are on the sweet side. All should be drunk as young as possible–preferably the current vintage.

Brut The standard for sparkling wine, usuallyá a mixture of Chardonnay and Pinot Noir.

Cabernet Sauvignon The strongest flavours are usually berries and fruit. California Cabernets can be medium to full-bodied, are normally dry, and can be tannic, a polite way to say astringent. 'Cab' has been the most fashionable and expensive red since the 1970s.

Chardonnay Light, simple flavours like apples, citrus, and flowers usually predominate. Winemakers delight in twisting Chardonnay to taste of nuts, butter, or oak. Advertising has made it the white wine of choice for people who don't know what they like.

Gewürztraminer This German grape has a unique mix of spice, flowers, and fruit. Gewürztraminer is usually made sweet to cover up a slight natural bitterness, but can be made dry, similar to Gewürztraminers from Alsace, on the French side of the Rhine. It also makes an intense, almost too-rich desert wine.

Merlot Merlot is softer than Cabernet, i.e., it has less tannin and more fruit flavour. It is traditionally mixed with 'Cab' to make a more drinkable wine, but has become popular on its own.

Pinot Noir Pinot is usually light and silky, and leaves a lingering freshness in the mouth.

Riesling Germany's other grape is a delicate mix of flowers and fruit, often made slightly sweet. It's the classic grape for sweet, heavy dessert wines.

Sauvignon Blanc/Fumé Blanc Same grape, different names. The wine is usually light and herbaceous – there's a hint of plant smells, sometimes newly mown hay.

Sparkling Wine Sparkler is California's version of Champagne, a name that can't be used in international commerce except by a select group of producers in the Champagne region of France. Look for labels stating 'méthode champenoise' or 'fermented in this bottle' for the best quality.

Zinfandel The search for the perfect 'Zin' is akin to the search for the Holy Grail. The wine is usually spicy with strong hints of berries, most often raspberries.

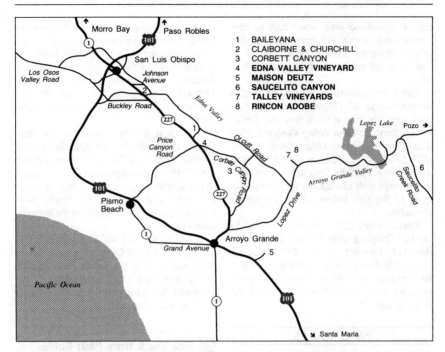

1 BAILEYANA
2 CLAIBORNE & CHURCHILL
3 CORBETT CANYON
4 **EDNA VALLEY VINEYARD**
5 **MAISON DEUTZ**
6 **SAUCELITO CANYON**
7 **TALLEY VINEYARDS**
8 **RINCON ADOBE**

Eleven miles (18 km) north of Nipomo is **Arroyo Grande**. **Arroyo Grande Chamber of Commerce**, *800 W. Branch, Arroyo Grande, CA 93421; tel: (805) 489-1488*, has free maps and bed and breakfast information. The main street, East Branch, is lined with historic buildings from the 1880s and later. The best stop in town is **Burnado'z Ice Cream Parlor**, *114 W. Branch*.

EDNA VALLEY WINERIES

The **Edna Valley** wine district stretches east and north of Arroyo Grande. Most of the dozen or so wineries are located near Lopez Dr. or Hwy 227, leading north to San Luis Obispo and rejoining Hwy 101.

Edna Valley Vintners, *2195 Corbett Canyon Rd, Arroyo Grande, CA 93420; tel: (805) 541-5868*, has information and winery maps. Maps are also available at hotels, restaurants, and tourist attractions between Santa Barbara and San Jose.

The Edna Valley opens onto the Pacific Ocean at Morro Bay, which keeps winters warm and

summers cool. Most vineyards are planted with Chardonnay grapes, which produce wines with rich, fruity flavours balanced by strong acids.

The high quality is no surprise. Mission San Luis Obispo, which once farmed the valley, was the richest California Mission on the strength of its wine production alone. Edna Valley still produces some of the best and most consistent wines in California, but only a few wineries are open for tours without prior arrangements. Allow a half-day for wine tasting.

Continue east on E. Branch, which becomes Lopez Dr. **Talley Vineyards**, *3031 Lopez Dr., Arroyo Grande, CA 93420; tel: (805) 489-0446*, started as a highly successful family vegetable farm. In 1982 the family planted a test vineyard on a steep hillside above the vegetable fields. Production has grown to about 5000 cases yearly. The tasting room is in the historic **Rincon Adobe**, 5 miles (8 km) east of Arroyo Grande, one of the oldest buildings in the county.

Saucelito Canyon Vineyards tasting room shares the Rincon adobe with Talley. The vineyards are inland beyond Lopez Lake, a popular recreational area, where high summer temperatures favour red wine grapes. The original Zinfandel vineyard was planted in 1880 and still produces intense, almost inky wine.

Turn back down Lopez Rd towards Arroyo Grande. At Hwy 227, Carpenter Canyon Rd, turn right. Turn right again at Biddle Ranch Rd, 7 miles (11 km) north, to **Edna Valley Vineyard**, *2585 Biddle Ranch Rd, San Luis Obispo, CA 93401; tel: (805) 544-9594*. Founded in the 1970s, Edna Valley Vineyard put the Edna Valley on modern winery maps with Chardonnay and Pinot Noir. Many of the best bottles remain surprisingly affordable.

Return to Hwy 227. Turn right (Edna Rd) to San Luis Obispo, 8 miles (13 km). To return to Hwy 101, turn left at Hwy 227 (Carpenter Canyon Rd). Drive 1 mile (1.6 km) to Price Canyon Rd. Turn right. Hwy 101 is 2 miles (3 km) south through a chequerboard of bucolic farmland and active oil wells.

The dusty, whitewashed exterior of the Mission is almost stark, but the interior glows with warm colours that reproduce the original tones. The museum is one of the best among the Missions, including a 17th-century wood carving of St Michael the Archangel and his dragon. The front courtyard is filled with an extensive cactus garden.

Just south of the Mission is the **Rios-Caledonia Adobe**, *PO Box 326, San Miguel, CA 93451; tel: (805) 467-3357*, which was built in the 1840s. It has been a rancho, stage-coach stop, rail hotel, bar, and now a State Historical Monument and museum. The shady picnic ground is especially inviting during the blistering summer months.

Return to Hwy 101 and continue north. The freeway runs through **Camp Roberts**, a US Army base, and parallels the Salinas River through rolling farm land. The broad river all but disappears during late summer, only to reappear with the first winter rains.

PASO ROBLES

Tourist Information: Paso Robles Chamber of Commerce, *1225 Park St, Paso Robles, CA 93446; tel: (805) 238-0506*.

Paso Robles was a railroad and hot springs spa resort in the last century. Today, it's the largest town in northern San Luis Obispo County. The town was named for the great stands of oak trees (*robles*) that once dotted the hills.

The **Call-Booth House Gallery**, *1315 Vine St, Paso Robles, CA 93446; tel: (805) 238-5473*, has revolving exhibitions by invited, mostly local, artists in a renovated Victorian cottage. **El Paso de Robles Area Pioneer Museum**, *2010 Riverside Ave, Paso Robles, CA 93446; tel: (805) 238-0506*, has turn-of-the-century farm, office, and home equipment. **Helen Moe's Antique Doll Museum**, 4 miles (6 km) north of downtown, *Hwy 101 and Wellsona Rd; tel: (805) 238-2740*, is one of the largest antique doll museums in the state.

Mission San Miguel Arcangel is 4 miles (6 km) north of Helen Moe's on the east side of Hwy 101, *801 Mission St, San Miguel, CA 93451; tel: (805) 467-3256*, in the tiny town of San Miguel.

 Side Track from Paso Robles

PASO ROBLES WINERIES

San Luis Obispo County's other wine area begins just before **Templeton**, 5 miles (8 km) north of Atascadero. The Paso Robles Chamber of Commerce has free winery maps.

Summer temperatures in the area hover near 35°C, favouring red grapes over white. Most wineries buy grapes from all over San Luis Obispo County to produce full lines of both red and white wines. Sweet wine fans can revel in the wide variety of Muscat Canelli wines, which often have a citrus tang beneath a heavy, almost honey taste.

Unfortunately, many wineries charge a tasting fee, but tours and picnic grounds are free. Exit at Vineyard Dr., just south of Templeton. Turn left and cross the freeway. The first winery is **Creston Vineyards**, *679 California Canyon (Hwy 58), Creston, CA 93432; tel: (805) 434-1399*. Tours by appointment only.

Pesenti Winery is 3 miles (5 km) beyond at *2900 Vineyard Dr., Templeton, CA 93465; tel:*

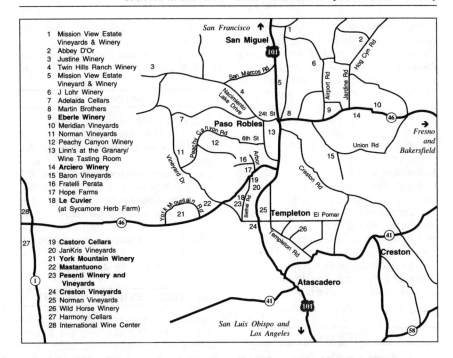

1 Mission View Estate
   Vineyards & Winery
2 Abbey D'Or
3 Justine Winery
4 Twin Hills Ranch Winery
5 Mission View Estate
   Vineyard & Winery
6 J Lohr Winery
7 Adelaida Cellars
8 Martin Brothers
9 **Eberle Winery**
10 Meridian Vineyards
11 Norman Vineyards
12 Peachy Canyon Winery
13 Linn's at the Granary/
   Wine Tasting Room
14 **Arciero Winery**
15 Baron Vineyards
16 Fratelli Perata
17 Hope Farms
18 **Le Cuvier**
   (at Sycamore Herb Farm)

19 **Castoro Cellars**
20 JanKris Vineyards
21 **York Mountain Winery**
22 **Mastantuono**
23 **Pesenti Winery and
   Vineyards**
24 Creston Vineyards
25 Norman Vineyards
26 Wild Horse Winery
27 Harmony Cellars
28 International Wine Center

(805) 434-1030. Winery and tasting room are open at 0800, probably the earliest tasting opportunity in the state. The family-owned winery reopened just months after Prohibition ended in 1933. Pesenti shows off the best of an old style of heavy, intense flavour that has fallen out of favour. The excellent wines are unfashionable, but great bargains. No picnic area.

Mastantuono is just beyond at *100 Oak View Rd, Templeton, CA 93465; tel: (805) 238-0676*. Zinfandel is the star, with other reds close behind. The walls are hung with local game trophies, most wearing silly hats. A shady white gazebo is perfect for picnics.

Turn left onto Hwy 46 and right onto York Mountain Rd. **York Mountain Winery**, *Route 2, Box 191, Templeton, CA 93465; tel: (805) 238-3925*. York Mountain Rd curves through a tiny forested valley and up the side of York Mountain to the winery, 4 miles (6 km) from Mastantuono. The 100-year old ranch and winery buildings are scenic; a fire burns in the tasting room most of the year to ward off the mountain chill. There's a

tasting fee, but the country scenery and old buildings are worth the drive.

Continue up York Mountain Rd to complete the semicircle back to Hwy 46. Turn left and drive 4 miles (6 km) to **Le Cuvier** at the **Sycamore Herb Farm**, *2485 Hwy 46 W, Paso Robles, CA 93446; tel: (805) 239-9235*. The winery and herb farm have a relaxing picnic area under spreading oak trees, but there is a charge for wine tasting.

Castoro Cellars is 2 miles (3 km) beyond, just off Hwy 46 at *1480 N. Bethel Rd, Templeton, CA 93465; tel: (805) 238-0725*. The tasting room is a garden room just off the owner's house, the wines consistent award winners. Like most Paso Robles wineries, reds are generally better than whites. There's a tasting charge, which is usually 'overlooked' for serious tasters.

JanKris Vineyards, just up Bethel Rd, *Route 2, Box 40, Bethel Rd, Templeton, CA 93465; tel: (805) 434-0319*, has a splendid century-old farmhouse for a tasting room, but charges for tasting.

Return to Hwy 46. Turn right to Hwy 101. Head north 6 miles (10 km) to Hwy 46 east. Exit eastbound. Drive 4 miles (6 km) to **Eberle Winery**, on the left-hand side of the road, *PO Box 2459, Paso Robles, CA 93447; tel: (805) 238-9607.* Specialities include Cabernet Sauvignon, Muscat Canelli, and a shady picnic ground overlooking the vineyards. Monthly winemaker gourmet dinners require advance reservations.

Turn left onto Hwy 46. Drive 2 miles (3 km) to **Arciero Winery**, on the right, *PO Box 1287, Paso Robles, CA 93447; tel: (805) 239-2562.* Great reds have emerged recently, especially Petite Sirah and Nebbiolo. The new winery has self-guided tours; the tasting room has a deli and a small formula auto racing museum, reflecting the owner's other passion in life. Plenty of parking, shaded picnic tables, and lawns where children can run off a little steam. Turn left onto Hwy 46 and return to Hwy 101 northbound.

KING CITY

Tourist Information: King City & Southern Monterey County Chamber of Commerce & Agriculture, *203 Broadway, King City, CA 93930; tel: (408) 385-3814.*

King City, 54 miles (86 km) north of Paso Robles, is the largest town in southern Monterey County. Early travellers to the Salinas Valley complained of having to stand up in their stirrups to see over the lush stands of wild oats and mustard. Ranching and farming have been a way of life ever since.

The **Agricultural and Rural Life Museum**, *1160 Broadway, King City, CA 93930; tel: (408) 385-5964,* features restored barns and other rural buildings filled with agricultural artifacts from early Mission days to modern wineries. From Hwy 101, take the Broadway exit and follow signs ½ mile (1 km) to the park.

Return to Hwy 101 northbound. Hwy 146, the turnoff for the western side of **Pinnacles National Monument**, is at Soledad, 20 miles (32 km) north of King City through rich agricultural lands. (see San Francisco–Visalia Route, p 262). **Mission Nuestra Señora de la Soledad**, is 3

miles (5 km) east of Soledad; tel: (408) 678-2586. The 1791 Mission has adobe ruins, a museum, and a restored chapel. Soledad is also the site of a state prison.

SALINAS

Salinas, 25 miles (40 km) north of Soledad, is the birthplace of John Steinbeck and the setting for many of his novels. First editions, letters, photos and other memorabilia are displayed in a special room at the **John Steinbeck Public Library**, *110 W. San Luis St, Salinas, CA 93902; tel: (408) 758-7311.* **Salinas Chamber of Commerce**, *119 E. Alisal St, Salinas, CA 93902; tel: (408) 424-7611.*

From Salinas, continue north on Hwy 101. If time permits, visit **Mission San Juan Bautista**, *5 miles (8 km) east on Hwy 156; tel: (408) 623-4881*, in the town of the same name.

MONTEREY COUNTY WINERIES

Wineries are scattered across from Santa Clara across the Santa Cruz Mountains and through Monterey County. More information from **Monterey Wine Country Associates**, *tel: (408) 375-9400*, **Santa Cruz Mountains Winegrowers Association**, *tel: (408) 479-9463*, and **Santa Clara Valley Winegrowers Association**, *tel: (408) 778-1555.* Along Hwy 101 **The Monterey Vineyard**, *Gonzales; tel: (408) 675-2481*, has a cool tasting room in which to escape the summer's heat.

SAN JUAN BAUTISTA

Tourist Information: San Juan Bautista Chamber of Commerce, *402A Third St, San Juan Bautista, CA 95045; tel: (408) 623-2454.*

Life in San Juan Bautista still revolves around the 1797 Mission, the largest and one of the most popular in California. The bear and coyote tracks in the floor tiles of the central aisle are real, apparently made while the tiles were drying outside nearly three centuries ago.

The square outside the Mission looks like a Spanish colonial plaza. It is now maintained as part of the **San Juan Bautista State Historic Park**; *tel: (408) 623-4881.* The park includes

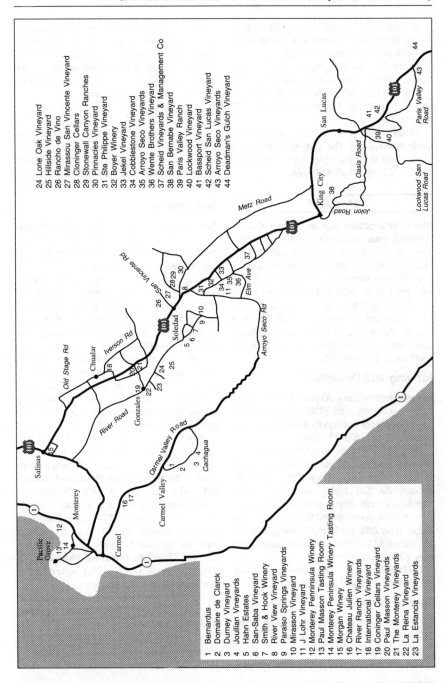

24 Lone Oak Vineyard
25 Hillside Vineyard
26 Rancho de Vino
27 Mirassou San Vincente Vineyard
28 Cloninger Cellars
29 Stonewall Canyon Ranches
30 Pinnacles Vineyard
31 Ste Philippe Vineyard
32 Boyer Winery
33 Jekel Vineyard
34 Cobblestone Vineyard
35 Arroyo Seco Vineyards
36 Wente Brothers Vineyard
37 Scheid Vineyards & Management Co
38 San Bernabe Vineyard
39 Paris Valley Ranch
40 Lockwood Vineyard
41 Bassport Vineyard
42 Scheid San Lucas Vineyard
43 Arroyo Seco Vineyards
44 Deadman's Gulch Vineyard

1 Bernardus
2 Domaine de Clarck
3 Durney Vineyard
4 Joullian Vineyards
5 Hahn Estates
6 San-Saba Vineyard
7 Smith & Hook Winery
8 River View Vineyard
9 Paraiso Springs Vineyards
10 Mirasson Vineyard
11 J Lohr Vineyard
12 Monterey Penninsula Winery
13 Paul Masson Tasting Room
14 Monterey Peninsula Winery Tasting Room
15 Morgan Winery
16 Chateau Julien Winery
17 River Ranch Vineyards
18 International Vineyard
19 Coninger Cellars Vineyard
20 Paul Masson Vineyards
21 The Monterey Vineyards
22 La Reina Vineyard
23 La Estancia Vineyards

three dozen other historic buildings dating back to the 1840s. A self-guided walk exploring the 12-block park takes about an hour. Return to Hwy 101. To go to Monterey/ Carmel, continue across the freeway on Hwy 156 to Hwy 1 and turn left. For San Jose, 45 miles (72 km) north and San Francisco, take Hwy 101 northbound.

Gilroy is best known for its late summer **Garlic Festival** and **The Outlets at Gilroy**, a major outlet shopping complex on *Leavesley Rd at Hwy 101; tel: (408) 848-7228.*

SAN JOSE

Tourist Information: San Jose Convention & Visitors Bureau, *333 W. San Carlos St, Ste 1000, San Jose, CA 95110; tel: (408) 295-9600 or (800) 726-5672.* The **Visitor Information Center** in the McEnery Convention Center lobby, *150 W. San Carlos St; tel: (408) 283-8833* is open Mon–Fri 0800–1730 and Sat–Sun 1100–1700. Other information centres are located at *San Jose International Airport, Terminal A and C baggage claim areas.* Event information is available 24 hours daily; tel: *(408) 295-2265.*

Arriving and Departing

San Jose International Airport, 3 miles (5 km) north of downtown; *tel: (408) 277-5366.* There is a **Thomas Cook Foreign Exchange** location in Terminal C; *tel: (408) 287-0748.*

Hwy 101 runs north along San Francisco Bay, the most direct route to San Francisco, and south to the Central Coast. **Hwy 280** runs north through the San Mateo Peninsula to San Francisco, a more direct route for destinations in western San Francisco and to the Golden Gate Bridge. **Hwy 880**, the Nimitz Freeway, runs up the east side of San Francisco Bay to connect with **Hwy 80** and Sacramento.

CalTrain has 52 daily commuter trains between San Jose and San Francisco.

Getting Around

San Jose is one of the safest major cities in the USA, but it's still a good idea to avoid lengthy downtown walks late at night.

The 20-mile (32 km) **Light Rail** streetcar system connects the Almaden Valley south of San Jose through downtown and north to the Great America theme park in Santa Clara; *tel: (408) 321-2300.* **Historic Trolleys** run on the downtown section of the light rail system on weekends, weather permitting.

Accommodation

All chains are represented in San Jose. The Convention and Visitors Bureau lists hotels and motels, but cannot make bookings. The nearest *AY* is **HI-Sanborn Park Hostel,** *15,808 Sanborn Rd, Saratoga, CA 95070; tel: (408) 7410166.*

Sightseeing

San Jose is spreading steadily southward along Hwy 101. The 22-mile (35 km) stretch north from **Morgan Hill** has become a dormitory town for **Silicon Valley** and **San Francisco.**

Traditionally the uncultured country cousin to San Francisco, San Jose has grown up. It is now the third largest city in California and 11th largest in the nation, bursting with a downtown renaissance of art, architecture, music, museums, and an effective public transport system.

The centre of San Jose is **Plaza Park**, heart of the original 1797 Spanish settlement and site of California's first state capital in 1849. Oval lawns surround a modernistic fountain. **McEnery Convention Center**, half a block from the park, is also framed by a fountain.

Across from Plaza Park is the golden sandstone US Post Office building from 1892. The former Post Office and an adjoining modern building form the **San Jose Museum of Modern Art**, *110 S. Market St; tel: (408) 294-2787.*

The Tech Museum of Innovation, *145 W. San Carlos; tel: (408) 279-7150*, is filled with interactive displays showing how technology, especially computer technology, affects everyday life. The **Children's Discovery Museum**, *180 Woz Way; tel: (408) 298-5437*, a 'petting zoo' of machines, gadgets and widgets.

The city's traditional attractions are outside the downtown area. The **Rosicrucian Egyptian Museum**, *1342 Naglee Ave; tel: (408) 947-3636*, presents pyramids, mummies, and metaphysical teachings from all ages. The gardens are filled with flowers framing obelisks, wall

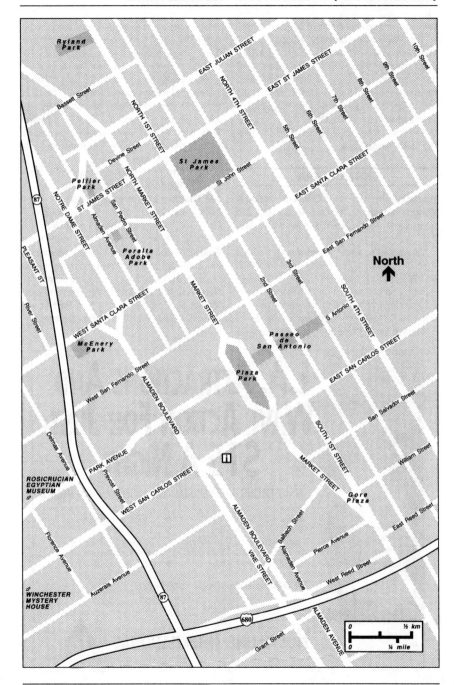

paintings, and reproductions of Egyptian deities. The **Winchester Mystery House**, *525 S. Winchester Blvd.; tel: (408) 247-2101* is a 160-room mansion filled with trick fireplaces, false doors, and stairways to nowhere. Builder Sarah Winchester believed that constant building could hold at bay the angry spirits of the thousands of victims of Winchester firearms.

San Jose blends imperceptibly into the next city north, **Santa Clara**.

SANTA CLARA

Tourist Information: Santa Clara Convention & Visitors Bureau, *2200 Laurelwood Rd, 2nd Floor, Santa Clara, CA 95052; tel: (408) 296-7111*.

Paramount's Great America, *on Great America Parkway east of Hwy 101; tel: (408) 847-988-1776 or (800) 969-3767*, is the San Francisco area's largest and liveliest family entertainment centre, with five roller coasters and a 1600-ft (484 m) white water raft ride.

Mission Santa Clara de Asis, *500 El Camino Real, on the Santa Clara University campus; tel: (408) 554-4023*, is a modern replica of the third Santa Clara Mission on the site, built in 1825. The original garden is in full bloom Apr–May.

Sunnyvale, the city north of Santa Clara, is the heart of **Silicon Valley**. The city claims more than 650 computer-related manufacturers. The airport on the east side of Hwy 101 is **Moffat Field**, a former Naval Air Station that has become a major NASA test facility. San Francisco Bay is visible behind Moffat.

Palo Alto, 2 miles (3 km) beyond Moffat is home to **Stanford University**, west of Hwy 101. **San Francisco International Airport** (SFO) is 8 miles (13 km) north of the San Mateo Bridge. From SFO, continue north on Hwy 101, the Bayshore Freeway. Follow signs toward the **Golden Gate Bridge** and take the **Mission St** exit. Turn right onto Mission St and move into the center lanes. Drive one long block to **South Van Ness Ave**. Turn left onto S. Van Ness and cross **Market St**. Continue 11 blocks to **Post St** and turn right. Drive 8 blocks. **Union Square** is on the right.

PALM SPRINGS

Palm Springs is a vision of hot-air balloons drifting above green golf courses, of mountains, desert, and date palms. Palm Springs describes both a city and the desert resort cities of the Coachella Valley, a quarter of a million people spread between I-10 and Highway 111. The chi-chi crowd enjoys the cool, dry desert climate between November and February, playing golf and tennis, shopping, and dining out to be seen.

The Hollywood film community discovered Palm Desert/Palm Springs, an hour's drive east of Los Angeles, in the 1930s. Tennis courts, hot springs and golf made passing the time a pleasure. The Agua Caliente Band of Cahuilla Indians were allowed to retain square miles of Palm Springs land laid out as in a chequerboard. Today, those developed land parcels are among the most valuable in the nation, while the tribe also retains rights to the wild, palm-studded Indian Canyons of the San Jacinto Mountains just south-west of town.

Tourist Information

Palm Springs Desert Resorts Convention and Visitors Bureau, The Atrium Design Centre, 69-930 Hwy 111, Suite 201, Rancho Mirage, CA 92270; tel: (619) 770-9000. Another **visitors centre** is at the **Palm Springs Regional Airport**, 3400 E. Tahquitz Canyon Way, open Mon–Tues 0800–1600, Wed–Fri 0800–2000, Sat 1000–1800, Sun 0900–1800.

Palm Springs Tourism, 401 S. Pavilion, Palm Springs, CA 92262; tel: (800) 347-7746 or (619) 778-8418.

Rancho Mirage Chamber of Commerce, 42-464 Rancho Mirage Lane, Rancho Mirage, CA 92270; tel: (619) 568-9351.

Palm Desert Chamber of Commerce, 72-990 Hwy 111, Palm Desert, CA 92260; tel: (800) 873-2428 or (619) 346-6111.

Desert Hot Springs Chamber of Commerce, 13560 Palm Dr., Box 848, Desert Hot Springs, CA 92240; tel: (800) 346-3347 or (619) 329-6403.

Arriving and Departing

Los Angeles is about 110 miles (176 km) west, Las Vegas 240 miles (384 km) north-east of Palm Springs. **Palm Springs Regional Airport**, 3400 E. Tahquitz Canyon Way, Palm Springs, CA 92262, is 1 mile (1.6 km) from downtown Palm Springs. Flights from Los Angeles, San Francisco, Oakland, San Jose, Mammoth Lakes, Lake Tahoe and Las Vegas. A taxi into Palm Springs is about $10; Rancho Mirage, $40. Most hotels have free or inexpensive airport shuttle service.

Getting Around

Highway 111 is the Coachella Valley's artery, leaving I-10 north-west of Palm Springs to continue 21 miles (34 km) to Indio near the Salton Sea. Hwy 111 is congested at rush hours and midday. Green and white street signs posted above the roadway mark major streets named after prominent residents, e.g. Bob Hope, Frank Sinatra, Dinah Shore, and Gene Autry.

Public Transport

The **SunBus** runs the length of the Coachella Valley from Desert Hot Springs to Coachella. Check on a day pass; single rides are 75 cents. Contact **Sunline Transit Agency**; tel: (619) 343-3451.

Driving

Cars can be hired at Palm Springs Regional airport. **Offroad Rentals & Tours**, tel: (619) 325-0376, hires 4X4s; **Magic Carpet Rides, Inc.**, tel: (619) 567-1170, hires Harley Davidson motorcycles.

Take water, snacks, warm clothing for evening chill, a hat, sun lotion, and closed shoes for protection against rocks, cacti, snakes and other desert denizens.

Living in Palm Springs

Accommodation

The Coachella Valley desert resort cities offer

hotel, motel and condominium accommodation, most priced according to proximity to golf courses and swimming pools. All lodging prices fall 50–70% during May–Nov. Book up to six months in advance for weekends during high season, Dec–April. If staying at a golf, tennis, or spa resort, arrange those activities in advance. Most hotel chains are represented, with moderately-priced accommodation. **Palm Springs Tourism**, *401 S. Pavilion, Palm Springs, CA 92262; tel: (800) 347-7746 or (619) 778-8418*, makes free bookings for 80 Palm Springs hotels.

The **Spa Hotel Resort & Mineral Springs**, *100 N. Indian Canyon Dr., Palm Springs, A 92262; tel: (800) 854-1279*, owned by the Agua Caliente Band of Cahuilla Indians, is expensive to pricey, but located in the heart of Palm Springs. **Two Bunch Palms**, *67-425 Two Bunch Palms Trail, Desert Hot Springs, CA 92240; tel: (800) 472-4334 or (619) 329-8791*, has drawn movie stars and celebrities to its pricey mineral hot springs since the '30s. Garbo and Marlon Brando are among the famous to have slept at the expensive **Ingleside Inn**, *200 W. Ramon Rd, Palm Springs, CA 92264; tel: (800) 772-6655 or (619) 325-0046*.

For fully-serviced, family-size villas adjacent to a water park, there's pricey **Oasis Water Resort**, *4190 E. Palm Canyon Dr., Palm Springs, CA 92264; tel: (800) 247-4664*. At the east end of the valley is **La Quinta Hotel**, *49-499 Eisenhower Dr., P.O. Box 69, La Quinta, CA 92253; tel: (800) 854-1271*, a 1926 Spanish hacienda-style resort surrounded by mountains which claims the area's first golf course. The moderate **Japanese Bed & Breakfast Inn**, *1677 North Via Miraleste; Palm Springs, CA 92262; tel: (619) 327-0705*, has futon beds, kimonos, and a choice of a Japanese or Western breakfast. There are also several naturist resorts. Moderate Palm Springs lodging is found along Belardo Road, one block west of Palm Canyon Dr.

Eating and Drinking

Endless restaurants in all price ranges line Hwy 111. There is no lack of Mexican, continental, steak, Chinese, Italian, Japanese, seafood or California cuisine eateries to choose from. For a list of better-known spots, pick up the free *Palm Springs Life's Desert Guide* at any hotel.

Old-fashioned red vinyl booths and vaguely Mexican wall murals draw a local Palm Springs lunch crowd at budget **Las Casuelas Original**, *368 N. Palm Canyon Dr., Palm Springs, CA 92262; tel: (619) 325-3213*. In Palm Desert, the **El Paseo** shopping street has many restaurants with al fresco dining. Golf pros show up at **B. B. O'Brien's Sports Cafe**, *72-185 Painters Path, Rancho Mirage, CA 92270; tel: (619) 346-5576*. Frank Sinatra is often spotted at **Dominick's Restaurant**, *70-030 Hwy 111, Rancho Mirage, CA 92270; tel: (619) 324-1711*.

Try tasty Thai food at **Siamese Gourmet Restaurant**, *4711 E. Palm Canyon Dr., Palm Springs, CA 92264; tel: (619) 328-0057*. **La La Java**, *245-A S. Palm Canyon Dr., Palm Springs, CA 92262; tel: (619) 322-6398*, near the historical museums, has excellent and cheap mocha iced coffee in a valley that prides itself on its coffee-houses.

The Coachella Valley's eastern end produces most of the US date crop. Make a pilgrimage to **Shields Date Gardens**, *80-225 Hwy 111, Indio, CA 92201; tel: (619) 347-0996*, for a cheap and scrumptious **date shake**. Watch a slide show on 'the sex life of the date', and enjoy the 1950s soda fountain atmosphere.

Communications

The Coachella Valley has a dozen **post offices**, including the main branch, at *333 E. Amado Rd, Palm Springs, CA; tel: (619) 325-9631*. Mail can be addressed to hotels.

Entertainment

Nightlife

Most nightclubs have a $5–10 cover charge. **Costa's Nightclub**, *Marriott's Desert Springs Resort & Spa, 74-855 Country Club Dr., Palm Desert, CA 92260; tel: (619) 341-1795*, has lagoon-side live bands, with no cover charge. **Chillers**, *262 S. Palm Canyon Dr., Palm Springs, CA; tel: (619) 325-3215*, has frozen drinks, bands, and dancing. **Zelda's Nightclub & Beachclub**, *169 N. Indian Canyon Dr., Palm*

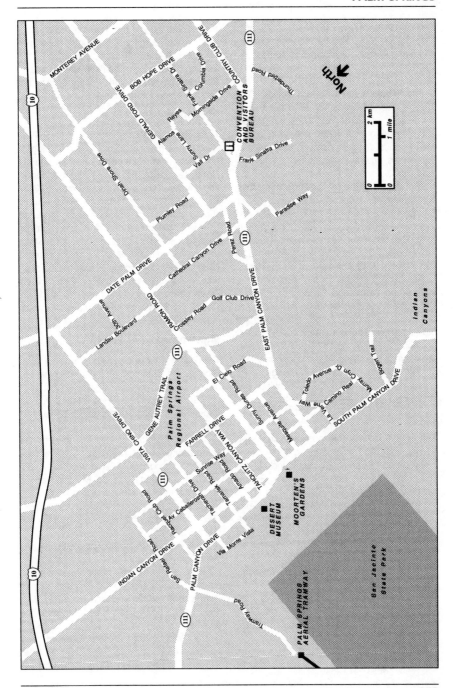

Springs, CA 92262; tel: (619) 325-2375, open Mon–Sat at 2000, also has dancing. Dancing and backgammon are featured at **Touche**, 42-250 Bob Hope Dr., Rancho Mirage, CA 92270; tel: (619) 773-1111, open 1830–0200.

The **Fabulous Palm Springs Follies**, Plaza Theatre, 128 S. Palm Canyon Dr., Palm Springs, CA 92262; tel: (619) 327-0225, has 50–80-year-olds performing music and song of the 1930s–1950s. Jugglers, dancers, banjo players, tap dancers, and vaudevilleans liven up the two-hour show.

McCallum Theatre for the Performing Arts, Bob Hope Cultural Center, 73-000 Fred Waring Dr., Palm Desert, CA; tel: (619) 340-2787, has year-round musical performances; the **Annenberg Theater**, Palm Springs Desert Museum, 101 Museum Dr., Palm Springs, CA; tel: (619) 325-7186 or (619) 325-4490, offers theatre.

Gambling is another form of entertainment. **Indio Bingo Palace and Casino**, Indio Springs Dr., Indio, CA 92202; tel: (619) 342-5000, has satellite horse betting, bingo, poker, and pai gow. **Shalimar Sports Center**, 46-350 Arabia St., Indio CA 92202; tel: (619) 863-8246, offers satellite horse gambling. A few miles north-west of Palm Springs is **Casino Morongo**, I-10, Cabazon, CA; tel: (800) 252-4499, which has bingo, card games, and satellite betting.

Sports

Golf is a Coachella Valley mania. Eighty-five courses and 1463 holes take advantage of a sunny climate. Famous golf events include the Bob Hope Chrysler Classic and Frank Sinatra Celebrity Invitational Golf Tournaments (Feb), the Nabisco Dinah Shore (Mar), and the Skins Game (Nov). To reserve hotel packages and tee times, call **Desert Golf Reservations**, tel: (619) 341-2662, **Gold a la Carte**, tel: (619) 324-5012, or **Golf Reservations of America**, tel: (800) TEE-TIME. The **Jude E. Poynter Golf Museum**, Victor J. LoBue Institute of Golf, College of the Desert, Fred Waring Dr. and San Pablo Ave, Palm Desert, CA 92260; tel: (619) 341-2941, open 0800–2000, has memorabilia, photographs, and golf-clubs.

Tennis is played on 600 courts. Major events include the Evert Cup Women's Tennis Tourna-

ment (February) and the Newsweek Champions Cup (March). Some private country clubs open for public tennis instruction, and offer Ladies' Days and Men's Days. The **Palm Springs Desert Resorts Convention and Visitors Bureau** has detailed tennis information.

Shopping

El Paseo, one block south of Hwy 111, in Palm Desert, is 2 miles (3.2 km) of trendy designer boutiques and restaurants. The **La Quinta Hotel**, La Quinta, has gift shops in a flower-lined arcade. Six blocks of downtown **Palm Canyon Drive** in Palm Springs mixes couture shops, restaurants, coffee-houses and art galleries. **Villagefest**, held each Thursday evening on Palm Canyon Dr., adds street vendors to the blend. Most of the desert resort cities have large air-conditioned shopping malls with major department stores. **Palm Desert Town Center**, Hwy 111 at Monterey Ave, Palm Desert, CA 92260; tel: (619) 346-2121, has an indoor public ice rink.

Sightseeing

The Coachella Valley cities are collectively called Palm Springs. Turn right off I-10 at the Hwy 111 turnoff, and follow the highway east until it rejoins I-10. Hwy 111 is called Palm Canyon Dr. through West Palm Springs and Palm Springs; from Rancho Mirage to Indio it is Hwy 111.

Turn right onto Tramway Rd. towards the **Palm Springs Aerial Tramway**, One Tramway Rd, Palm Springs, CA 92262; tel: (619) 325-1449. A 15-minute ride up **Mt San Jacinto** passes through five climactic zones from desert to alpine. It's much cooler at the top, at 8516 ft (2620 m), where the view encompasses the Coachella Valley.

Palm Canyon Dr. is one-way south; parallel Indian Canyon Dr. goes north. Palm Canyon Dr. has most of Palm Springs' historic interest areas, outdoor dining, and action. The red granite **Palm Springs Walk of Stars**, tel: (619) 322-1563, mimics Hollywood's famed stars set in the pavement.

The **Palm Springs Desert Museum**, 101 Museum Dr., Palm Springs, CA 92262; tel: (619) 325-7186, closed Mon, is a rich collection of

Native American basketry, Western American art, sculpture gardens, and dioramas of desert animals including rattlesnakes, desert tortoises, gila monsters and scorpions. The complex includes the **Annenberg Theater**. Due to the construction of a new wing, the museum will be closed for part of 1995.

On Palm Canyon Dr. is the **Plaza Theatre**, home of the Fabulous Palm Springs Follies (see 'Entertainment' on previous page). Next door at *134 S. Palm Canyon Dr.; tel: (619) 322-1877*, is trendy **Peabody's Jazz Studio & Coffee Bar**, Palm Springs' first coffee-house. The **Village Green Heritage Center**, *221-223 S. Palm Canyon Dr., Palm Springs, CA 92262; tel: (619) 323-8297*, has two historic houses, a 1930s general store, and a Native American cultural centre. The 1885 **McCallum Adobe**, considered Palm Springs oldest building, houses a small local history museum. The 1893 **Miss Cornelia White House**, built from railroad ties (sleepers), also has a small museum. **Ruddy's General Store Museum**; *tel: (619) 327-2156*, contains 6000 shelved and cased items that would have been sold in the 1930s and 1940s. The **Agua Caliente Cahuilla Cultural Center** has an excellent collection of basketry and photographs illustrating the tribe's history as owner of much of the region's land.

Moorten's Botanical Garden, *1701 S. Palm Canyon Dr., Palm Springs, CA 92264; tel: (619) 327-6555*, open Mon–Sat 0900–1630, Sun 1000–1600, has a nature trail through a cactus and desert plant arboretum.

Follow S. Palm Canyon Dr. to the **Indian Canyons**, three palm-studded, rocky river canyon oases owned by the **Agua Caliente Band of Cahuilla Indians**. These Native Americans own over 20% of Palm Springs land and much of the surrounding territory. Admission is charged to enter the canyons, open fall–winter 0800–1700, spring–summer 0800–1800. In **Palm Canyon**, the **Trading Post** has tribal art, pottery, baskets, and **Indian fry bread**. Fifteen-mile (24 km) long Palm Canyon follows a winding stream, and is accessible by foot or on horseback. **Andreas Canyon** has a scenic trail among wild rock formations, some with tribal rock art. In wilder **Murray Canyon**, watch

for Peninsula bighorn sheep and wild ponies.

Turning east on Palm Canyon Drive near Moorten's Botanical Garden, take **E. Palm Canyon Dr./Hwy 111**. Turn left on Country Club Dr. for 1½ miles (2.4 km), then left on Bob Hope Dr. **Heartland**, *39-600 Bob Hope Dr., Rancho Mirage, CA 92270; tel: (619) 324-3278*, closed Sun, is an interactive museum of the human heart, its structure, operation, and diseases!

El Paseo, Palm Desert's shopping street, parallels Hwy 111 for 2 miles (3.2 km). Turn right on Portola Ave and drive 1½ miles (2.4 km) to the **Living Desert**, *47-900 Portola Ave, Palm Desert, CA 92260; tel: (619) 346-5694*, closed mid-June–Aug. Twelve hundred acres (486 ha) of desert gardens from 10 North American regions are home to exotic animals like zebra and Arabian oryx as well as coyotes, bighorn sheep, Mexican wolves, eagles, javelina, mountain lions and other local species.

Palm Springs has activities from celebrity tours to sky diving. Guided, several hour, drive-by tours of celebrity homes are offered by Celebrity Tours; *tel: (619) 325-2682*, and Gray Line Tours; *tel: (619) 325-0974* or *(800) 635-1859*. **Carriage Trade Ltd.**; *tel: (619) 320-7832*, in downtown Palm Springs, uses horse-drawn carriages for celebrity home and historical tours. Tour the Coachella Valley and enjoy a Western barbecue with **Covered Wagon Tours**; *tel: (619) 347-2161*. Hire a bicycle, and explore the valley during the early morning or late afternoon.

Desert Adventures; *tel: (619) 864-6530*, has jeep tours into the San Jacinto Mountains. Ride a steed in the desert with **Smoke Tree Stables**; *tel: (619) 327-1372*. Hire a Harley Davidson motorcycle at **Magic Carpet Rides, Inc.**; *tel: (619) 567-1170*. Hike some of the desert foothills' 100 miles (160 km) of hiking paths with **Trail Discovery Tours**; *tel: (619) 325-4453*.

Skydive with **Parachutes Over Palm Springs**; *tel: (800) 535-5867* or *(619) 345-8321*. Be up before dawn in a hot-air balloon over the shimmering desert and golf courses. Or, take a bi-plane tour in a US Navy N3N-3, Tahore Aero South; *tel: (619) 345-3321*.

Sightseeing   **177**

PALM SPRINGS to DEATH VALLEY

Leave the desert resorts of Palm Springs for 292 miles (467 km) of true desert. This route traverses **Joshua Tree National Monument** *and* **East Mojave** *(pronounced moe-hah-vee)* **National Scenic Area** *to* **Death Valley National Monument**. *All three natural areas are proposed national parks. After filling the tank with petrol, take at least 2 days to cross these desert areas, staying or camping overnight in some of California's least-known areas.*

ROUTE

Drive south-east through the Coachella Valley on Hwy 111 from Palm Springs to the I-10 junction in Indio. Continue 24 miles (38 km) east on I-10, turn left going north on Cottonwood Spring Rd into **Joshua Tree National Monument**. Either continue directly to the Oasis Visitor Center at **Twentynine Palms,** just outside the monument's north side, or see more Joshua trees in the wetter western half of the monument by taking roads through Queen and Lost Horse Valleys to the town of Joshua Tree, before going 14 miles (22 km) east on Hwy 62 to Twentynine Palms.

Go left (north) on Adobe Rd, for 2 miles (3.2 km), then 16 miles (26 km) right (east) and 30 miles north on Amboy Rd to **Amboy**.

Amboy Rd skirts the south-east and eastern sides of the US Marine Corps Training Center, and salt processing at Bristol Dry Lake, before entering **Amboy**. Located on the **National Trails Highway**, the old **Route 66** of 1950s song and television fame, Amboy is a small town with a café, motel, and several daily freight trains passing through.

Two miles (3.2 km) south-west of town is **Amboy Crater**, a volcanic cinder cone offering hikers a view into the crater's interior from the 250-ft (77 m) high rim.

Go east 7 miles (11 km) on National Trails Hwy, then 11 miles (17.6 km) north (left) to enter **East Mojave National Scenic Area** on **Kelbaker Rd**. Go 57 miles (91 km) through **East Mojave National Scenic Area** to **Baker**.

Continue 48 miles (77 km) north on Hwy 127 to Tecopa. **Tecopa Hot Springs Park**, *PO Box 158, Tecopa, CA 92389; tel: (619) 852-4264*, is a 365-pitch campsite and nature preserve. There is an *AY* at Tecopa, **Desertaire Home Hostel**, *PO Box 306, Tecopa, CA 92389; tel: (619) 852-4580* for directions and reservations. Eight miles (13 km) north is **Shoshone**'s petrol, food, lodging, and ranger station. Two miles (3.2 km) beyond, turn left onto Hwy 178. Hwy 178 crosses 3315-ft (1020 m) Salsberry Pass before entering **Death Valley National Monument** at Furnace Creek. Death Valley is described more fully in the Los Angeles–Death Valley route, p. 80.

JOSHUA TREE NATIONAL MONUMENT

Tourist Information: Joshua Tree National Monument, *74485 National Monument Dr., Twentynine Palms, CA 92277-3597; tel: (619) 367-7511*. Alternatively, stop at the **Cottonwood Visitor Center** after entering Joshua Tree National Monument on Cottonwood Spring Rd.

Accommodation

Tent and RV camping are permitted in the monument's nine primitive campsites. Call **MISTIX**; *tel: (800) 444-7275* for reservations. All supplies – water, wood and petrol – must be brought in.

Sightseeing

The man-made palm oasis draws birds from afar. Rainfall in the monument is light, 7½ inches (20 cm) annually, most in July–Aug. Call ahead for wildflower bloom periods.

Driving through the National Monument, **Cottonwood Spring Rd** becomes **Pinto Basin Rd** and continues north-east, then north-west by a patch of thorny *ocotillo*, spiky flat-leaved bracts with thorns topped in spring by orange flowers.

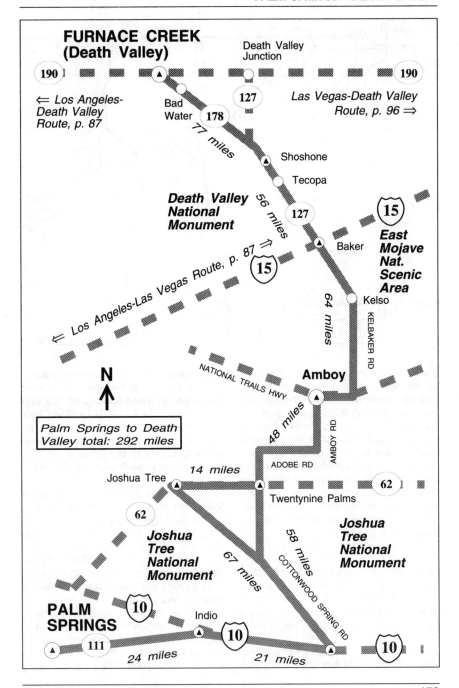

**FURNACE CREEK
(Death Valley)**

Death Valley
Junction

190

⇐ *Los Angeles-
Death Valley
Route, p. 87*

Bad
Water **178**

127

Las Vegas-Death Valley
Route, p. 96 ⇒

190

77 miles

Shoshone

Tecopa

*Death Valley
National
Monument*

56 miles

127

Baker

15

*East
Mojave
Nat.
Scenic
Area*

⇐ *Los Angeles-Las Vegas Route, p. 87* ⇒

15

Kelso

64 miles

KELBAKER RD

N

NATIONAL TRAILS HWY

Amboy

Palm Springs to Death
Valley total: 292 miles

48 miles

AMBOY RD

ADOBE RD

Joshua Tree

14 miles

62

Twentynine Palms

62

*Joshua
Tree
National
Monument*

67 miles

58 miles

COTTONWOOD SPRING RD

*Joshua
Tree
National
Monument*

**PALM
SPRINGS**

10

Indio

10

111

24 miles

21 miles

10

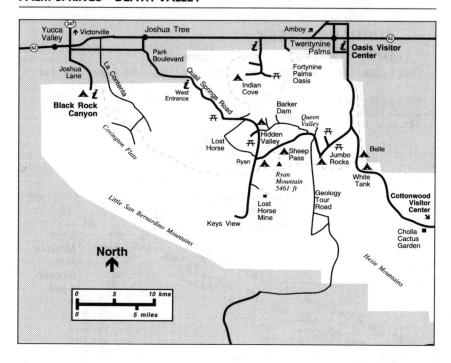

Stop just beyond at the **Cholla Cactus Garden** to see the spiny, bristling clumps of Bigelow 'jumping' *cholla* (pronounced *choy-uh*) cacti and huge-eared jackrabbits along a short self-guiding nature trail. Throughout the monument are ruins of gold mines, claims that played out quickly in the late 19th century. The route changes names to **El Dorado Mine Rd**, crossing a sweep of wilderness where the Mojave and Colorado Deserts meet. The ocotillo, cholla, and low, brushy, yellow-flowered creosote bush inhabit the arid **Colorado Desert**, which lies below 3000 ft (923 m).

With the Pinto Mountains on the right and the Hexie Range on the left, the route continues to rise into the wetter **Mojave Desert** and **Joshua trees** begin to appear. A Joshua tree's scraggly limbs are tufted with long, blade-like leaves, leading Mormon settlers to name them after the Biblical leader, Joshua, raising his arms to heaven.

If time is limited, pass the **Loop Rd** turnoff and continue north on **Gold Park** to the monument's

Oasis Visitor Center and **Twentynine Palms**.

To explore more of the monument, turn left onto **Loop Rd**. **Jumbo Rocks** surround a 130-pitch campsite. The 1.7-mile (2.7 km) Skull Rock Trail circles huge granite monoliths with signs explaining geology and flora. Continue on **Loop Rd** into **Queen Valley**, true Joshua tree country. The dirt **Geology Tour Road**, an 18 mile (29 km) round trip, turns to the left.

Loop Rd comes to a T-junction in **Lost Horse Valley**. Five miles (8 km) to the left (south) is 5185 ft (1595 m) **Keys View**, with vistas of the Coachella Valley, the San Jacinto and San Bernardino Mountain Ranges, and the Salton Sea. Right on Loop Rd is the 39-pitch **Hidden Valley Campground**, with trails around and up huge boulders. This **Wonderland of Rocks** is a climbing area boasting 4000 routes and hundreds of rock climbers and their entourages.

Continue north-west on Quail Springs Rd to the monument's west entrance, and on to the town of **Joshua Tree** at Hwy 62. Take Hwy 62 east to **Twentynine Palms**, which serves monument visitors and US Marine Corps (USMC) personnel stationed a few miles north at a desert training centre. **Twentynine Palms Chamber of Commerce**, *6136 Adobe Rd, Twentynine Palms, CA 92277; tel: (800) 533-7104 or (619) 367-3445*, has lodging lists and other information. There's a moderate *BW* motel and several others in the moderate–expensive range.

EAST MOJAVE NATIONAL SCENIC AREA

Tourist Information: Bureau of Land Management, *Needles Resource Area, Box 888, Needles, CA 92363; tel: (619) 326-3896*, has maps, a Mojave roads book, and information.

Accommodation

Lodging within the scenic area is limited to two campsites – 26-pitch Mid-Hills and 12-pitch Hole-In-The-Wall – east of Kelbaker Rd. You may pitch a tent legally within 300 ft (92 m) of any road, while staying more than 600 ft (185 m) away from water sources.

Sightseeing

The Mojave Desert is high desert, slightly wetter than the Colorado and Sonoran Deserts to the south and east. The scenic area shelters the endangered California State Reptile, the **desert tortoise**, and is a recreational area for off-road motorcycles and other all-terrain vehicles (ATV). Animal predators and motorised and armed humans have slashed the desert tortoise population by 90% in 50 years. Other Mojave Desert wildlife includes lizards, jackrabbits, kangaroo rats, hawks, owls, snakes and desert bighorn sheep. Joshua trees thrust spiky arms skyward as the wind blows constantly.

The **Granite Mountains** are left of Kelbaker Rd, offering challenging hiking trails and occasional desert bighorn sheep sightings. The **Providence Mountains** are on the right. Fifteen miles (24 km) up the road on the left via a 2.8 mile (4.5 km) access road are the **Kelso Dunes**. Twenty square miles (52 sq km) of fine white sand piled 500 ft (154 m) high create the third tallest dune system in North America. Plan on an effort-filled hour to walk to the top of the dunes, keeping watch for the serpentine signature of sidewinder rattlesnakes in the sand, and listening for 'singing' or 'booming' as sand scrapes down the dunes' leeward side.

Seven miles (11 km) north on Kelbaker Rd is **Kelso**, once a huge Union Pacific Railroad station site, now crumbling ruins. Pass the Kelso–Cima Rd turnoff which goes north-east to other remote sections of the scenic area. Pass through the **Devil's Playground**. Lava beds and a group of 32 cinder cones appear right of Kelbaker Rd. Exit the scenic area at **Baker**, where moderate accommodation is available at **Bun Boy Motel**, *PO Box 130, Baker, CA 92309; tel: (619) 733-4363*. Baker also claims the world's tallest thermometer, a 134-ft (41.2 m) neon, steel and plastic spike.

Desert Wildlife

The desert only *looks* empty and lifeless. Wildlife isn't as obvious as it is in the near-jungle of a redwood forest, but it's all around if you know what to look for.

California deserts are home to more than fifty types of mammals, from ¼ oz (4gm) bats to 200-lb (91 kg) mountain bighorn sheep. Over 200 species of birds haunt the air, from tiny hummingbirds to the great horned owl. There are reptiles, from lizards less than 4 in (10 cm) long, to rattlesnakes stretching more than 6 ft (2m). There are also oddities like the desert pupfish, and thousands of invertebrates from miniscule ants to giant, hairy scorpions.

The one thing they all have in common is some kind of adaptation that lets them survive extremes of heat, cold and dryness. Most creatures stay hidden during midday when ground temperatures can top 150°C (65°C) and late night when it drops to near freezing. Others hibernate in summer as well as winter to avoid the extremes. The best time to spot creatures of any size is during the more temperate hours around sunrise and sunset.

LONE PINE
to
SOUTH LAKE
TAHOE

The 334-mile (534 km) route between Lone Pine and South Lake Tahoe can be done in one exhausting summer day, but only at the expense of missing the highlights along the eastern escarpment of the Sierra Nevada. Two days is a reasonable minimum, with an overnight at Lee Vining, just north of Mono Lake. Better still, allow three to four days, with overnight stops at Bishop and Mammoth Lakes, June Lake, or Lee Vining. Least expensive petrol stops are Lone Pine, Bishop, and Lee Vining.

ROUTE

To reach **Mount Whitney** from **Lone Pine**, drive 0.7 miles (1 km) south on Hwy 395 to **Whitney Portal Rd** and turn right.

The route rejoins Hwy 395 via Movie Flat Road and Hogback Creek. Drive 4 miles (6 km) north to the town of **Manzanar**, and then continue along the Owens Valley on Hwy 395 for 5 miles (8 km) to reach **Independence**. Continue north on Hwy 395. At 13 miles (21 km) **Tinemaha Wildlife Viewpoint** is on the right, and the town of **Big Pine** is a further 13 miles (21 km) ahead.

Just north of Big Pine is the turnoff to Hwy 168 for **White Mountain Road** and the **Ancient Bristlecone Pine Forest**. Returning to Hwy 395, **Bishop** is 16 miles (26 km) north. Continue 39 miles (63 km), turning west to join Hwy 203, to visit **Mammoth Lakes**. Return once again to Hwy 395 and travel north to the intersection with Hwy 158 at **June Lake Junction**. Hwy 158 rejoins Hwy 395, forming the **June Lake Loop**.

North on Hwy 395, past the intersection with Hwy 120, is the town of **Lee Vining**; **Mono Lake**

lies to the east. The route travels north on Hwy 395 25 miles (39.6 km) to **Bridgeport** and a further 24 miles (38km) to **Walker**, before joining Hwy 207 to Genoa another 20 miles (32 km) north. For Genoa to **South Lake Tahoe**, see the Lake Tahoe Circuit, p. 196.

LONE PINE

Tourist Information: Lone Pine Chamber of Commerce, *104 N. Main St, Lone Pine, CA 93545; tel: (619) 876-4444.* For broad outdoor recreation information, visit the **Eastern Sierra Interagency Visitor Center**, *at the Hwy 395/136 junction, 2½ miles (4 km) south of Lone Pine; tel: (619) 876-4252.*

Accommodation and Food

There are a number of motels in town, including BW. The nearest camping is along Whitney Portal Rd, 0.7 miles (1 km) south of town.

Sierra Cantina, *123 North Main St; tel: (619) 876-5740*, has some of the best food at moderate prices. **Margie's Merry-Go-Round**, *212 S. Main St; tel: (619) 876-4115*, was John Wayne's favourite steak stop when he was here shooting a film.

Sightseeing

The **Indian Trading Post**, *137 S. Main St; tel: (619) 876-4641*, is a touristy gift shop with very ordinary souvenirs, but cinema buffs should stop and look at the frame around the front door. Gary Cooper, Errol Flynn, John Wayne and other film stars left their autographs in the wood. Later stars and autograph dealers have tried, unsuccessfully, to buy or even steal the door frame.

MOUNT WHITNEY

Tourist Information: Mount Whitney Ranger Station, *640 S. Main St, Lone Pine, CA 93545; tel: (619) 876-6200.*

Mt Whitney, the tallest mountain in the US south of Alaska, rises 14,494 ft (4392 m). The Whitney Portal parking area is 10½ miles (17 km) uphill at 7365 ft (2359 m). Enjoy the views of Mt Whitney on the way up Whitney Portal Road, for the mountain is hidden by trees at the top.

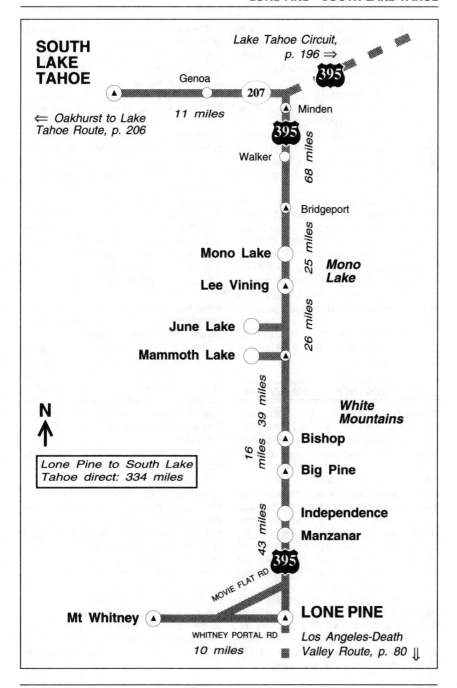

SOUTH LAKE TAHOE

Lake Tahoe Circuit, p. 196 ⇒

395

Genoa

207

⇐ *Oakhurst to Lake Tahoe Route, p. 206*

11 miles

Minden

395

Walker

68 miles

Bridgeport

Mono Lake

25 miles

Lee Vining

Mono Lake

June Lake

26 miles

Mammoth Lake

N
↑

White Mountains

39 miles

Bishop

16 miles

Lone Pine to South Lake Tahoe direct: 334 miles

Big Pine

Independence

43 miles

Manzanar

395

MOVIE FLAT RD

Mt Whitney

LONE PINE

WHITNEY PORTAL RD

Los Angeles-Death Valley Route, p. 80 ⇓

10 miles

Strong walkers have made the 22-mile (35 km) return trip to the Whitney summit in one very strenuous day. Instead of risking altitude sickness, more sensible visitors take 3 days.

Either way, the walk up Mt Whitney is not a solitary exercise. Mt Whitney is the most popular peak climb in the Sierra Nevada, possibly in the entire USA. And it seems that everybody wants to do it between mid-July and early October. Overnight walkers must have a free Forest Service permit; contact the Forest Service office in Lone Pine (see p. 182). Day walks do not yet require one.

Anyone interested in climbing Mt Whitney must request a lottery form early enough to meet the 1 Mar mail-in date for permit applications. Permits are required 22 May–15 Oct. Applications, by mail only, are accepted 1–31 May; the earliest postmarks get top priority. For the best chance, ask for a Sun–Thurs ascent. Fri and Sat are most in demand. Allow 4–6 weeks for a response. Permits must be picked up in person at the Forest Service office in Lone Pine between 0800 the day before the climb and 0800 the day of the climb. Permit holders who arrive late may lose their place.

MOUNT WHITNEY TO MANZANAR

Whitney Portal has other, less crowded attractions than Mount Whitney. Drive 2.3 miles (3.7 km) from the Hwy 395 junction, take **Horseshoe Meadows Rd** to the left to Horseshoe Meadows. The summit is a sparse pine forest in a shallow bowl-shaped meadow, but the drive is astounding. The paved road goes up. And up. And up again over a series of sharp switchbacks that seem as if they will never end. The views over nearby mountains, the Owens Valley, the pink, salt-encrusted dried bed of Lake Owens and Mt Whitney only get better with altitude. The end finally comes at about 10,000 ft (3048 m), before the equally tortuous drive back.

For a close look at the havoc wreaked by a recent earthquake, follow Whitney Portal Rd for ½ mile (1 km) from Hwy 395. Just past the aqueduct, turn right onto a dirt road. A third of a mile (0.5 km) later is a light grey ridge of boulders about 20 ft (6 m) high. Climb to the top.

The alluvial fan spreading from the east side of the reddish hills is cut by an earthquake scarp that appeared in 1872. In places, the surface dropped 21 ft (6.4 m). The 1872 earthquake was at least as strong as the quake that destroyed much of San Francisco in 1906, 8.25 on the Richter scale, but attracted little attention because the valley was so lightly populated. Twenty-nine people died, most of them crushed by the collapse of rough adobe buildings. Return to Whitney Portal Rd and turn right.

The reddish hills across the scarp are the **Alabama Hills**. If the weathered, rust-coloured rocks and sagebrush-covered hills look familiar, they probably are. From the 1920s through to the 1970s, a steady stream of cowboys, outlaws, cavalrymen, wagon trains and Indians (before they became Native Americans) galloped through these hills for thousands of cinema cameras. The parade finally slowed when Westerns faded in popularity in the late 1960s. **Movie Flat Rd** traces a 6-mile (9 km) route from Whitney Portal Rd to Hwy 395 that was once a favourite with the world's filmmakers.

The Alabama Hills were named by a group Confederate sympathisers who discovered gold in the hills behind Lone Pine during the American Civil War. The name isn't for the state, but after a Confederate gunboat. In retaliation, Union loyalists named mines just to the north **Kearsarge**, after the Union gunboat that sank the *Alabama*.

The ruddy hills and canyons cover 47 square miles (122 square km) with the white granite and dark green conifers of the Sierra Nevada as a constant backdrop. John Wayne made his starring debut in *The Big Trail* here in 1930. Other Westerns filmed here include feature films such as *How the West Was Won* and *Red River* and TV series like *The Lone Ranger*, *Hopalong Cassidy*, and *Bonanza*. More than one Western script writer borrowed from Lone Pine's genuine history. On at least one occasion, settlers attacked by angry Paiutes took refuge in nearby Fort Independence until a cavalry troop from Southern California could gallop to the rescue.

Other genres were filmed in the Alabama Hills. Almost all of the 1939 classic *Gunga Din*, and other British army epics were shot here.

More recently *Star Trek* film crews used the area in place of extraterrestrial real estate. From the dirt road to the earthquake scarp, turn right. Continue 2 miles (3 km) west to Movie Flat Rd. Turn right and head north. The paved road soon becomes gravel, but is easily passable by passenger cars. Stay on the main road; the side roads can get very rough and confusing. After 1½ miles (2 km) continue around the curve at a right turn and cross the large gully. At another intersection 3.7 miles (6 km) further on, continue around the curve to the right. Go ½ mile (0.6 km) further to a T-junction and turn left (north). At the intersection of Hogback Rd and Moffat Ranch Rd nearly a mile (1.5 km) beyond, go straight on. Follow Hogback Creek down to Old Hwy 395. Turn right on the main road, cross the cattle guard and aqueduct, then turn left to Hwy 395. Turn left. **Manzanar** is 4 miles (6.4 km) north.

OWENS VALLEY

The Owens Valley is a desert created by design to slake the insatiable thirst of Los Angeles. A century ago this long valley, between the eastern edge of the Sierra Nevada and the Inyo Mountains about 20 miles (32 km) to the east, had water in abundance and a promising future.

Native Americans from the Paiute tribe moved into the Valley somewhere between 40,000 and 13,000 years ago, hunting mastodons, bison, and other large mammals as well as abundant fish. As the last Ice Age ended and the climate became hotter and drier, the area around the Owens Valley turned to desert, but the valley itself remained an oasis. Streams flowed abundantly down the eastern Sierra, into the Owens River, and south into the Owens Lake.

The Owens Valley was 'discovered' by beaver hunters in 1834. They didn't find any beaver, but they did pioneer a route from Utah's Great Salt Lake into California. Their route, the California Trail, became an important artery into California for emigrants later in the century.

Most of the settlers passed through the Owens Valley, but a few stayed. By 1910, there were 4500 people in the Valley, raising dairy cattle and growing bumper crops of alfalfa, grapes, apples, corn, wheat and potatoes. A steamship plied the waters of Owens Lake, just south of Lone Pine. Then came William Mulholland and the Los Angeles Department of Water and Power (DWP).

Los Angeles needed water to continue growing, and the Owens Valley was the closest reliable source. The DWP, Mulholland, and assorted friends bought up most of the private land in the Owens Valley, usually by bringing lawsuits to force sales at bargain rates. They suborned local government, either through outright bribes or by making local officials rich through quasi-legal real estate schemes. The Jack Nicholson film *Chinatown* correctly portrayed Mulholland's methods, if not the precise history. The Owens Valley aqueduct opened in November 1913, sealing the area's fate.

Nearly all the water that once flowed through the Owens River now flowed beneath the mountains to Los Angeles. The steel blue waters of Owens Lake became a pink and white salt flat. As productive fields disappeared beneath drifting sand, most of the population drifted away. The city of Los Angeles said that the desertification of the Owens Valley was 'the greatest good for the greatest number.'

MANZANAR

Around the turn of the century, the tiny town of Manzanar was a thriving pear and apple growing town (the name is derived from the Spanish word for apple, *manzana*). The town died when Los Angeles sucked the Valley's water south and the orchards withered. Manzanar was resurrected during World War II, when the desolate, treeless area became an internment camp for about 10,000 Americans, most of them born in California. Their 'crime' was to be of Japanese ancestry during a period of rampant racism. To reach the site of the camp, turn left at the camp sign, just north of Manzanar Reward Rd. Go west 1.1 miles (1.8 km), then turn left and continue south for half a mile (1 km).

The camp was a complex of 600 flimsy wooden buildings, each 100 ft (30 m) long, covered with tar paper and set in military order across the barren plain. Most of the inmates had been prosperous farmers and merchants in coastal California communities. Many had owned their own businesses and homes; at Manzanar, a family of four could expect living space about 20 ft (6 m) on a side, subject to freezing winds in winter and blistering heat in summer. In 1944 the US Supreme Court ruled that internment was illegal. Manzanar and other Japanese-American camps were closed. Most of the buildings have long since disintegrated, leaving only a few foundations visible amidst the sagebrush and tumbleweeds. All that remains are a pair of ornamental gates (crafted by their inmate-builder to be a memorial to the injustice of internment), a garage that was once the camp auditorium and an obelisk in the camp cemetery.

INDEPENDENCE

The town of Independence is 5 miles (8 km) north of the Manzanar camp entrance. There is no tourist office, but the Lone Pine Chamber of Commerce has basic information for the town.

The **Eastern California Museum**, *155 Grant St; tel: (619) 878-0364*, has several exceptional collections and interpretive displays of Paiute and pioneer artifacts, natural history, photographs, rail and mining memorabilia, and a yard full of farming implements. A special section is devoted to the Japanese-American relocation program, the Manzanar camp, and the successful, decades-long battle to force the US government to pay reparation to inmates and their families.

Just behind the museum is **Little Pine Village**, a collection of original buildings moved to the site from around Independence. Several of the buildings have been restored and furnished, including a general store, blacksmithy, millinery, beauty and barber shop, and livery stable. A self-guided tour through outdoor displays of old farm and ranch implements gives a fair idea of the backbreaking labour that was required to wrest a living from the Owens Valley even before Los Angeles appropriated the water supply.

Just north of Independence is the **Mt Whitney State Fish Hatchery**; *tel: (619) 878-2272*. From Independence, take Hwy 395 2 miles (3 km) north to Fish Hatchery Rd. Turn left and drive 1 mile (1.6 km). This 1917 complex may be

the most beautiful fish hatchery in the world, an Old World-style monastery with a Tudor tower built of native stone and pleasant picnic grounds. The ruins of **Fort Independence**, established in 1862 to protect the Owens Valley from Native American attack, are near the hatchery turnoff. The fort was abandoned in 1877.

INDEPENDENCE TO BIG PINE

Continue 13 miles (21 km) north on Hwy 395 to the turnoff for the **Tinemaha Wildlife Viewpoint**, on the right. There is a sign some distance before the turnoff, but the dirt road headed east toward **Tinemaha Reservoir** is not marked. Follow signs to the north and up a small hill to the viewpoint. It's a good spot to see the Owens Valley stretching north and south, the Sierra Nevada to the west and the White Mountains to the east. **Tule elk** sometimes feed near the Owens River below the viewpoint in late afternoon or early morning.

The spreading antlers of tule elk were a common sight throughout the Central Valley and Coast Ranges in the early 19th century. By the turn of the century human population pressure and hunting had reduced the elk population to a small Central Valley herd. About 50 elk were brought to the Owens Valley in the 1930s and grew into the largest herd of free-roaming elk in California. The State now stages limited hunts to keep the herd to about 400. Autumn is the best time for viewing the elk, during rutting season when antlered males fight over small bands of cows. Males shed their antlers late each winter and calves are born in the spring.

The next town along Hwy 395 is **Big Pine**, 13 miles (21 km) north of the Tinemaha viewpoint.

BIG PINE

The town has a few motels and eating places, but no tourist office. The small **Palisade Glaciers** looming above Big Pine Canyon to the west are the southern-most living glaciers in North America. In glacier terms, that means the lower ends melt, break off into chunks, and otherwise disintegrate in summer while snow-turned-to-ice feeds into the upper end of the frozen river. For a closer look at the glaciers, turn left onto Glacier Lodge Rd. **Glacier Lodge**; tel: (619) 938-2837, several campgrounds, and the trailhead to the glaciers are 11 miles (18 km) west from Hwy 395.

Big Pine is also the gateway to the **Ancient Bristlecone Pine Forest**, 35 miles (56 km) and 7015 ft (2126 m) above the town. Turn right on Hwy 168 (Westgard Pass Rd). Death Valley Rd turns right (south-east) 2 miles (3 km) from the junction with Hwy 395. Continue straight on Hwy 168 for 11 miles (18 km) to **White Mountain Rd** and turn left. **Schulman Grove** is 22 miles (35 km) up the mountain side.

ANCIENT BRISTLECONE PINE FOREST

Summer is the best time to visit the bristlecones. The road to Schulman Grove is usually open from late June until sometime in October. It takes skis to visit any other time of the year.

Whatever the season, allow a full day for the trip up to the park. There are no services of any kind between Big Pine and the end of the road, so start with a full tank of petrol. Bring food, water (none is available on the mountain), good walking shoes, warm clothing (it can be shivery toward the top) and sun protection (sunburn takes just minutes at high altitude). Any vehicle in good condition should be able to make the drive, though most will cough and wheeze along the way from lack of oxygen – so will most humans. Caravans and large RVs shouldn't go beyond Schulman Grove, at 10,000 ft (3030 m).

Brochures and maps are available at the Cedar Flat entrance station, not far beyond the turn off Hwy 168. Four miles (6 km) later is the **Piñon Picnic Area** at 8000 ft (2424 m).

Next stop is the **Grandview Campground**, on the west side of the road. Take a few minutes to drive to the end of the campground, then walk ¼ mile (0.4 km) to a viewpoint near a pile of boulders. Both the Inyo Mountains and the Sierra crest are visible, making it one of the best places to watch the sunrise or sunset. An even better view is 2 miles (3 km) beyond the campsite on the west side of the road. **Sierra View**, at 9000 ft (2727 m), has a parking lot, toilets, and interpretive displays to explain the incredible vistas. Best times for photography are early and

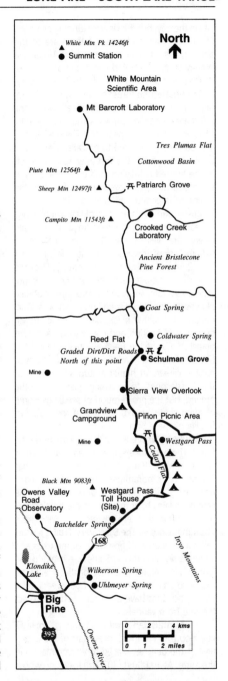

late in the day, but the view is stunning any time. On a clear day (and most of them are at this altitude) the panorama extends from Tioga Pass (Yosemite National Park) in the north to Mt Whitney in the south and east to Death Valley.

The **bristlecone forest** begins 1½ miles (3 km) beyond Sierra View. No camping is allowed in the forest area, including caravans and RVs. It's not a forest in traditional appearance. The bristlecones are too widely scattered to be called dense, but they're everywhere. The vast open spaces, set off by the twisted half-living, half-dead branches of the bristlecones, conveys a sense of visiting the top of an impossibly different world.

Bristlecone pines are the oldest living things on earth. Some of the trees in this mountain reserve are well over 4,000 years old. They're extremely slow growers at this altitude, around 1 inch (2.54 cm) in diameter per century. Over the centuries, the trees have been scoured by wind, sand, heat, rain, snow and ice to driftwood-like blond smoothness, relieved only by an occasional ribbon of healthy black bark leading to an explosion of needles and cones along a distant branch. Most of the trees are well under 25 ft (7.6 m), almost all gnarled and twisted. The even harsher climate at higher altitudes has reduced the bristlecones to crawling just above the ground, but the proliferation of seedlings (some of them centuries old) testifies to the stubborn fertility of these bizarre trees.

Schulman Grove is 1 mile (1.6 km) inside the forest. There are toilets, a picnic area, and a small visitor centre. Rangers at the centre offer interpretive programmes several times each day during the summer. A display outside the centre explains how the age of the bristlecones was determined. There are also two loop trails through the grove. The **Discovery Trail** is a short self-guided loop with fine views of the trees and surrounding mountains. Somewhere along the loop is Pine Alpha, the first bristlecone to be identified as more than 4000 years old. Identifying signs have been removed to protect the tree from vandals.

The **Methuselah Trail** is an easy 4½-mile (7 km) loop through the thickest part of the grove. Rest at the benches placed at viewpoints along the route. At 10,000 ft (3030 m) everyone who is not acclimatised to the altitude slows down. Just walking a few metres can be an effort, even for someone in good physical condition. Pushing too hard only brings on altitude sickness. If possible, allow half a day for the walk.

The **Patriarch Grove** is 13 miles (21 km) along a good gravel road beyond the Schulman Grove and 1000 ft (303 m) higher. The drive takes about 40 mins. At the end is another interpretive exhibit and two short self-guiding trails. Both trails are worth the effort, which, at 11,000 ft (3333 m) can be considerable. The road continues another 4.6 miles (7.4 km) to a locked gate below the University of California laboratories on Mt Barcroft, 12,470 ft (3779 m) and White Mountain, 14,496 ft (4393 m). The area beyond the gate is the **White Mountain Scientific Area,** devoted primarily to research on the effect of high altitude on humans. Do-it-yourself researchers can attempt the 15-mile (24 km) return walk to the peak of White Mountain. Camping is not allowed within the Scientific area.

BIG PINE TO BISHOP

Return to Hwy 395 and turn right to continue north. It's hard to notice much along the way except the awesome face of the Eastern Sierra rising on the left, but there are always a few surprises in store. The highway opens into four lanes 1 mile (1.6 km) north of Big Pine, although the speed limit remains 55 mph (88 kph).

Watch for grey dust devils any time of the year, stormy clouds of alkali dust as fine as flour blowing from the corpse of Lake Owens. The dust clouds are sometimes thick enough to create a driving hazard and occasionally bring on coughing fits. Elk can appear like ghosts from late afternoon through the night until early morning, suddenly looming from nowhere as they step from the sagebrush in matching camouflage colours.

BISHOP

Tourist Information: Bishop Chamber of Commerce, *690 N. Main St, Bishop, CA 93514; tel: (619) 873-8405.* For information on outdoor recreation, visit the **Inyo National**

Forest Headquarters, *873 N. Main St, Bishop, CA 93514; tel: (619) 873-5841*, which shares office space with the **Bureau of Land Management (BLM)**; *tel: (619) 872-4881*. The **White Mountain Ranger Station**, *798 N. Main St, Bishop, CA 93514; tel: (619) 873-4207* has the better selection of maps, permits, and information on walks, sights and campsites.

Accommodation and Food

A regional centre for outdoor recreation, Bishop is well supplied with lodging, including *BW, DI, VI*, and a host of other motels, RV parks, campsites, and bed and breakfasts. The nearest *AY* is **HI-Hilton Creek**, *Ror 1 Box U28, Crowley Lake, CA 93546; tel: (619) 935-4989*, 25 miles (40 km) north (see next page).

Jack's Waffle Shop, *437 N. Main St; tel: (619) 872-7971* is open 24 hours for budget meals. **Erick Schat's Bakery**, *763 N. Main St; tel: (619) 873-7156*, has the best budget bakery goods and light meals for a day's drive in either direction. For traditional American fare, the best bet is **Whiskey Creek**, *524 N. Main St; tel: (619) 873-7174*; budget breakfasts and lunches, moderate dinners. Traditional dinner houses include the **Brass Bell**, *635 N. Main St; tel: (619) 872-1200* and the **Firehouse Grill**, *2206 N. Sierra Hwy (Hwy 395 north of town); tel: (619) 873-4888*, both moderate to expensive.

Sightseeing

The biggest surprise is the town of Bishop itself, a splash of neon and civilisation in the midst of so much natural wonder. Tens of thousands of visitors descend on the town for celebrations in April, when trout fishing season opens, and again for Memorial Day and Labor Day.

The **Owens Valley Paiute-Shoshone Indian Culture Center**, *2300 W. Line Street, Bishop, CA 94514; tel: (619) 873-4478* on the reservation just outside of town, has exhibits covering traditional Native American food, shelter, tools and basketry. There are also occasional and highly unofficial demonstrations of traditional forms of gambling.

The **Chalfant Valley Petroglyph Loop** is a 40 mile (64 km) route through the rolling, sagebrush-covered Chalfant Valley. Several stops offer close-up looks at unusual (and unusually varied) petroglyphs created by the ancestors of present-day Paiutes. Most of the rock drawings are found at places where water used to be: springs, streams and lakes, most of them now dry, courtesy of Los Angeles. Some designs are abstract – spirals, mazes, undulating parallel lines. Many are clear depictions of deer, bighorn sheep, snakes, insects, and footprints of both animals and humans.

What the petroglyphs mean has been lost in the disintegration of Paiute culture. But since most of the carvings are along old hunting trails, many historians suggest that they are somehow related to good hunting luck. Others, like the symbols on modern walls, are probably graffiti. Modern graffiti and vandalism have become such a problem that the Bureau of Land Management office in Bishop sometimes restricts access to the petroglyphs. Check there for directions.

There's no question about directions to the **Laws Railroad Museum and Historical Site**, *Bishop Museum and Historical Society, PO Box 363, Bishop, CA 93514; tel: (619) 873-5950*. Open daily, 1000–1600 Easter–mid-Nov and weekends only during the winter. From Bishop, take US Hwy 6 north 4 miles (6 km) and east from the junction with Hwy 395 to Silver Canyon Rd. Follow Silver Canyon Rd ½ mile (1 km) east to the museum.

The museum covers 11 acres (4.5 ha) surrounding the Laws Station Railroad Depot. Laws was once an important stop on the narrow gauge Carson and Colorado Railroad running between Carson City and Keeler, on Lake Owens. The museum has the restored 1883 depot as well as the *Slim Princess*, the last steam locomotive to haul cars along the railroad, and several restored buildings from the town of Laws, which include a frontier physician's office and dispensary, the railroad agent's house, a library, an old Wells Fargo building, a blacksmith's shop, and the former post office. All have been carefully furnished with period antiques. Across the road is the newly old Drover's Cottage, built in 1966 for the Steve McQueen film *Nevada Smith*.

Death came to Laws in the 1930s. Diversion of water to Los Angeles decimated ranching and farming from Lake Owens to the north end of the

Bishop **189**

valley. There was nothing left for the Carson and Colorado Railroad to ship. The *Slim Princess* steamed into Laws for the last time in 1960.

BISHOP TO MAMMOTH LAKES

Return to Hwy 395 and turn right. Continue north. The road becomes four lanes again at the northern outskirts of Bishop and begins to climb above the **Pleasant Valley Reservoir**, a popular fishing spot. Twelve miles (20 km) beyond the start of the four-lane section is a popular scenic point, overlooking the Owens Gorge. The highway climbs another 2 miles (3 km) to Sherwin Summit, 7000 ft (2121 m). The section of highway over the summit is two lanes, widening to four lanes again just below the top.

Crowley Lake, another popular fishing reservoir, is just below the summit on the right side of the highway. Thousands of anglers swarm across the shores of the lake on the opening day of trout fishing season, the last Saturday in April. There are scenic viewpoints on both sides of the highway just north of the Hilton Creek exit. **Convict Lake**, 5 miles (8 km) north on Convict Lake Rd, is far more serene.

Harder to see is the **Long Valley Caldera**, a massive volcanic crater stretching from Crowley Lake north about 20 miles (32 km) to Obsidian Dome, north of Mammoth Lakes. It's one of the biggest volcanoes in western North America, and easily the most powerful, but virtually invisible to the untutored eye. The immense peak that once covered the area was blasted into dust about 700,000 years ago during a cataclysmic eruption. Ash and pumice spread at least 50 miles (80 km) in all directions in what vulcanologists say is probably the single most destructive volcanic event ever discovered.

MAMMOTH LAKES

Tourist Information: Mammoth Lakes Visitors Bureau, *PO Box 48, Mammoth Lakes, CA 93546; tel: (619) 934-8006 or (800) 367-6572, in Village Center Mall West, on Main St (Hwy 203), across from the post office.* For Forest Service and wilderness maps, permits, and information, visit the **Mammoth Ranger Station** at **Mammoth**

National Forest Visitor Center *off Hwy 203, PO Box 148, Mammoth Lakes, CA 93546; tel: (619) 934-2505.*

Accommodation

Mammoth has more lodging than any other area south of Reno, including the *AY* at Crowley Lake (see previous page), *M6, QI, VI,* and an endless parade of other motels, inns, dormitories, bed and breakfasts and RV parks. The traditional place to stay is the truly mammoth **Mammoth Mountain Inn**, almost on the ski slopes, *PO Box 353, Mammoth Lakes, CA 93546; tel: (619) 934-2581 or (800) 228-4947.* The Visitors Bureau has lodging lists but cannot make bookings.

Booking services include **800 Mammoth**, *tel: (800) 626-6684 or (619) 934-4541*, **Mammoth Accommodation Center**, *tel: (619) 934-6262*, **Mammoth Lakes Accommodations**, *tel: (619) 934-3931*, **Mammoth Reservation Bureau**, *tel: (619) 934-2528 or (800) 527-6273*, **Mammoth Sierra Reservations**, *tel: (619) 934-8372 or (800) 325-8415.* High season is at winter weekends, when Los Angeles skiers flock to Mammoth. Midweek winter prices are substantially lower. Summer rates are often 50% below the winter peak.

There are several Inyo National Forest campsites in the Mammoth Basin, including **Twin Lakes**, **Lake Mary**, and **Lake George**. Closer to town are **Pine City**, **Coldwater**, **Pine Glen** (wheelchair accessible), **New Shady Rest** and **Old Shady Rest**.

Eating and Drinking

Fast food joints have popped up like mushrooms after the first spring rain, but there is also a wide variety of real restaurants – Mammoth has the best selection of eateries on the eastern slope of the Sierra.

The best cheap-to-budget choice is **Blondie's Kitchen**, *in the Sierra Centre Mall on Old Mammoth Rd; tel: (619) 934-4048,* famed for gargantuan breakfasts served all day. Another budget favourite is **O'Kelly & Dunn Co.**, *Minaret Village Shopping Center on Old Mammoth Rd; tel: (619) 934-9316.* Dinners edge into the moderate price range. Beer lovers head for the **Brewhouse Grill** brewpub, *170 Mountain Blvd*

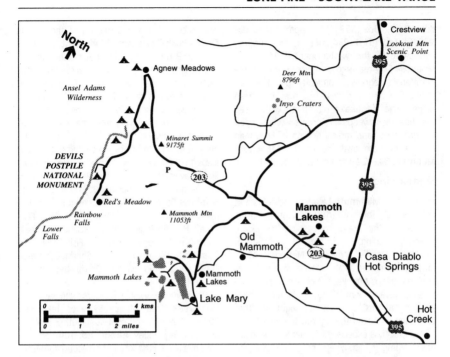

(behind Goodyear Tires); tel: (619) 934-8134. Great views from the deck, and there is live music (usually folk and bluegrass) most nights.

Best bakery (and sandwiches) in the area is **The Gourmet Grocer & Co.**, *Village Center West Mall, off Main St; tel: (619) 934-2997.* The local choice for steaks, prime rib and barbecued ribs is **Whiskey Creek**, *on Hwy 203; tel: (619) 934-2555,* but the moderate prices attract crowds most nights. For similar food and prices, but fewer people, try **Mogul**, *on Tavern; tel: (619) 934-3039.*

The most expensive (and maybe the best) restaurant in town is **The Lakefront Restaurant** at Tamarack Lodge; *tel: (619) 934-2442.* Make reservations for two reasons: the lodge is hard to find (on Lake Mary Rd, the extension of Hwy 203, north of town); and if there are no reservations for the ten tables, the chef goes home early.

Getting Around

The area is so popular in winter that public transport is almost mandatory. **Mammoth Area**

Shuttle (MAS) buses, *tel: (619) 934-2571,* run only during the ski season. Several lines connect the main base lodge and Mammoth village, other lines connect to base chairlifts.

In summer, almost everyone must ride the Forest Service Shuttle to areas beyond Mammoth Lakes, including **Agnew Meadows**, **Red's Meadow**, and **Devil's Postpile National Monument**. Backpackers *must* use the shuttle because backcountry permits prohibit driving into the valley or parking at trailheads. Campers with permits can drive in, with one very large caveat during the summer season: anyone driving in must do so before 0730 or after 1730. All other visitors must use the shuttle. The 2-hour return trip makes 10 stops.

For an Olympian view of the Mammoth Basin, ride the **gondola** to the top of **Mammoth Mountain**, 11,053 ft (3349 m) high. Most visitors ride the gondola back down, but it's possible to hike, or, in a new twist, bicycle down slopes that are reserved for skiers and snowboarders in winter. The **Mammoth Mountain**

Bike Park, *Box 353, Mammoth Lakes, CA 93546; tel: (619) 934-0606,* is the summer equivalent of the winter-oriented Mammoth Mountain Ski Area. Bike trails, like ski trails, come in different degrees of difficulty to suit all skill levels. The park's wildest bike trail has been named **The Kamikaze**, complete with steep switchbacks, sweeping corners, wide open straightaways, and radical downhills. Mountain bike rentals are available at the **Mammoth Mountain Bike Center**, next to the Main Lodge.

Sightseeing

The town of **Mammoth Lakes** provides lodging and services for winter and summer sports throughout the area, from skiing to hiking, camping, fishing, and general sightseeing, including **Devil's Postpile National Monument**. Mammoth is the closest major recreation area to Los Angeles, which accounts for the massive development of hotels, motels, urban-style restaurants, and jet set night life that continues unabated throughout the year.

Mammoth is especially popular with Angelenos for winter skiing, whether they're looking for alpine runs or cross-country challenges. The main alpine ski and snowboarding areas are **Mammoth Mountain Ski Area**; *tel: (619) 934-2571*, and the **June Mountain Ski Area**; *tel: (619) 648-7733*. Other winter activities include sleigh rides, dogsledding, snowmobiling, bobsledding, mountaineering, winter camping, and skating. For winter snow reports; *tel: (619) 934-6166.*

Summertime offers hiking, camping, boating, fishing, golf, hot-air ballooning, horse riding, skating, mountain and rock climbing, flying down mountain trails on bicycles, and lounging in natural hot springs. The one thing Mammoth doesn't have to offer is mountain solitude – on summer weekends, it can seem as if the entire population of the LA basin has moved to the mountains. Take the Mammoth Lakes exit, Hwy 203, west from Hwy 395.

The best driving view in the area is from atop **Minaret Summit**, *9175 ft (2780 m), 3½ miles (6 km) north-west of Mammoth Lakes on Hwy 203.* Private vehicles are not permitted beyond the summit vista point during the day during the summer months, but a regular shuttle provides easy access. The star attraction of the area is **Devil's Postpile National Monument**; *tel: (619) 934-2289,* 6.8 miles (11 km) beyond the summit. The highlight of this 800 acre (324 ha) monument is a sheer wall of symmetrical basaltic columns more than 60 ft (18 m) high. The three- to eight-sided columns, which look like stone piles driven into the earth, were formed by slowly cooling lava flows. The columns are a ½ mile (1 km) from the shuttle stop; a trail leads to the top of the formation, which looks like an oversized tile inlay. The Middle Fork of the San Joaquin River drops about 100 ft (30 m) at **Rainbow Falls**, 2 miles (3 km) by trail from the postpiles. Not far from Devil's Postpile is **Fish Creek Hot Springs**, with no facilities, no fees, and no restrictions. Follow the Fish Creek Trail from Red's Meadow past the Sharktooth Creek Trail, about 100 yards (91 m) beyond the campsite.

The favourite soak in the Mammoth Basin is at **Hot Creek**. From Mammoth Lakes, take Hwy 203 to Hwy 395 and continue south 3 miles (5 km) to **Long Valley Airport Rd**. Turn left and continue a ½ mile (1 km) to the second right turn, **Owens River Road**. The road becomes gravel beyond the **Hot Creek State Fish Hatchery**. Continue 2 miles (3 km) to the **Hot Creek Geothermal Area** and a small parking lot above a small valley. Hot Creek is a cold mountain stream running over vents bubbling with *very* hot water. Hot Creek is 'not recommended' for swimming or soaking by the Forest Service, but nobody seems to heed the warning. The trick is to find a spot that is comfortably warm but not scalding. Swimsuits are required; bring a towel and change in the toilets at the parking lot. And like anywhere else in Mammoth, don't expect to find solitude. Any sunset is likely to find a dozen or more sybarites up to their necks in hot water, many holding cold drinks above the ripples. Just don't settle too close to the hot water vents. A few bathers have actually been scalded to death in recent years by unexpected blasts of super-heated water.

MAMMOTH LAKES TO JUNE LAKE

Return to Hwy 395, turn right. The road reverts

to two lanes just north of the Mammoth Lakes exit and runs up the north end of Long Valley toward **Deadman Summit**, 8036 ft (2435 m). The section of highway over the steep summit is four lanes to allow for passing. For a good look back toward Mammoth, turn left onto **Glass Flow Rd** just north of the summit. A short, easy trail climbs about 600 ft (182 m) to the top of **Obsidian Dome**, a mass of black and colour-streaked volcanic glass. Wear good walking shoes: Native Americans used obsidian from the dome to make arrowheads and other razor-sharp cutting tools. Return to Hwy 395 and turn left. **June Lake Junction** is 1½ miles (3 km) north.

JUNE LAKE

Tourist Information: June Lake Chamber of Commerce, PO Box 2, June Lake, CA 93529; tel: (619) 648-7584.

Accommodation and Food

There are half a dozen motels and resorts, most of them in the town of June Lake or near the lake of the same name. The **Silver Lake Resort**, PO Box 116, June Lake, CA 93529; tel: (619) 648-7525, has tent and RV spaces as well as housekeeping cabins, restaurant, store, petrol station, rental boats, and a boat ramp.

There are also nearly a dozen campsites around the lakes, most of them run by the Forest Service. Some of the prettiest are near Silver Lake. The **Oh! Ridge** campsite, on June Lake, is accessible for the disabled and **Hartley Springs**, just south of June Lake Junction, is free.

For a quick snack, try **Schat's Dutch Bakery**, in the town of June Lake, for great sweet buns and fresh-baked bread.

Sightseeing

This 15-mile (24 km) loop passes a collection of high country lakes, campsites and summer homes in an alpine wonderland more than 7,600 ft (2,303 m) above sea level. The lakes bask in early morning sunlight, but the sawtoothed peaks and permanent snowcaps of the Ansel Adams Wilderness, just to the west, put the area into early shadow each afternoon. The heart-stopping scenery includes four lakes: Grant,

Silver, Gull, and June. All are popular for fishing and water recreation. Grant Lake, the largest, is the only lake open for water-skiing.

In winter, June Lake is a quieter alternative to the crowds skiing Mammoth. **June Mountain Ski Resort**, PO Box 146, June Lake, CA 93529; tel: (619) 648-7733, is owned by Mammoth Mountain; a single lift ticket is valid for both ski areas. Cross-country skiing is also available.

JUNE LAKE TO MONO LAKE/LEE VINING

Follow the June Lake Loop past all four lakes and return to Hwy 395. Turn left. Straight ahead across Hwy 120 are the **Mono Craters**, a dozen light grey volcanoes tinged with black. The explosion pits, cinder cones and lava flows are California's volcanic infants. Less than 60,000 years old, these are the state's youngest mountains, and usually judged the most likely to blow their tops in another round of eruptions. The slopes are largely barren.

The body of water to the east is **Mono Lake**. Three miles (5 km) north of the June Lake Junction is the junction with Hwy 120, coming down from **Yosemite National Park** and **Tioga Pass**. **Lee Vining** lies just beyond the Hwy 120 intersection.

MONO LAKE/LEE VINING

Tourist Information: Mono Lake/Lee Vining Chamber of Commerce, Hwy 395, PO Box 130, Lee Vining, CA 93541; tel: (619) 647-6595. **Mono Basin National Scenic Area Visitor Center**, just north of town to the right of Hwy 395; tel: (619) 647-6572, open daily 0900–1700 most of the year; to 2100 mid-June–Labor Day. The **Mono Lake Committee Information Center and Bookstore**, Hwy 395, PO Box 29, Lee Vining, CA 93541; tel: (619) 647-6386. This self-appointed group, pledged to salvage the lake, maintains an excellent information centre in the centre of town.

Accommodation and Food

Most of the motels and resorts in the area are in or around Lee Vining, including BW. Campsites

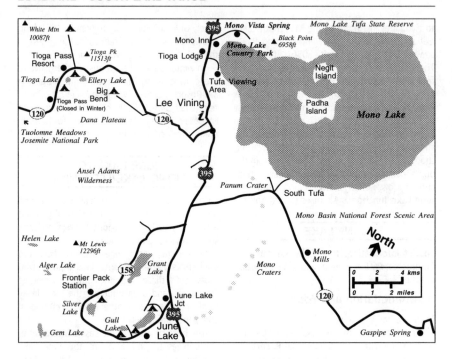

abound, but the most scenic is back along Hwy 120 toward Tioga Pass, **Big Bend Campground**, run by the Forest Service. Rough camping is also allowed in certain areas along the shores of Mono Lake above the 1941 shoreline and on the slopes of the Mono Craters. Ask rangers at the Visitor Center for suggestions and open areas.

For budget–moderate eating, try **Nicely's Restaurant**, *on Hwy 395; tel: (619) 647-6446.*

Sightseeing

The lake is deceptively calm amidst scattered pines, soft pumice sand and a wasteland of jagged stone towers rising from ragged beds of grasses clinging to impossibly salty soil. But for all the apparent calm, Mono Lake is the centre of one of the fiercest ecological battles of the century. The City of Los Angeles is facing a coalition of ardent environmentalists, local landowners, and government scientists.

The lake itself is well over 700,000 years old, possibly the oldest lake in North America. It's the nesting ground for about 85% of the California gull population, which feed on the four trillion or so brine shrimp and countless brine flies that hatch in the shallows each year. The lake is too salty and too alkaline to support other life. The jagged spires that dot the shoreline and the shallows, especially in the **South Tufa Area** are tufa, or limestone, that was deposited when hot, mineral-laden water bubbled from hot springs into the cooler lake water. Most of the spires have been exposed since the lake level began dropping in 1941.

The war over Mono Lake began in 1930 when Los Angeles voters decided to extend the Owens Valley aqueduct system north into the Mono Basin. Since the first aqueduct was opened in 1941, the lake level has dropped more than 40 ft (12 m), uncovering the dramatic tufa spires and significantly increasing the mineral content of the remaining waters. In the 1970s a band of lake and local property rights advocates began challenging the LA Department of Water and Power in court, in the press, and in public protests. The goal is to return the lake level to something approaching the 1941 level by halting diversion of Mono Basin water. So far, the DWP has been beaten to a stalemate and the battle continues.

For a close look at Mono Lake, start at the Visitor Center, 1 mile (1.5 km) north of town on Hwy 395. Reverse direction and drive 6 miles (19 km) south on Hwy 395 to the junction of Hwy 120 eastbound. Continue 3 miles (5 km) and turn left toward the **South Tufa Area**. Follow the dirt road 1 mile (1.6 km) toward the lake to a parking lot, then walk the ¼ mile (0.6 km) to the water line. The tufa spires tower like misshapen castle turrets, although they are quite fragile. Climbing and collecting are forbidden. Swimming is permitted; the best is Navy Beach, a 10 min walk to the east. The salty, highly alkaline water is very buoyant and extremely irritating to eyes and open wounds. There are no showers at the lake. Best times for photography are dawn and sunset. The two islands, light coloured Paoha Island and black Negit Island, are nesting sites for gulls and other birds.

MONO LAKE TO
SOUTH LAKE TAHOE

Return to Hwy 395 and turn right. Continue north. **Mono Lake County Park**, on the right 4½ miles (7 km) north of Lee Vining, has a pleasant picnic area overlooking Mono Lake. The best view of the lake is from atop Black Point, a 45 min scramble from the end of the road just beyond the park.

The valley floor is extremely dry, but it's easy to spot the many streams flowing down from the Sierra to the west. Every streambed is lined with aspens, a stark contrast of green (spring–late summer) or gold (autumn) against the sagebrush-covered hills.

Just beyond the park the highway begins climbing toward Conway Summit, 8138 ft (2467 m), 5½ miles (8.5 km) away. Six miles (9.5 km) below the summit is Hwy 270 leading to **Bodie State Historic Park**, *PO Box 515, Bridgeport, CA 93517; tel: (619) 647-6445*. Turn right onto Hwy 270, closed in winter, usually Nov–mid-April. The road is paved most of the way and is passable by passenger vehicles all the way to Bodie.

A century ago, a young girl wrote, 'Goodbye, God, we are going to Bodie'. What's left of the town sometimes evokes the same emotion, but more often it's a sense of amazement that the town ever prospered. In its heyday around the 1880s, the booming town had a population of 10,000 and over 30 mines. Citizens boasted that Bodie had the widest streets (all the way to the horizon), the meanest men, the worst climate, and the most disgusting whiskey in the West. Virgin Alley and Maiden Lane had neither. A local preacher called the town 'a sea of sin lashed by tempests of lust and passion'.

When the mines died, so did the town, along with the churches, red light district, newspaper, and general store. Most inhabitants simply walked away, leaving homes and businesses as though they were due to return. The 170 buildings that remain are preserved in a state of arrested decay, right down to a rusting child's wagon in the middle of an empty street. Visitors are free to wander the ghost town and peek through tattered lace curtains and discolouring glass at sagging bedsprings, dusty clothing, and store shelves still filled with merchandise. Pick up a self-guiding brochure at the **museum** in the old **Miner's Union Hall**. There is no smoking anywhere in Bodie because of high fire danger.

Return to Hwy 395. Turn right. **Bridgeport** is 6½ miles (10.5 km) north through a long, narrow valley filled with small ranches. From Bridgeport, the highway cuts diagonally through Long Valley toward the Sierra, over **Devil's Gate Summit**, 7519 ft (2278 m) and down into the Antelope Valley. As the valley narrows to the north, the highway follows a rushing creek, popular with trout fishermen hoping to catch dinner.

The tiny town of **Walker** is 24 miles (38 km) north of Bridgeport, with 300 people and the **Three Flags Trading Post**. The wooden Indian out front gives it a Disneyesque air of unreality. The even smaller towns of **Coleville** and **Topaz** lead to **Topaz Lake**, a windy lake straddling the California–Nevada border. The first Nevada casino, **Lake Topaz Casino Lodge**, is 1 mile (1.6 km) beyond the border. Hwy 395 continues another 20 miles (32 km) north to Hwy 207, the turnoff for Genoa. For the remainder of the route see Lake Tahoe Circuit, on the next page.

LAKE TAHOE CIRCUIT

To old-time Northern Californians, Lake Tahoe is simply 'The Lake', a sapphire-blue mirror fringed with rugged mountains, draped across the California–Nevada border. Tahoe is the largest alpine lake in North America, a rough oval 22 miles (35 km) long by 12 miles (19 km) wide. The lake averages nearly 990 ft (327 m) deep, its deepest point is 1545 ft (510 m) below the surface, and it holds enough water to flood the entire state to a depth of about 14 inches (36cm). On a calm day, the reflection of mountains, sky, and clouds is so rich and perfect that the originals seem like pale shadows.

Allow at least a half-day to drive and sightsee the 72 miles (115 km) around Tahoe, or two hours without stopping. The 28-mile (34 km) drive to Carson City and Virginia City takes about 45 minutes, but allow the better part of a day (or an overnight) for exploring.

The lake circuit begins at Stateline, but can be joined anywhere around the lake. **Drive Around Lake Tahoe**, for sale at most tourist-oriented shops around the lake, is an audio cassette guided tour of the lake circuit.

ROUTE

A clockwise route around the lake gives passengers the best views. From **Stateline**, and **South Lake Tahoe**, follow **Hwy 50** south-west to the junction with **Hwy 89**. Turn right onto Hwy 89. Continue north along the west shore to **Tahoe City**, then follow Hwy 28 north around the tip of the lake and south down the east shore, through **Incline Village**, to **Hwy 50**. Take Hwy 50 south to return to Stateline.

To visit Carson City and Virginia City if following the clockwise tour of the lake, travel south on Hwy 28 along the eastern shore of the lake as far as **Spooner Junction**. From Spooner Junction take Hwy 50 west.

The road climbs steeply from the lake, closely following the Emigrant Trail route from Nevada into the Tahoe Basin. The **Tahoe Rim Trail trailhead** is ½ mile (0.8 km) from the junction, just below **Spooner Summit**, 7146 ft (2358 m). The road sweeps down the nearly sheer eastern side of the mountains, providing magnificent vistas into Nevada. Clouds lose most of their moisture as snow and rain on the Tahoe side of the divide, leaving Nevada noticeably drier. In the Tahoe Basin, trees and underbrush are thick and lush at 6000 ft (1980 m). On the Nevada side, trees have all but disappeared by the same elevation except near streams running down from the peaks. Most of the mountainsides and the valley below are covered with dusty brush or the bright green of irrigated pastures.

Hwy 50 joins Hwy 395 9 miles (14 km) from the summit. To go directly to Carson City, the capital of Nevada, turn left onto Hwy 395. For a closer look at local history, turn right onto Hwy 395. Continue 1 mile (1.6 km) to **Jacks Valley Rd**, Hwy 206, and turn right toward **Genoa**, the first permanent settlement in Nevada, founded in 1851.

The **Genoa Courthouse Museum**, Main St; tel: (702) 782-4325, has replicas of an old schoolroom, courtroom, jail, and kitchen, plus Native American displays. **Mormon Station Historic State Park**, Main St at Hwy 57; tel: (702) 782-2590, is a reconstruction of the original log stockade and trading post, now a history museum. The museums are open only in summer, but the park picnic area is open all year. Take Hwy 57 to Hwy 395, 4 miles (6 km) east, and turn left toward **Carson City**.

Continue north on Hwy 395 to Williams St. Turn right onto Hwy 50 toward **Fallon** and continue 7 miles (11 km) to Hwy 341. Turn left toward **Virginia City**.

The road snakes up Gold Canyon, once among the richest silver and gold deposits in North America. The canyon is littered with abandoned mines and rusting equipment. Splotches of gold, red and yellow are 'tailings', piles of waste rock and dirt from mining operations. All land is private, much of it riddled

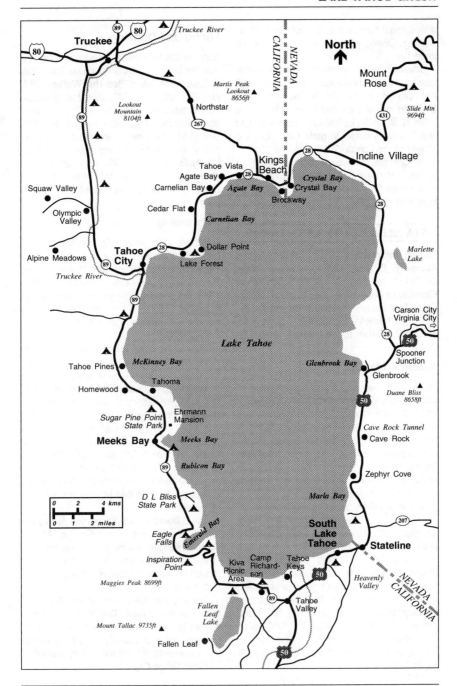

Lake Tahoe Map

with decrepit tunnels that can collapse without warning. Owners of active mines are jealously protective.

Silver City, now a collection of ramshackle houses and abandoned equipment, is 5 miles (8 km) from the junction. The **Golden Nugget Bar & Saloon**, one of the oldest hotels in Nevada, is in **Gold Hill**, 1 mile (1.6 km) uphill from Silver City and two miles below **Virginia City**, once the 'Queen of the Comstock.'

Retrace the route back to Lake Tahoe, or continue north on Hwy 341, which returns to Hwy 395 on the outskirts of Reno (Sacramento–Reno Route, p. 256).

STATELINE/SOUTH LAKE TAHOE

Tourist Information: Lake Tahoe Visitors Authority, *PO Box 16299, South Lake Tahoe, CA 96151; tel: (916) 544-5050*; **South Tahoe Chamber of Commerce**, *3066 Lake Tahoe Blvd, South Lake Tahoe, CA 96150; tel: (916) 541-5255*; and **Tahoe Visitors Center**, *4018 Hwy 50, South Lake Tahoe, CA 96150; tel: (916) 573-2674.*

Accommodation

South Shore has the largest concentration of glitzy hotels and resorts, starting with the casinos which abut the state line between California and Nevada. The Lake Tahoe Visitors Authority handles bookings; *tel: (800) 288-2463.* For the best bargains, consult the pink 'Datebook' Entertainment Section of the *Sunday San Francisco Chronicle and Examiner.* Lodging prices are generally lowest Sun–Thur.

Caesar's Tahoe, *Stateline, NV 89449; tel: (702) 588-3515*, **Harrah's Hotel & Casino**, *Stateline, NV 89449, tel: (702) 588-6611*, **Harvey's Resort Hotel**, *Stateline, NV 89449; tel: (702) 588-2411*, and **Horizon Casino Resort**, *Stateline, NV 89449; tel: (702) 588-6211* are the biggest, the brightest, and the first on the Nevada side; budget–expensive. The **Fantasy Inn**, *3696 Lake Tahoe Blvd, South Lake Tahoe, CA 96150; tel: (800) 367-7736*, is an adults-only hotel specialising in fantasy, romance, and weddings. Chains include *BW, DI, ES, M6*, and *TL*.

Eating and Drinking

Stateline casino buffets occasionally cost less than the fast food outlets along Lake Tahoe Blvd in South Lake Tahoe. **Red Hut Waffles**, *2723 Hwy 50; tel: (916) 541-9024*, has enormous budget breakfasts, especially waffles and omelettes. **Scooza!**, *1142 Ski Run Blvd; tel: (916) 542-0100*, has some of the most imaginative pizzas and pastas at the lake; moderate. **Llwelyn's**, *on the 19th floor at Harvey's Casino; tel: (702) 588-2411*, has spectacular views, great food, and possibly the highest prices.

Sightseeing

The chief indoor activities in Stateline or South Lake Tahoe are gambling, eating, and the **Lake Tahoe Historical Society and Museum**, *3058 Hwy 50, South Lake Tahoe, CA 96156; tel: (916) 541-5458.* The museum concentrates on Tahoe's natural and human history, including the oldest building still standing in the region, a toll house built in 1859.

Hwy 50, or **Lake Tahoe Blvd**, is lined with small sports equipment shops, bars and restaurants. On the California side, a maze of small, mostly run-down motels has been replaced by a few larger establishments (including *ES*) and a strip park along the lake front. **Ski Run Blvd**, 1 mile (1.6 km) inside California, is the first automobile access to the lake. The **Tahoe Queen**, *PO Box 14327, South Lake Tahoe, CA 95702; tel: (916) 541-3364 or (800) 238-2463*, a modern stern-wheel paddleboat, offers daily lake cruises from the **Ski Run Marina** at the foot of Ski Run Blvd.

The **El Dorado Beach Recreation Area** is one mile (1.6 km) beyond the Ski Run Marina. **Thomas Reagan Beach**, the largest patch of sand on the lake, is jammed with swimmers and sunbathers in summer and almost empty the rest of the year.

The highway leaves lake at the Recreation Area, turning toward **The Y**, the Y-shaped intersection of Hwys 50 and 89. Hwy 50 continues south and west toward Echo Summit and Sacramento. Hwy 89 turns north, toward the lake and **Tahoe City**.

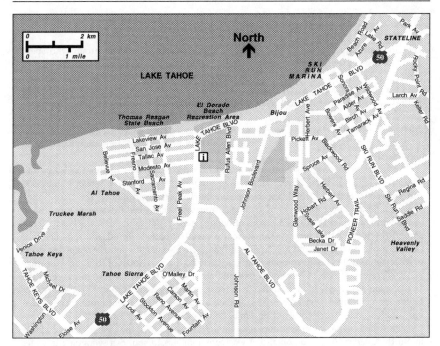

SOUTH LAKE TAHOE TO TAHOE CITY

The strip development lining Hwys 50 and 89 ends abruptly at the boundary of the **Tahoe Basin National Forest**, 1.2 miles (2 km) north of The Y, *PO Box 8465, South Lake Tahoe, CA 96158; tel: (916) 573-2600.* The **Headquarters**, *870 Emerald Bay Rd,* is open during business hours all year. The lake is occasionally visible through gaps in the trees and the forest seems relatively untouched. It's some of the best preserved forest along the lake, but it's all second growth.

Much of the road along the west shore is lined with a walking/cycling path. Two miles (3.2 km) north of the National Forest boundary are **Kiva Picnic Area**, and the turnoff and parking area for the **Tallac Historic Site**, *The Tahoe Tallac Association, Box 1595, South Lake Tahoe, CA 95705; tel: (916) 541-4975.* The site is open only in summer, but visitors can walk the area all year. Tallac is a 74-acre monument to Tahoe's days as an elite retreat before the highway around the

lake was completed in the 1930s. The site consists of three estates: the **Baldwin Estate**, now a museum; the **Pope-Tevis Mansion**; and **Valhalla**, a massive stone and timber home with a walk-in fireplace off the Great Hall. The buildings are being restored under Forest Service Supervision as money permits and emerging as a busy cultural centre. Local artists are showcased at regular exhibitions, part of a summer-long arts and music festival.

Just north of Tallac is a summer-only visitor centre and several self-guided nature walks. The **Rainbow Trail** drops below ground into a 'stream profile chamber' with glass walls onto Taylor Creek. It's a good stop any time of the year, but especially during Oct, when Kokanee salmon migrate upstream to spawn.

The highway begins climbing 2 miles (3.2 km) north of the visitor centre. A series of switchbacks offers wonderful views, but no lay-bys, as the road climbs to **Inspiration Point**, overlooking **Emerald Bay**. The Point has ample parking (rare along the lakeshore), toilets, and explanations of the history and geography of the Tahoe Basin.

Lake Tahoe

The original native people in the area were the Washoes, a peaceful group who spent summers near Lake Tahoe and winters in the warmer valleys along the western edge of Nevada, near what is now Genoa, Carson City, and Reno. US Army Capt John Fremont and his guide, Kit Carson, saw Tahoe in 1844. They were the first outsiders to spot the lake and return to tell about it. Most 49ers avoided the rugged terrain around Tahoe for easier routes across the Sierra Nevada, but the tide turned once the Comstock Lode was discovered beneath Virginia City. 'Bonanza Road', now Hwy 50, zigzagged through the mountains from Placerville to Lake Tahoe, then clung precariously along mountainsides to Virginia City.

The Comstock Lode was hard rock mining, hundreds of miles of tunnels drilled and blasted through solid rock. Every tunnel was supported by a massive timber framework, and between 1860 and 1890, the dense forests that once surrounded the Lake Tahoe vanished. So did immense stocks of giant lake trout and landlocked Kokanee salmon, fished to the brink of extinction to feed hordes of hungry miners. But as the Comstock played out around the turn of the century, Tahoe slowly reverted back to forest and fish. The lake became a playground for the rich from San Francisco, Sacramento and Los Angeles. Fleets of steamships hauled holidaymakers from one party to the next, most of them held on long-vanished private estates. Once roads into and around the Tahoe Basin were paved in the 1930s, middle class adventurers added their more modest holiday homes. The 1960 Winter Olympics at Squaw Valley (see p. 334) ignited a fury of development around Tahoe that only abated under strict construction limits that took effect in the late 1980s.

Lake Tahoe *isn't* as clean as it once was, though it's still one of the clearest, cleanest lakes in North America. A generation ago, it was commonplace to spot fish swimming in water more than 100 ft (33 m) deep. Today, visibility rarely passes 75 ft (25 m). Blame algae that thrive in water polluted with nutrients from lawns, gardens and septic systems. Millions of visitors crowd into summer and winter recreation facilities, jamming traffic. The best time to visit is late spring, when melting snows discourage skiers and other visitors, and autumn, after the summer crush and before the ski slopes open around Thanksgiving (late Nov).

The shallow, emerald green bay is one of the few sections of the lake that freezes in winter. The main body of Lake Tahoe is deep enough that freezing water from the surface sinks toward the bottom, pushing warmer water to the surface. The steady convection current keeps ice from forming in all but shallow protected shoreline areas.

Emerald Bay is almost completely filled by a glacial moraine, the pile of rock and gravel pushed ahead of an advancing glacier. At the head of the fjord-like bay is **Vikingsholm**, tel: (916) 541-3030, a heavily romanticised reproduction of a 9th-century Norse fortress with 38 rooms. The home is open for tours in summer, but the only way in is by boat or down a steep path that drops 600 ft (198 m) in 1 mile (1.6 km).

The walk back feels two or three times longer. When the house was built in 1928–29, the only access was by boat – the road ended near Inspiration Point. The estate included including a tea house (now a ruin) on Fannette Island, rising from the middle of Emerald Bay. It's an easier walk up to **Eagle Falls**, across the highway from the Bay.

No stopping is allowed for several miles north of Emerald Bay because the road is too narrow. **D.L. Bliss State Park**, Sierra State Parks, PO Drawer D, Tahoma, CA 96142; tel: (916) 525-7232, is one of the most popular parks on the lake. The beach fills up by noon in summer and campsites must be booked well in advance through **MISTIX**, tel: (800) 444-7275. Bliss is also headquarters for Emerald Bay and **Sugar Pine**

Point State Park, 6 miles (10 km) north. Sugar Pine has 2 miles (3.2 km) of rocky beach, but the real treasure is **Ehrmann Mansion**, the quintessential Tahoe summer house. The two-storey stone and pine Queen Anne-style house was built in 1903 by San Francisco banker Isaias Hellman, who called it Pine Lodge. The house, including a first-floor museum, is only open in summer. The grounds, open all year, offer an 1870 cabin, a nature centre, and nature tracks. Roadside and lakefront development increases north of Sugar Pine.

TAHOE CITY

Tourist Information: Tahoe North Visitors and Convention Bureau, PO Box 5578, Tahoe City, CA 96145; tel: (916) 583-3494 or (800) 824-6348; **Greater North Lake Tahoe Chamber of Commerce**; tel: (916) 581-6900.

Accommodation

North Shore is more relaxed and outdoors-oriented than casino-crazed South Shore, but no less crowded during peak summer and winter seasons. The CVB handles room bookings; tel: (800) 824-6348, a particularly useful service since North Shore accommodation, including TL, is in short supply. **Sunnyside Lodge and Restaurant**, 1850 West Lake Blvd; tel: (916) 583-7200, provides pricey old-style Tahoe atmosphere on the lake. Most rooms have private decks overlooking the water. **Tahoe City Inn**, 790 North Lake Blvd; tel: (800) 800-8246, is a long-time favourite, moderate off-season, pricey the rest of the year. **Cottage Inn**, just south of town at 1690 West Lake Blvd; tel: (916) 525-7333, is a moderate–pricey classic cluster of dark brown buildings with blue shutters and knotty pine interiors.

Eating and Drinking

Rosie's Café, 571 North Lake Blvd; tel: (916) 583-8504, has budget–moderate traditional fare such as ham and eggs and burgers. Locals like the **Fire Sign Café**, 2 miles (3 k) south of town, 1785 West Lake Blvd; tel: (916) 583-0871, for breakfast and lunch. **Hacienda del Lago**, 760 North Lake Blvd; tel: (916) 583-0358, is the local

hot spot for moderate Mexican food. Area resorts offer fine, if pricey, restaurants; bookings are essential. **Christy Hill**, 115 Grove St; tel: (916) 583-8551, in the Lakehouse Mall, usually gets the nod for the best California cuisine on the lake, expensive–pricey. **La Playa**, 7046 North Lake Blvd; tel: (916) 546-5903, is best for salads, seafood, and Sunday brunch; expensive.

Sightseeing

The best place to see monstrous trout is **Fanny Bridge** across the Truckee River in Tahoe City – named after the throngs of fish fans leaning over the bridge to watch the fish they aren't allowed to catch. There's not much to see in drought years, when the river slows to a trickle.

Rain or drought, the **Gatekeeper's Log Cabin Museum**, 130 West Lake Blvd; tel: (916) 583-1762, is one of the most popular attractions in town. The engineer responsible for maintaining the small dam at the mouth of the Truckee river once lived on the site. The reconstructed gatekeeper's cabin has displays on local and natural history, including Native American artifacts and historical photographs. The museum is open only in summer, the grounds and picnic area are open all year.

Spring–autumn, **North Tahoe Cruising**, 700 North Lake Blvd; tel: (916) 583-0141, offers water tours to Emerald Bay, a 'Shoreline Treasures' cruise past historical sites and modern lakefront estates on the west shore, as well as cocktail and dinner dance cruises.

More expansive views can be found at the top of the **Squaw Valley Cable Car**, 1960 Squaw Valley Rd; tel: (916) 583-6985. Like most Tahoe area ski resorts, Squaw Valley is pushing hard for summer business with walking, mountain biking, horse riding, and full use of spa/recreational facilities. Most resorts hire mountain bikes for use on ski slope access roads. They encourage cyclists to take the lift up and ride down, but fanatics are welcome to cycle up the mountain as well. **Porter's Ski and Sport**, tel: (916) 583-0293, and **CyclePaths**, tel: (916) 581-1171, have the best selection of hire mountain bikes as well as guided tours and suggestions for individual exploring. Mountain biking and walking are also allowed on nearly all of the old logging roads in the area; the Forest Service headquarters in South Lake Tahoe has maps and suggestions.

State parks around Tahoe offer short guided nature walks as well as longer treks. In winter, rangers swap hiking boots for snowshoes and cross country skis to continue their guided forest explorations.

Serious walkers should enquire about progress on the **Tahoe Rim Trail**, a volunteer effort to build and maintain 150 miles (240 km) of loop trail along the ridge lines surrounding the lake. The full loop is scheduled to be completed sometime this decade, with almost constant views of the lake as well as visits to the Sierra Nevada's largest bog, trees carved by Basque herders more than a century ago, and a major geothermal area. For information, contact **Tahoe Rim Trail**, *PO Box 10156, South Lake Tahoe, CA 96158; tel: (916) 577-0676.*

At Tahoe City, Hwy 89 turns away from the lake toward Squaw Valley, Truckee, and Quincy. Continue around the lake on Hwy 28. A **US Coast Guard Station** and public beach are two miles (3 km) beyond Tahoe City. **Carnelian Bay**, three miles (5 km) beyond the station, is an old resort town and marina. **Tahoe Vista**, just beyond, is one of the earliest resort towns on the lake, complete with comfortable, if slightly run-down resorts and motels.

The road begins to climb above the lake at **Rockway**, just before the California–Nevada state line. Lake views from Rockway are best in the morning. It's hard to miss the state line – the Nevada side of the forest suddenly sprouts casinos and large commercial developments.

INCLINE VILLAGE

Tourist Information: Incline Village Chamber of Commerce, *969 Tahoe Blvd, Incline Village, NV 89451; tel: (702) 831-4440 or (800) 468-2463.*

Accommodation

The **Tahoe North Convention and Visitors Bureau** *tel: (800) 824-6348*, handles bookings. Top of the line is the very pricey **Hyatt Regency Lake Tahoe Resort & Casino**, *Lakeshore At Country Club Dr; tel: (702) 832-1234.*

Sightseeing

Incline has a the best collection of fast food on the east shore, but the biggest draw is 1 mile (1.6 km) south of town. **Ponderosa Ranch**, *100 Ponderosa Ranch Rd; tel: (702) 831-0691*, is a Western theme park built around television and film sets used for the *Bonanza* series and later spinoffs. The park features tours of the Bonanza ranch house, complete with movable walls and ceilings to facilitate filming, and Hop Sing's kitchen, where the table is permanently set for Ben Cartwright and sons Hoss, Little Joe, and Adam. The park claims the world's largest collection of antique farm machinery, much of it on display in a reconstructed barn amidst television monitors playing a montage of *Bonanza* clips in more than a dozen languages. The cinematic mockup of Virginia City is a less interesting – the real thing is only 30 miles (48 km) away. A summer-only Haywagon Breakfast Ride offers spectacular views over Lake Tahoe on the way to an all-you-can eat pancake breakfast. The park is open May–Oct.

Lake Tahoe State Park begins just south of the Ponderosa Ranch, several miles of undeveloped shoreline dotted with house-sized boulders and occasional sandy beaches open to the public. The largest is **Sand Harbor**, with a small boat landing. A large meadow and wildlife viewing area is 5 miles (8 km) south of Sand Harbor, just before **Spooner Lake** and **Spooner Junction**, the junction with Hwy 50. Hwy 50 eastbound climbs toward Spooner Summit and drops down toward Carson City. Westbound, the highway continues south around Lake Tahoe. A vista point 5 miles (8 km) south of the junction offers an excellent view across the south end of the lake. **Cave Rock Tunnel** and **Cave Rock Cove** are just beyond. **Zephyr Cove** is 2½ miles (4 km) beyond the tunnel with a long, very popular beach surrounding a long pier. The pier is home to the **MS Dixie**, *760 Hwy 50, Zephyr Cove, NV 89448; tel: (702) 588-3508*, a genuine Mississippi stern-wheel paddle boat. One of the most popular cruises crosses the lake to Emerald Bay. Other offerings include breakfast, brunch, sunset, dinner, and dance cruises, and a south shore sightseeing trip.

CARSON CITY

Tourist Information: Carson City Chamber of Commerce Visitor Center, on the ground floor, *2180 South Carson St. Carson City, NV 89701; tel: (702) 882-7474*; and the **Carson City Convention & Visitors Bureau**, on the first floor; *tel: (702) 687-7410 or (800) 638-2321.*

Accommodation

Rooms may be in short supply when the state legislature is in session, but the rest of the year, Carson City is a small-town alternative to sleeping in Reno, 31 miles (50 km) north. Chains include *BW* and *DI*. **Downtowner Motor Inn**, *801 North Carson St; tel: (702) 882-1333 or (800) 364-4908*, is a good budget–moderate alternative.

Eating and Drinking

The best choice in town is **Adele's**, *1112 North Carson St; tel: (702) 882-3353*, with an enormous menu of Nevada-style California cuisine; moderate. The **Carson City Depot**, *111 East Telegraph; tel: (702) 884-4546*, a brewpub in the former bus depot, is a favourite with state government workers and downtown professionals.

Sightseeing

The Carson City Convention and Visitors Bureau publishes an excellent free brochure with self-guided walking and driving tours of the old part of town, west of Carson St. The tour includes the home used in John Wayne's last film, *The Shootist*. The **Nevada State Museum**, *600 South Carson St; tel: (702) 687-4810*, is in the old US Mint, where silver dollars were once produced. Exhibits include state historical relics, a reproduction ghost town, coins, and a walk-through mine.

The ornate **State Capitol Building**, *101 North Carson St*, is open during business hours. The **Brewery Arts Center**, *449 West King St; tel: (702) 883-1976*, is an arts centre housed in an old brewery. **Carson Hot Springs**, *1500 Hot Springs Rd; tel: (702) 882-0567*, is newly refurbished and newly popular.

The **Stewart Indian Museum**, *5366 Snyder Ave; Carson City, NV 89701; tel: (702) 882-1808*, once a school for Native Americans, highlights native cultures from the area. The museum trading post sells rugs, jewellery, beadwork, and other artworks.

Hwy 395, marked as Carson St closer to Carson City, is lined with small shopping malls and businesses. The **Nevada State Railroad Museum**, *2180 South Carson St; tel: (702) 687-6953*, is on the left, across the railroad tracks. The museum has more than 26 exhibits from the Virginia & Truckee Railroad, including several restored locomotives and a restored depot.

VIRGINIA CITY

Tourist Information: Virginia City Visitors Bureau; *tel: (702) 847-0177*; and the **Virginia City Chamber of Commerce**, *PO Box 464, Virginia City, NV 89440; tel: (702) 847-0311.*

Accommodation

Most visitors arrive en route or on a day trip. There are about 100 rooms scattered among a half-dozen inns, bed and breakfasts and motels, but advance bookings are essential in summer. The Chamber of Commerce has the most complete lodging list.

Eating and Drinking

Food is nourishment, not a fetish, in Virginia City. The choice runs toward pancakes, soup, sandwiches, and steaks, usually on C St, the main street. The **Union Brewery**, *28 North C St; no phone*, is the most unusual bar in town. The interior is a mass of dusty Nevadiana, from a collection of 'whorehouse miniatures', miniature spirit bottles once used to advertise Nevada's legal brothels, to ancient beer bottles, boxing gloves, road signs, and a Christmas tree hanging upside down from the ceiling festooned with cast-off bras.

Sightseeing

The Union Brewery is one of two monuments to the rowdy atmosphere that pervaded Virginia City in its heyday from 1860 to 1880. The other is the **Storey County Courthouse**, *B St near Union*, and its statue of Justice without her

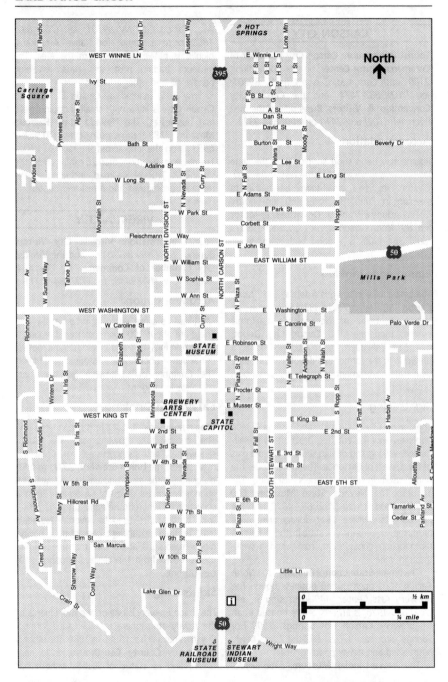

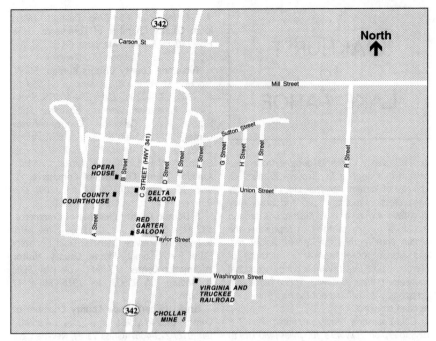

traditional blindfold. In the 1870s, the value of mining shares on the Virginia City Exchange exceeded the value of all US currency in circulation throughout the country. Justice, like everything else in the booming, boisterous city, was for sale. **Piper's Opera House**, *B and Union Sts; tel: (702) 847-0433*, was once the cultural centre of the entire West. Most of the interior furnishings and stage equipment is original.

That kind of opulence wasn't cheap, even in the 1880s. The 100-plus mines in and around Virginia City produced over $400 million in silver before the turn of the century – the slopes above, below, and beneath the town are riddled with unmapped mine shafts. The **Ponderosa Saloon**, *106 South C St; tel: (702) 847-0757*, offers guided tours of a small section of mine directly below the building. The **Chollar Mine**, *South F St; tel: (702) 847-0155*, offers a more extensive look at a far larger mine.

C Street is lined with historical buildings, most of them converted for the tourist trade. Mark Twain and Bret Harte, once reporters for the *Territorial Enterprise*, Nevada's first newspaper,

would recognise the buildings, if not the uses to which they have been put. The firehouse has become the **Comstock Firemen's Museum**, *125 South C St; tel: (702) 847-0717*. **The Delta**, *18 South C St; tel: (702) 847-0788*, and other saloons now cater to video poker players and museum goers. The few remaining gambling tables have become museum pieces.

Twain has his own museum. **Mark Twain's Museum of Memories**, *109 C St*, spreads through what was once the Nevada Bank of San Francisco, a livery stable, and Frederick's General Store. What was once the busiest red light district between San Francisco and St Louis has been reduced to a few museum cases in the **Red Garter Saloon**, *80 South C St; tel: (702) 847-0665*.

The **Virginia & Truckee Railroad**, *PO Box 467; tel: (702) 847-0380*, which once hauled, ore, bullion, freight and passengers, has been reborn as a tourist line to Gold Hill. The miners, gunslingers, lawmen, and saloon girls who fight, shout, and shoot it out along C St during the summer are all actors hired for the part.

Virginia City   **205**

OAKHURST to LAKE TAHOE

In 1848, sleepy California became front page news with a casual gold discovery 30 miles (48 km) east of Sacramento. Thousands left families and professions to take up pick and shovel. Hwy 49 follows a chain of Gold Rush towns through the Sierra Nevada foothills. In September the Mother Lode foothills sparkle with yellow, red, and orange foliage against a backdrop of evergreen pine forest. Winter brings occasional snow and traffic slowdowns. Spring bursts into green and wild daffodils dot the hills. Summer is hot and crowded.

Gold Country is heavily promoted. Plan 3–5 days to explore Hwy 49's 300 miles (480 km) to allow for low speed limits; winding, narrow roads; and summer traffic congestion.

ROUTE

Take Hwy 49 north from **Oakhurst to Nevada City**. Follow Hwy 20 to Hwy 80 at **Emigrant Gap**. Take Hwy 80 over **Donner Pass**. (Sacramento–Reno, p. 256, and Chester–Lake Tahoe, p. 330).

Turn right on Hwy 89 to the west shore of **Lake Tahoe** (see Lake Tahoe Circuit, p. 196). Oakhurst, Mariposa, Placerville and Auburn have the best petrol prices.

Tourist Information

Each county along Hwy 49 has information on local Gold Rush history, sights, accommodation and dining. Important towns and historic parks in each county are in parentheses. **Golden Chain Council of the Mother Lode,** PO Box 49, Newcastle, CA 95658; tel: (916) 663-2061, publishes a Mother Lode map. **Eastern Madera County Chamber of Commerce,** 49074 Civic Circle, PO Box 369, Oakhurst, CA

93644; tel: (209) 683-7766 (Oakhurst). **Mariposa County Chamber of Commerce,** 5158 Hwy 140, PO Box 425, Mariposa, CA 95338; tel: (209) 966-2456 (Mariposa, Coulterville).
Tuolumne County Visitors Bureau, 55 W. Stockton St, PO Box 4020, Sonora, CA 95370; tel: (209) 533-4420 or (209) 984-4636 (Chinese Camp, Jamestown, Sonora, Columbia State Historic Park). **Calaveras County Visitor Center,** 1211 S. Main St, PO Box 637, Angels Camp, CA 95222; tel: (209) 736-0049, (Angels Camp, Murphys, San Andreas, Mokelumne Hill). **Amador County Chamber of Commerce,** PO Box 596, Jackson, CA 95642; tel: (209) 223-0350 (Jackson, Sutter Creek, Plymouth).

El Dorado County Chamber of Commerce, 542 Main St, Placerville, CA 95667; tel: (916) 621-5885 (Placerville, Marshall Gold Discovery State Park/Coloma). **Placer County Visitor Information Center,** 13460 Lincoln Way, Suite A, Auburn, CA 95603; tel: (916) 887-2111 (Auburn).

Grass Valley/Nevada County Chamber of Commerce, 248 Mill St, Grass Valley, CA 95945; tel: (916) 273-4667 (Grass Valley, Nevada City).

Accommodation

Lodging is moderate–expensive. Gold Country has dozens of bed and breakfasts. And where there's a town, there's a Main St.

OAKHURST TO COULTERVILLE

The 'Golden Chain' route begins south of Yosemite in **Oakhurst** (Visalia–Yosemite, p. 267). A talking **grizzly bear statue,** Hwy 41 and Road 426, explains its species' history and forest fires. **Fresno Flats Historical Park;** tel: (209) 683-6570, preserves 19th-century Madera County buildings. **Sierraland,** PO Box 666, Oakhurst, CA 93644; tel: (209) 658-7007, has onstage country and western music. Antique shops and flea markets crowd the north end of town. Budget **Liberty Food Co.,** across Hwy 41 from BW Yosemite Gateway Inn, has sandwiches, salads and garlic chili popcorn. Elegant **Erna's Elderberry House,** 48688 Victoria Lane, PO Box 2413; tel: (209) 683-6800, offers moderate–pricey meals.

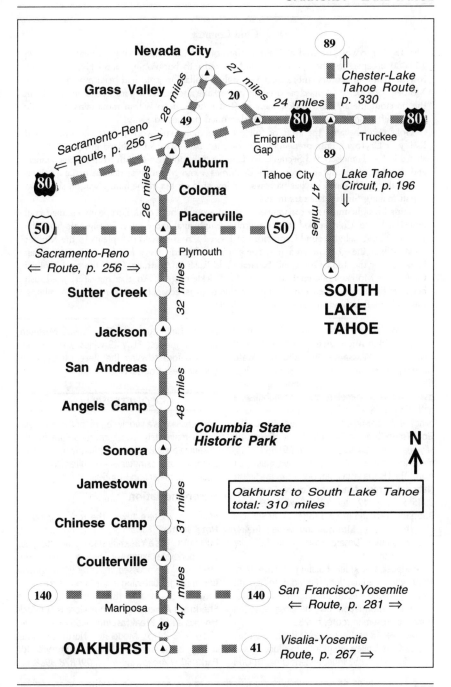

Nevada City

Grass Valley

27 miles

20

24 miles

28 miles

Sacramento-Reno
Route, p. 256 ⇒
⇐

49

80

Emigrant
Gap

89

Chester-Lake
Tahoe Route,
p. 330

Truckee

80

80

Auburn

89

26 miles

Coloma

Tahoe City

Lake Tahoe
Circuit, p. 196
⇓

Placerville

50

47 miles

50

Sacramento-Reno
⇐ Route, p. 256 ⇒

Plymouth

SOUTH
LAKE
TAHOE

Sutter Creek

32 miles

Jackson

San Andreas

Angels Camp

48 miles

Columbia State
Historic Park

Sonora

N
↑

Jamestown

31 miles

Oakhurst to South Lake Tahoe
total: 310 miles

Chinese Camp

Coulterville

47 miles

140

Mariposa

140

San Francisco-Yosemite
⇐ Route, p. 281 ⇒

49

OAKHURST

41

Visalia-Yosemite
Route, p. 267 ⇒

Gold Country

The 1848 discovery of gold at Coloma transformed California. Within a year, more than 100,000 prospectors and speculators had poured into burgeoning Sierra Nevada foothill towns. Within a century, more than $2½ billion dollars in gold had been mined from the Mother Lode. Early prospectors used only a pickaxe and pan to separate sand and grit from the precious metal. Hard rock miners blasted tunnels deep within mountains. Hydraulic mining left gold country hillsides pocked, eroded or washed away.

Gold fever became the stuff of folklore. Mining towns wore names like Rough and Ready or Drytown. Entrepreneurs made fortunes. Sam Brannan outfitted prospectors from stores in San Francisco and Sacramento. Levi Strauss took some cloth from Nîmes, France, and made practical, durable trousers – *de Nîmes* – known today as denims or Levi's. John Studebaker made miner's wheelbarrows and invested profits in the family wagon shop that began making Studebaker cars in 1904.

Ships brought miners – forty-niners – from around the world. Europeans escaped civil unrest at home, Chinese fled from government upheaval and famine. Immigrants from the US East Coast sailed around Cape Horn or forged across buffalo-rich plains to the Mother Lode. When the gold petered out, some miners stayed; many left for Sacramento, San Francisco, or the 1851 Ophir and Ballarat Gold Rush in Australia. Over the next century California's Mother Lode continued to yield a trickle of gold. Another miniature gold rush began in the 1980s, when a modern generation of prospectors began to rework the tailings, the rubble left behind in the golden mountains.

Six miles (10 km) north on Hwy 49, turn right on Road 628 in **Ahwahnee**. One mile (1.6 km) east is the **Wassama Roundhouse State Historical Park**, *tel: (209) 683-3631 or (209) 683-8194* open 1100-1600. Under spreading oaks is a Miwok cemetery and a roundhouse, a gathering place for religious ceremonies, gambling, and dancing. Return to Hwy 49. **Ol-Nip Gold Town Bed and Breakfast**, *45013 Hwy 49, Nipinnawasee, CA 93601; tel: (209) 683-2155*, moderate, has a restaurant and live music Sat night. The **Usona** vista point overlooks the **Sierra National Forest**. **Mariposa Coffee Company**, *2945 S. Hwy 49; tel: (209) 742-7339*, near **Bootjack**, has hand-ground coffee or the services of a chiropractor. **Mormon Bar** settlers futilely tried to establish 'Deseret State' under Salt Lake City's control.

Mariposa's wooden buildings survive from 1849 when Captain John Fremont shifted his property boundaries to include mining claims. For more information on Mariposa see San Francisco–Yosemite route, p. 285.

Five miles (8 km) north is **Mt Bullion**, on the way to **Bear Valley**, Fremont's headquarters in the 1850s. The 1852 Independent Order of Odd

Fellows Hall houses the **Oso** ('bear') **Museum**, open on request. Hwy 49 winds past oaks and pines before crossing the steep Merced River Canyon near **Coulterville**.

COULTERVILLE

Coulterville was a supply centre for the gold fields and a main stage-coach thoroughfare for the Yosemite area. Brothels, a Chinatown, saloons, a general store, cemeteries – Coulterville catered equally to miners and tourists.

Accommodation

Stay in a western town. The rock and adobe **Hotel Jeffrey**, *1 Main St; tel: (209) 464-3471*, built in 1851 as a Yosemite stage-coach stop, has 21 moderate–expensive rooms. The foyer 'wallpaper' is embossed tin. Enter the **Magnolia Bar** through bat-wing doors and strike up a conversation at the 1890s long bar. Above **Sherlock's Americana** antique store is **Sherlock Holmes Bed & Breakfast Inn**, *5006 Main St; tel: (209) 878-3915*. Moderate. North of Hotel Jeffrey is the budget 31-pitch **Coulterville RV Park**, *5009 Broadway; tel: (209) 878-3988*.

Eating and Drinking

Yosemite Sam's Grill, *5012 Main St; tel: (209) 878-9911*, has cheap, delicious pizza. A local gathering place, the former saloon, soft drink parlour and emporium is warmed by a wood-burning stove. Cowboys wearing worn leather chaps sidle up to the cherrywood bar. **Coulter Cafe**, *5015 Main St; tel: (209) 878-3947*, has cheap burgers and steaks. **The Banderita Restaurant**, *Jeffrey Hotel; tel: (209) 878-0228*, serves budget–moderate dinners.

Sightseeing

Whistling Billy, under the **Hanging Tree oak** in front of the Northern Mariposa County History Center, an 8-ton (7.3 tonne) locomotive, hauled up to 15 ore cars at once over a 4-mile (6.4 km) track. The **Northern Mariposa County History Center**, *Old Wells Fargo Bldg, corner of Hwys 49 and 132; tel: (209) 878-3015*, has antique guns, photographs, Worth's of Paris gowns, and silk robes and wall hangings from the homes of Chinese miners. At the 1851 adobe **Sun Sun Wo Company Store**, *Main and Kow Sts*, 1920s goods still sit on shelves, hiding an opium den in the back. **Candy's Place**, *Main St*, the bordello, is bedecked with a rosebush. Take in the **Coyote Howling** competition and fair in May or shoot-outs at the late Sept **Western Gunfighters Rendezvous**.

COULTERVILLE TO COLUMBIA

There are many vista points and lay-bys between Coulterville and **Chinese Camp**, 20 miles (32 km) north. Hwy 49 ascends a long slope, then turns narrow and winding while climbing a canyon wall. Tailing piles, 10 miles (16 km) from Coulterville on the right, are relics of dredging operations along **Moccasin Creek**. At **Moccasin** is an arm of **Don Pedro Lake**. Water pipes climb the hill behind the pink Spanish Colonial powerhouse. **Moccasin Creek Fish Hatchery** is open 0930–1600.

Chinese Camp is the ghost of the Gold Rush's largest Chinese settlement. The trees of heaven planted by wistful miners, the stone and brick post office (open, with old China Camp photographs when the Tuolumne County Visitors Bureau representative is present), and the restored St. Francis Xavier Church across Hwy 49 all recall the boom years. The 5000 Chinese residents scratched gold from the earth, chased from other areas by bigoted American miners. The Sam Yap and Yan Woo tongs, or clans, went to war in 1856. Each side fielded about 1000 armed men – the making of weapons had enriched blacksmiths around the countryside. At least four men were killed, and Chinese Camp's notoriety spread.

Hwy 49 swings right for 3 miles (5 km), then turns right again towards **Jamestown**. The **Chicken Ranch**, *6929 Chicken Ranch Rd, Jamestown, CA 95327; tel: (209) 984-3000*, has Thurs–Sun high-stakes bingo on the Miwok Reservation, south-west of Jamestown.

Main St, Jamestown runs parallel to Hwy 49 for a ½ mile (0.8 km). Turn left at Stockton St, 3½ miles (5.6 km) north-east, to continue on Hwy 49 into **Sonora**. Three miles (5 km) north, turn right on **Parrotts Ferry Rd**. Continue 2 miles (3.2 km) to **Columbia State Historic Park**.

JAMESTOWN

'Jimtown' was an early settlement, supply centre, and railway conduit in the Southern Mother Lode. Wooden storefronts with imposing balconies still line **Main St**.

Accommodation

The **Tuolumne County Lodging Association**, *PO Box 574, Jamestown, CA 95327; tel: (209) 533-4400*, has lodging information, but can't make bookings. Elegant historic hotels include the moderate **National Hotel**, *77 Main St; tel: (209) 984-3446*, the moderate to expensive **Jamestown Hotel**, *Main St; tel: (209) 984-3902*, and the **Palm Hotel**, *10382 Willow St; tel: (209) 984-3429*. The National and Jamestown Hotels have live music Fri and Sat nights.

Eating and Drinking

For ceiling fan atmosphere, try the moderate **National Hotel Restaurant**, *tel: (209)¹ 984-3446*. **Kamm's**, *18208 Main St; tel: (209) 984-3105*, serves budget Chinese food. Moderate

Willow Restaurant and Saloon, *Main St and Willow; tel: (209) 984-3998*, is a local favourite.

Sightseeing

Main St shops sell gold nugget jewellery. On weekends, there's a 20-min horse carriage ride around town; *tel: (209) 984-3125*. **Railtown 1897 State Historic Park**, *0.3 mile (0.5 km) down 5th Ave, PO Box 1250, Jamestown, CA 95327; tel: (209) 984-3953*, has rolling stock from the Sierra Railway. The cars hauled freight and lumber between the Sierra Nevada and the Central Valley. Tours explore the six-track working roundhouse, steam locomotives, railway cars and film production areas. Some of the equipment is familiar from cinema and television: *High Noon, My Little Chickadee, The Virginian*, and *Petticoat Junction*. The **Mother Lode Cannonball** steam train runs 1-hr tours spring–summer. **Keystone Special** tours include a barbecue dinner Sat, June–Sept.

Gold Prospecting Expeditions, *18170 Main St; tel: (209) 984-4653*, offers panning in front of the former livery stable; living history at Jimtown 1849 Gold-Mining Camp; training camps; and family gold panning trips.

SONORA

The Big Bonanza Mine, one of the richest of the Mother Lode, made Sonora a graceful town spread over several hills.

Accommodation

The **Tuolumne County Visitors Bureau** has lodging information, but does not make bookings. **Gold Country Inns of Tuolumne County**, *PO Box 462, Sonora, CA 95370; tel: (209) 533-1845*, books bed and breakfasts (moderate) . BW is represented. Moderate lodging includes the 1896 Spanish-style **Sonora Inn**, *160 S. Washington St; tel: (209) 532-2400*, the 1851 **Gunn House Motor Hotel**, *286 S. Washington St; tel: (209) 532-3421*; and secluded **Llamahall Guest Ranch**, *18170 Wards Ferry Rd; tel: (209) 532-7264*, with llamas and hot tubs.

Sightseeing

Old Sonora lies beneath **Piety Hill** and the 1860s

red **St James Episcopal Church**. Imposing storefronts line Washington St. The 1857 **Tuolumne County Jail** houses a gold collection and wagon train exhibit in the **Tuolumne County Museum and History Center**, *158 W. Bradford Ave; tel: (209) 532-1317*, closed Mon. Ask at the museum for a Victorian **Heritage Home Tour** walking tour brochure. **Quilter's Choice**, *564-B Stockton Rd; tel: (209) 532-4905*, sells handmade quilts.

COLUMBIA

Tourist Information: **Columbia State Historic Park**, *PO Box 151, Columbia, CA 95310; tel: (209) 532-4301*. The **visitor center** is in the **William Cavalier Museum**, *Main and State Sts*, open 1000–1630.

Accommodation

Book well in advance for both Main St hotels, restored to 1850s splendour. The moderate, two-storey properties offer breakfast and rooms (without bath). The **City Hotel**, *tel: (209) 532-1479*, and the **Fallon Hotel**, *tel: (209) 532-1470*, share a mailing address: *PO Box 1870*. Three RV parks are just outside town.

Eating and Drinking

The pricey **City Hotel** dining room has a wide reputation for good service, French-style meals with fresh California ingredients, and an extensive wine list. The adjacent **What Cheer Saloon** is a period libation parlour. The moderate **Columbia House Restaurant**, *Main St; tel: (209) 532-5134*, has all-American cuisine, like delicious pancakes. You can find Italian food, candy, ice cream, and old-fashioned sasparilla on Main St.

Sightseeing

Columbia, an 1850 Mother Lode latecomer, produced $87 million worth of gold. Burned in 1854 and 1857, it was rebuilt in brick, not wood. **Columbia State Historic Park** authentically evokes the Mother Lode era.

Columbia is an open-air museum. Park rangers, storekeepers, blacksmiths, miners and hotel staff dress in Gold Rush period costume: hooped skirts and bonnets for ladies; checked shirts, braces and boots for the men. Wooden boardwalks line the dirt Main St, closed to all but wagons, coaches, and pedestrians. Ride 'shotgun' position atop a real stage-coach, **Columbia Stage Line**, *PO Box 1777; tel: (209) 532-0663.* The **William Cavalier Museum** displays Gold Country photographs, panning equipment, and nuggets. The red brick **Wells Fargo Express** building has elegant gold assay equipment on the ground floor. The **Museum of the Gold Rush Press** displays the hyperbolised journalism of the last century. A smithy, barber, school, and buildings like the 1854 **Cheap Cash Store** create a *déjà vu* atmosphere. Summertime is melodrama season at the year-round **Fallon Theatre**, *PO Box 1849; tel: (209) 532-4644.* Columbia, too, has gold panning and gold mine tours, through **Matelot Gulch Mine Supply Store**, *PO Box 28; tel: (209) 532-9693*, closed Mon. **Bi-Plane Rides**, *Springfield Flying Service, 10767 Airport Rd; tel: (209) 532-4103*, leave from Columbia's small airport.

No one steps out of living history characterisation during **Columbia Diggins** in early June except into a hastily erected tent city. Ancient fire engines have pumping contests at **Firemen's Muster** in May.

COLUMBIA TO SUTTER CREEK

Continue on Hwy 49 into country lauded by Mark Twain in *The Celebrated Jumping Frog of Calaveras County*. A mile (1.6 km) beyond Tuttletown, on the right, is the turnoff to a replica of what may have been **Mark Twain's Cabin**, on **Jackass Hill**. Cross the high bridge over the **New Melones Reservoir** and drive through **Melones** and **Carson Hill** to **Frogtown**, venue for the May **Jumping Frog Jubilee**. Since 1928, trainers have spurred giant frogs to leap for prizes in the tongue-in-cheek spirit of Mark Twain's tale (a rival filled a boasting miner's frog with birdshot).

Ubiquitous frog merchandise blankets **Angels Camp**, named after a Gold Rush merchant, not heavenly beings. A prospector fired his muzzle-loading rifle at the ground, and split a gold-bearing quartz rock. Main St was dug up in the hunt for gold, though many buildings remain. The **Angels Hotel**, where Twain allegedly heard the jumping frog yarn, is now a hardware and auto parts emporium. **Calaveras County Visitor Center**, *1211 S. Main St, Angels Camp, CA 95222; tel: (209) 736-0049*, open 0900–1630, books lodging. The **Angels Camp Museum**, *753 Main St; tel: (209) 736-2963*, has mining equipment and bygone era wagons and buggies.

To pan a genuine gold claim, take Hwy 4 right to **Jensen's Pick & Shovel Ranch**, *4977 Parrotts Ferry Rd, Vallecito, CA 95222; tel: (209) 736-0287*. Just south is **Moaning Cavern**, *PO Box 78, Vallecito, CA 95251; tel: (209) 736-2708*, California's largest natural cavern, 236 steps down by staircase or abseiling (rappelling).

Continue east on Hwy 4 and turn left on Murphys Grade Rd to **Murphys**, a town of hospitable shops along a well-preserved main street. **Murphys Business Association**, *PO Box 2034, Murphys, CA 95247*, provides maps. Two brothers set up Murphy Diggins in 1848, but had better luck at shopkeeping. One married a Miwok Chief's daughter, the better to have the Native Americans collect gold. The brothers left as millionaires the next year. The 1856 **Murphys Hotel**, *457 Main St; tel: (209) 728-3444*, hosted Twain, Harte, and other celebrities while the front door collected bullet holes. The old hotel has a restaurant, bar, 9 moderate rooms with shared bathrooms, and motel rooms next door.

The **Calaveras Wine Association**, *PO Box 2492; tel: (800) 225-3674*, has information on six wineries within a 4-mile (6.4 km) radius of town. The huge **Mercer Caverns**, *PO Box 509; tel: (209) 728-2101*, are 1 mile (1.6 km) north.

Return via Murphys Grade Rd to Hwy 49 at **Altaville**. **San Andreas** is 13 miles (21 km) north; the historic district is east of the highway. In 1883 San Andreas saw the capture, trial and conviction of Charles Bolton, alias Black Bart, the highwayman who politely held up 28 stage-coaches with an unloaded gun and poems. The **Calaveras County Museum**, *30 N. Main St, San Andreas, CA 95249; tel: (209) 754-4023*, open 1000–1600, includes the old County Courthouse where Black Bart was tried, an exhibit of Miwok artifacts, and, out back, the old jail where Bolton was held.

Take scenic **Gold Strike Rd** north for 2½ miles (4 km) to rejoin Hwy 49. Turn right on Main St in

Columbia–Columbia to Sutter Creek

Mokelumne Hill. Moke Hill was called the liveliest town in the Mother Lode from 1848–1854, when Chileans, Frenchmen and Americans battled; today it looks frozen in time. The two-storey 1851 **Hotel Leger**, *8304 Main St, Mokelumne Hill, CA 95245; tel: (209) 286-1401*, has balconies on three sides, 13 rooms, an ancient bar, and **Nonno's Italian Restaurant**. Bull and bear fights were held out back. Moderate lodging and dining. Picnic in the tree-shaded park across from the Old French Quarter and Independent Order of Odd Fellows Hall. There's also a bakery, Wells Fargo Office, old county courthouse and wooden church.

Jackson began as a cattle watering hole. Hard rock mining began in 1856. The Kennedy and Argonaut mines were nearly a mile deep and operated until 1942. The ruins are visible on hills above Jackson, opposite the two surviving wooden **Kennedy Tailing Wheels**. In 1912 the wheels lifted mining rubble into in a series of flumes to move polluted gravel into a dumpsite. A scale model of the wheels, and mining techniques, are demonstrated at the **Amador County Museum**, *225 Church St, Jackson, CA 95642; tel: (209) 223-6386.*

The white 1894 **St Sava Serbian Orthodox Church**, *724 N. Main St; tel: (209) 223-2700*, serves as the faith's mother church; see the inside on Sun mornings.

The **Bed & Breakfast Referral Service of Amador County**; *tel: (209) 296-7778 or (800) 726-4667*, recommends Victorian inns. Jackson has a good choice of moderate motels, including BW. The **National Hotel**, *2 Water St; tel: (209) 223-0500*, has modest, budget–moderate rooms and weekend entertainment.

For Miwok culture, take Hwy 88 east 9 miles (14.4 km) to Pine Grove; turn left toward Volcano for 1½ miles (2.4 km) to **Chaw'se, Indian Grinding Rock State Park**, *14881 Pine Grove-Volcano Rd, Pine Grove, CA 95665; tel: (209) 296-7488*, open 1000–1700; for camping, contact **MISTIX**, *tel: (800) 444-7275*. Petroglyphs and grinding holes complement conical Miwok bark tents and a roundhouse replica. Mid-Mar–Apr, continue 6 miles (9.6 km) through **Volcano** to view 300,000 bulbs blooming on **Daffodil Hill**.

SUTTER CREEK

Architecturally, **Sutter Creek**'s 61 wood-frame and brick Gold Rush era buildings are splendid. **The Foxes in Sutter Creek**, *77 Main St; tel: (209) 267-5882*, is a fine, popular bed and breakfast; expensive. The 18-room **Sutter Creek Inn**, *75 Main St; tel: (209) 267-5606*, is moderate–expensive. There's moderate dining in beautiful Victorian dining rooms: **Sutter Creek Palace**, *76 Main St; tel: (209) 267-9852*, and **Pelargonium**, *1 Hanford St; tel: (209) 267-5008.*

Sightseeing

Gold was found in 1851. High wooden boardwalks protected miners against creek floods. An illustrated walking tour brochure is available in shops or from **Sutter Creek Merchants Association**, *PO Box 600, Sutter Creek, CA 95685*. Antiques, glass, pottery and crafts fill storefronts. The **1873 Knight Foundry**, *81 Eureka St; tel: (209) 267-1449*, open daily 0900–1600 for self-guided foundry and machine shop tours, used water power to make much of the heavy equipment that extracted gold from the Mother Lode. **Monteverde Concord Store Museum**, *3 Randolph St*, which functioned as a general store from 1898 to 1972, has many 1920s articles on its shelves.

SUTTER CREEK TO PLACERVILLE

North on Hwy 49, **Amador City** is another antiquer's paradise. **The Mine House Inn**, *14125 Hwy 49, Amador City, CA 95601; tel: (209) 267-5900*, the former 1880 Keystone Mine office, has 8 moderate bed and breakfast rooms named Vault, Assay, Mill Grinding, Retort, etc. The **Imperial Hotel**, *Main St; tel: (209) 267-9172*, in a two-storey red brick building, offers moderate lodging and dining and an old-fashioned saloon.

Pass through **Drytown** – more antique shops – to shabby **Plymouth**. Plymouth is the jumping-off point to the Sierra Foothills Shenandoah Valley wine area a few miles east. The **Amador Vintners Association**, *PO Box 718, Plymouth, CA 95669; tel: (209) 245-6942*, has a winery brochure for the **Shenandoah Valley**. The BW

Shenandoah Inn, *17674 Village Dr, Plymouth, CA 95669; tel: (209) 245-4498*, has moderate rooms.

North on Hwy 49, **Nashville** had the Mother Lode's first stamp mill. Little Gold Country atmosphere remains in **El Dorado** or in **Diamond Springs**, ½ mile (0.8 km) east. Turn left 3 miles (5 km) to **Placerville**.

PLACERVILLE

Tourist Information: El Dorado County and the **Placerville Downtown Association**; *tel: (916) 626-4990*, have tourist information. The **El Dorado Wine Country Association**, *PO Box 1614; tel: (916) 642-9717*, has local winery information. Lodging includes *BW* and *DI* and the moderate 1857 **Cary House Hotel**, *300 Main St, Placerville, CA 95667; tel: (916) 622-4271*.

Once called Hangtown for its final application of justice, the town gave its name to the **hangtown fry**, an omelette with oysters and bacon. Where the hanging tree stood in downtown Placerville, the **Hangman's Tree** building suspends an effigy. Hangtown's **Gold Bug Mine**, *Bedford Ave, 1 mile (1.6 km) north of Main St; tel: (916) 642-5232*, open June–Sept 1000–1600, offers self-guided tours through two shafts and a working stamp mill. The surrounding park has hiking and picnic areas. **Placerville City Hall**, *Main and Bedford Sts*, was the town's narrow brick and stone firehouse.

The **El Dorado County Historical Museum**, *100 Placerville Dr; tel: (916) 621-5865*, displays gold-era artefacts, a Studebaker miner's wheelbarrow, and a stage-coach. Placerville was an important stop for the **Pony Express** and later a transport point for silver from the Comstock Lode in Nevada. Hwy 50 runs through the town; traffic can be ferocious. Drive 7 miles (11 km) northwest to **Coloma**.

COLOMA

Tourist Information: Marshall Gold Discovery State Historic Park, *310 Back St, PO Box 265, Coloma, CA 95613; tel: (916) 622-3470*, open 1000–1700, on the **American River South Fork**.

California's identity was born here on January 24 1848, when John Sutter's sawmill construction supervisor, James Marshall, scooped some glinting flakes from the washings of a tailrace his crew was deepening. A full-size replica of **Sutter's Mill** is near the discovery site. Films and exhibits at the **Gold Discovery Museum** describe mining methods and the local Culluma tribe. Nearby are Chinese miners' buildings. Marshall's gravesite is marked with a monument (left off Hwy 49 to Sacramento St and Cold Springs Rd; right up **Monument Rd**).

The hot-air balloonist owner of the 1852 **Coloma Country Inn**, *345 High St; tel: (916) 622-6919*, offers lodging packages where guests ascend in a balloon or use the balloon gondola as a part-time raft on the American River! Seven rooms share a bath at the moderate, possibly haunted 1878 **Vineyard House**, *Cold Springs Rd; tel: (916) 622-2217*. An insane owner died in chains installed by his wife in the wine cellar, now the very popular **Vineyard House Saloon**. The **Old Coloma Theatre**; *tel: (916) 626-5282*, performs melodramas on summer weekends in the restaurant. Just north of the park is the moderate 1850 **Sierra Nevada House**, *at Lotus Rd, PO Box 496; tel: (916) 621-1649*. Isabella is the resident ghost here, angry over a spouse's philandering. The saloon has weekend entertainment. **Coloma Resort**, *6921 Mt Murphy Rd; tel: (916) 621-2267*, has camping.

AUBURN

It's 17 miles (27 km) to **Auburn**. The road rises to **Pilot Hill**, ornamented with the three-storey red brick **Bayley's Folly**, built as a railway hotel for the Central Pacific Railroad – which bypassed it. Modern wooden storefronts grace **Cool**. Hwy 49 slows to 15–30 mph (24–48 kph) near the Middle and North Forks of the American River.

Sprawling over several hills, **Auburn** is the junction of Hwys 49 and 80. Auburn became the largest Mother Lode city with the completion of the Transcontinental Railroad in the 1860s.

A wide variety of lodging includes *BW* and *HI*. Moderate **Victorian Hill House**, *195 Park St, Auburn, CA 95604; tel: (916) 885-5879*, overlooks Old Auburn. The bright pink, 15-room, 1900 mansion, **Power's Mansion Inn**,

164 Cleveland Ave, Auburn, CA 95603; tel: (916) 885-1166, is moderate–expensive.

To enter **Old Auburn** historic district, follow Lincoln Way instead of continuing north on Hwy 49. An Old Auburn walking tour map is available from the **Auburn Area Chamber of Commerce,** *in the railway depot, 601 Lincoln Way, Auburn, CA 95603; tel: (916) 885-5616,* open Mon–Fri 0900-1700. Inside the hilltop neo-classical **Placer County Courthouse,** *101 Maple St,* is the **Placer County Museum,** *tel: (916) 889-6500.* Antique and gift shops fill Old Auburn's rabbit warren, including **Lawyer's Row,** *on Commercial St.* The narrow, four-storey, red and white **Firehouse No. 1,** built in 1893, is capped with a steeple. The bell tolls daily at 0800, 1200 and 1700. The **Gold Country Museum,** *1273 High St (fairgrounds),* open Tues–Sun 1000–1600, displays quartz, gold, a walk-through mine, and Maidu and Chinese household objects. The **Shanghai Bar,** *289 Washington St; tel: (916) 823-2613,* saloon and restaurant, has old Chinese newspapers on the walls and plenty of atmosphere. Moderate.

North from Auburn the road rises 24 miles (38 km) gradually, entering forest near **Grass Valley.**

GRASS VALLEY

A **Grass Valley** farmer chasing a cow in the moonlight stubbed his toe on a gold nugget. Just before entering town, take the Empire Rd exit from Hwy 49 to **Empire Mine State Historic Park,** *10791 E. Empire St, Grass Valley, CA 95945; tel: (916) 273-8522.* The hard rock operation attracted Cornish miners, whose steam pumps emptied water from the 367 miles (587 km) of deep mineshafts. The 1850 mine owner's home and some businesses have been restored. The **Northstar Mining Museum and Pelton Wheel Exhibit**; *tel: (916) 273-4255,* open May–mid-Oct, is across Hwy 49.

Grass Valley accommodation ranges from *BW* to the moderate **Holiday Lodge,** *1221 E. Main St; tel: (916) 273-4406,* and the 1851 **Holbrooke Hotel,** *12 W. Main St; tel: (916) 273-1353.* Many of the Holbrooke's 28 rooms have balconies overlooking the historic part of town. Moderate–Expensive. **Historic Bed & Breakfast Inns,** *PO Box 2060, Nevada City, CA 95959; tel* *(916) 477-6634,* make bookings for 13 Grass Valley and Nevada City homes.

Hans' Pastry Shoppe, *141 E. Main S; tel: (916) 273-8500,* is the cheap breakfast spot, especially for muffins and coffee. **The Stewart House,** *124 Bank Street; tel: (916) 477-6368,* lovingly restored to Victorian splendour, serves moderate–pricey meals in parlour rooms.

Most buildings of historic interest are along Mill St, including the **Lola Montez House,** *248 Mill St,* owned by the flamboyant performer but now home to the **Nevada County Chamber of Commerce.** Montez' protege, **Lotta Crabtree,** grew up at **238 Mill St.** Streets parallel to Mill St have fine fancy Victorian buildings.

NEVADA CITY

Nevada City is 4 miles (6.4 km) north, a prosperous, attractive Victorian town. Free public parking and toilets are across the freeway from downtown. Nevada City is loaded with bed and breakfasts (see above). **The National Hotel,** *211 Broad St, Nevada City, CA 95959; tel: (916) 265-4551,* has 48 moderate–expensive rooms. Carriage rides start in front of the hotel. Shops have Western-style leather goods, antiques and crafts. The **Nevada City Chamber of Commerce,** *132 Main St, Nevada City, CA 95959; tel: (916) 265-2692,* has a walking tour brochure. **Firehouse No. 1** resembles white-iced wedding cake. It's the **Firehouse Museum,** *214 Main St; tel: (916) 265-5468,* containing Maidu artefacts, a Chinese joss house altar and mining tools. The **Miners Foundry Cultural Center,** *325 Spring St,* has a foundry exhibit, a radio station, and the **Nevada City Winery** tasting room, *321 Spring St; tel: (916) 265-9463,* open 1200–1700. **Nevada City Brewing Company,** *75 Bost Ave; tel: (916) 265-2446,* offers tours and tasting, Fri 1500–1700, Sat 1300–1700.

Take Hwy 20 north-east 5 miles (8 km) into **Tahoe National Forest**; a good picnic site is the Alpha and Omega marker just after entering the forest. Bad erosion from past mining is visible in several spots along the 22 miles (35 km) to the Emigrant Gap viewpoint. Follow Hwy 80 east. Turn right onto Hwy 89 and continue to **South Lake Tahoe.**

SAN FRANCISCO

For most of its recorded history, San Francisco has been 'The City' in California. It was The City the world encountered on the way to Gold Rush riches and The City where the successful few splurged on wine, women, real estate, and industry. Reinvention remains the favourite civic pastime, be it a personal past conveniently altered or a collective future that remains obscure. The City reinvented itself after earthquake and fire in 1906, then reinvented reality for the rest of the world. The Beatniks of the 1950s shook America; the 1960s and the Summer of Love shook the planet. This is the most ethnically diverse city in California, filled with fractious factions who have never got on but still manage to live together.

But despite frequent lapses, The City's historical touchstones of liberalism and tolerance remain intact. And freedom – including the freedom to make a mess of San Francisco – remains the semi-official rallying cry.

Tourist Information

San Francisco Convention & Visitors Bureau (SFCVB) Box 429097, San Francisco, CA 94142-9097; tel: (415) 391-2000 is open Mon–Fri 0830–1730. **Visitor Information Center,** 900 Market St at Powell, Hallidie Plaza, lower level (outside and left from Muni underground station), is open Mon–Fri 0900–1730, Sat to 1500, Sun 1000–1400. 24-hour recorded event information; tel: (415) 391-2001.

Weather

Mark Twain supposedly complained that the coldest winter of his life was June in San Francisco. June–Aug is often foggy, windy, and cold. Apr–May and Sept–Oct have the sunniest weather. Nov–Mar is frequently rainy.

Arriving and Departing

San Francisco International Airport (SFO), is 15 miles (25 km) south on US Hwy 101. Taxi to downtown, $25. **Airporter** bus to downtown hotels, $7.50 single. Door-to-door airport shuttle, $9 single. **SAMTRANS bus** to downtown, $0.85. Free shuttles to rental car locations and airport hotels.

Getting Around

San Francisco is just 7 miles (11.5 km) across, but hills are steep and parts of the city unsafe for pedestrians.

Avoid walking day or night in Hunters Point (the extreme south-east corner of the city), the Western Addition (Civic Center between downtown and Golden Gate Park), and on streets bordering public housing projects (council estates). The Tenderloin, between the Civic Center and the Union Square area, and public parks are unsafe to walk at night.

Public Transport

All major attractions can be reached – eventually – by Municipal Transit, **Muni,** tel: (415) 673-6864. **Buses** follow numbered routes along surface streets. **Streetcars,** which run underground in the city centre and above ground in outlying districts, follow lettered routes. **Cable cars** follow three routes:

California, California and Market Sts (beside the Hyatt Regency hotel) over Nob Hill to Van Ness Ave.

Hyde Street, Market and Powell Sts to Fisherman's Wharf via Nob Hill.

Mason, Market and Powell Sts through Chinatown and North Beach to the Fisherman's Wharf area.

Muni Passport (Visitor Information Center) provides unlimited travel and 26 admission discounts, from $6 for one day to $15 per week. Single bus/streetcar journeys: $1 adults; $0.35 seniors/children. Cable cars $2.

A transport map is in the front of the Yellow Pages section of the telephone book. The Visitor Information Center and hotel desks provide free transport guides. Maps are also posted at bus shelters and Muni underground stations.

Golden Gate Transit, tel: (415) 332-6600, provides bus services north across the Golden Gate Bridge to Marin County.

AC Transit, *tel: (510)-839-2882* provides bus service to the East Bay.

BART, (Bay Area Rapid Transit); *tel: (415) 788-2278*, links San Francisco with communities east and south, but does not extend to the airport.

SAMTRANS, *tel: (800) 660-4287*, provides bus service south to San Mateo County, including the airport.

Ferries

Blue & Gold Fleet, *tel: (415) 705-5555*, departs from the west side of Pier 39 with daily Bay tours and a ferry service to Gateway Center, Alameda.

Golden Gate Transit, *tel: (415) 332-6600*, depart by ferry from the Ferry Building at the Embarcadero end of Market Street to Larkspur and Sausalito, in Marin County.

Horn Blower, *tel: (415) 394-8900* offers dinner cruises from Pier 33.

Monte Carlo Cruises, *tel: (415) 433-4386* offers dinner and gambling (with play money) cruises, also from Pier 33.

Red & White Fleet, *tel: (415) 546-2628* offers daily Bay cruises, the only tours of Alcatraz, and ferry services to Angel Island, Marine World Africa USA, Muir Woods, Jack London Square (Oakland), and Vallejo. All boats depart from Pier 43½ at the east side of Fisherman's Wharf.

Driving

Coloured street signs point the way to key tourist areas:

A green outline of Italy for **North Beach**;
A red Chinese lantern for **Chinatown**;
An orange crab for **Fisherman's Wharf**;
A blue Victorian house for **Union Street**;
A white female statue for **Union Square**.

A car and a generous parking budget make touring easier. Street parking is nearly impossible in Chinatown, North Beach, Fisherman's Wharf and Union Square, and scarce elsewhere. Most parking metres accept $0.25 coins, good for 15–60 mins, depending on the neighbourhood.

Traffic wardens ('meter maids', whether male or female) generally ignore double- and triple-parked lorries to pursue parking violations by motorists. Car-hire companies bill unpaid parking fines and penalties to customer credit cards.

Garage (car park) parking prices range from $1 per hour for city-owned facilities to $20 per hour in the Financial District. Best bets are:

For downtown: **Stockton-Sutter (Streets) Garage**, near Union Square; **Fifth & Mission (Streets) Garage**, near the Powell Cable Car; **Civic Center (Plaza) Garage**, in front of City Hall.

For North Beach and Chinatown: **Police Garage**, 766 Vallejo St; **Portsmouth Square Garage**, Clay and Kearny Sts.

For Pier 39: Garage charges are exorbitant. Metered street parking in the area is tight, but possible.

Recreational vehicles are not allowed in garages due to height restrictions.

Weekend parking in Golden Gate Park is crowded, but easier away from the central museum area. Weekday parking problems are rare. Major Park roads are closed on Sundays for cycling and skating.

Living in San Francisco

Accommodation

San Francisco rooms range from youth hostels to familiar chains (Hilton, Sheraton, Holiday Inn, Pan-Pacific, etc.) and the ultimate in luxury (Ritz-Carlton, Mandarin Oriental, Huntington). Always book ahead. This is one of America's most popular tourist and convention cities.

SFCVB lists published hotel rates, but does not make bookings.

It's difficult to find a room for less than $80 a night, though weekend rates are lower. Some hotels offer discounts for Automobile Club members, senior citizens (over age 60), and children (under 18). Discounts are seldom publicised; ask upon booking if cheaper rooms or special rates are available, and ask again upon arrival.

San Francisco Reservations, *22 Second St, Fourth Floor, San Francisco, CA 94105; tel: (800) 677-1550*, makes free bookings for more than 225 local hotels. **Bed & Breakfast International**, *Box 282910, San Francisco, CA*

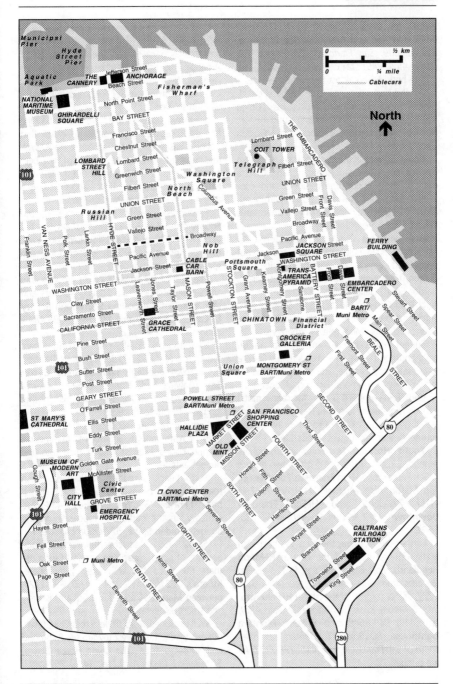

94128, tel: (800) 872-4500; fax: (415) 696-1699, and **Bed and Breakfast San Francisco**, *Box 420009, San Francisco, CA 94142; tel: (800) 452-8249; fax: (415) 921-2273*, are private bed and breakfast reservation services. For the best prices, contact the hotel direct. Hotels cluster downtown, mostly near Union Square, at Fisherman's Wharf and along the Van Ness-Lombard corridor leading to the Golden Gate Bridge.

Union Square is the best location without a car. It's near the main shopping and theatre districts, most major tourist sights, and convenient for public transport routes. With a car, allow $15 per day for parking. **Fisherman's Wharf** is tour group territory.

Best buys are 'boutique' hotels, recently renovated older buildings. Small rooms, but decor and service are smart. Try: Bedford, Carlton, Cartwright, Chancellor, The Fitzgerald, Harbor Court, Galleria Park, Juliana, Kensington Park, King George, Monticello, Shannon Court, Triton, Union Square, Villa Florence, Vintage Court, and York. Moderate to expensive.

Budget hotels line the margins of raffish neighbourhoods like the Tenderloin. They're clean, safe, comfortable, and sometimes charming. Try Mark Twain and Pickwick. Moderate.

Van Ness-Lombard is best for cars – motel parking is generally free. Van Ness and Lombard are busy streets; ask for a room in the back if you need peace and quiet. Moderate.

Youth Hostels: Hostelling International–American Youth Hostels (*AY*) offers two hostels in San Francisco: **HI-San Francisco/Fort Mason**, *Fort Mason, Bldg 240; tel: (415) 771-7277 or (415) 771-3645*, and **HI-San Francisco Downtown**, *312 Mason St; tel: (415) 788-5604*.

Further out of town, there are *AY* hostels in Marin County (north of the city) at **HI-Marin Headlands**, *Fort Barry, Building 941, Sausalito (8 miles from San Francisco); tel: (415) 331-2777*, and two south of the city, at **HI-Palo Alto**, *26870 Moody Road, Los Altos Hills (Palo Alto); tel: (415) 949-8648*, and **HI-Point Montara Lighthouse**, *PO Box 737, Montara (25 miles south of San Francisco); tel: (415) 728-7177*. All are budget.

Eating and Drinking

San Francisco calls itself the food capital of America. The title might be contested by Los Angeles, New York and New Orleans, but The City has been famous for food and drink since Gold Rush days.

California Cuisine tries to combine the freshest possible ingredients in ways that nobody has ever tried. Carpaccio made with raw tuna and sesame oil instead of raw beef and olive oil isn't to every taste, but the latest SF eatery is every bit as exciting – and expensive – as the newest entry in Paris or Rome.

Favourites change almost weekly, but **Square One**, *190 Pacific, Financial District; tel: (415) 788-1110*, and **Stars**, *150 Redwood Way, Civic Center; tel: (415) 861-7827* are long-term survivors. Expensive.

The best of Fisherman's Wharf includes crab and shrimp cocktails from sidewalk vendors, and sandwiches at the **Boudin Sourdough Bakery & Café**, *156 Jefferson; tel: (415) 928-1849*. Budget.

Elka (Miyako Hotel), *1625 Post St, Japantown; tel: (415) 922-7788* may serve the best fish in town. **Bentley's Seafood Grill & Oyster Bar**, (Galleria Park Hotel), *Sutter & Kearny, Downtown; tel: (415) 989-6895*, is another longtime favourite. Pricey.

Fortunately, San Francisco has the highest ratio of restaurants to inhabitants in America. Competition is keenest among moderate and budget eateries.

North Beach is redolent with garlic, fresh roasted coffee beans and sourdough French bread. **I Fratelli** *1896 Hyde; tel: (415) 474-8240* is heavy on the garlic and moderate on the budget. **Golden Spike**, *527 Columbus Ave; tel: (415) 421-4591*, has cheerfully served huge portions of pasta, meat, and antipasto for more than 60 years, in a homey atmosphere. **Kuleto's**, *221 Powell; tel: (415) 397-7720*, between Market St and Union Square, is lively and smart. Moderate.

Well-seasoned woks sizzle across Chinatown, but most locals head west toward the Richmond and Sunset districts. The **China House Bistro**, *501 Balboa (Richmond); tel: (415) 752-2802*, moderate, and **Eight Immortals**, *1433 Taravel (Sunset); tel: (415) 731-5515,* budget, are two of the best. Arrive early or expect to wait.

Asian restaurants line Clement, California, and Geary Sts around 19th Ave. Newly-arrived Russian immigrants are opening small restaurants on Geary between 22nd and 25th Aves. Budget.

The Mission District is a culinary cacophony, mixing Cuba with Mexico, Brazil, Chile, and every country in between. Best bets are taquerias along Valencia between 15th and 18th Sts. Cheap.

Brewpubs provide some of the best meals in town. **Gordon Biersch Brewing Company**, *2 Harrison, Embarcadero; tel: (415) 243-8246* is the largest and trendiest. The atmosphere is 1980s-style striving and the food overpriced, but the converted warehouse is cheery. Moderate. **Twenty Tank Brewery**, *316 11th St, SOMA; tel: (415) 255-9455,* is a friendly neighbourhood pub with heavy overtones of punk. SF's best beer and biggest sandwiches with no glitter or pretence. Budget. **San Francisco Brewing Company**, *155 Columbus, North Beach; tel: (415) 434-3344* caters to the Financial District. Small, often crowded, and definitely a place to be seen. Moderate.

Communications

There are more than four dozen post offices in the city. Mail can be addressed to your hotel.

Money

Thomas Cook Foreign Exchange branches are situated at *75 Geary St; tel: (415) 362 3452* and at *Pier 39 – Bldg M, Level 2, Pier 39, Space M-10; tel: (415) 362 6271.* Both will arrange travellers' cheque refunds.

Entertainment

There's no excuse to be bored in San Francisco. **Pier 39**, **The Anchorage** (near Fisherman's Wharf), and **The Cannery** specialise in buskers. The **Symphony**, *tel: (415) 431-5400,* **opera**, *tel: (415) 864-3330,* and **ballet**, *tel: (415) 703-9400* offer full seasons. Churches and cultural groups sponsor concerts.

The best single source of entertainment information is the pink 'Datebook' Entertainment section of the Sunday *San Francisco Examiner & Chronicle* newspaper. A 24-hour **SFCVB hotline**, *tel: (415) 391-2001,* provides selected information on events, theatre, dance, museum offerings and sport.

Theatre

For local flavour, try *Beach Blanket Babylon,* **Club Fugazi**, *678 Green, North Beach; tel: (415) 421-4222.* This musical parodies San Francisco, Hollywood, politicians, and current events with a fairy-tale plot and outrageous hats.

The **American Conservatory Theater** (ACT), *tel: (415) 749-2228,* keeps two stages busy. Touring companies stage the most successful New York productions. A host of small and experimental companies lure audiences with more provocative and more affordable productions.

Standing-room tickets are sometimes available for ballet and opera shortly before the performance. For assured seats at larger venues, contact the box office or **TIX**, a half-price ticket service on the east side of Union Square; *tel: (415) 433-7827.*

Music

San Francisco is a musical hot spot. Clubs cater to every taste, from the latest hip hop and rap to old line blues and ballads. Most clubs are in SOMA (see next page). For current information, check *SF Weekly* and *The Bay Guardian,* free weekly papers in racks around town.

Cinema

Evening and weekend programmes cost around $7 per person, but the first showing (bargain matinee) is often cheaper. Cinemas in the seedier section of Market St around 7th St offer bargain prices all day. Full programmes are published daily in the *Chronicle* (morning) and the *Examiner* (afternoon).

Shopping

San Francisco is a shopper's dream on any budget.

Top end names like **Neiman-Marcus**, *tel: (415) 362-3900,* **Saks Fifth Avenue**, *tel: (415)*

986-4300, and **Cartier**, *tel: (415) 397-3180* line Union Square.

Department stores are steps away: **Macy's**, *Union Square; tel: (415) 397-3333*, **The Emporium**, *835 Market; tel: (415) 764-2222*, and **Nordstrom**, *San Francisco Center, Fifth and Market Sts; tel: (415) 243-8500*.

Factory outlets are usually renovated warehouses. **Yerba Buena Square**, *899 Howard St; tel: (415) 543-1275*, has six floors of merchandise. **Six Sixty Center**, *660 Third St; tel: (415) 227-0464*, has 20 shops. The SFCVB has the latest names and locations.

Trendy: Chi-chi shoppers prowl **Union St** between Gough and Divisadero Sts. Pricey shops in stylish Victorian houses offer jewellery, marbled paper, clothing, antiques, furnishings and bric-a-brac from around the world.

The hip, or those who would like to be, gravitate to **Haight St**. The Haight's latest and seediest reincarnation provides a trendier-than-thou mix of fashion (male, female, and androgynous), food, and body piercing.

Duty-free Stores Don't bother. Stock is limited and prices inflated. Any large supermarket, department store or discount store has better prices.

Sightseeing

San Francisco is never 'Frisco'. For locals, the only proper diminutive is 'The City', with no apologies to London or New York. Precipitous hills and 750,000 people share 49 square miles (12,691 ha) that are periodically rearranged by earthquake and redevelopment.

Busy streets open into broad vistas of sea and sky. Modern architecture vies with 13,000 Victorian buildings, wooden homes built from the 1860s until the 1906 earthquake. The highly decorated buildings, some converted to offices and bed and breakfasts, are elaborately embellished with columns, bay windows, false cornices, towers, turrets, lacework and other artifices.

Neighbourhoods

Much of San Francisco's allure lies in its distinct neighbourhoods.

North Beach, bisected by Broadway and Columbus, was settled by Italians. A restaurant and entertainment district for more than a century, North Beach was also home to the 1950s beatniks. Poet Lawrence Ferlinghetti's **City Lights**, *261 Columbus; tel: (415) 362-8193*, invites patrons to browse books from cover to cover. **Vesuvio**, *255 Columbus; tel: (415) 362-3370*, is still the ultimate beat coffeehouse. More sedate cafés serve espresso, cappuccino, and other coffees from early morning until late night.

The ultimate North Beach experience is strolling up the narrow streets of Telegraph Hill to **Coit Tower** to look down on San Francisco.

Chinatown began as a shanty town of Chinese miners expelled from the gold fields around 1850. Spurred by wave after wave of immigrants, Sun Yat Sen planned the Chinese Nationalist Republic from Spofford Alley. Today Chinatown is the largest Chinese community outside Asia.

Grant Ave, Chinatown's official main street, is lined with import stores, tea-shops and T-shirt emporia. Stockton, one block west, is crowded with fresh vegetables, live fish, smoked ducks and other necessities of daily life.

Financial District, Chinatown east to San Francisco Bay, began life as the Barbary Coast, America's most infamous 19th-century red light district. Reduced to rubble in the 1906 earthquake, the neighbourhood was reborn as the financial heart of Western America.

SOMA, the South of Market Area, is a former industrial area that has become the hip artistic and nightlife centre. Boz Scaggs occasionally appears at his own club, **Slim's**, *333 11th St; tel: (415) 621-3330*. Factory outlet stores, with discounts up to 75%, are the newest wave.

The Marina, site of the 1915 Panama Pacific Exhibition, is an upmarket residential neighbourhood on the western edge of the Bay. The only survivor is the **Palace of Fine Arts**, now home to the **Exploratorium**. The Marina was devastated by the 1989 Loma Prieta earthquake and rebuilt.

The Presidio was the original San Francisco, a Spanish fort overlooking the Golden Gate, erected in 1776. The fort became a US Army base when the USA took California from Mexico in 1846. The Presidio became a National Park in Oct 1994.

The Mission is named after Mission Dolores, also founded in 1776. Spanish is the language of the streets, a swirling mix of every corner of Central and South America. Most blocks are adorned with bright wall murals painted by local residents. The messages are as bright as the colours: equality, ethnic pride, and hope.

Haight-Ashbury is less gaudy than during the 1967 Summer of Love, but still more counterculture than mainstream. The eclectic mix of Haight St shops is unique, with chic restaurants sandwiched between second-hand clothing shops and high-tech skateboards.

The Castro is America's most famous homosexual neighbourhood, but San Franciscans know it equally for the Art Deco glory of its local cinema, the Castro Theatre, 429 Castro St; tel: (415) 621-6120, and the meticulously restored Victorian houses ('Victorians').

Museums

A century of wealth has left San Francisco awash with museums.

City museums in Golden Gate Park include the Asian Art Museum, tel: (415) 668-8921 (rare jades, porcelains, bronzes and ceramics – this museum is scheduled to move to the Civic Center area in 1995–96); the M. H. de Young Memorial Museum, tel: (415) 750-3600 (American, Egyptian, Greek, Roman, African, Oceania), the California Academy of Sciences, tel: (415) 750-7145 (natural history, Steinhart Aquarium, and planetarium), the Conservatory of Flowers, tel: (415) 641-7978 (flower collections in imitation of Kew Gardens) and the Japanese Tea Garden, tel: (415) 668-0909. Admissions change with the exhibitions, but a $10 Culture Pass (Visitor Information Center and member museums) covers them all.

The Palace of the Legion of Honor (European art) in Lincoln Park will reopen in mid-1995 after renovation. The building resembles the Hotel de Salm in Paris.

Yerba Buena Gardens, between Market, Second, Harrison and Fifth Sts in SOMA, is the newest cultural venue: Ansel Adams Center,

250 4th St; tel: (415) 495-7000, (photography), Cartoon Art Museum, 665 3rd St; tel: (415) 546-9481 (cartoon history), The Center for the Arts, 701 Mission St; tel: (415) 512-1000 (modern art, film, sculpture, theatre) and the Museum of Modern Art, 151 3rd St; tel: (415) 357-4000.

Other notable museums include The Exploratorium, Marina Blvd and Lyon (Palace of Fine Arts); tel: (415) 561-0360 (interactive science for children), Musée Mechanique, 1090 Point Lobos Ave; tel: (415) 386-1170 (antique mechanical toys), San Francisco International Airport, tel: (415) 876-2100 (17 rotating exhibits) and the Wells Fargo Museum, 420 Montgomery; tel: (415) 396-2619 (Gold Rush and later California history).

Walking Tours

San Francisco is best seen afoot. Top walking tours include the free City Guides, tel: (415) 557-4266 (culture, history, architecture), Cruisin' the Castro, tel: (415) 550-8110 (living history of the Castro), Wok Wiz Chinatown Tours, tel: (415) 981-5588 (Chinatown secrets with chef and author Shirley Fong-Torres), Dashiell Hammett's Haunts, tel: (415) 564-7021 (hangouts of the mystery writer and Sam Spade), and Italians of North Beach, tel: (415) 397-8530 (food, history, and culture by chef and writer GraceAnn Walden).

Bay Cruises

See Getting Around, p. 216. The budget version is a commuter ferry from the Ferry Building at the foot of Market St. Bigger spenders can buy anything from a 45-minute excursion to a private overnight yacht charter.

Excursions cruise the waterfront, beneath the Golden Gate Bridge, past Alcatraz to the San Francisco-Oakland Bay Bridge, and back along The Embarcadero. Always take a jumper or a coat, and a hat. The winds which make San Francisco Bay a yachting mecca can bring shivers to the sunniest day.

Driving

See next chapter for the 49-mile classic driving tour.

Advertisement

SAN FRANCISCO 49-MILE DRIVE

The **49-Mile Drive** *was created for visitors to the 1939-40 Golden Gate International Exposition. Blue and white seagull signs still mark an outstanding city tour. Allow half a day or longer.*

UNION SQUARE TO PIER 39

This route begins on the north (Post St) side of **Union Square**, The City's primary hotel and shopping district.

Follow Post St (one way) to Grant Ave. Turn left. **Chinatown** begins two blocks north at a green-tiled gate topped with golden dragons.

Go left at California St along the cable car line up **Nob Hill**. The height was originally called Nabob Hill, after the palatial homes which crowned it from the 1860s to the 1906 earthquake. The only buildings to survive quake and fire were the Fairmont Hotel and the red stone Flood mansion, now the private Pacific Union Club. The modern Gothic towers of **Grace Cathedral** (Anglican) top the hill.

Turn right at Taylor St. Follow the tracks on Mason and Washington Sts to the red brick **Cable Car Barn**, *tel: (415) 474-1887, 1000–1700 daily.* An inside gallery overlooks 14-ft (4.2-metre) pulleys dragging steel cables beneath city streets at a constant 9 mph (15.2 kph). The cable car gripman operates levers which grab the cable to propel the car or release the cable and apply brakes to stop. Cable cars have the right of way over all other traffic.

Continue one block past the Barn on Washington to Powell St. Right one block to Clay St, then turn left. Five blocks ahead on the left is **Portsmouth Square**, where the US flag was first raised over San Francisco in 1846. Today it's the heart of Chinatown.

At Kearny St, turn left. On the right is **Jackson Square Historical District**, housing a handsome collection of 19th-century brick buildings. Most are occupied by art and antique dealers, apparel shops and solicitors. Park at the Portsmouth Square Garage to explore on foot.

Two blocks ahead, turn into Columbus Ave and **North Beach**. Coffee-houses and nightlife are concentrated around Columbus and Broadway. Straight ahead lie **Washington Square** and the imposing white basilica of Sts Peter and Paul.

At Broadway, turn right onto Grant Ave. On the right is **Telegraph Hill**, topped by **Coit Tower**, 212 ft (64 m) tall, giving stunning views of the city. The interior boasts Depression-era murals influenced by Diego Rivera. Hilltop parking is scarce; walk uphill or take bus 39.

At Lombard St, turn left, drive three blocks, then turn right onto Mason St toward **Pier 39**. Pier 39 is a 1000–ft (303 m) pier that has become one of America's most popular attractions, complete with shopping, restaurants, buskers, a carousel and barking sea lions. Cruise ships call at Pier 35, one pier east.

FISHERMAN'S WHARF AND ALCATRAZ

Continue left along Jefferson St to **Fisherman's Wharf**. Once home to a major fishing fleet, the Wharf is now a tourist and shopping venue. Try wharf-side crab or shrimp cocktails and sour-dough bread.

Alcatraz Island, formerly an infamous penitentiary, is 1½ miles (2.4 km) offshore. Tours leave from Pier 41: *tel: (800) 229-2784.* Bookings are advisable. Alcatraz was touted as America's only 'escape-proof' prison. Between 1934 and 1963, 1554 convicts spent an average of 8 years on Alcatraz. Only 36 ever tried to escape. Ten were killed in the attempt and 21 recaptured. The other 5 were never found.

The list of prisoners incarcerated on Alcatraz reads like a Who's Who of Hollywood celebrity criminals. Al 'Scarface' Capone arrived on The Rock inside an armoured car aboard a heavily guarded ferry. George 'Machine Gun' Kelly was carefully kept away from his favourite weapons. Robert Stroud became famous as 'The Birdman of Alcatraz' even though his research on bird diseases was done while serving time at the

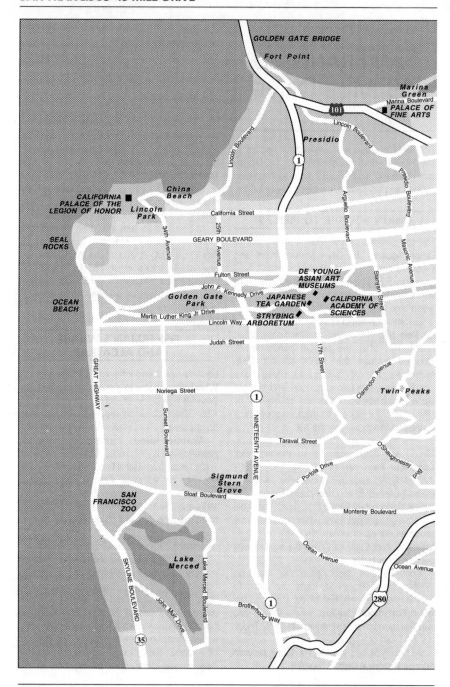

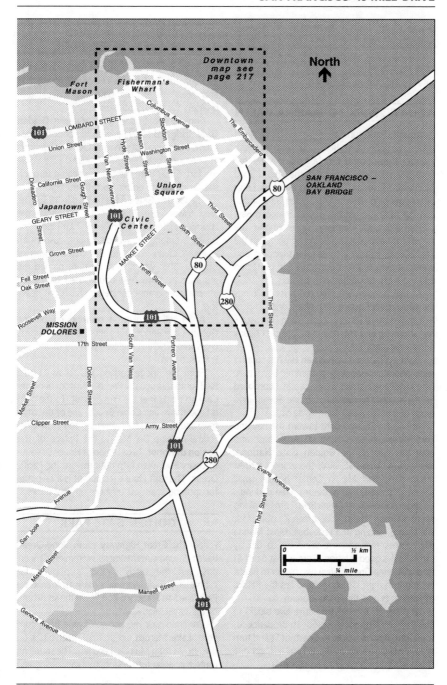

Leavenworth Federal Penitentiary in Kansas. Famous or not, only the country's most dangerous and most troublesome convicts were sent to Alcatraz. The place was designed for revenge, not rehabilitation.

AQUATIC PARK TO MARINA GREEN

At **Aquatic Park**, turn left, drive one block along Hyde St, right onto Beach St. Aquatic Park includes **Hyde Street Pier**, antique vessels that once plied local waters, and the ship-shaped **Maritime Museum**. The curving **Municipal Pier** offers sweeping views of the Golden Gate Bridge and the northern reaches of San Francisco Bay.

The red brick **Cannery**, once among the largest fruit and vegetable canning plants on the West Coast, is now a three-level shopping and entertainment centre. Courtyards and protected entrances are favourites with buskers.

At Polk St, turn left. The red brick buildings are **Ghirardelli Square**. The abandoned chocolate and mustard factory became San Francisco's first shopping and entertainment complex nearly thirty years ago.

Right at Francisco St. **Russian Hill** has country lanes and staircases with panoramic Bay views. 'The crookedest street in the world', **Lombard St**, makes nine hairpin turns in one flower-lined block descending east from Hyde St.

At Laguna St, turn right toward the Bay and **Fort Mason**, once a major US Army base and now the hub of the **Golden Gate National Recreation Area** (GGNRA), the world's largest urban park. Fort Mason Center houses small theatres, galleries and museums. Free parking.

Laguna St ends at Marina Blvd. Turn left along **Marina Green**. The bayside green is popular for kite flying, running and volleyball. Most Marina Blvd homes feature large windows to display carefully designed interiors. Turn left at Scott St (end of Marina Green), drive two blocks to Beach St, and turn right. Straight ahead lies the **Palace of Fine Arts** and the Exploratorium.

At Baker St, turn left and drive two blocks to Bay St. Turn left, go one block to Broderick St, turn right, go two blocks to Chestnut St and turn right. Chestnut ends at Lyon. Turn left, go one block, and turn right onto Lombard St.

THE PRESIDIO AND GOLDEN GATE BRIDGE

The Presidio of San Francisco National Park is 2¼ square miles (6 square km) of rolling parkland and ocean vistas. The base was once headquarters for the US 6th Army.

Continue to Lincoln Blvd and the **Golden Gate Bridge**. Directly beneath the bridge is **Fort Point**, one of the last surviving Civil War-era forts in America. Costumed guides recreate life inside the fort. Spray from the tides sweeping through the Golden Gate erupts 26 ft (8 m) high.

The Golden Gate Bridge opened in 1938. The twin towers rise 746 ft (246 m) above the churning waters. At 1.7 miles (2.7 km) long, the bridge is among the world's longest suspension spans. 'Golden' refers to the Golden Horn of Istanbul, after which John Fremont named the entrance in 1846. The bridge itself is painted international orange for better visibility in heavy fog.

A $3 toll is collected southbound on the Golden Gate Bridge, but pedestrians and cyclists cross free. There is metered parking at the San Francisco end.

From the Bridge parking lot, follow Lincoln Blvd south through the Presidio. Lincoln becomes Camino Del Mar at the Presidio exit. To the right is Seacliff Ave and **China Beach**, one of the city's few sandy beaches for swimming and picnicking. Follow Camino Del Mar to the **Palace of the Legion of Honor**. Take Legion of Honor Dr south to Geary Blvd, then turn right toward the Pacific Ocean. **The Cliff House** restaurant is a favourite for spotting seals just offshore on Seal Rocks.

GOLDEN GATE PARK

Follow **The Great Highway** south along Ocean Beach. Strong currents make swimming dangerous, but the sandy strand is popular for sunbathing. Twin windmills mark Golden Gate Park. The **San Francisco Zoo** lies at the south end of the Great Highway.

Continue past the zoo to Skyline Blvd; turn right. **Lake Merced**, an artificial reservoir, is on the left. At John Muir Dr, keep left. The shoreline route is popular for walking, running, biking and skating. At the end of the reservoir, turn left onto Lake Merced Blvd. San Francisco State University is on the right. Lake Merced Blvd becomes Sunset Blvd and runs north to **Golden Gate Park**. Originally barren sand dunes, the park offers winding, tree-lined drives, lawns, playgrounds, lakes, riding stables, a buffalo herd and museums (see 'Museums' section p. 221).

The **Japanese Tea Garden**, built in 1894, has a popular tea-house, pagoda, ponds, bridges and bonsai. **Strybing Arboretum** has an outstanding collection of California native plants.

Follow 49-Mile Drive signs through the park to Stanyan St. Turn right, drive seven blocks uphill to Parnassus Ave. Turn right past the University of California Medical Center. Turn left at Laguna Honda (bottom of the hill). Bear left onto Woodside Ave to Portola Dr., turn left onto Twin Peaks Dr. The scenic drive curves to the top of **Twin Peaks**. The 750-ft (227 m) summit offers windy vistas over San Francisco.

Follow Twin Peaks Blvd north to Clayton St, Roosevelt Way, and 14th St to Dolores St. Turn right. **The Castro** district is on the right. The **Mission District** extends left.

The original Spanish colony settled at **Mission Dolores** (16th and Dolores Sts) in 1776. The mission church was completed in 1791; Spanish-era leaders and 19th-century American notables are buried in the graveyard.

Continue on Dolores to Army St (one block past 25th St); turn left. Follow Army St under Hwy 101 toward San Francisco Bay. At Third St, turn left to Townsend St and right onto **The Embarcadero**.

THE EMBARCADERO

The Embarcadero is what remains of San Francisco's once-busy waterfront (most ship traffic now goes to Oakland, across the Bay, Los Angeles, or Seattle, Washington). The **San Francisco-Oakland Bay Bridge** is overhead.

At 7.9 miles (13.3 km) long, the Bay Bridge is one of the world's longest steel bridges. The $1 toll is collected westbound, on the Oakland side.

For a spectacular view back to San Francisco, drive part-way across the Bay Bridge to **Treasure Island**. From The Embarcadero, turn left onto Bryant St, right on Sterling St and onto the bridge to the Treasure Island exit. The Embarcadero continues to the **Ferry Building**, terminus for cross-Bay ferries since the 1890s.

The **Embarcadero Center**, five grey concrete skyscrapers marching inland from the Ferry Building, has dozens of shops and restaurants on the first three levels and thousands of offices tucked into the next thirty-odd floors. Shopping levels are connected by wide walkways lined with café tables in good weather.

Head north along The Embarcadero to Washington St, then turn left. Two blocks ahead is the neo-classical **US Customs** building, at Battery St. Turn left into the concrete canyons of the **Financial District**. Turn right onto Market St, the main downtown artery. **San Francisco Visitor Information Center** is at Hallidie Plaza, six blocks ahead.

CIVIC CENTER TO UNION SQUARE

Turn right at Hayes St (opposite 9th St) to Van Ness Ave and modernistic **Davies Symphony Hall** in the **Civic Center**. Turn right.

Other Civic Center structures include the copper-domed Beaux-Arts **City Hall**, Federal and State office buildings, **Civic Auditorium**, the **Public Library**, **Veterans War Memorial Building** (where the United Nations charter was signed in 1945), and the **War Memorial Opera House**. **Civic Center Plaza**, in front of City Hall, has a semi-permanent population of the homeless.

Turn left at Geary Blvd. Cathedral Hill is dominated by **St Mary's Cathedral**, dubbed The Washing Machine by architectural critics.

Turn right at Webster St, three blocks beyond St Mary's, into **Japantown**, or Nihonmachi. Peace Plaza Pagoda, at Japan Center, is the focal point for local Japanese festivals. The Center includes a hotel (The Miyako), a traditional spa (Kabuki Hot Springs), a cinema, restaurants and shops. Underground parking (off Post St) is reasonably priced.

Turn right onto Post. The **Haas-Lilienthal House**, *2007 Franklin St*, an 1886 Victorian building is open Sun, and Wed afternoons for tours. Union Square is nine blocks east on Post.

SAN FRANCISCO BAY AREA ROUTES

The San Francisco Bay Area is a kaleidoscope of images: redwood groves, wild seashore, cows grazing on rolling hills, a bayside corniche, a world-renowned university, ethnic neighbourhoods and awesome views of bay islands and skylines from any point in the hills.

The first of these routes explores Southern Marin County: Point Reyes National Seashore, groves of coastal redwoods, quaint towns, and Mediterranean-style Sausalito on San Francisco Bay. The East Bay cities of Oakland and Berkeley are in a separate route. It is possible to see the whole area in one long day with few stops, but touring is more enjoyable spread over two or more days. Use San Francisco as a central base, stay in a quaint bed and breakfast or camp in Marin County, or choose moderately priced East Bay accommodation.

MARIN COUNTY ROUTE

Bridge tolls, paid on re-entry to San Francisco, are $3 for the Golden Gate Bridge and $1 for the San Francisco–Oakland Bay Bridge.

Marin County traffic and crowds are heavy at weekends and holidays. Motorcyclists joyride along Hwy 1's twists and turns. Prior experience driving an RV is essential, as roads are narrow and speed limits sometimes drop to 15 mph (24 kph). Tour vehicles clog roads near Muir Woods National Monument. A map is vital, as some citizens of Marin's Hwy 1 towns 'disappear' signs to discourage visitors.

From San Francisco's Union Square take **Geary St** 8 blocks west. Turn right onto **Van Ness Ave, Hwy 101**, and go 17 blocks north. Turn left onto **Lombard St**, continue on Hwy 101 about 3 miles (5 km) onto **Golden Gate Bridge.**

Driving north to Marin County on Golden Gate Bridge, Alcatraz Island is on the right. The speed limit on the bridge is 45 mph (72 kph). Stay in the right-hand lane to exit to the **Vista Point** on the north side of the bridge for a magnificent view of San Francisco's skyline in clear weather.

Take Hwy 101, the Redwood Highway, through the Waldo Tunnel. Upon leaving the tunnel, descend the **Waldo Grade**. Turn right onto Hwy 1, the exit marked **Mill Valley-Stinson Beach**. No vehicles over 35 ft (10.8 m) long are permitted on the winding Hwy 1 route. At **Tamalpais Valley**, go left at the traffic lights, continuing on Hwy 1 through gum tree forests. Turn right on Panoramic Hwy for 1 mile (1.6 km), then turn left onto **Muir Woods Rd**, to enter **Mount Tamalpais State Park**. **Muir Woods National Monument** is 1 mile (1.6 km) south.

The circuit descends west on Muir Woods Rd down Frank Valley Canyon, to the junction with Hwy 1 at **Muir Beach**. The hamlet's houses are scattered amid pines and Monterey cypresses on streets named after Herman Melville's *Moby Dick*. The **Pelican Inn**, *Hwy 1, Muir Beach, CA 94965-9729; tel: (415) 383-6000*, closed Mon, looks and is British. The bed and breakfast is expensive; the wood-panelled Pelican Bar is 16th-century; and the dining room, candlelit with a beamed ceiling, serves excellent moderate lunches, dinner and Sunday brunch.

Hwy 1, the Shoreline Hwy, has many lay-bys as it follows the hills above the coast to **Stinson Beach**, *tel: (415) 868-0942 or (415) 868-1922* (weather, surf, and parking information for the Bay Area's most popular beach). Bicyclists are common on this narrow stretch of road. Surfers catch rollers gliding into wide Stinson Beach. Delis and general stores in town have picnic food. **Stinson Beach Grill**, *3465 Hwy 1, Stinson Beach, CA 94970; tel: (415) 868-2002*, has grilled local Tomales Bay oysters, tortillas and salsa. Budget.

The highway continues along **Bolinas Lagoon**, a haven for shorebirds and harbour seals among old oyster fences and piers. At the north end of the lagoon is the **Audubon Canyon Ranch**, *4900 Hwy 1, Stinson Beach; tel: (415) 868-9244*, open during the mid-Mar–mid-July nesting season, Sat–Sun 1000–1600. Blue herons and great egrets nest atop redwoods.

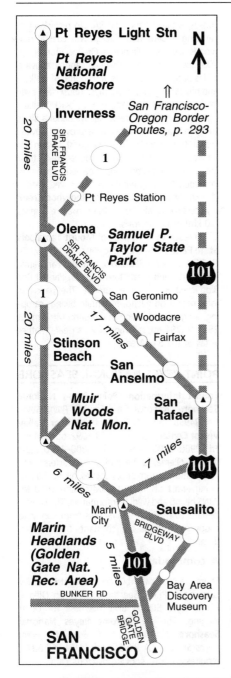

Avocets, sandpipers, harbor seals and leopard sharks share the lagoon, which is slowly turning into marshland.

Hwy 1 continues 9 miles (14 km) along the shoulder of the Olema Valley hills to **Olema**, with the Golden Gate National Recreation Area (GGNRA) on the right and **Point Reyes National Seashore (PRNS)** on the left. Turn left on Sir Francis Drake Blvd for the 40-mile (64 km) round trip to **Point Reyes Light Station**. Return to Hwy 1 at **Point Reyes Station** and turn right.

At **Olema**, turn left onto **Sir Francis Drake Blvd**. Four miles (6.4 km) east on Sir Francis Drake Blvd, in Lagunitas Canyon, is **Samuel P. Taylor State Park**, *PO Box 251, Lagunitas, CA 94938; tel: (415) 488-9897*, one of the first outdoor camping areas in the USA. Coastal Redwoods spread regally above campsites and picnic tables. Huge green elk clover lines the creek, while black-tailed deer roam the surrounding chaparral and grassland. Four miles (6.4 km) east at **San Geronimo**, turn left for ½ mile (0.8 km) on Nicasio Valley Rd, then walk into **Roy's Redwoods Open Space Preserve**. Experienced riders can take horses to the ridgetop overlooking PRNS. **DeBolt Trail Rides**, *tel: (415) 488-4490*.

Continue through **Woodacre** and **Fairfax** to **San Anselmo**. **San Anselmo Chamber of Commerce**, *1000 Sir Francis Drake Blvd, San Anselmo CA 94960; tel: (415) 454-2510*. The town claims over 130 antique dealers; **The Antique Dealers Association of San Anselmo**, *PO Box 684, San Anselmo, CA 94979; tel: (415) 454-6439*. Drake Blvd and Hwy 101 meet at **San Rafael**.

Seven miles (11 km) south, turn left on Bridgeway Blvd to **Sausalito**, driving along **Richardson Bay**. Follow Bridgeway south as it becomes 2nd St, then S. Alexander. To visit the children's **Bay Area Discovery Museum**, *557 E. Fort Baker; tel: (415) 332-7674*, continue on **East Rd**, or, take the Sausalito Lateral to Bunker Rd, cross under Hwy 101, and continue west to the **Marin Headlands**.

The **Marin Headlands**, *Golden Gate National Recreation Area, Bldg 1050, Ft Cronkhite, Sausalito, CA 94965; tel: (415) 331-1540*, include Forts Cronkhite and Barry; Nike Missile sites, operating during 1954–1974, but never used in action; and wildlife protection. The **California Marine Mammal Center**, *Bunker Rd, Fort Cronkhite; tel: (415) 289-7325,* open 1000–1600, pioneered rescue, rehabilitation, and release of harbour seals, sea lions, dolphins, porpoises, and whales. **Golden Gate Raptor Observatory**, *Fort Cronkhite; tel: (415) 331-0730,* conducts hawk watches, Aug–Dec. Bird-watching is spectacular in all seasons, as are the views from any bluff. Mountain biking is permitted. The *AY* **HI-Marin Headlands Hostel**, *Fort Barry, Building 941; tel: (415) 331-2777,* has budget lodging.

Return to Hwy 101 and cross the Golden Gate Bridge to San Francisco.

MARIN COUNTY

Tourist Information: **Marin County Chamber of Commerce and Visitors Bureau**, *30 N. San Pedro Rd, Suite 150, San Rafael, CA 94903: tel: (415) 472-7470.* **West Marin Chamber of Commerce**, *11431 Hwy 1, The Creamery Bldg, # 17, Point Reyes Station, CA 94956; tel: (415) 663-9232.*

Accommodation

In Western Marin County, most lodging is bed and breakfast. Most innkeepers require a 2-night stay if booking either Fri or Sat night. Several inn associations in Point Reyes Station make book-ings: **Inns of Marin**, *PO Box 547, Point Reyes Station, CA 94956; tel: 415-663-2000 or (800) 887-2880*; **Bed & Breakfast Cottages of Point Reyes**, *tel: (415) 663-9445,* expensive; **Coastal Lodging**, *PO Box 1162; tel: (415) 485-2678*; **Seashore Bed & Breakfasts of Marin**, *PO Box 1239; tel: (415) 663-9373.*

Money

Thomas Cook Foreign Exchange is at *The Village at Corte Madera, 1512 Redwood High-way, Corte Madera; tel: (415) 924-6001.*

MUIR WOODS

Muir Woods National Monument, *Mill Valley, CA 94941; tel: (415) 388-2595,* open 0800–sunset, is part of the GGNRA. No picnicking or camping is permitted. Old-growth coastal red-woods (see San Francisco–Oregon Border, p. 293) tower in a cathedral-like canopy above a series of fern-lined groves, a favourite of walkers and hikers. Fog may hover mysteriously like a veil in the branches high above. Blue-black Stellar's jays flit among the trees. Yellow banana slugs thrive in the damp, mossy undergrowth. In May, ladybirds (*Hippodamia convergens*) swarm on redwood bark, not quite camouflaged by their colour. Pacific salmon and steelhead spawn in Redwood Creek in winter. A flat, paved, 1-mile (1.6 km) **Main Trail Loop** along **Redwood Creek** is accessible to all. Above the grove are 6 miles (10 km) of hiking trails.

To reach the east peak of **Mount Tamalpais State Park**, *801 Panoramic Hwy, Mill Valley, CA 94941; tel: 415) 388-2070,* take the Panoramic Hwy north and west; turn right on Pantoll Rd/Ridgecrest Blvd to the summit. The park has information on hiking, mountain biking, camp-ing, lodging and dining in the park. Mt Tam, at 2571 ft (791 m), is famous for its clear-weather vistas of the Bay Area.

POINT REYES NATIONAL SEASHORE

Tourist Information: **Point Reyes National Seashore**, *National Park Service, Point Reyes CA 94956; tel: (415) 663-1092.* **Bear Valley Visitor Center**; *tel: (415) 663-1092,* open Mon–Fri 0900–1700, weekends 0800–1700, just beyond Olema, is the park headquarters, with information on camping, beaches, hiking, biking, riding and trails. Tune to AM station 1610 for PRNS hiking and wildlife information. The coastal climate can change in *minutes* from sunny to soupy fog. Winds are constant, trails often damp.

Accommodation

There are campsites, but no overnight car or RV camping in PRNS. See the sections on Olema, Point Reyes Station and Inverness for other lodging. The *AY* **HI-Point Reyes National Seashore**, *Limantour Road, Box 247, Point Reyes Station, CA 94956; tel: (415) 663-8811,* requires advance booking by credit card.

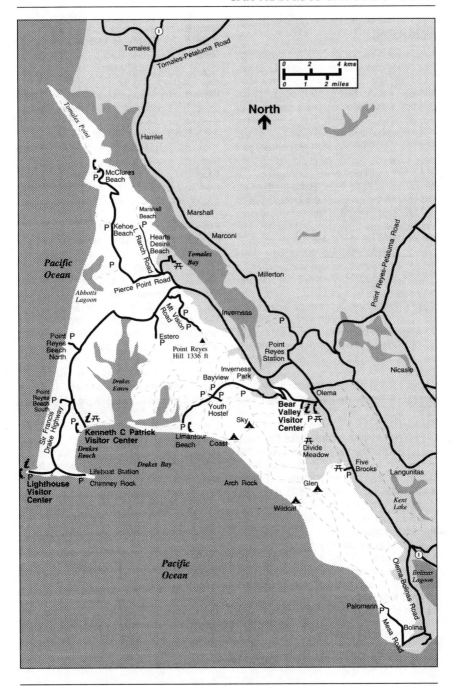

Sightseeing

Point Reyes National Seashore is a windswept, often foggy domain of wild cliffs, green pastures, and fairy tale remoteness. Traditional dairy farming and lumbering continue as hikers, bicyclists, horse riders, and beachcombers enjoy the natural beauty. Tule elk, deer, woodpeckers, foxes, mountain lions and red-tailed hawks roam wild. During winter migration gray whales pass close to shore. Native American culture, the USA's first true horse breed, earthquakes, and the mystery of Point Reyes' European discovery add spice to the flavour of this protected land.

The Miwoks fished and hunted the seashore's triangular wedge of land before the arrival of Sir Francis Drake on the *Golden Hinde* in 1579. Drake's exact landfall has yet to be proven, though it is assumed the ship was beached for repairs near present-day Drake's Estero (estuary), protected by the wide expanse of Drake's Bay. Drake's 'Nova Albion' was never reclaimed by the British. In 1603 the Spanish explorer Sebastian Vizcaino named the headlands after the Feast of the Three Kings, La Punta de Los Reyes. Settled in the 19th century, the land was ideal dairy pasturage.

The 1906 earthquake wrenched two San Andreas Fault plates beneath Point Reyes' Bear Valley. Buildings and land formations were displaced 16 ft (5 m), visible on the 0.6 mile (1 km) self-guided, paved, **Earthquake Trail Loop** across from the **Bear Valley Visitors Center**. The setting is bucolic – birds chirp, frogs croak, blackberries grow wild, and bay laurel trees scent the air. Blue posts mark the 1906 land shift; movement continues at 2 inches (5 cm) per year. A barn dragged 16 ft (5 m) off its foundation and an equally displaced fence are still visible.

At the **Morgan Horse Ranch**, *tel: (415) 663-1763*, next to the Visitors Center, this special US breed is trained for use by mounted park wardens. A ½ mile (0.8 km) from the Visitors Center is **Kule Loklo**, *tel: (415) 663-1092*, a re-creation of a Coastal Miwok encampment.

Point Reyes Light Station

Point Reyes Light Station awaits over bare hills 20 miles (32 km) west of Inverness on Sir Francis

Drake Blvd. The lighthouse is 300 steps below the **Point Reyes Headlands Visitors Center**, *tel: (415) 669-1534*. The stairs, open 1000–1630, may be closed in foul weather. On fair-weather days vistas are magnificent. Wardens describe this as the foggiest point on the continent's west coast. The **Lighthouse**, and **Chimney Rock** at the other end of the point, are crowded from late Dec–mid-Mar, grey whale watching season.

Six miles (10 km) back up Sir Francis Drake Blvd, turn right for 2 miles (3.2 km) to **Drake's Beach** and **monument**. Currents are strong and swift; be wary of the surf when beachcombing or tidepooling.

Inverness and Point Reyes Station

Inverness, named after an early settler's memories of Scotland, is a settlement of cottages and houses hidden among the trees, overlooking the tides of southern Tomales Bay. **Manka's Inverness Lodge**, *Argyle and Callender, Inverness, CA 94937; tel: (415) 669-1034*, a 1917 hunting lodge, has 8 expensive–pricey rooms and 4 cottages, and a popular restaurant serving specialities like wild boar, elk, wild pheasant, and local oysters; pricey. Inverness has no lack of restaurants; only fast food is absent. **Johnson's Oyster Company**, *17171 Sir Francis Drake Blvd; tel: (415) 669-1149*, open Tues–Sun 0800–1600, is a major oyster farm on Tomales Bay, with fresh and barbecued oysters.

Point Reyes Station has lots of surviving 1960s counterculture and quaint shops, and a bustling undertone. The **Station House Cafe**, *on Main St; tel: (415) 663-1515*, is the meeting place for locals, with average, moderately-priced meals. The **Bovine Bakery**, *tel: (415) 663-9420*, named after the countryside's dairies and its cow art, has excellent pastries and muffins.

Olema

Olema's three blocks are characterised by the 1876 six-room **Olema Inn**, *10,000 Sir Francis Drake Blvd, Olema, CA 94950; tel: (415) 663-9559*; expensive. High ceilings, skylights, and large, curtained windows make the moderate **Olema Inn Restaurant** bright, cheerful, and relaxed. Across the highway is the expensive **Point Reyes Seashore Lodge**, *10021 Hwy 1; tel:*

(415) 663-9000. The **Olema Ranch Campground**, *10155 Hwy 1; tel: (415) 663-8001*, is a budget choice and offers cyclists a discount.

SAN RAFAEL

Tourist Information: San Rafael Chamber of Commerce, *818 Fifth Ave, San Rafael, CA 94901; tel: (415) 454-4163.*

Mission San Rafael Arcangel, *1104 5th Ave; tel: (415) 454-8141*, is a replica of the 1817 Spanish mission that served as a hospital for San Francisco's Mission Dolores. A mansion that belonged to Arctic explorer Louise Boyd, the first woman to fly over the North Pole, houses local memorabilia in the **Marin County Historical Society Museum**, *1125 B St; tel: (415) 454-8538.* The **Marin County Civic Center**, *tel: (415) 499-7407*, offer tours of the Frank Lloyd Wright-designed building. For cultured dining, **Jazzed**, *816 4th St; tel: (415) 455-8077*, serves budget food to the non-smoking, alcohol-free tune of live jazz, Tues–Sun. Ales and porter top the brewpub list at the moderate **Pacific Tap and Grill**, *812 4th St; tel: (415) 457-9711.* **Bordenave's San Rafael French Bakery**, *1553 4th St; tel: (415) 453-2957*, has onion-cheese-tomato foccacia and sourdough, freshest before 1100.

San Quentin is California's oldest prison. An on-site museum includes antique handcuffs, a gallows, and a gas chamber: **San Quentin Museum**, *Dolores Way off Main St, Bldg. 106, San Quentin State Prison; tel: (415) 454-8808*, open 1000–1600; take Hwy 580 south-east off Hwy 101 for 2 miles (3.2 km). Ferries and windsurfers vie for space in Corte Madera Channel, just south of the prison.

SAUSALITO

Tourist Information: Sausalito Chamber of Commerce, *333 Caledonia St, PO Box 566, Sausalito, CA 94965; tel: (415) 332-0505.*

Accommodation

Two famous hotels with views perch on the hill above Bridgeway; both have main buildings and cottages. **Casa Madrona Hotel**, *801 Bridgeway; tel: (415) 332-0502 or (800) 288-0592*, includes breakfast. Expensive–pricey. The **Alta Mira**, *125 Buckley Ave; tel: (415) 332-1350*, is moderate–pricey. The Chamber of Commerce can recommend additional lodging.

Eating and Drinking

Sausalito has many restaurants with outstanding bay views. Vistas are most dramatic in daylight, when San Francisco sparkles across the bay. Book in advance for Sunday brunch. Expensive–pricey, the **Casa Madrona Restaurant**, *801 Bridgeway; tel: (415) 331-5888*, has ultra-fresh California cuisine with view windows above the marinas. **Café Madrona & Bakery** are adjacent; *tel: (415) 331-2253*; open 0730–1800. The **Alta Mira**, *tel: (415) 332-1350*, has view and American food. Pricey. Waterfront restaurants have great views, seafood, and are pricey. Two of the best are **Scoma's**, *588 Bridgeway; tel: (415) 332-9551*, and **The Spinnaker**, *100 Spinnaker Dr.; tel: (415) 332-1500.*

Sightseeing

In the 1870s, English sea captains in the grain trade saw Sausalito's setting as reminiscent of England. The captains brought their families, and San Francisco holidaymakers journeyed to Sausalito by ferry. All built country cottages on the hills. The Golden Gate Bridge made the ferries obsolete in 1937, but Sausalito revived as a shipyard town during World War II. In the 1950s, artists, writers and the 'beat' generation took up residence, many in waterfront houseboats. A bordello madam, Sally Stanford, opened a restaurant and was eventually elected mayor.

Sausalito today is trendy restaurants, cafés, boutiques, shopping complexes like **Village Fair**, *777 Bridgeway*, souvenir shops, galleries, marinas, floating homes, and humming toadfish – amorous fish, throbbing together in summer mating calls. The **Plaza de Vina Del Mar Park**, across from the **Sausalito Ferry Landing**, has a Spanish-style fountain and two stone elephants from the 1915 Pan Pacific Exposition. The **Bay Model**, *2100 Bridgeway; tel: (415) 332-3870*, open Tues–Sat 0900–1600, is a working scale model of San Francisco Bay's tidal action. A Marin-ship exhibit explains Sausalito's wartime shipyard activities.

Point Reyes National Seashore–San Rafael–Sausalito　　　**233**

EAST BAY AREA ROUTES

The **East Bay** area is easy to get to. Take **BART**, (see p. 216), to the centres of Berkeley and Oakland, as an alternative to driving.

Retrace the route through San Francisco to **Union Square** and take **Stockton St** south across **Market St** to **Folsom St**. Turn left. Get in the right-hand lane to turn right onto **Essex St** Drive one block, and cross **Harrison St** onto **I-80** across the **San Francisco-Oakland Bay Bridge**. Veer left onto Hwy 80/580 north for 2½ miles (4 km). Turn right onto **University Ave, Berkeley**. Return to I-80/580, and go south. Turn left onto the frontage road which parallels the freeway and go south to the bridge entrance, in west **Emeryville**. Continue south-east on Hwy 580 for 1 mile (1.6 km) south-east of the bridge exit. Turn right on Hwy 980 to downtown Oakland. To return, take Hwy 980 to Hwy 580, and take Hwy 80 over the San Francisco-Oakland Bay Bridge to **San Francisco**.

AMTRAK has moved some railway services from Oakland to Emeryville until a new station is built. **Colors**, *5900 Hollis St, Emeryville, CA 94608; tel: (510) 665-7100*, serves a tasty, budget soup or sandwich lunch.

BERKELEY

Tourist Information: **Berkeley Convention & Visitors Bureau**, (CVB) *1834 University Ave, 1st Floor, Berkeley CA 94703; tel: (510) 549-7040 or (800) 847-4823.* **University of California, Berkeley Campus Visitor Center**, *2200 University Ave; tel: (510) 642-5215.*

Accommodation

About 1000 rooms at all price levels are available in this university community. The Berkeley CVB has information on lodging.

Eating and Drinking

Chez Panisse, *1517 Shattuck Ave, Berkeley, CA 94709; tel: (510) 548-5525*, where California Cuisine sprang forth two decades ago, is still booked months in advance, serving pricey, inconsistent *prix fixe* meals. Budget **Triple Rock Brewery**, *1920 Shattuck Ave; tel (510)*

843-2739, has scrumptious sandwiches and beer. The **Gourmet Ghetto** along the 1500–1900 blocks of **Shattuck Ave**, is a food mecca for devotees, filled with fresh-ingredient and ethnic restaurants, coffee shops and bakeries. Stand in line for baguettes from **Acme Bread Co.**, *1601 San Pablo Ave; tel: (510) 524-1327*, probably the best bread in the region. **Spenger's Fish Grotto**, *1919 4th St; tel: (510) 845-7771*, serves hearty portions in a casual atmosphere. Budget–moderate. The largest sake brewery in the USA is **Takara Sake USA, Inc.**, *708 Addison St; tel: (510) 540-8250*, open 1200–1800.

Sightseeing

Berkeley is defined, confined, and refined by its centrepiece, the **University of California** campus (UCB). The academic lustre has been stronger in years past, but institutional research continues to churn out Nobel Prize winners and free-thinkers. In the mid-1960s a local effort saved People's Park; anti-Vietnam demonstrations, hippies, coffee-houses, and bookstores made street life colourful. Coffee-houses, book-sellers, and hippies remain, augmented by punks, grunge fans, and a solid middle class.

Towering above UCB is 307-ft (94 m) **Sather Tower**, known as the **Campanile**. Below its 61 bells is an observation platform with a magnificent view of the East Bay. Nine Nobel Prizes have been garnered by alumni of **Lawrence Berkeley Laboratory**; *tel: (510) 486-5122*, open for public tours of advanced X-ray technology, Mon 1000–1200, booked 1 week in advance. Many other campus buildings have specialist collections. On the south side is **Sather Gate**, the traditional green metal arch above the campus entrance. **Lawrence Hall of Science**, *Centennial Dr, UCB Campus; tel: (510) 642-5132*, has interactive science exhibits, using computers, life sciences, and astronomy to explain the natural world. Up the road is the **UC Botanical Garden**, *Centennial Dr. in Strawberry Cyn; tel: (510) 642-3343*, which cultivates world-class collections of cacti, old roses, redwoods and Chinese medicinal herbs.

Telegraph Ave, land of coffee-houses and bookstores, has been Berkeley's 'scene' for years. **Cody's Books**, *2454 Telegraph Ave; tel: (510)*

845-7852 carries volumes on anything from politics to computers, drawing both students and professors. On the pavement are street people, panhandlers and serious shoppers. In south-east Berkeley is the **Judah L. Magnes Museum**, *2911 Russell St; tel: (510) 549-6950*, displaying Jewish fine art, ceremonial objects, and rare books.

Berkeley's finest views are from **Grizzly Peak Blvd** and the benches high up in the 3000-plant **Berkeley Municipal Rose Garden**, *Euclid Ave and Eunice St*, with a sunset view over the Golden Gate Bridge.

OAKLAND

Tourist Information: **Oakland Convention & Visitors Bureau**, *1000 Broadway, Ste. 200, Oakland, CA 94607; tel: (510) 839-9000 or (800) 262-5526.*

Accommodation

Oakland has a wide variety of accommodation, including *BW* and *TL*, and *DI, HI, HL*, and *HY* near Oakland International Airport (south of this route). The white gleam against the hill is the pricey **Claremont Resort, Spa, & Tennis Club**, *Ashby & Domingo Aves, Oakland CA 94623-0363; tel: (510) 843-3000 or (800) 551-7266*. The **Lake Merritt Hotel**, *1800 Madison St, Oakland, CA 94612; tel: (510) 832-2300 or (800) 933-4683*, an Art Deco showplace overlooking a scenic lake, is expensive. The **Waterfront Plaza Hotel**, *10 Washington St, Oakland, CA 94607; tel: (510) 836-3800*, at Jack London Square, is close to the ferry landing; expensive.

Eating and Drinking

Pacific Coast Brewing Co., *906 Washington St; tel: (510) 836-2739* is a budget brewpub, with a long wooden bar, in Old Oakland. **Chinatown** eateries are good budget choices. Trendy restaurants and cafés are in the **Rockridge** district, on **College Ave** between 63rd and Alcatraz Sts. Ethnic choices range from Ethiopian to Cambodian.

Sightseeing

Cultural diversity is not just a slogan in Oakland, it's a fact. 43% African American, 14% Hispanic, and 14% Asian/Pacific Islander, Oakland has frequent neighbourhood and community festivals celebrating ethnic origins. Fall jazz and blues festivals, the Pointer Sisters and rap star Hammer are part of Oakland's musical heritage. Writers Jack London and Gertrude Stein were born in Oakland. The Port of Oakland is one of the busiest on the US Pacific Coast; huge cargo container cranes are visible from the Bay.

Jack London Square on the waterfront is a modern complex of shops, restaurants, and museums. The **Jack London Museum**, *30 Jack London Sq, Ste. 104; tel: (510) 451-8218*, is devoted to the writer and his contemporaries. The **Ebony Museum of Arts**, *tel: (510) 763-0745*, has African American art and culture.

Downtown **Old Oakland**, between Broadway and Clay St and 8th and 10th Sts, its meticulously restored blocks of Victorian buildings, now occupied by solicitors and other professionals. At street level are restaurants and art galleries. **G. B. Ratto & Co.**, or **Ratto's**, *821 Washington; tel: (510) 832-6503* is a deli and small restaurant with food products from all over – including California. Old Oakland has one of the liveliest **Farmer's Markets** in Northern California, *9th St and Broadway*, Fri, 0800–1330, where Asians from adjacent **Chinatown** sell and shop with other Oaklanders. Chinatown's boundaries are 6th and 8th Sts, and Broadway and Fallon. Chinatown is pan-Asian in ethnicity, with inhabitants from China, Korea, Cambodia, Vietnam, Laos, Thailand and the Philippines. Noodle shops, restaurants and produce markets are more relaxed, and economical, than in San Francisco's Chinatown.

The **Oakland Museum**, *1000 Oak St; tel: (510) 834-2413*, open Wed–Sat 1000–1700, Sun 1200–1900, is California's *de facto* state museum. Separate history, art and natural history displays, aided by computerised technology, rate comparison with the US Smithsonian Museum in Washington, D.C. The **Western Aerospace Museum**, *Bldg. 621, 8260 Boeing St, North Field, Oakland International Airport; tel: (510) 638-7100*, open Wed–Sun 1000–1600, shows-off Amelia Earhart's and Gen. Jimmy Doolittle's exploits from North Field in the pioneering days of flight, as well as a collection of vintage aircraft.

SAN FRANCISCO to NAPA VALLEY

The broad triangle of wine country, running from the town of Napa west to the mouth of the Russian River and north to Ukiah, boasts most of the wineries in California. Many wineries in Sonoma, Napa, Mendocino and Lake counties are open for tours; most offer tasting. To the world, though, 'Wine Country' is the counties of Napa and Sonoma, about an hour north of San Francisco.

Allow at least 2 days for the 216-mile (345 km) loop through the Russian River Valley, Dry Creek Valley, Alexander Valley, Napa Valley, Carneros, and Sonoma Valley. Three to four days is even better, although it's possible to visit one or two areas in a long day trip.

Best time to visit is mid-week during the spring and autumn. Try to avoid weekends, and the Napa Valley anytime during the summer. Traffic slows to a crawl and temperatures hit 40°C June–Aug.

ROUTE

Take Hwy 101 north from San Francisco towards **Rohnert Park**. Follow Hwy 116 north-west to **Guerneville**, on the **Russian River**. Follow Westside Road east to **Healdsburg**, then Dry Creek Road and Canyon Road to **Geyserville**. Take Hwy 128 south to **Napa**, follow Hwy 12 north to **Carneros**, **Sonoma**, and **Santa Rosa**, and return to **San Francisco** on Hwy 101 southbound.

SONOMA VALLEY

Take Hwy 101 50 miles (80 km) north to **Rohnert Park** and the Golf Course Dr. exit. Turn left onto Roberts Lake Rd. The **Sonoma County Wine &**

Visitors Center, 5000 Roberts Lake Rd, Rohnert Park, CA 94928; tel: (707) 586-3795, is open 1000–1800. The centre is the most complete source of wine information and gifts in the area. Interactive video kiosks design customised winery itineraries, complete with lodging, eating and recreation suggestions, or answer almost any question about tourist facilities in Sonoma County. The staff are especially good with novice's questions.

For accommodation bookings anywhere in Sonoma County tel: (800) 576-6662.

Cross beneath Hwy 101 and drive just under 1 mile (1.6 km) to **Stoney Point Rd.** Turn left. Continue 1½ miles (2.4 km) to **Hwy 116** and turn right. Hwy 116 is also called the Gravenstein Highway for the orchards of Gravenstein apples along the road. Roadside fruit stands sell Gravensteins and other local apples during the August–October harvest season. **Sonoma County Farm Trails**, PO Box 6032, Santa Rosa, CA 95406; tel: (707) 586-3276, produce a map, also available from the county visitor centre, which lists apple growers and other farm producers who welcome the public.

The highway runs through rolling countryside where apple orchards alternate with dairy pastures, herds of sheep and antique shops. Nearer Hwy 101, 'antique' can mean anything that looks well-used; nearer **Sebastopol**, antiques are more likely to be genuine and more expensive.

SEBASTOPOL

Tourist Information: Sebastopol Chamber of Commerce, 265 S. Main St, Sebastopol, CA 95472; tel: (707) 823-3032.

Accommodation and Food

There are many pleasant, moderate–expensive, bed and breakfasts in the area. The Chamber of Commerce has the most complete listing.

Grateful Bagel, 300 S. Main St, is a budget breakfast and lunch favourite. **East West Café**, 128 N. Main St; tel: (707) 829-2822, serves great budget meals all day. **Chez Peyo**, 2295 Gravenstein Hwy South; tel: (707) 823-1262 serves moderate French country fare at lunch and

101 ⇑ *San Francisco-Oregon Border Route, p. 293*

29

116

CANYON RD **Geyserville**

128 *24 miles*

DRY CREEK RD

WESTSIDE RD

11 miles

▲ **Calistoga**

Russian River

▲ **Healdsburg**

29

Guerneville ▲

7 miles

Napa Valley

Sebastopol

21 miles

▲ Santa Rosa

8 miles

116

STONEY POINT RD

12

▲ **St Helena**

23 miles

10 miles

Valley

▲ **Yountville**

Rohnert Park

Sonoma

▲ **12** ▲ **Napa**

Sonoma *12 miles*

50 miles

101

SAN FRANCISCO ▲

San Francisco to Napa round trip: 216 miles

N ↑

---

dinner, advance booking required. **Truffles**, *234 S. Main St; tel: (707) 823-3448*, has expensive Cajun and California specialities.

Sightseeing

Enmanji Buddhist Temple, *1200 Hwy 116* just south of town, is a calm, shady oasis beside the busy highway. The temple was brought to the USA from Japan for the 1933 World's Fair in Chicago. Just north of Sebastopol is **Buzzards Roost Ranch**, *1778 Facendini Lane; tel: (707) 823-2799*. Farm tours are hands-on, from learning to milk a goat to slopping (feeding) pigs and collecting chicken eggs.

Hwy 116 winds through central Sebastopol and into the countryside. Eight miles (13 km)

north is **Kozlowski Farms**, *5566 Gravenstein Hwy North, Forrestville, CA 95436; tel: (707) 887-1587*. The family farm offers cider and jam tasting. Almost next door is **Topolos at Russian River Vineyards**, *5700 Gravenstein Hwy North; tel: (707) 887-1575*. It's hard to miss Topolos, patterned on the weathered twin towers of a 19th-century kiln for drying hops – many wine country wineries put as much creativity (and money) into architecture as into winemaking. Best bets are Topolos' red wines and moderate Greek restaurant.

The best stop in **Forrestville**, 1 mile (1.6 km) beyond Topolos, is **Brother Juniper's Bakery**, *6544 Front St, Forrestville, CA 95436; tel: (707) 887-7908*. The bakery and café make some of the heartiest breads and sandwiches in Sonoma County. **California Carnivores**, *7020 Trenton-Healdsburg Rd, Forrestville, CA 95436; tel: (707)838-1630*, is a unique wine country stop. Located next to **Mark West Winery**, it is one of the largest carnivorous plant nurseries in Western North America. More than 350 species of plants that eat insects are on display, most of them for sale. Continue north on Hwy 116 toward the **Russian River**.

RUSSIAN RIVER

Tourist Information: Russian River Chamber of Commerce, *16,200 1st St, Guerneville, CA 95446; tel: (707) 869-9009*, has complete lists of accommodation, restaurants, and events.

Sunny valleys and hillsides are filled with vineyards, shadier areas are cloaked with oak and conifer forests. The river itself begins near Willits, to the north, and winds along Hwy 101 to Healdsburg, where it turns west toward the Pacific and about four dozen small wineries. Earlier in the century, The River, from Healdsburg west to Jenner, was a summer retreat for San Franciscans. In the 1970s, it became a favourite with the gay community. Today, it's a mixture of old-time cabins and new retreats, rickety inns and posh bed and breakfasts, family farmers and transplanted urbanites, all living along a river that floods in most years.

Guerneville is the closest the Russian River has to a capital. Most of the area's restaurants, bars and resorts are in a few short blocks on the north side of the river. Swimming and canoeing are favourite summertime activities, though the normally placid river can become a rampaging torrent in winter.

Follow Hwy 116 across the Russian River. Turn left and continue four miles (6 km) to **Korbel Champagne Cellars**, *13250 River Rd, Guerneville, CA 95446; tel: (707) 887-2294*. The flower gardens and ivy-covered brick buildings are worth a stop even if you aren't tasting. Three Bohemian brothers began as Russian River loggers in the 1860s, then planted grapes between the redwood stumps in the rich land near the river. The rest, along with the 1868 winery buildings, is very successful history.

Korbel's tour concentrates on the making of sparkling wine, though they also produce still wine and brandy.

Return to Guerneville and continue along the north side of the Russian River on Main River Rd, which becomes Westside Rd. Do not cross the river. Westside Rd is windy, narrow, rough and the main winery road through the Russian River Valley. Vineyards are gradually replacing dairy pastures and fruit orchards, but there are still a number of pre-wine-boom farms between the vineyards. **Hop Kiln**, *6050 Westside Rd, Healdsburg, CA 95448; tel: (707) 433-6491*, inside an old hop kiln, has better architecture than wine. **Ricciolo Winery**, next door, offers spectacular views across riverside vineyards from a shaded outdoor deck and picnic area. Ricciolo's slightly sweet whites are easy to drink, especially on a warm afternoon. Follow Westside Rd 7 miles (11 km) east to **Healdsburg**, at the confluence of the Russian River, Dry Creek, and Alexander Valleys.

HEALDSBURG

Tourist Information: Healdsburg Chamber of Commerce, *217 Healdsburg Ave, Healdsburg, CA 95448; tel: (707) 433-6935*.

Accommodation

There are well over a dozen choices in the area, including *BW*, but bed and breakfasts are the favourite. **Sonoma County Bed & Breakfast Inns Guide**, published by Sonoma County CVB, and **Wine Country Inns of Sonoma County**, *PO Box 51, Geyserville, CA 95441; tel: (707) 433-4743 or (800) 354-4743*, are the most complete listings. Most bed and breakfasts follow the motif established by the pink Victorian **Camellia Inn**, *211 North St; tel: (70) 433-8182*, one of the first, and still among the most elegant and popular, wine country bed and breakfasts. The pricey **Madrona Manor**, *1001 Westside Rd; tel: (707) 433-4231*, is tops for sleeping and eating.

Eating and Drinking

Restaurants come and go, but the number seems to hover around three dozen. **Downtown Bakery and Creamery**, *on The Plaza, 308 Center St; tel: (707) 431-2719*, has the best

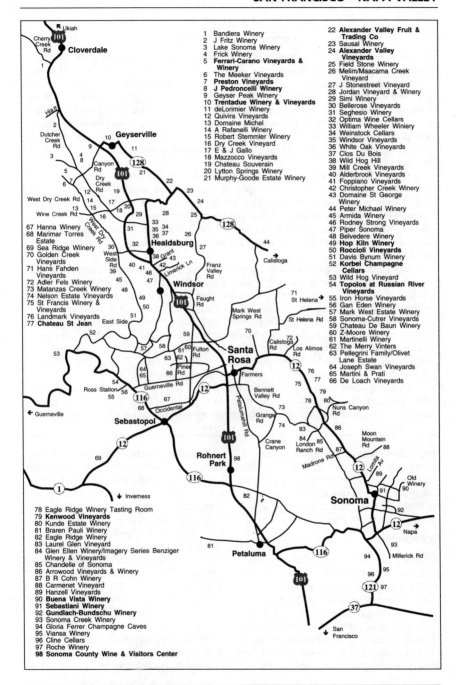

1 Bandiera Winery
2 J Fritz Winery
3 Lake Sonoma Winery
4 Frick Winery
5 **Ferrari-Carano Vineyards &
   Winery**
6 The Meeker Vineyards
7 **Preston Vineyards**
8 **J Pedroncelli Winery**
9 Geyser Peak Winery
10 **Trentadue Winery & Vineyards**
11 deLorimier Winery
12 Quivira Vineyards
13 Domaine Michel
14 A Rafanelli Winery
15 Robert Stemmler Winery
16 Dry Creek Vineyard
17 E & J Gallo
18 Mazzocco Vineyards
19 Chateau Souverain
20 Lytton Springs Winery
21 Murphy-Goode Estate Winery

22 **Alexander Valley Fruit &
   Trading Co**
23 Sausal Winery
24 **Alexander Valley
   Vineyards**
25 Field Stone Winery
26 Melim/Maacama Creek
   Vineyard
27 J Stonestreet Vineyard
28 Jordan Vineyard & Winery
29 Simi Winery
30 Bellerose Vineyards
31 Seghesio Winery
32 Optima Wine Cellars
33 William Wheeler Winiery
34 Weinstock Cellars
35 Windsor Vineyards
36 White Oak Vineyards
37 Clos Du Bois
38 Wild Hog Hill
39 Mill Creek Vineyards
40 Alderbrook Vineyards
41 Foppiano Vineyards
42 Christopher Creek Winery
43 Domaine St George
   Winery
44 Peter Michael Winery
45 Armida Winery
46 Rodney Strong Vineyards
47 Piper Sonoma
48 Belvedere Winery
49 **Hop Kiln Winery**
50 **Roccioli Vineyards**
51 Davis Bynum Winery
52 **Korbel Champagne
   Cellars**
53 Wild Hog Vineyard
54 **Topolos at Russian River
   Vineyards**
55 Iron Horse Vineyards
56 Gan Eden Winery
57 Mark West Estate Winery
58 Sonoma-Cutrer Vineyards
59 Chateau De Baun Winery
60 Z-Moore Winery
61 Martinelli Winery
62 The Merry Vinters
63 Pellegrini Family/Olivet
   Lane Estate
64 Joseph Swan Vineyards
65 Martini & Prati
66 De Loach Vineyards

67 Hanna Winery
68 Marimar Torres
   Estate
69 Sea Ridge Wiinery
70 Golden Creek
   Vineyards
71 Hans Fahden
   Vineyards
72 Adler Fels Winery
73 Matanzas Creek Winery
74 Nelson Estate Vineyards
75 St Francis Winery &
   Vineyards
76 Landmark Vineyards
77 **Chateau St Jean**

78 Eagle Ridge Winery Tasting Room
79 **Kenwood Vineyards**
80 Kunde Estate Winery
81 Braren Pauli Winery
82 Eagle Ridge Winery
83 Laurel Glen Vineyard
84 Glen Ellen Winery/Imagery Series Benziger
   Winery & Vineyards
85 Chandelle of Sonoma
86 Arrowood Vineyards & Winery
87 B R Cohn Winery
88 Carmenet Vineyard
89 Hanzell Vineyards
90 **Buena Vista Winery**
91 **Sebastiani Winery**
92 **Gundlach-Bundschu Winery**
93 Sonoma Creek Winery
94 Gloria Ferrer Champagne Caves
95 Viansa Winery
96 Cline Cellars
97 Roche Winery
98 **Sonoma County Wine & Visitors Center**

Sonoma and Napa Wines

The local wine industry recognises Agoston Haraszthy as the first to plant European varieties, which made his Buena Vista Winery in Sonoma famous. Samuele Sebastiani started a winery nearby in the town of Sonoma; winery and family remain major economic and political forces. In the Napa Valley, Charles Krug introduced Riesling and other European varieties in the 1860s, laying the foundation for what was to become California's most sophisticated and most successful wine region. Mark Twain, Robert Louis Stevenson, and Jack London were just a few of the writers who visited wine country and stayed to write about it. By the 1890s, California wines were besting French and German vintages in European competitions.

The 1906 San Francisco earthquake was a wine disaster. The quake and subsequent fire destroyed enormous stocks of wine aging in San Francisco warehouses and disrupted business for years. The quake also hit wineries, especially the unreinforced stone and masonry buildings so common in agricultural areas. By the time the industry was back on its feet, America was plunging into Prohibition. From 1919 to 1933, it was illegal to make, have, or consume wine (or any other alcoholic beverage) except for sacramental or medicinal purposes.

A few Napa and Sonoma wineries hung on, making cheap 'jug wine'. Consumers were small-town descendants of recent European immigrants. Urban wine drinkers wouldn't touch anything but French imports. Robert Mondavi and the few other 1940s and 1950s winemakers who dreamed of restoring the glory days were dismissed as dreamers. Half a century later, they're semi-saints. Their vision, with research help from the University of California, Davis, and new winemaking technology from bulk producers such as Gallo, gave California vintners more control over the art of turning grape juice into wine than any winemakers in the world. When Stag's Leap, from the Napa Valley, beat Mouton Rothschild in a Paris competition in 1976, the California wine rush was on.

Today, Napa and Sonoma produce less than 20% of California's wine, but garners 80% of the publicity. Most of the state's wine comes from producers in the Central Valley whose output is measured in millions of cases. In wine country quality counts more than quantity.

---

baked goods, pastries and ice cream around. **Bistro Ralph**, *109 Plaza St; tel: (707) 433-1381*, moderate–pricey, serves wonderfully prepared California Cuisine. **Samba Java**, *219 Center St; tel: (707) 433-5282*, budget–moderate, adds a Caribbean flair to the plaza.

Sightseeing

Healdsburg has long been the country cousin among wine country towns. It's more relaxed than Napa or Sonoma, less expensive, and offers easier access to more varied winery scenery than either of its larger competitors. More importantly, Healdsburg hasn't let the wine industry take over. Locals still gather at a favourite bakery over coffee each morning to talk about something other than grapes, wine and tourists.

Healdsburg Plaza is the heart of town, shaded by an unlikely combination of citrus trees, palms and redwoods. The plaza is well-stocked with benches and surrounded by shops and restaurants. Nearby blocks are filled with Victorian houses, most of them family homes. The Chamber of Commerce publishes an excellent self-guided walking tour map that includes historic downtown buildings and several wineries. **The Healdsburg Museum**, *221 Matheson St; tel: (707) 431-3325*, has a regional collection focusing on northern Sonoma County, including more than 8000 photographs.

One of the most traditional wine country activities is hot air ballooning. Residents aren't wild about the intermittent roar of flames heating air trapped inside the 150-ft (50 m) balloons, but drifting above vineyards as the sun slips over the hilltops can be a breathtaking experience for passengers. It can be an expensive experience, too: prices start around $150 per hour, including a post-flight breakfast with the traditional sparkling wine. Early French balloonists, who usually crashed into fields and orchards, carried a few bottles of champagne to calm irate farmers. Contact **Air Flambouyant**, *4714 Woodview Dr, Santa Rosa, CA 95405; tel: (707) 575-1955 or (800) 247-8439*, **Once In a Lifetime**, *PO Box 1263, Windsor, CA 95492*, or **Sonoma Thunder**, *4914 Snark Ave, Santa Rosa, CA 95409; tel: (707) 538-7359*. Launch sites, usually expansive winery lawns, change with the weather, and advance bookings are essential.

From Healdsburg, take Westside Rd beneath Hwy 101 to Kinley Rd and turn right. Follow Kinley Rd 1.3 miles (2 km) to Dry Creek Road. Turn left into the **Dry Creek Valley**, planted to vineyards for more than a century.

Many of the old vineyards survived Prohibition and are back in production. **Lambert Bridge**, *4085 W. Dry Creek Rd; tel: (7078) 433-5855*, uses many old growth lots. The tasting bar in one corner of a cathedral-sized redwood aging room is dwarfed by stacks of barrels. **Preston Vineyards**, *9282 W. Dry Creek Rd; tel: (707) 499-3372*, has a bocci ball court and one of the most scenic picnic areas in Dry Creek. **Ferrari-Carano**, *8761 Dry Creek Rd; tel: (707) 433-6700* makes one of the richest Chardonnays in the state, but may be the only Sonoma winery to charge for tasting.

Turn onto **Canyon Rd**, 9 miles (14 km) north of the Kinley Rd/Dry Creek Rd junction.

J. Pedroncelli Winery, *1220 Canyon Rd, Geyserville, CA 95441; tel: (707) 857-3619*, is one of the oldest family-owned wineries in the state. Cross beneath Hwy 101 onto Hwy 128. Follow Hwy 128 about 1 mile (1.6 km) to **Geyserville**, centre of the **Alexander Valley**.

GEYSERVILLE

Tourist Information: Geyserville Chamber of Commerce, *21035 Geyserville Ave, Geyserville, CA 95441; tel: (707) 857-3745*.

Hope-Bosworth House and **Hope-Merrill House**, *PO Box 42; tel: (707) 857-3356*, are the leading bed and breakfasts, lovingly restored to their original Victorian splendour. Moderate–expensive. **Catelli's The Rex**, *21047 Geyserville Ave; tel: (707) 587-9904*, is famous for copious budget–moderate Italian meals.

The geysers after which the town is named are off-limits inside a geothermal power plant. A viewpoint on **Geysers Road**, 14 miles (22 km) north of Hwy 128 overlooks steam vents and the plant. The turnoff is 5 miles (8 km) south of Geyserville. Good winery visits include **Trenta-due Winery**, *19170 Geyserville Ave; tel: (707) 433-3104*, **Alexander Valley Fruit & Trading Company**, *5110 Hwy 128; tel: (707) 433-1944*, and **Alexander Valley Vineyards**, *8644 Hwy 128; tel: (707) 433- 7209*. **Stage-A-Picnic**, *PO Box 536; tel: (707) 857-3619*, offers vineyard and winery tours by horsedrawn stage-coach.

Hwy 128 continues southwest, twisting up the flanks of **Mt St Helena**, looming above. The highway crosses into **Napa County** and drops down to **Calistoga**, at the head of the **Napa Valley**. Hwy 128 joins Hwy 29 at the south edge of town to become Hwy 29, the St Helena Hwy.

NAPA VALLEY

Tourist Information: The **Napa Valley Conference & Visitors Bureau**, *1310 Napa Town Center, Napa, CA 94559; tel: (707) 226-7459*, has general Napa Valley tourist information. The **Winery Hotline**, *tel: (707) 427-5500*, lists current winery news and events. **Napa Valley Cassette Guide**, *4076 Byway East; tel: 707 253-2929*, sells a 97-point Napa Valley tour guided by prerecorded cassette covering wineries, landmarks, and spots of local interest. The 2½ hour trip can be interrupted at any point.

The Napa Valley is becoming a wine theme park for people with serious money to spend. Prices are higher than in Sonoma County, crowds are bigger, and advance bookings are a necessity for almost everything. Crowds and prices increase to the south, or 'down valley', especially in summer. There's no getting around the prices, but you can avoid some of the crowds by following the **Silverado Trail** along the eastern edge of the valley and taking one of the many cross-valley roads back to Hwy 29 as needed. Many Napa wineries charge for tasting.

CALISTOGA

Tourist Information: Calistoga Chamber of Commerce, 1458 Lincoln, Calistoga, CA 94525; tel: (707) 942-6333.

Accommodation

The Napa County Fairgrounds, 1435 Oak St; tel: (707) 942-5111, has the only camping, although the Triple S Ranch, 4600 Mountain Home Ranch Rd; tel: (707) 942-6730, has small but moderate cabins. Moderate choices in town include Calistoga Inn, 1250 Lincoln Ave; tel: (707) 942-4101, Nance's Hot Springs, 1614 Lincoln Ave; tel: (707) 942-6211, Roman Spa, 1300 Washington; tel: (707) 942-4441 and Cl. Bed and Breakfast Exchange, 1458 Lincoln Ave; tel: (707) 942-2924, has current bed and breakfast information.

Eating and Drinking

Almost all the choices are along Lincoln Ave. Fellion's Delicatessen, 1359 Lincoln; tel: (707)-942-6144, and All Seasons Market and Café, 1400 Lincoln; tel: (707) 942-9111, are local favourites for budget breakfast/lunch and picnic makings. Best in town are Bosko's Ristorante, 1403 Lincoln; tel: (707) 942-9088, and Valeriano's, 1457 Lincoln; tel: (707) 942-0606, both with moderately priced Italian food. Napa Valley Brewing, 1250 Lincoln; tel: (707) 942-4101, has three beers to match the upmarket but moderately priced food.

Sightseeing

Calistoga sits atop an active geothermal area that bubbles to the surface as hot springs. Sam Brannan created the town in 1859, hoping to emulate the highly profitable hot springs of Saratoga, New York. Brannan ended up in San Francisco, but the Sam Brannan Cottage and the Sharpsteen Museum, 1311 Washington St; tel: (707) 942-5911, keep Brannan's historic contributions alive.

Calistoga is walkable, but cycling is trendy throughout the valley. Hire shops include Jules Culver Bicycles, 1287 Lincoln Ave; tel: (707) 942-0421' Palisades Mountain Sport, 1330 Gerrard; tel: (707) 942-4687 and St Helena Cyclery, 1156 Main St; tel: (707) 942-7736. The other way to sightsee is from the air with Calistoga Glider Rides, 1546 Lincoln Ave; tel: (707) 942-5000.

The town's other attractions are wineries and spas. The variations are endless, but the basic treatment includes a soak in hot volcanic mud, a hot mineral water bath and whirlpool, steam heat, blanket wrap, and massage. Modern fillips include herbal wraps or facials and enzyme baths (in tubs of decaying bark, bran and fibre.) Spa packages start about $50, depending on resort and options. Choices include Calistoga Spa Hot Springs, 1066 Washington; tel: (707) 942-6269, Indian Springs Spa, 1712 Lincoln; tel: (707) 942-4913, International Spa, 1300 Washington; tel: (707) 942-6122, and Dr. Wilkinson's Hot Springs, 1507 Lincoln; tel: (707) 942-4102.

California's best geyser is Old Faithful Geyser, 1299 Tubbs Lane; tel: (707) 942-6463. It erupts every 4 minutes, recent earthquakes permitting, in a 60-ft (19 m) blast of steam and water. Petrified Forest is 5 miles (8 km) west of town, 4100 Petrified Forest Rd, Calistoga; tel: (707) 942-6667. The best view of wine country is from atop Mt St Helena in the undeveloped Robert Louis Stevenson State Park, tel: (707) 942-4575, about 10 miles (16 km) north of town off Hwy 29. Stevenson honeymooned in an abandoned miner's cabin on the mountain in 1880, which provided material for Silverado Squatters and other books. He also penned the too oft-quoted 'bottled poetry' description of Napa wines. The 5-mile (8 km) return walk to the 4344-ft (1434 m) peak is debilitating in summer, but pleasant in autumn or spring. On clear days, the view extends from Mount Shasta in the north to San Francisco in the south.

The best picnic spot in the valley is Château Montelena, 1429 Tubbs Lane; tel: (707) 942-5105. A picnic pavilion surrounded by a formal Chinese lake (complete with half-sunken junk) can be booked in advance, or with great luck, on the spot. If not, the medieval French château

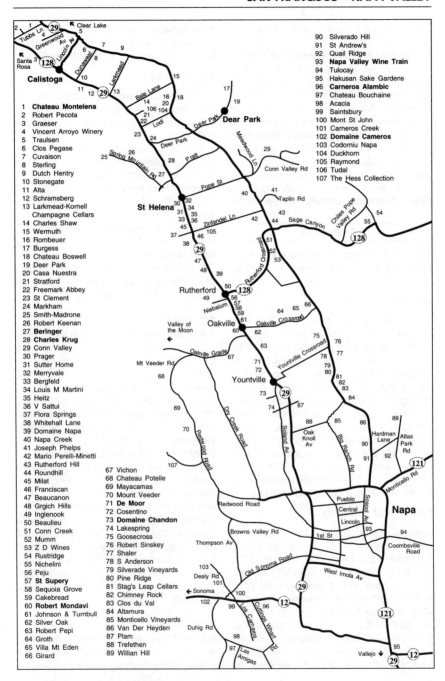

90 Silverado Hill
91 St Andrew's
92 Quail Ridge
93 **Napa Valley Wine Train**
94 Tulocay
95 Hakusan Sake Gardens
96 **Carneros Alambic**
97 Chateau Bouchaine
98 Acacia
99 Saintsbury
100 Mont St John
101 Carneros Creek
102 **Domaine Cameros**
103 Codorniu Napa
104 Duckhorn
105 Raymond
106 Tudal
107 The Hess Collection

1   **Chateau Montelena**
2   Robert Pecota
3   Graeser
4   Vincent Arroyo Winery
5   Traulsen
6   Clos Pegase
7   Cuvaison
8   Sterling
9   Dutch Hentry
10 Stonegate
11 Alta
12 Schramsberg
13 Larkmead-Kornell
    Champagne Cellars
14 Charles Shaw
15 Wermuth
16 Rombeuer
17 Burgess
18 Chateau Boswell
19 Deer Park
20 Casa Nuestra
21 Stratford
22 Freemark Abbey
23 St Clement
24 Markham
25 Smith-Madrone
26 Robert Keenan
27 **Beringer**
28 **Charles Krug**
29 Conn Valley
30 Prager
31 Sutter Home
32 Merryvale
33 Bergfeld
34 Louis M Martini
35 Heitz
36 V Sattui
37 Flora Springs
38 Whitehall Lane
39 Domaine Napa
40 Napa Creek
41 Joseph Phelps
42 Mario Perelli-Minetti
43 Rutherford Hill
44 Roundhill
45 Milat
46 Franciscan
47 Beaucanon
48 Grgich Hills
49 Inglenook
50 Beaulieu
51 Conn Creek
52 Mumm
53 Z D Wines
54 Rustridge
55 Nichelini
56 Peju
57 **St Supery**
58 Sequoia Grove
59 Cakebread
60 **Robert Mondavi**
61 Johnson & Turnbull
62 Silver Oak
63 Robert Pepi
64 Groth
65 Villa Mt Eden
66 Girard

67 Vichon
68 Chateau Potelle
69 Mayacamas
70 Mount Veeder
71 **De Moor**
72 Cosentino
73 **Domaine Chandon**
74 Lakespring
75 Goosecross
76 Robert Sinskey
77 Shaler
78 S Anderson
79 Silverade Vineyards
80 Pine Ridge
81 Stag's Leap Cellars
82 Chimney Rock
83 Clos du Val
84 Altamura
85 Monticello Vineyards
86 Van Der Heyden
87 Plam
88 Trefethen
89 Willian Hill

winery is worth the drive – so is the Cabernet Sauvignon.

Bale Grist Mill State Historic Park, *3801 St Helena Hwy; tel: (707) 963-2236*, is just south of town. The restored mill, the only grain mill in the Napa Valley when it was built in 1846, operates occasionally. The park is also welcome for its shaded walking paths. A 1-mile (1.6 km) History Trail leads to **Bothe-Napa Valley State Park**, *3801 St Helena Hwy; tel: (707) 942-4575*, with the only wooded campsite in the valley and several miles of shady walking paths. Napa Valley vineyards are thickest just south around **St Helena, Rutherford, Oakville**, and **Yountville**.

ST HELENA

Tourist Information: St Helena Chamber of Commerce, *1508 Main St, St Helena, CA 94574; tel: (707) 963-4456*.

Accommodation

There's plenty of room at the inn in St Helena, but the inns are expensive–pricey. Top of the line are **Auberge du Soleil**, *180 Rutherford Hill Rd, Rutherford, CA 94573; tel: (707) 963-1121* and **Meadowood Resort**, *900 Meadowood Land, St Helena, CA 94574; tel: (707) 963-3646*. Auberge is a sunny, Mediterranean retreat surrounded by olive groves and valley vistas; Meadowood surrounds a croquet pitch and golf course in a private valley with views up into oak-covered hills. Both have rabid devotees and raves for their pricey restaurants. The Chamber of Commerce is the best information source for the current bumper crop of bed and breakfasts.

Eating and Drinking

Upmarket restaurants come and go almost as quickly as bed and breakfasts. Survivors include **Tra Vigne**, *1050 Charter Oak Ave; tel: (707) 963-4444*, **Trilogy**, *1234 Main St; tel: (707) 963-8931* and **Terra**, *1345 Railroad Ave; tel: (707) 963-8931*, all very pricey. **Oakville Grocery Co.**, *7856 St Helena Hwy, Oakville, CA; tel: (707) 944-8802*, is the ultimate upmarket deli for picnic provisions. **Guigni's Grocery**, *1227 Main St; tel: (707) 963-3421* stocks fewer truffles and more practical items. **Napa Valley Olive Oil**

Manufacturer, *835 McCorkle Ave; tel: (707) 963-4173*, has a wonderful selection of breads, cheeses, and sausages, along with fine olive oil.

Sightseeing

The **Silverado Museum**, *1490 Library Lane; tel: (707) 963-3757*, has one of the world's best Robert Louis Stevenson collections with over 8000 items.

Ballooning is a well-tended mania. Companies include **Adventures Aloft**, *PO Box 2500, Yountville, CA 94599; tel: (707) 255-8688*, **Balloons Above the Valley**, *PO Box 3838, Napa, CA 94558; tel: (707) 253-2222*, **Balloon Aviation**, *PO Box 3298, Napa, CA 94558; tel: (707) 252-7067*, **Bonaventura Balloon Co.**, *133 Wall Rd, Napa, CA 94558; tel: (707) 944-2822*, **Napa Valley Balloons**, *PO Box 2860, Yountville, CA 94599; tel: (707) 253-2224* and **Napa's Great Balloon Escape**, *PO Box 4197, Napa, CA 94558; tel: (707) 253-0860*.

Best Tours

Robert Mondavi Winery, *7801 St Helena Hwy, Oakville, CA 94562; tel: (707) 963-9611*, may be the most famous winery in California. The modern mission-style buildings appear on millions of wine bottle labels every year. The wine is always decent, and the tour outstanding, especially for beginners. Arrive early or (particularly in summer) book in advance. **St Supéry Vineyards**, *8440 St Helena Hwy, Rutherford, CA 94562; tel: (707) 963-4507*, has both guided and self-guided tours. A model vineyard and winery calendar are enough to convince anyone that making fine wine is more work than art. A series of 'sniffers' give the key aromatic essences that make up wine's essential flavours. **Domaine Chandon**, *1 California Drive, Yountville, CA 94599; tel: (707) 944-2280*, has the most complete sparkling winery tour in the valley, also geared for beginners. There's always space on tours, but make restaurant bookings at least two weeks in advance.

Famous Stops

Beringer Vineyards, *2000 Main St, St Helena; tel: (707) 963-7115*, is one of the most popular wineries to visit. The tour includes caves (actually tunnels) dug into the hillside by Chinese labourers and used ever since. Tours end at the 17-room **Rhine House**, an ornate jewel on the National Register of Historic Places and also Beringer's tasting room. The summer crowds rival a sold-out rock concert, but winter visits are calm. The **Charles Krug Winery**, *2800 St Helena Hwy; tel: (707) 963-5057*, is the other contender for 'most popular winery tour', thanks to the myriad details imparted over 45 minutes.

YOUNTVILLE

Tourist Information: Yountville Chamber of Commerce, *PO Box 2064, Yountville, CA 94599; tel: (707) 944-2929*.

Eating and Drinking

The French Laundry, *Washington & Creek Sts; tel: (707) 944-2380*, is an old and pricey favourite for California cuisine. **The Diner**, *6476 Washington St; tel: (707) 944-2626*, is a budget hotspot for locals.

Sightseeing

Wineries are the lure, especially the visually striking **Domaine Chandon**. **DeMoor Winery**, *7481 St Helena Hwy; tel: (707) 944-2565*, is as popular for picnics as tasting. Shoppers can flex their credit cards at **Vintage 1870**, *6525 Washington St; tel: (707) 944-2451*, an old winery converted to a speciality shopping mall.

NAPA

Tourist Information: Napa Chamber of Commerce, *1556 1st St, Napa, CA 94559; tel: (707) 226-7455*, is open 0900-1700. A **Tourist Information Office**, *4076 Byway East; tel: (707) 253-2929*, is open 1000–1500.

Accommodation

Napa has more than half of the population of the Napa Valley and most of the hotels and motels, including *BW*, *M6* and *TL*. Best source for bed and breakfast information is **Napa Valley Reservations Unlimited**, *1819 Tanen; tel: (707) 252-1985*.

Basic camping is available at the **Napa Town & Country Fairgrounds**, *575 3rd St; tel: (707) 226-2164*.

Eating and Drinking

Napa is the only town in the valley with a full complement of fast food joints, but **Nation's Giant Hamburgers**, *1441 3rd St; tel: (707) 252-8500*, has the best burgers. **Table 29**, *4110 St Helena Hwy; tel: (707) 224-3300*, is new, moderate, and screamingly popular. **Willett's Brewing**, *902 Main St; tel: (707) 258-2337*, is a popular riverside brewpub.

Sightseeing

The easiest way to see the greatest number of wineries – from the outside – is aboard the **Napa Valley Wine Train**, *1275 McKinstry St, Napa; tel: (707) 226-2528*. The train makes daily lunch and dinner runs up and down the valley. Pricey, but there's no traffic. The **Napa County Historical Society Museum and Gallery**, *1219 1st St; tel: (707) 224-1739*, concentrates on local history.

Follow Hwy 29 1½ miles (2.4 km) south from Imola Ave. Turn right (east) onto Hwy 12/121 towards **Carneros**. Continue 1.5 miles (2.5 km) to Cuttings Wharf Rd. Turn left to **Carneros Alambic Distillery**, *1250 Cuttings Wharf Rd, Carneros; tel: (707) 253-9055*.

Carneros claims to be the first alambic (French pot still) brandy distillery in America and remains the largest to make brandy as it is made in Cognac, France. State law prohibits tasting of spirits, but there are daily tours and a brandy 'sniffing' to display the distinctive bouquet of fine California brandy.

Domaine Carneros, *1240 Duhig Rd; tel: 257-0101*, on the south side of the highway, specialises in sparkling wines.

Follow Hwy 12 west into Sonoma county and turn right onto Vineburg Rd 3 miles (5 km) beyond Domaine Carneros. Continue west until it becomes Napa Rd and follow it into **Sonoma**.

SONOMA

Tourist Information: Sonoma Valley Visitors Bureau, *453 First St, Sonoma, CA 95476; tel: (707) 996-1090*.

St Helena–Yountville–Napa–Sonoma

Accommodation

Sonoma is bed and breakfast country, but there are also *BW* and the elegant **Sonoma Mission Inn**, *PO Box 1447; tel: (707) 938-4250*, 8 acres (3.2 ha) of pricey spa indulgence wrapped around a hot mineral spring.

Eating and Drinking

Picnics are easy. **Sonoma French Bakery**, *468 First St East; tel: (707) 996-2691*, has the bread; **Sonoma Cheese Factory**, *2 Spain St; tel: (707) 996-1931*, has Sonoma's best selection of cheeses (the Sonoma Jacks are made locally) and deli items. **La Casa**, *121 Spain St East; tel: (707) 996-3406*, across from the mission, has budget–moderate Mexican fare. **Ristorante Piatti**, *405 First St West; tel: (707) 996-2351*, has handmade pastas.

Sightseeing

Strict building controls have kept the downtown intact, from the 8-acre (3.2 ha) **plaza** to surrounding rings of old adobes, historic buildings, trees and gardens. Sonoma was California's capital during a short bout of independence before the USA annexed California in 1847. Sonoma's California Republic lives on in the grizzly bear on the state flag.

Many of the historic buildings are part of **Sonoma State Historic Park**, *20 Spain St East; tel: (707) 938-1578*, with self-guided walking tours. Main buildings include **Mission San Francisco de Solano de Sonoma**; the **Blue Wing Inn**, the first hotel north of San Francisco; **Sonoma Barracks**, now a museum covering Native American through early American years; and the **General Mariano Vallejo Home**, furnished as though the town's last Mexican commandant might walk in the door.

Sonoma was also the birthplace of wine country. **Sebastiani Vineyards**, *389 Fourth St; tel: (707) 938-5532*, has part of the original mission vineyards as well as one of the most complete and relaxed winery tours imaginable. **Buena Vista Winery**, *18000 Old Winery Road, Sonoma; tel: (707) 938-1266*, is Agoston Haraszthy's original winery (see p. 240). **Gundlach-Bundschu Winery**, *2000 Denmark St; tel: (707) 938-5277*, has been in the family since the mid-1800s. The 17-mile (27 km) long Sonoma Valley now has about three dozen wineries.

Hwy 12 runs north-west through the 'Valley of the Moon', Jack London's name for the Sonoma Valley. His beloved Beauty Ranch has become **Jack London State Historic Park**, *2400 London Ranch Rd, Glen Ellen, CA 95442; tel: (707) 938-5216*. The park offers picnicking, a small museum, the ruins of London's dream **Wolf House**, and miles of walking or riding trails.

The hamlet of **Kenwood** is 3 miles (5 km) north of Glen Ellen. **Wine Country Wagons**, *PO Box 1069, Kenwood, CA 95452; tel: (707) 833-2724*, provides horse-drawn tours through the vineyards to visit local wineries, spring–autumn. **Château St Jean**, *8555 Sonoma Hwy (Hwy 12), Kenwood, CA 95452; tel: (707) 833-4134*, makes sparkling wines and excellent reds in a medieval-style building. **Kenwood Vineyards**, *9592 Sonoma Hwy; tel: (707) 833-5891*, is best known for outstanding reds. The pricey **Kenwood Restaurant**, *9900 Sonoma Hwy; tel: (707) 833-6326*, makes regular appearances on lists of America's best restaurants.

Take Hwy 12 for 10 miles (16 km) to Santa Rosa and follow Hwy 101 south to San Francisco.

Wine-tasting Tips

Anyone 21 or older can taste in California. Children are welcome in tasting rooms, but not at the bar. Most wineries provide non-alcoholic drinks for children and designated drivers.

Taste white wines, then reds, and finally sweet desert wines. The idea is to taste a wine, not to swill it. The waste buckets on the counter are practical, not ornamental. If a wine doesn't appeal, pour it out.

Most wineries have sales rooms. Posted prices usually apply to single bottle purchases. Discounts of 10–20% are standard on case purchases (12 bottles). And while buying at the winery is convenient, supermarkets and discount stores often undercut winery prices.

SAN FRANCISCO to SACRAMENTO

The direct route between San Francisco and Sacramento, I-80, is one of the most heavily travelled freeways in Northern California. The scenic route, which winds along back roads through the **Sacramento-San Joaquin River Delta**, *is all but unknown to most busy urbanites.*

→ Direct Route

Winding through downtown San Francisco to get to the Bay Bridge can be a slow, frustrating process during commuting hours. Try to begin (or end) the trip before 0730, from 0930 to 1530, or after 1900. The total trip is 96 miles (154 km) and takes just over 2 hrs in normal traffic.

From **Union Square**, take Stockton St south across Market St to Folsom St, behind Moscone Convention Center. Turn left. Turn right at Essex St, four blocks straight ahead, just after the freeway passes overhead. Drive one block and cross Harrison St onto the **Bay Bridge** entrance ramp.

The Bay Bridge is free eastbound, but costs $1 per vehicle westbound (into San Francisco). Views are limited by high railings. Eastbound traffic flows along the lower level of the two-tier bridge, westbound traffic on the upper deck.

The first section of the bridge is a suspension span, like the Golden Gate Bridge. At the end of the suspension span, the highway tunnels beneath **Yerba Buena Island** with an exit to **Treasure Island**. TI, as local traffic reporters call it, was built for the 1939 World's Fair and is now a Navy base and film studio. The road emerges from the ½ mile (1 km) tunnel onto the cantilever section of the bridge leading to the **East Bay** (see San Francisco Bay Area Routes, p. 234).

The eastern end of the Bay Bridge is appropriately called **The Maze** as the roadways twist over and under each other like strands of concrete spaghetti. Keep to the left two lanes, which merge onto I-80 eastbound, toward **Sacramento**. University Ave, the exit for **Berkeley** and the **University of California** is 1½ miles (2.5 km) beyond the merge.

Continue 18 miles (29 km) on I-80 to the **Carquinez Bridge**, spanning the mouth of the **Delta** at the **Carquinez Narrows**. The toll is $1, paid northbound only, at the north end of the bridge.

From the Carquinez Bridge, I-80 swings northeast through the final range of hills separating the San Francisco Bay Area from the Sacramento Valley. The block-like **Anheuser-Busch Brewery** sits 20 miles (32 km) beyond the bridge on the right at *3101 Busch Dr., Fairfield, CA 94533; tel: (707) 429-7595.* The brewery is open for public tours on the hour, 0900–1600, Tues–Sat. Children five years or under are not allowed on the production floor, nor is anyone wearing open-toe or open-heel shoes. **Travis Air Force Base**, a major staging point for US airborne troop movements, lies just beyond Fairfield.

The traditional stopping point between San Francisco and Sacramento is the **Nut Tree**, 15 miles (24 km) east of **Fairfield** at **Vacaville**. Exit on Nut Tree Rd. The Nut Tree has grown from a ramshackle fruit and nut stand beside a winding country highway into a major souvenir emporium, restaurant, playground and picnic area on the north side of I-80. A large collection of factory outlet stores has sprouted across the freeway.

The Nut Tree is in the Sacramento Valley, the flat agricultural heartland of California. The Valley was once a sea floor, but now produces a wide variety of vegetables, fruits, nuts and grains. The city of **Davis** is home to the **University of California, Davis** (UCD), one of the top agricultural research universities in the world. Many of the fields around the city are test plots for new crops, new varieties, and new equipment developed by UCD.

I-80 splits 11 miles (18 km) east of Davis. Traffic for Reno exits right to remain on I-80. Continue straight, following directions for

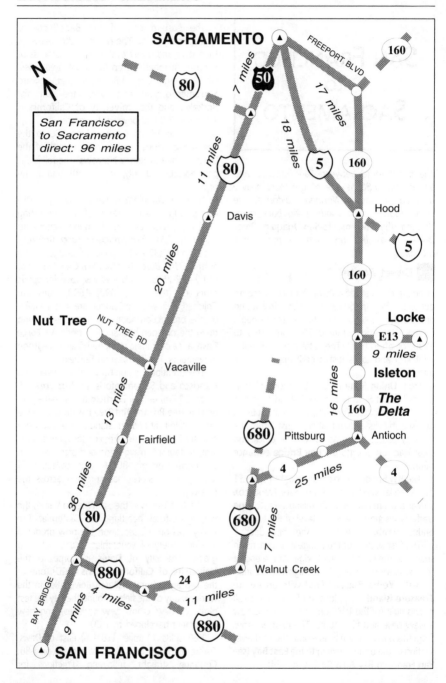

downtown **Sacramento** and South Lake Tahoe via Hwy 50. After the I-80 split, stay in the right two lanes, following signs for downtown Sacramento. Do not take Business 80, which bypasses downtown. Cross the Sacramento River. **Old Sacramento** is to the left, just over the river; the **State Capitol** is 11 blocks ahead on Capitol Mall.

⁓⁓ Scenic Route

Allow at least half a day to wind 110 miles (176 km) through the East Bay and the Delta to get to Sacramento. The most confusing and time-consuming part of the drive is getting out of San Francisco onto the Bay Bridge, so try to avoid rush hour departures or arrivals.

San Francisco to Pittsburg

Follow the Direct Route from Union Square onto the Bay Bridge and across San Francisco Bay into The Maze. Coming off the Bay Bridge, stay in the middle two lanes. Follow signs for Highway 24, Walnut Creek, and I-880. Merge onto I-880 and stay in the right hand lane. Four miles (6 km) later, exit right onto Hwy 24 eastbound toward **Walnut Creek**.

Hwy 24 runs through **Oakland** and north **Berkeley** toward the nearby hills. The BART (Bay Area Rapid Transit) line to Walnut Creek is sandwiched between the two sides of the freeway.

The **Caldecott Tunnel** is 5 miles (8 km) beyond the Hwy 24 junction. The tunnel has three two-lane bores, one in each direction and a middle bore that can be used for either direction. During morning commuting, the centre bore is used for westbound traffic; during the afternoon rush, for eastbound vehicles. The skeletal trees and open hillsides are a reminder of a wildfire which swept through the Oakland hills in the early 1990s, destroying thousands of homes.

Exiting the tunnel, Hwy 24 descends a long, gentle slope through heavily populated **Contra Costa County**. The freeway reaches a Y-junction 8 miles (13 km) from the tunnel exit. Merge left and take I-680 northbound toward **Concord** and **Sacramento**. Most hours of the day I-680 is filled with a steady stream of heavy lorries moving in both directions. Northern Contra Costa is flat and

crowded, much like the San Fernando Valley section of Los Angeles. Most Contra Costa residents commute elsewhere to work, creating massive traffic jams morning and afternoon.

Continue on I-680 for 7 miles (11 km) to Hwy 4 eastbound. Exit to the right on Hwy 4, also called the California Delta Highway, toward **Stockton** and **Pittsburg**.

The highway is lined with a patchwork of housing estates, shopping centres, industrial parks, and, along the Bay, storage tank farms and petrochemical plants. The Port Chicago Highway is 9 miles (14 km) beyond the Hwy 4 turnoff. The small mounds in the valley to the right of Hwy 4 are military ammunition bunkers. One of the largest non-nuclear blasts in history occurred at **Port Chicago** during World War II when an ammunition ship exploded.

The road tops a small hill 3 miles (5 km) beyond Port Chicago to reveal the Delta spread out in the distance beyond Pittsburg and Antioch. 13 miles (21 km) from the hilltop, Hwy 4 takes a sharp right toward Stockton. Continue straight as the road becomes Hwy 160 headed toward **Rio Vista**.

The Delta

One mile (1.6 km) beyond the intersection, Hwy 160 arches over the Delta via the **Antioch Bridge**. Toll is $1, collected northbound. The view from the top of the bridge, with the Delta to the right and the Bay to the left, is spectacular, but there is no stopping to admire the scenery.

The **Delta** is a patchwork of 'islands', irregular tracts of marsh that have been surrounded by tall levees, or dykes, and drained for agricultural use. Most levees are anchored by decades-old plantings of oaks, eucalyptus, palms and other trees. The water level in the winding waterways is several metres higher than the dry land behind the dykes. Hwy 160, and most other Delta roads, follow the tops of the levees, looking down on vast orchards and directly into first-floor windows.

The waterways of the Delta are open to the public for fishing and other recreational use. Larger islands have at least one shoreline picnic area, campground, and boat launching ramp. The orchards and fields behind the levees produce a variety of crops, including nuts, kiwis, peaches, pears, maize, and vegetables. During the late summer, many farms post 'U-Pick' signs, indicating ridiculously low prices for fruit and produce that buyers pick themselves.

The first drawbridge is 7 miles (11 km) beyond the Antioch Bridge. Flashing lights and barriers lowered across the road indicate that the bridge is raised (or is about to be raised) to permit vessels to pass along Three Mile Slough. Continue straight (do not cross the drawbridge) towards Isleton, 4 miles (6 km) away.

Isleton to Locke

Isleton calls itself the 'Crawdad Capitol of California'. Crawdads are freshwater crayfish, usually less than 6 in (15 cm) long, that live in the brackish and fresh waters of the Delta. Similar crustaceans are delicacies in Louisiana and Scandinavia.

The town itself is a typical Delta town, Main St lined with aging two- and three-storey brick buildings. Many carry Chinese names from days in the last century and early this century when the Delta was an isolated agricultural refuge for Chinese labourers forced from other parts of California by legalised racial discrimination. Much of the levee system was originally built by Chinese labour.

Hwy 160 turns left 2 miles (3 km) beyond Isleton. Continue straight on Sacramento County road E-13 toward the town of **Locke**. The levee is lined with dense groves of pines and euycalyptus that are filled with birds in all seasons. Locke is 9 miles (14 km) along E-13, sometimes known as River Road. Most traffic flows on the opposite side of the channel, along Hwy 160.

Locke, once one of the most important Chinese communities in the Delta, is now a dying town below the levee on Tyler Island. Most of the buildings that remain are inhabited by descendants of the original settlers. **Dai Loy Museum**, a former gambling den, has been restored and houses a good collection of Chinese emigrant artifacts. A joss house (temple) is nearby.

Hood to Sacramento

Turn back and rejoin Hwy 160. Hwy 160 crosses back over the waterway 6 miles (10 km) beyond

The Chinese in California

Three pigtailed Chinese men disembarked from the ship *Eagle* in San Francisco in 1848, fleeing famine, flood and civil unrest. Others followed, first to the gold fields, then to labour on the railroad. Their customs and determination to make a fortune before returning home to their ancestral villages set them apart from other immigrants who had left their Old Country forever.

In 1882 the US Congress passed the Chinese Exclusion Act, limiting immigration to those who could claim an immediate relative as a US citizen. Anti-Chinese riots led to ghetto-like China-towns. Detention of hopeful Chinese immigrants on Angel Island in San Francisco Bay led to delays of months or years, suicides, and mournful poetry on barrack walls. Despite persecution, the Chinese Golden Dragon has snaked his way through Chinatown to celebrate the coming of the new year since the 1860s.

Locke. Continue straight to the town of **Hood**, 11 miles (18 km) beyond Locke. For a quick trip into Sacramento, turn right at Hood to I-5 and take the freeway into downtown, about 10 mins. For a more leisurely pace, continue on Hwy 160 another 17 miles (27 km), about 30 mins.

The Delta comes to an abrupt end 10 miles (16 km) beyond Hood in a flurry of housing estates, shopping malls, and traffic signals. Continue straight on Hwy 160 past **Sacramento Executive Airport**, on the right; **William Land Park** on the left; and **Sacramento City College** on the right. Central Sacramento begins just beyond the railroad tracks with the old Victorian homes that once marked the outer suburbs of the city. At Broadway, Hwy 160 turns left and the street into the city centre becomes Freeport Blvd. *Do not* make the turn. Instead, continue straight on Freeport Blvd to L St. Turn left.

The **State Capitol** building is on the left at 11th and L Sts. For more information on Sacramento, see the next chapter.

SACRAMENTO

Sacramento is the bureaucratic centre of the State of California, the world's seventh largest economy. It's equally a slow-moving, humid, tree-lined downtown filled with turn-of-the-century buildings encircled by endless strip malls and shopping centres.

San Francisco lies south-west and Lake Tahoe is north-east, about 1½ hours' drive in either direction. The Sacramento River runs by the historic part of town, not far from the official government buildings. Sacramento is a transport hub for river traffic, rail freight, and lorries using an efficient maze of freeways.

Gold discovery in 1849 lured prospectors to Sacramento at the junction of the Sacramento and American Rivers. In 1850, California joined the United States of America. In 1854, Sacramento became the state capital and in the 1860s served as the westward terminus for the Pony Express and Transcontinental Railroad. The nearby University of California campus at Davis became world-famous for agricultural research and support for the state's wine industry. Agriculture flourishes, legislation passes, and Sacramentans quietly enjoy life.

Tourist Information

Sacramento Convention & Visitors Bureau, 1421 K St, Dept 100, Sacramento CA 95814; tel: (916) 264-7777, open Mon–Fri 0800–1700. **Sacramento Visitor Information Center**, 1104 Front St, Old Sacramento, CA 95814; tel: (916) 264-7777 or (916) 442-7644, weekends and holidays open 0900–1700, has information, maps, a post office and 24-hour automatic cash dispenser. **California Division of Tourism**, 801 K St, Suite 1600, Sacramento, CA 95814; tel: (916) 322-2882, open Mon–Fri 0800–1700.

Arriving and Departing

Sacramento Metro Airport is 10 miles (16 km) north-west of downtown Sacramento on I-5; tel: (916) 929-5411. Taxi to town averages $25; van is $10 single. **AMTRAK**, 4th and I Sts, Sacramento, CA 95814; tel: (800) 872-7245 or (916) 444-9131, has services from San Francisco (Emeryville) and San Diego/Los Angeles. **Greyhound Bus**, 7th and L Sts, Sacramento, CA 95814; tel: (916) 444-6800, serves some towns and major cities.

Getting Around

Sacramento's compact downtown centres around the State Capitol Building and Mall, Old Town Sacramento, and other public buildings between J and O Sts.

Public Transport

Sacramento Regional Transit, 1400 29th St, Sacramento, CA 95816; tel: (916) 321-2877, provides bus and light rail services on 60 routes, 0500–2200.

Driving

Unlike Los Angeles' freeway spaghetti, Sacramento's freeways cover the urban area efficiently. Lorries join pickups and private cars crowding the roads at rush hours. Traffic flows quickly on particularly smooth roads – being the capital has advantages.

I-80 originates 93 miles (149 km) south-west in San Francisco, dividing at the capital's outskirts. I-80 turns north, then east through northern suburbs towards Reno. Business-80 continues east, crosses the Sacramento River, and then turns north to rejoin I-80 just north-east of Watt Avenue. Further east, Business-80 becomes Hwy 50 which crosses Hwy 49 at Placerville, before continuing to South Lake Tahoe.

I-5 joins Hwy 99 7 miles (11 km) north of downtown Sacramento, and flanks Old Sacramento and downtown east of the Sacramento River. One mile (1.6 km) south of downtown, I-5 leaves Hwy 99 and continues south through the Central Valley to Mexico.

For 2 miles (3.2 km), Hwy 99 joins Business-80 going east, then Hwy 99 turns south along the Central Valley's east side to rejoin I-5 south of Bakersfield. Hwy 16 begins near downtown

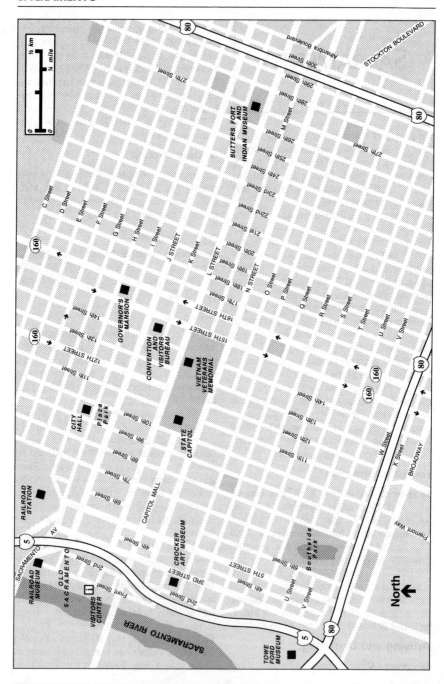

Sacramento as Folsom Blvd, and continues south-east to Hwy 49 at Plymouth.

Exits and interchanges between freeways come up quickly; it helps to know your destination, e.g. I-80 Reno versus Business-80, to choose the right direction.

Major downtown streets are one-way. Capitol Ave replaces M St. Locals say *eye* St for I St. Public parking is very inexpensive, and many businesses allow a few hours' free parking.

A 23-mile (37 km) **bicycle trail** follows the American River along the **American River Parkway**, starting 1 mile (1.6 km) north of downtown and winding east towards Lake Natoma.

Living in Sacramento

Accommodation

The state capital has lodging in all price ranges. For information, contact the **Sacramento Convention & Visitors Bureau**, or the **Sacramento Visitor Information Center**. **West Sacramento Hotel/Motel Association**, *PO Box 239, 1810 W. Capitol Ave, Sacramento CA 95691; tel: (916) 371-5052*, has economical accommodation next to I-80 within a few minutes' drive of downtown.

Most major hotel chains are represented. *AY* has **HI-Sacramento**, *900 H Street, Sacramento, CA 95814; tel: (916) 443-1691* (opening 1995, call to confirm), budget. The 44-stateroom **Delta King Hotel**, *1000 Front St, Old Sacramento, CA 95814; tel: (800) 825-5464*, a restored 1926 steam paddlewheel boat on the Sacramento River, with staterooms, restaurants, shops and a riverboat museum, is expensive.

Victorian-era mansions within walking distance of the State Capitol and Sacramento's main attractions offer bed and breakfast: **Abigail's Bed & Breakfast Inn**, *2120 G. St, Sacramento, CA 95816; tel: (800) 858-1568*, expensive, **Amber House**, *1315 22nd St, Sacramento, CA 95816; tel: (800) 755-6526*, moderate to pricey.

Hartley House, *700 22nd St, Sacramento, CA 95816; tel: (800) 831-5816*, moderate–expensive. **The Driver Mansion Inn**, *2109 21st*

St, Sacramento, CA 95818; tel: (916) 455-5243, pricey. **Sterling House**, *1300 H St, Sacramento, CA 95814; tel: (800) 365-7660*, expensive–pricey.

The **California Exposition & State Fairgrounds**, *1600 Exposition Blvd, Sacramento, CA 95815; tel: (916) 263-3187*, north-east of downtown on Business 80, has secure RV spaces for hire.

Eating and Drinking

When the best-known restaurant for a half-century is called Frank Fat's, the cuisine has to be straightforward and hearty. **Frank Fat's**, *806 L St, Sacramento, CA 95814; tel: (916) 442-7092*, is where politicians have gathered for good Chinese food and juicy steaks since the 1930s. Miraculously, nothing that's discussed appears in print. Book in advance, moderate to pricey.

The 1850s-style **Firehouse**, *1112 2nd St, Old Sacramento, CA 95814; tel: (916) 442-4772*, offers Continental cuisine, pricey. The **Pilothouse Restaurant**, *Delta King 1000 Front St, Old Sacramento, CA 95814; tel: (916) 441-4440*, is known for its Sunday brunch. Moderate–pricey; non-smoking.

The art deco Tower Theatre building shelters the **Tower Café**, *1518 Broadway, Sacramento CA 95818; tel: (916) 441-0222*, where art and European cuisine combine, moderate. The **4th Street Grille**, *400 L St, Sacramento, CA 95814; tel: (916) 448-2847*, uses pesticide-free produce in salads, pizzas, and pastas, moderate.

Mesquite-wood grilled meat is the fare at **The Texas Bar-B-Que**, *180 Otto Circle, Sacramento, CA; tel: (916) 424-3520*. Budget. Also budget are three brewpubs: **Hogshead Brew Pub**, *114 J St, Old Sacramento, CA 95814; tel: (916) 443-2739*, **Rubicon Brewing Company**, *2004 Capitol Ave, Sacramento, CA 95816; tel: (916) 448-7032*, and **River City Brewing Company**, *545 Downtown Plaza, Sacramento, CA 95814; tel: (916) 447-2739*.

Entertainment

Sacramento is a jazz centre on Memorial Day weekend at the end of May, when 100 traditional jazz bands attract over 100,000 spectators to the Dixieland **Sacramento Jazz Jubilee, Sacramento Traditional Jazz Society,** *2787 Del Monte St, West Sacramento, CA 95691; tel: (916) 372-5277.* The **California State Fair,** *California Exposition & State Fair, PO Box 15649, Sacramento, CA 95852; tel: (916) 263-3000,* presents cows, pies, horse shows and carnival rides in mid-Aug–early Sept.

For country and western music, try **Gaitlin Brothers Music City,** *645 Downtown Plaza, Sacramento, CA 95814; tel: (916) 447-5483.* **Jazzmen's Art of Pasta,** *1107 Front St, Unit 4, Old Sacramento, CA 95814; tel: (916) 441-6726,* has jazz and blues in an outdoor courtyard. The 1849 **Old Eagle Theatre,** *925 Front St, Old Sacramento, CA; tel: (916) 446-6761,* presents live theatrical productions.

Shopping

Among the best of Sacramento's mega-malls is **Arden Fair,** *1689 Arden Way, Sacramento, CA 95815; tel: (916) 920-4809,* north-east of downtown Sacramento off Business 80. Within a few blocks of the State Capitol and Old Sacramento is **Downtown Plaza,** *547 L St, Sacramento, CA 95814; tel: (916) 442-4000,* with cinemas, shops, Macy's and Weinstocks department stores, and nightly Rotunda laser shows.

In Old Sacramento are **Julia's Clown World,** *1181 I St, Old Sacramento, CA 95814; tel: (916) 443-5647,* and **Artists' Collaborative Gallery,** *1007 Second St, Old Sacramento, CA 95814; tel: (916) 444-3674,* with locally-made handicrafts and fine art, including outstanding pottery.

Hundreds of sellers deal at **Antique Plaza,** *(Sunrise Blvd exit east off Hwy 50) 11395 Folsom Blvd, Rancho Cordova, CA 95742; tel: (916) 852-8517.*

The **Blue Diamond Growers Retail Store,** *17th and C Sts, Sacramento, CA 95814; tel: (916) 446-8409,* has almond products from the world's largest almond processing plant.

Sightseeing

Sacramento's sights and entertainment are within a flat area demarcated by The State Capitol Building and the Mall on the east, and Old Sacramento on the western side along the river of the same name. Summertime's humid heat suggests driving to an area of interest and parking for several hours while exploring on foot.

Old Sacramento

Old Sacramento State Historic Park has inexpensive parking beneath I-5 and at the end of Front St. The self-guided walking tour of **Old Sac,** as locals call it, begins at the **Sacramento Visitor Information Center** on Front St.

The **Old Sacramento Citizens & Merchants Association,** *917 Front St; tel: (916) 443-0877,* also has area information. For Old Sac events, call the **Hotline;** *tel: (916) 558-3912.*

The Sacramento River flows south along the west side of Old Sac. The historic district is three blocks long by one block wide, with wooden kerbs and 300 restaurants, candy stores, gift and craft shops. Most buildings are 1850s-era. Interiors may have tin or wooden ceilings and brick walls – or may be very modern. Old Sac looks like an old Western town, with horse-drawn carriages – and automobiles incongruously parked by hitching posts.

The **walking tour** begins at the **Visitors Center,** the 1864 **California Steam Navigation Depot,** then proceeds north on Front St past Sacramento's oldest building, the 1852 **Lady Adams.** Providing miners' needs at his general stores, Sam **Brannan's Buildings** helped make him the state's first millionaire. The rebuilt canvas **Old Eagle Theatre** still hosts productions.

Museums

The **Discovery Museum,** *101 I St, Old Sacramento, CA 95814; tel: (916) 264 -7057,* closed Mon and Tues (winter), combines Sacramento history and science/technology with a planetarium in the original city administration building.

The jewel of Old Sac, and one of California's best museums, is the **California State Railroad Museum,** *125 I St, Old Sacramento, CA 95814; tel: (916) 448-4466,* open 1000–1700. The 1862 *Governor Stanford,* the Central Pacific's first steam locomotive, gleams. The *Sonoma* is a glittering black and brass locomotive surrounded by mirrors. The *Gold Coast* is an 1890s private car restored in 1948 style. The Canadian *St Hyacinthe* simulates a sleeping car's night-time roll along the tracks. Walk through a post office car, *under* a diesel locomotive, and see a room of model trains.

Outside, the **Central Pacific Passenger Depot** houses rolling stock undergoing restoration. The **Big Four Building**, or Huntington-Hopkins Hardware Store, was owned by the founders of the Central Pacific Railroad who schemed to build the Transcontinental Railroad's western section.

The **B.F. Hastings Building**, *at the corner of J and 2nd Sts*, served as the Pony Express terminus from 1860–1861 and as State Supreme Court chambers. Once the Old Sac Wells Fargo bank, assay, and stage-coach office, the Hastings Building is now the **Wells Fargo History Museum**, *1000 2nd St, Old Sacramento, CA 95814; tel: (916) 440-4263.*

The **Delta King Hotel**, *tel: (800) 825-5464*, has a riverboat museum. The paddlewheeler *Spirit of Sacramento, 110 L St, Old Sacramento, CA 95814; tel: (800) 433-0263*, offers river sightseeing and dining cruises.

The **Crocker Art Museum**, *216 O St, Sacramento, CA 95814; tel: (916) 264-5423*, open Tues–Sun 1000–1700, Thurs 1000–2100, is an 1873 Victorian mansion devoted to European and Californian art collections.

One of John Sutter's employees found gold at Sutter's mill in Coloma, 30 miles (48 km) east of **Sutter's Fort State Historic Park**, *27th and L Sts, Sacramento, CA 95816; tel: (916) 445-4422*, open 1000–1700. (See Oakhurst–Lake Tahoe Route, p. 206.) Sacramento's earliest settlement site has rooms furnished in the pre-Gold Rush era.

A block away is the **State Indian Museum**, *26th and K Sts, Sacramento, CA 95816; tel: (916) 324-0971*, open 1000–1700, with tribal artifacts.

For motor enthusiasts, **Towe Ford Museum**, *2200 Front St, Sacramento, CA 95818; tel: (916) 442-6802*, open 1000–1800, has 175 antique Ford cars and trucks. The **Sacramento Metropolitan Arts Commission**, *tel: (916) 264-5558* has information on public art walks. Even most light rail stations have modernistic public art.

Architecture

Sacramento historic architecture tour brochures for the *Capitol Area, Downtown*, and *Alkali Flat Residential District* are available from **Sacramento Heritage, Inc.**, *c/o Sacramento Housing and Redevelopment Agency, 630 I St, Sacramento, CA 95814; tel: (916) 440-1355.*

The Classical Revival 1861–1864 **State Capitol Building** nestles in a shady green 34-acre (14 ha) park and doubles as a **Museum**; *Capitol Mall and 10th St, Sacramento, CA 95814; tel: (916) 324-0333*; free hourly tours 0900–1600. California Senate and Assembly legislative sessions are open to the public. The capitol rotunda, which rises 120 ft (40 m) above the base of a sculpture of Queen Isabella and Christopher Columbus, has *trompe l'oeil* detail of cornucopias brimming with ripe fruits and vegetables. Symbolic grizzly bears are carved in newel posts and porticoes. Restored historic offices include the treasury, state library, and the 1906 earthquake-era governor's office.

The 1975–1982 restoration cost $68 million, one of the largest US state capitol restoration jobs ever undertaken. Floors were rotten, plaster was crumbling and the building was grimy. Artisans rediscovered techniques for applying plaster details – using a pastry tube applied by the craftsperson lying prone on a platform. Buttermilk coating, which can be washed off periodically and reapplied, was washed across painted details – both as protection and enhancement. Much of the furniture in the period offices was reclaimed from junk sales across the country.

Until Governor Ronald Reagan and wife Nancy declared it uncomfortable, the 1877 **Governor's Mansion**, *State Historic Park, 16th and H Sts, Sacramento, CA 95814; tel: (916) 323-3047 or (916) 324-0539*, had been the residence for 13 gubernatorial families. Hourly tours of the mansion, 1000–1600, reveal an eclectic collection of rooms decorated with eccentric taste.

SACRAMENTO to RENO

This central West–East route intersects with four other routes and the Lake Tahoe Circuit, making it a convenient link with journeys to the north or south of the state.

The 136-mile (218 km) direct journey takes 3 hrs. This route was followed by tens of thousands of immigrants to California after the 1849 Gold Rush. The first transcontinental railway line followed a similar course through the Sierra Nevada Mountains into Nevada.

The 'Big Four' who built the rail line convinced the US Congress that the Sierra Nevada begin near Rancho Cordova, 7 miles east of Sacramento – construction subsidies were far higher for mountain track than for rails across the flat Sacramento Valley. Following I-80, the foothills actually begin near Auburn, 34 miles east of Sacramento. This 1863 scam helped make the Big Four – Mark Hopkins, Collis Huntington, Leland Stanford and Charles Crocker – rich.

The scenic route to Reno follows Highway 50 to Lake Tahoe, one of the largest alpine lakes in North America, through a mini-Las Vegas across the Nevada border, then loops through mountains and gold mines. Much of the route is twisting two-lane highway with stunning views of mountains, lake and desert. The 162 miles (259 km) take 2–4 days. Lake Tahoe and Carson City are convenient stopping points.

ROUTES

 Direct Route

The most direct route between Sacramento and Reno is along I-80. Follow I-80 east from Sacramento over **Donner Summit** and through **Truckee** to Reno.

At **Auburn**, and again at Emigrant Gap, the direct route intersects with the Oakhurst–Lake Tahoe Route (see p. 206). At **Truckee** you can switch onto the Lake Tahoe Circuit (p. 196) south, or northwards onto the Chester–Lake Tahoe Route (p. 330).

Snowstorms can stretch the trip unpredictably in winter months. A November 1846 storm trapped a wagon train east of Donner Summit. 40 of the original 87 Donner Party survived until the February thaw by eating their companions.

Scenic Route

Follow Hwy 50 for 100 miles (160 km) east from Sacramento over Echo Summit to **South Lake Tahoe**. Continue 8 miles (13 km) around the south shore of Lake Tahoe to the intersection of Hwys 50 and 28.

Go right to stay on Hwy 50 to **Carson City**. At the bottom of the hill, 14 miles (22 km) later, turn left onto Hwy 395 and into Carson City, 3 miles (5 km) beyond. Details of this part of the route can be found in the Lake Tahoe Circuit chapter, p. 196. The Circuit runs along the same route as far as Reno.

At Williams St (Hwy 50), turn east toward **Fallon**. Follow Hwy 50 for 7½ miles (12 km), turn left onto Hwy 341. **Virginia City** is 8 miles (13 km) uphill.

From Virginia City continue 14 miles (22 km) on Hwy 341 to Hwy 395. Turn right. Follow Hwy 395 to S. Virginia Ave, where Hwy 395 becomes a freeway. Follow S. Virginia Ave left into downtown Reno, 7 miles (11 km), or take the freeway north to I-80, 6 miles (10 km), turn west, and follow I-80 3 miles (5 km) to downtown Reno at the Virginia Ave exit.

Traffic is slowest during holidays, weekends, and winter snowstorms.

SACRAMENTO TO SOUTH LAKE TAHOE

Hwy 50 is a freeway through increasingly rural suburbs south of downtown Sacramento. Commuter traffic can be heavy, but congestion clears quickly.

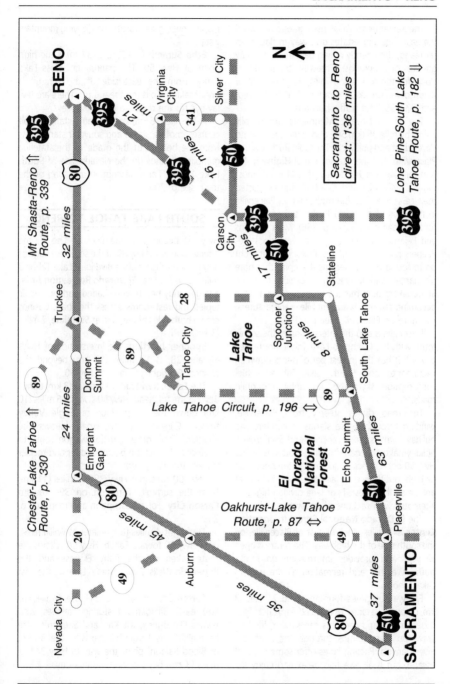

N

RENO

395

395

21 miles

Virginia
City

341

Silver City

80

395

19 miles

50

Mt Shasta-Reno
Route, p. 339

32 miles

Truckee

Carson
City

395

50

17 miles

Stateline

Sacramento to Reno
direct: 136 miles

Lone Pine–South Lake
Tahoe Route, p. 182 ⇓

395

Donner
Summit

89

28

Tahoe City

Lake
Tahoe

Spooner
Junction

8 miles

South Lake Tahoe

Chester–Lake Tahoe
Route, p. 330

89

24 miles

Emigrant
Gap

80

45 miles

20

Lake Tahoe Circuit, p. 196 ⇔

89

El
Dorado
National
Forest

Echo Summit

63 miles

49

Nevada City

49

Auburn

35 miles

Oakhurst–Lake Tahoe
Route, p. 87 ⇔

49

50

Placerville

37 miles

80

50

SACRAMENTO

The Sacramento Valley rises gradually toward the east. Housing estates give way to flat, open farmland, then gently rolling pastures broken by granite outcroppings. Freeway traffic barely slows for the first serious hills, 25 miles east of downtown. Check AM radio 1530 and 1140, and FM 105.1 for traffic bulletins.

The Sierra Nevada Mountains are usually visible by mile 35 (km 56), above the Sacramento Valley dust and pollution. The Gold Rush town of **Placerville**, and the intersection of **Highway 49**, is at mile 44 (km 70). Many of California's most famous industrial and financial figures started their careers as humble tradesmen in Placerville in the days of the Gold Rush. Two of the 'big four' railroad barons (see p. 256), Mark Hopkins and Leland Stanford, began as humble store-keepers here; local butcher Philip Armour went on to found the canned meat empire that bore his name; and it was in Placerville that the Studebakers built miner's wheelbarrows before becoming famous as automobile manufacturers. For more on Placerville, see p. 213.

Placerville is also the intersection of the scenic route with the Oakhurst–Lake Tahoe Route (see p. 206). It has the lowest petrol prices between Sacramento and South Lake Tahoe – fuel consumption skyrockets on uphill mountain roads.

The road climbs steeply from Placerville, winding through dense stands of conifers and holiday hamlets. San Francisco and Sacramento holidaymakers began building cottages along Hwy 50 decades ago. Food and petrol prices can be high, but there is no lack of places to pull over and smell the forest. Four-lane divided highway alternates with sections of freeway.

The **El Dorado National Forest Information Center** is 7 miles (11 km) east of Placerville, on the south side of the highway. The centre is open all year and provides information on roads, traffic, weather and recreation all the way to Lake Tahoe.

Freeway becomes four-lane road 2 miles (3 km) on and two lanes 18 miles (29 km) later. Tour buses, trucks and caravans can slow traffic to a crawl on steep climbs through the American River Canyon. Passing lanes offer some hope of escape, but if all else fails, relax and enjoy the rushing river, green forest and dizzying mountain vistas.

Echo Summit (7382 ft, 2237 m) is the high point of Hwy 50. The panorama across Lake Tahoe from the east side of the summit is breathtaking. So is the sheer drop. There are few lay-bys for the driver to enjoy the view.

A 10-mile (16 km) strip of petrol stations, golf courses, motels, stores and souvenir stands runs from the bottom of the grade to the stateline gambling casinos on the Nevada side of **South Lake Tahoe**. For a description and map of the town see p. 200.

SOUTH LAKE TAHOE TO RENO

Hwy 50 becomes Tahoe Blvd at **The Y**, the intersection with Hwy 89 at the southern edge of South Lake Tahoe. Tahoe Blvd joins Lake Tahoe 3 miles (5 km) later at **El Dorado Recreation Area**, a large sandy beach with shaded parking, picnic tables and rest-rooms across the road. Casinos crowd both sides of the road at **Stateline**, 2 miles (3 km) further.

Spooner Junction, the intersection of Hwys 50 and 28, is 12 miles (19 km) beyond the casinos. Go right to stay on Hwy 50.

The **Tahoe Rim Trail** is 1½ miles (3 km) uphill. Beyond the trailhead, Hwy 50 swoops 6 miles (10 km) down the steep slope of **Eagle Valley** toward Carson City. The road follows the Emigrant Trail, once a major wagon route to California. The terrain becomes drier and rockier toward the valley floor.

Hwy 50 runs into Hwy 395 7 miles (11 km) from the summit. Turn left on 395 toward **Carson City**. For a description and map, see p. 203.

Turn right 4 miles (6 km) later at Williams St, onto Hwy 50 toward Fallon. Hwy 50 follows the route taken by the Pony Express and the Butterfield-Wells Fargo Stage Line in the last century.

Carson City ends at Mound House, 6 miles (10 km) east. Billboards featuring ranches with names like Bunny, Kit Kat, and Sagebrush are brothel adverts. Larger billboards for the 'Bucket of Blood Saloon' point the way to Hwy 341, 2 miles (3 km) beyond, and Virginia City.

Turn left on 341. The **Nugget Chocolate Factory** offer free tours and candy tastings.

Highway 341 snakes up **Gold Canyon**, once among the richest silver and gold deposits in North America. The canyon is littered with abandoned mines and rusting equipment. Splotches of gold, red and yellow are 'tailings', piles of waste rock and dirt from mining operations. All land is private, much of it riddled with decrepit tunnels that can collapse without warning. Owners of active mines are jealously protective.

Silver City, now a collection of ramshackle houses and abandoned equipment, is 5 miles (8 km) up Hwy 341. One mile (1.6 km) beyond is **Gold Hill** and the Golden Nugget Bar & Saloon, one of the oldest hotels in Nevada. **Virginia City** is 2 miles (3 km) further. For a description and map, see p. 205.

Hwy 341 continues 14 miles (22 km) beyond Virginia City, winding through the mountains and down toward Hwy 395 and **Reno**. Turn right at Hwy 395 to Reno.

RENO

Tourist Information: Reno-Sparks Convention & Visitors Authority (RSCVA), PO Box 837, Reno, NV 89504; tel: (702) 827-7662, (800) 367-7366.

Visitor Centers: Reno Cannon International Airport; downtown Reno, 275 N. Virginia St; Reno Convention Center, 4590 S. Virginia St; Sparks, Pyramid Way and Victorian Ave. For road conditions, tel: (800) 752-1177.

Weather

Reno is a high desert valley (4490 ft, 1361 m), watered by rivers flowing from surrounding mountains. Summer temperatures hit 30°C, winter drops to -5°C. Snowfall is light in Reno itself, but heavy in the surrounding mountains. Always carry tyre chains in winter.

Arriving by Air

Reno Cannon International Airport is 10 mins from downtown. Taxi to downtown hotels $10. Bus 24 (RTC) is $1 into town, but routes avoid major hotels/casinos.

Accommodation

For reservations in the Reno area in all price ranges, tel: (800) 367-7366. Downtown casinos have the most plentiful rooms and sometimes the best prices. Special offers are listed in the pink Databook section of the Sunday San Francisco Chronicle & Examiner. Lowest prices are Sun–Thurs. Lower demand in Sparks, 4 miles (6 km) east on I-80, brings lower prices.

Eating and Drinking

Casinos have budget-priced meal specials that are barely more expensive than fast food. Check casino marquees and the RSCVA for the latest offerings.

Reno's best restaurant is **La Strada**, Eldorado Hotel & Casino, 345 N. Virginia St. Reservations tel: (702) 786-5700. It features Northern Italian dishes from the owners of the Ferrari-Carrano Winery in the Sonoma Valley. Expensive. **Le Moulin**, Peppermill Hotel & Casino, 2707 S. Virginia St does nearly as well with continental dishes. Reservations tel: (702) 826-2121. Expensive.

Basque restaurants have been local favourites for three generations. The best is **Louis' Basque Corner**, 301 E. 4th St; tel: (702) 323-7203. Budget lunch, moderate dinner.

Entertainment

Gambling is number one. Bingo and Keno offer the worst odds, followed by roulette, slot machines and craps. Blackjack and video poker give the closest Reno comes to an even break.

Most casinos offer free lessons during the day. The **Gambler's Bookstore**, 99 N. Virginia St; tel: (702) 786-6209, sells detailed guides.

Reno casinos are more relaxed than their Las Vegas counterparts. Beginners should find an uncrowded, low-limit table and ask the dealer for guidance – they're almost always sympathetic. Should you win, thank them by tipping with a couple of whatever denomination chips you're using.

Casino **showrooms** stage a variety of glittering musical reviews and headline entertainers. Tickets start around $15 per person, including two drinks. Look for discount coupons

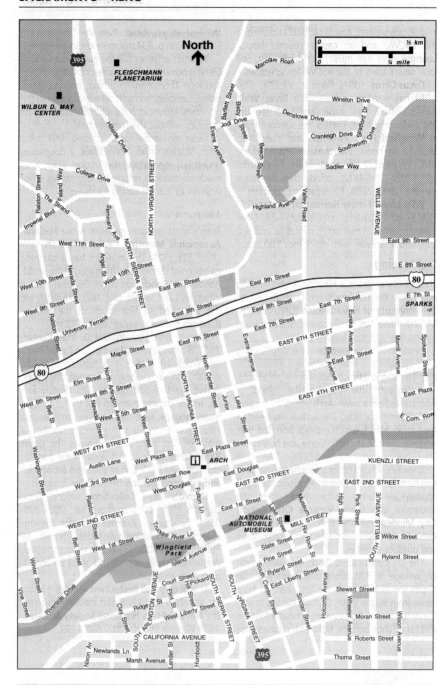

in local newspapers, tourist tabloids at casinos or the RSCVA, and in casino coupon books. **Lounges** offer free music, but drinks cost. See local newspapers or the RSCVA for schedules. **Circus Circus**, *500 N. Sierra St; tel: (800) 648-5010* has free circus acts. The **River Walk** provides more free music and fun; see the RSCVA for schedules. There's free summer music at **Wingfield Park**, *Arlington and Island Ave*, Mon–Fri at noon. **Fleischmann Planetarium**, UNR, 1½ miles (2 km) north of the Reno Arch; *tel: (702) 784-4812*, offers free telescope viewing, 1930–2030, Fri, weather permitting.

Wild Island Family Recreation Center, *250 Wild Island Ct., Sparks; tel: (702) 359-2927*, has a water park (summer only), miniature and real golf, and a raceway with mock Indy 500 cars.

Sightseeing

The old city centre is a nine-block grid running north from the **Truckee River**, beneath I-80, to the **University of Nevada-Reno** (UNR) campus. Modern Reno has mushroomed south toward Carson City and east toward Sparks.

Reno wants to be a northern Las Vegas, luring drive-up gamblers from Northern California the way Las Vegas attracts Southern Californians. 'The Biggest Little City in the World' is emblazoned on a neon **Arch** across N. Virginia St at Commercial Row. The arch is the heart of the casino district, which extends from the river north to Sixth St along N. Sierra and N. Virginia Sts.

The city's 40-odd casinos face heavy competition from Reno itself. New hotel/casinos and golf courses are luring visitors away from the traditional downtown. **Virginia City, Carson City, Minden** and other historic towns surround Reno. So do mountains packed with scenic drives and outdoor activities.

The dry climate lures sports enthusiasts with an average of 300 sunny days each year. Ski slopes for all skill levels are less than an hour away, from Squaw Valley Olympic classics to easy family fun slopes. Golf courses in nearby foothills and Lake Tahoe become Nordic ski courses once

the first snows arrive. (See the Chester–Lake Tahoe Route, p. 334, for more on Squaw Valley).

Summer activities run the gamut from biking (Reno is home to world champions Greg LeMond and Inga Thompson) to fishing, walking, horse riding, camping, and golf, all without leaving the city limits. Mountain recreation areas offer similar activities without the summer heat.

Older residential areas around UNR offer quiet, shaded walks. **River Walk**, a downtown pedestrian zone along the Truckee River, is as much an outdoor refuge for downtown office workers as it is for casino habituées.

Museums

Reno's most popular museum is the **National Automobile Museum**, *Lake and Mill Sts.; tel: (702) 333-9300*. The museum has a stunning collection of classic autos from around the world. **Ponderosa Ranch**, on Hwy 28 near Incline Village at Lake Tahoe; *tel: (702) 831-0691*, are the sets used to film much of the popular **Bonanza** television series (see p. 202).

Back in Reno, the **Wilbur D. May Center**, *1502 Washington St (Rancho San Rafael Park); tel: (702) 785-4064*, is a testament to idle wealth. Wilbur D. May wandered the globe during the first half of the 20th century and apparently bought every tourist trinket in sight from Bangkok to Brussels, Niger and Niagara Falls. Most ended up in his Reno ranch, now a museum. The complex also houses **The Great Basin Adventure**, an Old West theme park for children aged 2–12, and an extensive **arboretum and botanical garden** (free). Other freebies: **Harold's Gun Collection**, *second floor, Harold's Club*, by the Arch; *tel: (702) 329-0881*, is one of America's largest firearms collections, including weapons owned by Buffalo Bill, William S. Hart, and other famous Westerners. Anyone under 21 must be accompanied by an adult.

The **Liberty Bell Restaurant**, *4250 S. Virginia St; tel: (702) 825-1776*, slot machine museum. The **Nevada State Historical Society Museum**, *1650 Virginia St; tel: (702) 688-1190*.

SAN FRANCISCO to VISALIA

The heart of earthquake country is on display in wild displacements of land and jagged rocks thrown helter-skelter. Beginning in quake-prone urban San Francisco, this route follows the spine of some of the most active seismic faults on earth, through rural farmland, towering peaks and oilfields. To drive the 260-mile (416 km) route allow 1–2 days.

ROUTE

From San Francisco take Hwy 101 south to San Jose and **Gilroy** (see p.170).

Just south of Gilroy, the hills to the east and west flatten out, hawks circle overhead, and cattle ranches, orchards and flower fields appear. At 85 miles (136 km), turn left on a freeway overpass to the south-east onto state road 25. Where S25 leaves Hwy 101, roadside produce stands sell seasonal cherries, garlic, walnuts, apricots, corn and artichokes.

Continue 12 miles (19 km) to **Hollister** and 33 miles (53 km) further to **Pinnacles National Monument**. Between Hollister and Pinnacles National Monument, cattle ranches are scattered over rolling golden hills and valleys. California oaks and cows dot a landscape patrolled by hawks and crows. Stop en route and hear crickets whirr in the silence. Goats may wander across the road.

At 10 miles (16 km) beyond Hollister at Paicines, a sign warns that there are no services (petrol, accommodation or food) for 65 miles (104 km). Slow to 35 mph (56 kph) to wind uphill on narrow S25.

At mile 127 (km 203), turn right onto S146, driving south 3 miles (5 km) past quail, cottontail rabbits and wild turkeys to the east entrance of

Pinnacles National Monument. Slow to 25mph (40 kph).

From Pinnacles National Monument, take S146 3 miles (5 km) east to S25 and continue south through a valley flanked by deeply eroded sheer mountains to the east and layer upon layer of mountains off to the west. S25 becomes S198 37 miles (60 km) later, emerging into an awesome canyon with gigantic boulders thrown willy-nilly by nature. The road emerges from a narrow stretch of hills and depressions into California's **Central Valley**.

Continue 30 miles (48 km) beyond; **Coalinga** lies in the flatlands below, where summer heat rises to above 40°C.

Nine miles (15 km) north of Coalinga at **Arroyo de Cantua**, oil pumps painted like giraffes, butterflies, grasshoppers and dragons testify to Coalinga's oilfields. Here S198 turns eastward.

Travel 63 miles (101 km) east on S198, through **Hanford** and on to **Visalia**. From Visalia you can reach Yosemite (See Visalia–Yosemite Route, p. 267).

HOLLISTER

Tourist Information: **San Benito County Chamber of Commerce**, *649C San Benito St, Hollister, CA 95023; tel: (408) 637-5315.*

Accommodation and Food

Four miles south of Hollister on S25 is **Ridgemark Golf & Country Club**, *3800 Airline Hwy, Hollister, CA 95023; tel: (408) 637-8151.* 32 rooms. Moderate.

San Andreas Brewing, *737 San Benito St (on S25); tel: (408) 637-7074.* A microbrewery serving pub food in a 1940s-era tile-walled creamery building. Beers on draught – 5 cents during earthquakes – include Earthquake Pale, Seismic Ale, Earthquake Porter, Survivor Stout. Budget.

Sightseeing

San Benito County Historic and Recreation Park, *tel: (408) 628-3312.* At 105 miles (168 km) enter on the right, cross a shaded stream, to access the day-use picnic and barbecue area.

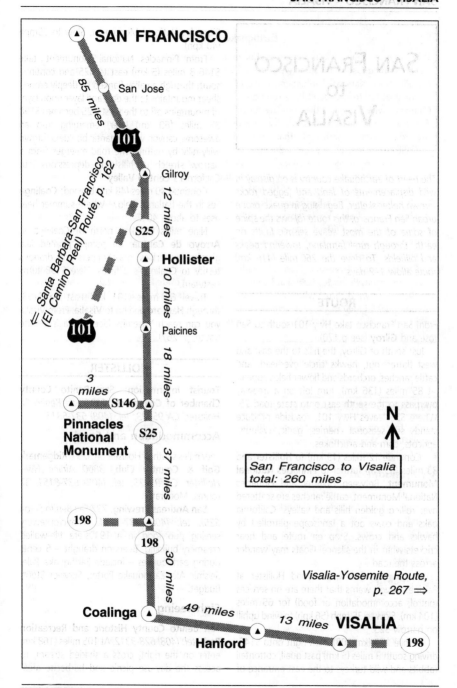

SAN FRANCISCO

San Jose

85 miles

101

Gilroy

12 miles

S25

Hollister

10 miles

← Santa Barbara-San Francisco
(El Camino Real) Route, p. 162

101

Paicines

18 miles

N
↑

3 miles

S146

Pinnacles
National
Monument

S25

37 miles

San Francisco to Visalia
total: 260 miles

198

198

30 miles

Visalia-Yosemite Route,
p. 267 ⇒

Coalinga

49 miles

13 miles VISALIA

Hanford

198

Earthquake Country

Why do more than 30 million people choose to live in a state where a shift of the earth can spell instant disaster? Pleasant weather and an abundance of astounding natural wonders, like Pinnacles National Monument, make up for the violence generated by earthquakes.

Most of California's fault lines run north-west to south-east. The coastal, western half of California where most of the population lives, is most susceptible to the earth's movements. The San Andreas Fault, historically one of the most lethal, runs from offshore of the Mendocino coast, south more than 1000 miles to near the Mexican border.

California's coastal cities are vulnerable: San Francisco abuts the San Andreas Fault, while Los Angeles is subject to shaking from the San Andreas and other faults. In 1906, San Francisco experienced California's most shocking – an 8.3 Richter scale earthquake followed by fires which destroyed most of the city (see San Francisco Bay Area Routes, p. 228, for the 0.7 mile-long 1906 Earthquake Trail along the San Andreas at Point Reyes National Seashore). The Loma Prieta quake in 1989 measured 7.0 and did major damage to San Francisco's Marina District and area freeways. Los Angeles' Northridge quake, in January 1994, measured 6.8 on the Richter scale, 40% less violent, yet it caused about $30 billion worth of damage.

On this route from San Francisco, Gilroy and Hollister sit on the seismically active Calaveras Fault. Pinnacles National Monument lies just beside the San Andreas Fault Zone. In 1983 an upward thrust which never broke the earth's surface rocked Coalinga with a 6.7 tremor. Such hidden thrust-faults create folds, which are obvious in the hills and depressions and in the winding roads leading to Coalinga.

Wander around old barns, stables and a blacksmith shop. $3 per vehicle.

PINNACLES NATIONAL MONUMENT

Tourist Information: Superintendent, Pinnacles National Monument, *Paicines, CA 95043; tel: (408) 389-4485.*

Accommodation

No lodging is available within the Monument's east side, but just outside is **Pinnacles Campground, Inc.**, *2400 Hwy 146, Paicines CA 95043; tel: (408) 389-4462,* with private camping and RV accommodation. No reservations taken. Budget.

Sightseeing

$4 entrance fee for 7 days. Although S146 enters the Monument on the west and east sides, there is no road built through the park.

The Monument is open all year, but to avoid winter rain and high summer temperatures, visit in autumn or spring.

Allow time to hike some of the 30 miles (48 km) of moderate to strenuous trails. Experienced rock climbers must bring their own equipment for technical climbs, and register in advance with Monument rangers. Climbing is permitted only from 2 Jul to 14 Jan, when birds are not nesting. Anyone can explore two talus caves, Bear Gulch Cave and Balconies Caves. Bear Gulch Cave is 0.7 miles (1.1 km) uphill from the Bear Gulch Visitor Center on the east side. Torches are required for cave exploration.

Drinking water is unavailable outside the Visitor Center and should be carried for all activities. Avoid rash-inducing red-leaved poison oak which grows abundantly in brushy and forested areas.

The Pinnacles thrust up like mounds of rosy brown clay boulders smashed together to rise sheer to more than 3300 ft (1007 m) on North Chalone Peak. The earth may feel in constant, subtle motion underfoot. The area is so seismically active that rangers barely notice Monument buildings move and shift.

The wild beauty of the crags and spires is the

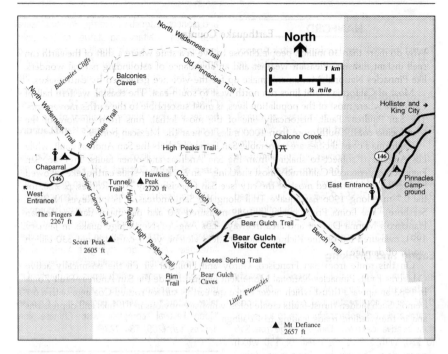

remnant of an eroded volcano that formed about 23 million years ago. The San Andreas Rift Zone plates ground against each other as the earth's interior thrust magma upwards into a volcanic crater. The Pacific Plate moved north-west, and today's Pinnacles are displaced 195 miles (312 km) from their original Lancaster location, north-east of Los Angeles. The 17,000-acre (6900 ha) of Pinnacles National Monument lies in the Gabilan Mountains, a part of the California Coast Range. Far from major cities, the Monument shelters over 100 bird species and over 500 different botanical varieties. Ungrazed land yields lush wildflower displays in spring, though the soil is fragile. Golden eagles soar on thermals near high peaks. Below, coveys of native California quail, the California state bird, scurry about.

COALINGA

Tourist Information: Coalinga Area Chamber of Commerce, 380 Coalinga Plaza, Coalinga, CA 93210; tel: (209) 935-2948.

Accommodation and Food

As S198 crosses I-5 15 miles (24 km) from Coalinga, the Harris Ranch complex is spread out below. Famous for its excellent beef, the Harris Ranch is one of the largest cattle operations in the USA. The **Harris Ranch Restaurant**, tel: (209) 935-0717, serves ranch-raised beef and produce. Moderate.

Take the Hanford-Lemoore offramp to the **Inn at Harris Ranch**, Rte 1, Box 777, Coalinga CA 93210; tel: (209) 935-0717. 123 rooms, tennis courts. Moderate to Expensive.

Sightseeing

'Coaling Station A', a Southern Pacific Railroad loading point for locally-mined coal, became 'Coalinga' as coal and oil boomed. No one expected the downed front porches, ripped foundations, and cracked streets generated by the 1983 6.7 Richter Scale earthquake.

R.C. Baker Memorial Museum, 297 W. Elm St; tel: (209) 935-1914, displays oilfield and ranch equipment, while ignoring quake events!

Pinnacles National Monument–Coalinga

HANFORD

Tourist Information: Hanford Visitor Agency, *200 Santa Fe, Suite D, Hanford, CA 93230; tel: (209) 582-0483.*

Accommodation

Hanford lodging ranges from basic to quaint. **Best Western Hanford Inn,** *755 Cadillac Lane* (11th Ave exit from S198), *Hanford, 93230; tel: (209) 583-7300,* is a convenient stopping point enroute. Moderate. **The Irwin Street Inn & Restaurant,** *522 N. Irwin St, Hanford, CA 93230; tel: (209) 584-9286,* combines 30 bed and breakfast rooms decorated with antiques, in four 1880-era Victorian houses, which share a garden jacuzzi. Expensive.

Eating and Drinking

In China Alley, the **Imperial Dynasty Restaurant,** *2 China Alley; tel: (209) 582-0196,* serves continental cuisine with traditional cream- and stock-enhanced sauces to a reservations-in-advance crowd. Dinners range from $15 to $30, with a 9-course meal for $50 which changes daily. Though the cuisine is not Asian, the 1880s building is filled with Chinese antiques and art. Downtown, the **Superior Dairy,** *325 N. Douty, tel: (209) 582-0481,* features local dairy and ice-cream products at a soda fountain, unchanged since 1929. The building, with pressed tin ceilings, counter and booths, is a throwback to the past. Cheap.

Sightseeing

Toward Hanford, cotton fields appear. The jewel of Courthouse Square in downtown Hanford is the golden-brick **Kings County Courthouse.** No longer used for legal proceedings, the renovated 1897 neo-classical, Italianate courthouse hides souvenir shops and dining establishments.

Four blocks away off Green Street is one-block-long **China Alley.** Compact buildings, including one with a first-storey 1893 **Taoist Temple** and ground-floor free museum with period rooms of Chinese artifacts, testify to what was once one of California's largest Chinese communities. The Chinese, brought to California to build the railroads, later bought small farms and pioneered agriculture in the Hanford-Visalia area. Incense, altars and statues of the Eight Immortals of Chinese tradition are among artifacts explained on guided tours; *tel: (209) 584-3236.* Centrepiece of the area is the **Imperial Dynasty Building,** owned by the Chinese Wing family since the 1880s. It now houses the non-Chinese restaurant of the same name. The 1910 Japanese **King's Hand Laundry** is still operational.

In early Oct Hanford celebrates the **Renaissance of Kings Cultural Arts Faire,** *tel: (209) 585-2525* on the Civic Auditorium grounds. It's 1521 Hanfordshire, where King Henry VIII, his court, various villagers and saucy wenches dance, play music on ancient instruments, harvest, sing, engage in mortal combat, and eat and imbibe. Attendees wear 'Tudor'-style garb. Various story lines for specific personalities are developed through the years, which lends continuity. On the same weekend, a free shuttle to China Alley takes visitors from Merrie England to a Chinese Moon Festival, complete with Chinese lion dances, *tel: (209) 584-3236.*

VISALIA

Tourist Information: Visalia Convention and Visitors Center (CVC), *720 W. Mineral King Ave, Visalia CA 93291; tel: (209) 734-5876.*

Accommodation

Lodging is plentiful in Visalia, frequently a jumping-off point for a visit to Sequoia, Kings Canyon and Yosemite National Parks. For tent or RV camping, **Visalia/South Fresno KOA,** *7480 Ave 308, Visalia, CA 93291,* 5 miles (8 km) northwest of Visalia; *tel: (209) 651-0544.* Budget.

Sightseeing

Walking tour maps from the Visalia CVC describe Victorian homes in this old and prosperous Central Valley town. The **Central California Chinese Cultural Center,** *500 S. Akers; tel: (209) 625-4545,* testifies to the region's Chinese history and art. Call in advance to visit the **Visalia Cooperative Cotton Gin,** *Ave 336 and Road 132; tel: (209) 732-1365,* Oct–Dec to see cotton being separated from its seeds. Free.

VISALIA
to
YOSEMITE

Conjoined national parks throw up craggy mountain vistas, raging river canyons, caverns, rocky outcroppings, towering sequoia trees; dense forests and meandering country roads. Follow the western side of the Southern Sierra Nevada Mountains north through groves of the world's tallest trees. Roads dotted with vista points snake through the parks; in summer, traffic can slow to a crawl. Allow at least three days to drive through Sequoia and Kings Canyon National Parks, including time for at least one hike through a sequoia grove.

ROUTE

The route rises quickly from Central Valley flatlands into the Sierra foothills, and winds through the western side of both parks.

The **basic itinerary** follows the same scenic roads to Centerville, and then splits into two alternative continuations. Along the way, there are two possible side tracks into the Sequoia and Kings Canyon National Parks, but they are open only in summer. From Centerville, finish the journey along the **direct continuation** if time is limited, if you prefer freeway driving, or if you are travelling between Nov and Apr. The summer-only **scenic continuation** completes the journey in a different direction, adding the countryside between Kings Canyon and Yosemite National Parks at a leisurely pace before barrelling towards Yosemite's wonders.

→ **Basic Route**

Follow Hwy 198 47 miles (82 km) east to **Three Rivers**. From here a **side track** to Mineral King, just south of Sequoia National Park, is possible, but only in summer months. The 21-mile (33.6

km) trip is the best driving access to the spine of the Sierras, a wild area that challenges the most adventurous hikers and pack horses. RVs are not permitted.

From Three Rivers enter Sequoia National Park 4 miles (6.4 km) beyond at **Ash Mountain**. Forty-two twisting miles (67 km) later, just beyond Lost Grove, the route along Hwy 198 enters the partially-logged-over Sequoia National Forest, in which it becomes known as the **Generals Highway**. Seven miles (11 km) north, the road enters Kings Canyon National Park.

At **Grant Grove**, allow an extra day if you want to negotiate the **side track** via Hwy 180 north and east to **Cedar Grove**, a 76-mile (122 km) return trip (summer only) through a sheer rock canyon twisting in and out of tunnels above the Kings River South Fork with scenery rivalling Arizona's Grand Canyon.

Resuming the basic route, From Grant Grove, continue west 38 miles (61 km) on Hwy 180 to Centerville. From here choose either the direct or the scenic continuation (see below).

Both options meet again at **Oakhurst**, from where you can begin the Oakhurst–Lake Tahoe Route (p. 206), by-passing Yosemite, if you wish.

Continue up Hwy 41 from Oakhurst to **Fish Camp**, just before you arrive at the Yosemite National Park South Entrance Station.

→ **Direct Continuation**

Following this route brings the total journey from Visalia to Yosemite to 247 miles (395 km). The route follows major highways from Kings Canyon to Fresno and continues north to Yosemite National Park.

Continue west from Centerville on the Kings Canyon Highway, Hwy 180, 50 miles (80 km) to **Fresno**. From Fresno, Hwy 41 climbs 60 miles (96 km) north to **Fish Camp**, just south of Yosemite National Park.

～ **Scenic Continuation**

At Centerville, turn right just beyond a dirt and gravel company onto Trimmer Springs Road. Continue north-east, skirting Pine Flat Reservoir Recreational Area, then turn left on Maxson Road, right on Watts Valley Road, left on Burrough Valley Road, and right on Toll House

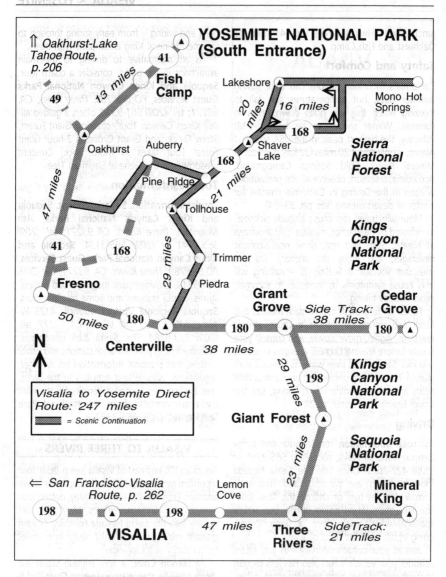

⇑ Oakhurst-Lake Tahoe Route, p. 206

YOSEMITE NATIONAL PARK (South Entrance)

Fish Camp

49 — 13 miles — 41

Lakeshore

16 miles — Mono Hot Springs

20 miles

168

Oakhurst   Auberry   Shaver Lake

168

Pine Ridge

21 miles

Sierra National Forest

41   168

Tollhouse

47 miles

Trimmer

Kings Canyon National Park

Fresno

29 miles

Piedra

50 miles   180

Grant Grove   Side Track: 38 miles   **Cedar Grove**

180   180   180

N ↑

Centerville   38 miles

29 miles

198

Kings Canyon National Park

Visalia to Yosemite Direct Route: 247 miles

▬ = Scenic Continuation

Giant Forest

23 miles

Sequoia National Park

⇐ San Francisco-Visalia Route, p. 262

Lemon Cove

Mineral King

198   198

VISALIA   47 miles   **Three Rivers**   SideTrack: 21 miles

Road until the junction with Hwy 168, a mile from Pine Ridge.

Hwy 168 to the north-east is 20 miles (32 km) of thick forests, mountain lakes, granite outcroppings and small resorts. In winter, the ski area caters to local visitors. A few miles from the end of Hwy 168 beyond Lakeshore (Huntington Lake), is Mono Hot Springs, recommended only for small cars and intrepid drivers in summer. Road and hot springs are closed in winter.

To continue towards Yosemite from the Hwy 168 junction, take Auberry Road west and north. Auberry Road changes names to Road 222, then Road 274, then Road 222 again, before the junction with Hwy 41. Take Hwy 41 north to Oakhurst and Fish Camp.

Safety and Comfort

California's mountain regions can bake during summer days, but temperatures can fall to freezing when the sun goes down, even in summer. Winter snow can be heavy – Mt Whitney, the highest peak in the USA south of Alaska, is only about 20 miles (32 km) due east of Mineral King's Cold Springs Campground. According to season, observe all the precautions advised in the Driving in California chapter for winter or desert driving (see pp. 33–34).

Mountain travel can cause altitude sickness, manifested by headaches, nausea, and shortness of breath. Stop and rest, drink non-alcoholic beverages, and enjoy the scenery. Do not overexert yourself if feeling ill – rushing will only cause symptoms to increase. In summer, avoid midday hiking.

Forest undergrowth can contain moulds and fungi and unfamiliar flora can cause allergic reactions. Again, move slowly, and consult your doctor before leaving home if allergies could lay you low. Stream and river water is infested with *giardia*. For avoiding unpleasant encounters with bears and other wildlife when hiking, see the Travel Essentials chapter, p. 20.

Driving

For **road information** for Sequoia and Kings Canyon National Parks, *tel: (209) 565-3351* or *(800) 427-7623*. Once into the Sierra Nevada foothills, roads are winding, and frequently narrow. Use lay-bys, or choose the slow lane. Use low gears when going uphill; use brakes sparingly when going down a slope. Drivers going uphill have the right of way.

Just as your oxygen decreases as you attain altitude, your vehicle's fuel also has less oxygen to work with. Allow extra time for stops, hikes, and altitude adjustment, and take it easy on your car. Petrol is much cheaper in Visalia or Fresno than anywhere else along this route.

Check under the bonnet before starting your engine. Beware of marmots – large, furry golden brown rodents which crawl into motor vehicle engine compartments and chew through hoses, belts and wiring – from early spring through to summer. Mineral King is rampant with them.

As an alternative to driving to the main attractions in the parks, consider a coach tour. **Sequoia and Kings Canyon National Parks Guest Services**, *PO Box 789, Three Rivers, CA, 93271; tel: (209) 561-3314*, offers a guided all-day Kings Canyon Tour, covering Giant Forest, Stony Creek, and Grant Grove. A 2-hour Giant Forest Tour takes in Moro Rock, Crescent Meadow and the General Sherman Tree.

Tourist Information

Tourist Information: Superintendent, Sequoia and Kings Canyon National Parks, *Ash Mountain, Three Rivers, CA 93271; tel: (209) 565-3341 or (209) 565-3134.* **Sequoia and Kings Canyon National Parks Guest Services**, *PO Box 789, Three Rivers, CA, 93271; tel: (209) 561-3314*, provides park lodging, food outlets, stores, petrol stations and some minibus tours. **Sequoia Regional Visitors Council**, *4125 W. Mineral King, Ste. 104, Visalia, CA 93277; tel: (209) 733-6284.* The *Sierra Bark* newspaper, available free at park entrance stations and visitor centres, has seasonal information on weather, regulations, wildlife and activities in the parks. Free backcountry camping permits for the joint parks are available from the **National Park Service**, *tel: (209) 565-3307.*

VISALIA TO THREE RIVERS

Ten miles (16 km) east of Visalia (see p. 266), four mountain ranges appear, sandwiched one above another. From the flat Central Valley, dotted with orange and tangerine groves, Hwy 198 rises quickly into the Sierra Nevada Foothills. Golden grasses, citrus, and dry oaks nestle in crannies below rocky outcroppings.

At **Lemon Cove**, a few antique stores are surrounded by orange trees. **Lemon Cove Bed & Breakfast**, *33038 Sierra Dr., Lemon Cove, CA 93244; tel: (209) 597-2555*, has nine moderately-priced, antique-filled rooms. Nineteen miles (30 km) from Visalia, a sign shows whether the road between Sequoia National Park and Grant Grove in Kings Canyon National Park is 'open' or 'closed'. If closed, Hwy 198 will take you to

Sequoia National Park; Hwy 180 will take you to Grant Grove in Kings Canyon National Park. One mile (1.6 km) further on the left is **Lake Kaweah** at the **Lemon Hill Recreation Area**. While surrounding hills are desert-dry, the shining blue lake is subject to rapid filling from rainstorms.

Hwy 198 becomes the Sierra Highway as mountain peaks shaped like buttes appear to the north. To the left, birds flit through the Kaweah River Valley, and huge hawks circle above the lake's picnic-perfect **Slick Rock Recreation Area**.

THREE RIVERS

At an elevation of about 1000 ft (308 m), the south, middle and east forks of the **Kaweah River** come together in this foothill town spread along both sides of Hwy 198. River swimming and fishing are favourite local pastimes. Founded in the 1880s as the Kaweah Utopian community, Three Rivers (population 1400) survives as the gateway to Kings Canyon Sequoia National Parks and nearby Mineral King.

Accommodation

The town offers motels and RV parks, catering to park visitors who wish to stay outside the parks or cannot secure accommodation inside. Lodging runs from budget to moderate; all accommodation has swimming pools to offset summer heat. Typical of the budget range is the **Sequoia Motel**, *43000 Sierra Dr., Three Rivers, CA 93271; tel: (209) 561-4453* and **Three Rivers Motel & RV Park**, *43365 Sierra Dr., Three Rivers, CA 93271; tel: (209) 561-4413*. **The Gateway Lodge**, *45978 Sierra Dr., Three Rivers CA 93271; tel: (209) 561-4133* and **Buckeye Tree Lodge**, *46000 Sierra Dr., Three Rivers CA 92371,; tel: (209) 561-4611* are set amid huge boulders along the Kaweah River.

Eating and Drinking

Try the cakes but avoid greasy eggs at **We Three Bakery**, *43368 Sierra Dr., Three Rivers, CA 93271; tel: (209) 561-4761* for breakfast; soup and sandwiches at the **Staff of Life**, *41651 Sierra Dr., Three Rivers, CA 93271; tel: (209) 561-4937*, for lunch on a budget; and a steak for a moderate dinner at the **Gateway Restaurant & Lodge**, *45978 Sierra Dr., Three Rivers, CA 93271; tel: (209) 561-4133*, or other roadside eateries.

◣ Side Track from Three Rivers

A few miles outside of town is the turnoff for Mineral King Road, Mountain Rd. 375A, prohibited to RVs at any time and closed in winter. The return trip is 42 miles (68 km), over curving, alternating dirt and paved roads to Cold Springs Campground, staging point for wilderness walkers and horse pack tours, and back.

MINERAL KING

Sub-alpine Mineral King closes with the first snowfall, generally around the American Thanksgiving in late November. Water is turned off in campsites in mid-October. The area re-opens by Memorial Day, the last weekend of May, depending on snowfall. Carry water, as it may be scarce or unavailable.

In 1965, Walt Disney tried to turn Mineral King's rough wilderness into a ski resort. Thirteen years of litigation later, the wilderness was preserved, and in 1978 it was added to Sequoia National Park.

Hwy 198 winds for 5 miles (8 km) north-east of Three Rivers before reaching the turnoff for Mineral King. A sign warns 'no RVs or trailers', 'winding road' and '90 mins to Mineral King Area'. Don't believe for a moment that you'll be able to drive the 21 miles (34 km) in that time; the narrow 2-lane road twists into corkscrews, on and off paved track. Safety around blind curves and sharp turns dictates driving no more than 10–25 mph (16-40 kph). Passengers fearing heights should be warned that there are few verges, and the canyon wall drops precipitously. The uncut forest is thick and grey boulders crop up alongside the road at every turn. The river canyon is not U-shaped, but appears to be receding layers of mountains to the east. Yucca plants mix crazily with oaks and conifers, all clinging precariously to mountainsides. Six miles (9.6 km) east of Hwy 198 is the scenic **Kaweah River Oak Grove Bridge**, built in 1932. Three miles (5 km) further, waterfalls flow over holes etched in rocky slabs by time.

For the first 10 miles (16 km), until it enters Sequoia National Park, the road follows the Kaweah River's East Fork. Black-tailed deer, quail, and even fuzzy brown tarantulas roam these mountains. There is a ranger station at **Lookout Point** at the park entrance. Five miles (8 km) beyond are the first **giant sequoia trees**, set off by whitish peaks rising above the forest.

Stop and smell the rich, damp forest at **Redwood Creek**, where a sign explains the surrounding sequoias. Thick green moss grows on the northern side of the sequoias' intense torch-like orange–red bark.

Two miles (3.2 km) beyond, the road becomes uneven and sandy, then reverts to paved road later at **Atwell Mill**. Yokut Indians used the area as a summer campsite 2000 years ago. In 1873, silver mining was attempted in Mineral King, 6 miles (9.6 km) to the east. By 1879, the 698-turn Mineral King Road had been laid for miners' wagons, but in the early 1880s, the mining boom in the area collapsed. At 6650 ft (2046 m), the 23 campsite pitches are in high forest among huge sequoia stumps and are highly desirable. Bear and mountain lion (also called cougar, bobcat, or puma) roam the area.

Pass Cabin Cove before coming to **Silver City**. A general store has camping, backpacking and fishing supplies, area maps, books, postcards, stamps, a postbox, souvenirs, showers, petrol, and the adjacent **Silver City Bakery and Restaurant**. The **Silver City High Sierra Rustic Family Resort**, *2420 E Hillcrest Ave, Visalia CA 93292; tel: (209) 734-4109* (late Sept–late May), or *PO Box 56, Three Rivers, CA 93271; tel: (209) 561-3223* (late May–late Sept), has lantern-lit cabins and three chalets, moderate to expensive.

Mineral King Ranger Station, *tel: (209) 565-3768*, is just 1 mile (1.6 km) up the road past the 37-site **Cold Springs Campground**. At 7500 ft (2308 m), this is the end of the road. Horseback and hay wagon rides, and overnight to 7-day wilderness horse pack trips are offered by **Bedell Pack Trains**, *PO Box 61, Three Rivers, CA 93271; tel: (209) 561-3404* (summer), *(209) 561-4142* (winter).

The sheer golden mountains of Sawtooth Pass rise to the east. According to experienced hikers, where eastward mountains rise to more than 10,000 ft (3077 m), hiking is 'hardcore', tougher than most other places in the state, and only for the experienced who want to 'entertain themselves in nature'. The attraction is to hike the Great Divide along the **John Muir Pacific Crest Trail** to see the east side of the Sierra Nevada Mountains, plateaux, and untouched forests. Obtain backcountry permits from ranger stations in advance. A ¼-mile (0.4 km) self-guided Cold Springs nature trail, to see birds and wildflowers in season, takes 45 mins.

SEQUOIA NATIONAL PARK

Highway 198 continues 4 miles (6.4 km) northeast of Three Rivers to the entrance to Sequoia National Park at Ash Mountain Park Headquarters.

Tourist Information: Two ranger stations, at **Ash Mountain/Foothills**, *tel: (209) 565-3134*, and **Lodgepole**, tel: *(209) 565-3782*, provide information, backcountry permits, and exhibits. When approaching the park, tune your radio to 1610 AM for general park information. There are 26 sequoia groves in America's second national park, founded in 1890 to protect the trees and forests from overgrazing by cattle and sheep.

Pay entrance fees, and pick up a park brochure. Some 2½ miles (4 km) into the park, pass under – or drive around if vehicle is taller than 7ft 9in (2.3 m) – **Tunnel Rock**, a huge boulder fallen to form an arch over the road. At a lay-by 3 miles (5 km) beyond, the peak of Mt Stewart is visible.

Stop 7 miles (11 km) from the park entrance at **Hospital Rock**, named when a Caucasian hunter was treated here in 1873. The Patwisha tribe of Western Mono, or Monache natives, and Penutian-speaking Yokuts inhabited the area, leaving red pictographs on rocks just to the north of the parking lot. Three-quarters of a mile (1.2 km) below the pictographs in a secluded canyon is **Buckeye Flat Campground**, with a magnificent view of peaks to the northeast.

Use a lay-by off Hwy 198 to take a picture of **Moro Rock**, a bare grey granite dome which juts

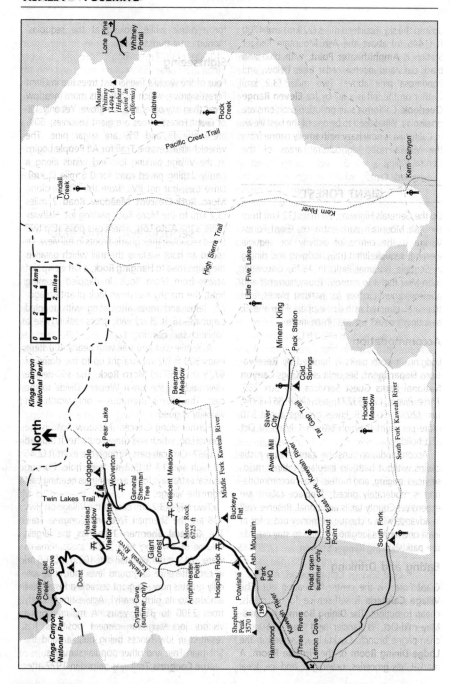

Sequoia National Park Map

up into the sky. Fourteen miles (22 km) and 4700 ft (1446 m) above the Ash Mountain Ranger Station is **Amphitheater Point**, with blue and black oaks and incense cedar trees below, and Ponderosa pine above. Two miles (3.2 km) further on the left is a lay-by for **Eleven Range Overlook**. California's air pollution problems are on display. What used to be one of the best views in California is now hazy with smelly ozone from the Visalia-Fresno agricultural areas of the Central Valley.

GIANT FOREST

Up the Generals Highway, 20 miles (32 km) from the Ash Mountain park entrance, Giant Forest Village is the centre of activity for sequoia viewing, sequoia-lined trails, lodging and dining in Sequoia National Park. In 1875, discoverer John Muir had it to himself. Today, summer and autumn crowds jockey for parking places, and trails are crammed with day-trippers. Plan ahead, as lodging books up well in advance.

Accommodation

Lodging in both parks is handled by **Reservations Department, Sequoia and Kings Canyon National Parks Guest Services**, *PO Box 789, Three Rivers, CA, 93271; tel: (209) 561-3314, fax: (209) 561-3135*. Prices average about $10 more per night for high season 1 May–10 Oct and holidays.

Accommodation runs the gamut from rustic cabins without bath, to fireplace cabins, maid-serviced lodging, and motels. Most accommodation is moderately priced; fireplace cabins are expensive. County tax is additional. Reserve well in advance with a cheque or money order for at least one night's lodging, or plan to stay outside the park(s).

Eating and Drinking

Giant Forest is the centre for eating out. The **Village Cafeteria** is self-service for all meals, cheap to budget. The **Dining Room**, open mid-May–mid-Oct, is fancier and has a Sunday champagne brunch. Cocktails are served in the **Lodge Dining Room** or the **Fireside Room**. A market has groceries, beverages, and ice, ideal for a picnic while looking at the sequoias' monumental trunks.

Sightseeing

Four of the world's five largest trees live in Giant Forest's grove, which also boasts more meadow areas than any other sequoia grove. Yet only 1% of Giant Forest's trees are giant sequoias; 60% are white fir and 9% are sugar pine. The wheelchair-accessible **Trail for All People** begins at the Village parking lot, and winds along a gently-sloping paved road for 0.6 mile (1 km). Drive cars, but not RVs, from the Village along **Moro Rock-Crescent Meadow Road** 2 miles (3.2 km) to the Moro Rock parking lot. Halfway there is the **Auto Log**, where cars pose atop two felled sequoias, their gnarled roots in full view. Or spend an hour walking the trail which parallels the same road to **Hanging Rock**, a flat viewpoint across from Moro Rock. In dappled morning light, the marshy meadows look phantasmagoric, ferns and moss alternating with toppled sequoias' 15 ft (5 m) wide roots looking like a Salvador Dali painting.

A ¼-mile (0.4 km) trail with nearly 400 steps leads 300 ft (92 m) straight up to the dome of 6725 ft (2069 m) **Moro Rock**. The 360-degree view takes in the Great Western Divide to the east. The hike is strenuous – only worth it if visibility is good.

Further along Crescent Meadow Road is the Tunnel Log, which was carved out after it toppled in 1937. Cars can pass through the eight ft (2.46 m) high and 17 ft (5.2 m) wide hole. Plan on several extra days to hike other trails heading east from the Village.

Two miles (3.2 km) east of the Village on Hwy 198 are the Sherman Tree and Congress Trail. The **General Sherman Tree** has the largest volume of anything alive: 1975 measurements were 274.9 ft (84.6 m) tall and 102.6 ft (31.5 m) in circumference at ground level (but undoubtedly greater now – a giant sequoia adds a small amount to its girth yearly). Age estimates vary from 2300 to 3500 years. A million annual visitors jockeying for camera positions has resulted in low fences being built around the Sherman Tree and other popular sequoias.

The **Congress Trail** was named in 1922 after

the collective US legislative assemblies, the House and Senate. Plan on 2 hrs to follow the 2-mile (3.2 km) loop path from the **Sherman Tree** to the **Chief Sequoyah Tree, President Tree, Senate** and **House** Groups, **General Lee Tree**, and **McKinley Tree.** Ancient fires and recent controlled burns cause the sequoias to propagate, sometimes in double or triple trunks; their resinless bark prevents destruction by fire. Young trees resemble Christmas trees, with drooping bough tips.

Just up Hwy 198 is **Wolverton** picnic area, a staging site for horse riding and winter skiing. **Sequoia and Kings Canyon National Parks Guest Services**, *PO Box 789, Three Rivers, CA, 93271; tel: (209) 561-3314.*

Almost 5 miles (8 km) north of Giant Forest Village is **Lodgepole (park) Visitor Center.** The **Lodgepole Market** sells groceries and ice cream; a cafeteria and **Lodge Restaurant** offer food;

and there are showers and a laundry. The **Lodgepole Campground**, open mid-May–Sept, has 260 places. Petrol is exorbitant. Take a picnic to **Halstead Meadow**, 4 miles (6.4 km) north on Hwy 198. Another 218 camping pitches are open from Memorial Day to Labor Day at **Dorst Campground. Lost Grove** on the northern edge of Sequoia National Park is one of 26 sequoia groves in the park. Some 400 trees are spread over 54 acres (21.85 ha).

For a few miles, the Generals Highway traverses Sequoia National Forest. Fewer sequoia trees are apparent; the forest is fairly uniform, indicating reforestation. **Stony Creek** has a picnic area and a lodge/restaurant, market and gift shop. Moderate **Stony Creek Lodge, Sequoia and Kings Canyon National Parks Guest Services**, *PO Box 789, Three Rivers, CA, 93271; tel: (209) 561-3314,* open summer only, has eleven carpeted rooms with private showers.

Giant Sequoias

Sequoiadendron giganteum, shorter than California's coastal redwoods, live up to 3200 years, weigh up to 2.7 million lb (5940 tonnes), have red bark up to 31 in (79 cm) thick, yet reproduce only from oat-flake like seeds. Instinctively, one looks up the cinnamon-red trunk, to be bewildered by tufts of green foliage high up the tree. The top is often obscured by height and greenery. Sequoias are found in 75 groves, though two or three may appear to cluster together. Age and size make sequoias seem immortal – disease and fire barely faze the growth. Yet the shallow tap root can allow a tree to topple in high winds or when soil is over-moist or disturbed.

Logging for grapestakes, shakes and fence posts before the mid-1880s left individual trees scattered within the 5000–7000 ft (1538–2154 m) elevation where sequoias can grow in the Sierras. Shepherds' flocks and mining prospectors had weakened the land. Many trees shattered when cut, or were too bulky to get out of the mountains. Naturalist-explorer John Muir's writings finally resulted in protection for many of the remaining Big Giants in nature reserves from 1885 onwards.

Sequoias are probably named after the Native American Se-quo-yah who devised a written alphabet for his Cherokee people . Four of the world's five largest trees stand in Giant Forest, in Sequoia National Park; the largest is the General Sherman Tree near Giant Forest Village.

Giant Forest in Sequoia National Park, Grant Grove in Kings Canyon National Park and the Mariposa Grove near Hwy 41 in south Yosemite National Park have walking paths through the towering sequoias.

Photographers' note: It is tempting to get the souvenir 'we were here' picture in sequoia areas. Even lying flat on the ground with a wide angle lens, it may be impossible to get the tops of these giants in the picture. Be content with posing people against the red trunks, or aim up at the top of a group of trees with part of one specimen's trunk showing.

All-season **Montecito-Sequoia Lodge**; tel: (800) 227-9900, has 38 rooms and some cabins. Moderate prices include an all-you-can-eat buffet dinner, snacks and non-alcoholic drinks in the cosy central lodge log cabin. Summer visitors row on a man-made lake and winter cross-country skiers gravitate to the lodge's balcony overlooking a red fir forest.

At **Kings Canyon Overlook**, a sign claims that it is a view of the second largest roadless landscape in the lower 48 US states. Spread to the north and north-east is Kings Canyon National Park and Monarch and John Muir Wilderness areas. **Redwood Mountain Overlook**, 2 miles (3.2 km) west on Hwy 198, provides a view to the south, where air pollution may be heavy. **Redwood Mountain Grove**, the largest of the 75 sequoia groups, is here. Enter Kings Canyon National Park.

KINGS CANYON NATIONAL PARK

On Epiphany, 6 Jan 1806, Spanish explorer Gabriel Moraga's expedition discovered a major river. In honour of the holy day, the raging waterway was named *El Rio de los Santos Reyes*, 'the river of the Holy Kings', the Magi who visited the infant Jesus.

John Muir visited the Kings River Canyon in 1873, impressed by its resemblance to Yosemite Valley. Grazing rapidly wrought havoc on the ground, and sawmills chewed up those sequoias which hadn't shattered on impact when felled. In four years, Muir noted, the large **Converse Grove** of sequoias was levelled to one survivor.

When Sequoia National Park was established in 1890, followed by Yosemite National Park a week later, the US Congress designated the General Grant National Park to protect the Grant Grove sequoias. Fifty years later, in 1940, Kings Canyon National Park was established, incorporating Grant Grove. The wilderness between Yosemite and Sequoia National Parks was preserved.

GRANT GROVE

At the junction of Hwy 198 and 180, turn right (east) to Grant Grove. The **Grant Grove (park)**

Visitor Center; tel: (209) 335-2856, is open daily from 0800–1700, and has the best-stocked parks bookshop. **Cross-country skiing** opens with the first snowfall and continues until mid-April, **Sequoia and Kings Canyon National Parks Guest Services**, PO Box 789, Three Rivers, CA, 93271; tel: (209) 561-3314. A gift shop, post office, and petrol station are in Grant Grove Village.

Accommodation

The **Grant Grove Lodge**, Sequoia and Kings Canyon National Parks Guest Services, PO Box 789, Three Rivers, CA 93271; tel: (209) 561-3314, has cabins with and without baths. Moderate. The three Grant Grove campsites are within a ¼ mile (0.4 km) of Grant Grove's small village: 113-place **Azalea** is open year-round; 184-place **Sunset** and 67-place **Crystal Springs** are open Memorial Day–Sept.

Eating and Drinking

Grant Grove Coffee Shop serves meals year-round, 0700–2100. **Grant Grove Market** sells groceries and beverages. Both are run by **Sequoia and Kings Canyon National Parks Guest Services**, PO Box 789, Three Rivers, CA, 93271; tel: (209) 561-3314.

Sightseeing

Grant Grove is Kings Canyon National Park's magnificent sequoia group. The **General Grant Grove**, less than 1 mile (1.6 km) northwest of the Grant Grove Visitor Center, has a 0.3 mile (0.5 km) self-guided walking trail.

The **General Grant Tree** is the third-largest living thing, and has the greatest base diameter of any sequoia. It is a living National Shrine and War Memorial, and more happily, is also the country's official Christmas Tree. A nearby bench affords the best view of the fenced-off giant. Diagonal patterns snake up the trunk of the **Oregon Tree**. Climb through a 3 ft (1 m) hole in the weathered-looking **Fallen Monarch**, which has been a house and hotel/saloon at various times. There are about 80 giant sequoias on or near the General Grant Grove. The **Happy Family** cluster next to the parking lot offers red trunks as a fiery background for pictures.

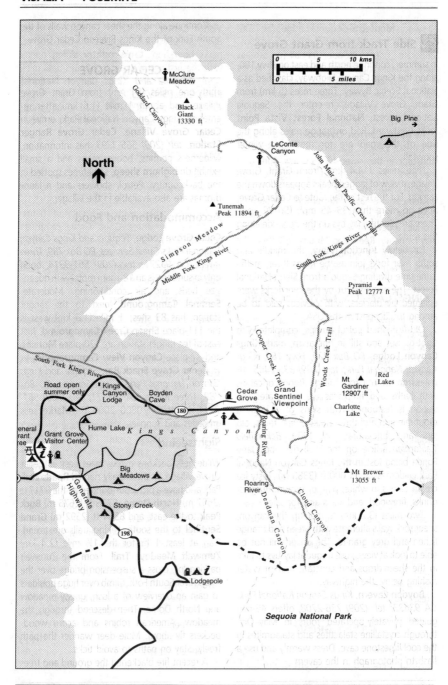

0   5   10 kms

0   5 miles

McClure
Meadow

Goddard Canyon

Black
Giant
13330 ft

Big Pine →

LeConte
Canyon

John Muir and Pacific Crest Trails

North

Tunemah
Peak 11894 ft

Simpson Meadow

Middle Fork Kings River

South Fork Kings River

Pyramid
Peak 12777 ft

Cooper Creek Trail

Woods Creek Trail

South Fork Kings River

Road open
summer only

Kings
Canyon
Lodge

Boyden
Cave

180

Cedar
Grove

Grand
Sentinel
Viewpoint

Mt
Gardiner
12907 ft

Red
Lakes

Charlotte
Lake

General
Grant
Tree

Grant Grove
Visitor Center

Hume Lake

K i n g s   C a n y o n

Roaring River

Big
Meadows

Generals
Highway

Roaring
River

Deadman Canyon

Cloud Canyon

Mt Brewer
13055 ft

Stony Creek

198

Lodgepole

Sequoia National Park

Side Track from Grant Grove

In summer, continue north and east on Hwy 180, along the Kings Canyon Highway, classified as a National Scenic Byway. Three miles (5 km) from Grant Grove Village, re-enter the Sequoia National Forest. **National Forest Vista Point** looks westward. Red or orange poles along the side of the road are for measuring winter snowfall.

Nine miles (14.4 km) from Grant Grove Village, a view of jagged peaks appears down the canyon. For the rest of the route to Cedar Grove, drive no more than 35–45 mph (56–72 kph). There are plentiful lay-bys on the view side along this route.

Far below **Junction View**, the middle and south river forks join as the Kings River, at the same time dividing Sequoia from Sierra National Forest. The canyons cut by the river forks were enlarged by glaciers, with crevices said to be among the deepest in the USA.

Old-fashioned petrol pumps, complete with sight-glasses and still in operation, mark **Kings Canyon Lodge**, *PO Box 820, Hwy 180, Kings Canyon National Park; tel: (209) 335-2405*, 16 miles from Grant Grove Village. Rooms or cabins with baths and fireplaces are moderate. The saloon is festooned with skins of a bear, a mountain lion and three snakes, deer racks, old jars and bric-a-brac. A 1989 *Bakersfield Californian* article on the wall describes Jane Fonda being lost in the Kings Canyon National Park wilderness at 11,000 ft (3385 m). Tasty ice cream comes in white, pink or brown. Burgers, drinks, firewood, and ice is also for sale.

Two miles (3.2 km) further up the canyon, sheer rock walls alternate with green and orange lichen and grey granite. The driver will not be able to look at views; use frequent lay-bys to take in the sheer drops and constant roar of water rushing below the highway.

Boyden Cavern, *Kings Canyon National Park, CA 93633; tel: (209) 736-2708*, offers 45-min guided privately-operated tours in May–Oct. through crystalline stalactites and stalagmites in the cool limestone cave. Dress warmly and use a flash to photograph in the cavern.

Continue along the sheer canyon walls of the South Fork of the Kings River to Cedar Grove.

CEDAR GROVE

Thirty-one miles (51 km) from Grant Grove Village, and about 1 mile (1.6 km) after re-entering Kings Canyon National Park, arrive in **Cedar Grove Village. Cedar Grove Ranger Station**, *tel: (209) 565-3793*, has information, wilderness permits, books, maps and a small exhibit on **bighorn sheep**, sometimes spotted in the backcountry. Petrol, showers and a laundromat are also available in the village.

Accommodation and Food

Cedar Grove Lodge, *Sequoia and Kings Canyon National Parks Guest Services, PO Box 789, Three Rivers, CA 93271; tel: (209) 561-3314*, open only in summer, is an 18-room motel with queen-size beds and air conditioning. Moderate. **Sentinel Campground**, next to the ranger station, has 83 sites; 1 mile (1.6 km) west is the 111-place **Sheep Creek Campground**. Just east of the ranger station are 120-place **Moraine** and 37-place **Canyon View Campgrounds**.

Cedar Grove Snack Bar, *Sequoia and Kings Canyon National Parks Guest Services, PO Box 789, Three Rivers, CA, 93271; tel: (209) 561-3314*, is open daily 0800–2000. The **Market** sells groceries and supplies.

Sightseeing

Wilderness beckons a few miles east of Cedar Grove Village, at the literally-named **Roads End**. Park and have a picnic surrounded by the 8717 ft (2657 m) **North Dome**, 8776 ft (2675 m) **Buck Peak** to the east, and 8504-ft (2592 m) **Grand Sentinel** to the south. Hiking trails are taxing. Plan at least 1 hr for the 1½ mile (2.4 km) **Zumwalt Meadow Trail**. From the Zumwalt parking lot, cross a suspension bridge over the Kings River South Fork. Climb over huge boulders to gain an overview of a lush, grassy meadow and North Dome. Then descend through the meadow. American robins and acorn woodpeckers fly about. Mule deer wander the path freely. Stay on paths to avoid ticks.

A recent fire blackened the ground and trees

along the 2.6 mile (4 km) **Motor Nature Trail,** which runs from east to west past Cedar Grove Village. The speed limit is 10 mph (16 kph) along a way that is often a narrow, washboard dirt road. Retrace the route back to Grant Grove.

GRANT GROVE TO CENTERVILLE

From Grant Grove, continue on Hwy 180. **Big Stump Basin** is a 1-mile (1.6 km) trail around remnants of felled or burned sequoia trunks, a monument to the destruction of a grove before national park status protected such trees. Exit the park to Sequoia National Forest 3 miles (5 km) from Grant Grove. Rangers will ask for a paid receipt for entrance to the park, and may search vehicles for illicit goods.

Twenty miles (32 km) from Grant Grove is **Clingan's Junction,** the western end of Highway 180's 50 miles (80 km) of National Scenic Byway. Mountains give way to small, dusty, oak-lined foothills in the descent towards the Central Valley. Clingan's Junction is a full-service hamlet: a deli, a restaurant, a pizza joint, a feed store, a shop selling fishing tackle, bait, crickets, and oak firewood, a beauty salon and an antique dealer augment the petrol station. Four miles further is **Squaw Valley,** nestled in grassy pastures and oaks. Hwy 180 continues west to **Centerville.** From Centerville either take the scenic continuation or continue along Hwy 180 to Fresno.

CENTERVILLE TO OAKHURST SCENIC CONTINUATION

At Centerville turn right on **Trimmer Springs Rd,** just beyond a dirt and gravel company, to continue on the scenic route. The farms on either side of the road look like a stereotype of the Central Valley: cows grazing in bucolic pastures behind miles of white fences; orange groves hedged with palm trees; well-to-do farmhouses with battered trucks and shiny, sleek town cars parked beneath spreading oak trees. Most of the road is straight, but there are occasional sharp turns to follow property lines.

The road suddenly begins climbing into the Sierra Foothills 5 miles (8 km) beyond the Hwy

180 junction. The **Kings River** winds between the same hills, easily accessible with the four-wheel drive vehicles so popular in the area. During trout fishing season, it isn't unusual to see fishermen (and women) relaxing in chairs under a shady tree or even sitting in the shallow riffles near the bank to keep cool.

Pass the turnoff for **Wonder Valley,** another small community, and continue north toward **Piedra.** Cattle wander the open range and occasionally decide to stop on the highway. A couple of blasts from the horn is usually enough to convince them to move off to the verge.

The highway takes a sharp left 5 miles (8 km) beyond Piedra toward **Pine Flat Lake** and **Trimmer. Kirkman's Overlook,** 5 miles (8 km) beyond the turn on the right, offers an expansive view of the foothills reservoir. If the lake level is down, however, it looks more like a dirty disaster than a prime recreation area with boating, fishing, camping and walking. There are numerous lay-bys to allow faster traffic to pass. The major lake facilities, including a boat ramp and houseboat rentals, are near the junction of Trimmer Springs Rd and Maxson Rd.

Turn left on Maxson Rd, up a short, steep hill. The **Trimmer Ranger Station** is at the summit, 1 mile (1.6 km) beyond the turn. From the Ranger Station, the little-used, single-track road winds down into the next valley. Be cautious at blind corners; local drivers, almost the only traffic on Maxson Rd, don't expect to meet oncoming vehicles and may stray onto the wrong side of the road. Turn right 4 miles (6 km) beyond the Ranger Station onto **Burroughs Valley Rd.** Continue 7½ miles (12 km) to **Toll House Rd** and turn right.

The town of **Tollhouse** is 2½ miles (4 km) beyond the junction. The town has a post office, petrol (expensive), a small market and a café.The road out of Tollhouse winds sharply uphill, following ridgetops where possible, but often cut into the steep hillsides. The many lay-bys offer grand vistas back down the valley, but beware of the many unmarked switchbacks.

Toll House Rd ends at Hwy 168, at Pine Ridge, 7 miles (11 km) beyond Tollhouse. Turn right onto Hwy 168. The four-lane section of road lasts little more than 1 mile (1.6 km). The forest surround-ing the highway is thick, but conifers slowly replace oak trees as the altitude increases from 2100 ft (640 m) at Tollhouse to 5300 ft (1615 m) at **Shaver Lake**, 12 miles (19 km) beyond. There are frequent delays for road repairs during the short spring–autumn working season. If the traffic halt lasts more than a few minutes, turn the engine off to avoid wasting petrol and contributing to the air pollution that drifts up from the Central Valley.

The small town of **Shaver Lake** offers complete services, from petrol to real estate sales. The lake is just beyond, dark blue waters surrounded by deep green pine forests and speckled grey granite outcroppings. Most of the shoreline is lined with private homes and moorings. Officially known as Big Creek 2A Hydroelectric Project, Shaver Lake and much of the surrounding forest is owned by Southern California Edison (SCE), which supplies electrical power to Southern California. The marina is open Apr–Oct.

Follow the highway around to the right just beyond the marina to **Tamarak Ridge**, 7244 ft (2208 m), and down to **Huntington Lake**, 16 miles (26 km) from Shaver Lake. Huntington is also an SCE reservoir.

The steep, twisting road to **Mono Hot Springs** is to the right from the north end of Huntington Lake. The Mono road is not recommended for RVs, caravans, timid drivers, or nervous passengers.

For a slow, scenic return to the Yosemite route, follow the road around Huntington Lake back to Shaver Lake, 20 miles (32 km) and 45–60 mins over an extremely narrow road.

For an easier return, retrace the route on Hwy 168. Either way, continue past Shaver Lake on Hwy 168. Turn right onto Auberry Rd, 1½ miles (2.5 km) beyond the four-lane section of road. Auberry Rd immediately begins climbing toward the tiny towns of **Auberry** and **New Auberry**. Just beyond New Auberry the road becomes Powerhouse Rd and continues climbing.

To continue on the **direct route**, drive west on Hwy 180 along the Blossom Trail. In the Central Valley flatlands near Fresno, citrus groves appear, then plums, cotton, olives, grapes, and apple orchards.

FRESNO

Tourist Information: Fresno Convention and Visitors Bureau (CVB), *808 M St, Fresno, CA 93721; tel: (800) 788-0836 or (209) 233-0836, open Mon–Fri, 0800–1700.*

Getting Around

Fresno can be a jumping off point for exploring Yosemite, Kings Canyon and Sequoia National Parks. The **Fresno Air Terminal**, *5175 Clinton Way, Fresno, CA 93727; tel: 209 251-6051*, is the regional airport. **Fresno Transit**; *tel: (209) 488-1122* provides local transportation. **S.A.V.E. Company**; *tel: (209) 275-1295*, has airport transport and taxi service. Most car hire companies have local offices.

Accommodation and Food

Lodging runs the entire price range. Chains include *BW, HI, HJ, HL, HY, M6, MA,* and *RM;* the Fresno CVB has a list of accommodation.

Try some of the ethnic food brought by settlers in this part of the central Valley. For Armenian cooking, there's **George's Shish Kebab**, *2405 Capitol St, Fresno; tel: (209) 264-9433*. Moderate. In the USA, Basque food means heaped portions of country cooking served family-style in tureens or on platters at budget to moderate prices: try **Santa Fe**, *935 Santa Fe Ave, Fresno; tel: (209) 266-2170*. Cheap to budget is **Butterfield Brewing, Bar & Grill**, *777 E. Olive Ave, Fresno, CA 93728; tel: (209) 264-5521*, serving burgers, salads, pasta and ribs, with brewed ales and home-made Butterfield Classic Root Beer.

Sightseeing

Fresno is in California's agricultural heartland, producing one-third of all US grapes, 55% of its nectarines, figs, cotton, and turkeys.

Fresno is hot in the summer, perfect for the 250-some commercial crops that yield $3 billion annually. The original barren area was transformed into wheatfields by irrigation canals in 1885, ten years after a grape producer accidentally forgot his fruit on the vines, and ended up with raisins. Most California raisins come from the vineyards around the city.

Native son **William Saroyan**, author of *The Human Comedy* and the play *The Time of Your Life*, was the son of Armenian immigrants; he deftly fictionalised the city to portray the newcomers' experiences. Saroyan sites, including his childhood home at *3204 E. El Monte Way*, are prominently marked throughout Fresno, and acknowledged in an annual May festival. For a self-guided **Saroyan Walking Tour** brochure, contact **William Saroyan Festival**, *920 E. Yale Ave, Fresno, CA 93704; tel: (209) 221-1441*.

An eclectic collection of offerings, including a permanent collection of Saroyan works, is at the **Fresno Metropolitan Museum of Art, History, and Science**, *1555 Van Ness Ave, Fresno, CA 93721; tel: (209) 441-1444*, open Wed, 1100–1900, Thurs–Sun, 1100–1700. Other attractions are 16th-century and 17th-century still life and *trompe d'oeil* paintings, Ansel Adams photographs, and Asian collections. The **Fresno Art Museum**, *Radio Park, 2233 N. First St, Fresno, CA 93703; tel: (209) 485-4810*, open Tues–Sun, 1000–1700, has changing American and Mexican art exhibitions.

Kearney Mansion Museum, *7160 W. Kearney Blvd, Fresno, CA 93706; tel: (209) 441-0862*, open Fri–Sun, 1300–1600, is the lovingly restored 1900–1903 French Renaissance-style mansion, and château-style servant's quarters of 'The Raisin King of California', Martin Theodore Kearney. Seven miles (11 km) west of downtown Fresno, it is surrounded by a park. The only remaining example of early architecture in the area is the 1889 Queen Anne-style **Meux House Museum**, *1000 R St, PO Box 70, Fresno, CA 93707; tel: (209) 233-8007*, open Fri–Sun, 1200–1530, built by a prominent physician. The **Tower Theatre**, *816 E. Olive St; tel: (209) 485-9050*, is an Art Deco beacon for jazz and legitimate theatre productions performed in the restored cinema house. The surrounding neighbourhood is the **Tower District**.

For a look at the area's abundant agriculture, **Simonian Farms**, *2629 S. Clovis Ave, Fresno, CA 93725; tel: (209) 237-2294*, open daily, 0800–sunset, is a third-generation 1901 family farm producing a hundred fruit and vegetable varieties. Antique farm equipment adds atmosphere.

Fill up with some of the cheapest petrol in the state before leaving Fresno. On the **direct route**, continue north on Hwy 41, the Southern Yosemite Highway, to Oakhurst, leaving the San Joaquin Valley for the oak-strewn foothills and cattle pastures. **Southern Yosemite Visitors Bureau**, *PO Box 1401, Oakhurst, CA 93644; tel: (209) 683-4636*, and **Eastern Madera County Chamber of Commerce**, *49074 Civic Circle, PO Box 369, Oakhurst, CA 93644; tel: (209) 683-7766*, have information on local attractions and accommodation. The **Yosemite Apple Growers Assn**, *PO Box 2687, Oakhurst, CA 93644*, has an apple farm guide.

Descend Deadwood Mountain into **Oakhurst. Fresno Flats Historical Park**, *School Rd, 427 Hwy 41, PO Box 451, Oakhurst, CA 93644; tel: (209) 683-6570*, open Wed–Sun in summer, weekends in other seasons, is a schoolhouse museum with other period buildings containing century-old memorabilia. The Taylor 'dog trot' house, a merchant's home, an 1880s jail, a smithy, barns and wooden wagons add interest to this picnic spot. Summer melodramas are offered at the **Golden Chain Theatre**, *PO Box 604, Oakhurst, CA 93644; tel: (209) 683-7112*. Petrol prices skyrocket once you approach a national park – make sure the tank is full.

OAKHURST

For more on Oakhurst, see the Oakhurst–Lake Tahoe Route, pp. 206–214.

FISH CAMP

Fish Camp's most famous attraction is the **Yosemite Mt Sugar Pine Railroad**, *56001 Hwy 41, Fish Camp, CA 93623; tel: (209) 683-7273*. Steam trains and jenny 'Model A' powered railcars operate along a 4-mile (6.4 km) return track in the Sierra National Forest – weather and snow permitting. Fish Camp is jammed with highway-side motels, bed and breakfasts, and dining, all likely to be comparable to or even cheaper than Wawona or Yosemite National Park concession prices. See p. 286 for Yosemite National Park.

SAN FRANCISCO
to
YOSEMITE

Leave the urban San Francisco Bay Area behind for the rural hills and dormitory communities of the East Bay, where windmills and vineyards enliven the countryside. Head south along the agricultural northern Central Valley, then drive east from Merced to Mariposa, the gateway to Yosemite National Park and the southern Gold Country.

It's a half-day non-stop drive from San Francisco to the approach to Yosemite National Park on this 196 mile (313 km) route. With stops, overnight in Merced or Mariposa before tackling the drive to Yosemite.

ROUTE

From Union Square in San Francisco, take Stockton St three blocks south. Cross Market St and continue three blocks on Fourth St, then turn left onto Folsom St for another 2½ blocks. From the right-hand lane, turn right onto Essex St. One block south, cross Harrison St to the onramp and go east on I-80 over the **San Francisco–Oakland Bay Bridge** to **Oakland**.

Take the Hwy 24 exit and move quickly to the East Bay and beyond Oakland (San Francisco Bay Area Routes, p. 234) through the Caldecott Tunnel, which physically divides the bayside flatlands from the interior valleys.

About 1 mile (1.6 km) south-east of the Caldecott Tunnel is the 381-acre (154 ha) **Robert Sibley Volcanic Regional Preserve**, *East Bay Regional Parks; 2950 Peralta Oaks Ct, P.O. Box 5381, Oakland, CA 94605-0381; tel: (510) 635-0135*. Take the Fish Ranch Rd exit, north above the tunnel. At Grizzly Peak Blvd, go 2.4 miles (4 km) south to Skyline Blvd, and the Visitors Center entrance. Drive or hike up 1763-ft (542 m)

Roundtop Mountain, the centre of volcanic activity 10 million years ago. Lava flows, vents, tufas and other volcanic geology spread below.

Back on Hwy 24 on the left, is the **Bruns Memorial Amphitheatre**, *100 Gateway Blvd, Orinda, CA 94563; tel: (510) 548-9666*, home of the **California Shakespeare Festival**. Architecture resembles Elizabethan theatres; plays are performed in summer Wed–Sun. About 1 mile (1.6 km) east is **Orinda**. (**Orinda Chamber of Commerce**, *2 Theatre Sq; tel: (510) 254-3909*). Orinda's Art Deco cinema, the **Orinda Theatre**, *4 Orinda Theatre Square; tel: (510) 254-9060*, is the centrepiece of a thriving downtown shopping and dining scene.

Take the Acalanes Ave exit in Lafayette, then turn left on Mt Diablo Blvd to Entrance Rd. Paved and unpaved trails circle the **Lafayette Reservoir**, *tel: (510) 284-9669*. The recreation area has fishing, boating and a visitors' center with insect displays and an aquarium.

Continue on Hwy 24 to **Walnut Creek**. Follow Hwy 680 south-east through **Alamo** and **Danville**. Continue on Hwy 680 through **San Ramon** and **Dublin**. Turn left (east) on Hwy 580 to **Livermore**.

From Livermore, return to Hwy 580 and continue east, up the **Altamont Pass**. A windfarm forest of wind turbines, modern metal windmills, creates electricity without fossil fuel, though the winds are sufficient to keep them turning only between May and Sept. Continue east on Hwy 205 to **Tracy**. East of Tracy, turn left on I-5 for 2 miles (3.2 km), then go right on Hwy 120 for 6 miles (10 km). **Manteca** is on the left.

Turn right and follow Hwy 99 south past **Ripon** to **Salida**. You can break up the drive with almond tasting at **Blue Diamond Growers**, *4800 Sisk Rd, Salida, CA 95368; tel: (209) 545-3222*. Continue to **Modesto**, on the **Tuolumne River**.

Continue on Hwy 99 south. Next down the Central Valley are **Ceres** and **Turlock**. (**Turlock Chamber of Commerce**, *115 Golden State Blvd, Turlock, CA 95380; tel: (209) 632-2221*). One of the Valley's prides is the free **Castle Air Museum**, *PO Box 488, Atwater, CA 95301; tel: (209) 723-2178*, open 1000–1600, at the edge of Castle Air Force Base. Off-duty US Air

Route   **281**

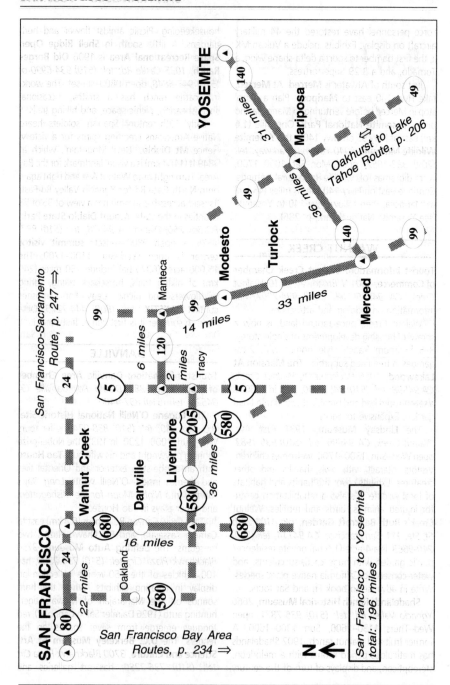

YOSEMITE

140

31 miles

Mariposa

49

Oakhurst to Lake
Tahoe Route, p. 206

49

Modesto

Turlock

140

36 miles

99

33 miles

Merced

Manteca

99

14 miles

99

San Francisco-Sacramento
Route, p. 247 ⇒

120

6 miles

2 miles

Tracy

24

5

5

24

205

580

Livermore

Walnut Creek

Danville

36 miles

580

680

580

SAN FRANCISCO

680

16 miles

24

Oakland

580

22 miles

80

San Francisco Bay Area
Routes, p. 234 ⇒

San Francisco to Yosemite
total: 196 miles

N ←

Force personnel have restored the 44 military aircraft on display. Exhibits include a Vulcan MK II, the first bomber to sport a delta-shape wing, a Tornado, and a B-29 Superfortress.

Just south of Atwater is **Merced**. At **Merced**, take Hwy 140 east to **Mariposa**. Plan a petrol stop in Merced before venturing to Mariposa and on to **Yosemite National Park**. One mile (1.6 km) east of Hwy 99 on Hwy 140 is the **Yosemite Wildlife Museum**, *2040 Yosemite Parkway; tel: (209) 383-1052*, open Mon–Sat 1000–1700, with dioramas of wildlife in natural settings. Continue east on Hwy 140 for 28 miles (45 km) to Mariposa, then follow Hwy 140 to Yosemite (see Yosemite National Park, p. 286).

WALNUT CREEK

Tourist Information: Walnut Creek Chamber of Commerce, *1501 N. Broadway, #110, Walnut Creek, CA 94596; tel: (510) 934-2007*, has information on lodging and attractions.

Walnut Creek, once rancho land, is now a sprawl of housing developments of single-storey, 3–5 bedroom 'ranch'-style homes with 2-car garages in tree-lined suburbia. **The Mansion At Lakewood**, *1056 Hacienda Dr, Walnut Creek, CA 94598; tel: (510) 945-3600*, built in 1860, is a seven-room bed and breakfast with a tree-lined garden. Expensive to pricey.

The **Lindsay Museum**, *1931 First Ave, Walnut Creek, CA 94596; tel: (510) 935-1983*, open Wed–Sun, 1300–1700, welcomes children. Visitors interact with owls, hawks and other creatures. Exhibits cover the habits and habitats of local wildlife. It's also a rehabilitation centre for injured animals, birds and reptiles. Walnut Creek's **Ruth Bancroft Garden**, *c/o 4104 24th St, Ste. 111, San Francisco, CA 94114; tel: (510) 210-9663*, is a 4-acre (1.6 ha) private residence/public garden with huge cacti, succulents, and water-conserving California native plant species. Write in advance to book Fri and Sat tours.

Shadelands Ranch Historical Museum, *2660 Ygnacio Valley Rd; tel: (510) 935-7871*, open Wed–Thurs 1130–1600, Sun 1300–1600. A former fruit and walnut ranch, 1902 Shadelands has meticulous period rooms with a melodeon, stereopticon, and displays of turn-of-the-century

housekeeping. Picnic amidst flower and herb gardens. A little south in **Shell Ridge Open Space Recreational Area** is 1906 **Old Borges Ranch**, *1035 Castle Rd; tel: (510) 934-6990 or (510) 943-5848*, open 0800–sunset. The working cattle ranch has a smithy, occasional sheepshearing, picnic space, and hiking trails.

Early 19th-century Spanish soldiers heard Native Americans crediting spirits for a victory. Hence **Mt Diablo**, 'Devil Mountain', which at 3849 ft (1184 km) is a visual landmark for the Bay Area. Turn right onto Walnut Ave and right again onto North Gate Rd for Ygnacio Valley Rd East. Its road-accessible summit has a view of 35 of 58 counties in the state. **Mount Diablo State Park**, *PO Box 250, Diablo CA 94528; tel: (510) 837-2525*, is open 0800–sunset; **summit visitor center** is open Wed–Sun 1100–1700. The 15,000 acres (6070 ha) include 150 miles (240 km) of hiking trails, horseback riding, spring wildflowers and picnic areas. For campsites contact **MISTIX**, *tel: (800) 444-7275*, Oct–May; in summer it is first come, first served.

DANVILLE

Tourist Information: Danville Area Chamber of Commerce, *380 Diablo Rd, Danville CA 94526; tel: (510) 837-4400*.

The **Eugene O'Neill National Historic Site**, *P.O. Box 280; tel: (510) 838-0249*, offer tours Wed–Sun, 1000, 1230. In 1937, the Nobel-prize winning playwright and his wife built **Tao House** with an adobe-style exterior and Oriental tiles and themes inside. O'Neill wrote *Long Day's Journey Into Night*, *Moon for the Misbegotten*, and other plays in Tao House.

Take Crow Canyon Rd 4 miles (6.4 km) east to Camino Tassajara, and Blackhawk Plaza's two museums. The **Behring Auto Museum**, *3750 Blackhawk Plaza Cir; tel: (510) 736-2280*, has 100 vehicles of the 250-vehicle collection on display in rotating exhibits. When the horn sounds on the Maharajah of Mewa's tiger-hunting auto (1926 Daimler Salon Cabriolet), red tongues emerge from silver snakes on the fenders. The **U.C. Berkeley Museum of Art, Science and Culture**, *3700 Blackhawk Plaza Cir; tel: (510) 736-2280*, has art galleries and anthropology exhibits, including fossils of camels, mastodons and other animals which roamed Blackhawk Quarry 9 million years ago.

LIVERMORE

Tourist Information: Livermore Chamber of Commerce, *2157 First St, Livermore, CA 94550; tel: (510) 373-2121.*

The Livermore Valley was one of the original wine regions, known for its morning fog, gravel soil – and Sauvignon Blanc, Semillon, and Petite Sirah wines. Chateau d'Yquem provided some of the original vine cuttings. **Wente Bros Estate Winery**, *5565 Tesla Rd; tel: (510) 447-3603*, founded 1883, is the oldest family-owned winery in California. **Wente Sparkling Wine Cellars**, *5050 Arroyo Rd; tel: (510) 447-3694*, then named Cresta Blanca Winery, received the first international recognition for California wines at the 1889 Paris Exposition. **Wente Brothers Restaurant**, *5050 Arroyo Rd; tel: (510) 447-3696*, serves moderate–pricey California cuisine. **Concannon Vineyard**, 4950 Tesla Rd; tel: (510) 447-3760, was started in the 1880s to produce sacramental wine. All three wineries are open Mon–Sat 1000–1630, Sun 1100–1630.

Orchid Ranch, *1330 Isabel Ave; tel: (510) 447-7171*, open Tues–Sun 1000–1700, has nine greenhouses devoted to these flowers. The jewel-like brick **Shiva-Vishnu Temple**, *Arrowhead Dr; tel: (510) 449-6255*, is an unexpected Hindu temple complex in the middle of a suburban housing area. On the profane side is **Lawrence Livermore National Laboratory Visitors Center**, *PO Box 808, N. Greenville Rd; tel: (510) 422-9797* (if not a US citizen, book 45 days in advance; *tel: (510) 423-0545)*. The lab remains controversial for its history of nuclear research and toxic waste, but has upbeat exhibits on energy and the environment.

MODESTO

Tourist Information: Modesto Convention and Visitors Bureau, *1114 J St, Modesto CA 95353; tel: (209) 577-5757*, has information on lodging, including *HI, M6,* and *RM.*

Entering Modesto is to enter the heart of California, geographically central and agriculturally rich. **Gallo Winery** produces about 25% of table wine enjoyed in the USA. Modesto 'arrived' with George Lucas' film *American Graffiti*, a look back at his 1950s home town (though the film was not actually made in Modesto).

St Stan's Brewery & Restaurant, *821 L St. (Hwy 132), Modesto CA 95354; tel: (209) 524-4782*, serves ales, lagers and German Alt-style beer under the motto, 'conceived in heaven, brewed in California'. The time-warped **A & W Drive In**, *14th and G Sts; tel: (209) 522-7700*, has 1950s-style root beer and hang-the-tray-on-the-car-door burger service by rollerskating carhops.

The **McHenry Mansion**, *906 15th St, Modesto CA 95354; tel: (209) 577-5341*, open Tues–Thurs, Sun 1300–1600, Fri 1200–1500, is a grande dame Italianate Victorian, cluttered with period objects as it was when built by a local rancher-banker in 1883. Down the street, the old library has become the **McHenry Museum**, *1402 I St, Modesto CA 95354; tel: (209) 577-5366*, open Tues–Sun 1200–1600. A doctor's office, school, and country store are among rooms showing ranching life a century ago. The **Great Valley Museum of Natural History**, *100 Stoddard Ave, Modesto CA 95350; tel: (209) 575-6196*, also has exhibits on the indigenous Miwok and Yokut native peoples.

MERCED

Tourist Information: Merced Conference and Visitors Bureau, *690 W. 16th St, Merced, CA 95340; tel: (800) 446-5353 or (209) 384-3333*, open Mon–Fri 0830–1700, has information on lodging, including *BW* and *TL*, and provides a guide to Merced's history.

The 1875 **County Courthouse**, *21st and N Sts*, houses the county museum's local history exhibits in restored offices and court chambers. The exterior bears a striking resemblance to the California State Capitol Building in Sacramento, and is set in a lovely, shady park. Dinner is an excuse to see a collection of cattle branding irons and soak up Western atmosphere at **The Branding Iron Restaurant**, *640 W. 16th St; tel: (209) 722-1822*. Moderate–pricey.

MARIPOSA

Tourist Information: Mariposa County Chamber of Commerce, at the North Hwy 49/Hwy 140 junction, PO Box 425, Mariposa, CA 95338; tel: (209) 966-2456. The **Mariposa Ranger District**, at the South Hwy 49/Hwy 140 junction, PO Box 747, Mariposa, CA 95338; tel: (209) 966-3638, has information on camping, walking, and other outdoor activities.

Accommodation

Mariposa is close enough to Yosemite to attract summer crowds, so there are a reasonable number of motels, inns, and bed and breakfasts in the area, including AY and BW. Advance bookings are required in summer and strongly recommended the rest of the year. For bed and breakfast bookings, contact the **Yosemite-Mariposa Bed and Breakfast Association**, PO Box 1100, Mariposa, CA 95338; tel: (209) 742-7666. The Chamber of Commerce has a lodgings list, but cannot make bookings.

Eating and Drinking

Best bet for Mexican food is **Castillo's**, 4995 5th St; tel: (209) 742-4413, budget prices. A local favourite, also budget, is the **Country Pantry**, 5029 Charles St; tel: (209) 966-4097.

Sightseeing

This small town (the name means 'butterfly' in Spanish) is the most southerly of the major Gold Rush camps, when it was called Logtown. Captain John Fremont put Mariposa on the map by purchasing a nearby Mexican land grant in 1847. His purchase didn't include Logtown, but when gold was discovered two years later, he redrew the grant boundaries to include the mine and renamed the town to bolster his scheme. The hills surrounding Mariposa are filled with ghost towns, most of them abandoned even before they could be recorded on the maps of the day. The wide, peaceful streets and old homes make it a pleasant stop.

Visitors aren't encouraged to look for Fremont's **Mariposa Mine**, which sits, unmarked, on a hillside behind **St Joseph's Catholic Church** cemetery. Since the gold rush

went flat, Mariposa has been a relative backwater. The local motto has long been 'if it isn't broken, use it'. The **Old Mariposa Jail**, on Bullion St between 4th and 5th Sts with natural rock walls 2 ft (61 cm) thick, was the local lock-up until 1960, then turned to other uses.

The blindingly white **Mariposa County Courthouse**, on Bullion St between 9th and 10th Sts; tel: (209) 966-2456, has been the seat of local government since it was built in 1854, making it the oldest government building in California still in use. Whatever government action there is happens at the courthouse, Mon–Fri, 0800–1700. Furnishings on the first floor are original, including simple benches and a potbellied wood stove. The ground floor is more utilitarian.

The **Mariposa County Historical Center**, 12th and Jessie Sts; tel: (209) 966-2924, is an excellent free museum in the same building as the public library. The collection includes Gold Rush relics, printing and mining equipment, an old apothecary, lady's boudoir, Miwok dwellings, a sheriff's office, and a miner's cabin, all with authentic furnishings. A miniature stamp mill with the interior exposed shows how gold ore was ground to powder for processing. A genuine five-stamp mill is outside, next to the mule-powered Mexican arrastra, or grinding wheel, that was used to grind ore for processing and corn for tortillas. **Mariposa Mining Supply**, 5027 Hwy 140, Mariposa, CA 95338; tel: (209) 966-356 has equipment and gold mining tours.

One of the world's largest gem and mineral collections is the **California State Mining and Mineral Museum**, at the county fairgrounds on Hwy 49, 1 mile (1.6 km) south of town, PO Box 1192, Mariposa, CA 95338; tel: (209) 742-7625, open Wed–Mon, 1000–1800. The mines around Mariposa were some of the richest in the Mother Lode; the museum's collection of more than 20,000 minerals, gold, diamonds, and other gems reflects the wealth that flowed through the town. Most of the exhibits are drawn from the over a century old California State mineral collection. Other exhibits include an assay office, stamp mill, and hard rock mine replica. The gift shop sells fine mineral specimens from around the world.

Mariposa

YOSEMITE NATIONAL PARK

Each year hundreds of thousands of visitors spend a week, often more, in Yosemite National Park, one of the natural wonders of the world. Even a cursory dash through the park's major sites takes a full day. Better still, allow a full day (or more) in Yosemite Valley and second day for the spring–autumn drive on Hwy 120 over Tioga Pass to Mono Lake.

Heavy snow closes the road over Tioga in winter, usually from mid-November until mid-May. Hwy 140 from Mariposa into Yosemite seldom closes. The park may be at its best in winter, when trees and waterfalls are rimmed with ice and the daily visitor count is in the hundreds rather than the tens of thousands. In autumn, winter, and spring, carry tyre chains in case of unexpected snowstorms.

Tourist Information

Yosemite Valley Visitors Center, *at the west end of Yosemite Village Mall; tel: (209) 372-0299,* open 0900-1700 daily. Must-haves are the park brochure and the current *Yosemite Magazine*, both free at park entrances.

For advance information, contact **Yosemite National Park**, *PO Box 577, Yosemite National Park, CA 95389; tel: (209) 372-0264/2000* for recorded visitor and road information. Information is also available from the **Western Region Information Center**, *National Park Service, Bldg 201, Fort Mason, San Francisco CA 94123; tel: (415) 556-0560.* **Caltrans** provides road information, *tel: (800) 427-7623.* The **Yosemite Snow Phone** has winter snow reports; *tel: (209) 372-1000.*

The **Yosemite Mountaineering School**, *Yosemite National Park, CA 95389; tel: (209) 372-1244,* has rock climbing information and

rentals as well as lessons. Beginners' climbing lessons are offered daily, intermediate classes on weekends and alternate weekdays. Call for advanced classes. Reservations are recommended, but there is occasional space for walk-in students.

Arriving

From San Francisco, follow the San Francisco–Yosemite Route (p. 281) through Mariposa. The park entrance is 32 miles (51 km) from Mariposa. The highway follows the Merced River canyon upstream into Yosemite. In summer the river is a placid trickle. During May and June, the spring snow melt turns the river into a raging torrent that froths and foams its way through the twisting canyon. The ledge on the opposite side of the river from the highway was the roadbed for a narrow-gauge railroad that once ran into Yosemite.

The most direct route into the park from Southern California is the **South Entrance Station**, following the Visalia–Yosemite Route (p. 267). The road divides just beyond the entrance station: to the right is the **Mariposa Grove** of sequoia redwoods; to the left is **Wawona** and the road to Yosemite Valley. The Valley is 35 miles (56 km) north of the South Entrance Station.

Getting Around

A one-way anti-clockwise loop road provides access to the Valley. Most of the road is lined with parking spaces on one or both sides. A paved walking/cycling trail runs parallel to the road.

Automobile is the main means of transport in the park, but the National Park Service is trying to change deeply ingrained habits and reduce traffic. Free shuttle buses circle Yosemite Valley all year. Seasonal shuttles (also free) serve other attractions such as the Badger Pass ski area, the Mariposa Grove of Giant Sequoias, and trailheads between Yosemite Valley and Mono Lake. Bicycles and walking are highly encouraged.

Accommodation

Yosemite Concession Services Corp., *Central Reservations, 5410 East Home, Fresno, CA*

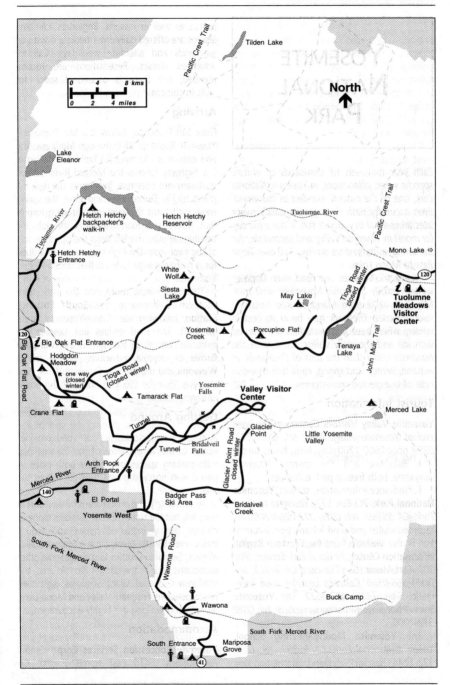

93727; tel: (209) 252-4848, controls nearly all lodging within the park. Reservations are accepted up to 366 days in advance and *are essential all year*. Choices include the pricey **Ahwahnee Hotel**, expensive **Wawona Hotel**, and moderate **Yosemite Lodge**, **White Wolf Lodge**, **Tuolumne Meadows Lodge** and **Camp Curry**. Only the Ahwahnee and Yosemite Lodge are open in winter.

Private accommodation includes **Yosemite West Condominiums** *near Badger Pass; tel: (209) 372-4240*, and **The Redwoods**, *PO Box 2085, Wawona, CA 95389; tel: (209) 375-6666*, a development of one- to five-bedroom homes. Other alternatives include **Fish Camp**, **Oakhurst**, and **Mariposa**. Winter lodging in surrounding communities is seldom a problem, but in summer unbooked space is extremely rare within several hours drive of Yosemite.

Campsite reservations are handled by **MISTIX**, *PO Box 85705, San Diego, CA 92138; tel: (800) 365-2267*. Advance reservations are essential in all seasons. During May–Sept, the Camp Curry **Campground Reservation Office** sometimes has last-minute cancellations, but demand is intense.

Backcountry camping is by permit only, obtainable from the visitor centre. Write as far in advance as possible. Half of the permits allotted for most wilderness areas are assigned in advance, the other half on a first-come, first-served basis during the season.

Eating and Drinking

Yosemite Concession Services Corp. controls food and drink as well as lodging. **The Ahwahnee Hotel's** cathedral-like dining room is pricey, dressy, and better for breakfast and lunch than at dinner – except for special events such as the **Vintners' Holidays** and the **Chefs' Holidays**, when dinners are outstanding.

The **Wawona Hotel**, at the south end of the park, is moderately priced and more casual than the Ahwahnee. Sunday Brunch is particularly good. The **Yosemite Lodge** has a budget-priced cafeteria and a moderate restaurant. The least expensive eatery in the park is the cheap–budget **Village Grill**, in Yosemite Village, with basic burgers and sandwiches. **Degnans Deli** and **The Loft** are variations on a similar theme. For picnics, the **Village Store** is a full grocery store, but supplies are markedly more expensive than outside the park. **Curry Village** and **Tuolumne Meadows** both have grills open until the first snowfall; the **Badger Pass Lodge** offers simple meals in winter only.

Sightseeing

Waves of glaciers carved Yosemite into a colossal landscape that captivated a Scottish immigrant and itinerant mountain wanderer named John Muir more than a century ago. It's a wild wonder of soaring granite, deep gorges, mountain meadows, and silent peaks that seem to touch the sky. Even Yosemite's trees are larger than life – **giant sequoias** in park groves are among the largest living organisms on the planet. **Yosemite Falls**, thundering 2425 ft (739 m) to the valley floor, is the tallest waterfall in North America and the fifth tallest in the world.

There are really three Yosemites within the park: Yosemite Valley, with the greatest concentration of attractions and visitors; the south park and Tioga Pass Rd, which are almost as crowded; and the back country, which is relatively untouched.

In retrospect, it's easy to blame Muir for the steadily growing popularity that has chipped away at Yosemite's beauty. His efforts were largely responsible for putting the spectacular landscape into a national park and preserving it. But his success at protecting Yosemite was due primarily to his success at promoting the place as unique in all the world. And Muir was one of the best promoters California has ever seen. Once word got out, people from around the world came to test his tales of astounding beauty, including the very first Thomas Cook tour of America in the 1870s. A century ago, it was a trickle of visitors. Today, park rangers warn of 'loving Yosemite to death'.

A torrent of around 4 million people pours into Yosemite every year. In summer, a transient city of 50,000 appears, complete with trash, traffic, smog, crime, drugs, noise, and a rootless population. Despite National Park Service efforts to limit the impact of visitors, congestion is the rule. Anyone who wants to enjoy even the

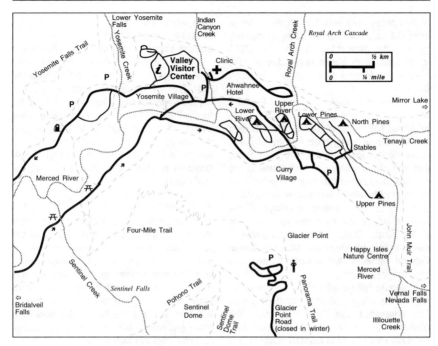

Labels on map: Lower Yosemite Falls, Yosemite Falls Trail, Yosemite Creek, Indian Canyon Creek, Royal Arch Creek, Royal Arch Cascade, Valley Visitor Center, Clinic, Yosemite Village, Ahwahnee Hotel, Mirror Lake, Lower River, Upper River, Lower Pines, North Pines, Tenaya Creek, Stables, Merced River, Curry Village, Upper Pines, John Muir Trail, Four-Mile Trail, Glacier Point, Happy Isles Nature Centre, Merced River, Sentinel Creek, Sentinel Falls, Pohono Trail, Panorama Trail, Vernal Falls, Nevada Falls, Bridalveil Falls, Sentinel Dome, Sentinel Dome Trail, Glacier Point Road (closed in winter), Illilouette Creek

0   ½ km
0   ¼ mile

semblance of solitude should plan to escape into the back country on foot as quickly as possible. Otherwise, visit early in the spring, late in the autumn, or, better still, in mid-winter, when crowds are at an absolute minimum. In any season, do whatever it takes to avoid visiting at weekends or holidays.

It's also wise to keep a distance from park animals. They can react unpredictably if approached too closely or surrounded. Black bears also frequent the valley in search of human food. Follow park recommendations for storing food out of bears' way. If a bear is spotted, alert park rangers.

Events

The biggest event of the Yosemite year is the **Bracebridge Dinner** at the Ahwahnee, a 1927 brainstorm from photographer Ansel Adams and friends. The three-hour pageant is modelled on the story of Squire Bracebridge in *The Sketch Book of Geoffrey Crayon, Gent.*, by Washington Irving. Look for a seven-course, full-dress processional 'English' feast with fish, peacock

pie, boar's head, baron of beef, and more. The entire event is accompanied by much poetic and musical silliness under the direction of The Lord of Misrule. Advance tickets for the five daily dinner seatings go quickly, so apply to the Yosemite Concession Services Corp. in early November for the next year.

The park boosts winter business with three-day seminars and demonstrations hosted by famous chefs at the **Chefs' Holidays** and equally famous California vintners at the **Vintners' Holidays**. The vintners normally come to Yosemite before Christmas, the chefs in January. Advance registration with the Yosemite Concession Services Corp. is required. Seminars and demos are free, but the final banquet dinners are pricey – and worth every penny.

Yosemite Valley

Yosemite has an activity for almost every interest, most of them centred on the Valley. For better or for worse, nearly all of the sights that made Yosemite famous line the sheer Valley walls, up to 3200 ft (975 m) high. On a busy summer day,

50,000 people may pass through the 7 square miles (18 square km) of the Valley, completely ignoring the other 1182 square miles (3061 square km) of park. **Yosemite Meadow** and the meandering **Merced River** occupy the valley floor.

Entering the Valley as Hwy 140 from Maricopa, the one-way loop road passes **Bridalveil Fall**, **Sentinel Dome**, the **wedding chapel**, **housekeeping tents** (on the left), and **Curry Village** before curving to the left at the east end of the valley with **Half Dome** in the distance. The road runs through campsites, then passes the **Ahwahnee Hotel** beneath the Valley wall, and comes to **Yosemite Village**. Village facilities include the **Park Headquarters** and **Valley Visitor Center**, **stores**, **restaurants**, a **medical clinic**, **bicycle rental**, **Museum**, **Indian Cultural Museum**, **Art Activity Center**, and other services.

Yosemite Fall cascades down the Valley wall beyond the Village, almost across the highway from **Yosemite Lodge**. The road continues to a connector for the return loop, or beyond, past the sheer rock face of **El Capitan** rising 7569 ft (2307m) above, and another return connector.

Glacier Point, perched some 3214 ft (977 m) above the valley floor, offers spectacular views of the Valley, Yosemite Falls, Half Dome and much of the park. However, it's a circuitous 25-mile (40 km) drive to get there. Leave the Valley by the Wawona Rd (Hwy 41) and turn left onto the Glacier Point Rd (closed in winter beyond the Badger Pass Ski Area) about 5 miles (8 km) after leaving the Valley. From the car park at the end of the road it's a short, easy (and well-trodden) walk to Glacier Point itself. A 1-mile (1.6 km) walk from the parking area leads to Sentinel Dome, 8122 ft (2476 m), 908 ft (275 m) above Glacier Point. On full moon nights the Valley below becomes a fairyland.

Walks

Start early to avoid the crowds, no matter what the season. It's a good idea to take water, since none is available on most trails. The most popular walks are the paved ½-mile (1 km) trails to **Lower Yosemite Fall** and **Bridalveil Fall**, on opposite sides of the Valley. The return walk to **Mirror Lake**, which reflects surrounding mountains, is 2 miles (3 km), most of it flat. With occasional help, all three trails can be navigated by wheelchairs.

One of the more popular longer Valley walks is the 3 mile (5 km) return hike up the **Vernal Fall Mist Trail** to **Vernal Fall**. Two miles (3 km) beyond is **Nevada Falls**. Most visitors take all day for the 7-mile (11 km) return trip because of the altitude. A special treat for the truly fit and determined is the 17-mile (27 km) return walk up the granite hemisphere forming the back of **Half Dome**. Steel cables anchored in the rock help the final ascent.

South Yosemite

To reach the **Mariposa Grove**, travelling from the south, turn right immediately beyond the South Entrance Station and follow the winding road 4 miles (6 km) east to the paved parking area. The road is closed to all caravans and RVs more than 25 ft in length because of restricted parking space. If grove parking is full, drive to Wawona and take the free shuttle back. The grove has toilets, drinking water, a museum, souvenir shop and walking trail.

Split rail fences protect the shallow roots of the giant sequoias that dot the parking area. The main grove is a two-minute stroll down a walking trail. During the summer an open air tram tours the grove. Near the start of the trail is the **Fallen Monarch**, immortalised in an 1899 photograph of an entire US Cavalry troop, including horses, posing atop the tree. **Grizzly Giant** is an estimated 2700 years old, one of the oldest living sequoias. The huge limb far up on the south side of the trunk is nearly 7 ft (2 m) in diameter, larger than any non-Sequoia tree in the area.

About 150 ft (46 m) beyond the Grizzly Giant is the **California Tunnel Tree**, cut in 1895 to allow stage-coaches to pass through. Millions of visitors passed through the **Wawona Tunnel Tree** between 1881, when it was cut open, and 1969, when it collapsed under the weight of a record snowpack. Weakened by the gigantic hole in its base, the tree may have died 1000 years prematurely. The **Mariposa Grove Museum** is on the site of a cabin built in 1861 by Galen Clark, the first official Guardian when the Yosemite Valley and Mariposa Grove were set aside as a state reserve in 1864. Yosemite became a National Park in 1890. The museum focuses on the natural history of the sequoias.

Return to Hwy 41. Follow the road past the entrance station to **Wawona Basin**. The valley, now largely taken over by a golf course, was a Native American encampment and site of a roadside hostel built by Galen Clark in 1857. Clark's Station was an overnight stop between Mariposa and the Yosemite Valley. The white Victorian gingerbread **Wawona Hotel** was built in 1875 and is still a popular holiday destination.

The golf course, directly across the highway from the hotel, is as popular with grazing deer and hunting coyotes as it is with golfers, especially in early morning and late afternoon. Coyotes shy away from humans but deer frequently cross to the hotel grounds in search of hand-outs. Biscuits, crisps and other human treats are harmful to the deer's health. Deer have also been known to bite the hands that feed them.

Just beyond the hotel is the **Yosemite Pioneer History Center**, which concentrates on the human history of Yosemite. The museum features a collection of historic cabins and other buildings moved to the site, plus several stage-coaches. There are stage-coach rides and living history demonstrations during the summer months.

Continue north on Hwy 41 toward Yosemite Valley, 27 miles (43 km) ahead. Fire scars are visible on both sides of the road in several places, the result of nearly a century of ruthless fire suppression in Yosemite. Until the 1960s, forest managers didn't realise that fire is an integral part of Sierra forests. Many forest species, including redwoods, need fire to regenerate. The seeds need the bare soil created by natural fires in order to germinate, and open sunlight to grow. Historically, late summer fires swept through these forests every 7 to 20 years, burning out undergrowth and fallen branches and leaving a layer of rich ash atop the bare soil. Years of fire suppression allowed underbrush, fallen limbs, and shade-tolerant trees to proliferate. When fires did start, they burned fiercely through the dense brush and down

wood that had built up. Instead of rejuvenating the forest, fire destroyed everything in its path, leaving vast tracts of charred tree trunks.

The solution is controlled fire, called 'management fires', set by park personnel during damp autumn weather when winds are calm. Watch for signs which warn of management fires ahead. *Any other fires should be reported to park personnel by dialling 911 from any telephone.*

Continue north on Hwy 41. The road follows the western boundary of the park, winding from the crest of one ridge to the next. 12 miles (19 km) beyond Wawona is a left turn toward **Yosemite West**, a private development just outside the park boundaries. The turnoff for **Badger Pass** and **Glacier Point** is a ½ mile (1 km) beyond Yosemite West. Turn right onto **Glacier Point Rd.** The narrow, winding road is closed to caravans and RVs, but coach tours leave from Yosemite Village during the summer.

Glacier Point Rd twists through forests of pine and fir. The road is open all year as far as the **Badger Pass Ski Area**. Badger Pass was the first commercial ski area in California. Most runs are beginner and intermediate. Park rangers also lead snowshoe walks into the deep snows that blanket the surrounding forests. The less energetic can ride snow cats, large tracked vehicles with open air seating, along forest roads. The remainder of the road is closed in winter, but cross-country skiers continue all the way to Glacier Point, overlooking Yosemite Valley, 3214 ft (977 m) below (see p. 290).

Return to Hwy 42 and turn right toward Yosemite Valley. **Inspiration Point** is 6 miles (10 km) beyond the junction, with a fine view of the **Gates of Yosemite**. The **Cathedral Rocks** are on the right, **El Capitan** on the left, with **Half Dome** rising 8842 ft (2695 m) in the background. Continue downhill through the tunnel to **Tunnel View**, the official viewpoint into Yosemite Valley. **Bridalveil Fall** is visible on the right. The view is on the left side of the road, but there is parking on both sides. Watch for pedestrians crossing the highway who are more intent on the view than oncoming traffic. The parking area for Bridalveil Fall, and the beginning of the Valley floor loop, is 1½ miles (3 km) below Tunnel View.

Sightseeing

Tioga Pass

Hwy 120, the **Tioga Pass Rd**, crosses the park from east to west and provides the only access from the eastern side of the Sierra. Most of the two-lane road is more scenic than vexing, but traffic can be heavy, especially on midsummer weekends. Allow 2 hrs for the 70-mile (112 km) drive without any stops.

From Yosemite Village, follow the Valley loop road 6½ miles (10.5 km), passing **El Capitan** on the right. An excellent **valley view** across the Merced River is on the left side of the road just beyond El Capitan. At the junction with Hwy 140, bear to the right on Big Oak Flat Rd toward Tioga Pass. The road begins climbing almost immediately, affording broad views across the Merced River canyon. There is an **observation point** just beyond the first tunnel. Turn right onto Hwy 120 7 miles (11 km) after the viewpoint, following signs for **Yosemite Institute, Tuolumne Grove, Tuolumne Meadows**, and **Tioga Pass**.

Or, for a look at what could have happened to Yosemite, continue on Big Oak Flat Rd to the **Big Oak Flat Entrance**. Turn right onto Evergreen Rd toward **Camp Mather**. Go straight to Hetch Hetchy Rd, re-enter Yosemite at the **Hetch Hetchy Entrance**, and continue to **Hetch Hetchy**. Hetch Hetchy Valley was the visual equal of Yosemite Valley until it was dammed and drowned to provide electricity and drinking water for San Francisco in 1913. The National Park Service was created in 1916, charged to preserve and protect National Park lands from similar commercial attacks in the future. Return to the Tioga Pass Rd. The 52 mile (83 km) return trip takes about two hours.

The **Yosemite Institute** is an outdoor education institute on the left side of the highway above the **Tuolumne Grove** of sequoias. Walk down to the grove (summer or winter) along a 1- mile (1.6 km) return trail. The grove contains 20 sequoias, including the **Dead Giant**, a tunnel tree that broke in two several years ago. Highway 120 is closed just beyond the grove in winter.

The road continues climbing beyond the grove, following low ridges and shallow valleys between peaks topping more than 10,000 ft (3048 m). The best guide to the sights, facilities, and geography on the drive is the *Yosemite Road Guide*, published by the Yosemite Association and on sale throughout the park. Most lay-bys and vista points have picnic tables and explanatory signs keyed to local geography, plants, or animals.

Siesta Lake, 14 miles (22 km) beyond the Tuolumne Grove, is a favourite photographic stop. The shallow lake, on the right side of the road, mirrors the surrounding forests and mountain peaks. **White Wolf**, 1 mile (1.6 km) beyond, has summer camping and eating facilities. **Tenaya Lake**, another 14 miles (22 km), is a favourite for fishing.

The highlight of the Tioga Pass Rd is **Tuolumne Meadows**, 6 miles (10 km) from Tenaya Lake. The high country meadows, 8600 ft (2621 m), are popular for camping, walking, fishing, and as a departure point for mountain climbing and backcountry exploration. Rangers at the **Visitor Center** conduct daily walks and evening educational programmes in summer. Petrol, groceries, a restaurant, post office, guides, horses, and other services are also available in summer.

The highway continues climbing toward **Tioga Pass**, 9945 ft (3031 m) and the **Tioga Pass Entrance Station** just beyond. Private food, petrol, and lodging facilities, as overpriced as any inside Yosemite, begin about 2 miles (3 km) below the park entrance. The last 12 miles (19 km) of highway take long, sweeping turns down the eastern side of the Sierra Nevada, with magnificent vistas up and down the **Lee Vining Canyon National Scenic Byway**. Watch for a viewpoint on the right side of the road overlooking **Tioga Lake**, 5 miles (8 km) below the entrance station. The panoramas across Mono Basin and beyond are magical, especially in the warm sunlight of late afternoon.

The 7% slope provides an exciting ride, swooping down the mountainside, but it can be extremely hard on the brakes, especially for RVs and caravans. The best driving tactic is to shift into low gear at Tioga Pass and use the brakes sparingly. The junction with Hwy 395 is 8 miles (13 km) beyond Tioga Lake. **Mono Lake** (see p.193) is straight ahead.

SAN FRANCISCO to OREGON BORDER

The route from San Francisco north to the Oregon border covers two of the state's most talked about and least seen areas, the coastal redwoods and the wild North Coast. Either route can be driven in one muscle-cramping, mind-numbing day, as long as you don't stop for the magnificent scenery or historic towns along the way. For sleep and safety as well as the scenery, allow at least 5 days to drive one way.

ROUTES

There are two alternative routes, either direct by Hwy 101 or following the coast for part of the way on Hwy 1. The two routes rejoin at Leggett. In addition, there is a third circuit which follows part of the coastal route and then returns you to San Francisco via the Anderson Valley. This chapter covers the towns on the direct route first, then goes back to describe those along the coastal route, with a final description of the Anderson valley wine region.

→ Direct Route

Take Hwy 101 north for 362 miles (579 km) from San Francisco to **Crescent City** near the Oregon border. Overnight near Santa Rosa, Ukiah, Garberville, Eureka, and Crescent City.

⌇⌇> Coastal Route

Take Hwy 101 north from San Francisco to the **Hwy 1 exit**, 3 miles (5 km) beyond the Golden Gate Bridge. Follow Hwy 1 north 188 miles (300 km) to **Leggett**. Rejoin Hwy 101 and the direct route. Overnight in West Marin County and near Mendocino, Fort Bragg, Garberville, Eureka, and Crescent City.

→ Anderson Valley Circuit

Follow the scenic route for 118 miles (189 km) as far as **Hwy 128**, just north of **Elk**. Take Hwy 128 through the **Anderson Valley** to **Hwy 101**, 57 miles (91 km) south and return to San Francisco, 86 miles (138 km) south. Allow at least 2 days, overnighting near Mendocino or in the Anderson Valley.

MARIN COUNTY

Tourist Information: Marin County Visitors Bureau, *30 N San Pedro Rd, Ste. 150, San Rafael, CA 94903; tel: (415) 472-7470.* For further descriptions of Marin County, see p. 228 (Marin County Route).

Take Hwy 101 out of San Francisco, over the Golden Gate Bridge. The freeway drops down a steep hill just north of San Rafael past the **Marin Civic Center**; *tel: (415) 499-7407,* on the right, the last major project by eccentric architect Frank Lloyd Wright. The pastiche of mission-style arches, blue tile roof, and futuristic gold tower houses Marin County's administrative offices and jail.

The population thins beyond San Rafael, an occasional hillside still visible between housing estates. **Novato** is a combination of sprawling dormitory estates and an old farming community. The historic **Old Town** area, centred around the **Novato History Museum**, *815 De Long Ave; tel: (415) 897-4320,* has antique tools, photographs, and relics.

The **Marin Museum of the American Indian**, *2200 Novato Blvd; tel: (415) 897-4064,* displays artifacts from Miwok and Pomo tribes that once lived in the area. **Olompali State Historic Park**, *PO Box 1400, Novato, CA 94948; tel: (415) 897-9963,* is 3 miles (5 km) north of Novato on Hwy 101 on the west side of the highway. The 700-acre (283 ha) ranch was a major Native American trading village before the Spanish arrived. A silver sixpence, circa 1567, discovered on the site suggests that Sir Francis Drake and his crew visited the area. Museum exhibits cover the Miwoks as well as later Spanish Colonial and Victorian ranching eras. Continue 4 miles (6 km) north into **Sonoma County**.

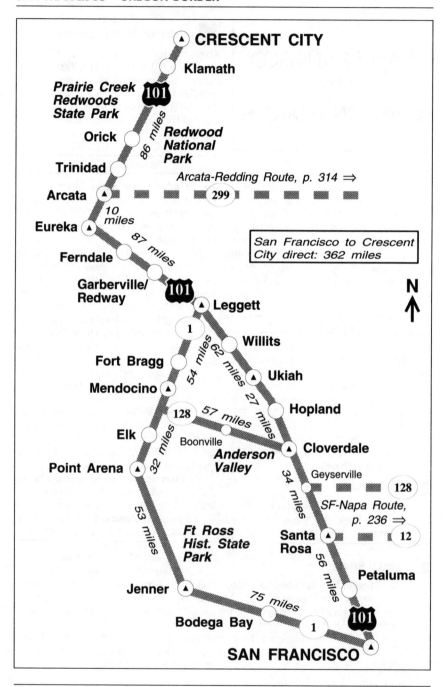

CRESCENT CITY

Klamath

101

Prairie Creek
Redwoods
State Park

Orick

86 miles

Redwood
National
Park

Trinidad

Arcata

Arcata-Redding Route, p. 314 ⇒

299

10 miles

Eureka

87 miles

Ferndale

San Francisco to Crescent
City direct: 362 miles

Garberville/
Redway

101

N
↑

Leggett

1

62 miles

Willits

Fort Bragg

54 miles

Ukiah

Mendocino

27 miles

Hopland

128

57 miles

Elk

Boonville

Anderson
Valley

Cloverdale

Point Arena

32 miles

Geyserville

128

34 miles

SF-Napa Route,
p. 236 ⇒

53 miles

Ft Ross
Hist. State
Park

Santa
Rosa

12

Petaluma

56 miles

Jenner

75 miles

Bodega Bay

1

101

SAN FRANCISCO

PETALUMA

Tourist Information: Sonoma County Convention and Visitors Bureau, *500 Roberts Lake Road, Rohnert Park, CA 94928; tel: (707) 586-8100 or 800-326-7666;* and the **Petaluma Chamber of Commerce**, *215 Howard St, Petaluma, CA 94952; tel: (707) 762-2785.*

Accommodation and Food

Petaluma has *BW* and *QI*, but few other choices. For free bookings in Petaluma and the rest of Sonoma County; *tel: (800) 5-SONOMA (800-576-6662).*

The **Creamery Store**, *711 Western Ave; tel: (707) 778-1234*, has budget picnic makings plus tours of the California Cooperative Creamery cheese plant and more than 600 'cow' gifts. **Dempsey's Alehouse**, in the Golden Eagle Center, *50 E Washington; tel: (707) 765-9694*, is a budget–moderate brewpub. Everything is homemade, including the spicy nuts and jerky. The **Petaluma Queen**, *255 Weller St; tel: (707) 762-2100*, is pricey because all meals on this sternwheel riverboat include a cruise on the Petaluma River. **Cattleman's Restaurant**, *Hwy 101 at Penngrove; tel: (707) 763-4114*, moderate, specialises in enormous steaks. The **Marin French Cheese Co.**, *7500 Red Hill Rd; tel: (707) 762-6001*, has fine local brie and camembert cheeses and factory tours. **Sonoma County Farm Trails**; *PO Box 6032, Santa Rosa, CA 95406; tel: (707) 586-3276*, has a free driving guide to county farm products.

Sightseeing

Old Petaluma, west of the freeway, has one of the finest collections of iron front Victorian commercial buildings in the country. Scores of stately Victorian homes stand on tree-shaded streets. Many neighbourhoods are so quintessentially 'American' that Petaluma has become a cinematic favourite. Famous Petaluma films include *American Graffiti*, *Peggy Sue Got Married*, and *Basic Instinct*, plus political adverts.

The town began as *Casa Grande*, the two-storey adobe headquarters for Rancho Petaluma, Gen. Mariano Vallejo's 1836 bastion against Russian fur traders at Fort Ross. The adobe is the centrepiece of **Petaluma Adobe State Historic Park**, *3325 Adobe Rd; tel: (707) 778-4398*, furnished with period candles, tools, leather goods, clothing, and furniture. In the late 19th century, a local inventor perfected a chicken incubator and Petaluma became 'The World's Egg Basket.' **Petaluma Historical Library and Museum**, *20 4th St; tel: (707) 762-4871*, covers life in the quietly prosperous 19th-century river and farming community. Most of the old downtown survived long enough to become a Historic District. The Chamber of Commerce publishes two self-guided walking maps: *Streets of Petaluma* concentrates on the riverside downtown area and *Victorian Homes of Petaluma* covers cafés, bookstores, antique shops, and houses in six nearby blocks.

Hwy 101 plunges into farmland and gum groves on the way to **Santa Rosa** and the **Wine Country** (for more on wineries, see San Francisco–Napa Valley Route, p. 236).

SANTA ROSA

Tourist Information: Greater Santa Rosa Conference & Visitors Bureau, *637 First St, Santa Rosa, CA 95404; tel: (707) 577-8674.*

Accommodation

Santa Rosa has dozens of bed and breakfasts, hotels, and motels, including *BW, DI, M6,* and *TL*. For bookings; *tel: 800-576-6662*. The **Wine County Inns of Sonoma County** brochure, *PO Box 51, Geyserville, CA 95441; tel: (707) 433-4231*, is a good B&B guide. The closest camping is at **Spring Lake**, *5585 Newanga Ave; tel: (707) 539-8092*, on the eastern edge of town.

Eating and Drinking

All the familiar fast food joints are in Santa Rosa. So is **Santa Rosa Brewing**, *458 B St, Santa Rosa, CA 95401; tel: (707) 544-4677*, with budget gourmet burgers and pizza to accompany beer made on the ground floor. **Mixx**, *135 Fourth St; tel: (707) 573-1344)*, budget–moderate, offers a constantly changing parade of sandwiches, fresh seafood, venison, pasta, and sinfully rich deserts. Mixx is among several eateries in **Railroad Square**.

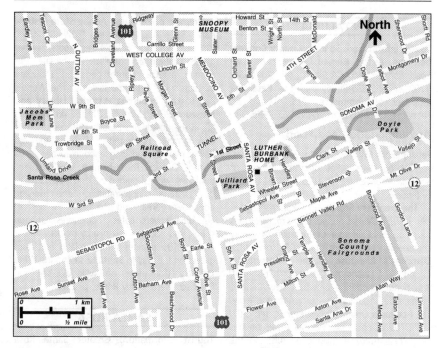

Sightseeing

Most downtown buildings disappeared in the 1906 San Francisco earthquake; most of the survivors perished beneath the wrecker's ball in later decades. The **Railroad Square Historic District**, *west of Hwy 101 between the railroad tracks, 3rd St, and 6th St,* is a restored 1920s shopping and entertainment area. The depot was one of the few buildings to survive the 1906 quake. **Luther Burbank Home & Gardens**, *Santa Rosa and Sonoma Aves, PO Box 1678, Santa Rosa, CA 95402; tel: (707) 524-5445,* preserves the gardens and home of the plant wizard who introduced more than 800 different fruits, nuts, grains, vegetables, and flowers. Burbank's restored horticultural garden is open all year; the house, with original furnishings, is open April–mid-October for guided tours. **Smith and Hawken**, *360 Sutton Place, Santa Rosa, CA 95401; tel: (707) 585-9481,* has the best garden tools money can buy and great bargains on overstocks and seconds.

The **Church of One Tree/Ripley Museum,** *across from the Burbank Gardens, 492 Sonoma Ave, Santa Rosa, CA 95401; tel: (707) 524-5233,* is a Gothic church built of wood from a single coastal redwood tree. The church, made famous by Robert L. Ripley in his 'Believe It Or Not!' newspaper column, is now a museum devoted to Ripley, one of Santa Rosa's more noted citizens. Charles Schulz, creator of the *Peanuts* cartoon series, owns **Redwood Empire Ice Arena**, *Steele Lane, tel: (707) 546-7147,* and the **Snoopy Museum**, next door; *tel: (707) 546-3385.*

Vineyards begin appearing along the freeway north of Santa Rosa. For a closer (and slower) look at wineries and vineyards, follow **Old Redwood Highway**, roughly paralleling the freeway for 28 miles (45 km) through **Healdsburg** and **Geyserville** (see San Francisco–Napa Valley Route, p. 236) to **Cloverdale**.

CLOVERDALE

Tourist Information: Cloverdale Chamber of Commerce, *132 S. Cloverdale Blvd, Cloverdale, CA 95425; tel: (7078) 894-4470.*

Hwy 101 narrows into Cloverdale Blvd, the main street through town. Local police wait for northbound drivers maintaining highway speeds into town, which can lead to expensive traffic fines. A by-pass is planned.

The **Cloverdale Historical Museum**, *215 North Cloverdale Blvd; tel: (707) 894-2067*, displays local memorabilia, including an old-time general store. Hwy 128 from the Anderson Valley joins Hwy 101 north of Cloverdale (see p. 296)

Hwy 101 climbs through forested foothills immediately north of Cloverdale, then drops into **Mendocino County** and a broad valley surrounding **Hopland**, 14 miles (22 km) north.

HOPLAND

Tourist Information: Hopland Chamber of Commerce, *PO Box 677, Hopland, CA 95449; tel: (707) 744-1171* and the **Mendocino County Convention and Visitors Bureau**, *PO Box 244, Ukiah, CA 95482; tel: (707) 462-3091*. **Mendocino County Vintners Association**, *PO Box 1409, Ukiah, CA 95482; tel: (707) 463-1704*.

Accommodation

The best (and almost the only) choice is the moderate **Thatcher Inn**, *13401 South Hwy 101; tel: (707) 4744-1890*. This restored Victorian bed and breakfast has an excellent restaurant, a lavish collection of single malt Scotch whiskies, and a cosy, club-style library.

Eating and Drinking

The **Mendocino Brewing Co.**, *13351 South Hwy 101; tel: (707) 744-1361*, was California's first modern brewpub when it opened in 1983. The beer is unremarkable, but a summer afternoon beneath the trellised hops in the garden is always welcome. The other choice is a sandwich from the deli at **Fetzer Vineyards**, *13500 South Hwy 101, Hopland, CA 95449; tel: (707) 744-1737*. **The Cheesecake Lady**, on Hwy 101; *tel: (707) 744-1441* has great cheesecake and other desserts.

Sightseeing

Fetzer Winery's ivy-covered brick buildings (with an extensive tasting room) are the centre of town. Other nearby wineries include **McDowell Valley Vineyards**, *3811 Hwy 175; tel: (707) 744-1053*; **Milano Winery**, *14594 South Hwy 101; tel: (707) 744-1396*; and **Dunnewood**, *13450 Hwy 101; tel: (707) 744-1728*. **Jepson Vineyards**, two miles (3 km) north at *10400 South Hwy 101; tel: (707) 468-8936*, also produces sparking wine and fine brandy. All are open for tastings; tours are by appointment only. Another 20 or so wineries are near Hwy 101, north to **Ukiah**, and in the **Redwood Valley**.

UKIAH

Tourist Information: Ukiah Chamber of Commerce, *495 East Perkins, Ukiah, CA 95482; tel: (707) 462-4705*.

Accommodation

Ukiah has a fair number of motels, including *BW*, *M6*, and *TL*. Best bets for bed and breakfast include **Oak Knoll**, *858 Sanel Dr; tel: (707) 468-5646*, and **Sanford House**, *306 South Pine; tel: (707) 4626-1653*, both moderate. The renovated **Vichy Springs Resort and Inn**, *2605 Vichy Springs Rd; tel: (707) 462-9515*, a mineral springs resort that rated raves from Robert Louis Stevenson, and remains popular for its relaxed atmosphere and moderate prices.

Lake Mendocino, *1160 Lake Mendocino Dr; tel: (707) 462-7581*, has camping.

Eating and Drinking

The familiar fast food choices are visible from the freeway. **Angel's Mexican Food**, *499 North State St; tel: (707) 463-3735* offers budget Mexican dishes. **North State Café**, *247 North State St; tel: (707) 462-3726*, serves budget breakfast and lunch, moderate dinner, with grilled meat and fish, pasta, and pizzas. **City of Ten Thousand Buddhas**, *end of Talmage Rd; tel: (707) 462-0939* serves cheap–budget vegetarian fare at a Buddhist university and monastery. Stop at the administration office for directions.

Schat's Courthouse Bakery and Café, *113 West Perkins St; tel: (707) 462-1670* is a wildly popular budget lunch eatery.

Sightseeing

'Ukiah' means 'deep valley' in the language of the Pomo, the Native Americans who once inhabited the area. Today, they're most visible at the **Pomo Visitor Center,** *north end of Lake Mendocino,* and the **Grace Hudson Museum and Sun House,** *431 Main St; tel: (707) 462-3370,* housing Hudson's Pomo portraits as well as one of the best Native American basket and artifact collections in North America. Historical buildings include the 1891 **Palace Hotel,** *272 North State St* and **Moore's Flour Mill,** *South State St.* The **Mendocino County Historical Society,** *603 West Perkins; tel: (707) 462-6969* has tour information.

Hot springs and wineries are the other major attractions. **Vichy Springs Resort** is a state historical landmark and popular getaway. **Orr Hot Springs,** 14 miles (22 km) northwest, *13201 Orr Springs Rd; tel: (707) 462-6277* is a very private (the winding road discourages visitors) and mostly nude spa dating back to stage-coach days.

The **Mendocino County Vintners Association,** *PO Box 1409, Ukiah, CA 95482; tel: (707) 463-1704,* produces winery tour maps. **Parducci Wine Cellars,** *501 Parducci Rd; tel: (707) 462-3828,* offers tours and an excellent winemaking video as well as tasting, sales, and a shady picnic area. **Weibel Champagne Cellars,** 5 miles (8 km) north, *7051 North State St; tel: (707) 485-0321,* has tasting and picnicking. **Alambic Inc.,** *PO Box 175, Ukiah, CA 95482; tel: (707) 462-3221* produces brandies to match the finest French Cognacs. Most local wineries are in **Redwood Valley,** seven miles (11 km) north of Ukiah. Hwy 101 winds 14 miles (22 km) through a succession of small valleys and hills to **Willits**.

WILLITS

Tourist Information: Willits Chamber of Commerce, *239 South Main St, Willits, CA 95490; tel: (707) 459-7910.*

Hwy 20, the only road inland from Fort Bragg, ends at Willits. So does the **Skunk Train,** *PO Box 907, Fort Bragg, CA 95437; tel: (707) 964-6371,* chugging through some of the most rugged scenery in Northern California from Fort Bragg, 40 miles (64 km) west (see p. 312). **Willits Station,** *East Commercial Street,* is slightly frumpy for modern tastes, but was carefully built of the finest redwood lumber the railroad once carried. The **Mendocino County Museum,** *400 East Commercial St; tel: (707) 459-2736,* is a storehouse of the past, including oral histories, Pomo and Yuki baskets, handmade quilts, and other local artifacts.

One of California's more eccentric characters, stage-coach robber Black Bart, worked the steep slopes of **Ridgewood Summit,** just south of Willits. The well-dressed bandit always left his victims with a bit of doggerel in return for their valuables. The large rock opposite the **White Deer Lodge,** *16580 North Hwy 101, Ridgewood summit, CA 95490; tel: (707) 459-4047,* was his favourite local hiding spot.

Towns become smaller north of Willits, fewer, and farther between. Hwy 101 follows rivers and creeks, then climbs ridges to drop into the next northbound valley or canyon. The road jumps from freeway to four-lane to two-lane and back again, depending on how difficult local geography makes road-building.

Towns like **Laytonville,** 24 miles (38 km) north of Willits, are in no hurry to see the freeway extended. Roadside businesses such as the **Cottage Motel,** *44901 Hwy 101, Laytonville, CA 95454; tel: (707) 984-6480* and **Laytonville Farms,** *43701 North Hwy 101; tel: (707) 984-8448,* survive on tourist traffic. Attractions in the area include the **Eel River,** with salmon, steelhead, and trout fishing in season, and large tracts of forest with deer, quail, and wild boar.

The highway climbs into the **Coast Range** toward **Rattlesnake Summit,** 1790 ft (591 m), 8 miles (13 km) north of Laytonville. The road expands to four lanes just beyond the summit and drops into **Leggett** and the Highway 1 junction. Old Hwy 101, renamed Hwy 271, winds through the Eel River Canyon to Hwy 1, just west of modern 101.

LEGGETT

This small, one-time lumber town is sometimes

called the Gateway to the Redwoods. The first of a long string of redwoods parks, **Standish-Hickey State Recreation Area**, *PO Box 208, Leggett, CA 95455; tel: (707) 925-6482* and **Smithe Redwoods State Reserve**; *tel: (707) 247-3318*, are just north of town. Road signs begin calling Hwy 101 'The Redwood Highway.'

Accommodation

Eel River Redwoods AYH Hostel, *70400 Hwy 101, Leggett, CA 95455; tel: (707) 925-6469*, is open all year. The few motels in town cater mainly to hunters and fishermen.

Full-sized cars can drive through the **Chandelier Tree** at **Drive-Thru Tree Park**, *Drive Thru Tree Rd and Hwy 1; tel: (707) 925-6464*. The tree towers 315 ft (104 m) tall and is 21 ft (6.9 m) in diameter at the base. The park also holds 200 acres (81 ha) of virgin redwood forest. Hwy 101 continues north through the **Eel River Canyon**.

Sightseeing

The Redwood Highway has several attractions along the lines of the Drive Thru Tree. **The World Famous Tree House**, 3 miles (5 km) north of Leggett, has a room 21 ft by 27 ft (6.9 m x 8.9 m) with a 50-ft (16.5 m) ceiling inside a living tree 250 ft (82.5 m) tall.

Just north is **Confusion Hill**, a miniature railroad through a redwood grove to a hilltop where optical illusions seem to tilt the force of gravity on its ear.

Confusion Hill is a good introduction to **Humboldt County**, where many things seem a little off centre. Rough coastal waters occasionally turn into fairytale cities, complete with towers, spires, gates, and moats. It's the fog, which is more common than sunshine in every season. The area was spotted by Sir Francis Drake and other early Europeans, but remained

---

Coastal Redwoods

Sequoia sempervirens, coastal redwoods, are the tallest living trees in the world. Heights of 300 ft (99 m) are common, the tallest yet measured is 368 ft (121 m). When the Spanish came to California, coastal redwoods were common as far south as Santa Cruz; 150 years of logging has pushed the species to the brink of extinction outside protected park areas.

Coastal redwoods grow in sheltered, foggy areas, clustered in dense groves, branches and shallow roots intertwined for support. Fog collects on the dense tangle of branches and needles, dripping onto the mat of roots just below the surface. It's an efficient system to support fast growth (200 ft, 66 m, per century), not so efficient to support the trees themselves. The tall, top-heavy redwoods easily fall victim to heavy winds and soil erosion.

Fortunately, coastal redwoods seldom die. When trees fall (or are cut), a ring of bright green shoots quickly appears around the base of the old tree, creating a fairy circle of new trees. Walking into these rings a few centuries later is like entering a series of living, intertwined cathedrals, the sunlight filtering down in focused beams or the branches shrouded in silent, drifting mist.

Native Americans generally avoided the deep redwood forests, considering them the realm of spirits and ancestors. It's easy to see why. Not only do the dense forests *look* ethereal, the trees themselves are amazingly resilient. If a redwood falls, the roots regenerate. If it doesn't fall, almost nothing can kill it. The bark is over 1 ft (30 cm) thick and resistant to fire. The wood itself resists insects, fungus, water, and decay. If the interior is burned or cut away, the tree survives.

The same characteristics make redwood a valuable timber resource. Timber companies are harvesting, i.e, cutting, as quickly as possible. Environmental groups are working just as feverishly to block further harvest through legal action, legislation, and buying forests. Either way, the Northern California timber industry seems destined to run out of trees in the relatively near future.

---

untouched by outsiders for nearly three centuries – the rocky coast has few beaches and fewer natural harbours. The deep, rich soil that produced the lush redwood forests is notoriously unstable. Landslides are common, even without help from poorly built roads and eager loggers. Geological faults could bring quakes to equal anything the world has seen this century. The coast northward is exposed to tsunamis, or tidal waves, produced by earthquakes elsewhere around the Pacific Ocean.

All this natural uncertainty has helped limit human intrusion. Hwy 101 is not just main highway, it's often the *only* highway, parts of it still only two lanes wide, including the section through **Richardson Grove State Park**, *PO Box E, Garberville, CA 95440; tel: (707) 247-3318*. The park has over 800 acres (324 ha) of redwood groves and three extremely popular campgrounds. Advance bookings through **MISTIX**; *tel: (800) 444-7275*, are essential in summer, but few visitors hike beyond the campgrounds. The **Seven Parks Natural History Association**, in the Visitor Center at **Grove Lodge**, *1600 Hwy 101*, has a good selection of redwood-related books, maps, and gifts.

Just north of the park is the **Benbow Inn**, *445 Lake Benbow Dr, Garberville, CA 95440; tel: (707) 923-2124*, overlooking the Eel River. The Tudor-style country inn (expensive rooms, moderate–pricey restaurant) counts Herbert Hoover, Charles Laughton and Eleanor Roosevelt among past guests.

Benbow Lake State Recreation Area, *Garberville, CA 95440; tel: (707) 923-3238*, has camping, picnicking, hiking, sailing, canoeing, and windsurfing. Summer activities include a jazz festival, a Shakespeare festival, and an arts fair. Summer campsites go quickly; book through **MISTIX**; *tel: (800) 444-7275*, or try the private **Benbow RV Resort**, *7000 Benbow Valley Dr, Garberville, CA 95440; tel: (707) 923-2777*.

GARBERVILLE/REDWAY

Tourist Information: Garberville/Redway Chamber of Commerce, *773 Redwood Dr, Garberville, CA 95542; tel: (707) 923-2613*.

Accommodation and Food

Most of Garberville is within two blocks of Business 101, Redwood Drive, including *BW* and other motels.

The moderate **Mateel Café**, *478 Redwood Dr.; tel: (707) 923-2030*, is a local food mecca. **Sicilito's**, *445 Conger Lane,; tel: (707) 923-2814*, has budget–moderate Italian, Mexican, and pizza.

Sightseeing

Garberville was once called the marijuana capital of the world, a title locals would rather forget. The crop brought prosperity and unwelcome law enforcement attention from as far away as Washington, DC. Conversation now leans toward hunting, fishing, redwoods, and the early August **Reggae on the River**, *tel: (707) 923-3368*, the largest reggae music festival on the West Coast. Two small sections of **Humboldt Redwoods State Park** are just north.

The **Avenue of the Giants**, *Avenue of the Giants Association, PO Box 1000, Miranda, CA 95553; tel: (707) 923-2555*, begins 7 miles (11 km) north of Garberville. This 33-mile (53 km) strip of old Hwy 101 (now Hwy 254) winds through some of the largest surviving groves of redwoods in Humboldt and Del Norte Counties. Most of the redwoods along the Avenue are within the boundaries of **Humboldt Redwoods State Park**, *PO Box 100, Weott, CA 95571; tel: (707) 946-2409*. The park contains over 50,000 acres (20,235 ha), including 17,000 acres (6880 ha) of old growth redwoods.

A few sections of the Avenue remain in private hands. The owners, primarily timber companies, have kept a visual screen of trees along the Avenue as part of an ongoing campaign to convince the public that logging has no negative impacts. For a look at the same countryside when the loggers have finished, follow any road east from the Avenue, especially along the northern end of the drive from Redcrest. Redwoods are quickly replaced by bare, often heavily eroded slopes or plantations of Douglas fir.

Park lands along the Avenue are filled with picnic areas, campgrounds, and walking trails.

Self-guided driving tour brochures are available at both ends of the Avenue. The park headquarters and visitors centre are located next to the **Burlington Campground**, near the town of **Weott**, in the middle of the Avenue. Advance campground bookings are necessary during the summer; **MISTIX**; *tel: (800) 444-7275.*

Private lands along the Avenue have their own attractions. **One Log House**, *Phillipsville, CA 95559; tel: (707) 943-3258*, is a 2100-year old redwood hollowed out into a single room 7 ft (2.3 m) tall and 32 ft (10.6 m) long and mounted on wheels in 1946. The **Chimney Tree, Hobbiton, USA**, also in Phillipsville, *tel: 923-2265*, is a redwood gutted by fire in 1914 and still thriving amidst a miniature theme park based on J.R.R. Tolkien's *The Hobbit.*

One of California's oldest tourist traps is the **Shrine Drive-Thru Tree**, *Meyers Flat; tel: (707) 943-3154*. Wagon travellers used to pull their vehicles through the same burned-out gap in the base of the tree.

The towns along the Avenue were once dependent on the lumber industry. Today, the remaining residents of **Phillipsville, Miranda, Myers Flat, Weott, Redcrest**, and **Pepperwood** depend on the tourist trade. Most towns offer petrol, food, and lodging, although prices are higher than in Garberville, to the south, or Fortuna, to the north. In the 1950s, there were dozens of lumber mills in these Eel River towns. The sole survivor, Eel River Sawmills, in Redcrest, is not open for tours.

The **Pacific Lumber Company (PALCO)**, *PO Box 37, Scotia, CA 95565; tel: (707) 764-2222*, owns a demonstration forest on the east side of Hwy 101 at the north end of the Avenue of the Giants. **Scotia**, 3 miles (5 km) north, is PALCO's company town. PALCO traditionally looked after employees from conception to death in return for unquestioning loyalty. Whether the decades-old bargain can withstand modern economic stresses (including a debt-ridden buyout) is open to question, but mill and town remain.

PALCO's self-guided **mill tour** is one of the most impressive industrial tours in California. Pick up free tickets at the mill office during the winter and the **Scotia Museum** in summer, both on Main St. The one-hour tour starts with debark-ing, where thundering jets of steam blast the bark from giant logs, and ends with stacks of finished lumber ready to be shipped around the world. Comfortable walking shoes are a must, ear plugs a good idea. The Museum is a stylised Greek temple, with redwood logs replacing marble columns. The former bank building houses history exhibits on PALCO and the local lumber industry. The **Scotia Inn**, Mill and Main Sts, *PO Box 248, Scotia, CA 95565; tel: (707) 764-5683* is a moderate–pricey hotel once used by company executives. The moderate restaurant is among the best on the north coast.

Rio Dell, just across the Eel River from Scotia, was home for non-PALCO workers in the area. **Rio Dell/Scotia Chamber of Commerce**, *715 Wildwood Ave, Rio Dell, CA 95562; tel: (707) 764-3436*. Both towns were heavily damaged in an April 1992 earthquake and have been largely rebuilt.

From Rio Dell, take Blue Slide Rd north and east as it becomes Grizzly Bluff Rd. **Ferndale** is 11 twisting miles (18 km) north over heavily forested mountains and across one of the finest dairy pasturages in the state and is probably the most completely preserved and restored Victorian village in California.

FERNDALE

Tourist Information: Ferndale Chamber of Commerce, *PO Box 325, Ferndale, CA 95536; tel: (707) 786-4477.*

Accommodation and Food

This is bed and breakfast country; advance bookings are essential all year. The Chamber of Commerce has the latest listing. Alternatively, you can stay in nearby Eureka. The **Humboldt County Fairgrounds**, off *Van Ness at 5th; tel: (707) 786-9511* has tent and RV spaces except during the late summer rodeo, racing and county fair season.

The **Ferndale Meat Company**, *376 Main St; tel: (707) 786-4501*, makes a good selection of local smoked sausages and other meats for picnics. **Victorian Inn**, *400 Ocean Ave; tel: (707) 725-9686* has moderate lunches and dinners amidst Henry Ford memorabilia.

Sightseeing

Not much more than six blocks long by three blocks wide, Ferndale is filled with 'butterfat palaces', elegant Victorian homes and commercial buildings erected by the very successful dairy farmers who settled the area in the 1860s. The entire village is a California Historical Landmark. The easiest way to see Ferndale is on foot. The Chamber of Commerce publishes a free guide to historic buildings, which comprises almost every structure in town.

If time is short, concentrate on the three blocks of **Main St** between Ocean and Shaw Sts, the historic commercial centre. Highlights include the **Golden Gait Mercantile**, 421 Main, the **Bank of America**, 394 Main, and **The Ferndale Enterprise**, 334 Main.

The best known building is the **Gingerbread Mansion**, 400 Berding; tel: (707) 786-4000, a Queen Anne–Eastlake Stick dripping with gingerbread, frosting, and almost every other ornamentation obtainable, surrounded by a formal English-style garden. The mansion is a popular, and pricey, bed and breakfast. Tours are given for non-guests. The **Ferndale Museum**, Shaw and Third Sts; tel: (707) 786-4466, explores local history in great detail.

Follow Main St north toward **Eureka** through pastures and dairy cows half-hidden in the tall grass. Cross the Eel River and turn left on **Eel River Dr.** to **Loleta** and the **Loleta Cheese Factory**, 252 Loleta Dr, Loleta, CA 95551; tel: (707) 733-5470. The factory sells a 14 different cheeses made from local milk, including smoked salmon, jalapeno, and garlic.

Continue north on Eel River Rd to **Hookton Rd** and the **Humboldt Bay National Wildlife Refuge**, 1020 Ranch Rd, Loleta, CA 95551; tel: (707) 733-5406. More than 200 species of birds visit the refuge yearly. Peak viewing season for waterbirds and birds of prey is Sept–Mar; black brant and migratory shorebirds peak mid-Mar–late Apr; egrets, gulls, terns, cormorants, pelicans, and herons are common in summer.

Return to Hwy 101 on Hookton Rd and continue north 10 miles (16 km) to **Eureka**. The cheapest petrol in the area is along Broadway on the south end of town.

EUREKA

Tourist Information: Eureka Chamber of Commerce, 2112 Broadway, Eureka, CA 95501; tel: (707) 442-3738; and **Eureka/ Humboldt County Convention and Visitors Bureau**, 1034 2nd St, Eureka, CA 95501; tel: (707) 443-5097.

Accommodation

Eureka, the largest city on the North Coast, has the best choice of bed and breakfasts, hotels, and motels. Chains include BW, CI, RM, and TL. **Broadway** is 'motel row.' Other reasonable motels are along 4th St. **Eureka B&B Reservation Service**, PO Box 207, Eureka, CA 95502; tel: (707) 441-1215, books several local bed and breakfasts. The expensive **Eureka Inn**, 7th and F Sts; tel: (707) 442-6441, is a National Historic Landmark with all the modern luxuries. **The Carter House Inn**, 1033 3rd St, tel: (707) 445-1390, moderate–expensive, is a new bed and breakfast built to 1884 plans for a Victorian mansion.

Eating and Drinking

Seafood lovers are in luck: Fisherman's Wharf is the real thing, not a tourist trap. The cheap–moderate **Eureka Seafood Grotto**, 6th and Broadway; tel: (707) 443-2075, has been the locals' choice for years. **Café Marina**, Woodley Island; tel: (707) 443-2233, **Lazio's Seafood Restaurant**, 327 2nd St; tel: (707) 443-9717, and **The Sea Grill**, 316 E St; tel: (707) 443-7187, are other local favourites. The **Lost Coast Brewery and Café**, 617 4th St; tel: (707) 445-4480, keeps beer fans happy.

The Samoa Cookhouse, on the Samoa Peninsula; tel: (707) 442-1659, may be the last genuine loggers' cookhouse still serving. 'All you can eat' means enormous piles of surprisingly tasty pancakes, steaks, fried chicken, ham, turkey, vegetables, and pie, served family-style. Breakfast crowds are light, but go early at weekends. Expect to wait an hour for lunch or dinner in summer: budget–moderate. The attached museum is free. Follow Hwy 101 north to the Samoa Bridge, turn left, and left again to the town of Samoa.

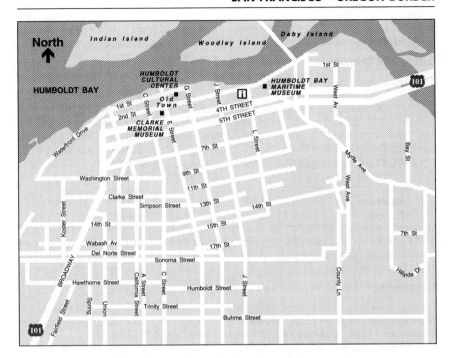

Sightseeing

Humboldt Bay, 10 miles (16 km) long, becomes **Arcata Bay** at the north, forming California's largest natural harbour north of San Francisco. Exhibits at the **Humboldt Bay Maritime Museum**, *1410 2nd St; tel: (707) 445-1910*, describe the bay and estuary. The museum's **M/V Madaket**, a 1910 Humboldt Bay ferry, explores the same waters on lunch, afternoon, or dinner cruises. Once a rich lumber town, Eureka has an equally rich heritage of fine Victorian buildings – a six-hour Chamber of Commerce tour passes a good portion of Eureka's 100 or so Victorians and 1000-plus 'architecturally significant' buildings. The Chamber also offers a free self-guided Victorian tour.

Old Town Eureka, 1st–3rd and C–G Sts, along the Bay, is the heart of Victorian and artsy Eureka. The Gothic, dollar-green **Carson Mansion**, at M and 2nd Sts, was built for local lumber baron William Carson. The mansion is a private club and closed to the public. **Clarke**

Memorial Museum, *240 E St; tel: (707) 443-1947*, concentrates on regional history, including notable collections of Native American basketry and ceremonial regalia. The **Humboldt Cultural Center**, *422 1st St; tel: (707) 442-2611*, explores the modern cultural diversity of the North Coast in an 1875 building that was once a ship's chandlery. Follow Hwy 101 north along the shores of Humboldt and Arcata Bay, but expect to encounter fog during the summer and rain during the winter.

ARCATA

Tourist Information: Arcata Chamber of Commerce, *1062 G St, Arcata, CA 95521; tel: (707) 822-3619*.

Accommodation

There's a better choice in Eureka, 10 miles (16 km) south, but Arcata prices are slightly lower. Chains include *BW, CI, M6*, and *QI*, plus bed and breakfasts. Tops in town is the moderate **Hotel**

Arcata, *708 9th St; tel: (707) 826-0217*, a nicely renovated historical landmark on the plaza.

Eating and Drinking

What Arcata doesn't have in accommodation it has in restaurants, thanks to Humboldt State University. **Wildflower Café and Bakery**, *1604 G St; tel: (707) 822-0360*, serves great bakery items and light meals at budget prices. **Humboldt Brewery**, *856 10th St; tel: (707) 826-2739*, has a following equally devoted to the blues, country, and folk musicians who play most evenings and to the budget-priced beer and food. **Casa de Que Pasa**, *854 9th St; tel: (707) 822-3441*, serves large portions of budget–moderate Mexican food. **Ottavio's**, *686 F St; tel: (707) 822-4021*, has moderately-priced gourmet fare from around the world. Most restaurants in Arcata are non-smoking.

Sightseeing

The high point of each year is the three-day **World Championship Great Arcata to Ferndale Cross-Country Kinetic Sculpture Race**, *PO Box 916, Ferndale, CA 95536; tel: (707) 725-3851*. The vague rules are open to a wild variety of interpretation: people-powered moving 'sculptures' (help from wind, water, or gravity is allowed) must float, roll, flounder, or otherwise move through 38 miles (49 km) of water, sand, and slime between Arcata and Ferndale. The ultimate prize is not first, but the Aurea Mediocritas, for the sculpture finishing closest to the middle. Why? First and last are extremes, while perfection lies in the middle.

Redwood Park and the **Arcata Community Forest**, east of downtown and the freeway, have 620 acres (251 ha) of redwood groves and conifer forests with 17 miles (27 km) of walking trails. Nearby **Humboldt State University** has a good **arboretum**, **fish hatchery**, and **art gallery**. The University's **Natural History Museum**, *13th and G St; tel: (707) 826-4479*, has local natural history displays as well as an impressive fossil collection. The downtown **plaza** has palm trees and plenty of people-watching from benches or surrounding cafés. **Jacoby's Storehouse**, *8th and H Sts.*, a stone and brick gem which houses several businesses, is one of

21 historic buildings on a self-guided architectural tour. Maps are available from the Chamber of Commerce.

Arcata Marsh and Wildlife Preserve, along Arcata Bay at the south end of town, is a redeveloped landfill and sewage treatment area with more than 200 bird species. The Audubon Society offers guided walks every Saturday; the **North Coast Environmental Center**, *879 9th St; tel: (707) 822-6918*, has details. **The Lanphere-Christensen Dunes Preserve**, *6800 Lanphere Rd; tel: (707) 822-6378*, is a 213-acre (86 ha) preserve on the Samoa Peninsula near the Mad River Slough. The preserve is open for public tours Saturday mornings.

Hwy 101 curves west toward the Pacific Ocean north of Arcata. **McKinleyville** is an Arcata suburb, but **McKinleyville Vista Point** has good whale-watching during the winter migration months. Just north is **Clam Beach County Park**, a good spot to search for agates and moonstones. **Little River State Beach**; *tel: (707) 677-3570*, next door, has broad sandy beaches and good sand dunes.

Arcata is the starting point for the Arcata–Redding Route, p. 314.

TRINIDAD

Tourist Information: Greater Trinidad Chamber of Commerce, *PO Box 356, Trinidad, CA 95570; tel: (707) 677-0591*.

Accommodation

The most reasonable lodging is just north of town at **Patrick's Point State Park**, *4159 Patrick's Point Dr; tel: (707) 677-3570*, with three campgrounds. Summer bookings are necessary – **MISTIX**; *tel: (800) 444-7275*. There are several moderate lodges and motels between Patrick's Point and Trinidad, including **Bishop Pine Lodge**, *1481 Patrick's Point Dr.; tel: (707) 677-3314*, **Shadow Lodge**, *687 Patrick's Point Dr.; tel: (707) 677-0532*, and **Trinidad Inn**, *1170 Patrick's Point Dr.; tel: (707) 677-3349*. Bed and breakfasts run to the expensive: **Trinidad Bed & Breakfast**, *560 Edwards St; tel: (707) 677-0840* and the **Lost Whale**, *3452 Patrick's Point Dr.; tel: (707) 677-3425*.

Eating and Drinking

The moderate **Larrupin Café**, *1150 Westhaven Dr.; tel: (707) 677-0230*, barbecues everything from oysters to ribs for appreciative crowds. **The Seascape Restaurant**, *at the Trinidad pier; tel: (707) 677-3762*, lures locals with hearty, budget-priced breakfasts and moderate, no-nonsense seafood for lunch and dinner.

Sightseeing

The main sight is the sea. **Trinidad Head** looms above a small harbour and fishing fleet; **Trinidad Memorial Lighthouse** looms above Main St from the cliff above the harbour. The **Humboldt State University Marine Lab & Aquarium**, *Edwards and Ewing Sts; tel: (707) 677-3671*, is open to the public.

Beachcombing is excellent at **Trinidad State Beach**, just north of town, but the real lure is **Patrick's Point State Park**, 6 miles (10 km) beyond. Native Americans once followed tracks around rocky **Patrick's Point**, an excellent whale-watching spot. The 2-mile (3 km) **Rim Trail** has fine ocean vistas, but stay back from the crumbly cliff edge. Sea lions are common along the southern part of the park near **Palmer's Point**. Park meadows blaze with wildflowers in the spring. Elsewhere, azaleas, berry bushes, and mushrooms grow in wild profusion.

Just north of Patrick's Point is **Humboldt Lagoons State Park**, a quartet of beaches : **Big Lagoon**, **Dry Lagoon**, **Stone Lagoon** and **Freshwater Lagoon**. RVs are a permanent fixture along Freshwater Lagoon. There's good beachcombing, fishing, surfing, and windsurfing, but leave swimming to the seals and sea lions – they're equipped for the frigid water and pounding surf. The **Visitors Center**, *Stone Lagoon*, is open only in summer.

REDWOOD NATIONAL PARK

Tourist Information: Redwood National Park, *1111 Second St, Crescent City, CA 95531; tel: (707) 464-6101*; and the **Orick Redwood National Park Information Center**, north of Freshwater Lagoon on the west side of Hwy 101, PO Box 234, Orick, CA 95555; tel: (707) 488-

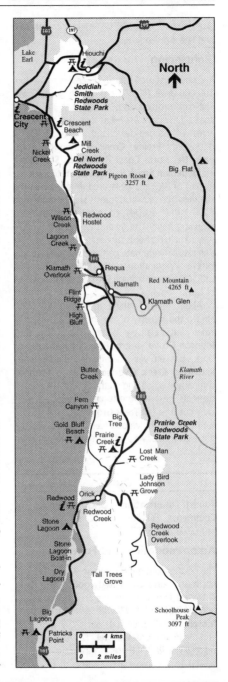

Trinidad–Redwood National Park–Redwood National Park Map   **305**

3461. For the least fog, visit mid-Sept–early-Nov and late Apr–early Jun.

Sightseeing

Redwood National Park (RNP) covers more than 100,000 acres (40,407 ha) on the North Coast. The park protects 28,000 acres (11,332 ha) of coastal redwoods as well as tens of thousands of acres of logged-over land which is being reforested. **Prairie Creek Redwoods State Park**, **Del Norte Coast Redwoods State Park** and **Jedediah Smith Redwoods State Park** are all part of RNP and all layered in fog during the summer. The redwood forests shelter more than 1000 other species of plants and animals, including banana slugs and two of the world's only remaining herds of wapiti, or Roosevelt elk (the rest are in remote parts of Olympic National Park in Washington state). RNP was the first UNESCO World Heritage Site on the Pacific Coast of North America.

About the only thing to 'do' in RNP is to absorb the majesty of which nature is capable when left relatively alone. The **Lady Bird Johnson Grove**, east of Hwy 101 just north of Orick, has an easy, self-guided nature walk. **Redwood Creek Overlook** offers a textbook comparison of logging methods, with devastated clearcuts next to forests where selected trees were cut. The **Tall Trees Grove** is a 3-mile (5 km) walk from the Redwood Creek trailhead. Visit the grove on foot or via shuttle from the information centre.

ORICK

Tourist Information: Orick Chamber of Commerce, *PO Box 234, Orick, CA 95555; tel: (707) 488-6755.*

Accommodation and Food

The best lodging bet is camping 9 miles (11 km) north at **Prairie Creek Redwoods State Park**. There are few motels in the area: **Orick Motel and RV Park**, *tel: (707) 488-3501;* **Park Woods Motel**, *121440 Hwy 101; tel: (707) 488-5175;* and the **Prairie Creek Motel**, *123749 Hwy 101; tel: (707) 488-3841,* are all moderate.

The food choices aren't much more varied.

Rolf's Park Café, next to the Prairie Creek Motel; *tel: (707) 488-3841,* serves huge budget breakfasts and lunches and moderate dinners. The **Palm Café** has budget meals and the **Orick Market** sells basic picnic supplies.

Orick is also home to souvenir shops specialising in oversized sculptures chewed from redwood logs by chainsaw. The **Prairie Creek Fish Hatchery** is 3½ miles (6 km) north on Hwy 101.

PRAIRIE CREEK REDWOODS STATE PARK

Tourist Information: Prairie Creek Redwoods State Park, *Orick, CA 95555; tel: (707) 488-2171.* Take the **Elk Prairie Parkway** exit off Hwy 101 just north of **Lost Man Creek**, a seldom-visited picnic area surrounded by deep forests, and the fish hatchery.

Roosevelt elk herds are a permanent hazard, especially near the main campground entrance at **Elk Prairie**. Drivers tend to come to an abrupt halt at the sight of these huge creatures calmly grazing near the road. Another herd grazes the meadows above the 11 miles (18 km) of **Gold Bluff Beach**, accessible by car (caravans not recommended) or on foot. The rest of the park is the closest California has to rainforest. A stunning array of plants starts with a carpet of green moss and oxalis so delicate the leaves fold up at the first touch of sunshine, then builds to ferns, rhododendrons, shrubs, hemlocks and Sitka spruce, with coastal redwoods towering above them all. **Fern Canyon** is an easy 1-mile (1.6 km) return hike near Gold Bluffs along a tinkling stream. Sixty-foot (19 m) rock walls are carpeted with dozens of species of ferns. The **Brown Creek Trail**, north of the visitor centre, is rich in rhododendrons. The park is busy in summer, nearly deserted mid-Sept–mid-May.

The parkway (old Hwy 101) rejoins the 8-mile (13 km) Hwy 101 bypass just beyond the park and 5.5 miles (9 km) south of the small town of **Klamath** and the **Klamath River**. For a more scenic drive, take **Alder Camp Rd** west just before leaving the park. Continue along the wild and nearly deserted coastline to the Klamath River, then follow the river upstream to Hwy 101.

Part of the road is unpaved and not recommended for caravans, but is fine for cars and RVs.

KLAMATH

Tourist Information: Klamath Chamber of Commerce, *1661 West Klamath Beach Rd, Klamath, CA 95548; tel: (707) 482-7165.*

Accommodation

There are more than 2000 camping and RV places in the area, but few motels. The moderate **Motel Trees**, *PO Box 309; tel: (707) 482-3152,* across Hwy 101 from the Trees of Mystery, is among the largest. **Requa Inn**, *451 Requa Rd; tel: (707) 482-8205,* moderate, is the best bed and breakfast and restaurant in the region. The views are equally good at the **HI-Redwood Hostel**, *14480 Hwy 101, Klamath, CA 95548; tel: (707) 482-8256,* 9 miles (14 km) north of town.

Sightseeing

The Klamath is a traditional fishing river, once for Native Americans, now for anyone who can put a boat on the river during salmon season. The old town was washed away by floodwaters in 1964 and has become a blackberry patch. The new town is on higher ground. **Tour Thru Tree**, *430 Hwy 169; tel: (707) 482-5971,* just east of town, was opened for drive-through traffic by a chain saw in 1976.

Two miles (3 km) north of Klamath, **Requa Rd** west from Hwy 101 offers a 5-mile (8 km) return overlook of the wild coastline. It's impossible to miss **Trees of Mystery**, 2 miles (3 km) north, *15500 Hwy 101; tel: (707) 482-5613,* with kitschy statues of Paul Bunyan and Babe the Blue Ox looming over a huge parking lot. The free **End of the Trail Indian Museum** has Native artifacts from across North America. The **Trail of Tall Tales** charges admission to walk in redwood groves that are more crowded than anything in Prairie Creek Park.

The **Vista Point** 3 miles (5 km) north, just north of the Redwood Hostel, has great coastal views and useful information displays. The coastline north of Klamath, plus about 6000 inland acres (2428 ha) are part of **Del Norte**

Coast Redwoods State Park, *PO Drawer J, Crescent City, CA 95531; tel: (707) 458-3115.* Park campsites close because of winter rains, but walking trails are open all year. Hwy 101 descends toward Crescent City beyond the park, passing a well-kept **demonstration forest**, *Rellim Redwood Co, PO Box 247, Crescent City, CA 95531; tel: (707) 464-3144.* The self-guiding walking tour and detailed explanation of reforestation are worth a stop.

CRESCENT CITY

Tourist Information: Crescent City-Del Norte Chamber of Commerce, *1001 Front St, Crescent City, CA 95531; tel: (707) 464-3174.*

Accommodation

Crescent City has several moderate bed and breakfasts and motels, including *BW* and *TL*.

Eating and Drinking

Supermarkets provide the usual picnic possibilities, but **Rumiano Cheese Company**, *9th and E Sts; tel: (707) 465-1535,* and the **Crescent Meat Company**, *1298 Elk Valley Rd; tel: (707) 464-6767,* offer more interesting fare. **Ship Ashore**, *12370 Hwy 101; tel: (707) 487-3141,* in Smith River, is a local seafood favourite – don't be put off by the touristy beached ship in the parking lot. **Harbor View Grotto**, *155 Citizen's Dock Rd; tel: (707) 464-3815,* is also popular locally.

Sightseeing

An attractive waterfront park is what remains of the old wharf after a 1964 tsunami (tidal wave) and a 1972 typhoon. **Battery Point Lighthouse**, on a small island near the north end of the bay, is open when weather and tides permit. The **Del Norte Historical Society Museum**, *577 H St; tel; (707) 464-3922,* chronicles local history from Native Americans through Gold Rush, lumbering, and tsunami. **Pebble Beach Dr.**, from the end of 9th St, looks over the **Point Saint George Lighthouse**, now deactivated, on an island offshore. Beachcombing and agate hunting are good when the seas are calm, but avoid the beaches when the surf is high. **Lake Earl** and **Lake Talawa**, just north of town off Lake Earl

Drive, are part of the **Pacific Flyway**. More than 250 species of birds visit or live in the 5000 acres (2024 ha) of marsh, dunes, ponds, and coastal lakes.

Most of the lilies sold in the United States are grown between Crescent City and the Oregon border, 28 miles (45 km) north. Nearby is **Pelican Bay State Prison** (not open for voluntary visits), home to California's violent criminals.

Jedediah Smith Redwoods State Park, *PO Drawer J, Crescent City, CA 95531; tel: (707) 464-9533*, begins 4 miles (6 km) east of Crescent City on Hwy 199. Few visitors venture off Hwy 101, so Jed Smith is almost unvisited, even in summer. Most park campsites are along the Smith River, away from most summer fog. The river has sandy beaches and sunny swimming. Walking tracks visit quiet redwood groves. The 30-minute **Stout Grove Trail** combines fine swimming and the area's tallest trees. The **Hiouchi Trail** is best for rhododendrons and huckleberries (tiny wild blueberries); the **Simpson and Peterson Trails** combine into an easy 2-mile (3 km) loop through redwoods and ferns.

To reach the Oregon border, return to Hwy 101 and turn north. The highway runs through 24 miles (38 km) of rolling lily fields above the coastline to the **Agricultural Inspection Station** just south of the Oregon state line.

SAN FRANCISCO TO BODEGA BAY

The beginning of the coastal route alternative follows the Marin County Route, p. 228. Continue north on Hwy 1 through rolling dairy pastures toward the shores of **Tomales Bay**. On clear days (most likely mid-Sept–mid-May), the town of **Inverness** is visible across the Bay. The **Tomales Bay Oyster Co.**, *15479 Hwy 1, Pt Reyes Station, CA 94956; tel: 415-663-1242*, on the bay 6 miles (10 km) north of Pt Reyes Station, sells live oysters and clams. Much of the bay shore is part of **Tomales Bay State Park**, *Star Rte, Inverness, CA 94937; tel: (415) 669-1140*, including the **Marconi Conference Center**; *tel: (415) 663-9020*. The magnificently refurbished old hotel was once owned by Guglielmo Marconi, inventor of the wireless.

Marshall, a small bayside village, was once a major fishing and oystering port for San Francisco. The hills beyond, like much of the Northern California coast, are covered with gorse, an unstoppable transplant from England that has become a major pest despite masses of golden flowers every spring. **Tomales**, 10 miles (16 km) north of Marshall, is a small farming community with bucolic views, numerous original Victorians, and successful businesses transplanted from the bustle of San Francisco. The **Tomales Bakery**, *on Hwy 101; tel: (707) 878-2429*, serves fresh bread, pastries, and generous cups of inky espresso.

Just beyond the Sonoma County boundary and **Americano Creek**, Hwy 1 turns sharply left toward the tiny town of **Valley Ford** and the coast. The Sonoma coast is even wilder than the western shores of Pt Reyes. Sandy beaches are isolated accidents of nature along a succession of increasingly steep cliffs. Undertows, riptides, and jagged rocks that would be spectacular along any other shore are commonplace. The crowds, and the fog, are thickest in summer. By Sept–Oct, both have disappeared.

BODEGA BAY

Tourist Information: Bodega Bay Chamber of Commerce, *850 Coast Hwy 1, Bodega Bay, CA 94923; tel: (707) 875-3422*.

Accommodation

Bodega Bay is a popular holiday destination from the San Francisco area, filled with inns, bed and breakfasts, and motels – including *BW* and *HI*. **The Inn at the Tides**, *800 Coast Hwy; tel: (707) 875-2751*, expensive–pricey, is the best-known. **Bodega Bay Lodge**, (BW), *103 Coast Hwy; tel: (707) 875-3525*, and **Bodega Coast Inn**, *521 Coast Hwy; tel: (707) 875-2217*, are in the same price range. Check with the Chamber of Commerce for current bed and breakfast possibilities. The closest camping is at **Doran Beach County Park**, *PO Box 372; tel: (707) 875-3540*, on the southern edge of the bay.

Eating and Drinking

The Tides Wharf Restaurant, *on the wharf; tel: (707) 875-3652*, is homegrown favourite that has moved upmarket. For a more relaxed atmosphere, move next door to **Lucas Wharf Restaurant**, tel: (707) 875-3522, and **Lucas Wharf Deli and Fish Market**, tel: (707) 875-3562.

Sightseeing

Bodega Bay was the beleaguered town in Alfred Hitchcock's The Birds. Fortunately, the ever-present seabirds are mostly interested in soaring above the bay and the looming bulk of **Bodega Head**. That leaves visitors free to explore the beaches, the headlands, the tidepools, and the growing number of galleries and gift shops along Hwy 1.

Bodega also has the cheapest petrol between San Francisco and Fort Bragg.

BODEGA BAY TO JENNER

Most of the 13 miles (21 km) of coastline north to **Jenner** is part of **Sonoma Coast State Beaches**, Salmon Creek Ranger Station, Bodega Bay, CA 94923; tel: (707) 875-3483, including Bodega Head. The **University of California Bodega Bay Marine Station** is open to the public on Saturdays. Five miles (8 km) of walking tracks wander the **Bodega Dunes**, near the north end of the bay. At the opposite end of the headland is 'the biggest hole in the head', a gigantic water-filled hole once destined to house a nuclear power station. Local residents raised an environmental storm against the proposed plant – the San Andreas earthquake fault passes just 4 miles (6.4 km) away.

The coast north is a series of beaches separated by jutting headlands, tidepools, rock arches, and 'sea stacks', isolated rocks that may be as tall as the headlands. Beachcombing, fishing and sunbathing are wonderful, but swimming is deadly. Scuba and free diving (for abalone) are possible in a few protected areas. **Portuguese Beach**, a sandy beach between rocky headlands, has the best rock and surf fishing. **Rock Point**, a headland, has the best picnic views. **Shell Beach** is best for beachcombing and surfside strolling. **Goat Rock Beach**, near the north end of the park, is at the end of a delightfully snaky road down from Hwy 1.

JENNER

Jenner overlooks the mouth of the **Russian River**. Just beyond the hamlet is a lay-by overlooking a sandbar in mid-river. What look like logs are actually seals and sea lions resting on the sand. Seals swim upstream as far as Monte Rio in search of fish.

The cliffs become even more rugged beyond the Russian River, the views even more spectacular, and the surf even more dangerous. The best view south is from the **Sonoma Coast Vista Trail** rest area on the west side of Hwy 1 5 miles (8 km) north of Jenner. Point Reyes is clearly visible from the vista point, fog permitting. The rest of the year, an information sign points you in the right direction (left).

Fort Ross State Historic Park, 19005 Coast Highway 1, Jenner, CA 95450; tel: (707) 847-3286, is 6 miles (10 km) north of the vista point. First established in 1812, Ross Colony (the original name) was the edge of a Russian empire that once stretched from St Petersburg to Alaska and south nearly to San Francisco. The colonists raised grain and vegetables for their Alaskan compatriots (not very successfully) and hunted (extremely successfully) for sea otter pelts. In its heyday, the stockade was the center of a thriving village of nearly 100 buildings and a mixture of Russians, Alaskan Natives, local Natives, and others. As far as anyone knows, the 40 cannon inside the stockade were never fired except on ceremonial occasions. When Russian authorities sold the stockade to John Sutter in Sacramento, the local Pomo community held an official mourning ceremony.

Most of Fort Ross is reconstructed from the original plans found in a Moscow archive. The **Visitor Center and Museum** have an excellent slide programme and introductory exhibits to set the stage for an **audio tour** of the fort. The Orthodox **chapel** is a pilgrimage site for Russians. The Commandant's quarters, barracks, and other buildings are furnished as though the original inhabitants had just walked out the door.

Benjamin Buffano's unfinished **Peace Sculpture** rises above the **Timber Cove Inn**, 21780 North Coast Highway One, Jenner, CA 95450; tel: (707) 847-3231. Rooms are expensive–pricey, but anyone can stop to peer up at Buffano's last, and unfinished, sculpture.

Salt Point State Park, *25050 Highway 1, Jenner, CA 95450; tel: (707) 847-3221*, is filled with rugged outcroppings wreathed in spray, forests of stunted trees, wind-sculpted sandstone, and one of California's first marine sanctuaries. The park also has extensive dunes, several Pomo village sites, fishing, berrying and mushrooming (in season) and a pleasant campsite. Bookings are essential in summer, contact **MISTIX**; *tel: (800) 444-7275*.

Kruse Rhododendron Preserve; *tel: (707) 865-2391* is part of Salt Point. The 317-acre (128 ha) preserve is a natural garden of native rhododendrons up to 30 ft (9 m) tall beneath the shade of second-growth redwoods. Peak bloom is April–May; telephone for current predictions. **Salt Point Lodge**, *23255 Highway 1, Jenner, CA 95450; tel: (707) 847-3234*, has moderate lodging and budget–moderate meals nearby. Farther north is **Sea Ranch** and the pricey **Sea Ranch Lodge**, *60 Shore Walk Dr, Sea Ranch, CA 95497; tel: (707) 785-2371*.

JENNER TO ELK

Tourist Information: Mendocino Coast Chamber of Commerce, *PO Box 1141, Fort Bragg, CA 95437; tel: (707) 961-6300*.

Gualala is 8 twisting miles (13 km) north of Sea Ranch. The old lumber town has been renovated for modern tourists, including the 1903 **Gualala Hotel**; *tel: (707) 884-3441*, budget–moderate. Bar and restaurant are loud, lively, and friendly. For a more sedate view of the coast, check into **Saint Orres**, 3 miles (5 km) north, *PO Box 523, Gualala, CA 95445; tel: (707) 884-3303*. Music literati call a visit 'sitting in the dacha the bay', but the Russian-influenced redwood, copper, and stained glass hotel-restaurant is one of the most relaxed places on the Mendocino coast. Prices are moderate–pricey. Bookings are a must.

The coastline angles another 14 miles (22 km) westward through coastside pastures to **Point Arena**, both a lighthouse and one of California's smallest cities. Most of the town lies along Hwy 1, a strip of historic buildings. **Point Arena**

Light Station, *PO Box 11, Point Arena, CA 95468; tel: (707) 882-2777*, is 2½ miles (4 km) north at the end of Lighthouse Rd. The white, smokestack-shaped 115-ft (38 m) tower replaces an ornate brick structure that collapsed during the 1906 San Francisco earthquake. The lighthouse is now automated, but is open for tours from the museum at its base. The former Coast Guard houses are now holiday rentals.

Elk, 17 miles (27 km) north, is another ex-logging town that could never afford to rebuild after the timber industry died. Most of the old buildings have been renovated. **Greenwood Creek Beach State Park**, in the centre of town, is the site of the mill and port from Elk's lumber days. It's also a popular push-off for sea kayakers. Bed and breakfasts as well as restaurants cluster at the expensive–pricey end of the spectrum.

The increasingly rugged, windswept coastline north of Elk is interrupted by a string of small towns, all former lumber ports finding new life as tourist havens. The clifftops were once heavily forested, but were logged and turned to pasture a century ago.

MENDOCINO

Tourist Information: Mendocino Coast Chamber of Commerce, *PO Box 1141, Fort Bragg, CA 95437; tel: (707) 961-6300*.

Accommodation and Food

Mendocino is filled with bed and breakfasts and restaurants, most at the upper end of the price range. Advance bookings are mandatory.

Sightseeing

San Francisco artists rescued Mendocino as the lumber industry died in the 1950s. They may have succeeded too well. The town looks like a film set (it has been one, many times), picture-perfect New England-style buildings perched on the edge of the swirling Pacific Ocean. The whole community is a National Historic Preservation District, its original buildings intact, beautifully renovated, and almost invisible behind the crowds.

Most of the artists have long since departed, pushed out by rising living costs. In their place are shops and galleries catering to the tourist trade rather than serious buyers. The town recovers a degree of its original charm in November and January, the only months visitors don't swamp the fewer than 1000 residents.

Mendocino Art Center, *45200 Little Lake St, Mendocino, CA 95460; tel: (707) 937-5818*, remains the centre for arts and artists throughout the county. **The Gallery** and **The Showcase** exhibit local as well as outside artists. The free *Arts and Entertainment* magazine lists almost every event in the county. The centre can also suggest local galleries more devoted to serious art.

Mendocino Historical Research, Inc., *PO Box 922; tel: (707) 937-5791*, offers guided historical walks. Their **Kelly House**, *Main St*, is the official museum. Equally impressive is the **Mendocino Hotel**, *45080 Main St; tel: (707) 937-0511*.

If the weather is reasonable, **Mendocino Headlands State Park**, *PO Box 440; tel: (707) 937-5804*, is a refreshing respite. Start at park headquarters, the **Ford House**, on Main St, then continue along the sandstone cliffs sculpted by wind and wave.

Russian Gulch State Park, just north of Mendocino, is another defunct lumber port. The park has 1200 acres (486 ha) of redwoods, rhododendrons, azaleas, ferns, berry bushes, trees, fishing, and camping.

Jug Handle State Reserve, just north of the Caspar Headlands, is a prime example of an ecological staircase. A succession of ancient marine terraces, each about 100 ft (33 m) above the other, is home to a different set of plants, from salt-tolerant wildflowers near the water to redwoods high above.

FORT BRAGG

Tourist Information: Fort Bragg Chamber of Commerce, *PO Box 1141, Fort Bragg, CA 95437; tel: (707) 961-6300*.

Accommodation and Food

Fort Bragg is the largest town on the coast between San Francisco and Eureka, but Mendocino, 11 miles (18 km) south, gets most of the visitors. There are a handful of motels, including

Mendocino–Fort Bragg–Mendocino Coast Map

BW, and a number of bed and breakfasts. Prices are considerably more reasonable than in Mendocino.

Fort Bragg has the best collection of fast food chains on the coast. The **North Coast Brewing Co.**, *444 North Main St; tel: (707) 964-2739*, is usually crowded for the beer and robust budget–moderate meals. For fresh-off-the-boat seafood, locals head to **Noyo**, the fishing harbour just south of town.

Sightseeing

Fort Bragg is Mendocino without culture vulture crowds and inflated prices. Main St is lined with Victorians, renovated for local use as much as for the tourist trade – merchants decided it was faster, cheaper, and more attractive to refurbish than to rebuild. A Chamber of Commerce historic walking guide covers more than two dozen downtown buildings, including the 1924 **Railroad Depot**, *401 North Main St*. The depot is home to the **Skunk Train**, *PO Box 907; tel: (707) 964-6371*, which still runs through the mountains to Willits, on Hwy 101. The depot and **Railroad Museum** share space with retail shops and several restaurants. The 2½-hr **History Bus Tour**, *tel: (707) 964-8687*, also leaves from the depot. The **Guest House Museum and Fort Building**, *343 North Main St; tel: (707) 961-2825*, displays the history of Fort Bragg and the timber industry in photographs and artifacts. Two miles south of town, near the Hwy 1–Hwy 20 junction, is **Mendocino Coast Botanical Gardens**, *18220 North Highway 1; tel: (707) 964-4352*, 47 lush acres (19 ha) of rhododendrons, fuchsias, ferns, camellias, roses, and more. Several commercial rhododendron nurseries are located along the first few miles of Hwy 20.

ANDERSON VALLEY

Tourist Information: Anderson Valley Chamber of Commerce, *PO Box 275, Boonville, CA 95415; tel: (707) 895-2379*, and **Anderson Valley Winegrowers Association**, *PO Box 63, Philo, CA 95466*.

It would be trite to say the Anderson Valley wine region is like Napa and Sonoma 20 years ago. It would also be wrong. The Valley is closer to Napa and Sonoma of 40 years ago, when vineyards shared the hillsides with fruit orchards, pastures, and vegetable plots. The dozen-plus wineries are relatively small; most are extremely successful with cool-climate grapes: Pinot Noir, Chardonnay, Gewürztraminer, and White Riesling. Morning fog keeps temperatures far lower than a few miles inland near Cloverdale and Ukiah. And they offer far more than grapes.

The west end of Anderson Valley is 11 miles (18 km) inland from the Mendocino coast. Hwy 128 follows the **Navarro River** and the **Navarro River Redwoods State Park**, *Mendocino Area Parks, PO Box 440, Mendocino, CA 95460; tel: (707) 937-5804*, a narrow strip along the valley floor. **Paul Dimmick Wayside Campground**, 8 miles (13 km) from the coast, has pleasant riverside campsites beneath a broad canopy of redwoods and fragrant California bay laurel trees. The first vineyards appear just south of **Navarro**.

Handley Cellars, *PO Box 66, Philo, CA 95466; tel: (707) 895-3876*, 2 miles (3 km) beyond Navarro, is bright with yellow lilies and a wisteria arbour. The wines are equally bright and drinkable. **Roederer Estate**, *4501 Hwy 128; tel: (707) 895-2288*, and **Husch Vineyards**, *4400 Hwy 128; tel: (707) 895-3216*, are on opposite sides of the highway 1½ miles (2.5 km) beyond. The interior of the Husch tasting room is filled with spicy Pinot Noirs and round, buttery Chardonnays. A self-guided vineyard tour gives a good indication of how much hard work and patience go into good wine. Roederer, a low, modern building of unpainted wood, is owned by the French champagne house of the same name. Their California sparkling wines follow the same bright style.

Kendall-Jackson, *5500 Hwy 128; tel: (707) 895-3623*, **Greenwood Ridge**, *5501 Hwy 128; tel: (707) 895-2002*, and **Navarro**, *Box 47; tel: (707) 895-3686*, are clustered just down the road. Kendall-Jackson, on a hillside to the west of Hwy 128, has spectacular vineyard views from the tasting room and picnic area. Wines from other Kendall-Jackson wineries (Cambria, J. Stonestreet, Edmeades Estate, La Crema) are also available. The modernistic Greenwood Ridge tasting room is home to the annual California

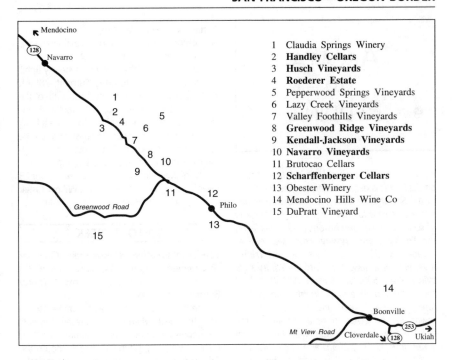

Mendocino
128
Navarro

1 Claudia Springs Winery
2 **Handley Cellars**
3 **Husch Vineyards**
4 **Roederer Estate**
5 Pepperwood Springs Vineyards
6 Lazy Creek Vineyards
7 Valley Foothills Vineyards
8 **Greenwood Ridge Vineyards**
9 **Kendall-Jackson Vineyards**
10 **Navarro Vineyards**
11 Brutocao Cellars
12 **Scharffenberger Cellars**
13 Obester Winery
14 Mendocino Hills Wine Co
15 DuPratt Vineyard

Greenwood Road

Philo

Boonville

Mt View Road   Cloverdale   253   Ukiah

Wine Tasting Championship. Navarro, next door, is surrounded by one of the most spectacular gardens in the valley.

Just down the road is **Gowan's Oak Tree**, a roadside stand specialising in local produce and antique apple varieties, followed by **Scharffenberger Cellars**, PO Box 2; tel: (707) 895-2920, just north of Philo. Scharffenberger, now owned by France's Champagne Pommey, is among the finest California sparkling wines. **The Tin Man**, 3 miles south near **Boonville**, specializes in obscure apple varieties from local orchards.

Accommodation

There are a dozen or so bed and breakfasts and hotels in the Valley as well as camping at Dimmick Campground and **Hendy Woods State Park**, both north of Philo. The moderate **Boonville Hotel**, Boonville, CA 95415; tel: (707) 895-2210 has finely finished rooms – the two largest are over the bar, which can be a little noisy.

Eating and Drinking

The **Boonville Hotel** also has superb moderate meals. The **Buckhorn Saloon**, across the street; tel: (707) 895-2337 is more casual, as befits a brew pub. Locals go for the food as well as the beer. While you're there, check out **Boontling**, a creative dialect that is rapidly disappearing. Bright lighters are people from the city. Walter levy is a telephone, named for Walter, who had the first one in the Valley, but a pay telephone is a bucky walter, named for the early 20th century five-cent coin it first took to use one. If it's any consolation, most of the people who created Boontling are now in their codgiehood, as in old codgers.

Boonville is near the east end of the Anderson Valley detour and 27 winding miles (43 km) from Hwy 101. To return to San Francisco, turn south onto Hwy 101 to **Cloverdale** and the **Golden Gate Bridge**.

ARCATA to REDDING

*It's possible to drive all of Hwy 299 from Arcata on the Pacific coast, to Redding at the north end of the Sacramento Valley, in just over 3 hours. Allow at least a full day for 138 miles (221 km) of scenic beauties and historical treasures lining the **Trinity Scenic Byway**. From sea level at Arcata, Hwy 299 winds above the wild **Trinity River** with vast views north into the **Trinity Alps Wilderness**, 500,000 acres (202,350 ha) of snowcapped granite peaks looming above lush forests and jewel-like mountain lakes. Gold Rush towns dot the region, some abandoned, some alive and well, some inundated by modern water projects. Hwy 299 is also one of the few east–west highways that crosses the Coast Range in Northern California.*

ROUTE

From Hwy 101 in Arcata, follow Hwy 299 east. (For a description of Arcata, see p. 303). The road begins climbing immediately. **Blue Lake**, 6 miles (10 km) uphill from Arcata, is a tiny town in farm and lumber country. Weathered barns and silos are picturesque pieces set against a large lumber mill and power plant fuelled by mill waste. Smoke from the power plant frequently mixes with fog blowing in from the coast. The one thing Blue Lake doesn't have is a lake. The Mad River changed its course years ago, slowly turning the lake into a marsh.

The **Mad River Fish Hatchery** produces more than a million salmon every year as well as trout and steelhead. The **Blue Lake Museum**, in the *Arcata and Mad River Depot, Railroad Ave, Blue Lake, CA; tel: (707) 668-5655,* is filled with local memorabilia. Hours are irregular, so call for an appointment. Locals called the railroad the

Annie & Mary Railroad, after two early bookkeepers. The pair also gave their names to a local festival in early August.

From Blue Lake, the road twists steeply uphill for 21 miles (34 km) to **Berry Summit**, 2859 ft (944 m). A vista point is located just south of the highway. The view extends back to the Pacific Ocean, though it's more common to see a bank of grey fog hanging over the coastline than the ocean itself. Redwood Creek splashes through the canyon directly below the summit.

The highway follows Willow Creek east for 23 miles (37 km) down to the town of **Willow Creek** at the junction of Hwy 96.

WILLOW CREEK

Tourist Information: **Willow Creek Chamber of Commerce**, *PO Box 704, Willow Creek, CA 95573; tel: (916) 629-2693.* **Lower Trinity Ranger District**, *tel: (916) 629-2118.*

The town is best known as a summer escape from the coast, when the ever-present fog gets too depressing to bear. Warm summer weather makes swimming, rafting, and canoeing on the **Trinity River** popular attractions. Accommodation and restaurants tend toward the basic.

Willow Creek is also the heart of **Bigfoot** Country. Bigfoot is Northern California's version of the yeti reputed to haunt the higher elevations of the Himalayas. There are no Bigfoot photographs, just 150 years of sightings – not all of them after too many hours in the nearest bar. See p. 316 for more on Bigfoot. True or imaginary, Bigfoot has become a local icon, with his name appearing on everything from the **Big Foot Golf Course** to local restaurants and handicraft shops.

The Trinity River, which flows north along Hwy 96 and south-east along Hwy 299, is fishing and rafting country. Trout season opens in April. Fishing permits and tackle are available at sporting goods shops throughout the area. The Trinity was once among California's finest wild rivers, but dams built near Redding in the 1960s dramatically altered the river – for the worse, as locals still proclaim to one and all.

Rafting companies in Willow Creek, Redding, and Mount Shasta offer trips along the Trinity,

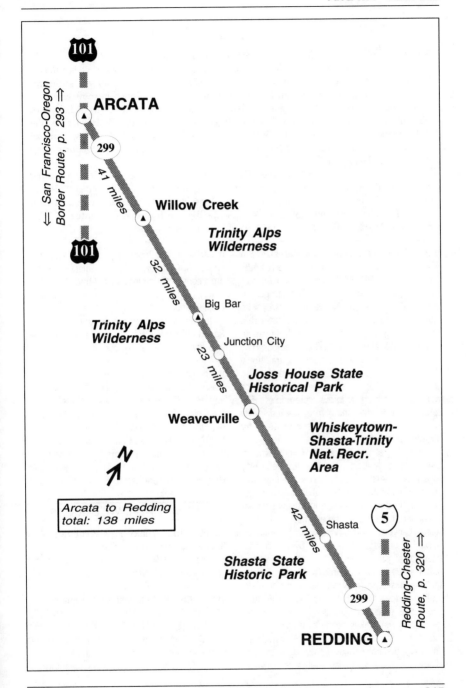

101

⇐ San Francisco-Oregon Border Route, p. 293 ⇒

ARCATA

299

41 miles

101

Willow Creek

Trinity Alps Wilderness

32 miles

Big Bar

Trinity Alps Wilderness

Junction City

23 miles

Joss House State Historical Park

Weaverville

Whiskeytown-Shasta-Trinity Nat. Recr. Area

N

Arcata to Redding total: 138 miles

42 miles

Shasta

5

Redding-Chester Route, p. 320 ⇒

Shasta State Historic Park

299

REDDING

Bigfoot

Bigfoot is the local equivalent of the Himalayan Yeti, an oversized, hairy humanoid with prodigious strength and a child-like temperament. Native Americans across Northwest California and Southwest Oregon called the creature Sasquatch, but later arrivals settled for the more prosaic name taken from gigantic footprints reportedly found in snow and mud.

Bigfoot has never been photographed, but reported sightings continue to trickle out of the wilderness. Most sightings have emerged from the **Yolla Bolly-Middle Eel Wilderness Area**, south-east of Weaverville off Hwy 36. The **Trinity Alps**, north of Hwy 299, are another hotbed of Bigfoot sightings, but there are occasional reports along the length of Hwy 299.

Look for a creature male or female, about 8 ft (2.6 m) tall, covered with long, matted body hair, usually black or dark brown. Bigfoot is reputed to be friendly and curious, but terribly shy — and terribly strong if provoked. Most Bigfoot stories are recounted with tongue firmly in cheek, but should you see one, the **Bigfoot Information Center**, *PO Box 632, The Dalles*, or *tel: (503) 298-5877*, would like to hear the details.

Mar–Oct. **Kimtu Outdoors Adventures**, *PO Box 938, Willow Creek, CA 95573; tel: (916) 629-3843 or (800) 562-8475*, provides an unusual twist on the ordinary river run. The company is owned and staffed by Native Americans, who offer one- and two-day tours of the historically rich Tish Tang Gorge on the Hoopa Reservation, 11 miles (18 km) north of Willow Creek on Hwy 96. Trips include introductions to traditional Hoopa culture, visits to the Hoopa Museum, an ancient village, and local sweat lodges, which were used during religious ceremonies. The company offers everything from relaxed family float trips to spine-jarring Class V white water throughout Northern California.

Hwy 299 follows the Trinity River upstream toward its headwaters in the heart of the **Trinity Alps Wilderness**, directly north of the highway. There isn't a single traffic signal or parking meter in Trinity County, a situation local residents are trying hard to preserve. The emphasis is on *wild*: steep canyons with white water foaming through rapids interrupted by occasional stretches of calm green water; dramatic waterfalls; rounded valleys scoured by ancient glaciers; sharp peaks with snowcaps that never melt; open meadows filled with wildflowers into July; and dense, unlogged forests.

The highway takes nearly as many twists as the river on its journey east from Willow Creek. The road generally follows the ridgetops high above the river, but occasionally dips down to water level. The highway is icy and slippery in winter, hot and dry in late summer. Forest fires are a constant summer worry. About 15% of the Trinity Alps Wilderness burned in a 1987 conflagration.

It wasn't the first fire in the area. **Burnt Ranch**, 16 miles (26 km) beyond Willow Creek, was named after farmhouses that were burned in an 1853 attack by Native Americans upset at the damage done by gold miners. One of many reasons for their anger probably lived in **Big Bar**, another 16 miles (26 km) east. There were at least nine Gold Rush towns calling themselves Big Bar, but this one was home to 'Commodore Ligne'. The self-made Commodore gained fame by selling gold mining claims, then driving buyers away with a shotgun and selling the claims again. He was finally banished to San Quentin Prison.

TRINITY ALPS WILDERNESS

Tourist Office: Trinity Alps Wilderness Area Big Bar Ranger Station, *Star Rt. 1, Box 10, Big Bar, CA 96010; tel: (916) 623-6106*, has information and permits for the Wilderness. For more general information, contact the **Trinity County Chamber of Commerce**, *317 Main St, Weaverville, CA 96093; tel: (916) 623-6101 or (800) 421-7259*. Ask for the *Trinity Heritage Scenic Byway* auto tour brochure and map, which covers Hwy 299 in detail.

The Trinity Alps aren't as tall as major Cascade

or Sierra Nevada Peaks, but they're wetter, which means more snow in winter and much lusher vegetation all year long. The climate is so good that marijuana growers have flocked to the wilderness and nearby river canyons to plant their illegal, but highly profitable, crops. Federal and State police officials claim that years of airborne assaults have made the area safe for public use. Residents say aggressive police tactics present the greatest danger to public safety.

Either way, it's a good idea to check conditions locally before venturing into the back country. Ranger stations, guide companies, and outdoor equipment suppliers know which areas it might be politic to avoid, but don't ask too many questions.

The most popular stretch of the Trinity River for rafting is Big Bar to Pigeon Flat. Class II and Class III rapids are sprinkled through a scenic stretch of canyon, punctuated by long pools of crystal clear water. The gentle rapids, wild enough for thrills but reassuringly safe, are a favourite with families. Choices include traditional rafts or inflatable kayaks. **Trinity River Rafting**, *PO Box 572, Big Bar, CA 96010; tel: (916) 623-3033 or (800) 307-4837*. The **Big Bar District Ranger Station**, *tel: (916) 623-6106*, has information on other commercial outfitters, as well as rafting, canoeing, hiking, camping, fishing and other activities.

The North Fork of the Trinity River joins the main river at the ghost town of **Helena**. The town was settled in 1849 by French Canadian prospectors, who fared better as farmers than as miners. The high point came in 1855, when the town had more than 200 acres (81 ha) of fruit orchards. All that remains are a few gnarled trees and brick buildings.

The confluence of the North Fork and the main river is a favourite summer swimming spot and starting point for river trips. To enter the Trinity Alps Wilderness, follow East Fork Road north to the Hobo Gulch Trailhead. The trail follows the pristine North Fork north into the Wilderness.

Junction City was known as Milltown when it was a bustling centre for local ranches and miners in the 1850s and 1860s. Just north on Canyon Creek was the smaller town of Canyon

City, known more popularly as Raggedy Ass. One mile (1.6 km) north was Dedrick, home of the area's richest gold producers, the Bailey, Silver Gray and Globe Mines. It's possible to walk up Canyon Creek to ruins of the two towns and mines, but there is no vehicle access. Check local conditions at the Big Bar Ranger Station or in Weaverville before attempting the hike.

The Trinity River turns south at Junction City. Hwy 299 continues east to **Oregon Mountain Summit**, 2897 ft (956 m), and a historical marker for **La Grange Mine**. Scars from La Grange, one of the largest hydraulic mines in the world, are still clearly visible. One of the original cast iron monitors, or nozzles, slowly flaking into rusty oblivion, stands next to the marker. The highway drops steeply down to **Weaverville** from the east side of Oregon Mountain.

WEAVERVILLE

Tourist Information: **Trinity County Chamber of Commerce**, *317 Main St, Weaverville, CA 96093; tel: (916) 623-6101 or (800) 421-7259*. For general prerecorded information about Trinity area camping and outdoor recreation; *tel: (916) 246-5338*. For more details, visit the **Forest Service Weaverville Ranger District Office**, *on Hwy 299, PO Box 1190, Weaverville, CA 96093; tel: (916) 623-2121*, open daily 0800–1700 in summer, weekdays 0800–1700 the rest of the year.

Accommodation

There are several budget–moderate motels in town as well as **The Weaverville Hotel**, *201 Main St, Weaverville, CA 96093; tel: (916) 623-3121*, a pleasant, old fashioned hotel with moderate rates. **Granny's House Bed and Breakfast**, *313 Taylor, Weaverville, CA 96093; tel: (916) 623-2756* is a small Queen Anne-style bed and breakfast with moderate rates. There are also an RV park in town and several campsites at Trinity Lake, just east of town.

Eating and Drinking

The Mustard Seed, *252 S Main St; tel: (916) 623-2922* is a good budget choice for breakfast and lunch. Other popular spots include **La**

Grange Café, *Hwy 299, just west of downtown; tel: (916) 623-5325*, budget at breakfast and lunch, moderate at dinner, and the **Brewery**, *401 S Main St; tel: (916) 623-3000*, budget–moderate lunches and dinners in the 1855 Pacific Brewery building. An old horse buggy is hanging from the ceiling, a mannequin is dressed like a dancehall harlot, and an old stove is surrounded by (empty) whiskey jugs and beer kegs.

Weaverville is Trinity County's version of urban life, a combination of the 1950s and the 1850s. Neat brick and wood frame homes are surrounded by tidy picket fences covered with flowering vines. The town centre, a few short blocks along Hwy 299, is filled with Gold Rush buildings fitted with spiral staircases running up the outside. Local custom dictated different owners for ground floor businesses and first and second floor flats.

The **Weaverville Drugstore**, *219 Main St*, is the oldest working apothecary shop in California. Prescriptions are still filled behind a modern counter in the back, but the display of early remedies, potions, and apothecary equipment is more interesting. **Big Ben's Doll Museum**, *on Main St; tel: (916) 623-6383*, is open Apr–mid-Dec, or by appointment. The Chamber of Commerce's free *Walking Tour of Historic Weaverville* brochure features a complete inventory of historic buildings and sights, which includes most of the town.

It's hard to reconcile today's peaceful village with life during the Gold Rush, when Weaverville was the largest and most violent settlement in the region. In March 1851 a trio of suspected mule thieves was not just lynched but scalped by local vigilantes. In 1854 two Chinese Tongs staged a bloody battle near what is now Weaverville High School. According to newspaper accounts, 800 fighters attacked each other with home-made knives and pitchforks to the wild cheering and feverish betting of local miners. The final two combatants reportedly stabbed each other repeatedly with hand-forged pitchforks until one fell to the ground, dead. The victor died of his wounds two weeks later.

Half of Weaverville's Gold Rush-era residents were Chinese, lured by the same dreams of wealth that drew miners from around the globe.

The Chinese community built a small Taoist temple in 1853, which burned in 1873. The replacement temple has been in use since it was dedicated in 1874, making it California's oldest Chinese temple in continuous use as well as the centrepiece of **Joss House State Historic Park**, *Oregon and Main Sts; tel: (916) 623-5284*. The temple is draped with antique pennants; and Chinese New Year offerings lie on a massive, hand-carved altar. Ancient votive figures are dressed in rich silks and brocades. An antechamber preserves the temple keeper's office and living area which is decorated with the names of hundreds of local residents whose donations rebuilt the temple in 1874.

Park and temple are open daily, 1000–1700. Rangers give tours on the half-hour in summer, on the hour in winter. The park also contains a small museum covering early Chinese life in Weaverville. The local Chinese population has fallen from a high of about 2500 in the 1850s to nearly zero today.

The **J.J. 'Jake' Jackson Memorial Museum**, *across the parking lot from the Joss House Park; tel: (916) 623-5211*, is the county historical museum. The brick building contains an excellent collection of firearms, mining equipment, Native American baskets, Chinese artifacts, and other regional exhibits. Outdoor displays include a working stamp mill, an original miner's cabin from La Grange, and a reconstructed blacksmithy and tin shop. The museum is free, but donations are expected.

WHISKEYTOWN-SHASTA-TRINITY NATIONAL RECREATION AREA

Most visitors come to Weaverville to visit the **Whiskeytown-Shasta-Trinity National Recreation Area**. For a map of the area, see the map of the entire Mt Shasta region on p. 325. The recreation area includes **Shasta Lake** (see p. 323) as well as three lakes near Weaverville: **Trinity Lake** and **Lewiston Reservoir**, just east of Weaverville, and **Whiskeytown Lake**, 32 miles (51 km) east towards Redding. The three Weaverville-area lakes were created in the 1960s, an engineering project that local residents refuse to forgive or to forget.

Trinity Lake is officially called **Claire Engle Lake**, after the senator who was largely responsible for the project. The lake is universally called Trinity, for the wild river which once rushed through the valley past Whiskeytown, Minersville, Stringtown, and other Gold Rush settlements which are now under water. The lake is warm enough for swimming in summer and is popular for fishing all year. The 150 miles (240 km) of shoreline offer numerous campsites. The lake is 7 miles (11 km) north of Weaverville on Hwy 3.

Lewiston Reservoir is a cold-water lake just below Trinity Dam. The cold waters offer good trout fishing, but are chilly for swimming. There are also several campsites, some of them free because they lack drinking water. The **Trinity River Fish Hatchery**, just below Lewiston Dam, may be the most automated salmon and steelhead hatchery in the world. To reach hatchery and lake, follow Hwy 299 19 miles (30 km) east from Weaverville to **Trinity Dam Blvd**. Turn left and follow the winding road 6 miles (10 km) north.

The highest point on Hwy 299, **Buckhorn Summit**, 3215 ft (1059 m), is 4 miles (6 km) east of the junction with Trinity Dam Blvd. Trinity Mountain Rd turns left toward **French Gulch**, 9 miles (14 km) east of the summit. The town is 3 miles (5 km) north. Like Helena, French Gulch was founded by French Canadian prospectors, but the tiny town managed to survive into the modern era. Most of the scenic town is made up of extremely well-maintained historic buildings.

The area around the junction of Hwy 299 and Trinity Mountain Rd is protected in the **Tower House Historic District**, named after local developer Levi Tower and his Tower House Hotel. Both played prominent roles in the development of mining, agriculture, and industry along the Trinity River. The hotel burned in 1919. An abandoned mine, flumes, and other water works are visible along the **Camden Water Ditch Trail**, across Hwy 299 from Trinity Mountain Rd.

Whiskeytown Lake is 1–2 miles (1.6–3.2 km) east of Trinity Mountain Rd, depending on the lake level. Hwy 299 follows the north shore of the lake for 7 miles (11 km) to the turnoff for

Whiskeytown, a few hundred yards to the left. The original Whiskeytown was drowned by the lake; the general store and post office are modern. Continue 3 miles (5 km) to John F. Kennedy Memorial Drive. Turn right and follow the Drive ½ mile (1 km) to the **Whiskeytown Headquarters and Visitor Center**, PO Box 188, Whiskeytown, CA 96095; tel: (916) 241-6584.

Gold put Whiskeytown on the map (the name comes from a mule that fell off a nearby cliff, much to the consternation of miners awaiting the cargo of whiskey), and there's still gold to be found. Recreational gold panning is allowed in the area around Whiskeytown Lake, but a free permit from park headquarters or the visitor centre is required. Other popular activities include fishing, camping, boating, scuba diving, horse riding, walking, and hunting. The lake is just 8 miles (13 km) from Redding and is often crowded.

Shasta State Historic Park, PO Box 2430, Shasta, CA 96087; tel: (916) 243-8194, straddles Hwy 299, 5 miles (8 km) east of the Whiskeytown Lake visitor centre turnoff. At first glance, the roofless brick walls and empty building lots look like candidates for (or possibly victims of) urban renewal. In the 1850s, Shasta City was the largest, richest, and busiest town at the northern end of the Sacramento Valley. Main St, now Hwy 299, was choked with the dust of up to 100 freight wagons, 2000 pack mules, and hundreds of drunken miners every evening of the week. The town faded almost overnight when the railroad came to Redding in 1872, but more than 20 buildings or foundations remain.

The **Old Courthouse** has been restored as an excellent local museum. The interior has been returned to the 1860s, with jail cells and court room in their original locations. Other rooms house collections of local art and artifacts. In the back is a reconstructed double gallows, complete with gallows poetry. Beyond a shaded picnic area is the **Trinity River Barn**, an 1850s barn moved from its original site to save it from flooding by the Trinity Dam. All of the major structural joints are held together with wooden pegs. An original stage-coach and other antique pieces are displayed in and around the barn. Continue east 3 miles (5 km) on Hwy 299 to **Redding** (see p. 322).

REDDING to CHESTER

The I-5 between Redding and Mount Shasta City is the most spectacular 60 miles (96 km) of freeway ever built in California. The highway parallels the western slopes of the Sierra Nevada, with the towering peaks of Mt Lassen or Mt Shasta, and often both, visible for much of the drive. The only way to improve upon the scenery is to turn east into the Sierra at Mount Shasta and take Hwy 89 south through the heart of the mountains to Chester. At more than 8500 ft (2575 m), the road over Mt Lassen is among the highest frequently travelled roads in the state. Allow 3–4 days for the 209 miles (334 km), although it can be done in 2 tiring days.

ROUTE

From Redding take I-5 northbound. The freeway begins climbing into the mountains toward **Shasta Lake**.

Continue north on I-5 to **Castle Crags State Park**, at the Castella exit, 26 miles (42 km) north of O'Brien; *PO Box 80, Castella, CA 96017; tel: (916) 235-2684*. The silver-grey granite Crags, jutting 6000 ft (1818 m) tall just west of I-5, are the south-eastern rampart of the Klamath Mountains. The rugged climb to the top is for experts only, but an easy trail leads from a parking area to a hilltop picnic spot overlooking both the Crags and Mt Shasta. Best views are late afternoon when the setting sun can turn the Crags and Mt Shasta a deep, smouldering orange. Continue 6 miles (10 km) north on I-5 to **Dunsmuir**, once an important railroad centre and now a local trout fishing centre. **Dunsmuir Chamber of Commerce**, *4841 Dunsmuir Ave, Dunsmuir, CA 96025; tel: (916) 235-2177*. **Mount Shasta City** is 8 miles (13 km) north.

At Mt Shasta City you can switch to the Mt Shasta–Reno Route (see p. 339) to tour the extreme north-east of California.

From Mount Shasta City take I-5 back south 2 miles (3 km) to Hwy 89. Take Hwy 89 south toward **McCloud**. Hwy 89 is a two-lane highway that delves into the maze of north–south valleys and low passes that penetrate the mountainous heart of Northern California. Much of the road is straight, but there are a few slower sections with frequent curves and long uphill slopes. Lay-bys are common along the slow stretches. Use them: State law requires slow-moving vehicles that are delaying five or more other vehicles to pull over at the first safe spot and allow traffic to pass. To visit McCloud turn left onto Minnesota St, then right onto Main St, now marked as **Historic McCloud**.

Return to Hwy 89 and turn left to continue southbound. To visit the **Falls of the McCloud River**, turn right 6 miles (10 km) south of McCloud onto River Rd at the sign for Fowlers Campground. The lower falls are 1.3 miles (2 km) down River Rd. A stairway from the picnic area leads down to the falls.

To reach the **upper falls**, turn left onto a dirt road ½ mile (1 km) from Hwy 89 and continue 1.3 miles (2 km) to the upper falls overlook. Other unpaved roads in the area are not advisable for passenger vehicles or RVs. Return to Hwy 89.

A viewpoint on the right, 2 miles (3 km) south of the McCloud River Falls turnoff, offers an unobstructed view of the entire length of Mt Shasta. Trees in the foreground have been removed to give the mountain an unreal air of looming high above trackless forests. The tree line, the altitude above which trees cannot survive, is clearly visible about two-thirds of the way up the mountain. **Dead Horse Summit**, 4505 ft (1365 m) is 12 miles (19 km) beyond the viewpoint.

The road descends slowly through the thick pine forests, running straight for several miles before making a gentle curve and returning to another straight run. Logging truck drivers use the long straight ways to make up speed and time lost on slower sections with more curves. They generally have good safety records, but frequently tailgate, i.e. drive as close to the preceding vehicle as possible, to suggest that cars and RVs either speed up or make way.

The highway climbs out of the lava flows and back into thick forests toward **Eskimo Hill Summit**, 5933 ft (1798 m). Hwy 44 turns right toward Redding 1 mile (1.6 km) beyond the summit. Hwy 89 continues straight toward Lassen Volcanic National Park, another mile (1.6 km) up the mountain.

Hwy 36 from Red Bluff joins Hwy 89 at 4 miles (6 km) south of the park. Continue straight on Hwy 89 to **Morgan Summit**, 5750 ft (1742 m). The road drops sharply from the summit into

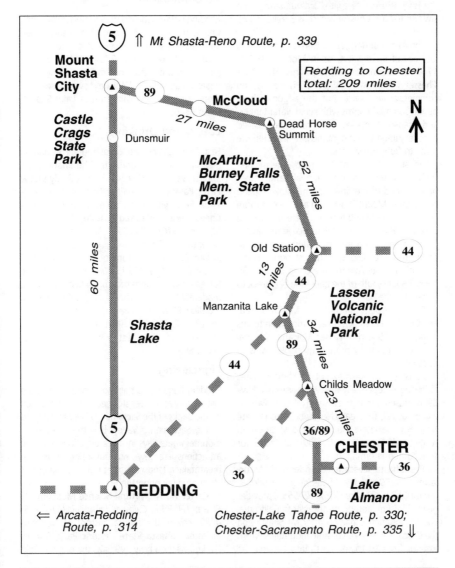

Route–Route Map

Childs Meadows, 4 miles (6 km) south. The wide, open valley has several small motels and lodges. The area is extremely popular during the summer months with Sacramento Valley residents escaping the heavy lowland heat.

The highway winds 18 miles (28 km) through heavy conifer forests toward **Lake Almanor** and the Hwy 36/Hwy 89 split. Continue straight on Hwy 36 toward **Chester**, which is 3 miles (5 km) ahead.

The **Almanor Ranger Station** is 1½ miles (2.5 km) ahead on the left, open Mon–Fri, 0800–1700 for information. Directly across Hwy 36 is **Chester Municipal Airport**. There is no commercial air service, but the airport is busy during summer months with aerial water tankers and transport planes for firefighters (called 'smoke jumpers') who parachute into remote areas to fight forest fires.

. The slowest part of the road, the section through Lassen Volcanic National Park, comes near the end of the drive. If time allows, spend one night in Mount Shasta and at least one more night in or around the park. There are several park campsites, but no indoor accommodation. Non-campers can overnight in Burney, just west of the route, or Old Station, just north of the park. It's also possible to drive on to Chester, 30 miles (48 km) south of the park, and backtrack to Lassen for the day.

Fill up on petrol in Redding, Mount Shasta, and Chester. Prices skyrocket in mountain towns along Hwy 89 and in Lassen Volcanic National Park, but return to more reasonable levels in Chester.

I-5 is open all year except for short closures following exceptionally heavy snowstorms. Hwy 89 is closed through Lassen National Park in winter, usually from early November through late May. For the latest road conditions, crucial in winter, call **Caltrans**, *tel: (800) 427-7623* for prerecorded information.

The **Shasta Cascade Wonderland Association**, *14250 Holiday Rd, Redding, CA 96003; tel: (800) 326-6944 or (916) 275-5555*, provides general information on north-eastern California. The organisation is named after Mt Shasta and the Cascade Range of volcanic mountains which extends from Mt Lassen north into Canada.

REDDING

Tourist Information: Redding Convention & Visitors Bureau (CVB), *777 Auditorium Dr, Redding, CA 96001; tel: (916) 225-4100 or (800) 874-7562.*

Accommodation

Redding is well-supplied with motels and motels. Chains include *BW*, *M6*, and *VI*, plus several bed and breakfasts. The cheapest motels are south of town on Market St (Hwy 273). Redding CVB has lodging lists, but does not make bookings. The nearest camping is **Whiskeytown Lake**, but there are also many campsites at **Lake Shasta**, north of town.

Eating and Drinking

Fast food chains are ubiquitous. For budget meals in a real restaurant, try **The Shack**, *1235 Eureka Way; tel: (916) 241-5126* or **Andy's Cow Patty Palace**, *2105 Hilltop Dr.; tel: (916) 221-7422*. Best sweets and light meals in town are at **Cheesecakes Unlimited & Café**, *1334 Market St; tel: (916) 244-6670*, just north of the Downtown Redding Mall, also budget. The **Italian Cottage**, in front of Motel 6 at *1630 Hilltop Dr.; tel: (916) 225-4062*, is a good choice for all meals – budget for breakfast and lunch, moderate for dinner. The best restaurant in town is **Bello's Place**, *3055 Bechelli Lane (at Hartnell); tel: (916) 223-1636*, with very good Italian food and one of the best wine lists north of Sacramento.

Sightseeing

Redding began as a railroad boom town in the last century and never stopped growing. Perched on the banks of the Sacramento River at the head of the Sacramento Valley, it is the gateway to mountain getaways in three directions. Cultural attractions are few, not surprising given the breathtaking landscape that pulls people out of town at every opportunity.

Carter House Natural Science Museum, *48 Quartz Hill Rd in Caldwell Park; tel: (916) 225-4125*, covers the natural history of Northern California. **Shasta State Historic Park**, 6 miles (10 km) west on Hwy 299, was the original Gold

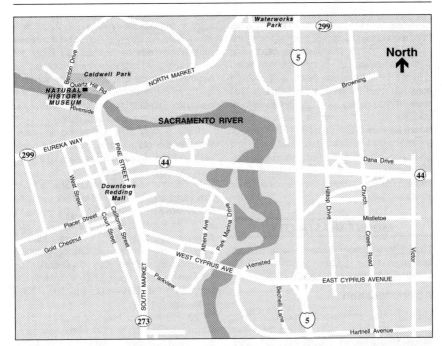

Rush town in the area, now being restored. For details see p. 319. **Waterworks Park**, ¼ mile (0.5 km) east of Hwy 299 at 151 North Boulder Dr., *tel: (916) 246-9550*, a massive water park, is a welcome relief from oppressive summer heat.

SHASTA LAKE

When it's full, Shasta Lake has more shoreline than San Francisco Bay and a surface area of more than 30,000 acres (13,410 ha), all of it used by the 2 million or so visitors who visit the lake every year. The lake was created between 1938 and 1945 to tame the Sacramento, Pit, and McCloud Rivers for hydroelectric power and irrigation water for the Central Valley.

The gigantic lake is a mecca for water skiing, fishing, and houseboating, but it's not the best spot to commune with nature. Not only is it usually crowded, but the ring of naked red soil above the current water level gives Shasta Lake the look of a large bathtub very badly in need of cleaning.

To reach the dam, take the Shasta Dam Blvd exit, 8 miles (13 km) north of Redding. The dam is 6 miles (10 km) west of I-5. Walk across the dam for a close-up look at the second largest concrete dam in the USA: 602 ft (182 m) high, 3460 ft (1048 m) long, and 883 ft (141 m) thick at the base. To the east are five endless arms of blue-green water, accompanied by the thunder of water cascading over the spillway. It's possible to see three Shastas at once from the dam and the viewpoint: lake, dam, and mountain. The free **Visitor Center**, *tel: (916) 275-4463*, tells the story of this engineering feat with exhibits and a short film. Open Mon–Fri 0730–1700 and Sat 0830–1700 during the summer. Winter hours vary. Tours of the dam are available during occasional open days. The Shasta Cascade Wonderland Assn and the Redding CVB have information on recreation, lodging, and houseboat rentals.

The **Lake Shasta Caverns**, *PO Box 801, O'Brien, CA 96070; tel: (916) 238-2341*, are a spectacular example of what water can do as it trickles through rock. The Cathedral Room is decorated with soaring 'waterfalls' of calcium carbonate 60 ft (18 m) tall and 20 ft (6 m) wide. In other rooms, stalagmites reach up from the cavern floor to fuse with stalactites descending from the ceiling to create delicate, fluted columns. The Spaghetti Patch is a swirling mass of multi-coloured mineral straws that seem to defy gravity. The tour is well-lit, with concrete steps and guardrails. Two-hour excursions leave from O'Brien, 6 miles (10 km) north of the Shasta Dam Blvd exit, starting with a 15-min catamaran trip across the lake and an exhilarating bus ride up an 800 ft (242 m) hill to the cave entrance. Bring a pullover; the caverns are chilly all year.

MOUNT SHASTA CITY

Tourist Information: Mount Shasta Visitors Bureau, *300 Pine St, Mount Shasta, CA 96067; tel: (916) 926-4865 or (800) 926-4865.*

Accommodation

There are more than a dozen motels in town, including *BW* (visible from I-5) and the luxury **Mount Shasta Resort,** *1000 Siskiyou Lake Blvd, Mount Shasta, CA 96067; tel: (916) 926-3030.* There are another dozen bed and breakfasts, holiday chalets, and cabins, plus campgrounds and RV parks. The Chamber of Commerce can provide a list of overnight lodging, but cannot make bookings. High season is summer and autumn (for hunting and fishing).

Eating and Drinking

Mount Shasta has the best selection north of Redding, with nearly three dozen restaurants in all price categories. Mount Shasta Resort is easily the most expensive; fast food outlets are concentrated on Lake St near the I-5 exit. Best value in town is **Subs 'n Such,** *520 W. Lake St at the Central Mt Shasta exit; tel: (916) 926-3427,* bargain prices for freshly prepared and oversized soups, sandwiches, and sweets. The local beer is produced by **Etna Brewery,** in the town of Etna, a 90-min drive to the north-west.

Sightseeing

Mount Shasta, as the town is usually called, is a former railroad and lumber centre that has successfully made the transition into the modern world. The town is the gateway to Mt Shasta and surrounding recreational areas, an important fishing centre, and the staging area for New Age pilgrimages to the purported energy vortexes, harmonic convergences and power points on nearby Mt Shasta. There is also alpine skiing in the wintertime at a small local resort.

There is very little sightseeing in town, although the old downtown has been nicely preserved and renovated for modern boutiques, book stores and galleries.

Just west of I-5 are the **Mount Shasta State Fish Hatchery,** *tel: (916) 926-2215,* and the **Sisson Museum,** *tel: (916) 926-5505, both at 1 North Old Stage Rd, Mount Shasta, CA 96067.* To reach both, take Lake St west, over I-5, and cross Old Stage Rd into the Hatchery grounds. The Hatchery is open daily, 0700–dusk. The Museum is open 1000–1700, early May–30 Sept; Mon–Sat 1200–1600 and Sun 1300–1600. Both are free.

The 100-year old Hatchery produces 5–10 million trout annually to stock lakes and streams throughout Northern California. The entire operation is open for self-guided tours, from indoor troughs holding clouds of minnow-sized trout to outdoor holding tanks filled with trophy-sized specimens. Fish food is available to feed outdoor trout. Sisson Museum (Sisson was an early name for the town) contains relics and curiosities from early life in the area.

In winter, skiing is available at **Mount Shasta Ski Park,** 10 miles (16 km) east of I-5 via Hwy 89 and Ski Park Highway. The ski lift is open in summer for sightseers, mountain bikers, and hikers.

Mount Shasta City Park, at the north end of town just west of Mount Shasta Blvd, contains the headwaters of the Sacramento River. **Big Spring** gushes icy clear water from a lava tube that originates deep within Mt Shasta.

It is also possible to **climb** 14,162 ft (4292 m) **Mt Shasta** in 8–12 hours, depending on the weather. Most climbers make the attempt in June and July, but killer blizzards can descend without warning even on the hottest day. There is no trail, and all climbers must carry an ice axe and crampons to traverse hard snow and ice

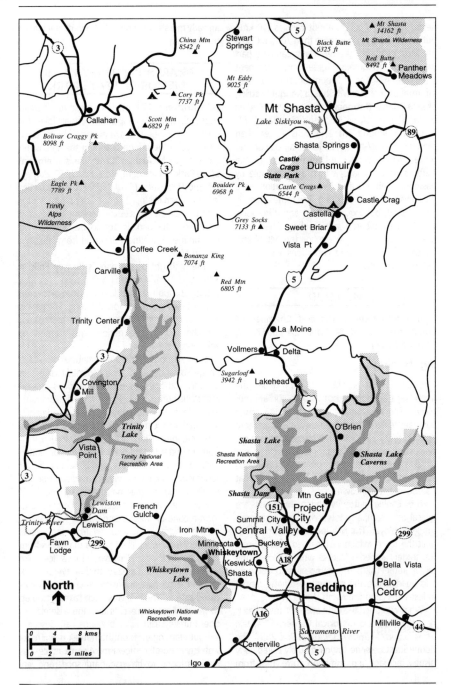

North

↑

fields. The climb covers about 6 miles (10 km), but the elevation gain is more than 7000 ft (2120 m). Most climbers take two days, camping part way up the mountain. Guides and equipment rental are available in Mount Shasta. For more information, contact **Mt Shasta Ranger District, Shasta-Trinity National Forests**, *204 W Alma St, Mt Shasta, CA 96067; tel: (916) 926-4511.*

Driving around Mt Shasta is easier than climbing it. A 77-mile (123 km), half-day driving route circumnavigates the peak. Most of the route is on dirt roads, which are navigable by passenger vehicles and RVs with caution once the snows melt in late spring. The route is largely uninhabited, but logging trucks and other local vehicles use the back roads regularly. Check with the Chamber of Commerce or the Mt Shasta Ranger station for road conditions and a map before setting out.

McCLOUD

Tourist Information: McCloud Chamber of Commerce, *Main St, McCloud, CA 96057; tel: (916) 964-2471.*

Sightseeing

McCloud is just 9 miles (14 km) from the unending traffic of I-5, but could be on another planet. The tiny hamlet was built as a lumber company town in the last century. It is still remote enough that heavy winter snows sometimes cut power and telephone lines for days at a time, but a trickle of urban refugees from the San Francisco area and Southern California has revived what had been a dying town.

The cookie cutter wooden buildings are typical of a company town built by, and for, a single employer. The McCloud River Lumber Co. built the town, which was named after a Scots fur trader named McLeod who explored the region in the 1820s. The company sold the town and buildings to the residents after the timber industry declined following World War II.

What was once the lumbermen's union hall is now the **McCloud Historical Center**, *520 Main St, McCloud CA 96057; tel: (916) 964-2604.* The Center has preserved much of the town's early history, including a house-sized drive wheel from an early mill steam engine that dwarfs the rear of the building.

McARTHUR-BURNEY FALLS MEMORIAL STATE PARK

Lake Britton is 17 miles (27 km) south of Dead Horse Summit, a popular artificial lake for boating, fishing and swimming. 1½ miles (2 km) beyond the bridge spanning the lake is the entrance to **McArthur-Burney Falls Memorial State Park**, on the right, *Rt. 1, Box 1260, Burney, CA 96013; tel: (916) 335-2777.* Activities include picnicking, hiking, camping, visitor centre, and a concession selling food and souvenirs. The park is apt to be busy during the summer and almost deserted from late Sept to mid-May.

The highlight of the park is **Burney Falls**, a 129 ft (39 m) waterfall with twin cascades cutting through several layers of moss-covered lava in a lush evergreen forest setting. The park is half-way between Mt Shasta and Mt Lassen, and, like the rest of the region, was formed by volcanoes.

Unlike more explosively famous Cascade Range volcanoes, including Mount St Helens in Oregon and Mt Lassen, the volcanoes around McArthur-Burney Falls Park were less dramatic and less violent. The many small, steep-sided hills around the park are actually volcanoes, known as 'cinder cones'. They are formed when a vent from an underground pool of magma, or molten rock, opens to the surface, and large amounts of superheated steam and watery magma pour out. Small chunks of magma shoot skyward, cool quickly in the air, and fall back to the ground to form a cone of porous cinder rock.

The magma which flowed from local vents was very thin, much like the lava that flows from volcanoes in Hawaii. This type of lava flows like water, covering vast areas with thin layers of rock to form large plateaus with very gentle slopes called shields. The highway from Lake Britton up to the park entrance cuts through a shield. So does Burney Falls.

Even the open forest that makes for easy walking is due to volcanism. As lava cools, gas bubbles form, which makes the solid rock very porous. When water hits the surface, either as rain or as melting snow, it passes down through the rock instead of running off. The relatively dry soil near the surface inhibits the growth of plants and bushes with shallow roots, but offers fertile ground for deep-rooted trees. The resulting forest is very open and easy to see and walk through.

The park offers several short, self-guided nature walks. The easy **Falls Trail Loop**, winds 1 mile (1.6 km) to the bottom of the falls and back up the other side. The 1½-mile (2.4 km) **Headwaters Loop** heads upstream from the falls beyond the point where the underground water source that keeps the water flowing year round emerges from the lava flows. The **Pioneer Cemetery Trail** is a 1½-mile (2.4 km) return trip along the original wagon road to Burney Falls. The Burney Falls Cemetery is the final resting place for many of the original white settlers of the area. A large Native American burial site is nearby.

The intersection of Hwy 299 is 6 miles (10 km) south of the park. The road is ribbed with warning bumps to alert drivers of the approaching traffic signal, but many drivers still career through the intersection instead of stopping. Cross with care and continue south on Hwy 89.

The town of **Burney** is 6 miles (10 km) west on Hwy 299. It has the best selection of lodging north of Lassen Volcanic National Park, although the choices are few. **Burney Chamber of Commerce**, *37477 Main St, Burney, CA 96013; tel: (916) 335-2111*. There's no reason to detour into Burney unless looking for accommodation before continuing on to Lassen Volcanic National Park the following day.

The first town south of the Hwy 299 intersection is **Hat Creek**, 8 miles (13 km) from the traffic signal. Named after the creek which flows through the valley, the town is one of many tiny farming communities which line Hwy 89. Most of the ranches raise horses or cattle. **Rancheria Angus**, 7 miles (11 km) south of Hat Creek, has turned part of its Angus cattle pasture into an RV park.

The ground begins rising again beyond Rancheria Angus, offering the last clear glimpses of Mt Shasta in the distance. As the ground rises,

it also becomes more open. Rough lava flows lie just beneath a layer of soil too thin and porous to support large trees. Dense forests and sparkling creeks lined with rich pastures occupy the gaps between lava flows.

The 250 people who live in **Old Station** make it the biggest town in Deer Valley, 7 miles (11 km) south of Rancheria Angus. Hwy 44 joins Hwy 89 from the east. Dual road numbers toward Lassen Volcanic National Park can make road signs confusing .

Deer Valley is dotted with campsites. Old Station has the nearest lodging to Lassen Volcanic National Park. The two choices are **Rim Rock Ranch**, *13275 Hwy 89, Old Station, CA 96071; tel: (916) 335-7114*, and the **Hat Creek Resort**, *PO Box 115, Old Creek CA 96071; tel: (916) 335-7121*, just down the highway.

At the south end of Deer Valley is a vista point on the left, 2 miles (3 km) beyond Old Station. There's a picnic area, a short nature trail, an exhibit showing how the barren lava flows were reforested about 50 years ago, and a magnificent panorama south to Mt Lassen, source of all the surrounding lava.

LASSEN VOLCANIC NATIONAL PARK

The park covers 106,000 acres (42,898 ha) of volcanic mountains where the Cascade Range joins the Sierra Nevada. The only route through Lassen Park is Hwy 89, which can be accessed from the north or the south. Access from the west is by Hwy 44 from Redding, which joins Hwy 89 north of the park, or by Hwy 36 from Red Bluff, which joins Hwy 89 south of the park. From the east (Hwy 395), take either Hwy 44 or Hwy 36 from Susanville to Hwy 89, then turn into the park.

The park entry fee is good for seven days; keep the receipt to show upon entering or leaving. The speed limit is 35 mph (56 kph) unless otherwise posted, which is too fast for many of the steep switchback turns. The visitor centre and park museum are located at the north entrance, but a concession store (Lassen Chalet) at the south entrance has basic visitor information. Pick up the official map and guide, free upon entering the park, and the *Road Guide to Lassen Volcanic*

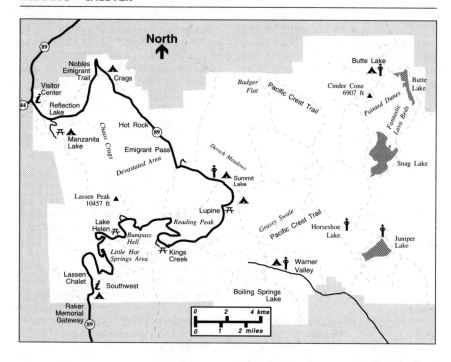

National Park, for sale at the park. Roadside markers are keyed to the Road Guide.

The park is open all year, but Hwy 89 is not kept open after the first heavy snowfall beyond the district ranger's office, 1 mile (1.6 km) from the north entrance, or the Lassen Chalet, just beyond the southern entrance. The road is usually open from early June until early November. There are five campsites in the park, but no other lodging. *PO Box 100, Mineral, CA 96063; tel: (916) 595-4444.*

Prominent park features include **Lassen Peak**, 10,457 ft (3169 m) and several smaller volcanoes, plus lava flows, fumaroles, hot springs, boiling lakes, mudpots, verdant meadows, and a vibrant display of high mountain wildflowers in springtime, around mid-July. And that's just what can be seen from the 37-mile (59 km) drive through the park.

Mt Lassen is the hard core (or plug) of a much larger volcano which has been eroded away over the past several thousand years. The mountain was quiet until the spring of 1914, when a series of small eruptions began. In 1915 a blast sent a mushroom cloud of ash 7 miles (11 km) into the stratosphere and tongues of lava and boiling mud roaring down the slopes. Hwy 89, Lassen Park Road, winds around three sides of Lassen Peak, affording constant views of the volcano and its power.

Manzanita Lake (marker 66 on the official *Road Guide*), on the right just inside the park boundary, was formed by an enormous rockfall during an eruption about 1200 years ago. The lower end of **Reflection Lake**, (marker 65) on the left, is a favourite spot for photographers during the late afternoon and early evenings when Mt Lassen is reflected in the calm waters. **Loomis Museum**, (marker 64) 1 mile (1.6 km) from the entrance, was built during the 1920s. It was built by Benjamin Loomis, who achieved international fame for his 1914–21 photographs of Mt Lassen's last eruption. Manzanita Lake Campground is to the right at the far end of the museum parking area.

Nobles Emigrant Trail (marker 60) passed

through the park 2 miles (3 km) from Manzanita Lake, briefly following the same route as the current road. The Trail was used by thousands of migrants from the Eastern USA into Northern California in the 1850s and 1860s. The trail is still visible to the north-east through the chaparral.

The **Devastation Area** (markers 50 and 44), 6 miles (10 km) from the Emigrant Trail, is a 2.6-mile (4 km) wide swath of destruction from the 1915 blast. Although new growth has hidden much of the damage, it is still possible to see the remains of huge trees toppled like matchsticks and bark ripped from tree trunks 18 ft (5.5 m) above the ground level by flowing mud.

As the road curves up and around the mountainside from the Devastation Area, the forest becomes thicker and the trees larger. Even the biggest trees have a curve at the base, called a snow bend, the result of being bent low as saplings by the weight of up to 50 ft (15 m) of snow every winter.

The **Lassen Peak Trail** parking lot is 19 miles (30 km) from the Emigrant Trail. The trail is a well-graded climb from 8500 ft (2576 m) to 10,457 ft (3169 m) in 2½ miles (4 km). Most hikers take about 4 hrs for the return trip. There is no water or shade on the trail, and the high mountain sun is blistering. Carry water, snacks, a hat, dark glasses and sun block, and wear long sleeves against serious sunburn.

Mt Shasta is clearly visible from the peak, 75 miles (120 km) north. The first woman known to have climbed to the summit of Mt Lassen, Helen Brodt, was the namesake for **Lake Helen**, a deep blue glacial lake 1 mile (1.6 km) down the highway from the parking lot. The lake is frozen eight months of the year.

Just around the curve from Lake Helen is the parking lot for **Bumpass Hell**, one of Lassen's main attractions. A 3 mile (5 km) return trail leads to a self-guided walk through a geothermal basin filled with boiling waters, gurgling mud, and steam tinged with the unmistakable smell of sulphur. Mineral stains turn water, mud, and rocks into an ever-changing rainbow.

The wide trail into Bumpass Hell offers scenic views across much of the park. Once in the thermal basin, the trail becomes a boardwalk set above the bubbling mud. Much of what looks like solid ground is actually a fragile mineral crust over boiling water and mud. *Do not leave the boardwalks*. Bumpass Hell was named after Kendall Vanhook Bumpass, a Danish miner who broke through the thin crust into a thermal pool. The leg that plunged into the boiling pool cooked and had to be amputated.

A miniature alternative to Bumpass Hell is the **Sulfur Works**, 8 miles (13 km) downhill next to the roadway. An easy boardwalk winds through several small fumaroles and mudpots on the hillside to the right of the highway. On the left, a large fumarole produces a steady plume of sulphuric steam that blows erratically with the winds. **Lassen Chalet**, a campsite, and the **South Entrance** are 2 miles (3 km) down the mountainside.

CHESTER

Tourist Information: Chester & Lake Almanor Chamber of Commerce, *529 Main St, Chester, CA 96020; tel: (916) 258-2426.*

Accommodation

There are about two dozen motels and resorts in the Chester/Lake Almanor area, plus several bed and breakfasts. The Chamber of Commerce can provide lodging lists, but does not make bookings.

Sightseeing

This tiny town is a relic from two generations ago when the mountain economy was dependent on timber, ranching, and firefighting, and hunting and fishing were more for survival than for recreation. Tourism has become the economic mainstay of the area, but rough-and-tumble attitudes still reflect the earlier era. Chester has the largest concentration of lodging near Lassen Volcanic National Park and is the gateway for recreation on and around **Lake Almanor**.

For a somewhat more urbanised atmosphere with outdoor beer gardens and soft folk music instead of smoky bars with driving country and western music, continue 44 miles (70 km) to **Quincy**. Quincy and Lake Almanor are both described on p. 333 as part of the Chester–Lake Tahoe Route.

CHESTER to LAKE TAHOE

It's possible to drive the 132 miles (211 km) from Chester to Lake Tahoe in less than 3 hrs, but it's safer to allow half a day for the occasional scenic overlook and stretch break. There are no breathtaking vistas along the way, but the pleasant mountain drive along country highways goes a long way towards explaining why Californians themselves comprise the vast majority of visitors to the Sierra Nevada Mountains. Adding side trips could stretch the journey to Lake Tahoe to 2–3 days.

ROUTE

From Chester (see p. 329), drive 3 miles (5 km) west on Hwy 89/36 and turn left to follow Hwy 89 southbound. The highway parallels the west shore of **Lake Almanor**, most of which is privately owned.

To detour around the **eastern shore of Lake Almanor**, take Hwy 36 east from Chester 5 miles (8 km) to Plumas County Rd A-13. Turn right and continue to another 5 miles (8 km) to Hwy 147. Turn right. Hwy 147 southbound follows the lake shore for 7 miles (11 km) to the town of **Canyon Dam**, where it joins Hwy 89.

To reach the **western shore** of Lake Almanor, turn onto Prattville Reservoir Rd from Hwy 89, 7 miles (11 km) south of the Hwy 89/36 junction. The Lake is 2 miles (3 km) downhill. Turn right onto Almanor Dr. West. (Watch out for deer and children crossing the residential road.) **Camp Prattville Resort**, *2913 Almanor Dr. West, Prattville, CA 95923; tel: (916) 259-2464*, is an RV park with a restaurant and outdoor deck that offer stunning views across the lake.

Continue south on Almanor Dr. West to Hwy 89, a total of 3 miles (5 km). Turn left onto Hwy

89. The highway crosses the spillway for Lake Almanor Dam 3 miles (5 km) later, then runs slowly uphill through yellow pine forests toward the town of **Canyon Dam**. The highest point on the road south from Almanor, 4 miles (6 km) south of Canyon Dam, is just 4000 ft (1212 m), less than half the altitude of the road over Mt Lassen. From here, the road drops gently through a succession of small valleys filled with verdant meadows and low rolling hills.

The rusting ruins of abandoned lumber mills loom over most valleys, put out of business over the past 30 years by rising costs, decreasing supply of harvestable timber and increasingly strict air pollution controls.

Most mills once burned their sawdust and waste wood in tall tapering burners, capped with screen spark arresters to prevent forest fires. The burners efficiently reduced the heaps of sawdust and scrap wood produced by busy mills. Many more advanced mills used heat from their burners to heat water that was piped to company buildings and homes for winter heat and year-round hot water. But the constant burning obscured the surrounding mountains with a pall of blue smoke most of the year. As the burning was halted, visibility increased dramatically, but the cost of hauling waste away over winding mountain roads forced mills to scale back production or close entirely. A few consolidated lumber mills now process the timber that was once handled by dozens of local operations. Tourism has become the economic lifeline of the mountains.

Hwy 89 is joined by Hwy 70 at Spanish River, 20 miles (32 km) beyond Canyon Dam. Turn left onto the main highway toward **Quincy**.

Continue south on Hwy 89/70 through **East Quincy**, the more modern portion of the town, and on through the **Indian-American Valley**, 1 mile (1.6 km) beyond, filled with horse ranches. The **Massack Rest Area** is 2 miles (3 km) further with picnic tables, toilets, and local information. **Lee Summit**, 4439 ft (1345 m) is 5 miles (8 km) up a steep slope. The extended slope down from Lee Summit leads to Long Valley, lined with small resorts, holiday cabins, RV parks, and campsites in all price ranges.

Toward the end of the valley, Plumas County

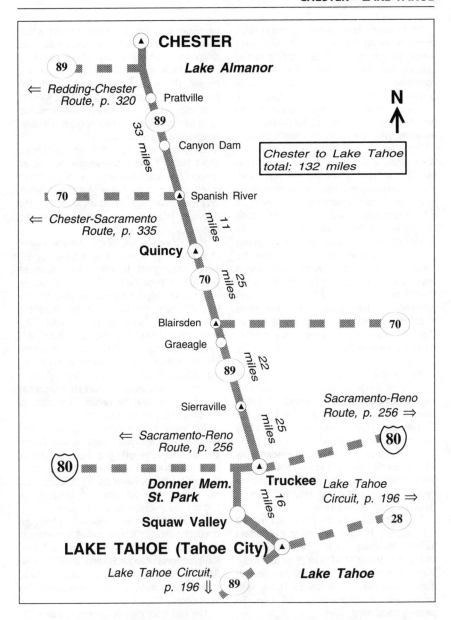

CHESTER

Lake Almanor

89

⇐ *Redding-Chester Route, p. 320*

Prattville

N ↑

89

33 miles

Canyon Dam

Chester to Lake Tahoe
total: 132 miles

70

Spanish River

⇐ *Chester-Sacramento Route, p. 335*

11 miles

Quincy

70

25 miles

Blairsden

70

Graeagle

22 miles

89

Sierraville

Sacramento-Reno Route, p. 256 ⇒

25 miles

⇐ *Sacramento-Reno Route, p. 256*

80

80

Donner Mem. St. Park

Truckee Lake Tahoe

Lake Tahoe Circuit, p. 196 ⇒

16 miles

28

Squaw Valley

LAKE TAHOE (Tahoe City)

Lake Tahoe Circuit, p. 196 ⇓

89

Lake Tahoe

Rd A-14 turns right toward **Plumas-Eureka State Park**, *310 Johnsville Rd, Blairsden, CA 96103; tel: (916) 836-2380*, 4 miles (6 km) uphill. Within the park are the historic mining town of Johnsville and the partially restored Plumas-Eureka stamp mill, a campsite, several alpine lakes and what may be the birthplace of competitive downhill skiing in the United States.

Gold was first discovered in the area in 1851, prompting a rush that produced the three large mining companies and three booming mining towns. The three mines were eventually consolidated under British ownership. Johnsville became the principal town, largely because of the stamp mill, which pounded ore mined from mountain tunnels into dust so the gold could be extracted. When the mines were finally closed in 1943, about 65 miles (104 km) of tunnels had been carved into Eureka Peak, rising directly behind. The building housing the park head-quarters and museum was once a mine bunk-house. Part of the old tramway is still standing. It is believed to have served as the world's first ski lift. Mining operations slowed in winter on account of the deep snows. According to period photographs and written accounts from the 1860s and 1870s, bored miners began racing from Eureka Lake 1700 ft (515 m) down the steep slope on skis up to 12 ft (3.6 m) long, and wagering on the results. From the times recorded, it seems racers hit speeds of 80 mph (128 kph) in the quest for prize money of $250, then rode the mine tram back to the top for the next race.

Park rangers strongly advise campsite reservations from mid-June to Labor Day; tel: (800) 444-7275 up to eight weeks in advance of arrival. Space is generally available at other times, but the campsite is closed from early October to May on account of heavy snow.

At the end of Long Valley is **Blairsden**. Hwy 70 becomes the primary road and continues east toward Hallelujah Junction and the Mt Shasta–Reno route (see p. 347) and Hwy 395. Hwy 89 continues south toward Lake Tahoe.

Train buffs may want to detour onto Hwy 70 approximately 10 miles (16 km) to the **Portola Railroad Museum**, PO Box 608, Portola, CA 96122; tel: (916) 832-4131 or (916) 832-4737. The museum has one of the largest collections of diesel locomotives in the United States, with more than 30 locomotives, and over 80 passenger and freight cars.

The museum is a hands-on project staffed by volunteers. Unlike most rail museums, this one encourages visitors to climb into the locomotives, sit in the engineer's chair, walk through freight or

passenger cars, tour the cabooses, and watch restoration at close range. The museum also hires driving time on its vintage diesel switching engines. Each hire includes a private instructor if needed. The museum has about 12,000 ft (3.6 km) of track in a former Western Pacific Railroad switching yard. There are no age restrictions, and up to four people can share a single engine hire. Reservations are required.

Continue straight on Hwy 89 southbound about 1 mile (1.6 km) to **Graeagle**. The former lumber town has been reborn as a golf resort based on a vaguely Native American theme. Watch out for golfers strolling across the highway. Information is available from the Plumas County Visitors Bureau.

From Graeagle, Hwy 89 rolls through a series of small valleys separated by increasingly tall passes. The highest, 10 miles (16 km) south of Graeagle, is **Yuba Pass**, 5334 ft (1616 m). Six miles (10 km) beyond the summit, Hwy 49 joins Hwy 89 from the west, running from the Oakhurst–Lake Tahoe route (p. 206). The combined highway skirts the valley floor, with verdant meadows stretching out on one side. Steep mountain slopes rise almost within touching distance of the other side of the highway.

The two roads separate 5 miles (8 km) later at a traffic signal near **Sierraville**. Turn right to remain on Hwy 89 southbound.

The valley is filled with cattle, mostly Red Angus and Red Brangus, a cross between Angus and Brahma. The offspring have the heavy shoulders associated with Brahma cattle in India, but lack the hump. Power poles and fence posts are popular look-out and resting spots for vultures and several varieties of hawks.

Sierraville, less than ½ mile (1 km) from the stoplight, was once a breadbasket for miners in the nearby mountains. Today, it has a **Tahoe National Forest Ranger Station**, tel: (916) 994-3401. The office is open on weekdays, but basic information is posted on signboards outside the front doors.

The road quickly winds up to more than 6000 ft (1818 m), then drops down to meet the Little Truckee River and a succession of other small streams that have cut valleys through the rugged mountains. Hwy 89 crosses I-80 22 miles (35 km) from Sierraville and continues on to **Truckee**. (At this point the route intersects the direct portion of the Sacramento–Reno Route, p. 256, and it is only a short distance west along the I-80 to Emigrant Gap, at one end of the Oakhurst–Lake Tahoe Route, p. 206.)

From Truckee, Hwy 89 winds along the Truckee River on the way to **Tahoe City** and **Lake Tahoe**. The turnoff for **Squaw Valley** is 9 miles (14 km) from Truckee. Turn right and follow Squaw Valley Rd 2 miles (3 km) to the resort area.

Hwy 89 reaches **Lake Tahoe** (see p. 196) at **Tahoe City**, 3½ miles (6 km) beyond Alpine.

LAKE ALMANOR

Tourist Information: Chester & Lake Almanor Chamber of Commerce, *520 Main St, Chester, CA 96020; tel: (916) 258-2426.*

The Lake, as frequent visitors call it, is an artificial reservoir, created early in the century to produce electricity for the giant Pacific Gas & Electric Co. Despite its mundane beginnings, Almanor looks like a tiny Lake Tahoe – apart from the bathtub ring effect of naked soil between the fluctuating waterline and the permanent forest higher up the shore. The lake can feel unbelievably lonely despite its nearness to major cities in the Sacramento Valley – heavy advertising and gambling casinos lure most lake-bound visitors to Shasta Lake and Lake Tahoe. Even in mid-summer, there are days when Almanor's mirrored surface is undisturbed by a single outboard motor wake, though sails drift across the waters whenever a breeze comes up.

The appeal of Lake Almanor includes cool, clean air, brisk water for swimming and water skiing, good fishing, and uncrowded boating. The western side, along Hwy 89, is more relaxed, rustic, and longer established. The eastern shore offers new homes for holidaymakers and permanent residents as well as several very expensive resort developments.

QUINCY

Tourist Information: Quincy Main Street Chamber of Commerce, *PO Box 3829, Quincy, CA 95971; tel: (916) 283-0188,* and

the **Plumas County Visitors Bureau**, *91 Church St, Quincy, CA 95971; tel: (916) 283-2247.*

Accommodation and Food

There are about a dozen motels and bed and breakfasts to choose from. The best is **The Feather Bed**, a bed and breakfast just behind the Courthouse at *542 Jackson St, Quincy, CA 95971; tel: (916) 283-0102.*

The best spot to pass a quiet afternoon is **The Loft**, *Main St; tel: (916) 283-0126,* which has live music and an outdoor beer garden as well as a full restaurant. **Morning Thunder**, *557 Lawrence St, Quincy, CA 95971; tel: (916) 283-1310,* has good Mexican and American fare; budget for breakfast and lunch, moderate at dinner. **Moon's Restaurant**, just down the street; *tel: (916) 283-0765,* has the best Italian food in the area.

Sightseeing

The town sits in a broad grassy valley, cleared decades ago when Quincy was a thriving lumber centre. It's easy to see just how profitable lumbering could be. White stone facings and soaring pillars make the four-storey **County Courthouse**, *Main St,* one of the most imposing buildings in the northern Sierra.

The modern era has been equally kind to Quincy. As the lumber industry was shrinking, urbanites seeking the calm of small town life began trickling in, keeping the population level and the tax base relatively healthy. Modern Quincy is an old-fashioned mountain town with an unexpectedly polished veneer, including some surprisingly good restaurants. Look out for the **murals** at the corner of Main and Bradley Sts, just beyond the courthouse, showing two vital threads in local history. Quincy Drug shows a Native American ceremony in the valley before the arrival of white settlers; the Pizza Factory has a logging and sawmill scene.

Don't miss the **Plumas County Museum**, *500 Jackson St, Quincy, CA 95971; tel: (916) 283-6320,* directly behind the Courthouse. The museum has a solid collection of mining and logging artifacts and a fine group of Native American baskets woven by the Maidu, who once inhabited the area.

TRUCKEE

Tourist Information: Truckee-Donner Chamber of Commerce, *PO Box 2757, Truckee, CA 96160; tel: (916) 587-2757 or (800) 548-8388.*

Accommodation

Truckee proper has *BW* and a scattering of other motels. Most accommodation is at Lake Tahoe (see p. 196).

Sightseeing

Truckee grew up during the heady days of the transcontinental railroad. Its original Wild West ambience survived the years so well that Charlie Chaplin chose the town as the ideal location to shoot his film *The Gold Rush*. It was one of the snowiest winters on record.

The town's saloons did a roaring business with the Hollywood film crew, business which continued unabated through the years of Prohibition. A lively red-light district was spawned and supported by the railroad, then by long-distance truck drivers hauling freight in and out of California. The brothels weren't closed down until just before foreign journalists were due to arrive for the 1960 Winter Olympic Games at nearby Squaw Valley. Today, the biggest draw is the **Tahoe Truckee Factory Stores** mall, *Donner Pass Rd, near the I-80 interchange.*

- - - - - - - - - - - - - - - - - - -

◠ Side Track from Truckee

To reach **Donner Memorial State Park**, *PO Box 549, Truckee, CA 96160; tel: (916) 587-3841,* follow Donner Pass Rd (or I-80) 2 miles (3 km) toward **Donner Lake**. Follow signs to the park.

The park is a summertime favourite for camping, water sports, and short walks, but the real reason to visit is the **Emigrant Trail Museum**. The museum tells the story of the Donner Party's hungry winter of 1846–47, the construction of the Central Pacific Railroad through the area in the 1860s, and the natural history of the region. The museum is free to campers and park picnickers with a park receipt; everyone else pays a separate entry fee.

- - - - - - - - - - - - - - - - - - -

SQUAW VALLEY

Tourist Office: Squaw Valley USA, *PO Box 2007, Olympic Valley, CA 96146; tel: (916) 583-6985 or (800) 545-4350.*

Accommodation

The choices are expensive, expensive and expensive. Unless you have money to burn, stay at a more reasonable place near the lake and drive in for the day.

Sightseeing

This is the most famous of all Tahoe area ski resorts, with some of the world's finest alpine skiing. Squaw also has some of Tahoe's most crowded skiing, thanks to a publicity hangover from 1960, a steady advertising barrage and a full plate of winter offerings: expert, intermediate, beginner, and night skiing, snowboarding, and a restricted area for disabled skiers. There's even a climbing wall at the tram building to help pass the time while waiting for the interminable weekend tram queues to inch forward.

Even non-skiers flock to the resort to ride the tram to the top of Squaw Peak, 8909 ft (2700 m), for the spectacular views of Lake Tahoe (the tram is open in summer, too). Equally astounding is the Bath and Tennis Club atop the mountain, with spas, a swimming lagoon, tennis courts that are heated for winter play, and an outdoor winter-only ice skating rink.

Squaw, like other ski resorts, has been pushing summer activities in recent years to boost its annual income. The Squaw Peak tram is open for sightseers and resort restaurants do a booming business. On a more practical level, Squaw's hiking trails are hard to beat anywhere in the Tahoe area, and relatively uncrowded because the area's fame rests so heavily on winter sports.

Alpine Meadows, *PO Box 5279, Tahoe City, CA 96145; tel: (916) 583-4232,* is 1½ miles (2.5 km) beyond Squaw Valley toward Lake Tahoe. With six bowls, Alpine has far more skiable terrain than Squaw Valley, with far fewer skiers – which is why locals tend to ski here and leave Squaw to the tourists. Summer activities are limited.

CHESTER
to
SACRAMENTO

Allow at least 4 hrs for the 163 miles (260 km) from Chester down to the Sacramento Valley and Sacramento. The actual drive takes about 3 hrs, but there are enough sights along the way, especially in the scenic Feather River Canyon south to Oroville, to spend a full day. Best places to buy petrol are Chester and Oroville.

ROUTE

Leaving Chester, follow the Chester–Lake Tahoe route (see p. 330) 33 miles (59 km) to the Hwy 89/70 junction. Turn right onto Hwy 70 toward **Sacramento**. The highway snakes above the **Feather River**, past **Twain** and **Belden**.

The highway begins climbing up the side of the canyon 20 miles (32 km) beyond **Belden** and crosses high above the river on a narrow concrete bridge. The railroad crosses at the same spot near the canyon floor. There are no observation points near the bridge, but look for an unofficial lay-by on the right about 1 mile (1.6 km) beyond the bridge. Park and walk across the road for a look at the unusual juxtaposition of road and rail bridges crossing the same river almost at right angles, one more than 300 ft above the other. The view is an afternoon favourite with postcard photographers.

Hwy 70 leaves the river behind 10 miles (16 km) beyond the double bridge. Six miles (10 km) after the two-lane road expands to four lanes, just beyond the highway bridge over **Lake Oroville**, turn left onto Cherokee Road. Follow signs for the town of Cherokee and the covered bridge.

Continue up Cherokee Rd for 4 miles (6 km) to Derrick Rd. Turn left and continue ½ mile (1 km) to the **covered bridge** and **Oregon City**.

From Oregon City return to Cherokee Rd and turn left. Continue 11 miles (18 km) to **Oroville**. Immediately after crossing the Feather River, turn right onto Montgomery St and continue into the city centre.

From Oroville return to Hwy 70 and continue south toward **Marysville** through rolling farm country. Most of the orchards are olives, walnuts, cherries, peaches and pears. During the late summer and early autumn, many growers set up stands along the highway to sell, at bargain prices, fruit that is too ripe to withstand rough handling on the way to supermarkets .

To navigate through Marysville, follow signs for Hwy 70 past Ellis Lake towards Sacramento, 39 miles (62 km) south. Hwy 70 becomes a freeway at the Yuba River bridge. Six miles (10 km) later, it reverts to an ordinary highway. Much of the land on either side of the road is planted with rice, the reason behind California's enduring zeal for pursuing rice exports to Japan. Traffic becomes much heavier 17 miles (27 km) later when Hwy 70 joins Hwy 99.

Hwy 99 is Main Street for the entire Central Valley and is heavily travelled by lorries and agricultural equipment. The highway becomes freeway 9 miles (14 km) later and continues another 9 miles (14 km) into downtown **Sacramento**.

FEATHER RIVER

The course of the Feather River is one of the most scenic canyon drives in California. The river is never out of sight, sometimes roaring and foaming through immense rapids, sometimes sliding silently through vast, limpid pools teeming with trout. Trees near the river turn flaming red and gold during the autumn months, a striking contrast with the blue-green water and dark green conifers. The road is kept open all winter, but tyre chains may be required.

Hwy 70 opened in 1937 as an all-weather alternative to Hwy 80 (now I-80) over Donner Summit, which was subject to frequent winter closures. Cutting the 78 miles (125 km) of roadway through the Sierra Nevada from Oroville to Quincy cost 8 million Depression dollars. It was a massive sum at the time, for a massive project:

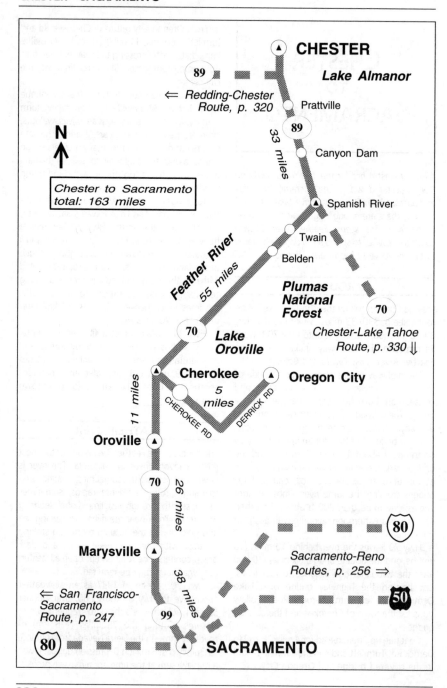

CHESTER

Lake Almanor

89

⇐ Redding-Chester
Route, p. 320

Prattville

89

33 miles

Canyon Dam

Spanish River

N
↑

Chester to Sacramento
total: 163 miles

Twain

Belden

Feather River
55 miles

Plumas
National
Forest

70

Chester-Lake Tahoe
Route, p. 330 ⇓

70

Lake
Oroville

Cherokee

5
miles

Oregon City

CHEROKEE RD

DERRICK RD

11 miles

Oroville

70

26 miles

80

Sacramento-Reno
Routes, p. 256 ⇒

Marysville

50

38 miles

⇐ San Francisco-
Sacramento
Route, p. 247

99

80

SACRAMENTO

workers removed 7½ million cubic yards (5.7 million cubic metres) of rock, bored three tunnels through solid granite, and built seven bridges. The Pacific Gas & Electric Co. promptly pounced on the newly accessible river and built a number of hydroelectric generating plants which are still in operation beside the road.

Turn left 8 miles (13 km) west from the Hwy 89/70 junction to the town of **Twain**. Once a thriving rail and lumber town, Twain now has a store and RV park, plus a well-stocked information kiosk just outside the store.

The Feather River, like most waterways in the Sierra, was first discovered by the Spanish (it was named after the huge rafts of wild pigeon feathers that once drifted downstream) but not seriously explored until the Gold Rush. One of the richer gold strikes was made near **Belden**, 12 miles (19 km) downstream from Twain. Between 1849 and 1852 more than 250,000 ounces (7.1 tonnes) of gold was mined from the riverbed between Belden and Bar, 4 miles (6 km) upstream. Small finds are still made.

Belden Town is now a small resort across a bright orange bridge over the river from the highway. The resort has RV and camping spaces, overpriced petrol, and a restful view of the canyon from a small restaurant or picnic tables. An official rest area offers a similar view from the highway, complete with broad shade trees, drinking water, picnic tables, toilets, and traffic noise instead of the sounds of the river.

The road continues along the canyon floor, winding through tunnels and passing giant brown or green pipes that drop water from high country reservoirs through turbines inside riverside powerhouses. The tall canyon walls keep the road in shade much of the day. Rock climbing is allowed, but climbers must keep at least 15 ft (4.5 m) from the roadway.

CHEROKEE

The narrow road curves up the side of Table Mountain, a flat-topped mountain overlooking the Sacramento Valley. Along the way, look for remains of stone walls built with lava boulders moved out of the way by miners and used as boundary markers by later landowners. The remains of Cherokee are 1½ miles (2.5 km) beyond the turnoff from Hwy 70.

The town of Cherokee was the original Gold Rush settlement in the area. The town was founded in 1853 by Cherokee Indians and their New England-born school teacher, who led them from Oklahoma west to California in search of gold. They found a rich vein along the western side of Table Mountain, but white settlers in the area heard of the strike and forced the Native Americans off their claims. The new owners named the settlement Cherokee.

From 1870 to 1886 it was a boom town with 17 saloons, eight hotels, a school, racetrack, brewery, and even two churches. By 1881, the Spring Valley Hydraulic Gold Mining Company was in 24-hour operation, thanks to the electric lights that had recently been installed. Diamonds were also discovered.

The hydraulic miners used gigantic water nozzles, called monitors, to direct 40 million gallons (151 million litres) of water against the sides of Table Mountain each day, literally washing the mountain away – the hydraulic mining scars are still visible. It was a highly profitable mine, but the destruction wrought by millions of cubic metres of tailings, or rubble, washed onto farms and rivers downstream by the operation led to the banning of hydraulic mining in California a few years later.

It was good training for mine operators. Louis Glass, the mine secretary and telegraph agent, went on to found Pacific Telephone & Telegraph, California's first telephone company. Gardner Williams, mine superintendent, sailed for South Africa, where he helped Cecil Rhodes consolidate the Kimberly Diamond Mines into DeBeers Limited, which he managed for nearly 20 years.

All that remains today are the barren, ragged cliffs left by the hydraulic operation, a few stone foundations built by Welsh miners, and an old boarding house that has become a museum. The **Cherokee Museum**, open weekends 1100–1500, has a small collection of local artifacts.

OREGON CITY

Oregon City, founded in 1848 by a band of immigrants from the state of Oregon, has all but disappeared. The school, now a museum (tel: (916) 533-5316 for tours by appointment), and a 1984 replica of an old covered bridge are all that remain. The new bridge is a faithful copy of the original, with the addition of structural steel supports. The founder of Oregon City, Peter Burnett, became the first civil Governor of California.

OROVILLE

Tourist Information: Oroville Area Chamber of Commerce, 1789 Montgomery St, Oroville, CA 95965; tel: (916) 533-2542 or (800) 655-GOLD (4653).

Sightseeing

The most obvious thing about Oroville is the desolate heaps of rocks and gravel surrounding the small town. They're tailings, the remains of dredging operations that ripped topsoil from the fertile Feather River floodplain in search of gold well over a century ago. When the gold boom faded, Oroville went with it.

The town picked up during a 1960s construction project that created **Lake Oroville**, only to falter when the dam was completed in 1967. Oroville has one of the best-preserved and most attractive old city centres in the state because no one could afford to knock it down and rebuild. Stately gardens and old homes are worth the time it takes to cruise through. Newer parts of town (including petrol stations) lie to the south, along Oro Dam Blvd.

Liet Sheng Kong, the **Temple of Many Gods**, Elma and Broderick Sts; tel: (916) 538-2496, is a reminder of how important China was to the building of California. The 1863 temple was built by subscription from a local Chinese community of 10,000 (the total modern population is only 12,000) with financial help from the Emperor of China. The temple is a museum as well as an active place of worship for Confucianism, Buddhism, and Taoism.

The **Judge C.F. Lott Historic Home in Sank Park**, 1067 Montgomery St, Oroville, CA 95965; tel: (916) 538-2415, is a Victorian Gothic revival house set in a formal gazebo garden. The house

is a museum reflecting the early days of Oroville, including furniture, paintings, rugs, textiles, clothing, silver, and glassware, 1849–1910.

Lake Oroville supplies water to local farmers, the Central Valley and Southern California, controls flooding, generates electricity, and provides boating, fishing, and camping opportunities on a five-fingered lake. The lake also necessitated construction of the **Feather River Fish Hatchery**, 5 Table Mountain Blvd; tel: (916) 538-2222, to perpetuate the salmon and steelhead spawn that was blocked by the dam. Best time to visit is in the autumn, during the annual spawning run, but the hatchery is open all year.

The **Lake Oroville Visitor Center**, tel: (916) 538-2200, is 7 miles (11 km) north-east of Hwy 162, then 1½ miles (2.5 km) north and overlooks the lake and dam. Displays chronicle the Gold Rush, local Native American tribes, and development of the California Water Project, of which the lake is a major part. To visit the dam power plant tel: (916) 534-2306.

MARYSVILLE

Tourist Information: Yuba-Sutter Chamber of Commerce, 10th and E Sts, Marysville, CA 95901; tel: (916) 743-6501.

Sightseeing

A Gold Rush town founded by Chilean miners, most of modern Marysville is connected to nearby Beale Air Force Base. When Beale lost its SR-71 spy planes a few years ago, Marysville lost much of its economic base.

The **Bok Kai Temple** stands on the levee at the foot of D St; tel: (916) 742-5486 for permission to visit. It is the only temple in the United States dedicated to the Chinese river god of good fortune. Another pleasant spot is **Ellis Lake**, a small, quiet lake in the midst of a spaghetti of highways from several different directions weaving through town.

SACRAMENTO

For a description of Sacramento, see p. 251.

MOUNT SHASTA
to
RENO

Allow at least 2 days, preferably 3–4 days, to drive the 355 miles (568 km) through California's remote north-east corner. Modoc County, which abuts Oregon and Nevada, has the population of a small town, but scattered across tens of thousands of square miles. There aren't many man-made attractions (or facilities) along the route, but it's filled with soaring mountains, wildlife refuges, vast forests and empty deserts stretching to the horizon.

ROUTE

Head north from **Mount Shasta City** (see p. 324) along the I-5. At **Weed**, turn off north-east onto Hwy 97. Follow Hwy 97 past **Dorris** and up to the California–Oregon border. Turn right at the junction with Hwy 161 and head east, parallel with the border. The road passes **Klamath Basin National Wildlife Refuge** and joins Hwy 139 at 2 miles (3 km) past the Visitor Center. Turn right onto Hwy 139 and continue to **Tulelake**.

Three miles south of Tulelake turn right onto Modoc County Rd 111 and into **Lava Beds National Monument**. From the end of County 111, 14 miles (22 km) further on, take Nat. Forest Hwy 97 for 2 miles (3 km) back to Hwy 139.

Continue south down Hwy 139 for 22 miles (36 km) to the junction with Hwy 299. Turn right at **Canby**. At **Alturas**, 18 miles (29 km) further on, turn south onto Hwy 395. The road goes to **Honey Lake**, where an abrupt change of direction on Hwy 395 takes you into and out of **Susanville**, 107 miles (171 km) from Alturas, unless you take a short-cut along County Rd A3, rejoining Hwy 395 further south. Hwy 395 takes you another 66 miles (104 km) into **Reno**.

For general information, contact the **Shasta**

Cascade Wonderland Association, *14250 Holiday Rd, Redding, CA 96003; tel: (916) 275-5555.*

Fill up with petrol in Mount Shasta. Prices rise dramatically in mountain communities. For a two-day trip, stop overnight at Lava Beds National Monument (camping only), in the town of Tulelake or at Tionesta. To stretch the trip, spend more than one night at Lava Beds or add a night in Alturas.

MOUNT SHASTA CITY TO WEED

Take I-5 north from Mount Shasta City. The speed limit jumps to 65 mph (104 kph) just north of town. The mountain on the right, almost within touching distance of the freeway, is **Black Butte**, 6325 ft (1917 m). A steep 2½-mile (4 km) trail leads to the top, which affords spectacular views of Mt Shasta towering to the east, Mount Shasta City and the Sacramento River canyon to the south, the Klamath Mountains to the west, and the town of Weed to the north.

To reach the trailhead from Mount Shasta City, follow Alma St east past Sisson Elementary School to the stop sign. Turn left onto Everitt Memorial Hwy for 2 miles (3 km). Turn left at the Penny Pines sign and follow the dirt road to the right for 2½ miles (4 km). When the dirt road crosses beneath the power line, take a smaller dirt road to the left. The trailhead parking area is ½ mile (1 km) ahead.

Continue 5½ miles (9 km) to the Central **Weed** exit, also marked as Hwy 97 toward Klamath Falls. Follow Hwy 97 into town.

WEED

Tourist Information: Weed Chamber of Commerce, *34 Main St, Weed, CA 96094; tel: (916) 938-4624*, on the left, just beyond the 'Weed' arch at the corner with Hwy 97.

The town was named after a lumber baron who picked the windiest spot in the area to build a mill so his newly sawn lumber would season quickly. The late 1800s downtown remains largely intact.

The highway bypasses the town centre, although the Weed lumber mill and cemetery are visible on the right. To explore Weed, go left on Main St from the Chamber of Commerce. To continue on, turn right from the Chamber of Commerce and right again back to Hwy 97 toward Klamath Falls.

WEED TO THE KLAMATH BASIN

The road begins climbing 3 miles (5 km) beyond Weed into the hills around Mt Shasta. The landscape alternates between lush conifer forest and low brush clinging to lava flows. Ancient volcanic activity is visible on all sides, from barren lava flows to naked cinder cones thrusting into the sky. To reach the **Lake Shastina Recreation Area** for fishing, boating, and camping, turn left 4 miles (6 km) beyond the lumber mill and cemetery.

Shortly after the Lake Shastina turnoff, the highway begins climbing sharply around the north flank of Mt Shasta. There are numerous lay-bys for slow traffic and gazing at the ever-changing views of Mt Shasta. Views are generally best in morning because the peak is frequently obscured by clouds later in the day. The landscape shifts almost minute by minute between forest, brush, alpine meadow, bare lava, rolling hills, and naked volcanic cliffs. The **Emigrant Trail**, the route used by 19th-century emigrants who crossed North America on foot and in wagon trains, followed the same route 10 miles (16 km) beyond Lake Shastina. A historical marker is on the right-hand side of the highway. There is a view point with a good panorama of Mt Shasta on the left side of the highway 4 miles (6 km) beyond the historical marker.

Grass Lake Summit, 5101 ft (1546 m) is 1 mile (1.6 km) beyond the vista point. The broad valley, much of it a shallow marsh, looks like a lake of grass. Ranchers graze cattle in the valley as early settlers did more than a century ago. The highway crosses the marshy ground atop a small levee that leads to a large rest area at the far end of the valley.

The road climbs back into the mountains immediately beyond the rest area. **Hebron Summit**, 5202 ft (1576 m), leads into **Butte Valley**, another expanse of flat agricultural land. The valley sparkles emerald green where irrigated; the unirrigated areas are covered by dusty chaparral brush. The first town in the valley, **Macdoel**, 10 miles (16 km) from Hebron Summit, is a major metropolis of 600 inhabitants. Bald eagles from the nearby Bear Valley National Wildlife Refuge in Oregon sometimes hunt over the valley.

The Butte Valley Airport is 5 miles (8 km) beyond Macdoel. The only sign of activity is a windsock whipping in the almost constant breeze above a dirt landing strip. Railroad tracks parallel the highway across the valley; small lorries often ride the rails. Maintenance crews use customised pickups that have been fitted with small railroad guide wheels which fold out of the way for road use.

The **California Agricultural Inspection Station** is located at **Dorris**, 10 miles (16 km) north of Macdoel. All southbound traffic must stop. Dorris has a small lumber mill, grain elevators, and a very few small shops.

The California–Oregon border is 4 miles (6 km) north of Dorris. Just before the border, turn right onto Hwy 161 eastbound toward Tulelake, the **Klamath National Wildlife Refuges** and the **Tule Lake National Wildlife Refuge**. The area is part of the **Modoc Plateau**, a vast region of ancient volcanoes, sand dunes turned to rock, sheer cliffs, and marshes, all beneath the brooding sentinels of Mt Shasta and Mt Lassen. Native peoples called Modoc 'the smiles of God'. Before the marshes were drained for agriculture earlier in this century, it was a rich land, filled with game, wild birds, forests, rivers, and shallow lakes between the rugged lava flows.

Today, cowboys still ride the range and belly up to small town bars, and locals still haven't forgiven 60 Native Americans for holding 600 Army troops at bay a century ago in a doomed effort to regain ancestral lands (see p. 345).

KLAMATH BASIN NATIONAL WILDLIFE REFUGE

Tourist Office: Klamath Basin National Wildlife Refuge, *Route 1, Box 74, Tule Lake, CA 96134; tel: (916) 667-2231.* The **Visitor Center**, on *Hill Rd,* east of the town of Tule Lake, is open Mon–Fri 0800–1630; Sat–Sun 0800–1600.

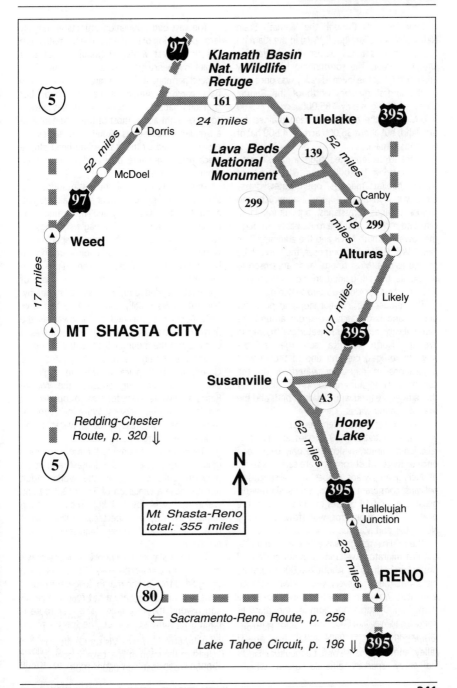

97 Klamath Basin Nat. Wildlife Refuge

5

161
24 miles

Dorris

52 miles

McDoel

▲ Tulelake **395**

Lava Beds National Monument

139
52 miles

97

Canby

299

▲ Weed

18 miles

299

▲ Alturas

17 miles

Likely

MT SHASTA CITY

107 miles

395

Susanville ▲

A3

Redding-Chester Route, p. 320 ⇓

Honey Lake

62 miles

N ↑

5

Mt Shasta-Reno total: 355 miles

395

Hallelujah Junction

23 miles

RENO

80

⇐ Sacramento-Reno Route, p. 256

Lake Tahoe Circuit, p. 196 ⇓ **395**

Hwy 161 cuts through the Klamath Basin National Wildlife Refuges (NWRs) in the Klamath Basin, which spreads across the California–Oregon border. The surrounding hills are dry and barren, but the lowland valley was once one of the largest marshes north of the Central Valley, covering nearly 185,000 acres (74,700 ha). Most of the marsh has been drained for farmland, but about 36,000 acres (14,500 ha) of wetlands remain.

There are six separate refuges in the Klamath Basin, covering 151,000 acres (61,000 ha) of varying habitat: marshes, open water, grassy meadows, coniferous forests, sagebrush and juniper uplands, grasslands, agricultural land, cliffs and rocky slopes. The route passes through the Lower Klamath NWR and the adjoining Tule Lake NWR. For touring purposes, the two can be treated as one. Most refuge lands are closed to the public, but self-guided driving tours provide limited access for close-up bird-watching.

The refuges are a major stopping point for birds – and bird-watchers – from around the world. Every north–south waterfowl flyway in Western North America converges at the Klamath refuges, creating one of the densest populations of migratory waterfowl on the continent. From autumn to spring, skies over the refuges are filled with clouds of birds and the roar of beating wings.

253 species have been verified as regular visitors; an additional 39 species are listed as 'accidental' visitors which have only been seen once or twice. Most common are several species of duck, geese, swans, grebes, several species of pelicans, cormorants, herons, egrets, shorebirds, gulls, terns and 14 species of birds of prey. The peak viewing times for waterfowl are early November and March.

The original refuge was established in 1908, the first migratory wetlands to be given federal protection in the USA. About 700,000 migratory birds visit the area every year, down from an estimated 7 million a half-century ago. More than 45,000 ducks are born in the marshes annually, as well as 2600 Canada geese and tens of thousands of other marsh and shore birds. The refuges also have one of the world's last nesting colonies of white pelicans.

The vast bird population attracts an equally large population of predators. The Klamath Basin has the largest wintering population of bald eagles in America outside Alaska, and one of the largest permanent populations anywhere. The bald eagle is America's national bird, but shrinking habitat has turned what was once a common sight across most of the continent into an endangered species. Adult bald eagles are easily identified by the stark white head atop a black body. Immature bald eagles are mottled white and brown.

The northern part of the Basin supports a sizeable breeding population of bald eagles, about four dozen nesting pairs. The nesting areas are closed to the public, but eagle sightings are common throughout the area, especially in winter. Migrating eagles begin arriving in November; the highest concentration is in January and February, when 500 or more of the white-headed birds of prey roost nearby. Migrant eagles usually leave by late March or early April, many headed as far away as northern reaches of the Northwest Territories in Canada and the mountains of central Mexico.

Because nesting and roosting areas are closed, the best place to observe eagles is along self-guided tour routes in the Wildlife Refuges. In winter, look for areas of open water amidst the frozen marshes. Waterfowl concentrate in the few areas of open water, luring eagles to the same open waters.

The Basin is also home to the more common golden eagle, one of the largest and most powerful birds of prey in the world. Adult females have a wingspan of 7½ ft (2.3 m) and weigh up to 14 lbs (6.4 kg). Their courtship displays are filled with spectacular roller-coaster dives, loops, and other high-speed aerial acrobatics.

The first vista point overlooking the marsh is 7 miles (11 km) beyond the Hwy 161 turnoff. For a self-guided **tour of the marsh**, follow the brown signs and turn right onto a dirt road 2 miles (3 km) beyond the vista point. The tour route is open from sunrise to sunset. The speed limit on the gravel road is 35 mph (56 kph), which is too fast on curves and corners. The road follows dykes and levees with almost no verge to provide a safety margin in case of skids on the loose surface.

The roads are little travelled, so birds show little fear of humans or their vehicles. Watch for birds on the road, especially in springtime, when waterfowl may be escorting hatchlings from one pond to another. It's also a good idea to walk only on the roadway, not on the verges. The verges are soft, and the edge of the dropoff into the water is hidden by thick vegetation, but the roadside grasses are an important nesting site for many birds. With no stops, the 10-mile (16 km) route takes about 40 mins.

To reach the **Wildlife Refuge Visitor Center**, turn right at Westside Grocery onto Hill Rd. The centre is 4 miles (6 km) down Hill Rd. Exhibits cover the natural history of the area and the conversion from marsh to farmland. A shaded picnic area is in front of the centre; a short trail leads up a hill behind the to a view point with an excellent view north over the marshes.

TULELAKE

Tourist Information: Tulelake Chamber of Commerce, PO Box 592, Main St, Tulelake, CA 96134; tel: (916) 667-5178.

Accommodation

Ellis Motel, 2238 Hwy 139, Tulelake, CA 96134; tel: (916) 667-5242; **Park Motel**, Hwy 139, Tulelake, CA 96134; tel: (916) 667-5190; **Tulelake Hotel**, 156 Main St, Tulelake, CA 96134; tel: (916) 667-2913.

Sightseeing

The town of about 1000 represents one-third of the population of the entire basin. Three very basic motels are the only lodging north of Lava Beds National Monument (cabins are available in Tionesta, 14 miles (22 km) south-east of Lava Beds). Town and lake are both named after the tules, a type of reed, which grow in nearby shallow waters. The only attraction in town is the **Tulelake Horseradish Co.**, 619 Main St, Tulelake, CA 96134; tel: (916) 667-5319, with demonstrations of how raw horseradish is turned into the fiery condiment. Souvenirs and a variety of horseradish products are for sale.

Continue south on Hwy 139. The **Tule Lake Ranger Station, Modoc National Forest**, is directly across the highway from a towering grain elevator. Continue 3 miles (5 km) on Hwy 139 to Modoc County Rd 111, just after crossing the railroad tracks. Turn right, following brown signs for **Lava Beds National Monument**.

Continue south through Lava Beds. The road swings down the hillside almost immediately upon leaving the Visitor Center area and comes to a dead end 14 miles (22 km) later. Turn left onto National Forest Highway 97 toward Hwy 139. The tiny town of Tionesta is just beyond the turn. Petrol is expensive, but the eight cabins at **Hawk's Nest**, Star Route, Tulelake, CA 96134; tel: (916) 664-3187, are the only lodging south of the park. The cabins are simple, but supplied with cooking facilities, including full-sized refrigerators and enormous enamelled stoves that could grace a museum display. Advance reservations are strongly advised. High season is late summer, when forest fire-fighting crews move in, and autumn, hunting season.

LAVA BEDS NATIONAL MONUMENT

Tourist Office: Lava Beds National Monument Headquarters, PO Box 867, Tulelake, CA 96134; tel: (916) 667-2283. The park **Visitor Center** and campsite are at Indian Well, near the south-east entrance.

The 72 square miles (186 square km) of the monument is dry, rugged, inhospitable, and breathtakingly beautiful. The landscape is a jumble of lava flows, cinder cones, chimneys, caves, and low hills, only slightly softened by sagebrush and mountain juniper trees. Several caves are open for unguided exploration, a rarity in liability-plagued America. Snow has been recorded in every month of the year, but it can also be blazingly hot in summer. Expect snow and dense white fog, called **tule fog**, in the winter. The elevation gradually rises from 4000 ft (1212 m) at the north end, near Tule Lake, to 5700 ft (1727 m) near the visitor center at the south end of the monument.

Bubonic plague is endemic amongst wildlife in the area. Ground squirrels and other rodents living on the Modoc plateau carry fleas which

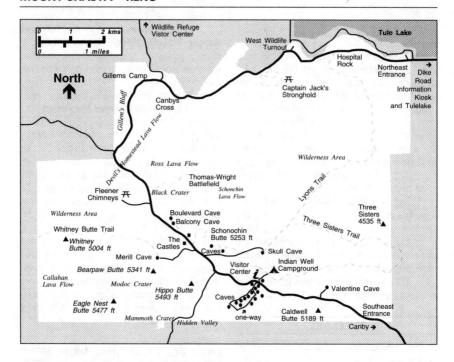

harbour the plague bacterium. The plague-infested fleas don't leave the rodents (a permanent meal) unless another warm body is within a few inches, so avoid contact.

One mile (1.6 km) beyond the turnoff from Hwy 139, turn left onto Modoc County Rd 111. Follow the brown signs toward **Petroglyph Point**, 5 miles (8 km) down the gravel road. A wire fence protects more than 5000 petroglyphs, images carved into the base of a towering cliff. Their meaning is unknown, but geological evidence suggests that they were cut between 4500 and 2500 years ago. Japanese characters carved in rocks near the south end of the cliff are relics of a World War II internment camp at Newell, about 4 miles (6 km) away. Return to County Rd 111.

The road runs just south of Tule Lake National Wildlife Refuge, visible to the right. Continue 7 miles (11 km) to **Captain Jack's Stronghold**. This isolated, desolate patch of lava was the scene of the most expensive war the US government ever launched against its own Native population, and

the only Indian War ever fought in California. A 30–60 min self-guided trail explores the formation and battle site.

Leaving Captain Jack's Stronghold, turn left. **Canby's Cross**, the site of the ambush of the Peace Commission, is 2 miles (3 km) west. A half mile (1 km) beyond the cross, Hill Rd joins the highway from the Klamath National Wildlife Refuges Visitor Center. Directly ahead is **Gillem's Bluff**, site of the main US army camp during the Modoc war. The road turns south and climbs the side of the bluff. A view point on the left, 2 miles (3 km) after the turn, overlooks **The Devil's Homestead**, a flow of rough lava, called aa lava, that poured down along the base of the bluff from the south. Signs at a second view point 1 mile (1.5 km) ahead, where the road crosses the flow, explain the different types of lava that erupted in the area.

The turnoff for **Fleener's Chimneys** is 2 miles (3 km) beyond the aa flow, to the right. The chimneys are hollow cones formed when volcanic vents threw up globs of lava, building

The Modoc War

The Modoc plateau was the scene of 30 years of on-again, off-again skirmishes between Native Americans and settlers moving first through, and then into, the area. Wagon trains frightened away game necessary for survival. Native Americans correctly blamed settlers for bringing epidemics of smallpox and other diseases which decimated local populations. Young warriors took to raiding wagon trains and settlements for survival as well as revenge. Estimates of the day, not always very accurate, say that about 400 settlers had been killed by 1858.

In 1864 the US Bureau of Indian Affairs negotiated a peace treaty with the Modocs. The Modocs agreed to leave their ancestral lands and settle on the Klamath Reservation in Southern Oregon in return for cash and supplies. But the Modocs and the Klamaths were traditional enemies; the Klamaths blocked the Modocs from hunting grounds. Starving, the Modocs drifted back toward the only home they knew. A young chief, Kentipoos, named 'Captain Jack' by whites, emerged as a leader, vowing to keep his people on their ancestral lands and hold the Americans at bay in the lava beds south of Tule Lake.

In November, 1872, soldiers sent to return the Modocs to the reservation ended up fleeing with 13 dead or wounded instead. The Modocs fulfilled a vow to kill every man in the Tulelake Valley if attacked, then settled into the lava beds to await an army counterattack.

In January, 1873, about 300 soldiers moved into position around what came to called 'Captain Jack's Stronghold' and attacked at dawn. It was a disastrous defeat. About 60 Modocs easily held the troops at bay, fighting from the rugged lava caves and trenches that made the area a natural fort. The Army brought in more troops, but was unable to dislodge the Modocs. Kentipoos built on the success by giving interviews to leading newspaper reporters from as far away as London, creating a wave of public sympathy across America.

It came to a sudden end in April. A militant Modoc faction forced Kentipoos into staging an ambush that killed two members of the Army's Peace Commission, including the commanding general, E.R.S. Canby. Army troops renewed the attack and entered the stronghold two days later. The Modocs had retreated on foot and finally surrendered in late May. Kentipoos was captured and hanged.

---

tall tubes. The hollow chimneys are up to 100 ft (30 m) deep. A pleasant picnic area is nearby.

Schonchin Butte, 5253 ft (1601 m) is 15 miles (24 km) beyond Chimneys. Turn left into the dirt access road. The road leads 1 mile (1.5 km) around and part way up the Butte to a tiny parking area. A walking trail leads another $3/4$ mile (1.2 km) up to a fire lookout at the top. The views are spectacular, especially since visibility in the area tops 100 miles (160 km) about 75% of the year. The road up the butte is *not recommended* for RVs or caravans because the turnaround area at the top is extremely small.

The road climbs toward the south, slowly moving away from naked lava flows into areas more heavily covered with brush and small trees.

Near the **Indian Well Visitor Center**, 22 miles (35 km) beyond Schonchin Butte, there is enough soil to support occasional patches of forest. Watch for deer on roadways around the Visitor Center and campsite, especially at dusk and dawn, their natural feeding times.

The Visitor Center has the usual excellent collection of books on the area and evening programs in the summer, but **Mushpot Cave** is a special offering. It is the only lit cave at Lava Beds, complete with a paved trail and interpretive displays underground. The accessible portion of the cave is less than ½ mile (1 km) long, but it's a good introduction to Lava Bed's most unusual feature, its caves, which are actually lava tubes.

Lava tubes, formed by rivers of thin, super-

The Modoc War–Lava Beds Nat. Mon.

heated lava that cool on the outside but continue to flow inside the new walls, are common enough in volcanic areas. But Lava Beds has more than 200 tubes, and the sheer number is unusual. Many have permanent deposits of ice and all are cool, no matter how hot it gets outdoors. The youngest caves are about 30,000 years old.

Cave Loop Road, a 24-mile (38 km) one-way circuit, offers access to most of the Lava Beds caves which can be explored without a permit. There are more than a dozen caves on the loop, all with parking areas and clearly marked ladders from the surface down into the lava tube. No water and no toilet facilities are available anywhere on the loop road.

The caves are quite safe (there are few side caves and it's hard to get lost), but it's not a good idea to go exploring alone. Trails and lights have not been installed except in Mushpot Cave, so falls sometimes occur.

It's also pitch black underground. Once away from the entrance, there is no light whatsoever, which sometimes unnerves people who have never experienced absolute darkness or caves before. Having someone else around helps ease the fright and, if necessary, the scramble back to daylight.

Most of the passageways are tall enough to walk upright, but it's necessary to crawl through a few low spots. The lava is extremely rough and hard, so park rangers recommend that everyone wears some sort of hard hat underground. The Visitor Center sells plastic hard hats for about $3. Solid shoes are also advisable. Some of the tube floors are smooth, but most quite rough and uneven.

The best guide is *Lava Beds Caves*, a small volume filled with maps, photos, and detailed cave explanations, for sale at the Visitor Center. Rangers conduct guided walks every afternoon during the summer months, often visiting caves which are normally closed to the public.

On your own or with a ranger, it's wise to carry two lights per person, one as a main light and one as a backup when the main light fails – which always seems to happen to at least one person in every group. The Visitor Center loans powerful torches, but collects a deposit to ensure

their return. More importantly, borrowing a torch is an easy way to let the rangers know a group is going underground. If the torches don't come back, it's time to mount a search party.

LAVA BEDS TO ALTURAS

Continue 2 miles (3 km) to Hwy 139. Turn right toward **Canby** and **Alturas**. All southbound traffic must stop at the **California Agricultural Inspection Station** 5 miles (8 km) beyond the turn onto Hwy 139. As the highway goes southeast, away from Lava Beds, the countryside becomes softer and more rolling, with fewer ragged lava flows visible on the surface.

Hwy 139 joins Hwy 299, 22 miles (36 km) beyond the Agricultural Inspection station. Turn left, toward Alturas. The town of **Canby** is just beyond the junction, in the middle of a large agricultural valley. Hwy 299 is a main north–south route with almost as many RVs as seagulls during the prime summer holiday months. The population slowly builds toward Alturas, with a growing number white fences, bright red barns, and isolated farm houses shaded by huge trees. **Alturas** is 18 miles (29 km) beyond Canby. Turn left at the traffic signal to join Hwy 395.

ALTURAS

Tourist Information: Alturas Chamber of Commerce, *522 S. Main St, Alturas, CA 96101; tel: (916) 233-4434.*

Accommodation

Alturas has the best choice of lodging, *BW* and about a dozen other motels, RV parks, and bed and breakfasts. The Chamber of Commerce can provide lodging lists, but cannot make bookings.

Eating and Drinking

The restaurant selection is the best between Mount Shasta and Reno. **The Brass Rail**, *Lakeview Hwy; tel: (916) 233-2906*, has solid Basque food, popular with locals. The hottest spot in town (or anywhere else nearby) is the **Niles Hotel & Saloon**, *304 S. Main; tel: (9160 233-3411*. The food is stolid American meat-and-potatoes fare, but the atmosphere lives up the claims on the whitewashed walls fronting on Main St: 'A Veritable Buffalo Bill Cody Wild West Show'. The advertising is accurate. The saloon could be a frontier museum, with patrons fresh off the range to match. Even if you're only driving through town, don't miss it.

Sightseeing

With the only traffic signals in all of Modoc County, Alturas is the biggest town for hours in any direction. Highlights are some wonderful old buildings, a museum, and what may be the nearest thing to a real Wild West saloon to survive into the late 20th century.

The **Modoc County Museum**, *600 S. Main St; tel: (916) 233-2944* is directly across the street from the Chamber of Commerce. The museum has an eclectic display of more than 400 firearms, 500 Native American baskets, plus miscellaneous paraphernalia from the local past. A steam locomotive is parked behind the museum.

The **Elks Hall**, *619 N. Main St* is easily the most striking building in town. Built in 1917 as the headquarters for the Nevada, California and Oregon Railroad (more often called the Narrow, Cantankerous and Ornery), the pastiche of Mission and Colonial Revival looks more Hollywood than Wild West. For a look at other historic buildings, pick up a self-guided **historic tour** guide at the Chamber of Commerce.

Headquarters for the **Modoc National Wildlife Refuge**, *PO Box 1610, Alturas, CA 96101; tel: (916) 233-3572*, is approximately 3 miles (5 km) to the east on County Rd 56. Follow the brown signs and turn left just beyond the Pit River bridge at the south end of Main St. Bird-watching is especially good near the headquarters.

ALTURAS TO RENO

Continue south on Hwy 395 through a flat, marshy valley. Much of the land on both sides of the highway is part of the Modoc National Wildlife Refuge. The road climbs out of the valley 15 miles (24 km) south of Alturas and drops into a similar valley. The well-watered valley floor looks to be a likely spot for a town amidst the dry hills, and the tiny valley town is called **Likely**.

Beyond Likely, the road climbs 10 miles (16 km) to **Sage Hen Summit**, 5566 ft (1687 m). The pattern of valley and pass repeats for the next 50 miles (80 km) to **Honey Lake**, a seasonal lake that becomes an alkali marsh most summers.

Hwy 395 takes an abrupt right turn above Honey Lake. At the petrol station 6 miles (10 km) beyond the turn, go left onto Lassen County Road A3 to bypass **Susanville**. To visit Susanville, and the first fast food outlets since Mount Shasta, continue straight on Hwy 395. A3 runs 9 miles (14 km) through gentle farmland wedged between the alkali flats of Honey Lake and the dry heights of the eastern side of the Sierra Nevada.

At Hwy 395, turn left toward Reno. Look for a popular rest stop on the left, 2 miles (3 km) beyond the junction, with plenty of shade, drinking water, toilets, and a pleasant view of Honey Lake and the mountains. Hwy 395 is the main route skirting the eastern slope of the Sierra Nevada. Farms and small towns line the highway, which is seldom deserted. Local traffic can be heavy at times, but most long-distance lorries prefer I-5, in the Central Valley. The road climbs to a final, unmarked summit south of Honey Lake, then descends into Long Valley for the final run into the Reno basin. Hwy 70 runs west toward Portola and Quincy from **Hallelujah Junction**, 44 miles (70 km) from the Honey Lake rest area. The junction was named by early travellers who rejoiced that they had finally crossed the Nevada desert and were about to climb into the lush pastures of the Sierra Nevada.

Hwy 395 becomes a freeway at the junction, which also has the first petrol station since Honey Lake. Northbound traffic must stop at the **Agricultural Inspection Station** 3 miles (5 km) south of Hallelujah Junction. The **Nevada border** is 5 miles (8 km) south of the inspection station. The first casino, appropriately enough, is called **Bordertown**. The outskirts of Reno lie just beyond. To reach the city centre casino area, take the Business 395 exit, 11 miles (18 km) south of Bordertown. Business 395 becomes Virginia Ave and passes the **University of Nevada, Reno (UNR)** planetarium and campus 4 miles (6 km) later. I-80, and Reno city centre (see p. 259), are 1 mile (1.6 km) beyond the UNR campus.

INDEX

References are to page numbers; *italic* numbers denote the page number of a map in the text; **bold** numbers refer to the map page and grid square of the colour road maps at the end of the book. For example, San Diego 100–108, *101*, **6:A10** shows where to find the text description of San Diego (pp. 100 to 108), the city map (p. 101) and the position of San Diego on the colour road maps (map page 6, grid square A10). Due to overlap, some places appear on two pages of the road maps and thus have two map references.

READER SURVEY
Fill in this form and you can win a set of full-colour guidebooks!

If you enjoyed using this book – or if you didn't – please help us to improve future editions, by taking part in our reader survey. Every returned form will be acknowledged, and to show our appreciation for your help we will give you the chance to win a set of Thomas Cook illustrated guidebooks for your travel bookshelf. Just take a few minutes to complete and return this form to us.

When did you buy this book?

Where did you buy it? (Please give town/city and if possible name of retailer)

Did you/do you intend to travel in California in 1995/96?
☐ Have travelled   ☐ Will travel 1995   ☐ Will travel 1996

If so, which cities, national parks and other locations did you/do you intend mainly to visit?

When did you/do you intend to travel?

For how long (approx.)?   How many people in your party?

Did you/will you travel: ☐ Making all your arrangements independently?
                                  ☐ On a fly-drive package?

Please give brief details:

Did you/do you intend to use this book:
☐ For planning your trip?   ☐ During the trip itself?   ☐ Both?

Did you/do you intend to also purchase any of the following travel publications for your trip?
☐ Thomas Cook Travellers: California
☐ A road map/atlas (please specify)
☐ Other guidebooks (please specify)

Please rate the following features of On the Road around California for their value to you
(Circle the 1 for 'little or no use,' 2 for 'useful,' 3 for 'very useful'):

The 'Travel Essentials' section on pages 10–31	1	2	3
The 'Driving in California' section on pages 32–39	1	2	3
The touring itineraries on pages 44–52	1	2	3
The recommended driving routes throughout the book	1	2	3
Information on towns and cities, National Parks, etc	1	2	3
The maps of cities, parks, wineries, etc	1	2	3
The colour planning map	1	2	3

READER SURVEY

Please use this space to tell us about any features that in your opinion could be changed, improved, or added in future editions of the book, or any other comments you would like to make concerning the book:

....

....

....

....

Your age category:

☐ Under 30   ☐ 30–50   ☐ over 50

Your name: Mr/Mrs/Ms   (First name or initials)
(Last name)

Your full address (please include postal code or zip code):

....

....

Your daytime telephone number:

Please detach this page and send it to: The Project Editor, On the Road around California, Thomas Cook Publishing, PO Box 227, Peterborough PE3 6SB, United Kingdom.

North American readers: Please mail replies to: E. Taylor, On the Road around California, Passport Books, 4255 West Touhy Avenue, Lincolnwood (Chicago), Illinois 60646-1975, USA.

Over £200/$300** worth of guidebooks to be won!

*All surveys returned to us before 28 April 1995 and again before 31 October 1995 will be entered for a prize draw on those dates. The senders of the first **three** replies drawn on each occasion will each be invited to make their personal selection of any six books from the Thomas Cook Travellers* range of guidebooks, worth over £40/$75**, to be sent to them free of charge. With dozens of cities and countries to choose from, this new, full colour series of guides covers the major tourist destinations of the world. Each book, retail price £6.99/$12.95**, offers 192 pages of sightseeing, background information, and travel tips.*

*North American readers please note: in the United States this range is published by Passport Books under the name 'Passport's Illustrated Guides from Thomas Cook'. North American winners will receive the US editions of their selected books.
**Prices correct at time of going to press.

Prizewinners will be notified as soon as possible after the closing date and asked to select from the list of titles. Offer is subject to availability of titles on the dates of the draws. A list of winners will be available on receipt of a stamped self-addressed envelope.